HANDBOOKS

BAJA

NIKKI GOTH ITOI

CENTRAL BAJA

Sea of Cortez

(Gulf of California)

Parque Natural
Isla Angel de la Guarda

Isla Angel de la Guarda

Canal de Ballenas

Isla Partida

Isla Raza

Isla Salsipuedes

Isla Las Ánimas

Isla San Lorenzo

Isla Coronado

Bahía de los Angeles

Bahía de las Ánimas

Bahía San Rafael

Bahía San Francisquito

Bahía Santa Teresa

San Francisquito

Punta Final

Bahía de Calamajué

Sierra de la Asamblea

Bahía de los Angeles

San Borja

SAN FRANCISCO BORJA
1762-1818

Parque Natural del Desierto Central

SANTA GERTRUDIS
1752-1822

Laguna Chapala

Valle de los Cirios

Rosarito

10

Rancho San Ignacito

Parque Natural del Desierto Central

Nuevo Chapala

Parador Punta Prieta

Punta Prieta

Jesús María

Ejido Morelos

El Arco

BAJA CALIFORNIA

Laguna de San José

EAGLE MONUMENT

Guerrero Negro

Bahía Santa Rosalillita

Punta Santa Rosalillita

Punta Rosarito

Morro Santo Domingo

Laguna Manuela

Punta Cono

Punta María

Bahía Santa María

Punta Negra

Laguna Ojo de Liebre

Parque Natural de la Ballena Gris

Pico Gill

Isla Cedros

Cerro de Cedros

Cedros

Cedros

To Islas San Benito

Isla Natividad

Punta Eugenia

Bahía de Sebastián Vizcaíno

Playa Malarrimo

PENINSUL

Pico Veracruz

Bahía Tortugas

Bahía Thurloe

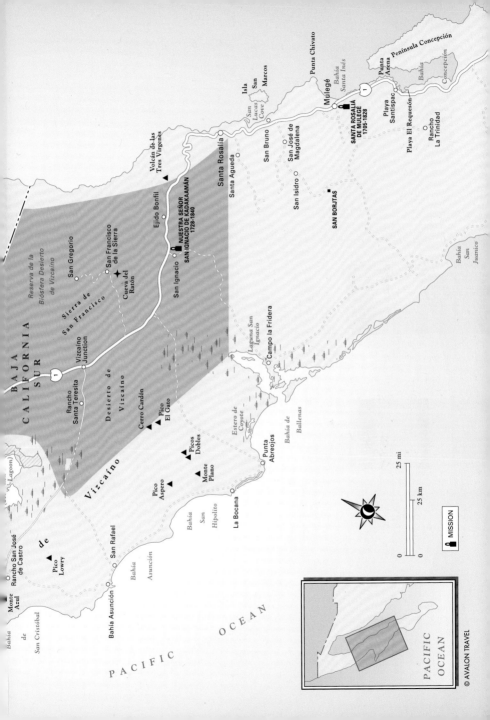

PACIFIC OCEAN

© AVALON TRAVEL

BAJA CALIFORNIA SUR

Reserva de la Biósfera Desierto de Vizcaíno

Desierto de Vizcaíno

Vizcaíno

Sierra de San Francisco

Península Concepción

Bahía Concepción

PACIFIC OCEAN

Punta Arena

Playa Santispac

Playa El Requesón

Rancho La Trinidad

SANTA ROSALÍA DE MULEGÉ
1705-1828

Mulegé

Punta Chivato

Bahía Santa Inés

San Marcos

Isla San

Lucas Cove

Punta

SAN BORJITAS

San José de Magdalena

San Isidro

San Bruno

Santa Águeda

Santa Rosalía

NUESTRA SEÑOR
SAN IGNACIO DE KADAKAAMAN
1728-1840

San Ignacio

Ejido Bonfil

Volcán de las Tres Vírgenes

San Francisco de la Sierra

Cueva del Ratón

San Gregorio

Laguna San Ignacio

Campo la Fridera

Estero de Coyote

Bahía de Ballenas

Bahía San Juanico

Punta Abreojos

La Bocana

Picos Dobles

Pico El Gato

Cerro Cardón

Monte Plano

Pico Áspero

Bahía San Hipólito

San Rafael

Bahía Asunción

Bahía Asunción

Pico Lowry

Rancho San José de Castro

Monte Azul

Bahía de San Cristóbal

Vizcaíno Junction

Rancho Santa Teresita

Lagoon

1

1

1

25 mi

25 km

MISSION

PACIFIC OCEAN

SOUTHERN BAJA

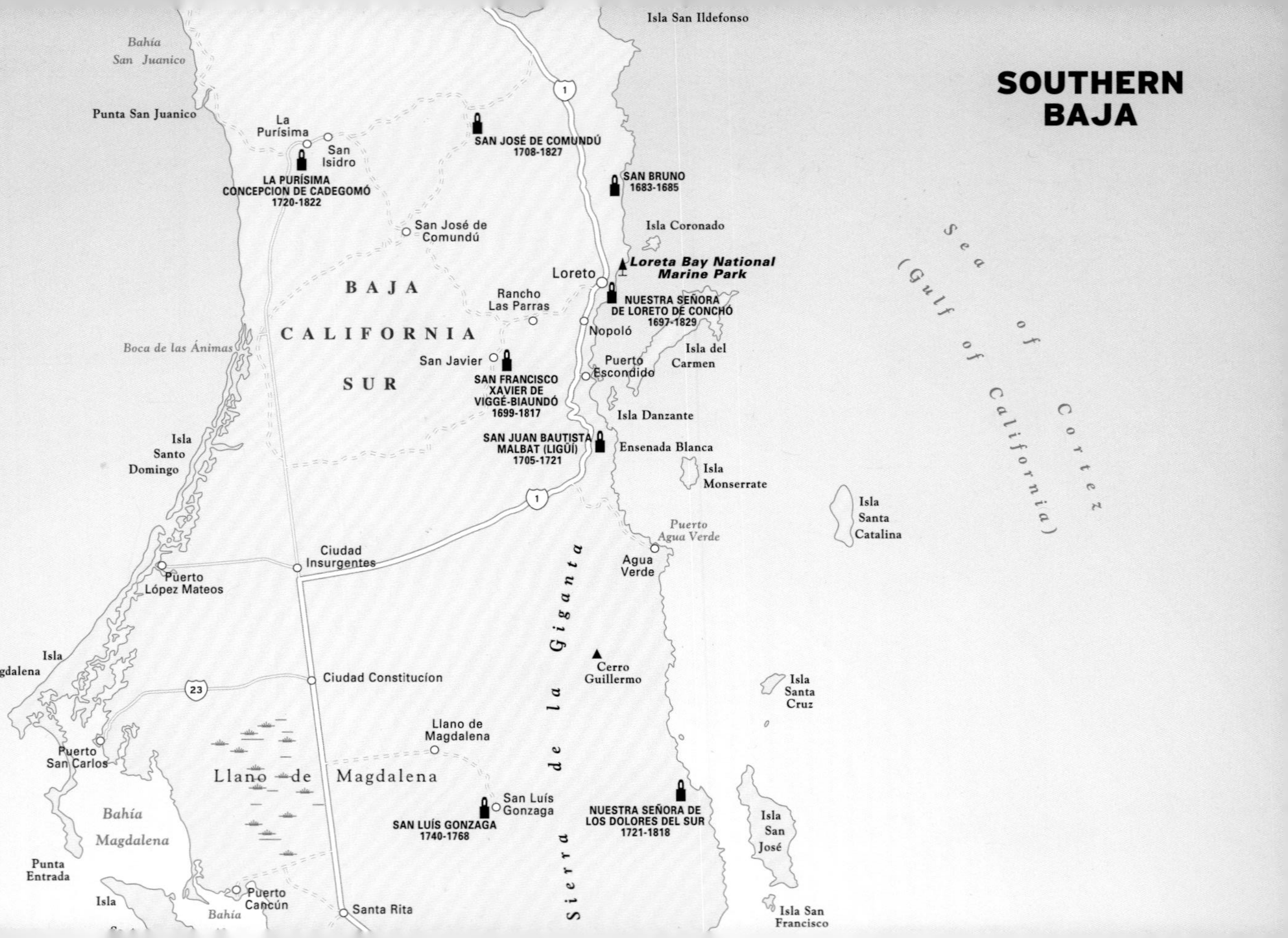

S e a   o f   C o r t e z

(G u l f   o f   C a l i f o r n i a)

Isla San Ildefonso

Isla
Santa
Catalina

Isla
Santa
Cruz

Isla
San
José

Isla San
Francisco

SAN BRUNO
1683-1685

Isla Coronado

★ Loreta Bay National
   Marine Park

NUESTRA SEÑORA
DE LORETO DE CONCHÓ
1697-1829

Nopoló

Isla del
Carmen

Puerto
Escondido

Isla Danzante

Ensenada Blanca

Isla
Monserrate

Puerto
Agua Verde

NUESTRA SEÑORA DE
LOS DOLORES DEL SUR
1721-1818

Loreto

Agua
Verde

1

SAN JOSÉ DE COMUNDÚ
1708-1827

Rancho
Las Parras

SAN FRANCISCO
XAVIER DE
VIGGE-BIAUNDÓ
1699-1817

SAN JUAN BAUTISTA
MALIBAT (LIGÜÍ)
1705-1721

Cerro
Guillermo

Sierra   de   la   Gigante

Sierra   de   la   Gigante

San José de
Comundú

San Javier

1

San Luis
Gonzaga

B A J A

Llano de
Magdalena

SAN LUIS GONZAGA
1740-1768

La
Purísima

San
Isidro

LA PURÍSIMA
CONCEPCIÓN DE CADEGOMÓ
1720-1822

C A L I F O R N I A

S U R

Ciudad
Insurgentes

Ciudad Constitución

Santa Rita

Bahía
San Juanico

Punta San Juanico

Boca de las Ánimas

Isla
Santo
Domingo

Puerto
López Mateos

23

Puerto
San Carlos

Llano   de   Magdalena

Bahía
Magdalena

Puerto
Cancún

Bahía

Isla

Isla
Magdalena

Punta
Entrada

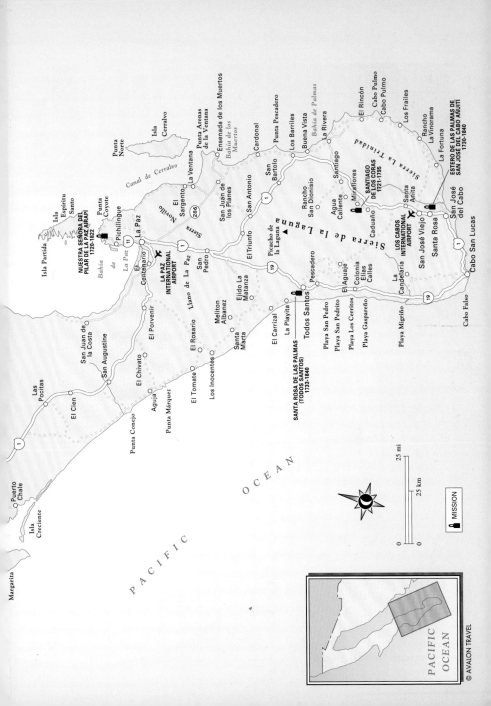

Contents

Discover Baja

All travelers who make the journey to the tip of the Baja California peninsula remember their first taste of the "real" Baja: the first night spent sleeping in a hammock under a palm shelter by the sea. That chance encounter of a baby sea turtle release. A plunge into a sparkling freshwater pool high in the mountains. The farmer who helped fix a flat tire. Hooking a red snapper from a line cast into the surf.

The typical pattern of discovery goes something like this: Fly to Los Cabos for a short trip to see if Baja is for you. Return for a longer vacation a year later with family or friends in tow. Then plan a sabbatical, take a leave of absence, retire early, or volunteer to shuttle supplies to a local charity – any excuse to spend the first of many seasons exploring every beach and town from Ensenada to Cabo San Lucas.

The Baja California that appeals to these travelers is a land of extremes: a few large cities mixed in with dozens of tiny settlements; desert, tropical, coastal, and mountain environments; communities made up of native Baja California families, mainland Mexican immigrants, and foreign expatriates; historic missions and contemporary art galleries; luxury resorts and rustic fish camps; *pangas* and cruisers and 100-foot yachts.

The earliest Spanish explorers believed Baja to be an island. They were wrong about the geography, but their maps captured the spirit of

the place. Though we know better now, much of the 800-mile-long peninsula that was once known as Antigua California continues to exist happily outside the mainstream — even as paved highways, international airports, and information technology keep trying to link it to the outside world.

From the multicultural border zone to the tourism-oriented Los Cabos Corridor, the peninsula's two states, Baja California (Norte) and Baja California Sur, offer contrasting visitor experiences. But wherever you go, you'll find plenty of opportunity for outdoor recreation. Kayaking, scuba diving, surfing, sportfishing, kiteboarding, and windsurfing rank among the most popular coastal activities. The interior offers terrain suitable for mountain biking, horseback riding, and wilderness hiking. And when you've worn yourself out in the water or on land, you can shift your focus to cultural experiences and culinary adventure.

Traveling around Baja is about collecting moments — and forming friendships — that will stay with you forever.

Planning Your Trip

▶ WHERE TO GO

Tijuana, Rosarito, and Tecate

As the peninsula's largest city, Tijuana is a high-risk, high-reward place. Outstanding cuisine, trendsetting nightclubs, and bargain shopping attract loyal weekenders from Southern California. But the stories you hear of drug and sex trafficking, corrupt cops, rip-off artists, and predatory cab drivers are not urban legend. On the Pacific coast to the south, Rosarito draws surfers and college students on spring break. East of Tijuana, Tecate offers a more relaxed border crossing, pleasant town plaza, and the namesake Tecate beer.

Ensenada to El Rosario

South of the border region, Ensenada has hopping clubs and bars at its north end and a quiet and more upscale *malecón* (waterfront promenade) downtown. Nearby are the boutique wineries of the Valle de Guadalupe and empty beaches along Bahía de San Quintín. El Rosario marks the gateway to the desert that makes up the peninsula's interior.

Mexicali to San Felipe

Mexicali is the state capital of Baja California (Norte), a regional center of agricultural commerce, and a supply depot for travelers passing through to points south. Its Chinesca district offers a Mexican twist on Chinese cuisine. Nearby are hot springs in the Cañon de Guadalupe and a sizable expat community in San Felipe on the Sea of Cortez. You can hike among towering cacti in the Valle de los Gigantes or camp on secluded beaches near Puertecitos and Bahía San Luis Gonzaga.

Desierto Central to Bahía de los Angeles

Here begins the quintessential Baja. You'll drive through miles of undisturbed desert terrain. Stop to stretch your legs in Cataviña and walk among the boulders. Head west to find waves

Ensenada coastline

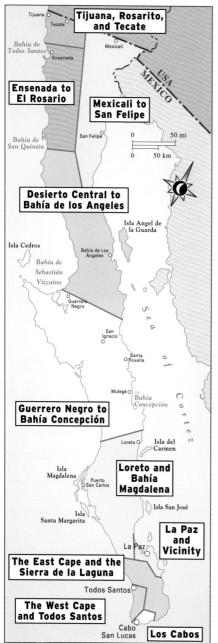

at The Wall or east to explore the timeless fishing outpost of Bahía de los Angeles on the Sea of Cortez.

Guerrero Negro to Bahía Concepción

Guerrero Negro marks the state line between Baja California (Norte) and Baja California Sur. From mission towns to mining towns and prehistoric rock art sites, this region is rich with opportunities for cultural exploration. On the Pacific coast are two lagoons where gray whales come to bear their calves. On the Gulf coast, the shallow bays of Bahía Concepción are ideal for paddling, snorkeling, and cruising.

Loreto and Bahía Magdalena

The site of the first permanent Jesuit mission, Loreto has a deep-rooted history. Today, it has become a government-sponsored tourist corridor that entertains visitors with full-service resorts, sportfishing charters, and a national marine park. Nearby, San Javier gives a taste of life in the isolated interior. Across the peninsula, on the Pacific, gray whales congregate in Bahía Magdalena during the winter months.

La Paz and Vicinity

Known for its beautiful sunsets and malecón, La Paz is an authentic Mexican city with a strong mainland influence. White-sand beaches along the Pichilingue Peninsula invite relaxation, while the protected islands offshore support a rare and fragile ecosystem.

The East Cape and the Sierra de la Laguna

Travelers with a passion for water sports and a willingness to rough it will find paradise along the Gulf coast. This is a place of solar

IF YOU HAVE . . .

- **FOUR DAYS:** Plan a weekend getaway in Valle de Guadalupe wine country, Loreto, La Paz, or San José del Cabo. These destinations are all close to major international airports.

- **SEVEN DAYS:** With a full week, you can complete the Los Cabos–East Cape–La Paz–West Cape loop, book a liveaboard diving or sailing trip, or explore part of the Spanish mission trail.

- **THREE WEEKS:** Three weeks is ample time for driving down the peninsula and back, making stops at all the key towns along the way. It's also enough time to get to know one place really well, so you might opt to rent a condo in Loreto, Todos Santos, La Paz, or Los Cabos and spend your days exploring the immediate vicinity.

- **THREE MONTHS:** Travelers with time on their hands can manage to visit just about every out-of-the-way place, including the peaks of the sierras, Bahía de Los Angeles, the Vizcaíno Peninsula, Laguna San Ignacio, and Candelaria, plus many of the lesser-known islands, such as Isla Cedros, Isla San Marcos, and Isla Cerralvo.

distinctive rock formation on Playa Balandra near La Paz

power, dirt roads, *panga* boats, and *palapa* restaurants. The Sea of Cortez offers secluded beaches, steady winds, abundant game fish, a living coral reef, and 30-meter visibility underwater. Inland, the Sierra de la Laguna attracts hikers and horseback riders with cascading waterfalls and 2,100-meter peaks.

Los Cabos
Los Cabos (The Capes) refers to the towns of San José del Cabo and Cabo San Lucas at the tip of the Baja Peninsula. One entertains the young and young at heart, while the other offers a more sophisticated scene of gourmet restaurants and fine art.

The West Cape and Todos Santos
Along the Pacific coast, a rugged shoreline extends from Cabo San Lucas north to the growing artist community of Todos Santos. The West Cape remains the least-developed stretch of coastline on either side of the peninsula south of La Paz.

▶ WHEN TO GO

Northwestern Baja

Northwestern Baja enjoys a mild Pacific climate, which makes it comfortable year-round. High season is May–October, when the sun shines the brightest and beaches are warmest. To get away from the crowds and enjoy low-season prices, visit October–April. December–February can be chilly and cloudy.

High Sierras

Summer is the season to hike in the sierras, as temperatures stay comfortably cool above 1,500 meters (5,000 ft.). Expect a winter-like climate at higher elevations October–April.

Deserts

The desert is prettiest after the rainy season, usually in November, when flowering cacti fill the landscape with splashes of color. Daytime temperatures are dangerously hot May–October, but the rest of the year is fine for exploration. Remember that nights in the desert can be cold at any time of year.

cirio in Baja's extensive desert

Sea of Cortez Coast

Along Baja's Gulf coast, moderate temperatures prevail October–mid-June. In summer and early fall, the weather can be uncomfortably hot and many businesses close while their owners flee to cooler temperatures in the north. The busiest tourist season is

pangas in a harbor on the Sea of Cortez

November–March, even though for most visitors, the northern stretch of coastline is too cold for swimming at this time. You can pursue a variety of water sports year-round from Loreto to Cabo, even in the winter. Fishing and diving are best in summer.

Los Cabos

The tip of the Baja Peninsula, from San José del Cabo to Cabo San Lucas, is pleasantly warm throughout the year. Like elsewhere in Southern Baja, August and September tend to be extremely hot. But the Pacific Ocean helps to keep summer temperatures a little lower at the cape than along the Sea of Cortez.

Land's End in Cabo San Lucas

► BEFORE YOU GO

Passports and Other Documents

Passports are now required for U.S. citizens. If you are driving your own vehicle, bring two copies of your Mexican auto liability insurance policy, plus roadmaps and at least a basic auto repair kit.

Transportation

Buy round-trip airfare to San Diego, Tijuana, Loreto, La Paz, or Los Cabos, or arrange to reach the border by car or by boat. Reserve a rental car for pickup at the airport, or plan to take a shuttle or taxi into town and use public transportation to get around.

a local burro looking for food

Explore Baja

▶ BEST OF BAJA ROAD TRIP

The road may be paved now and fuel much easier to come by than in the early days of peninsular travel, but Baja California remains a classic route for travelers who enjoy the thrill of a long road trip. All you need is ample time, a reliable vehicle, and an ability to cope with unpredictable situations. This itinerary follows Mexico 1 from the border crossing in Tijuana to the Los Cabos tourist corridor at the southern tip of the peninsula, 1,600 kilometers away, with a few options for side trips and off-highway scenic drives along the way.

Day 1

Cross the U.S.–Mexico border at San Ysidro early in the day and head south through Tijuana with an optional sightseeing stop to tour Baja Studios and Xploration. Try a lobster roll in Puerto Nuevo (30 km from Tijuana). Make your way to Ensenada by afternoon (116 km from Tijuana). Walk the downtown promenade and spend the night at one of the modest hotels in town.

Day 2

Spend the day wine-tasting in the rural Valle de Guadalupe, a half-hour drive from downtown Ensenada, then pack the car and return to Mexico 1 to continue the drive south. Before Maneadero, take the turnoff to La Bufadora to watch seawater explode out of a blowhole in the rocks.

Reach San Quintín or El Rosario by nightfall. At low tide, dig for clams along Playa Santa María. If you're in a hurry to reach destinations farther south and have the stamina for a long day of driving, you can skip some of these northern attractions and overnight at Guerrero Negro instead.

Day 3

Buy fresh tortillas and stock up on water and groceries in San Quintín or El Rosario, then

You can find hand-embroidered dresses for sale on Ensenada's downtown promenade.

prepare to make the four-hour trip across the desert. A smorgasbord of cacti—some of them 13 meters tall and hundreds of years old—extends from highway to horizon in all directions. Giant boulder piles, roadside shrines, and jagged peaks of the Sierra de la Asamblea complete the picture. Fill up on gas in Cataviña if the station is open, and stay overnight if daylight is waning; otherwise, continue to Guerrero Negro.

Day 4

Back on Mexico 1, a 145-kilometer drive from Guerrero Negro leads to the palm oasis of San Ignacio. You can tour the historic mission, arrange a guided trip to nearby cave paintings, or in winter head west to Laguna San Ignacio to see the gray whales.

Days 5-6

Today's journey brings the first glimpse of the Sea of Cortez as you descend into the historic silver mining town of Santa Rosalía (74 km from San Ignacio). Walk the busy streets and note the French influence that lingers from its days as a company town. In the afternoon, follow Mexico 1 to Mulegé, 134 kilometers farther south. Spend a couple nights at a bed-and-breakfast along the river, or camp on a beach along Bahía Concepción. Spend the next two days wandering the town; book a day of diving through Cortez Explorers; snorkel the beaches along Bahía Concepción; or arrange a guided tour of the nearby cave paintings.

Days 7-9

Pack up for the 135-kilometer (2.5-hr) drive south to Loreto. Settle in for a few days to enjoy the wealth of outdoor recreation at your doorstep. A national marine park, historic mission, and pleasant *malecón* await exploration.

Side trip: Visit one of the best-preserved Jesuit missions on the peninsula in the tiny

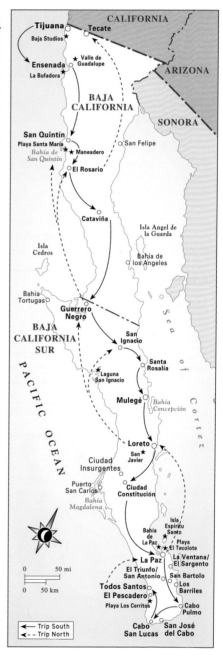

Misión San Francisco Xavier de Viggé-Bianndó in San Javier

village of San Javier, a 36-kilometer drive southwest of Loreto.

Day 10

This is a travel day to La Paz, 367 kilometers south on Mexico 1. Allow six hours for the trip, including a brief stop for gas and food in the agricultural supply center of Ciudad Constitución. Book a room near the *malecón* in La Paz in time to catch the sunset.

Side trip: During whale-watching season (Nov.–Mar.), Puerto San Carlos on Bahía Magdalena is worth a side trip west from Ciudad Insurgentes (57 km).

Day 11

Spend at least one day at the beach or in the water. Explore the pristine beaches along Bahía de La Paz, finishing the day at breezy Playa El Tecolote, 30 minutes from downtown. Or book a day of diving or kayaking and snorkeling at Isla Espíritu Santo.

Day 12

Shop for souvenirs, supplies, and gifts in the morning, then stock up on groceries, and prepare to begin the loop around the southernmost part of Baja. Next up: the

East Cape. It's a 90-minute drive through the mountains and mining-turned-farming towns of El Triunfo, San Antonio, and San Bartolo. Los Barriles (paved roads only) has several modest hotels, RV campgrounds, a windsurfing camp, and some private vacation rentals; a half-hour farther south, Cabo Pulmo has more primitive lodging in solar-powered *casitas* and three dive operators. In between are a handful of fishing lodges and private vacation rentals.

Side trip: During the windy season

Hotel Palmas de Cortez in Los Barriles

covered beach chairs in Cabo San Lucas

(Nov.–Mar.), add one day of travel and drive 40 kilometers southeast from La Paz along BCS 286 to Bahía de La Ventana and the neighboring villages of La Ventana and El Sargento. Watch the colorful sails of kiteboarders and windsurfers gliding through the chop; or pile in a *panga* for a day of diving at Isla Cerralvo across the channel. Return to Mexico 1 via the newly paved road that connects San Juan de los Planes to San Antonio.

Day 13

Spend today playing on, in, or near the Sea of Cortez, then continue the cape loop to the southernmost tip of the peninsula. Prepare for culture shock as you enter the scenic Los Cabos Corridor. After two weeks of relative isolation, the mega-resorts and developed tourist infrastructure of San José del Cabo and Cabo San Lucas may come as a surprise. Wander the streets surrounding the plaza and Boulevard Mijares to get a feel for San José del Cabo. Browse the art galleries and Mexican fire opal stores downtown and splurge on a late lunch or early dinner at a restaurant that specializes in *alta cocina mexicana*. Continue along the Transpeninsular Highway to Cabo San Lucas if you're in the mood for late-night entertainment.

Day 14

Snorkel at Playa Chileno or Playa Santa María on the Corridor. Book a massage at one of the five-star resorts if the mood strikes and budget allows. Tour the marina and downtown area of Cabo San Lucas, and take a water taxi to Playa del Amor and El Arco at Land's End. Stay the night to enjoy the lively bar and disco scene around town.

Day 15

Now it's time to point the GPS north and explore the West Cape and Todos Santos. Follow Mexico 19 out of Cabo San Lucas. Look for surf, or just have a picnic at one of the rugged beaches west of the highway. Continue north to Km 64 and Playa Los Cerritos. Swim, boogie board, or surf at one of the only sheltered beaches along the West Cape. Then make your way to accommodations on the beach in El Pescadero (Km 62)

ISLAND HOPPING

Whether you are already a pro or are picking up a paddle for the very first time, kayaks are a perfect way to experience Sea of Cortez marinelife up close. Whales, flying mantas, and sea turtles are just some of the creatures you might see from the surface. Throw on a mask and fins, and an entire world becomes visible below. Beach camping on uninhabited islands completes the experience. Overnight trips can take a couple of days, a full week, or more; organized trips are an appealing option, especially for novices.

Mobulas are a common sight in the Sea of Cortez.

WHERE TO GO

Mulegé to Loreto
Many kayakers begin their Baja expedition paddling the islands of **Carmen** and **Danzante,** offshore from Loreto, for a week or more. Protected by land on three sides, 14-mile-long **Bahía Concepción** between Mulegé and Loreto is a good choice for novice kayakers who want to try a multiday paddle. It takes 5-7 days to complete the coastal trip from Mulegé to Loreto.

Loreto to La Paz
A more ambitious coastal route begins in Loreto and ends in La Paz, taking in the island of **Espíritu Santo** at the finish. This 65-mile paddle usually takes 8-10 days. For a shorter trip, make La Paz your home base and spend two or three days camping on the islands offshore.

Bahía de los Angeles
With its many islets and islands, Bahía de los Ángeles appeals to kayakers of all levels, though the strong channel currents require some caution.

Pacific Coast
Conditions are much rougher on the Pacific, even in the most protected parts of the coast. Experienced kayakers head to **Punta Banda,** an inlet-scalloped cape near Ensenada. **Bahía Magdalena,** a large, protected bay in southern Baja, attracts many kayakers during the winter whale-watching season.

WHEN TO GO
Temperatures are hottest July-September, and winds are strongest November-February, making March-May the best months for a long-distance paddle. Whale-watching trips take place on the Pacific coast November-March.

---

or in the town of Todos Santos, a few kilometers farther north.

Day 16
Head northwest across the *huerta* to *el otro lado,* the other side of Todos Santos, where you can catch waves, cast a fishing line in the surf, or simply stroll the beach at Playa La Pastora. In winter, watch for flying mantas and whales breaching just offshore. Around 3 P.M., drive south to Punta Lobos to watch local fishermen unload their fresh catch, and buy some *dorado* (mahi mahi) or *huachinango* (red snapper) for dinner.

Days 17-18
Complete the cape loop along Mexico 19 by returning to La Paz, where you'll pick up

Mexico 1 again. Now it's time to begin retracing your steps, filling in any missed sights or optional side trips along the way. Spend the first night in Loreto, after a seven-hour drive, and the next in San Ignacio (5 hrs) or Guerrero Negro (7 hrs).

Days 19-20
Leave the state of Baja California Sur early in the morning, and head back across the desert to El Rosario (5 hrs) or San Quintín (6 hrs).

Day 21
Follow Mexico 1 north to the last military checkpoint at Maneadero. At El Sauzal, north of Ensenada, choose between the toll road north to Tijuana, or Mexico 3, which heads northeast to Tecate (105 km). Savor one last meal of tacos and *cerveza*. Then cross the border and leave Baja behind, for now.

San Ignacio

▶ AROUND THE CAPE IN SEVEN DAYS

Travelers with a week or longer can experience the many dimensions of the lower Baja peninsula by making a circular route around the region via paved highways Mexico 1 and Mexico 19. Extending a total distance of approximately 564 kilometers, this route takes visitors along the lower slopes of the Sierra de la Laguna, through the sierra's former mining towns, across the plains of La Paz, and along the coastlines of the East and West Capes as well as the Corridor between San José del Cabo and Cabo San Lucas.

It's possible to complete the loop by bus, but expect to do a fair amount of walking to get from the stops along the highway to the scenic coastal areas. A rental car affords more flexibility and convenience, and you can park easily in all of the towns along the route.

This loop can be comfortably driven in two or three days, but since there are many towns worth exploring and activities to enjoy at each stop, most travelers prefer to allow a week or longer. For more of an adventure, consider widening the loop by taking the sandy Camino Rural Costero (Rural Coastal Road).

Day 1
Arrive at Los Cabos International Airport (SJD); transfer to a hotel in downtown San José del Cabo and spend the evening around town. Browse the art galleries and Mexican fire opal stores downtown before sitting down to a leisurely dinner at a restaurant serving *alta cocina mexicana.*

Day 2
Drive to Cabo Pulmo via Mexico 1 (1–1.5 hrs), exiting at La Ribera and heading east

SCUBA DIVING TIPS

Certified divers have some difficult choices to make when planning a trip to the Sea of Cortez. Wherever you go, you'll encounter one of the world's richest marine ecosystems, with sea lions, sea turtles, whale sharks, manta rays, amberjacks, and schooling hammerheads all living among the islands, seamounts, and bays in the sea. Water temperatures are comfortable most of the year; visibility rarely falls below six meters and can exceed 30 meters on the best of days.

Dive operators in all of the locations listed here provide expert services. For those who are seriously dedicated to the sport, live-aboard trips are another option.

WHERE TO DIVE

Cabo San Lucas

One option is to stay close to the lively scene in Cabo San Lucas. Short boat rides are an advantage to diving here; crowds and noise from harbor traffic are the main deterrents.

A **deep submarine canyon** just 45 meters offshore offers exciting underwater topography for experienced divers. The canyon is known for its "sandfalls" – streams of falling sand channeled between rocks along the canyon walls. But even when the rivers aren't running, the dive offers varied marine life, large and small.

Another popular dive from San Lucas begins in the surge under a sea lion colony on the Sea of Cortez side of **Land's End** and concludes with an underwater swim around to the Pacific side.

Cabo Pulmo

Alternatively, you can sacrifice nightlife and amenities to explore the **living coral reef** and national marine park offshore from Cabo Pulmo in the East Cape region. The coral attracts a wide variety of fish of all sizes and colors; other smaller reefs, as well as shipwrecks, lie in the general vicinity. Drift dives are common here, and boat rides are short. Several sites, including a sea lion colony, are ideal for novices.

La Paz

The islands and seamounts offshore from La Paz harbor some of the most exciting under-

Two schools of fish converge in Cabo Pulmo.

water topography and the largest marine creatures in the sea. Boat rides are long – an hour or more – and currents tend to be strong at these sites. The reward is the chance to experience the deep blue and to spot some of the largest pelagics in the sea. An advanced dive site called **El Bajo** is famous for its summer population of giant manta rays and schooling hammerhead sharks. Beginners will enjoy dives in the bays around Isla Espíritu Santo and the sea lion colony at Los Islotes.

Loreto and Bahía Concepción

Loreto offers access to **Isla Coronado,** among other islands, and the wreck of a 120-foot **sunken freighter.** Wall dives and underwater caves are additional highlights of the diving in this location. Proximity to historic missions and rock-art sites are another reason to choose to travel to Central Baja. To the north, the protected inlets of **Bahía Concepción** offer opportunities for snorkeling calm and clear waters.

WHEN TO DIVE

From La Paz south, onshore water temperatures are around 21°C (70°F) in winter and 29°C (85°F) in summer and early fall. Water visibility is best July–October, when it exceeds 30 meters (100 ft); this is also when the air temperature is warmest, often reaching well over 32°C (90°F).

La Paz's *malecón* at sunset

to pick up the coastal road. The last few kilometers will be on dirt road. Head straight for the beach and spend the rest of the day snorkeling the live coral reef that comes all the way into shore. Order fish tacos and an icy *michelada* for dinner at La Palapa restaurant on the beach, or try Restaurant El Caballero for a wide variety of Mexican dishes prepared by a professional chef. Book your activity of choice for the next morning: Fishing, kayaking, and diving top the list.

Side trip: At Santiago, head west to reach the Cañon de la Zorra and a 10-meter waterfall, just a 10-minute walk from the parking lot.

Day 3

Spend the morning out at sea, and in the afternoon continue north along Mexico 1 to La Paz (1.5–2 hrs). Check in to a downtown hotel and walk the *malecón* at sunset. Seek out seafood at Mariscos Moyeyo's or *arranchera* at Rancho Viejo, then head to Casa de Villa or Las Varitas for drinks and live music.

Day 4

Take a *panga* shuttle to Isla Espíritu Santo for a day of kayaking and snorkeling, or book a day of diving. Alternatively, paddle or drive to a few of the beaches along the Pichilingue Peninsula. Enjoy the views from one of the waterfront seafood restaurants at Playa El Tecolote. Spend the next morning exploring the Museo Regional de Antropología e Historia in downtown La Paz, and shopping for pottery and other crafts.

Depart La Paz in the afternoon, heading south on Mexico 1 to Mexico 19, which leads to Todos Santos (1 hr). Check in to a hotel in town, such as the Todos Santos Inn, or a vacation rental near the beach, such as Los Colibrís. For dinner, choose casual Mexican fare at Miguel's or Barajas Tacos, or something more upscale at Tres Gallines.

Day 5

Walk the historic district in Todos Santos, with brick buildings and colorful facades that date back to the town's status as Baja's sugarcane capital in the late 19th century. Admire the artwork in a few of the town's dozen galleries. Drive north along the coast to Playa La Pastora or south along Mexico 19 to Playa Los Cerritos, at Km 64, to stroll the beach in the afternoon. Continue south along Mexico 19 to reach Cabo San Lucas before dark (1 hr). Check in to a hotel in downtown Cabo San Lucas or a resort along the Corridor, such as the Sheraton Hacienda del Mar. Make a reservation at Nick-San Restaurant for an outstanding sushi experience.

Day 6

Hire a water taxi, paddle a kayak, or rent a WaveRunner to visit Playa del Amor, or plan a day of fishing or diving out of Cabo San Lucas. Wander the shops and enjoy afternoon cocktails at The Nowhere Bar or the Giggling Marlin along the marina. Take a nap so you can rally for the nightlife at Cabo Wabo or El Squid Roe after dark.

Get a massage on the beach in Cabo San Lucas.

Day 7

Schedule a massage for your last morning in paradise. Take a dip in the pool, hit the shops, and return to the airport with sand in your shoes.

► FOUR-DAY GETAWAYS

Winter blues got you down? Looking to escape muggy summer days at home? A long weekend in the dry Baja sun may be just the answer. Travelers based in the western United States can reach San Diego, Ensenada, Loreto, La Paz, or Los Cabos by air in a matter of hours. From these international airports, a variety of weekend itineraries are possible. Here are just three of the options.

Wine Country

DAY 1

Cross the U.S.–Mexico border at San Ysidro after the morning rush hour and head south through Tijuana and onto the toll road. Stop in Rosarito for lunch at El Nido. Sit in the shaded back patio if it's not too hot and try the locally raised quail and venison dishes. Walk off lunch by cutting through the Rosarito Beach Hotel and onto the pier that runs 600 yards out over the Pacific. If you have extra time, take the *libre* south out of Rosarito and stop in the housewares stores along the roadside in Popotla.

The total driving time from Tijuana to Ensenada will be less than two hours on the *cuota* and around 2.5 hours on the *libre,* depending on traffic. When you arrive in Ensenada, check into the Corona Hotel. Hit the downtown area for dinner, and then head north to Hussong's Cantina for a beer. If the spirit moves you, walk to the corner and join

Taste some of Mexico's finest wines on the Ruta del Vino in Valle de Guadalupe.

the party at Papas and Beer until the wee hours of the morning.

DAY 2

If you weren't out too late and you've called ahead, hop on a chartered fishing boat with Sergio's Sportfishing Center. Back on the docks, take your catch to a vendor in the Mercado de Mariscos to have them cook up a custom batch of fish tacos.

Spend the afternoon strolling the shops along López Mateos and visit La Esquina de Bodegas for some preliminary wine tasting. In the late afternoon make your way north out of Ensenada to Route 3. A green overhead sign will welcome you to the Ruta del Vino. Check into the Tuscan-style La Villa del Valle for the next two nights, and grab a casual dinner at La Casa Vieja.

DAY 3

After breakfast at the Villa, hang out by the pool until Steve Dryden, your personal guide, arrives in a custom motor coach. He'll take you on a tour of some of the leading Baja wineries, including L. A. Cetto, Monte Xanic, and Chateau Camou. Carefully choose the single bottle you're allowed to take back home.

You'll appreciate the designated driver on your way to a truly unique dining experience at Restaurant Laja. Retreat to the Villa del Valle for some much-earned rest.

DAY 4

An after-breakfast massage at the hotel will prepare you for the drive home. If you have time, goof off at Xploration and grab a lobster roll in Puerto Nuevo on your way north. Get to the border crossing before 3 P.M. on a weekday. If you're crossing on a Sunday, you'll have plenty of time to reflect on your trip as you crawl through traffic back into the United States.

Loreto

DAY 1

Arrive mid-day at Loreto International Airport and transfer to a hotel, bed-and-breakfast, or vacation rental in town. Stroll the *malecón* and plaza at sunset. Mingle with local expats over dinner at the Mita Gourmet or sample the legendary fish tacos at El Rey del Taco.

DAY 2

Rise early to spend the day fishing, kayaking, diving, or touring the islands in the Loreto Bay National Marine Park directly offshore. Then reward yourself with a meal of hearty Argentinean fare at Pachamama and drinks at the second-story, open-air Bar Eclipse.

DAY 3

Visit one of the best-preserved Jesuit missions on the peninsula in the tiny village of San Javier, a 36-kilometer drive southwest of Loreto. Finish the day with a meal at Del Borracho Saloon and Grill.

DAY 4

Take an early morning walk along the waterfront. Browse the shops near the plaza for souvenirs. Take one last dip in the pool, and off you go.

SEASIDE ROMANCE

Weddings, honeymoons, and anniversaries often inspire a quiet retreat. Sunset beach walks, couples' spa treatments, shopping for fine art or jewelry, dinner by candlelight, and movies on the beach are just a few of the ways to celebrate the occasion. With swim-up bars, private soaking tubs, and full-service spas, several resorts along the Los Cabos Corridor excel in creating that intimate setting. Farther afield, bohemian Todos Santos adds a layer of art and culture to the romance.

MOST ROMANTIC RESORTS

- Spacious luxury suites at **Dreams Los Cabos** in the Corridor's Cabo Real development are a favorite for celebrating special occasions.

- Select linens for your bed from a menu when you check in at **Las Ventanas al Paraíso,** then enjoy a private movie showing on the beach at night.

- The remote setting on the Pacific coast and no-kids policy of **Pueblo Bonito Pacifica** appeals to those in search of a quieter Los Cabos experience.

BEST CANDLELIGHT DINNERS

- In the heart of downtown La Paz, **Las Tres Vírgenes** serves creative *bajacaliforniano* cuisine.

- **La Panga Antigua,** in San José del Cabo, offers contemporary Mexican cuisine in an outdoor courtyard setting.

- At the Marquis Los Cabos along the Corridor, **Canto del Mar** seats just 21 guests for an elegant French dinner.

MOST INTIMATE BOUTIQUE HOTELS

- Watch stunning sunsets from the pool or bar at **Posada de las Flores,** on the *malecón* in La Paz.

- Enjoy the natural surroundings of a freshwater lagoon at secluded **Posada la Poza,** in Todos Santos.

- Relax in contemporary European style at **Casa Natalia,** in the heart of downtown San José del Cabo.

BEST BEACHES TO WALK AT SUNSET

- Watch surfers catch their last waves of the day at **Playa Costa Azul,** just outside of San José del Cabo.

- See the sun melt into the Pacific from **Playa Solmar,** which runs along the southwestern edge of the Cape.

- Observe the wildlife in action along the **Estero San José,** just outside San José del Cabo, or at **Playa Las Pocitas,** near Todos Santos.

BEST SPAS

- Enjoy treatment rooms with a view at the **Marquis Los Cabos.**

- Heavenly body wraps and ocean-side massages set the mood at the **Westin Los Cabos,** near San José del Cabo.

- Soak in the indoor steam caves and waterfalls at **Esperanza,** close to Cabo San Lucas.

SHOPAHOLICS, REJOICE

- Browse **contemporary fine art** on display in the galleries of Todos Santos and San José del Cabo.

- Find a **Mexican fire opal** in one of San José's jewelry shops.

- Watch artisans making ceramics at **Ibarra's Pottery** in La Paz.

beachside seating in San José del Cabo

San José del Cabo

DAY 1

Arrive at Los Cabos International Airport (SJD); transfer to a hotel in downtown San José or a resort along the Corridor. Consider El Encanto Suites for modest accommodations or Casa Natalia for something more upscale. A condo at Playa Costa Azul on the outskirts of San José is another good option. If it's Thursday, browse open galleries on the weekly evening Art Walk in downtown San José. Savor the tastes of *alta cocina mexicana* at one of San José's stylish restaurants, such as La Panga Antigua, Tequila Restaurant, or Don Emiliano.

DAY 2

Grab a pastry for breakfast at the French Riviera. Relax with a good novel by the pool. Later, walk or kayak along the Estero San José; snorkel the rock reefs at Playa Chileno or Playa Santa María, looking for green moray eels, spotted eagle rays, and schools of tropical fish; or catch some waves at Playa Costa Azul. Book a sunset horseback riding tour along the beach that fronts the hotel zone in San José del Cabo. In the evening, order a refreshing *michelada* followed by a seafood dinner at an oceanview restaurant along the Corridor, such as Puerta Vieja or Sunset da Mona Lisa. Finish the evening at Morgan's Restaurant and Cellar near the plaza in San José.

DAY 3

Head out for a day of fishing from La Playita or surfing at Playa Costa Azul. Alternatively, you could travel to Cabo San Lucas to go diving. Or browse the many interior design shops in San José. Better yet, sign up for a massage at one of the luxurious spas at the Westin Los Cabos, Marquis Los Cabos, or Esperanza Resort.

Head to Carnitas Los Michoacanos to order *carnitas* by the kilo, or try the stone bowls filled with flank steak and avocado at Guacamaya. Afterward, head to the Tropicana Bar and Grill on Boulevard Mijares for live Cuban-style music.

DAY 4

Last chance to work on a tan by the pool. Stroll Boulevard Mijares one last time to pick up gifts and souvenirs at Sol Dorado or Antigua Los Cabos. Pack your bags and leave in time for lunch at Mariscos Mazatlán II on your way to the airport.

TIJUANA, ROSARITO, AND TECATE

Whether you end up loving it or hating it, northwestern Baja makes a vivid first impression. As a dynamic border zone between Mexico and the United States, the region encompassing Tijuana, Rosarito, and Tecate has a complex, multicultural identity shaped by rapid economic growth, immigration, and the harsh reality of sharing a border with a much wealthier country. The change in scenery as you cross from Alta to Baja California is shocking and depressing. The lush green lawns and newly paved streets of San Diego become dusty roads and shantytowns on the outskirts of Tijuana, with signs of industrial pollution all around. Downtown Tijuana has modern skyscrapers, glitzy shopping malls, and wealthy residential neighborhoods, but you have to walk or drive through the less attractive parts of the city to get to them.

As the gateway to Baja California, Tijuana lures hundreds of thousands of visitors a day to cross the border and spend their dollars. They come to shop, eat, and party. Some go home that day, others stay the weekend, and a few simply pass through on their way to coastal attractions farther south. Caesar salad, Tecate beer, Nortec music, and trendsetting nightclubs all are part of the experience.

Fewer than 80 kilometers east of the metropolis of Tijuana, laid-back Tecate is the oldest border town in Baja and maintains the feel of an authentic Mexican community.

South along the coast, beachside Rosarito is a favored weekend getaway for San Diego and

HIGHLIGHTS

PACIFIC OCEAN

UNITED STATES

San Diego

Zona Río
Tijuana

Rosarito Beach

Rosarito

Tecate

Baja Studios

Tecate Brewery

Parque Hidalgo

Ensenada

MEXICO

Punta Banda

0   20 mi

0   20 km

Puerto San Isidro

PACIFIC OCEAN

◖ **Zona Río:** The trendsetting clubs in Tijuana's upscale Zona Río pack thousands of people onto their dance floors every night (page 32).

◖ **Rosarito Beach:** A string of mega-clubs along Rosarito Beach provide 24/7 entertainment for college students from the United States during the annual spring break holiday (page 43).

◖ **Baja Studios:** The Hollywood theme park Xploration allows visitors to go behind the scenes of a working movie house to learn how to produce a blockbuster film (page 47).

◖ **Parque Hidalgo:** Food and festivities center around Tecate's shady plaza, making it a suitable launch point for a northern Baja adventure (page 51).

◖ **Tecate Brewery:** While in Tecate, tour the plant that produces Baja's most popular brew. Located on the site of the original keg brewery, today's operation uses modern, high-tech equipment to produce 40 million liters per month (page 52).

LOOK FOR ◖ TO FIND RECOMMENDED SIGHTS, ACTIVITIES, DINING, AND LODGING.

Los Angeles residents, except during March and April, when spring breakers from across the western United States come to town.

The news of gruesome murders, kidnappings, and military interventions in all three of these cities in 2008 and 2009 has deterred many would-be travelers from visiting the border. Day-trippers, partiers, eco-tourists, and seasonal snowbirds decided to go elsewhere for the winter 2008 and 2009 seasons. Faced with extremely low demand, many outfitters have had to cancel longstanding trips to the region. It's a cycle that's going to be difficult to reverse.

But for every traveler who has decided Northern Baja is too risky, there are others who are following through on their plans. And most

of them are getting through the border region trouble-free. The violence is real, and it's scary, but it's not the whole story.

PLANNING YOUR TIME

Many travelers prefer to limit time in the border region in order to maximize time at Southern Baja destinations; however, Tijuana, Rosarito, and Tecate each have their own appeal. You might spend a day, a weekend, or, in the case of Rosarito, a whole week enjoying the culture and adjusting to the change of pace.

A popular weekend itinerary involves crossing from San Diego into Tijuana, heading south to Rosarito and Ensenada, then northeast via Mexico 3 and the Ruta del Vino (Wine Route) to exit at Tecate.

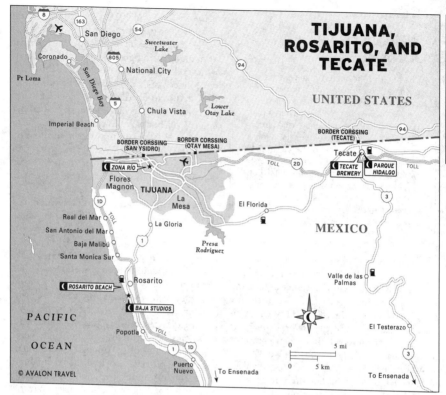

If you're heading all the way to Baja California Sur, you can cover the length of Baja California (Norte) from Tijuana to Guerrero Negro in one long day, or, more comfortably, with a stopover in San Quintín or El Rosario.

Northwestern Baja enjoys a dry and comfortable climate year-round, much like Southern California. The beaches between Rosarito and Ensenada are warmest and most crowded July–September. Winter months tend to be cold and cloudy.

Tijuana and Vicinity

Straddling the Río Tijuana, now a canal, which empties into the Pacific Ocean, Tijuana encompasses a population of around 2.5 million (estimates range from 1.6 million to 3.5 million). Its urban sprawl covers deep canyons, hills, and plateaus in the northwest corner of Mexico. Most visitors come for the shopping, dining, and clubbing, but the city also draws people who want to drink underage, buy prescription medications over the counter, and visit its legal red-light district.

HISTORY

It may be hard to imagine today, but Tijuana wasn't always a border town. The Treaty of Hidalgo, signed in 1848, ceded Alta California

WHAT'S IN A NAME?

The origin of the name Tijuana is a matter of some dispute. In pre-Hispanic times, the Yumano tribes that lived here called the valley Ti-wan (Near the Sea), a name that the Spanish later changed to Tijuan on their early maps of the peninsula. A local ranch that dates back to the early 19th century called itself Rancho Tia Juana (Aunt Jane), which sounded similar but was easier to pronounce. Americans living in California adopted this pronunciation, and stuck to it, long after the city's name was officially decided as Tijuana.

between 1950 and 1970. An era of industrial development fueled the next wave of growth, with international companies opening hundreds of manufacturing plants called maquiladoras, which take advantage of cheaper labor costs to produce goods for export. Without the infrastructure to handle such explosive growth, Tijuana faced severe housing shortages and pollution. Collaboration between the United States and Mexico led to improvements through the end of the 20th century, and today, the standard of living is much improved—to the point where tens of thousands of U.S. nationals have made Tijuana their permanent residence.

Present-day Tijuana is a multicultural, cosmopolitan city facing a host of socio-economic challenges. Its dozens of universities draw students from all over the country. As the fourth-largest city in Mexico (after Mexico City, Guadalajara, and Monterrey), it also has the busiest international border crossing in the world, through which 40 million people pass each year. Tijuana has one of the highest income per capita of any city in the country, but as a border zone, it also must cope with a sizable immigrant population (legal and illegal, foreign and national), widespread poverty, and deep-rooted organized crime. In 2008, the city reported more than 800 murders, or 56.8 per 100,000 people, a rate that is lower than the comparable figure for several U.S. cities, but more than twice the number reported for 2007.

At its heart, multicultural, cosmopolitan Tijuana remains a young city searching to find its place in the world. Even as it struggles to cope with systemic crime and poverty, this urban community finds itself at the forefront of global trends in music and art. If it can find a way to harness and nurture that creative, edgy spirit, while at the same time restoring law and order, Tijuana could re-emerge as an economic and cultural leader in the region.

to the United States and commenced Tijuana's rapid transformation from an insignificant cattle ranching settlement to a center of tourism, industry, and immigration. It was officially founded as Tijuana in 1889. Many U.S. citizens first heard of the city in 1911, one year after the Mexican Revolution, when a group of revolutionaries briefly occupied the town.

When the Panama-California fair took place in San Deigo in 1916, Tijuana put itself on the global tourism map, drawing a number of attendees over to the border for a concurrent Traditional Mexican Fair. With its lineup of arts and crafts, local foods, hot springs, horse racing, and boxing matches, the city made a lasting impression.

The U.S. Prohibition era brought foreigners over the border in greater numbers to drink and gamble. In 1928, the historic Agua Caliente hotel, casino, and spa opened to entertain elite Hollywood types, and the resort quickly became an icon of the growing city. The party lasted until 1935 when then-President Cárdenas outlawed gambling and closed Mexico's casinos, causing a severe recession.

By this point, however, the city was primed for growth through tourism and domestic immigration, and its population tripled from 1940 to 1950, from approximately 20,000 to more than 60,000, then exploded by 600 percent

SIGHTS
◖ Zona Río

Officially called the Zona Urbana Río Tijuana, this part of the city borders the Tijuana River/Canal across from the *palacio municipal*. The

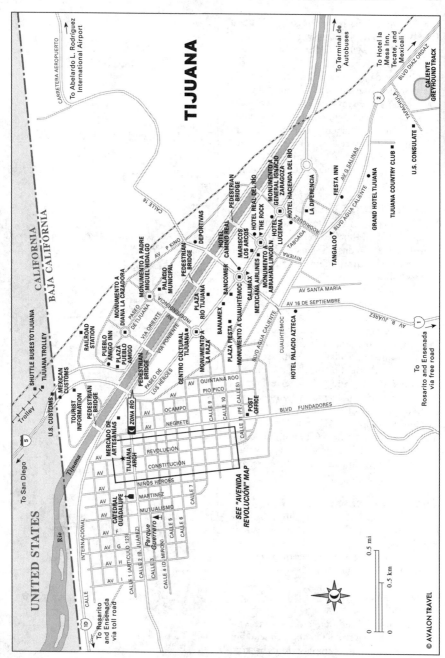

© AVALON TRAVEL

heart of the district is the **Plaza Río Tijuana** (Paseo de los Héroes btw Av. Independencia/Blvd. Cuahutémoc), with dozens of shops and restaurants, several hotels, and some of the city's hottest dance clubs. In fact, the Zona Río boasts some of the largest and liveliest clubs in the world. A day trip here might encompass bargain shopping, a gourmet dinner and musical performance, and a night of drinking and dancing until the wee hours of the morning.

The Tijuana Cultural Center is a block away from the Plaza Réo Tijuana, across Avenida Independencia.

Centro Cultural Tijuana

Well-known Mexican architects Pedro Ramírez Vásquez and Manuel Rosen Morrison designed Tijuana's industrial-looking landmark, the Centro Cultural Tijuana (Paseo de los Héroes and Av. Independencia, tel. 664/684-1111, www.cecut.gob.mx), with a giant, white spherical planetarium (now an IMAX theater). The government-sponsored complex opened in 1982 with the goals of strengthening national identity in Northern Baja and promoting cultural tourism. Today, its 1,000-seat performing-arts theater hosts the Baja California Orchestra (OBC) and other performances (with some outdoor events in summer), and the **Museo de las Californias,** with historical, anthropological, and archaeological exhibits (Tues.–Fri. 10 A.M.–6:30 P.M., Sat.–Sun. 10 A.M.–4 P.M., US$2). The center also has a café, bookstore, and shops. Tickets are sold daily 10 A.M.–6 P.M.

Avenida Revolución

More shopping, dining, and nightlife are to be found along an eight-block stretch of Avenida Revolución (La Revo, in San Diego–speak), where the clubs are oriented toward a younger, Southern California crowd.

Tijuana Arch and Monumental Clock

This controversial addition to the skyline is located at Avenida Revolución and Primera, but it is visible from most of the city. To its backers,

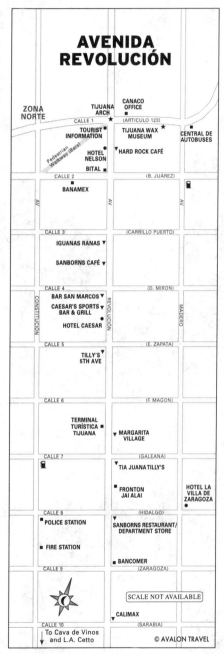

AVENIDA REVOLUCIÓN

© AVALON TRAVEL

it's the symbolic gateway to Baja, but to most locals it's a visual hangover from the Y2K celebration. Either way, it's a good landmark to meet your friends after a long night in TJ.

SPORTS AND RECREATION
Golf
Founded in 1927 as part of the Agua Caliente Club complex, the **Club Campestre Tijuana,** or Tijuana Country Club (Blvd. Agua Caliente, tel. 664/681-7855, U.S. tel. 888/217-1165, www.tijuanacountryclub.com), off Boulevard Agua Caliente has a 6,800-yard, par-72, 18-hole course. The Mexican Open is played here on occasion. Greens fees are US$18–45. The club has a driving range and pro shop and offers golf lessons.

Baseball
Los Potros (The Colts, www.potrosdetijuana.com, US$10) play competitors in the Mexican-Pacific League as well as visiting teams from the United States and Central America. The 15,000-seat **Estadio de los Potros** (tel. 664/625-1056) is located off Boulevard Los Insurgentes near the Otay-Mesa border crossing. The season runs from the end of the American World Series through late January. Tickets often sell out, and parking is a challenge, so consider taking a cab.

ENTERTAINMENT AND EVENTS
There are myriad ways to spend an evening out in Tijuana, from professional sporting events and cultural performances to a night of drinking and clubbing.

Bullfighting
Traditional bullfights, though an increasingly controversial pastime, take place in the **Plaza de Toros Monumental** at the beach (La Playas de Tijuana, tel. 664/680-1808, www.plaza-monumental.com, US$10–50), off the toll road to Ensenada.

Dance Clubs
Most of Tijuana's top dance clubs enforce a dress code of no jeans or sneakers, and some insist on even more formal attire. The clubs begin to fill up around midnight and often stay open until dawn. The later the hour, the louder the music.

Trendy and formal, **Tangaloo** (Monterrey 3215, tel. 664/681-8091, www.tangaloo.com.mx), off Boulevard Agua Caliente, has taken over from Baby Rock as the hottest place to see and be seen. Dress accordingly, and pick a back-up option, as it may be impossible to get in. **Club Balak** (Plaza Pueblo Amigo, Vía Oriente, tel. 664/682-9222, plays Nortec DJ music, a fusion of classic *norteña* and techno music. **The Rock** (formerly Baby Rock, Av. Diego Rivera 1482, tel. 664/622-3800, daily until dawn) has been a favorite for many years for its laser-light shows and attentive staff.

A younger crowd frequents the clubs along Avenida Revolución—known locally as La Revo. Choices include **Club Animale** (Calle 3 and Av. Revolución), **Iguanas Ranas** (Calle 3 and Av. Revolución), **Tilly's** (Calle 7A and Av. Revolución, tel. 664/685-1612, weekends till 2 A.M.), and **Margarita Village** (Av. Revolución 702 and 1020, tel. 664/685-3862).

Mike's Disco (Av. Revolución 122, tel. 664/685-3534, nightly till 5 A.M.), on the east side of Revolución at Calle 6, is a gay and lesbian dance club with drag shows on weekends. On nearby Calle 7, **Los Equipales** (Calle 7/Galeana 8236 at Av. Revolución, tel. 664/688-3006) is similar.

Bars
If dance music isn't your thing, Avenida Revolución has lots of bars—some historic, some divey, some fancy. Mariachi bands do their rounds, and the scene is usually a mix of locals, expats, and out-of-towners. **Bar San Marcos** (Calle 5 at Avenida Revolución, tel. 664/688-2794), adjoining Caesar's Sports Bar & Grill, has survived since its heyday in the 1950s. The Nortec Collective has composed a song about the **El Dandy Del Sur** (Calle 6 and Av. Revolución, tel. 664/688-0052), where the drinks keep flowing until dawn.

Large and loud, **La Cantina de los Remedios** (Av. Diego Riviera 2476, tel. 664/634-3087) in the Zona Río, is a chain with similar res-taurant/bars in several cities on the mainland. Complimentary valet parking is a plus.

Tijuana's **Zona Norte,** from Calle 1 down-town north almost to the border, is the city's red-light district; it's best to avoid this area, especially at night.

SHOPPING

The majority of Tijuana visitors come to shop in the free trade zone (up to US$400). You'll find a long list of goods for sale, from arts and crafts souvenirs and hand-embroidered dresses to name-brand apparel and discount prescription drugs. You can pay with U.S. dollars anywhere in the city; some stores will also accept credit cards. Most of the stores along Avenida Revolución have someone who speaks English on staff.

Avenida Revolución between Calle 2 and Calle 9 has a concentration of upscale bou-tiques. For example, **Tolan** (Av. Revolución 1111 at Calle 7, tel. 664/688-3637) carries a nice selection of glassware, pottery, and other high-end arts and crafts. For a wider selec-tion of pottery at lower prices than the bou-tiques, head to the **Mercado de Artesanías** (Av. Ocampo and Calle 2). Across from the Tijuana Cultural Center at Paseo de los Héroes and Avenida Independencia, **Mercado Hidalgo** is a more traditional farmers market with fresh produce and other foods.

Plaza Río Tijuana (Paseo de los Héroes btw Via Poniente/Blvd. Cuauhtémoc, www. plazariotijuana.com.mx) in the Zona Río, is a modern shopping mall with more than 100 businesses. The main department stores here include Comercial Mexicana, Dax, Solo Un Precio, and Dorian's. You can buy everything from a pair of glasses to jewelry and fine art.

A number of tile and furniture stores line Boulevard Agua Caliente between Avenida Revolución and the Caliente Greyhound Track. You can buy high-quality pieces made of wood or wrought iron at much lower prices than you'd pay in the United States or Canada. Just be sure to check the latest U.S. Customs regulations before filling up your car.

San Diego residents frequent **Sanborns** de-partment store (Av. Revolución 1102 at Calle 8, tel. 664/688-1433, www.sanborns.com/mx) for English-language books, arts and crafts, medi-cations, and liquor.

Tijuanenses buy their shoes, liquor, medica-tions, and other day-to-day items on Avenida Constitución, one block west of Avenida Revolución. Prices are accordingly lower.

For last-minute souvenirs, or to pass the time at the border, browse the kitschy crafts in the indoor/outdoor **Plaza Viva Tijuana** (Av. Frontera and Av. de la Amistad), just before the border gate.

ACCOMMODATIONS

The hotel business in Tijuana is not well devel-oped for a city of its size because the vast ma-jority of visitors do not spend the night. The nicer places cater to business travelers from elsewhere in Mexico and overseas.

Under US$50

Safe and clean budget hotels are hard to find in downtown Tijuana. If you need to keep costs down, consider staying at the **Hostal Barnes** (Calle Relampago 1230, Seccion Dorado, no tel.), located outside of the downtown area at Playas Tijuana. It offers safe accommodations for US$10–15 per person. Private one- or two-bed rooms instead of dorm-style makes it a steal, but you'd have to bus or cab to La Revolución. If you can hold out for Ensenada, you can get nicer accommodations for a few bucks more.

In town, there are a couple of options for US$25 a night if all you need is a place to crash and shower after a night of partying on La Revo. **Hotel Lafayette** (Av. Revolución btw Calles 3/4, tel. 664/685-3940) is right in the center of the ac-tion, so you won't have to walk far to get home. But for the same price, **Catalina Hotel** (Calle 5 #2039 at Madero, tel. 664/685-9748) gets you off the main drag. Otherwise, it's a big jump up in cost to the lower-end business hotels.

US$50-100

Well-worn and centrally located **Hotel Nelson** (Av. Revolución 151, tel. 664/685-4302, fax

664/685-4304, US$50) has 92 clean, heated rooms with satellite TV and phones. Pack your earplugs. **Motel León** (Calle 7/Galeana 1937, west of Revolución, tel. 664/685-6320, US$90–110) offers 70 clean rooms with free, secure parking (though limited availability). **Hotel Palacio Azteca** (Av. 16 de Septiembre/Blvd. Cuauhtémoc Sur 213, off Blvd. Agua Caliente, tel. 664/681-8100, toll-free U.S. tel. 888/901-372, www.hotelpalacioazteca.com, US$80) provides above-average accommodations with large TVs, as well as heat and air-conditioning. Guests may use laundry facilities, as well as a swimming pool and parking lot.

Renovated in 2008, **Hotel Real del Río** (Calle J. M. Velazco 1409, tel. 664/634-3100, www.realdelrio.com, US$75) is a good value for business travelers, though street noise can be a nuisance.

C **Hotel Hacienda del Río** (Blvd. Sánchez Taboada 10606, tel. 664/684-8644, U.S. tel. 800/303-2684, www.bajainn.com, US$69) is reliable and modern business-oriented establishment with its own restaurant/bar, heated pool, fitness center, and business center. Choose from 130 large rooms and suites, which feature satellite TV, Internet access, and climate control. Ask for rooms at the back of the hotel facing the pool, since the front rooms are at ground level and face the road.

If you're driving and want to stay within walking distance of La Revolución, try the **Hotel La Villa de Zaragoza** (Av. Madero 1120 btw Calles 7/8, tel. 664/685-1832, www.hotellavilla.biz, US$60). Rooms are hit or miss, but your best bet is to ask for one of the garden rooms. Amenities include heat/air-conditioning, TVs, phones, parking, and laundry. Nonsmoking and accessible rooms are available. The security guards do a good job, but the front desk staff can be surly.

US$100-150

Your best choice in this price range is located in the Zona Río: C **Hotel Lucerna** (Av. Paseo de los Héroes 10902, tel. 664/633-3900, U.S./Canada tel. 800/582-3762, www.hotel-lucerna.

com.mx, US$120) has all of the amenities one would expect from a large, international business hotel: restaurants, pools, gardens, fitness center, and car rental desk. Ask for a room in the annex if one is available.

The **Grand Hotel Tijuana** (Blvd. Agua Caliente 4500, tel. 664/681-7000, U.S./Canada tel. 800/472-6385, www.grandhoteltij.com.mx, US$120) was one of Tijuana's first skyscrapers. With 22 floors and more than 400 rooms, it is a full-service resort, but the walls are thin and you can easily hear what your neighbor is watching on TV. The shopping area here has a ghost-town feel.

US$150-250

Business travelers and well-off weekenders like the **Hotel Camino Real** (Paseo de los Héroes 10305 and Cuauhtémoc, tel. 664/633-4000, U.S. tel. 800/722-6466, www.caminoreal.com, US$150) chain for its luxury amenities, such as marble baths and high-end toiletries; however, experiences at this property have been inconsistent in recent years. The rooms are underwhelming, but the staff generally makes up for it with top-tier service. Maria Bonita, its relatively new restaurant specializing in *alta cocina mexicana,* is open Monday–Saturday 1 P.M.–1 A.M. and Sunday 1–5 P.M.

FOOD

Aside from its shopping, bars, and nightlife, Tijuana is a culinary destination in its own right, with everything from cheap eats to haute cuisine.

Avenida Revolución and Vicinity

Caesar salad was invented in Tijuana by Italian-Mexican brothers Alex and Caesar Cardini in 1924. C **Caesar's Sports Bar & Grill** (Calle 5 at Avenida Revolución, tel. 664/685-1664, daily for lunch and dinner, mains US$10–15), located next to the Caesar Hotel, still carries on the tradition. A server prepares the salad at your table, and the key ingredient is coddled eggs, instead of raw.

The **Sanborns** department store chain has several of its popular *cafeterías* around town

(Av. Revolución at Calle 8, Av. Revolución btw Calles 3/4, Av. Revolución 737, and Plaza Río, tel. 664/668-1462, daily for breakfast, lunch, and dinner, mains US$10–15). The food is good, and so are the prices.

In business since 1947 under a couple different names, **Tia Juana Tilly's** (Calle 7 at Av. Revolución, tel. 664/685-6024, reservations tel. 664/685-1213, www.tiajuanatillys.com.mx, daily noon–midnight, Fri. and Sat. until 3 A.M., mains US$15 and up) is popular with locals and San Diego folks for Mexican dinners, as well as steaks and seafood. The friendly staff makes visitors feel welcome.

Zona Río

If you only have time for one "nice" dinner in Tijuana, call **La Diferencia** (Blvd. Sanchez Taboada 10611, Rio Tijuana, tel. 664/634-3346, www.ladiferencia.com.mx, Mon.–Thurs. noon–10:30 P.M., Fri.–Sat. noon–midnight, Sun. noon–8 P.M., US$10–23) for a reservation. The seasonally available Chile en Nogada or the duck with hibiscus flower *(jamaica)* sauce are standouts on an all-around excellent menu. Attentive service and a contemporary setting make the meal.

For truly authentic Mexican cuisine, **La Casa de Mole Poblano** (Blvd. Paseo de los Héroes 1501, tel. 664/634-6920, daily 10 A.M.–11 P.M., mains under US$10) matches its chili-chocolate, chili-almond, and sesame-seed sauces with a variety of meat and poultry. The high ceilings, ivy, and mariachi bands create an upbeat and family-friendly environment popular with locals.

A highlight on the menu at **Mariscos Los Arcos** (Blvd. Sánchez Taboada at Diego Rivera, tel. 664/686-4757, daily 8 A.M.–10 P.M., Thurs.–Sat. till midnight) is Mazatlán-style *pescado zarandeado*—a whole fish rubbed in herbs and spices, then seared and broiled.

Vips Restaurant Cafetería (Blvd. Sánchez Taboada 10750, tel. 664/634-6196, daily 7 A.M.–10 P.M., mains under US$10) is part of a large coffee-shop chain, and it offers a long list of breakfast and lunch fare, including Mexican plates. The locals like it, and it's affordable.

Agua Caliente

Check the specials menu on the blackboard on your way in at **La Querencia** (Escuadron 201 No. 3110 Sanchez Taboada at Blvd. Salinas, tel. 664/972-9940, www.laquerenciatj.com, mains US$10–25). It's easy to get distracted by the strange combination of safari decor and industrial chic. The lamb chops are well prepared and not oversauced. Just make sure your cab driver doesn't mistake it for the well-known La Diferencia.

Carnitas Uruapán (Blvd. Díaz Ordaz 550 opposite Plaza Patria, tel. 664/681-6181, daily 7 A.M.–5 A.M., mains US$10–15, cash only) sells housemade carnitas by the kilo for family-style dining. Sides include rice, beans, salsa, and guacamole.

Groceries

The two main grocery store chains in Tijuana are **Calimax** (Paseo de los Héroes, east of Blvd. Cuauhtémoc) and **Gigante** (Blvd. Aqua Caliente directly across from the greyhound racetrack or Juárez btw Calles 2/3). The Walmart-like **Ley** (Plaza Pueblo Amigo) has just about everything a traveler could need.

INFORMATION AND SERVICES
Tourist Assistance

The **Tourist Information Booth** (Av. Revolución at Calle 1, tel. 664/688-0555, Mon.–Fri. 8 A.M.–8 P.M., Sat.–Sun. 10 A.M.–3 P.M.) has a bilingual staff and the usual collection of maps and brochures covering Northern Baja. Additional booths are at the border crossing and the airport. The **Tijuana Convention and Visitors Bureau** (COTUCO, main office Paseo de los Héroes 9365-201, Zona Río, tel. 664/684-0537 or 664/684-0538, www.tijuanaonline.org. daily 9 A.M.–6 P.M.) has Visitor Information Centers set up at the pedestrian border crossing, the airport, and on Avenida Revolución between Calles 3/4. The privately run **Tijuana Tourism Board** (Blvd. Agua Caliente 4558-1108, tel. 664/686-1103, toll-free U.S./Canada tel. 888/775-2417, www.seetijuana.com) represents a group of local businesses.

The **Cámara Nacional de Comercio, Servicios y Turismo de Tijuana** (CANACO, Av. Revolución at Calle 1, tel. 664/684-0537, www.canacotijuana.com, Mon.–Fri. 9 A.M.–7 P.M.) has tourist information, mailing supplies, restrooms, and a public telephone.

For any questions that these organizations cannot answer, or for legal assistance, contact the **State Secretary of Tourism** (SECTUR, Plaza Patria, 3rd floor, Blvd. Díaz Ordaz, tel. 664/688-0555).

Money

You can use U.S. dollars just about everywhere in Tijuana, except for bus fare. The city has numerous ATMs, including a Banamex southeast of Plaza Fiesta and Plaza Zapato on Paseo de los Héroes. For currency exchange, a number of *casas de cambio* are set up along the pedestrian path from the border.

Post and Telephone

Tijuana's main post office (Calle 11 at Av. Negrete) is open Monday–Friday 8 A.M.–7 P.M.

Internet Access

Many hotels and coffee shops now have wireless Internet service for their patrons. Look along the northern end of Avenida Revolución if you need an Internet café.

Immigration and Customs

The Tijuana/San Ysidro border crossing processes all immigration and customs paperwork (daily 24/7)

Foreign Consulates

Visit the **U.S. Consulate** (Tapachula 96, Col. Hipódromo, tel. 664/622-7400, Mon.–Fri. 8 A.M.–5 P.M., closed U.S. and Mexican holidays) for help with lost or expired U.S. passports or visa issues. Other consulates in town include: **Canada** (Germán Gedovius 10411-101, Condominio del Parque, Zona Río, tel. 664/684-0461, Mon.–Fri. 9 A.M.–1 P.M.); **France** (Av. Revolución 1651, 3rd floor, tel. 664/681-3133, btdmex@telnor.net); **Germany**

TIJUANA PHONE NUMBERS

- Tijuana area code: 664
- Fire Department: 068
- General Hospital: 684-0922
- Green Angels: 624-3479
- Highway Patrol: 682-5285
- Immigration: 682-3439
- Police: 060
- Red Cross: 066
- State Police: 685-4444
- State Tourism Office: 688-0555
- Tourist Assistance: 078

(Cantera 400, Building 304, tel. 664/680-2512); and **United Kingdom** (Blvd. Salinas 1500, Col. Aviación, La Mesa, tel. 664/686-5320, fax 664/681-8402).

Green Angels

Mexico's Green Angels automotive emergency assistance service maintains headquarters at the Otay Mesa border crossing (Edificio Federal Garita, tel. 664/624-3479).

GETTING THERE
By Air

Tijuana has an international airport in Mesa de Otay, about 10 kilometers northeast of downtown: **Abelardo L. Rodríguez International Airport** (TIJ, tel. 664/607-8200, http://tijuana.aeropuertosgap.com.mx). Several international and discount airlines offer service to/from Tijuana, including:

- **Aeroméxico** (Plaza Río Tijuana 12-A1, Paseo de los Héroes, tel. 664/638-8444 or 800/021-4010, toll-free U.S. tel. 800/237-6639, www.aeromexico.com
- **Mexicana** (Edificio Fontana, Diego Rivera

UNITED STATES-MEXICO BORDER CROSSINGS

Crossing	Hours
Calexico (Mexicali) East	6 A.M.-midnight
Calexico (Mexicali) West	24 hrs/day
Los Algodones	6 A.M.-10 P.M.
Otay Mesa (Tijuana)	24 hrs/day
San Ysidro (Tijuana)	24 hrs/day
Tecate	5 A.M.-11 P.M.

Visit the U.S. Customs Border Protection website at http://apps.cbp.gov/bwt/index.asp to check border wait times before you cross.

1511 at Av. Paseo de los Héroes, tel. 664/634-6566, airport tel. 664/682-4184 or 800/509-8960, toll-free U.S./Canada tel. 800/531-7921)

- **Aero California** (Plaza Río Tijuana C-20, Paseo de los Héroes, tel. 664/684-2876, toll-free U.S. tel. 800/237-6225)

- Monterrey-based **Aviacsa** (Blvd. Sánchez Taboada 4499, Plaza Guadalupe 6, tel. 664/622-5024, airport tel. 664/683-8202 or 800/711-6733, toll-free U.S. tel. 888/528-4227, www.aviacsa.com)

- **Volaris** (www.volaris.com.mx) is one of a handful of low-cost carriers that fly in and out of Tijuana—an increasingly appealing way to mitigate the rising cost of airfare from LAX. It opened for business in 2006, and the best part about flying with this airline is that it runs a shuttle from the San Diego train station to the Tijuana airport (US$15), so travelers don't have to deal with driving themselves through the busy streets of Tijuana. From the shuttle pickup, it's a 30-minute drive to the airport, including a short stop at the border. The planes are new, and most of your fellow passengers will be gringos in the know. This is a great way to

get to La Paz and Los Cabos in Baja California Sur.

- The airport has food, books, and gift shops, plus an ATM and parking garage.

- TIJ is an official port of entry for foreign pilots. Check with **Baja Bush Pilots** (www.bajabushpilots.com) for current information.

- **Airport Transportation:** Taxi service between the airport and any destination within the city limits costs US$12 for up to five passengers, and slightly less to the Central de Autobuses. Public buses signed "Centro" offer frequent connections to the downtown area (US$0.60 pp).

By Bus

Tijuana's **Central de Autobuses de Tijuana** is located five kilometers east of the city on Lázaro Cárdenas at Boulevard Arroyo Alamar (tel. 664/621-2982). It has a restaurant, *lonchería,* telephone service, immigration office, and currency exchange. **Transportes Norte de Sonora** (TNS) and **Autotransportes de Baja California** (ABC, tel. 664/621-2668, www.abc.com.mx) offer connections east to Mexicali

(US$9–12, nine buses/day) and the Mexican mainland. **Transportes de Pacífico** and **Chihuahuenses** offer more frequent connections to destinations on the mainland.

ABC's (tel. 664/621-2668, www.abc.com.mx) *ejecutivo* buses depart for Ensenada every half-hour 6 A.M.–midnight from the second Central de Autobuses (Av. Madero and Calle 1). Regular buses (no air-conditioning) leave for Ensenada from **Plaza Viva** at the border. ABC offers both *ejecutivo* and regular bus service to San Felipe as well.

Autotransportes Aguila offers intercity service to points south, including El Rosario, Santa Rosalía, and La Paz.

Greyhound (toll-free U.S. tel. 800/231-2222) buses from San Diego and Los Angeles arrive at the Tres Estrellas de Oro terminal (Av. México and Av. Madero, tel. 664/688-0082), which also has frequent ABC buses to Tecate.

Mexicoach out of San Ysidro has its own station at the Terminal Turística Tijuana (Av. Revolución btw Calles 6/7).

By Taxi

Taxi service from the border to downtown is about US$5 (flat rate); to Rosarito US$35 (one-way); to Ensenada US$100.

By Car

Most visitors heading to Tijuana by car cross at San Ysidro. You don't need a permit for your vehicle unless you plan to continue on to the mainland. You do need a validated tourist permit if you plan to go south of Maneadero or stay longer than 72 hours anywhere on the peninsula. A Mexican auto insurance policy is essential.

On Foot

A popular way to get to Tijuana from Southern California is to park at San Ysidro and walk across the border. The route is well marked and it takes about 15–20 minutes to get to Avenida Revolución this way. If you don't want to drive to the border, you can take the **Tijuana Trolley** (www.sdmts.com, daily 5 A.M.–12:40 A.M., US$2.50) from San Diego instead.

GETTING AROUND
By Bus

Tijuana has a complex bus system that can be useful for budget travelers or anyone who'd rather not have to negotiate with a taxi driver. As with other cities in Baja, the end destination of the bus is displayed in the windshield. You need pesos for the fare (around US$0.50). Walk along Avenida Constitución to find buses arriving and departing from the downtown area.

By Taxi

Taxi rides within the downtown area should cost less than US$5, and under US$15 to the airport or Central de Autobuses. You can pay in U.S. dollars. The yellow taxis that shuttle pedestrians from the border to downtown are a special breed. Drivers often ask more than the going rate of US$8, and they often get kickbacks from certain businesses downtown, so they may try to discourage you from going to the place you request. To avoid this hassle, consider taking a shuttle bus from the Tijuana Trolley terminal in San Ysidro to Avenida Revolución (US$1 pp).

Route taxis (*taxis de ruta*) are similar to buses, except the vehicles are station wagons that can hold up to 12 passengers and they stop wherever someone flags them down, which makes for more flexible transportation. Rates are slightly higher than the going bus fare.

By Car
RENTAL CARS

You can rent from any of several international chains, including Avis, Budget, Central, Dollar, Hertz, and National. Rates are lower here than in neighboring Ensenada or Mexicali. Reserve ahead, since fleets are small. When you arrive at the counter, you'll need to give a major credit card (not a debit card) as a deposit on the rental.

DRIVING

Traffic in Tijuana is heavy, though not insurmountable. Parking is another challenge. If you're used to navigating urban environments in the United States, you can probably figure it out here. Street parking is difficult along Avenida Revolución, but there are several pay lots open 24/7 for US$5 per day.

LEAVING TIJUANA
To the United States
To return to San Ysidro and Southern California, head north on Avenida Revolución and follow signs to San Diego. Avenida Padre Kino, north of the downtown area, is an alternative when traffic is heaviest. It connects you to the east lanes of the border crossing, which tend to be less crowded.

South to Rosarito and Ensenada
The 100-kilometer route from Tijuana to Ensenada is easy to follow. Most travelers these days take the four-lane toll road (cuota), Mexico 1-D, south, but you can also choose the two-lane libre (free road), which is the original Mexico 1. The toll road hugs the coast more closely, but offers fewer opportunities for stops.

To get on the toll road from downtown Tijuana, get on Calle 3 heading west and look for signs to Ensenada; traffic may crawl until the toll-road entrance near Playas de Tijuana. There are three tolls (casetas de cobro, US$2–3 each for regular passenger vehicles) along the way. You can pay in dollars or pesos, and your change may come in either currency depending on what the toll collector has on hand.

If you can manage to find it from downtown Tijuana, the libre follows an inland route at first and meets the coast at Rosarito. It then parallels the shore until La Misión, when it heads into the mountains again. Access to the free road is not well marked downtown. Drive south along Avenida Revolución until it joins Boulevard Agua Caliente and watch for a sign that says A Rosarito (To Rosarito) and points right. Pass the Calimax store on the right and take the next right turn onto Boulevard Cuauhtémoc, which leads eventually to Mexico 1.

East to Tecate and Mexicali
If you want to travel east on the libre, take Boulevard Agua Caliente southeast. It will turn into Boulevard Díaz Ordaz and then Mexico 2. If you want to take the toll road to Tecate, follow the signs for the airport, not the signs for Tecate, which direct you toward the free road.

ISLAS LOS CORONADOS
A group of islands called Los Coronados lie within sight of shore 11 kilometers west of San Antonio de Mar, which is 12 kilometers south of Tijuana. The islands have a colorful past that includes pirates, rum-running, and a Prohibition-era casino known as the Coronado Islands Yacht Club. Steep terrain makes the islands impractical for habitation, but the Mexican navy maintains an outpost on one of them.

Geography and Natural History
The islands are the peaks of a submerged mountain range. The southernmost island is the largest at three kilometers long and 204 meters high. The northern island, Coronado del Norte, is one kilometer long and 142 meters high. The two islands in the middle are little more than rocky outcroppings. Since no one is allowed to land on the islands, they are popular nesting sites for brown pelicans and more 160 other species of birds. There is a large sea lion colony on the west side of Coronado del Norte.

Fishing and Diving
From April–October, yellowtail fishing is excellent around the islands. There are rock cod, bonito, calicos, and halibut.

Los Coronados offers good visibility for diving and playful sea lions. There aren't many large fish, but there are plentiful moray eels and schooling small fish. The main sites are the Lobster Shack, off the northeastern coast of Coronado del Norte, and the Keyhole archway at the south end of the same island. No regular dive boats frequent the islands, but San Diego–based **Horizon Charters** (U.S. tel. 858/277-7823, www.horizoncharters.com) will run a charter trip.

Rosarito and Vicinity

Once a quiet ranching community, Rosarito (pop. 73,000) has become something of a mini Las Vegas, only without the casinos. Development began in the 1920s with the opening of El Rosario Resort and Country Club, and reached a feverish pitch in the 1990s, when Fox Studios came to town. Rosarito's fate as a party town was sealed when the Hotel Festival Plaza built a huge entertainment complex right on the waterfront. The town's greatest appeal today—as then—is its long, sandy beach, which the high-rise hotels and luxury condos are slowly crowding out.

Until 1995, Rosarito belonged to the *municipio* (county) of Tijuana, and played a major role in funding the larger city's annual budget. Rosarito residents lobbied for 15 years to create their own *municipio,* so they could use the city's relatively high income to develop its own infrastructure and services rather than supporting Tijuana.

Tourism drives Rosarito's economy today, but like Tijuana and Tecate, the town has been severely affected by the wave of drug-related violence sweeping through northwestern Baja. To their credit, local authorities have taken steps to improve security, but many longtime Rosarito fans are staying away temporarily because it just doesn't seem worth the risk of being in the wrong place at the wrong time.

Many first-time visitors to Rosarito return home disappointed in the overall scene and their accommodations. This is a party town; on weekends and any day in the summer, the clubs rock until dawn. And chances are you will hear the music from your room, especially if you stay anywhere close to the main strip. March and April bring hoards of college kids on spring break, while an older crowd from Mexico and the United States visits during the peak summer months. If you know what you're in for, it can be a fun time, but if you're looking for a quiet escape in a boutique hotel, this definitely isn't the place.

Between Rosarito and Ensenada are a few beaches, coves, surf spots, and residential communities, collectively dubbed the Gold Coast by marketing-minded real estate developers.

SIGHTS
◖ Rosarito Beach
The action in Rosarito centers around the beach—an eight-kilometer-long stretch of sand. You can swim, snorkel, or surf here, but most people just come to relax on the beach and party at the clubs. North of the pier are several mega-clubs that provide beach chairs and drinks by day and DJ music at night. During the annual spring break holiday, college students from the United States invade the town and take full advantage of the 18-year-old drinking age. Horseback riding used to be another popular pastime, but it was banned in 2006. You can rent ATVs, fish from the pier, or just people-watch as you sunbathe.

Rosarito Beach Hotel
There are a few truly iconic hotels in Baja, and the Rosarito Beach Hotel (south end of Blvd. Juárez, tel. 661/612-1111, toll-free U.S. tel. 800/343-8582, www.rosaritobeachhotel.com) is one of them. It started as the only place to stay in Rosarito in the 1920s. During the 1940s and '50s, it became popular with the Hollywood crowd, counting Mickey Rooney, Lana Turner, and Orson Welles among its regulars.

The founder's nephew, a recent mayor of the town, became the new owner of the hotel in 1974. It has grown from 12 to 280 rooms, and its dramatic ocean pier anchors the Rosarito beach vista. The 500-meter pier (daily 10 A.M.–6 P.M.) is popular for sportfishing, but the height makes landing fish from the surface far below a challenge and the activity can be sporadic. Admission to the pier is US$1 for adults, free for children under 12. Fishing from the pier costs US$5 for the public.

TIJUANA

© PAUL ITOI

Rosarito Beach Hotel

SPORTS AND RECREATION
Surfing
There are at least 25 named surf breaks between Rosarito and Ensenada, far too many to cover in detail here. Some are over-hyped and packed with boards; others are consistent yet never crowded. Whether you are a beginner or an advanced surfer, you can probably find a spot that works for your skill level. For info break by break, pick up a copy of *The Surfer's Guide to Baja.*

ENTERTAINMENT AND EVENTS
Bars and Nightclubs
The best-known mega-club in town is **Papas and Beer** (Eucalipto 400 at Coronado, tel. 661/612/0444, www.papasandbeer.com), a huge entertainment center and nightclub covering about 4,600 square meters of sand with multiple bars, dance areas, and beach volleyball; the low cover charge keeps it packed on warm summer nights, but it's empty in winter. Papas and Beer celebrated its 25th anniversary in 2008. It has satellite locations in Ensenada and La Paz.

The open-bar policy at **Iggy's,** next to the Rosarito Beach Hotel, for the price of the cover (negotiable), can seem like a deal, but the drinks are often watered down. You can overcome that problem by working with the same bartender and tipping well. The crowds seem to pass by Señor Frogs located on Juárez and head straight for the beachside clubs.

Rene's Sports Bar (Km 28, Mexico 1, tel. 661/612-1061), next to Paraíso Ortiz at the south end of town, has pool tables and TVs for watching the game.

Festivals and Events
Aside from spring break, the best-known event in Rosarito is the **Rosarito-Ensenada 50-Mile Bicycle Ride,** which takes places twice a year, in April and September, and attracts thousands of cyclists. For more information, contact **Bicycling West** in San Diego (U.S. tel. 619/424-6084, www.rosaritoensenada.com). Even if you can't beat the course record of 2 hours and 13 minutes, you'll still have a great time.

The **Festival del Vino y la Langosta** (Festival of Wine and Lobster) takes place

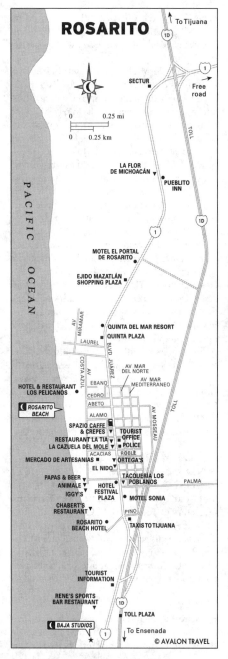

in October; call the local restaurant association, Cámara Nacional de la Industria Restaurantera (CANIRAC, tel. 661/612-0700), for information.

SHOPPING

Rosarito offers much of the same shopping you'll find in Tijuana, just on a smaller scale. There are handicrafts, furniture stores, leather shops, and art galleries.

For souvenirs, head to the **Mercado de Artesanías** (daily 9 A.M.–6 P.M.), on the west side of Boulevard Juárez, about midway between the Quinta del Mar and Rosarito Beach Hotel. This crafts market has hundreds of vendors selling all kinds of Mexican-made arts and crafts. Shop around and bargain to get a fair price for any items you buy. For beachwear and boutique shops, browse the many shopping plazas around town.

ACCOMMODATIONS

Most of Rosarito's hotels line busy Boulevard Juárez, which runs parallel to the beach. Condos and vacation homes are another option for travelers who want to cook some of their own meals. Contact the tourist office at the north end of town (Blvd. Juárez, tel./fax 661/612-0200, www.sectur.gob.mx, Mon.–Fri. 9 A.M.–7 P.M., weekends 10 A.M.–4 P.M.).

US$50-100

Originally built by the same family that established the Rosarito Beach Hotel and Rene's Sports Bar, **Motel Paraíso Ortiz** (Km. 28, Carr. Libre a Ensenada, tel. 661/612-1020, US$45–65) consists of simple beach cottages close to, but not on the beach, behind the Rosarito Beach Hotel. Comfortably removed from the noise of the main strip, **Hotel Los Pelicanos** (Ebano 113, tel. 661/612-0445, US$65) has 39 large rooms, all with heat and TV. On the north side of town, **Hotel Quinta Terranova** (Blvd. Juárez 25500, tel./fax 661/612-1650, www.hotelquintaterranova.iwarp.com, US$65–109) is pet friendly, as long as your pooch is well behaved and you bring proof of current vaccinations.

US$100-150

The **Rosarito Beach Hotel** (south end of Blvd. Juárez, tel. 661/612-1111, U.S. tel. 800/343-8582, www.rosaritobeachhotel.com, US$129) has evolved into an enormous complex over the years. Given the piecemeal construction of the hotel, the rooms can vary in age and decor. The newly opened Pacifico Tower has modern rooms. There have been enough complaints regarding the overall service and cleanliness that it merits a mention.

North of the Rosarito Beach Hotel, the **Hotel Festival Plaza** (Blvd. Juárez 1207, tel. 661/612-2950, U.S. tel. 888/295-9669, www.festival-plazahotel.com, US$100–160) is still the party epicenter in Rosarito for summer and spring break. Its proximity to the beach clubs keeps drawing the crowds, but in recent years readers have reported thefts and incidences of bedbugs and general disrepair at the hotel. The valet parking system is of particular concern, since you have to leave your keys with the staff. The hotel/entertainment complex includes a Ferris wheel and tequila bar, plus restaurants, clubs, and a heated swimming pool. The 114-room hotel section has basic rooms that have been frat-partied nearly to death. Suites, condos, and *casitas* are better, though pricier, options. Service tends to be a little better in the off-season. Wrist bands are required to enter the hotel, so you won't be able to invite that special someone back to your room unless they are staying at the hotel already.

FOOD

Most of Rosarito's many dining options are crowded along Boulevard Juárez. You can find everything from tacos to steak to seafood. Much of the food is adapted to gringo tastes. The larger hotels have their own restaurants as well.

◖ El Nido (Blvd. Juárez 67, tel. 661/612-1430, http://elnidorosarito.net, daily 8 A.M.–midnight, US$6–23), has great atmosphere and the food to back it up. The beef is grilled over an open fire. For breakfast, try the quail eggs and venison *machaca*. The restaurant's owner raises his own quail and red deer.

La Cazuela del Mole (Blvd. Juárez at Calle René Ortiz, tel. 661/612-2910, Wed.–Mon. noon–8 P.M., mains US$5), specializes in authentic sauces called *moles,* as well as house-made tamales.

La Flor de Michoacán (Blvd. Juárez 291, tel. 661/612-1858, daily 8 A.M.–10 P.M., mains US$5–10) still makes outstanding carnitas, and you can order them by the kilo (US$23–25 includes the usual sides of beans, guacamole, salsa, and tortillas).

Ortega's Place (Blvd. Juárez 200, tel. 661/612-0022, daily for breakfast, lunch, and dinner, mains US$15) is one of the original Puerto Nuevo lobster places, now with a restaurant in Rosarito. It still offers the lobster, but the buffet is more popular. Champagne brunch is a Sunday tradition.

Tacquería Los Poblanos (daily 11 A.M.–1 A.M.), on Boulevard Juárez across from the Festival Plaza, serves up spicy but good *tacos al pastor* for US$1.

Restaurant La Tia (daily 8 A.M.–3:30 P.M.) sits across from the Pemex on the southwest side of Calle Ciprés, packed with locals and not a tourist in sight. It serves *birria,* chicken, or beef in chipotle sauce. Plates start at US$5.

For espresso drinks, **Cappuchino's Coffee and Pastry House,** is the place, diagonally across the street from Hotel Festival Plaza. Internet access is available. **Spazio Caffe & Crepes** (daily 8–10 P.M., US$4–6), across from the Banamex behind the Extra market on the southwest side of Juárez, is another option.

INFORMATION AND SERVICES
Tourist Assistance

The national **Secretaría de Turismo** (Secretary of Tourism or SECTUR, Calle Juan Ruiz de Alarcón 1572, Zona Río, tel. 664/682-3367, www.discoverbajacalifornia.com, Mon.–Fri. 9 A.M.–7 P.M., weekends 10 A.M.–4 P.M.) distributes information about local sights, accommodations, and restaurants.

Money

Rosarito has plenty of ATMs these days. For example, Banamex and Serfín have branches on Boulevard Juárez near the Hotel Festival Plaza.

GETTING THERE AND AROUND

Taxis de ruta make the 40-minute trip between Tijuana and Rosarito for about US$2 per person. You can hail one on Boulevard Juárez. These taxis can also provide service to the coastal towns south of Rosarito. The white-and-red taxis you see around town offer local service only.

Mexicoach (tel. 664/685-1470, U.S. tel. 619/428-9517, www.mexicoach.com) also runs shuttles between Tijuana and Rosarito (US$14 pp).

You can take the toll road (Mexico 1-D) or the free road (Mexico 1) from Tijuana to Rosarito. The distance is about the same, but the toll road is faster and easier to find.

If you're driving north out of Rosarito, follow the sign toward San Diego; the one for Tijuana puts you on the highway heading south to Ensenada.

Small shuttles called *calafias* are another way to get around locally on Boulevard Juárez. The fare is only a few pesos.

POPOTLA

Fifteen minutes south of Rosarito (6.5 km), around Km 33, a concrete arch in need of a paint job marks the entrance to Popotla, known for its collection of seafood vendors and other food stands. Menus are based on the catch of the day, which lands right there at the beach. It doesn't get much fresher than this, and prices are a little lower than what you'll pay in Rosarito or Puerto Nuevo. The stands begin serving around 11 A.M. daily. Turn off the *libre* just after you see the Xploration sign and studio.

◖ Baja Studios

In the 1990s, Twentieth Century Fox chose Popotla as the site for a massive US$25 million film studio, custom-designed for the production of its blockbuster, *Titanic*. Once the film was released, Fox decided to keep the studio and make it available to other filmmakers. Additional movies filmed here include *Master and Commander* (2003) and *Pearl Harbor*

(2001). Disney reportedly plans to film the next *Chronicles of Narnia* at Baja Studios.

A more recent addition to the complex, **Xploration** (Km 32.5, Mexico 1, tel. 661/612-4294, U.S. tel. 866/369-2252, www.xploration.com.mx, Wed.–Fri. 9 A.M.–5:30 P.M., Sat.–Sun. 10 A.M.–6:30 P.M., adult US$12, seniors and children 3–11 US$9, under three free), gives movie buffs an inside look at a working studio in a theme park–style experience.

The studio is about five kilometers south of Rosarito between Mexico 1-D and the beach. Exit the toll road at the exit for La Paloma, Popotla, and Calafia, and get on the *pibre* heading south. Look for the entrance at Km 32.8 on the *libre,* just before the arch that leads to the village of Popotla.

Accommodations

Near Popotla, **Las Rocas Resort and Spa** (Km 37.5, Mexico 1, tel. 661/614-0354, toll-free U.S./Canada tel. 888/527-7622, www.lasrocas.com, US$160) has a rustic feel with views of a popular surf break, fireplaces, and kitchenettes in its rooms. The rooms can be hit or miss, so ask to see one before you commit. Amenities include secured parking, cable TV, a restaurant, swimming pool, and hot tub. The hotel's on-site spa provides a full menu of treatments, such as massage and facials, and a steam room.

PUERTO NUEVO

Foodie alert: Baja's self-proclaimed lobster capital awaits in Puerto Nuevo at Km 44 at the north end of Bahía Descanso. Harvests have dwindled since the first in-home restaurants opened in the 1940s and '50s, and the scene is too touristy for some (mediocre food), but the village's lobster tradition is still going strong. Choose from dozens of seafood restaurants steps from the ocean (most listed at www.puertonuevolobster.com), which feature the signature lobster platter, with rice, beans, and tortillas on the side. There are a few different styles of presentation, including deep fried and grilled, *ranchera* style with tomatoes and chili, or just plain boiled.

© PAUL ITOI

Puerto Nuevo

If you happen to be traveling in mid-October, stop by for the **Festival del Vino y la Langosta** (Festival of Wine and Lobster, US$25 pp), which takes place in Puerto Nuevo's restaurant zone.

It's easy to find your way around the village, as it consists of only three blocks. Four streets run parallel to the ocean, and they are bound by the Avenida Rentaria (one-way toward the beach) to the north and Calle Barracuda (one-way toward the highway) to the south.

Misión El Descanso

Misión El Descanso (1817–1834) is one of the least-visited mission sites on the peninsula. It was founded by Dominican Padre Tomás de Ahumada in 1817, after the flood that washed away the crops at Misión San Miguel, just 13 kilometers to the south. The two missions were closely linked for the short time that El Descanso was in operation. A modern church is built on top of the original mission foundation.

Accommodations

The **Grand Baja Resort** (Km 44.5, Mexico 1, tel. 661/614-1493, U.S. tel. 877/315-1002, www.grandbaja.com, US$79–275), just south of Puerto Nuevo overlooks the Pacific Ocean. The views are great; the rest is not. Most units are in need of repairs, and the beds and linens are old. This is not the place for neat freaks.

A better bet is a rental home or condo in the **☾ Las Gaviotas** (one bedroom US$100–150) gated community, located eight miles south of Rosarito. Several property managers offer rentals in this development. Visit www.las-gaviotas or www.golasgaviotas.com for current listings.

Food

Prices are the same at most of the lobster houses, ranging US$15–30 for main dishes, and you'll need to pay in cash. Hours are generally 10 A.M.–8 P.M. weekdays, with later hours on Friday and Saturday nights. **Puerto Nuevo I** (S/N Av. Rentaria, no tel.) is the original Puerto Nuevo restaurant and still a perennial favorite. Next door, **Puerto Nuevo II** (Av. Rentaria 2, tel. 661/614-1454) is more upscale. These family-run places have been serving lobster for many years: **Chela's** (Arpon 15, tel. 661/614-1058), **La Escondida** (Anzuelo/

Paseo del Mar, no tel.), **El Galeón** (Anzuelo, no tel.) and **La Perlita** (Barracuda just west of the highway, tel. 661/614-1276).

LA FONDA AND LA MISIÓN

Mexico 1 *(libre)* and Mexico 1-D (toll road) diverge between La Fonda (a.k.a. K-58 or La Salina), on the coast at the southern end of Bahía Descanso, and La Misión, to the southeast (and not to be confused with Playa La Misión, which is a little south of La Fonda on Bahía Descanso). La Fonda offers the best beaches in the area, several of which have surfable waves. Take exit for La Misión–Alisitos from the toll road at Km 59.

Misión San Miguel Arcángel de la Frontera

East of the highway, historic Misión San Miguel Arcángel de la Frontera (1788–1833) is part of the Spanish mission trail in Baja. Dominican Padre Luis Salles came here from Misión Santo Tomás to the south, in search of a strategic point of connection between the Baja California missions and the newer Alta California missions that were under construction. Relatively little is known about the mission today, but it did grow corn and wheat and had around 400 indigenous people at its peak. A flood in 1816 destroyed much of the mission, and it was abandoned in 1833, at which point the population had declined to only 25. The scant remains of its adobe compound— just two walls in a present day schoolyard— are now protected by the Instituto Nacional de Antropología e Historia (INAH).

Accommodations and Food

La Fonda Hotel (Km. 59.5 Mex 1-D Rosarito– Ensenada Toll Road, tel. 646/155-0307, www.lafondamexico.com, US$85) is a quirky area classic. There are standard rooms as well as multi-room apartments with fireplaces and kitchenettes (US$100–150). Movement around the cliffside hotel involves numerous steep staircases, so if mobility is an issue, make sure to ask the front desk for an accessible room. The restaurant serves reliably tasty seafood and steaks (mains US$12–25). Make sure to get a good seat on the terrace for the sunset, and if it gets chilly, the waiters bring small blankets and turn on the patio heaters.

Alisitos K-58 Surf Camp (Km. 58 Mex 1-D Rosarito–Ensenada Toll Road, tel. 646/155-0120, U.S. tel. 949/313-7059, www.alisitosk58.com, US$16) is a board shop and campground that can accommodate RVs. Amenities are few (flush toilets and cold showers), but the beach is a good one, and you can't complain about the price.

The **Poco Cielo Bed and Breakfast** (Km 59, tel. 646/155-0606, U.S. tel. 760/670-3336, www.pococielo.com, pococielo@yahoo.com) has four well-appointed rooms that are true to their themes down to the construction of the walls, murals, sinks, and sculpted entry rooms. A private stairwell leads down to the beach, and a new restaurant margaritas for US$7. It's a little Disneyland, but the good service and friendly owner make it a good choice for those looking to escape the bustle of Ensenada and Rosarito.

Baja Seasons (Km 72, tel. 646/155-4015, toll-free U.S. tel. 800/754-4190, www.bajaseasons.com) is a full-service resort with villas (US$140–250), motel rooms (US$80–120), and campsites suitable for tents or RVs (US$72 oceanfront or US$48 interior). You can only get to the park from the southbound toll road. Make a U-turn if you're driving north from the Ensenada area.

SAN MIGUEL AND EL SAUZAL

San Miguel and El Sauzal are neighboring communities on the Pacific coast, known primarily these days for good surf. In fact, San Miguel might be Baja's most consistent point break. It's located just south of the third toll booth on Mexico 1. Parking is US$5, and the crowds will be on it if the surf is good. Get there early to catch it before the onshores start up in the late morning.

Accommodations and Camping

◖ **Hostel Sauzal** (Av. L 344, tel. 646/174-6381, http://hostelsauzal.tripod.com, $15 pp) has been the starting point for many a Baja backpacking trip. It offers rare ocean-view hostel accommodations in dorm room bunks. Rates include bed linens, storage lockers, hot showers, continental breakfast, and bike/surfboard storage. Its four rooms have desks for writing letters and updating travel journals; plus there is a small library containing books, maps, and magazines. To find the hostel from the toll road southbound, go through the tollbooth at San Miguel and continue on the highway for about three more kilometers, passing under the footbridge. Next, turn left at a stoplight after the Pemex. Go two blocks and turn right; then one block more and turn left up a dirt road. The hostel is the third house on the right.

Several of the beaches along this stretch allow tent and RV camping for less than US$15 per night.

Tecate and Vicinity

Mountainous Tecate (pop. 120,000) sits at an elevation of 514 meters (1,690 ft) in the Sierra Juárez, which makes for a pleasant climate year-round. The highest peak nearby is the Mount Cuchimá, which straddles the U.S.–Mexico border. Protected by its geography from its industrial neighbors of Tijuana and Mexicali—and also from the extreme climates of the Pacific coast and San Felipe Desert—Tecate is an oasis of sorts along the international border zone. Fresh air and clean spring water led to the establishment of Tecate's two most famous enterprises: the Tecate Brewery and Rancho La Puerta health spa.

The town today is a quiet farming center, but it has also developed something an artistic side, with a small community of painters and writers in residence. Beyond the city limits, several rancho resorts and numerous aquatic recreation parks offer accommodations and entertainment.

Mexican-American writer Daniel Reveles

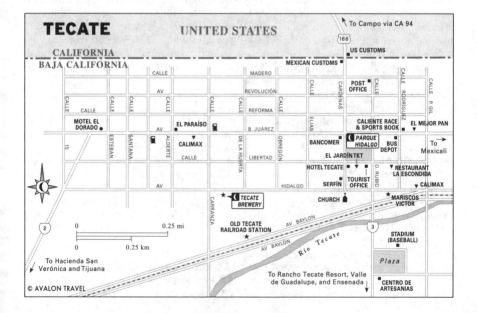

has written several books of short stories that take place in Tecate. They can be an enjoyable way to get acquainted with the town.

HISTORY

In its earliest history, the fertile valley and abundant water supply here supported a group of Yuma, who called the area Zacate (the most likely origin of the name Tecate). They believed the 1,520-meter Cerro Cuchumá (also spelled Kuchumaa) had important spiritual significance.

In the early 19th century, Mexicans began cultivating the land, and in the 1830s, a Peruvian named Juan Bandini founded the town with a land grant from the Mexican government. Later in the century, the government built a railroad to connect the three emerging border towns of Tijuana, Tecate, and Mexicali, and Tecate became the capital of its own Mexican municipality in 1892.

The most significant development in the city's history took place in 1943, when the Tecate Brewery opened for business. As the border zone industrialized later in the century, Tecate gained a number of maquiladoras, east of the city on Mexico 2. The economy today is mainly driven by farming, though tourism and manufacturing play smaller roles.

SIGHTS
◖ Parque Hidalgo

Tecate has five main parks within its limits, and the most popular is shady Parque Hidalgo (Av. Juárez and Calle Lázaro Cárdenas, Zona Centro). Built in 1952, this small park is the center of town life and gives the visitor a good sense of the place. A pretty gazebo and wrought-iron benches invite quiet contemplation. Eat ice cream and watch the locals play a game of dominoes. Note the statue of Miguel Hidalgo, the Dolores priest who issued the call for Mexican independence in 1810, in the southeast corner of the park. Surrounding the park are local government offices, restaurants, taco stands, and a few shops selling *artesanias*.

© JIMCLINE.COM

Tecate Brewery

◖ Tecate Brewery

Entreprenaur Alberto Aldrete came up with the idea for a brewery to complement his malt-making business. He ran out of money 10 years after creating Tecate beer, but a Monterrey businessman, Eugenio Garza Sada, bought the label and added it to the lineup offered by Cervecería Cuauhtémoc.

Canned Tecate is brewed in Monterrey, but bottles and kegs are made only in its name-sake Tecate. If you've tried Tecate beer only in the United States, chances are you haven't experienced the real thing. Exported Tecate is made in Monterrey (not from the pure spring water of Tecate) and with a lower alcohol content than domestically consumed Tecate (3.2 percent compared to 3.6 percent).

The brewery today (Dr. Arturo Guerra 70, tel. 665/654-9478, www.ccm.com.mx, Mon.–Fri. 10 A.M.–noon and 3–4:30 P.M., Sat. 9–10:30 A.M.) occupies the same site as the original keg brewery; high-tech German equipment is used to produce 40 million liters per month and ship to 100 countries around the world.

Old Tecate Railroad Station

Built in 1915, the Old Tecate Railroad Station was part of a line that connected San Diego to Yuma, Arizona, and played an important role in the industrial development of the area. In its time, the station held a waiting room, office, and small warehouse on its ground floor, and a residence for the station master above. The station is now part of a small historic district, which includes the Tecate Brewery and is protected by the city.

The **Pacific Southwest Railway Museum** (State Hwy 94 and Forest Gate Rd., Campo, CA, U.S. weekend tel. 619/478-9937, U.S. weekday tel. 619/465-7776, www.sdrm.org, US$43) offers occasional Saturday rail trips from its Campo depot (80 minutes by car from downtown San Diego) to Tecate, 1.25-hour ride. Trains leave Campo at 10:30 A.M. and return at 4:30 P.M. In summer, twilight trips depart Campo at 3 P.M. and return at 9 P.M. Reservations are required. Credit cards and PayPal are accepted.

Walking Tour

A two-hour self-guided walking tour of Tecate begins on Avenida Juárez heading east from Parque Miguel Hidalgo. Cross Rubio and Rodríguez at Rodriguez and look for El Major Pan de Tecate Bakery on the next block. Retrace your steps to the park and cross through it to find the alley called Callejón Libertad and temporary art exhibits in the **Baja California Cultural Institute** (ICBC, Av. Ortiz Rubio and Callejon Libertad s/n, Zona Centro, no tel., Mon.–Fri. 8 A.M.–7 P.M., Sat. 9 A.M.–1 P.M.). Next door is the state tourism office. Continue walking toward the park along Lázaro Cárdenas, and look for the 1941 Iglesia de Nuestra Señora de Guadalupe at the intersection with Avenida Hidalgo. Turn left out of the church and follow Avenida Hidalgo to Calle Elías Calles, where you'll find the Tecate Brewery. Back on Elías Calles, turn right to follow the railroad tracks to the Old Tecate Railroad Station. The tour concludes back at the park.

Rancho La Puerta

Aside from its beer, Tecate is known the world over for its exclusive fitness resort and spa, Rancho La Puerta (U.S. tel. 760/744-4222 or toll-free U.S. tel. 800/443-7565, www.rancholapuerta.com). Founded in the 1940s at the base of Mount Cuchumá/Kuchumaa, the resort has hosted the likes of Madonna, Steven Seagal, Jodie Foster, and Oprah Winfrey. Well ahead of their time, the resort's founders advocated a simple and health-oriented retreat in a beautiful natural setting as an antidote to the busy modern lifestyle. Participants come for a week at a time to hike in the sierra, soak in the hot springs, learn to cook new foods, and enjoy eating fresh produce from the organic farm.

The addition of the **Saturdays at the Ranch** program has opened the resort up to a wider audience. These one-day visits include fitness, spa, and culinary components, all packed into a single 12-hour day that begins and ends in San Diego (tel. 665/654-9155, U.S. tel. 800/443-7565, 8 A.M.–8 P.M., US$195 pp, spa treatments cost extra).

ENTERTAINMENT AND EVENTS

Nightlife is virtually non-existent in Tecate, but in the daytime, off-road races provide a popular pastime for locals and visitors alike. The Santa Veronica Offroad Park and Roadway (www.ranchosantaveronica.com, haciendasantaveronica@hotmail.com), at Rancho Santa Veronica, 30 kilometers east of Tecate off Mexico 2, produces a few such events each year, including the **Gran Carrera de Tecate,** a three-day festival held in late May. The **Gran Carrera de Caballos** is more popular among locals. It takes place on the last weekend in March.

The **SCORE Tecate Baja 500** occurs in June and early November (U.S. tel. 818/225-8402).

During the second week of October, the city celebrates the **Fiesta de la Fundación de Tecate,** which commemorates Tecate's founding in a multiday festival of parades, live music, and (rare in Baja) fireworks.

SHOPPING

There are a few shops near the plaza, but the best place to browse for souvenirs is the **Centro de Artesanias de Tecate** (Calzada Universidad near Parque Adolfo López Mateos, Mon.–Fri. 8:30 A.M.–6 P.M., Sat. 10 A.M.–3 P.M.). Originally a workshop for glassblowing, the center sells a full range of pottery, jewelry, and other crafts.

ACCOMMODATIONS AND CAMPING
Hotels and Motels
UNDER US$50

Hotel Tecate (Cardenas y Callejón Libertad No. 20, tel. 665/654-1116, US$35) has 12 simple rooms, but only a few had TVs at last check. The rooms that overlook the plaza have better lighting.

Centrally located **El Paraíso** (Aldrete 83 at Av. Juárez, tel. 665/654-1716, US$25 pp) has 38 clean rooms with air-conditioning and hot showers. The management also provides space heaters for chilly winter nights. There is secure parking in an underground garage.

La Hacienda (Av. Juárez 861, tel. 665/654-1250, US$40) offers clean and safe accommodations on the outskirts of town. Rooms have air-conditioning and cable TV, and there is secure parking. It has a restaurant that's open 8 A.M.–4 P.M. daily, except for Monday when it closes at noon. A cab ride to the town center costs about US$5.

US$50-100

Two blocks west of the Paraíso, **El Dorado** (Av. Juárez 160, tel. 665/654-1333, eldorado@yahoo.com.mx, US$57) is a non-descript two-story motel on the west side of town at Avenida Juárez and Calle Esteban. Its large rooms have air-conditioning, heat, TV, and phone. Off-street parking is available.

On the road to Ensenada, just outside of town, the **Hotel Rosita Resort Inn** (Km 3.6, Carr. Tecate-Ensenada, tel. 665/103-0093, www.rositaresortinn.com.mx, US$50–100) has 52 rooms and suites with modern amenities like air-conditioning, phone, cable TV, and high-speed Internet. Its restaurant serves Mexican specialties, and the recreation area has a swimming pool. Secure parking is another feature.

Ranch Resorts

Popular with the ATV and motorcycle crowds, **Hacienda Santa Verónica** (Km 95, Carr. Tijuana-Mexicali Cuota/Mexico 2-D, tel. 665/521-0017 or -0018, U.S. tel. 888/556-6288, www.ranchosantaveronica.com, US$70) is located about 30 kilometers east of Tecate. Mission-style accommodations (52 rooms and 8 suites) have fireplaces and patios, and meal plans are an option. Activities include tennis, off-road riding (quad rentals US$40/hr), horseback riding, swimming, volleyball, and basketball, and you can come for just the day (8 A.M.–10:30 P.M.) Its campground/RV park is open to the public. To find the resort, exit at Km 106 from the free road and follow the signs; there is no exit for the ranch from the toll road.

Rancho Los Chabacanos (Km. 118 Carr. Mexicali-Tecate, tel. 665/655-1624, U.S.

tel. 619/565-1183, www.rancholoschabacanos. com, US$95–285) has a distinct colonial feel in both its hacienda-style architecture and the surrounding eco-preserve. There are no TVs or phones in its 17 casitas, though Wi-Fi is an option. Guests enjoy black mud treatments and steam treatments in the on-site spa.

Stays at **Rancho La Puerta** (U.S. tel. 760/744-4222 or toll-free U.S. tel. 800/443-7565, www.rancholapuerta.com) are a full week, and include all meals. Accommodations are in cottages or suites—most with fireplaces and each with its own private garden—and the resort can hold 150 guests at a time. Organic produce comes from the resort's own farm.

All-inclusive prices range from US$2,780 per week for a studio with bath to US$4,205 for a two-bedroom villa suite. Summer rates (late June–early September) are lower.

Camping and RV Parks

Rancho Ojai (tel. 665/655-3014, www.rancho-ojai.com) offers cabins, RV sites with full hookups, and cabins on their working ranch. This is a family-friendly place that is popular with up-scale Tijuana and Tecate residents, who come for the immaculate cabins, pool, and miniature golf. Rancho Ojai is part of the KOA network, and has been voted one of top KOA campgrounds in the world. Cabins with shared bath are US$68, US$90 with private bath, and US$135 with private bath and kitchenette. The ranch is 21 kilometers east of Tecate on Mexico 2. Exit the toll road at El Hongo and drive west on Mexico 2 for eight kilometers to the Rancho Ojai gates.

Rancho Santa Verónica (30 km east of Tecate at Km 98, Mexico 2, U.S. tel. 888/556-6288, haciendasantaveronica@hotmail.com, www.ranchosantaveronica.com, US$20) also has full-hookup slots and tent spaces. Guests may use any of the ranch's recreational facilities.

FOOD

There is no better place in Baja to try your first real tacos than the stands near Tecate's Hidalgo Park. Each one does this Mexican standard a little differently; Mexicans tend to eat tacos for their evening meal, but the taquerías are usually open from late morning until late in the evening. **Taquería Los Amigos** (Callejón Libertad and Rubio, no tel.) is one of the busiest, and the carne asada in particular is excellent.

For a place where the people-watching can be better than the food (and the food is good), try **El Jardín TKT (Tecate)** (no tel., daily 6 A.M.–noon, mains under US$10) located on the south side of the plaza. They serve inexpensive Mexican standards for breakfast, lunch, and dinner. Outside seating is available during warm weather. The chile verde is excellent.

Mariscos Victor (Av. Hidalgo 284, no tel., from 7 A.M. for breakfast, lunch, and dinner, mains US$5–10) makes dependable seafood dishes and ranch-style entrées like *machaca* and *bistek*.

With a history dating back to 1969, **El Mejor Pan de Tecate** (Av. Juárez 331, btw Rodríguez/Portes Gil, tel. 665/654-0040, www.elmejorpandetecate.com) has impressed many a visitor with its handmade brick-oven breads—some of the best you'll find anywhere in Baja.

Groceries

Several *tiendas* on Avenida Juárez and Avenida Hidalgo stock the basics; a **Calimax** supermarket on Avenida Juárez near the Calle Carranza intersection has more selection.

INFORMATION AND SERVICES
Tourist Assistance

The **Secretaría de Turismo** (Secretary of Tourism or SECTUR, tel. 665/654-1095, www.tecatemexico.com.mx, Mon.–Fri. 9 A.M.–7 P.M., Sat. 9 A.M.–3 P.M., Sun. 10 A.M.–2 P.M.) is located on the south side of Parque Hidalgo, next door to the police station. Or stop by the smaller booth at the border crossing (Lázaro Cárdenas and Madero).

Money

Most places in Tecate accept U.S. currency. There's a money exchange in Tecate,

© PABLO NOBILI
a typical shoe-shine stand in downtown Tecate

California, in the same plaza as the U.S. post office and Western Union.

The Banamex on Avenida Juárez and Serfín on Calle Cárdenas both have ATMs and currency exchange services.

Post Office
Tecate's post office is on the corner of Calles Madero and Ortiz Rubio.

Immigration and Customs
The immigration and customs offices at the border crossing are open daily 6 A.M.–midnight.

GETTING THERE
By Bus
Tecate's bus depot is on Avenida Juárez at Calle Rodríguez; it has a snack bar and long-distance telephone service. **ABC** (tel. 664/621-2668, www.abc.com.mx) has regular connections to Mexicali, Tijuana, and Ensenada.

By Car
From San Diego, take I-805 to CA 94 and follow this highway southeast for 66 kilometers to the exit for Tecate. From Arizona, pick up CA 94 from I-8 west. Plan to arrive between 5 A.M.–11 P.M. when the border gate is open.

Be sure to buy a Mexican auto insurance policy online or at the border before you cross into Mexico. Temporary vehicle import permits (required for driving on the mainland, but not in Baja), are issued Monday–Saturday 8 A.M.–4 P.M. at the customs office.

Two Baja, California, state highways pass through Tecate: Mexico 2 (to Tijuana or Mexicali) and Mexico 3 (to Ensenada). The toll road (US$10) between Tijuana and Tecate, Mexico 2-D, parallels the border.

By Rail
The **Pacific Southwest Railway Museum** (State Hwy 94 and Forest Gate Rd., Campo, CA, U.S. weekend tel. 619/478-9937, U.S. weekday tel. 619/465-7776, www.sdrm.org, US$43) offers a periodic rail tour to the Old Tecate Railroad Station (one-day or twilight).

By Foot
For a day trip, you can park in any number of lots on the U.S. side of the border and walk over to Tecate.

MEXICO 3 TO ENSENADA
Mexico 3 is a two-lane state highway that begins in Tecate, follows the foothills of the Sierra Juárez to the Valle del Guadalupe Wine Country, and ends near Ensenada. This route makes a longer, but pleasant alternative to the coastal road from Tijuana.

ENSENADA TO EL ROSARIO

Whether they are on a cruise from Los Angeles, driving from San Diego, or passing through on the way to points south, many travelers find themselves in Ensenada for an afternoon or longer. Those who venture away from the commercial port and busy tourist zone into the town center find a surprisingly pleasant Mexican town to explore.

Beyond the border region but still within easy reach of San Diego, Ensenada has an identity all its own. Cruise ships bring tourists by the thousands. They roam the *malecón* by day and return to their ships at night, leaving the town to the locals and visitors who've driven themselves from the other side of the border for an overnight getaway.

Accordingly, the first few blocks along the busy waterfront are crowded with tourist shops and services. But a few blocks inland, Ensenada transforms into a regional center of commerce with a much more local—and inviting—feel. Ranches, fisheries, and wineries all conduct their business here. Students come to study at several universities. And travelers from mainland Mexico come to explore the wine country in the nearby Valle de Guadalupe. A Dominican mission, Russian colony, and beautiful coastline add to Ensenada's appeal.

South of Ensenada, Mexico 1 meanders through a series of farming communities, including the rolling hills and vineyards of the Valle de Santo Tomás. Legendary sportfishing and surfable waves await all the way south to San Quintín. El Rosario, at the southern end of this region, marks the gateway to the vast central desert and the Valle de los Cirios.

HIGHLIGHTS

(Riviera del Pacífico: For a slice of Ensenada history, walk the grounds of the former Playa Ensenada Hotel and Casino, once run by American boxer Jack Dempsey and now the city's cultural center (page 60).

(La Bufadora: One of the more touristy attractions in Northern Baja, this blowhole is an easy excursion from Ensenada. Visitors congregate around the top of a cavern to watch spumes shoot 30 meters in the air (page 73).

(Ruta del Vino: Taste Mexico's finest vintages at the growing number of boutique wineries in the rural Valle de Guadalupe along Mexico 3 between Ensenada and Tecate (page 75).

(Valle de Santo Tomás: Mexico 1 passes rolling hills carpeted in green, a historic winery, and mission ruins in this grape- and olive-growing region (page 81).

(Parque Nacional Sierra San Pedro Mártir: The tallest peaks on the peninsula offer a refreshing contrast to Baja's desert scenery (page 85).

LOOK FOR (TO FIND RECOMMENDED SIGHTS, ACTIVITIES, DINING, AND LODGING.

ENSENADA TO EL ROSARIO

© 123RF.COM/CONNIE WADE

Ensenada coastline

Away from the Pacific coast, hikers and backpackers can explore two mountain ranges, the Sierra Juárez and the Sierra de San Pedro Mártir, which has the tallest peak on the Baja Peninsula, an internationally known observatory, and nearly 69,000 hectares of untouched wilderness.

PLANNING YOUR TIME

Half a day is plenty of time to get a feel for Ensenada. If you have a car, you might spend a few hours or an entire day visiting wineries along the Ruta del Vino. Anglers will be content to spend a week or more plying the waters of Bahía San Quintín.

For sierra-bound visitors, the best hiking seasons are mid-April–mid-June (good for wildflowers) and late September–early November (when quaking aspens put on a show).

Ensenada and Vicinity

More travelers visit Ensenada than any other town on the Baja Peninsula outside of the border region, but this is not a purpose-built resort destination. Thanks to the commercial fishing, aquaculture, and agriculture industries, Ensenada has grown to become the third-largest city in Baja. Farms in the area grow olives and grapes on land, and yellowtail and halibut in the water. Ensenada's port does more business than any other on the peninsula.

Most first-time visitors begin their tour of Ensenada with a stroll along Avenida López Mateos near the waterfront. But if you walk a few blocks away from the harbor, across Avenida Juárez, you'll find yourself in a much quieter, residential part of town with more local-style shops and restaurants.

HISTORY

Spanish explorers Juan Cabrillo (1542) and Sebastián Vizcaíno (1602) were the first Europeans to land at Ensenada, and the first ranches were established through a land grant from Spain in the early 1800s. One of these ranches, Rancho Ensenada, became the inspiration for the town's name. Ensenada experienced dramatic growth when gold was discovered in 1870 and the town transformed into a mining center.

From 1882 to 1915, Ensenada served as the capital city of the Territory of Baja California. U.S. Prohibition fueled another boom in the 1920s, which saw the opening of the historic Ensenada Hotel and Casino, but this time the prosperity was short-lived due to the repeal of Prohibition and the onset of the Great Depression.

In the 1950s, travelers from the United States began visiting Ensenada to take advantage of the sportfishing opportunities, and the city became known as the Yellowtail Capital of the World.

Today, Ensenada is the capital city of the *municipio* (county) of Ensenada, which extends

© PAUL ITOI

Ensenada's *malecón* features a giant Mexican flag.

south to the border with Baja California Sur. Around 40,000 expats are permanent residents in the area. The economy is driven by fishing and aquaculture, fish processing, farming, and the import/export trade. The addition of a cruise ship pier and village, plus a scenic *malecón* further enhanced the city's appeal to visitors.

SIGHTS
◖ Riviera del Pacífico

During the U.S. Prohibition era, heavyweight boxing celebrity Jack Dempsey built a massive resort on the Ensenada waterfront called the Playa Ensenada Hotel and Casino. On opening night in 1929, Bing Crosby and the Xavier Cugat Orchestra entertained the crowd. A local singer named Margarita Carmen Cansino joined the orchestra—and later changed her name to Rita Hayworth. A symbol of Ensenada's newfound prosperity, the resort thrived for a few years until the repeal of Prohibition and the onset of the Great Depression sent most of the gamblers home. Management tried reopening the hotel as the

© AVALON TRAVEL

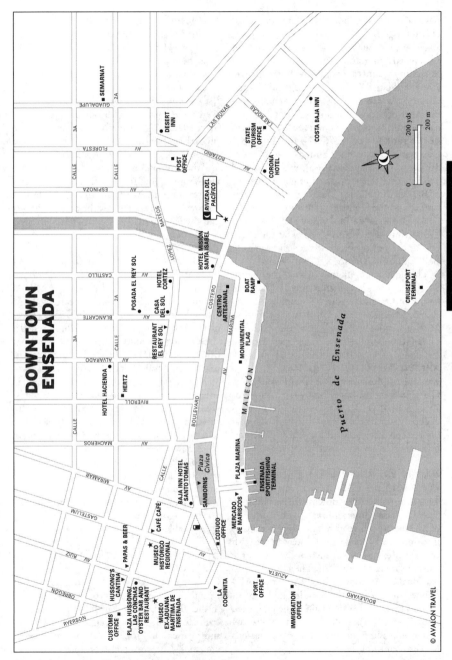

ENSENADA TO EL ROSARIO

DOWNTOWN ENSENADA

Puerto de Ensenada

© AVALON TRAVEL

200 yds
200 m

Riviera del Pacífico, but by 1938, the doors had closed for good.

Forty years later, the Mexican government intervened and restored the legendary building as the city's **Centro Social Cívico y Cultural Riviera** (Social, Civic, and Cultural Center, corner of Av. Costero/Riviera). It contains government offices and a public library, as well as a small museum, the **Museo de Historia de Ensenada** (tel. 646/177-0594, Mon.–Sat. 9:30 A.M.–2 P.M. and 3–5 P.M., Sun. 10 A.M.–5 P.M., by donation), with historical exhibits that represent the indigenous people of Baja California, the era of European exploration, and the Dominican missions.

The **Galería de la Cuidad** (tel. 646/177-3130, Mon.–Fri. 9 A.M.–6 P.M.), at the north end of the building, showcases the works of Baja California artists.

Throughout the building, much of the original tile and paintings have been preserved. The street-level **Bar Andaluz** features a mural by Alfredo Ramos Martínez (1871–1946), who established Mexico City's Las Escuelas de Pintura al Aire Libre (Schools of Painting in the Open Air).

Museo Histórico Regional

Ensenada's Museum of Regional History (Av. Gastelum near Av. López Mateos, tel. 646/178-2531, Tues.–Sun. 10 A.M.–5 P.M., by donation) occupies a former 1886 military garrison that housed the Ensenada jail until 1986. The permanent collection consists of native artifacts.

Museo Ex-Aduana Marítima de Ensenada

This historic building downtown was built by the U.S.-based International Land Company of Mexico, which acquired much of the coastline from the Mexican government in the 19th century. Mexico's Aduana Marítima (Maritime Customs) took over in 1922. Then the Instituto Nacional de Antropología e Historia (INAH) stepped in to restore the building and convert it into a museum (Av. Ryerson/Calle Uribe, tel. 646/178-2531, Tues.–Sun. 9 A.M.–4 P.M., by donation). Temporary exhibits cover various Mexican cultural themes.

Malecón

Ensenada's *malecón,* built in the 1990s, is a relatively new fixture on the waterfront. With its giant Mexican flag and bay views, the promenade is a good place to get your bearings before a walk around town. At the north end of the *malecón* are the sportfishing terminal and *mercado de mariscos* (seafood market). Near here, **Plaza Cívica** features statues of three pivotal figures in Mexican history: Benito Juárez (Mexico's first president), Padre Miguel Hidalgo (initiator of the Mexican Revolution), and Venustiano Carranza (first president after the revolution). At the south end, across the narrow Bahía Ensenada, is the cruise ship pier and the Riviera del Pacífico.

Wineries

Ensenada has a long history in the grape-growing/winemaking business and a growing reputation for bottling world-class vintages. Most of the vineyards are located in the nearby Valle de Guadalupe, but several operations have offices and/or tasting rooms in downtown Ensenada.

Bodegas de Santo Tomás (Av. Miramar 666, tel. 646/178-3333, bstwines@hotmail.com, Mon.–Sat. 10 A.M.–9 P.M., Sun. 10 A.M.–5 P.M.) is a good place to get acquainted with the local varietals. As Mexico's oldest winery, its roots go back to the Dominican mission in the Valle de Santo Tomás. The winery offered its first wine to the public in 1888 and moved its winemaking headquarters to Ensenada in 1934. Recently, the company has been shifting its equipment back to Santo Tomás, but the tasting room and wine store in Ensenada remain open to visitors. Short, English-language tours of the facility are available.

SPORTS AND RECREATION
Fishing

Commercial fishing has taken its toll since Ensenada's heyday as a sportfishing getaway in the 1950s and '60s. But a day on a *panga* or cruiser can still yield a decent catch in the peak summer season. Lingcod, rockfish, and bonito are among the most common species.

© PAUL ITOI

Bodegas de Santo Tomás, Mexico's oldest winery

For an old-school fishing experience, hire a *panga* at the Ensenada Sportfishing Terminal near the north end of the harbor or at Punta Banda, south of Ensenada. **Sergio's Sportfishing Center** (tel./fax 646/178-2185, toll-free U.S. tel. 800/336-5454, www.sergiosfishing.com, US$50 pp) is a good choice if you're looking for a six-pack boat. **Gordo's Sportfishing** (tel. 646/178-3515 or 646/178-2377, www.gordossportfishing.com) has larger open party boats and offshore tuna rigs. Be prepared to be badgered by sportfishing salesmen as you walk along the marina to book with any of the outfitters.

Note: By law, anyone who goes out on a fishing boat needs to buy a license, even if you don't plan to fish.

Boating

Marina Coral (radio VHF 71, tel. 646/175-0000, toll-free U.S. tel. 800/862-9020, www.hotelcoral.com), has 500 yacht slips to 135 feet and a floating fuel dock. The marina has a full suite of shore services, including hookups, lockers, restrooms, telephones, and wireless Internet.

Ensenada Cruiseport Village Marina (tel. 646/173-4141, fax 646/173-4151, U.S. tel. 877/219-5822, www.ecpvmarina.com) has 210 slips to 60 feet, LOA and recently renovated laundry and other shore facilities.

As Ensenada is an official Mexican port of entry, arriving boaters must check in with the port captain on Boulevard Azueta. Ensenada's Marina Coral offers the *Ventanilla Unica* (Single Window) service. Boaters can get their tourist cards and TIP (Temporary Import Permits) and pay at the adjoining bank machine. It's open Monday through Friday 8 A.M.–5 P.M.

Surfing

By the time you've reached the surf spots around Ensenada, you've distanced yourself beyond the reach most of the weekend warriors from San Diego. Ensenada has several surf shops located on the north end of town. The **Baja Board Shop** (Loc. 720-4 Costero, Plaza Bocarelli, tel. 646/175-7218, chimbo@hotmail.com) that is often listed as north of town is now located on Boulevard Costero.

San Miguel might be Baja's most consistent point break. It's located just south of the toll booth on Mexico 1. Parking is US$5 and the crowds will be on it if the surf is good. Get there early to catch it before the onshores start up in the late morning. There are several spots as you drive south that are less consistent.

Isla Todos Santos is located 20 kilometers offshore of Ensenada. Killers is located on the northwest side of the island, and breaks on winter swells coming from the northwest. Because of its direct exposure to the north, and a deep water canyon that channels the long period swell, Killers can get huge and is not for the uninitiated. You can hire a boat from the Ensenada harbor for a ride to the island for around US$100.

Diving

There is little shore diving around Ensenada, but boat trips take divers to explore several underwater pinnacles.

Almar Dive Shop (Av. Macheros 149, tel. 646/178-3013, almardive@hotmail.com) offers rental gear and lessons. **Dale's La Bufadora Dive Shop** (Rancho La Bufadora, tel. 646/154-2092, www.labufadoradive.com, open weekends or by appointment) rents gear and does boat trips to the pinnacles just offshore.

Whale-Watching

Sergio's Sportfishing Center (tel./fax 646/178-2185, toll-free U.S. tel. 800/336-5454, www.sergiosfishing.com) and **Gordo's** (tel. 646/178-3515 or 646/178-2377, fax 646/174-04810, www.gordossportfishing.com) offer whale-watching boat tours late December–late March. You won't get as close to the whales here as you can in the gray whale birthing lagoons farther south, but it's still a pleasant way to get out on the water if you're not interested in fishing or diving.

Spa Services

Choose from a variety of treatments and service packages at the spa at **Hotel Coral & Marina** (Km 103 Carr. Tijuana-Ensenada #3421, Zona Playitas, tel. 646/175-0000, toll-free U.S. tel. 800/862-9020, www.hotelcoral.com, Mon.–Sat. 8 A.M.–8 P.M., Sun. 8 A.M.–6 P.M.). Services include Swedish massage, body wraps, and facials.

Cruises

You can visit Ensenada as part of a four-day cruise along the Pacific coast with Royal Caribbean's **Monarch of the Seas** (toll-free U.S. tel. 800/327-6700, www.royalcaribbean.com, US$219–379). The ship departs from Los Angeles. Carnival (www.carnival.com) offers three- and four-day Baja trips aboard the **Paradise** at comparable prices.

Organized Tours

La Jolla, California–based **Baja California Tours** (U.S. tel. 858/454-7166 or toll-free U.S. tel. 800/336-5454, www.bajaspecials.com, bajatours@aol.com, office hours Mon.–Fri. 10 A.M.–4 P.M.) books day trips to Ensenada and the Valle de Guadalupe, as well as points north and south.

ENTERTAINMENT AND EVENTS
Nightlife

Most of the evening entertainment takes place along Avenida López Mateos and Boulevard Costero between Calle Sanginés and Avenida Macheros. Some of the hotels and bars host live music, and there are a few discos, but it's nothing compared to what you'll find in Tijuana.

Ensenada's best-known bar has been serving patrons since 1892. Opened by German immigrant Johan Hussong, 🎵 **Hussong's Cantina** (Av. Ruiz 113, tel. 646/178-3210, www.cantina-hussongs.com, daily 10 A.M.–1 A.M.) has been a gathering place for expats and locals ever since, and many veteran Baja travelers kick off each road trip down the peninsula with a Tecate, Bohemia, or XX beer here. Late afternoon is the best time to beat the rowdy crowds.

Two-story **Papas and Beer** (Av. Ruiz and López Mateos, tel. 646/174-0145, www.papasandbeer.com, daily noon–3 A.M.), across the street, has less character but is also a little mellower. Next door to Papas, **Oxidos** (Av. Ruiz and López Mateos, tel. 646/178-8827, daily 8 A.M.–midnight) is a lounge-like place with a dance floor.

El Patio (López Mateos 1088, tel. 646/178-3866, www.elpatiobar.com, Mon.–Tues. 6 P.M.–midnight, Wed.–Thurs 1 P.M.–midnight, Fri.–Sat. 1 P.M.–2 A.M., Sun. 1 P.M.–midnight) is the place to sample some high-end tequila and watch the game in a garden patio setting.

Festivals and Events
FEBRUARY
Ensenada puts on a good show for **Carnaval,** during the six days before Ash Wednesday. The festivities include parades, amusement rides, live music, costumes, and lots of food and drink.

APRIL
Thousands of cyclists ride in the **Rosarito-Ensenada 50-Mile Fun Bicycle Ride** (tel. 619/424-6084, www.rosaritoensenada.com) each April. Register online in advance (US$35) or on the day of the event (US$40).

The **Tommy Bahama Newport-Ensenada Race** (www.nosa.org) is a regatta in which hundreds of yachts sail from Southern California to Ensenada.

JUNE
SCORE International and Tecate beer sponsor the annual **Baja 500** (U.S. tel. 818/225-8402, www.score-international.com) off-road race starting in Ensenada.

JULY
Beach volleyball players from all over the world compete for sizable cash prizes in the **Baja Volleyball Open** (www.bajaopen.com) held at Playa Hermosa.

AUGUST
The wine country celebrates the **Fiesta de la Vendimia Bajacaliforniana** (Baja California Wine Harvest Festival, tel. 646/174-0170, www.caniracensenada.com), with 10 days of wine-tasting, winery tours, and gourmet

cooking at the wineries around town and in the Valle de Guadalupe. Admission prices vary by location.

SEPTEMBER
J. D. Hussong Baja International Chili Cookoff & Salsa Contest (tel. 646/174-4575, www.hussongs.com/chilicookoff.html, US$10) takes place on a Saturday afternoon at the Quintas Papagayo Resort. Chili connoisseurs battle for the opportunity to attend the annual International Chili Society's World Championship in Omaha, Nebraska. This is one of the most popular events in Ensenada each year.

OCTOBER
The local restaurant association CANIRAC organizes the popular **Feria Internacional del Pescado y el Marisco** (International Seafood Fair, tel. 646/174-0448 or 646/174-0435, www.caniracensenada.com), featuring restaurants from Ensenada and as far away as Tijuana and Southern California.

Pro surfers compete in a two-day **Mexican Surf Fiesta** at Playa de San Miguel (tel. 858/586-9173, www.mexicansurffiesta.com, surfiesta@yahoo.com).

NOVEMBER
The **SCORE-Tecate Baja 1000** (U.S. tel. 818/225-8402, www.score-international.com) off-road race takes over much of the Baja Peninsula for a week each November. On alternate years, the course goes all the way to La Paz. If you happen to be driving Mexico 1 during the week of the race (or the two weeks leading up to it), you'll see clouds of dust following the motorcycles, trucks, and dune buggies that are on the dirt course. And they'll probably be traveling much faster than traffic on the paved highway.

SHOPPING
Ensenada shopping is more international and upscale than what you'll find in Tijuana, a reflection of the sorts of things that cruise ship passengers like to buy. The stores along Avenida

ENSENADA TO EL ROSARIO

© KATHRYN LATENDRESSE

hand-embroidered dresses for sale

López Mateos and Boulevard Costero have an assortment of souvenirs and beachwear. Some of the most popular purchases are silver jewelry, leather goods, pottery, fine art, and accessories for the beach. In general, prices drop the farther you get from the waterfront.

The **Centro Artesanal** (Blvd. Costero 1094 at the end of Av. Castillo) has arts and crafts from all over Mexico.

Open since 1988, **Galería de Pérez Meillón** (Centro Artesanal, Loc. 40, Blvd. Costero 1094 and Av. Castillo, tel. 646/175-7848, adalbertopm@hotmail.com, daily 9 A.M.–5 P.M.) specializes in Mata Ortiz pottery, made by Native Americans from a small village in the mainland state of Chihuahua. Owner Adalberto Pérez Meillón selects each piece directly from the artists. He also carries a variety of other Native American handcrafts, as well as works by contemporary artists living in Baja California and mainland Mexico.

The wide variety of *artesanías* and friendly English-speaking staff create a pleasant shopping experience at **Bazar Casa Ramírez** (Av. López Mateos 496-3, tel. 646/178-8209,

bramirez717@hotmail.com). This large family-run shop contains high-quality crafts from all over Mexico, including Talavera pottery, wrought-iron sculptures, decorative mirrors, and works of carved wood and blown glass. For silver jewelry from Taxco, try **Arriaga de Taxco** (two locations on Avenida López Matéos 821 and 865, tel. 646/174-0704, sterling@telnor.net, Mon.–Fri. 10 A.M.–7 P.M., Sat. until 8 P.M., Sun. until 6 P.M.).

Los Globos (Calle 9 three blocks east of Av. Reforma, daily 9 A.M.–6 P.M.) is a flea market with vendors selling housewares, furniture, apparel, and more. Weekends are best.

For leather goods, try **Nuevo México Lindo** (Av. López Mateos 688, tel. 646/178-1381). It specializes in saddles and related gear but also has handbags.

A few fine art galleries have sprung up around town, including **Galería La Esquina de Bodegas** (Av. Miramar and Calle 8, tel. 646/178-3557, Sun.–Fri. 8 A.M.–10 P.M.), which is located across from Bodegas de Santo Tomás, and shows the works of Mexican and international artists.

Shopping Centers

Ensenada has several large shopping plazas, including **Centro Comercial Misión** (Calle 11 and Av. Reforma), with a Gigante supermarket, Banamex ATM, Lavamática Express, Smart and Final, and Cinema Gemelos.

ACCOMMODATIONS
Downtown

Ensenada's hotels are concentrated along Avenida López Mateos and Boulevard Costero. Late-night noise is a concern here, especially if you end up in a room that faces the street. Also, many of the longtime favorite establishments have let standards slip in recent years to the point where we can no longer recommend them. Aside from peak travel times of July–August, Carnaval (February), and U.S. college spring break (March), hotels are rarely full and rates are negotiable.

The high season in Ensenada is May–September, and weekdays are generally slower than weekends year-round. Rates below do not include 12 percent tax, unless specified. Some places also add a 10 percent service charge to the nightly rate.

UNDER US$50

Hotel Hacienda (Calle 2 #211 at Alvarado, tel. 646/178-2344, US$40) has a good location just one full block from the main drag. Traffic noise is an issue for the rooms that face Calle 2, but all of the rooms are well maintained and clean.

Three blocks north of Hussong's Cantina, **Hotel Ritz** (Av. Ruiz 379 at Calle 4, tel. 646/174-0501, fax 646/178-3262, US$32) appeals to travelers who don't need off-street parking and who prefer to stay a comfortable distance from the main tourist drag (but still within the downtown area). Rooms on the lower level are dark; balconies on the more expensive second and third stories are a nice feature.

US$50-100

The northernmost property in the small **Desert Inn** (Av. Floresta at Bucaneros, tel. 646/176-2601, toll-free U.S. tel. 800/346-3942, www.

desertinns.com, US$70–122) chain of hotels in Baja has 50 rooms in a three-story building. Rooms come with air-conditioning, heat, TV, and phone. There are a restaurant and pool on-site but no off-street parking. It's adequate enough for a place to crash, but certainly nothing special.

Hotel Misión Santa Isabel (Blvd. Costero 1119 btw Av. Castillo/Av. López Mateos, tel. 646/178-3616, fax 646/178-3345, US$39–139) is a large, mission-style building with clean rooms and friendly service—something that seems increasingly hard to find in Ensenada accommodations. Its 57 guestrooms have colonial-style wood furnishings, with modern amenities such as air-conditioning, heat, satellite TV, and direct-dial phones. The welcoming grounds include a restaurant/bar, gift shop, and one of the cleaner swimming pools in town; secure parking is another plus.

Rooms in the mission-style **Casa del Sol Hotel** (Av. López Mateos 1001, tel. 646/178-1570, U.S. tel. 877/316-1684, www.casadelsolmexico.net, US$65–120) come with tiled baths, air-conditioning, TV, phone, and Wi-Fi. Services include secure parking and the on-site Bistro Café Sutaza and Essence Spa, with a full menu of treatments. Your morning coffee is on the house.

Suites are a good value at the **Baja Inn Hotel Santo Tomás** (Blvd. Costero 609 at Av. Miramar, tel. 646/178-1503 or 800/026-6999, toll-free U.S. tel. 800/303-2684, www.bajainn. com, US$80), which is part of the same group of Baja Inn hotels. Its 80 clean rooms have air-conditioning, heat, and satellite TV, and there's secure parking and a restaurant.

US$100-150

The well-run **Hotel Cortez** (Av. López Mateos 1089, tel. 646/178-2307 or 800/026-6999, toll-free U.S. tel. 800/303-2684, www.bajainn. com, US$65–110) has 75 rooms in a two-story colonial-style building with an attractive lobby. Amenities include air-conditioning, heat, direct-dial phones, and cable TV. Nonsmoking rooms are available. The hotel also has a heated pool, restaurant/bar, and secure parking.

US$150-250

The recently renovated five-story, 93-room **C Corona Hotel** (Blvd. Costero 1442, tel. 646/176-0901, www.hotelcorona.com.mx, US$159) gives you an in-town location that's removed from the worst of the noise. Rooms feature bay views, balconies, satellite TV, air-conditioning, and heat. The spa is well appointed and clean. The bar has the feel of a hip ski bar in Switzerland. The secure parking out front can handle any size rig. You can even back your car up to the ground-floor rooms at the front of the hotel.

Popular with the yachting crowd, the **Hotel Coral & Marina** (Km 103, exit Mexico 1 at Ensenada Centro, tel. 646/175-0000, toll-free U.S. tel. 800/862-9020, www.hotelcoral.com, US$150 and up) has a full-service marina in addition to clean and contemporary accommodations. Its suites have balconies overlooking the marina. There is a restaurant serving *alta cocina mexicana,* plus a long list of guest services such as a nightclub, heated indoor and outdoor pools, hot tub, sauna, lighted tennis courts, and parking garage. The place is kid friendly, to boot.

Posada El Rey Sol (Av. Blancarte 130, tel. 646/178-1601, U.S. tel. 888/311-6871, www.posadaelreysol.com, US$80–110) has 52 good-sized rooms, and a heated pool, spa, restaurant, bar, and enclosed parking. It's a block from the waterfront, with a friendly and helpful staff.

Out of Town
US$100-150

Overlooking the Pacific Ocean five kilometers north of town, **Punta Morro Hotel and Suites** (Mexico 1, Km 106, tel. 646/178-3507, toll-free U.S. tel. 800/526-6676, www.punta-morro.com, US$250) has clean and quiet suites, from studios to three-bedroom units. Highlights include well-equipped kitchens, fireplaces, and terraces. The food and spa aren't at the same level as the accommodations, however.

Ocean views are the best part about a night's stay at **Las Rosas Hotel and Spa** (Km. 105.5, Ensenada Road, tel. 646/174-4595 or 866/447-6727, fax 646/175-9031, www.lasrosas.com,

Posada El Rey Sol

© PAUL ITOI

US$150), which is located six kilometers north of town on Mexico 1. The tradeoffs are small baths and no air-conditioning. Amenities include a restaurant with somewhat pricey food, pool, hot tub, sauna, exercise center, and tennis court.

OVER US$250

At the highest end of the spectrum, **Casa Natalie** (Km 103.3, tel. 646/174-7373, toll-free U.S. tel. 800/562-8254, www.casanatalie.com, US$180–395), located near the Hotel Coral & Marina has five suites furnished to a level rarely seen in Baja. Three more rooms opened in 2007. If you can drag yourself away from the infinity pool, this would be the ideal home base for a weekend of wine tasting in the Guadalupe Valley.

FOOD

Fish tacos and seafood cocktails top the list of foods to try in Ensenada (or anywhere in coastal Baja, for that matter). One of the best places to try these local delights is the **Mercado de Mariscos** (Seafood Market, Blvd. Costero at Av. Miramar, daily late morning–early evening), behind the Plaza Marina on the waterfront. You can also buy fresh fish here to cook yourself.

Mexican

Manzanilla (Blvd Teniente Azueta 139, tel. 646/175-7073, www.rmanzanilla.com, Wed.–Sat. noon–midnight, US$10–30) has become one of Ensenada's top restaurants. Guests are greeted by the co-owner, and the restaurant is known for its rib eye, raw fish, and local wines. The restaurant uses local organic ingredients and seafood.

Rinconcito Oaxaqueño (no tel., daily 9 A.M.–5 P.M.), off Diamante and a block south of Reforma, serves authentic Oaxacan cuisine. You can order nopales, *chicharron,* or carne asada in a taco or plate from US$1–5. If they are in season, and you're an adventurous eater, try the grasshoppers *(chapulines)* washed down with an ice cold Dos Equis.

Acambaro (El Refugio Ensenadense) (Av.

MEXICAN-STYLE EGGS

Mexican-style egg-and-beans plates come in many different styles. They typically are served as a late breakfast or brunch on weekends and holidays. Here are some of the preparations you may see on the menu:

- *huevos revueltos:* scrambled eggs

- *huevos duros:* hard-boiled eggs

- *huevos escafaldos:* soft-boiled eggs

- *huevos estrellados:* eggs fried sunny side up

- *huevos a la Mexicana/huevos mexicanos:* eggs scrambled with chopped tomato, onion, and chilies

- *huevos rancheros:* fried eggs served on a tortilla

- *huevos divorciados:* two *huevos estrellados* separated by beans, each egg usually topped with a different salsa

- *con chorizo:* with ground sausage

- *con machaca:* with dried, shredded meat

- *con tocino:* with bacon

- *con jamón:* with ham

Iturbide 528 off Av. Juárez btw Calles 5/6, tel. 646/176-5235, daily for breakfast, lunch, and dinner, mains US$10–15) serves tasty Mexican dishes in a rustic wood and brick setting. Plates arrive with the works: limes, oregano, and salsa.

A group of restaurants along Avenida Lópes Mateos specializes in roast chickens: **Hacienda del Charro** (Av. López Mateos 454, tel. 646/178-2114, daily for lunch and dinner till 11:30 P.M.) is the best one along this strip, also offering chicken tamales and *pollo pipián* (chicken cooked in a pumpkin-seed mole). The tangy flavor of homemade *agua de jamaica* (hibiscus) balances the savory chicken.

Las Cazuelas Restaurant Bar (Sanginés 6 near Blvd. Costero, tel. 646/176-1044, daily 7 A.M.–11 P.M., mains US$10–25) is an old standby serving border-style cuisine, including *codorniz* (quail), seafood, steaks, ribs, and hearty Mexican breakfasts.

The most unique food experience in Ensenada is still offered at **❰ El Taco de Huitzilopochtli** (Av. de las Rosas 5, Col. Valle Verde, tel. 646/174-2381, Sat.–Sun. 9 A.M.–5 P.M., mains under US$10). The house specialty is *mixiote,* which is lamb wrapped in maguey leaves and then baked for 16 hours in a wood-fired oven. They start the process on Friday, and the food isn't ready until Saturday morning. The menu is limited only by your sense of adventure. You can order *huitlacoche* (corn fungus tacos) or *huanzontle,* a reedy vegetable. The easiest way to get there is to take a taxi from downtown, and you'll appreciate not having to drive if you're there when the owner breaks out the "house" tequila.

On the corner of Espinoza and Juárez, **Tacos Fénix** (daily noon–8 P.M.) serves up some of the town's best seafood tacos out of a stand across from the Calimax. Shrimp tacos are light and crispy, and they cost US$1–1.50 each.

Seafood

Las Conchas Oyster Bar and Restaurant (tel. 646/175-7375, daily for lunch and dinner, mains US$15 and up), in Plaza Hussong, draws a crowd for oysters *(ostiones)* and other seafood specialties. It's a popular place, so expect to wait for a table.

Tacos el Fenix (Av. Espinosa at Av. Juárez, no tel., daily 8 A.M.–8 P.M.) prepares fish and prawn tacos for US$1 each.

Asian

La Cochinita (Paseo Hidalgo next to Maritime Customs, tel. 646/178-5445, www.lacochinita.com.mx, daily lunch and dinner) is a Baja chain that specializes in Mexican-style Japanese food. There are a dozen locations in Ensenada and more in major cities throughout the peninsula.

© CARMEL TSABAR

the happy meeting of corn and flour at a local *tortillería*

Cafés

Stop in for a quick bite at **El Faro Café** (no tel., mains under US$10), before a day of sportfishing. Located next to Gordo's Sportfishing, behind Plaza Marina on the waterfront, it opens early at 4:30 A.M. and serves breakfast only.

Pueblo Café Deli (Av. Ruiz 96, tel. 646/178-8055, daily 8 A.M.–midnight) serves espresso drinks, plus breakfast foods, Mexican fare, salads, pastries, wine, and beer.

Dependable **Sanborns Café** (Plaza Marina, Blvd. Costero, tel. 646/174-0971, daily 7:30 A.M.–10 P.M., mains US$10–15) always has a number of soups, salads, sandwiches, breakfasts, and Mexican dishes on the menu.

Café Café (Av. López Mateos 496, tel. 646/178-8209, daily from 9 A.M.) is a combination coffee house/art gallery that also hosts occasional cultural events and performances.

European

El Rey Sol (Av. López Mateos 1000 at Av. Blancarte, tel. 646/178-1733, daily 7:30 A.M.–10:30 P.M., mains US$20 and up) is an Ensenada institution for fine French cuisine. The restaurant was founded in 1947 by a native of Santa Rosalía (a town in southern Baja that was built by a French mining company) named Doña Pepita, who studied at the Cordon Bleu cooking school in France. Whether you choose a seafood, poultry, or meat entrée, it will arrive with fresh herbs and vegetables from the family's ranch in the Valle de Santo Tomás, south of Ensenada.

In the Bodegas de Santo Tomás building, **La Embotelladora Vieja** (Av. Miramar 666 at Calle 7, tel. 646/174-0807, Mon. and Wed. noon–11 P.M., Thurs.–Sat. noon–11 P.M., Sun. noon–5 P.M., mains US$20 and up), has a Mediterranean menu and an international wine list.

Groceries

The **Gigante** at Avenidas Reforma and Delante is the largest supermarket in town and the easiest to find on your way through. Stop here to pick up just about anything you left behind at home.

Avenida Diamante has a string of local *panaderías, tortillerías,* and *dulcerías.* Vendors along the highway south of town sell fresh tamales, as well as local olives, chilies, and honey.

INFORMATION AND SERVICES

Tourist Assistance

The **Baja California State Tourism Secretariat** (Blvd. Costero and Calle Las Rocas, tel. 646/172-3022, Mon.–Fri. 8 A.M.–5 P.M., Sat.–Sun. 10 A.M.–3 P.M.) has a wealth of information regarding local events, restaurants, and accommodations, as well as for the entire state. The staff speaks English and will be happy to help.

The **Ensenada Tourism Trust** (Blvd. Lázaro Cárdenas 609-5, tel. 646/178-8578 or 800/025-3991, toll-free U.S. tel. 800/310-9687, www.enjoyensenada.com) has much of the same information.

Money

There are several ATMs in town, including a Banamex at Avenida Juárez and Riveroll and a

---

ENSENADA PHONE NUMBERS

- Ensenada area code: 646
- Customs: 174-0897
- Fire Department: 068
- Green Angels: 176-4675
- Highway Patrol: 176-1311
- Immigration: 174-0164
- IMSS Hospital: 172-4500
- ISSSTE Hospital: 176-5276
- Police: 060
- Red Cross: 066
- State Police: 061
- State Tourism Office: 172-3022
- Tourist Assistance: 078

ENSENADA TO EL ROSARIO

Banca Serfín at Avenida Ruiz 290. Most banks in Ensenada refer visitors to a *casa de cambio* for foreign-exchange services. Several shopping centers along Avenida Juárez and Avenida Reforma feature money-changing booths or storefronts.

Post and Telephone

There is a post office at the corner of Avenidas López Mateos and Rotario (Riviera), across from the Desert Inn (Mon.–Fri. 8 A.M.–6 P.M., Sat. 9 A.M.–1 P.M.). Public telephones are a better deal for local and long-distance calls than hotel phones.

Immigration

If you plan to travel south of Maneadero and haven't validated your tourist card yet, you'll need to pay a visit to the Ensenada immigration office (tel. 646/174-0164, daily 9 A.M.–5 P.M.), next to the port captain's office (COTP) on Avenida Azueta. Look for the turnoff near the waterfront at the northern entrance into town.

Parking here can be a challenge, since there is no public lot for the office, and most of the curbs nearby are painted red. Consider parking farther away and walking in.

If you run into any problems getting your tourist permit here, go to the state tourism office (Blvd. Costero and Calle Las Rocas, tel. 646/172-3022) and ask for help from the SECTUR *delegado*.

Language Schools

Colegio de Idiomas de Baja California (Baja California Language College, Av. Riveroll 1287, tel. 646/174-1741, U.S. tel. 619/758-9711 or 877/444-2252, www.bajacal.com) teaches 30-hour Spanish classes for US$279. Classes are small groups and courses take one week to complete.

The **Center of Languages and Latin American Studies** (Calle Felipe Angeles #15, tel. 646/178-7600, www.spanishschoolbaja. com) also has a one-week program (US$280), with discounts for four or more weeks. Materials, homestays, meals, and registration cost extra.

Emergencies

The **Clínica Hospital ISSSTE** (Calle Sanginés and Av. Pedro Loyola, tel. 646/176-5276) offers 24/7 emergency medical services. For ambulance service, call **Cruz Roja** (tel. 066). If you need emergency treatment at San Diego medical facilities, contact **TransMedic Ambulance** (842-3 Av. Ruiz, tel. 646/178-1400), a 24/7 emergency service that offers air and land transportation to San Diego.

GETTING THERE
By Air

Ensenada's **Aeropuerto El Ciprés** (tel. 646/177-4503) is located three kilometers south of town off Mexico 1. It is a military base and an official Mexican airport of entry with a paved airstrip; however, only two regional airlines currently offer regular service. If you aren't flying your own plane or travel to and from Guerrero Negro or Isla Cedros, this airport isn't going to be of much use.

By Bus

Autotransportes de Baja California (ABC) offers intercity connections on air-conditioned buses, departing from the Central de Autobuses terminal at Avenida Riveroll and Calle 11 (tel. 646/178-6680). Buses leave this terminal twice a day for points south, including San Quintín (4 hours), Guerrero Negro (8 hours), Santa Rosalía (12 hours), Loreto (15 hours), and La Paz (20 hours).

Buses without air conditioning leave from the smaller terminal at Avenida Riveroll and Calle 8 (tel. 646/177-0909, every hour to Tijuana from 5 A.M.–9:30 P.M.).

The **Transportes Norte de Sonora** (TNS, Tijuana tel. 664/688-1979) and **Estrellas de Oro** (Tijuana, tel. 664/683-5022) companies all offer connection to Guaymas, Los Mochis, Mazatlán, Guadalajara, and Mexico City on the mainland.

By Car

Ensenada marks the end of the toll road, Mexico 1-D, from Tijuana. From here until Los Cabos, Mexico 1 is a paved, two-lane highway that's narrow and without a shoulder for much of its length.

Mexico 3 from Tecate also passes through Ensenada on its way to the Sierra Juárez and the intersection with Mexico 5 near San Felipe. Here's how to pick up Mexico 3 heading east out of Ensenada: Take Avenida Juárez to Avenida Reforma at the Benito Juárez statue. Cross Avenida Reforma and follow the street called Calzada Cortés until it turns left and becomes Mexico 3.

GETTING AROUND
By Bus

Ensenada's compact tourism zone can be managed by foot, but a number of public buses do run along the main streets (US$0.50). The route is usually given as a street name posted in the window.

By Taxi

Taxis can be found along Avenidas López Mateos or Juárez, and at the bus depot on Calle

11 at Avenida Riveroll. Trips within the city should cost under US$10. Negotiate the fare before you get in. A taxi ride to La Bufadora costs US$10–15.

By Car and Motor Scooter
RENTAL CARS AND MOTOR SCOOTERS
Since it doesn't have an international airport, Ensenada has less demand for rental cars, and fewer agencies means higher prices. Most visitors either drive their own car, take the bus, or rent a car in San Diego. Only a few of the major chains still allow cars to be driven into Mexico (Avis and Hertz are two that do; you'll have to buy Mexican auto insurance when you pick up the vehicle at the San Diego airport). **Fiesta Rent-A-Car** (Blvd. Costero 1442, in the lobby of Hotel Corona, tel. 646/176-3344) is one local option. If you don't mind prepaying and not knowing which company you will rent from, you can also book a car through a discount service like HotWire. com. Rates at press time started at US$35 per day (without Mexican auto insurance).

At the south end of Plaza Cívica, **Chavo's Sport Rentals** (Gaviotas #256, tel. 646/212-7677 or 646/201-5942) rents Yamaha motor scooters and ATVs for around US$20 per hour.

DRIVING
Ensenada is a big city with busy streets, but it's not impossible to navigate. Just take your time, watch for signs, and stop at every intersection, whether you see a stop sign or not. Absolutely do not speed or drink while driving.

ESTERO BEACH
Twelve kilometers south of Ensenada, the Río San Carlos meets Bahía de Todos Santos to form an estuary environment. The beach here isn't the prettiest that Baja has to offer (unless you're into tidal flats), but it tends not to be too crowded, except in the middle of the summer. Turn off Mexico 1 7.5 kilometers south of the Gigante at Avenidas Reforma and Delante.

Accommodations
There are a few motels near the beach, but the Estero Beach Resort or its attached RV park are the best options if you want to spend the night. The well-worn and family-oriented **Estero Beach Resort Hotel** (Km 14, Carretera Transpeninsular, tel. 646/176-6225 or 646/176-6230, U.S. tel. 619/335-1145, www.hotelesterobeach.com, US$80–120) has 100 rooms and suites, most of which have views of the beach and are set amidst landscaped grounds of grass and palms. This is a full-service resort, but think Super 8 more than Crowne Plaza, and you'll be pleasantly surprised. Families who fall in love with the place tend to return every year until their kids are grown. Guest services include tennis courts, boat rentals, horseback riding, a swimming pool, playground, restaurant/bar, general store, and small historical museum. The adjoining RV park has 60 spaces with full hookups and grassy campsites (US$35–45). This place is popular with caravans, so book early. Campers are allowed to use the hotel facilities. There are several less expensive campgrounds and trailer parks along the beach.

Getting There
City buses signed for the Chapultepec neighborhood run between downtown Ensenada and the estuary.

PUNTA BANDA
The estuary at the south end of Bahía Todos Santos is protected by a sharp, rocky peninsula that extends northwest and ends at a cape called Cabo Banda. The name Punta Banda is used to reference the peninsula, the cape, and a settlement on the bay.

A large-scale real estate development is scheduled to open in 2011 with 100 villas and 40 home sites, starting at US$3 million. The par-70 golf course will be closed to the public, so if you want to play the Tiger Woods–designed course, you'll need to pony up for a home site or be invited by someone who has.

◖ La Bufadora
If you miss the chance to see gray whales spouting offshore Punta Banda, this blowhole on the south side of the peninsula is

not a bad substitute. A frequent stop on the tour bus circuit—and popular with locals as well—La Bufadora (The Snorter) creates a spectacular display as incoming swells push seawater into an underground canyon and out through a hole in the rocks. The resulting explosion of water and spray reaches heights of 25–30 meters. The sight has been developed with a small visitor center and restrooms. A number of food vendors line the road to the parking area.

Water Sports
Dale's La Bufadora Dive Shop (Rancho La Bufadora, tel. 646/154-2092, www.labufadoradive.com, open weekends or by appointment) is a multi-sport operation on tiny Bahía Papalote that offers *panga* fishing (US$35 per person, min. two people), unguided dive trips (US$35 per person, min. two people), and kayak rentals (US$20 per half-day, US$30 per full-day).

La Bufadora is an excellent place to begin a scuba diving tour of the Baja Peninsula if you don't mind cold water. Its pinnacles, kelp beds, and giant green anemones make for memorable dives. Conditions in the bay are best for intermediate to advanced divers, as there is a good amount of surge except on the calmest of days. Currents keep the water here a few degrees colder than temperatures in San Diego. You'll need lots of neoprene or, preferably, a dry suit to be comfortable. You can rent gear and reserve a boat from Dale's, or through the Almar dive shop in Ensenada (Av. Macheros 149, tel. 646/178-3013, almardive@hotmail.com).

Another option for fishing is **Vonny's Fleet** (tel. 646/154-2046, www.vonnysfleet.com,

U$139/boat up to three people), which launches *pangas* from the beach at Punta Banda.

Camping and RV Parks
La Jolla Beach Camp (Km 12.5 BCN 23, La Jolla, tel. 646/154-2005, US$15) is a large, basic park that faces Bahía de Todos Santos. Its 200 sites come with use of hot showers, boat ramp, tennis court, and dump station (no hookups, except for a few sites with electricity). The park also has its own market and restaurant.

Next door, smaller **Villarino RV Park** (Km 13 BCN 23, La Jolla, Ensenada, tel. 646/154-2004, US$22–28) has a little more character, plus some of its sites have full hookups. The park has clean restrooms, hot showers, picnic tables, a boat ramp, boat rentals, restaurant, and market. The office is open daily 9 A.M.–noon and 1–5 P.M.

Three *ejido*-run campgrounds on the peninsula have restrooms and water, but no other facilities (US$5).

You can walk to Dale's La Bufadora Dive Shop from **Rancho La Bufadora** (tel. 646/178-7172, US$15), which overlooks Bahía Papalote. It has primitive campsites, and there are flush toilets and 24/7 security.

Getting There
To get to Punta Banda from Ensenada by car, follow Mexico 1 about 25 kilometers south to BCN 23, a right turn that comes before Maneadero. Take this road west through the retirement community of La Jolla and along the peninsula. The road will climb over the rocks and around to south-facing La Bufadora. A taxi ride from Ensenada to La Bufadora runs about US$15–20.

Valle de Guadalupe

The scenic Guadalupe Valley follows the Río Guadalupe between Ensenada and Tecate on Mexico 3, with a small town at Km 77.

MISIÓN NUESTRA SEÑORA DE GUADALUPE DEL NORTE

Padre Félix Caballero established the last of nine Dominican missions (1834–1840) in Baja in 1834, 24 kilometers east of the next closest mission (San Miguel), above the Río Guadalupe. The missions were already on the decline at this point, but the new settlement became a successful farm and ranch with 400 indigenous people under its tutelage, if only for a few short years. The mission ruins are not recognizable today.

COLONIA RUSA

After the Mexican government secularized the mission properties, a group of Russian pacifists called the Molokans (milk-drinkers, who abstained from drinking alcohol), fled the Russian Orthodox Church and purchased the land surrounding this settlement to start a new colony in 1905.

The original families planted crops and vineyards, raised livestock, built adobe houses, and went about their simple way of life.

In 1938, then-president Cárdenas seized all foreign-owned property in the country, and 3,000 Mexicans arrived to take over the colony, renaming it Francisco Zarco. Only a few of the original Russian families stayed in the area, but the area retains a Russian look and feel. Some of the Molokan homes have survived the years, and tombstones in the town cemetery have Russian enscriptions.

The neighboring **Museo Comunitario del Valle de Guadalupe** (Tues.–Sun. 10 A.M.–6 P.M., by donation) and **Museo Histórico del Valle de Guadalupe** (Tues.–Sun. 10 A.M.–5 P.M., by donation) display historical artifacts, such as clothing, photos, and tools. To find the cemetery (across from the Monte Xanic winery) and museums, turn off the highway at Francisco Zarco and follow the paved road to its end. Turn right and go another 150 meters.

◖ RUTA DEL VINO

The Valle de Guadalupe is an internationally recognized winemaking region that has been gaining attention from Southern California residents and the U.S. travel press in recent years. Baja California wines are shipped all over Mexico and Western Europe, but because of U.S. and Canadian trade policies, they weren't exported north of the border until recent years. They're still difficult to find in Canada and the United States.

The highest concentration of wineries—more than two-dozen at last count—are located in the 23-kilometer-long Valle de Guadalupe, located off Mexico 3, northeast of Ensenada. The introduction of stainless steel tanks and temperature-controlled barrels at many of these vineyards have helped put Baja wines on the map. But you can still enjoy personal service and, often, time with the winemakers themselves as you make your way through the valley. Spring and summer are the most popular time to visit, though Mexican holiday weekends also draw a crowd.

You might start your tour at the west end of Guadalupe Valley in the village of San Antonio de las Minas. At **Vinisterra** (Km 94.5, tel. 646/178-3350, www.vinisterra.com, Sat. 11 A.M.–4:30 P.M., Sun. 11 A.M.–3 P.M.), Abelardo and Patricia Macouzet Rodriguez offer a cabernet sauvignon–merlot blend, tempranillo, and other award-winning wines.

Inquire about the award-winning merlot at family-owned **Viña de Liceaga** (Km 93.5, tel. 646/155-3091, www.vinosliceaga.com, Mon.–Fri. 8 A.M.–3 P.M., Sat.–Sun. 11 A.M.–3 P.M.). Choose from several tasting options for US$3–5. Reservations are recommended. Nearby, contemporary **Casa de Piedra** (Km 93.5, tel. 646/155-3097, www.vinoscasadepiedra.com) offers tastings in a farmhouse setting.

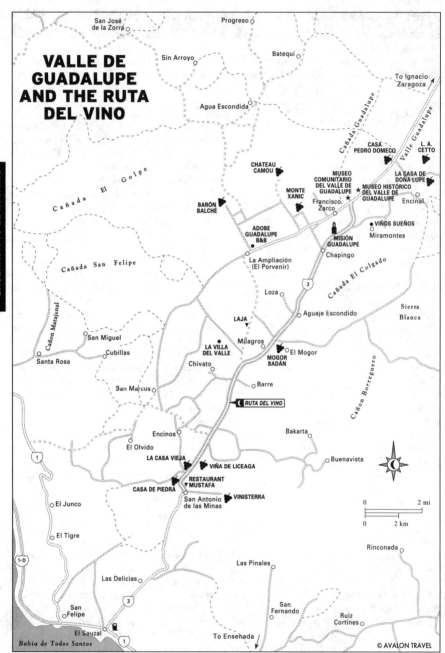

VALLE DE GUADALUPE AND THE RUTA DEL VINO

San José de la Zorra
Progreso
Sin Arroyo
Batequí
To Ignacio Zaragoza
Agua Escondida
Cañada Guadalupe
Valle Guadalupe
CASA PEDRO DOMECQ
L. A. CETTO
Cañada El Golpe
CHATEAU CAMOU
MUSEO COMUNITARIO DEL VALLE DE GUADALUPE
LA CASA DE DOÑA LUPE
MUSEO HISTÓRICO DEL VALLE DE GUADALUPE
MONTE XANIC
Francisco Zarco
Encinal
BARÓN BALCHÉ
ADOBE GUADALUPE B&B
VIÑOS SUEÑOS
Miramontes
Cañada San Felipe
MISIÓN GUADALUPE
La Ampliación (El Porvenir)
Chapingo
Loza
Cañada El Colgado
3
Aguaje Escondido
Sierra Blanca
San Miguel
Cubillas
LAJA
Milagros
LA VILLA DEL VALLE
El Mogor
MOGOR BADÁN
Santa Rosa
Cañon Matajanal
Chivato
Cañón Borrguero
San Marcos
Barre
RUTA DEL VINO
Encinos
Bakarta
El Olvido
LA CASA VIEJA
VIÑA DE LICEAGA
Buenavista
1
CASA DE PIEDRA
RESTAURANT MUSTAFA
VINISTERRA
San Antonio de las Minas
El Junco
Rinconada
El Tigre
1-D
Las Pinales
Las Delicias
San Fernando
Ruiz Cortines
San Felipe
3
El Sauzal
1
Bahía de Todos Santos
To Ensenada

0   2 mi
0   2 km

© AVALON TRAVEL

BAJA CALIFORNIA'S WINE TIMELINE

Though it's a relatively new phenomenon to many foreign wine connoisseurs, Baja California's wine history dates back several centuries.

- **Early 16th century:** Hernán Cortés introduces Spanish vines to Mexico.

- **1597:** The Jesuits set up a winery in the present-day state of Coahuila.

- **1697:** Padre Juan Ugarte transplants the cuttings to Misión San Javier.

- **1791:** Dominican Padre José Lorieto establishes Misión Santo Tomás de Aquino, introducing the first vines of Spanish origin to the Valle de Santo Tomás, 45 kilometers south of Ensenada.

- **1888:** Italian miner Francisco Andronequi assumes control of the former mission vineyard and renames it Bodegas de Santo Tomás.

- **1906:** A Russian Christian sect acquires a tract of land in the Valle de Guadalupe and plants more vineyards, which prove to grow exceptionally well in the hot, dry Baja climate.

- **1939:** A former general from the Mexican Revolution, Abelardo Lujan Rodríguez, buys Bodegas de Santo Tomás and moves its headquarters north to Ensenada.

- **Early 1960s:** Rodríguez hires a winemaker from the internationally renowned school for viticulture and oenology at the University of California at Davis, who introduces new varietals as well as modern winemaking technology.

- **1972:** Pedro Domecq, a maker of brandy from Spain, establishes a wine-making operation in the Valle de Guadalupe, creating a buzz for Baja wines within the international wine community.

- **1990s:** Boutique wineries including Monte Xanic and Chateau de Camou (Viñas de Camou) raise the bar even higher, establishing credibility and visibility for the emerging wine region.

- **2007:** Baja California wineries account for approximately 90 percent of all wine made in the country.

Reservations are required. Once a year, it offers a four-weekend wine-making seminar. **La Casa Vieja** (Km 93.5, tel. 646/155-3153, lacasavieja.baja@hotmail.com) opens daily at 9 A.M. and closes at sunset, or whenever the crowd disperses. In addition to offering tastings, this winery has a deli, arts and crafts store, and information center on-site.

Chateau Camou (tel. 646/177-2221 or 646/177-3303, www.chateau-camou.com.mx, Mon.–Sat. 8 A.M.–3 P.M., Sun. 9 A.M.–2 P.M.) specializes in expensive Bordeaux-style reds. It offers three tasting/tour options: Try four wines and a tour for US$5, six tastings and a tour for US$10, or a tour with the winemaker and a complete tasting including a barrel sample for US$40.

Next up, **Mogor Badán** (Km 86.5, tel. 646/177-1484, abadan@cicese.mx) is a combination organic produce farm, vineyard, and winery with tours, tastings, and shopping. Reservations are required. Baja's most acclaimed winery, **Monte Xanic** (tel. 646/174-7055, www.montexanic.com, Mon.–Fri. 9 A.M.–4 P.M., Sat. 8 A.M.–noon), produces 50,000 cases of wine per year, and many of its labels have won awards in the United States, Canada, and Mexico. The winery charges US$4 for tasting whites and an additional US$4 for reds. Reservations are required.

Housed in an adobe brick building, **Barón Balché** (El Porvenir, tel. 646/183-9501, www.baronbalche.com, daily 10 A.M.–4 P.M.) is another boutique winery using the latest technology to make wine—10,000 cases a year.

The largest winery in the region—and in all of Latin America—Italian-owned **L. A. Cetto** (Km 73.5, tel. 646/155-2179, www.cettowines.com or www.lacetto.com, daily 10 A.M.–3 P.M.) has gardens and a picnic area, as well as an inviting tasting room. You can tour the winery without reservations, and there are no tasting or tour fees. Past L. A. Cetto, **La Casa de Doña Lupe** (Rancho La Gotita, Francisco Zarco, tel. 646/155-2323, www.donalupe.com, daily 9 A.M.–7 P.M.) tempts visitors with home-baked goods, as well as farm-fresh cheese, honey, and produce and organically grown wines. In the same vicinity, you'll pay US$2.50 to taste the tempranillo, graciano, and mazuelo varietals at **Casa Pedro Domecq** (Km 73.5, tel. 646/155-2333, www.vinosdomecq.com.mx, Mon.–Fri. 10 A.M.–4 P.M., Sat. 10 A.M.–5 P.M.). The fee includes a cellar tour, plus use of a picnic area on the grounds.

Also at Domecq, **GaleríAH** (Mexico 3, Km 73, tel. 646/175-3132, www.galeriah.com.mx) represents contemporary artists from Mexico around the world.

Baja Wine Country Tours

Local resident Steve Dryden (U.S. tel. 619/300-4976, www.mexicowinetours.com) offers wine-tasting tours by private van or motor coach. Day-long bus tours depart from San Diego and include tastings at three wineries and lunch at Mustafa's Moroccan Restaurant. Steve is a former Napa Valley winery manager with extensive knowledge of the Mexican wine industry, as well as the Kumiai people, Russian (Molokan) history, and the culture and history of Baja California. To follow the action in Baja's wine country, read his *Baja Times* column online (www.bajatimes.com/bajawine.asp).

Fiesta de la Vendimía Bajacaliforniana

Each August, the Valle de Guadalupe wineries celebrate a 10-day winemaking festival with tastings, food/wine pairings, vineyard tours, and the requisite music and dancing, in the valley and in downtown Ensenada. For information on upcoming festivals, call 646/174-0170 or Bodegas de Santo Tomás in Ensenada (tel. 646/178-3333) or contact CANIRAC, the Ensenada restaurant association (www.caniracensenada.com).

ACCOMMODATIONS AND CAMPING
Under US$50

Budget travelers can rent a cottage for US$35 a night at **Viños Sueños** (tel. 646/179-4763, daily 9 A.M.–5 P.M.) winery in Francisco Zarco.

US$50-100

Warm colors set the tone in affordable rooms at **El Mezon del Vino** (tel. 664/162-9010, www.elmezondelvino.com, US$60 weekdays, US$80 weekends, suites US$150). Book an in-room massage for US$45. The hotel has a restaurant (weekends 8 A.M.–7 P.M.) for wine-tasting as well as breakfast and lunch.

US$100-250

Tuscan-style **La Villa del Valle** (6 km. west of Mexico 3 from Km. 88 btw San Antonio de las Minas and Ejido El Porvenirtel. 646/183-9249, U.S. tel. 818/207-7130, www.lavilladelvalle.com, US$175) stands atop a hill on 28 hectares with sweeping views of surrounding vineyards, orchards, and gardens. Four of its six rooms have private balconies; all have luxury linens and many more elegant touches. In between tastings, guests relax by the pool or soak in the hot tub, book a massage on-site, or play a game of bocce ball. Rates include full breakfast, an afternoon glass of wine and *botanas,* and Wi-Fi access. There is a two-night minimum on weekends.

Near the Monte Xanic and Chateau Camou wineries, the **Adobe Guadalupe B&B** (Francisco Zarco, tel. 646/155-2094, www.adobeguadalupe.com, US$168) was the first winery to offer accommodations in the valley. The 24-hectare winery offers six guestrooms in a rambling adobe-walled, hacienda-style complex. Rates include a complete breakfast served at a common table in the huge kitchen. Other meals may be arranged per cost. In recent years, some guests have complained of overly protective dogs roaming common areas of the inn (reportedly, they do bite) and less-than-attentive service. Also note that double beds are twins pushed together.

Camping

You can camp on an 32-hectare farm at **Bibayoff-Bodegas Valle de Guadalupe** (tel. 646/177-2722, bibayoff@telnor.net), run by a Russian family in San Antonio de las Minas. Exit Mexico 3 at El Tigre and follow the dirt road to Rancho Bibayoff. The Kumiai have opened a campground just north of L. A. Cetto Winery. Some say it resembles a California state park at the turn of the 20th century. Sites cost US$5, and services include firewood, water, showers, and a general store. Guided hikes, horseback riding, cultural displays, and crafts are also available. Reservations are required. Contact Horacio Moncada at tel. 646/178-8093 or 646/118-9113.

FOOD

The valley now has a few well-known restaurants to go with its boutique wineries: Around 22 kilometers northeast of Ensenada, perched on a hill just north of the small community of San Antonio de las Minas, **Restaurant Mustafa** (Km 93, tel. 646/155-3185, Wed.–Mon. 8 A.M.–7 P.M., mains US$7–12) serves Moroccan-influenced dishes, including lamb shish-kebab and chicken breast stuffed with spinach and cheese, along with a menu of Mexican specialties. In San Antonio itself, **El Mesón** is popular for breakfast and lunch; it's closed on Thursday. The owner is an admirer of British aviation artist Robert Taylor and displays Taylor's work on the restaurant walls.

Visiting gourmands praise **Restaurant Laja** (Km 83, tel. 646/155-2556, www.lajamexico.com, prix fixe menu US$52 or US$72) for farm-fresh cuisine on par with California's celebrated Chez Panisse and French Laundry restaurants. The brainchild of former Four Seasons chef Jair Téllez, the restaurant is located about 50 meters off Mexico 3 via a washboard road, in a private home with white walls and a red tile roof.

In Francisco Zarco, **Doña Chuy's** (Km. 83 Mexico 3, Francisco Zarco, no tel., mains under US$10) has reasonably priced Mexican plates, and **La Cabaña de las Lomas** (Km 91.5, Cajeme St., tel. 646/155-3033, www.lacabanadelaslomas. com, Fri.–Sun. 8 A.M.–5 P.M.) prepares northern Mexican specialties such as fresh quail.

Mercado La Chica and **Abarrotes C. R.,** both in Francisco Zarco, can meet basic needs for food and supplies.

GETTING THERE

The Valle de Guadalupe is less than a two-hour drive (113 km) south of San Diego on the toll road from Tijuana to Ensenada. After paying the last toll, watch for a sign to Tecate via Mexico 3 and the Ruta del Vino. Travel east on Mexico 3 for 11 kilometers until you drop down into the Baja wine country at San Antonio de las Minas. This is the western end of the Guadalupe Valley wine region, which extends 22 kilometers east toward Tecate, ending near Km 73.5 at L. A. Cetto and Domecq wineries.

Sierra Juárez

The least-traveled highway on the Baja Peninsula, Mexico 3, connects Ensenada to Mexico 5 and San Felipe on the Sea of Cortez. Along the way, it passes a Dominican mission site, provides access to a small national park, Constitución de 1857, and crosses the Sierra Juárez via the San Matías Pass.

There are four places to buy gas along the route: Ojos Negros (Km 39), Independencia (Km 94), as well as Lázaro Cárdenas and

Francisco R. Serrano, closer to the east end of the highway.

PARQUE NACIONAL CONSTITUCIÓN DE 1857

This 5,000-hectare park covers a sub-alpine plateau in the center of the Sierra Juárez range. Granite boulders and Ponderosa pines ring its two natural lakes, Laguna La Chica and Laguna Juárez (Laguna Hanson). The latter has campsites (US$5) with fire pits and grills, but there are no marked hiking trails in the park.

The park is generally deserted except during Semana Santa (the week before Easter), when off-roaders invade. Be prepared for snow in winter.

Getting There
The easiest access road to the park heads northeast off Mexico 3 at Km 55 near Ojos Negros. This route is mostly paved now, and is passable for most vehicles, except after winter storms.

If you don't want to retrace your steps to Mexico 3, you can continue on the access road heading northeast to the other side of the park, and meet Mexico 2 60 kilometers from Laguna Hanson, near La Rumorosa.

MISIÓN SANTA CATALINA VIRGEN Y MÁRTIR
Padre José Loriente founded this mission (1797–1840) to the west of a strategic mountain pass that led to the San Felipe desert and the Colorado River beyond. At 1,067 meters, the mission was built to serve as a fort, protecting the coastal missions against raids from indigenous people to the east. At one time, it claimed the most converts of any Dominican mission on the peninsula, but it was destroyed in 1840 in a rebel attack. Only traces of the mission walls remain in the present-day village of Santa Catarina, which is eight kilometers east of Independencia (Km 94) along a graded dirt road.

Maneadero to Vicente Guerrero

Between Ensenada and San Quintín, Mexico 1 meanders inland along low mesas, through the fertile valley of Santo Tomás, and on south past a series of ranchos and agricultural supply towns. Four Dominican mission sites dot the highway along the way.

MANEADERO
Once you pass into the farming town of Maneadero, 20 kilometers south of Ensenada, you've reached the end of the "free zone" and will need immigration papers (tourist card or visa) to proceed farther south. The military often has a checkpoint set up here, and the *topes* (speed bumps) are plentiful, so take it slow.

Accommodations and Camping
Las Cañadas Campamento (Km 31–32, tel. 646/153-1055, toll-free U.S. tel. 800/027-3828, www.lascanadas.com, US$16 pp) originally opened as a day-use swimming complex in the summer, but it also has a few campsites with full hookups and lakeside tent camping, both of which are open year-round. Basic cabins rent for US$65 per night; bring your own linens.

LA BOCANA AND PUERTO SANTO TOMÁS
The first opportunity for off-road exploration south of Ensenada comes at Km 46–47, where a gravel road heads west, following the Cañon Santo Tomás to the coast. Sheltered by Punta Santo Tomás to the north, the fishing settlements of La Bocana and Puerto Santo Tomás have free camping on the beach and cabins for rent. *Panga* fishing and kayak fishing are popular activities, with rock cod and snapper among the common catches. There is a boat launch for small watercraft, and the kelp beds in the bay could make for an interesting dive if you have your own equipment.

There are a couple of *tiendas,* but don't count on much. You're off the grid here, so phones and other power-intensive amenities aren't going to be available. Cell phones don't get much of a signal either. It takes about an hour and a half to get to Puerto Santo Tomás by car.

Surfing
Surfers find occasional reef and point breaks in Bahía Santo Tomás and at Punta China to the south (turn left when you reach the coastal

road and La Bocana). But the waves are more consistent and the rides often longer at the next point south, Punta San José. Popular with surfers from San Diego, the point has free cliffside camping above the surf, with outhouses but no services. There are two ways to reach San José. The best road leaves the highway just south of the Pemex in Santo Tomás. Go about 23 kilometers and bear right at the fork; continue another 16 kilometers to the lighthouse and camping area. Alternatively, if you have a high-clearance vehicle you might attempt an ungraded road that branches south from the Cañon Puerto Santo Tomás road, about 20.5 kilometers west of Mexico 1. From the turnoff, it's about 11 kilometers of rough driving to the break. Inquire in town about the road conditions before you choose this route.

Accommodations

The **Puerto Santo Tomás Resort** (Ensenada message tel. 646/154-9415, www.puertosantotomas.com, realbaja@starband.net) has rustic cabins (US$40–50) and larger houses (US$100–150) for rent, as well as campsites (US$14, includes showers and toilets) and a cantina serving Mexican and seafood dishes. You need to book ahead to eat here so the management can get the supplies it needs in time for your arrival. *Panga* fishing rates are US$130–160 per day. To find the resort, look for a road sign for Puerto Santo Tomás between Km 46–47 and turn right about 45 meters after the sign. (If you reach the village of Santo Tomás on Mexico 1, you've passed the turn.) Follow this road 29 kilometers west, staying right each time the road forks. The road meets the coast at La Bocana (The Mouth). Turn right (north) and follow the road over a small hill and along the coast for about five kilometers to Puerto Santo Tomás.

◖ VALLE DE SANTO TOMÁS

You know you've entered the agricultural valley of Santo Tomás (pop. 400) when you start to see rolling hills covered in a carpet of brilliant green, rows of grapevines, olive groves, and fields of wildflowers.

Misíon Santo Tomás de Aquino

Dominican Padre José Loriente established this mission (1791–1849) midway between Misíon San Miguel to the north and San Vicente to the south. He planted to raise livestock and planted the first mission crops, including olives and grapes. The mission's wine became known all over the peninsula, and the Bodegas de Santo Tomás continues the tradition today.

The mission had a prosperous but turbulent history. Indigenous people here were less receptive to missionary efforts than those the Jesuits had first encountered in Southern Baja, and two of the resident priests would be murdered before the mission was secularized in 1849.

There are two places to see what little remains of the mission ruins (a few adobe mounds, barely recognizable). The Dominicans built the original buildings west of Mexico 1, on a low mesa off the gravel road that parallels the Cañon Santo Tomás. Later, the community moved to the present-day village of Santo Tomás, east of the highway and north of the Palomar Trailer Park.

Bodegas de Santo Tomás

Founded in 1888, this winery (Rancho los Dolores, Mexico 1, Km 49, Ensenada office tel. 646/178-3333, daily 11 A.M.–3 P.M.) owns the majority of the vineyards in the Valle de Santo Tomás and also has an office in Ensenada. It makes a highly regarded wine called Duetto, through a partnership with Wente Vineyard of California. The winery offers group tours by reservation only.

Accommodations and Food

A mainstay on the Northern Baja travel circuit for more than half a century, **El Palomar** (Mexico 1, Km 51–52, Santo Tomás, tel. 646/153-8002, www.elpalomar.ws, edgaryarce@hotmail.com) consists of a restaurant (daily 7 A.M.–10 P.M., mains start at US$7), motel (US$18 pp), campground with two swimming pools, and Pemex station. The campsites and pool are in an olive grove on the east side of the highway (and you have to descend a steep driveway to get there), but the office, restaurant, motel, and Pemex are on the west side at the base of a hill as you come around a bend in the road. RV camping costs US$16.50 per night for two people (full hook-ups) and includes two free margaritas.

ERÉNDIRA AND PUERTO SAN ISIDRO

For another side trip to the coast, turn west from Mexico 1 at Km 78 on the paved road that leads out to the Ejido Eréndira. There is a sign for Coyote Cal's at the turn. The road winds 24 kilometers through a canyon to the nondescript village of Eréndira (pop. 1,500). Head north along the dirt road five kilometers to Coyote Cal's hostel, at the end of the power lines.

Three more kilometers north along the coast will bring you to Punta Cabras. South of this point, Half Moon Bay is protected from the prevailing northwest winds and catches the summertime south swells. Long Beach, to the north of the point, catches most swells and offers plenty of peaks, unless the onshore winds are killing it. There have been numerous reports of thefts in the area around River's Mouth, but you can leave valuables at Coyote Cal's for safekeeping.

Fishing

About 1.5 kilometers north of Eréndira, you'll find San Isidro Cove. The buildings on the cliff on the north side above the boat ramp are **Castro's Place** (tel. 646/176-2897). Vicente Castro starting fishing the area in 1949, and now his kids run the operation. They use a rusty tractor to tow their *pangas* in and out of the cove. With experienced captains, the bottom fishing in this area is a no-brainer and a *panga*-load of four anglers can fill a 100-quart cooler in a day. Surface fishing for yellowtail and dorado is possible, but the best opportunities are on the bottom. Castro's provides bait, licenses, and gear, but you can use your own if you prefer. There are also clean cabins with bunks for US$25–30 per night, and you can camp for a nominal fee.

Accommodations

Coyote Cal's Mexico Hostels (Ejido Eréndira, tel. 646/154-4080, www.coyotecals.com) is turning into a classic Baja meeting place for surfers, European backpackers, and touring motorcyclists. One of the reasons for its popularity is that there is a room for every budget. You can camp out front on the "beach" (a sandy front yard) for US$10, plus US$3 for breakfast (mid-sized RVs okay if self-contained). On the other end of the spectrum, there's the top-floor Crow's Nest room for US$60 per night (three-night minimum, reserve online) with panoramic views of the surrounding cliffs and ocean. Bunks go for a reasonable US$15–18 per person and private rooms are US$45–50 per couple. The hostel also rents surfboards, mountain bikes, and snorkeling gear. Its new Barefoot Cantina serves XX lager, Sol, and Tecate beer, as well as a menu of mixed drinks. The cantina does not serve meals, however, so plan to buy your own supplies in Ensenada on the way down.

Getting There

Many budget travelers reach Coyote Cal's without their own transportation. Bus fare from Ensenada costs about US$11 and drops you off at Km 78. From here, you need to hitch a ride (easy to do, according to those who've done it). Catch the bus before 2 P.M. to reach the hostel before dark. Alternatively, stay on the bus until San Vicente. When you depart, look across the street and to the left of the Pemex for Mimi Hotel. Inquire here about taxi service (tel. 646/165-6747, available 24/7 for US$25–30) to the hostel. You'll need to speak Spanish to arrange the ride.

A third option is to hire a station wagon taxi from Ensenada (US$75 flat fee, negotiate before you get in and tell the driver the trip will include about five kilometers of dirt road driving, to avoid extra costs). The taxi can stop at the Calimax store, where you can buy food, and then bring you directly to the hostel.

SAN VICENTE

The next valley south of Santo Tomás is almost as picturesque, with more agricultural crops and the Llano Colorado (Reddish Plain) beyond it. The town itself (pop. 3,500) is a small-sized commercial center, with a few restaurants and stores, as well as an ABC bus terminal—all right along the highway. The only real point of interest here is the historic Dominican mission of San Vicente Ferrer, located one kilometer north of town, at Km 88.

Misión San Vicente Ferrer

Founded by Padres Miguel Hidalgo and Joaquín Valero in 1780, this mission (1780–1833) and military outpost played an important role in connecting the Baja California missions to the newer settlements in Alta California. It also had one of the largest building complexes of any Dominican mission. In 1997, Mexico's Instituto Nacional de Antropología e Historia (INAH) began an archeological dig to uncover, reinforce, and protect the remaining mission ruins. Today, the site is lined with gravel paths and the adobe walls are covered in a waterproof layer. To find the mission site, look for a dirt road heading west off Mexico 1, just south of Km 88.

COLONET AND SAN ANTONIO DEL MAR

The farming town of Colonet has a Pemex and handful of places to eat and shop. Use it as a supply station for trips to the coast or into the sierra. There aren't any sights of interest in the town proper.

Almost due west of Colonet, San Antonio del Mar is a remote beach camp on an estuary with a few homes and trailers. The exposed, sandy beach faces west, and there are good shore fishing and decent beachbreaks in both directions. This is a good bet to escape the crowds. Stock up on supplies and fill your tank with gas in Colonet. Primitive camping with no facilities costs US$5 per night. Turn off Mexico 1 at Km 126, a little north of town and just before the bridge. From here, it's 12.5 kilometers to the coast.

Bahía Colonet (14 km southwest) is supposedly a target for development as part of the Escalera Nautica project, but nothing has

materialized to date. The north point of this bay, Cabo Colonet, breaks on northwest swells. On the bay itself, **Cuatro Casas** is one of the more crowded longboarding breaks along this stretch of coastline. It is also a fickle spot that doesn't break consistently.

Crime warning: An armed robbery of a surf instructor and longtime Baja traveler was widely reported in the San Diego press in 2007. He was camping with his girlfriend in a deserted spot along the coast after getting lost on the road to Cuatro Casas after dark. Take precautions when exploring this area. Leave your valuables behind, travel in groups, camp at the hostel, and don't be conspicuous.

Accommodations and Camping

On an exposed bluff overlooking the break, **Cuatro Casas Hostel Surf** (U.S. tel. 619/756-0639, www.myspace.com/cuatrocasas) has a variety of clean rooms starting at US$15 in a large house, and camping for US$5. The parking area is fenced, and the owner has a bright spotlight on the roof to ward off would-be intruders. In recent years, we've seen short-sighted fishermen out front using bleach to ferret out octopuses from their holes in the tidepools.

To find Cuatro Casas coming from the north on Mexico 1, drive 13.8 kilometers south of Colonet to a Pemex on the left and then another kilometer and a half on the highway after that toward the intersection with the paved road to San Telmo. After you pass a yellow auto parts store, turn right onto a dirt road that leads to the coast (12.9 km). Call or text the owner, Richard, for reservations.

PUNTA SAN JACINTO

Nine kilometers west of Camalú on Mexico 1 via a wide, graded dirt road, Punta San Jacinto offers surfing and primitive camping on a sandy but exposed beach. The turnoff to Punta San Jacinto comes between Km 149–150 on Mexico 1.

The town of Camalú, beginning at Km 157, can meet most basic traveler needs with its several markets, pharmacies, and eateries. There is also an auto mechanic and Pemex station with diesel fuel. Directly west of town (turn right at the stoplight north of the Pemex and drive straight out to the beach), Punta Camalú is a worthwhile right point break, reportedly more consistent than Cuatro Casas to the north.

Surfing
The surf is found at the site of a huge freighter, *Isla del Carmen,* that is beached on the sand. It's a soft wave, but a good choice for days when the northwest swell is huge. **Baja Surf Adventures** (toll-free U.S. tel. 800/428-7873, www.bajasurfadventures.com, baja.bill@gmail. com) runs a solar-powered resort here providing lessons and basic accommodations for up to 16 guests.

Camping
You can camp for free on the sand dunes behind the beach, but it's not recommended since crime in this area is a real concern.

VICENTE GUERRERO
As a regional hub for agricultural commerce, Colonia Vicente Guerrero (pop. 10,600) has a post office, police station, and medical clinic, as well as a grocery store, ATMs, and several places to eat. The Pemex is open around the clock. ABC buses stop here, and there are three RV parks in town.

Migrant workers from mainland Mexico tend to crops of tomatoes and strawberries in the surrounding fields. On the coast, surf-casting is a popular pastime for locals and visitors alike.

Misión Santo Domingo de la Frontera
Padres Miguel Hidalgo and Manuel García founded the second Dominican mission

(1775–1839) in Baja near the Arroyo Santo Domingo, northeast of Vicente Guerrero. Although it occupied a strategic location, with ample freshwater and easy coastal access, the mission grew slowly at first. It produced large quantities of corn and wheat and traded otter furs with ships that came to nearby San Quintín. But the indigenous people suffered from disease, and the mission was abandoned in 1839.

During its life, the mission occupied three sites in the Vicente Guerrero area. Ruins at the third and final site are among the most recognizable of all the ruins on the peninsula. Mexico's INAH agency has protected the site by reinforcing the crumbling adobe walls, putting a fence around the mission quadrangle, and adding an entry kiosk. A building on-site now contains a small collection of items from the mission era.

Accommodations and Camping
RV caravans often spend the night at **Posada Don Diego RV Park and Restaurant** (off Mexico 1 at Km 174, tel. 616/166-2181, www. posadadondiego.com, posadadondiego@yahoo. com, daily 8 A.M.–9 P.M.). Under its current ownership since 1979, this park has 100 campsites (50 with full hookups for US$11, the rest with electricity and water only for US$10), plus four motel-style rooms for US$35. There are also a three-bedroom house and four trailers for rent. On-site activities include basketball and volleyball. Its restaurant serves Mexican plates, a full lineup of steaks, baby back ribs, and seafood dishes, all at reasonable prices. Breakfast mains cost US$3.50–9 and dinners are US$7–14.

To find Posada Don Diego, go about a kilometer and a half south of the only stoplight in town Vicente Guerrero and turn right (west) just before the propane plant.

Sierra de San Pedro Mártir

For true wilderness seekers, the highest mountain range on the Baja Peninsula offers a dramatic change from the desert and coastal scenery below. Lodgepole pines, quaking aspens, and the endemic San Pedro Mártir cypress are just a few of the unusual trees that have attached themselves to the slopes and canyons of the Sierra de San Pedro Mártir. The rare *borregón* (bighorn sheep) lives in the range, and the California condor was recently reintroduced.

At 3,095 meters, the tallest peak in the range, Picacho del Diablo (Devil's Peak), also goes by the names Cerro de la Encantada (Enchanted Mountain) and La Providencia (Providence). Its two granite peaks are often capped with snow in winter. Experienced backpackers typically approach the summit from the eastern side in a three-day trip.

◖ PARQUE NACIONAL SIERRA SAN PEDRO MÁRTIR

Founded by a presidential decree in 1974, this 68,796-hectare national park centers around the San Pedro Mártir Plateau (elevation 1,800 m), which covers approximately 70 kilometers by 15 kilometers at the north end of the range. Given its remote location, it is one of the least visited national parks in all of Mexico, which can make a trip here all the more enjoyable.

The park entrance is located 78 kilometers from Mexico 1 via a paved road that heads west from Mexico 1 at San Telmo; follow signs marked Observatorio. The park is open daily 7 A.M.–7 P.M., and the entry fee is US$7.50 per vehicle. Another way to access the Sierra de San Pedro Mártir is via a rough dirt road (high clearance required) through the farming town of Valle de la Trinidad, off Mexico 3 (Km 121). This route is 48-kilometers long and takes you to the northern boundary of the national park.

OBSERVATORIO ASTRONÓMICO NACIONAL

Clear air and nonexistent light pollution led the Mexican government to choose Cerro de la Cúpula (elevation 2,830 m) as the location for a

PARQUE NACIONAL SIERRA SAN PEDRO MÁRTIR

To Ensenada · San Vicente · MISIÓN SAN VICENTE · Valle de Trinidad · 3 · 5 · Sea of Cortez · Valle Santa Clara · RANCHO VILLA DEL SOL · Laguna Diablo (dry) · San Rafael · MIKE'S SKY RANCH · RANCHO SANTA CLARA · Río · Colonet · NATIONAL OBSERVATORY · San Telmo · RANCHO MELING · Cañón del Diablo · Picacho del Diablo · Valle San Felipe · San Felipe · Punta Colonet · Río · San Telmo · PARK ENTRANCE · Camalú · Santo Domingo · MISIÓN SAN PEDRO MÁRTIR · Sierra San Pedro Mártir · PACIFIC OCEAN · MISIÓN SANTO DOMINGO · Río · To San Quintín · 0 20 mi · 0 20 km

© AVALON TRAVEL

MAJOR BAJA CALIFORNIA MOUNTAIN RANGES

Range	Highest Peak	Summit Elevation
Sierra de San Pedro Mártir	Picacho del Diablo	3,095 meters (10,154 ft)
Sierra de la Laguna	Picacho de la Laguna	2,161 meters (7,090 ft)
Sierra de San Francisco	Pico Santa Monica	2,104 meters (6,904 ft)
Sierra San Borja	Pico Echeverría	1,907 meters (6,258 ft)
Sierra Juárez	Cerro Torre Blanco	1,800 meters (5,904 ft)
Sierra de la Giganta	Cerro La Giganta	1,765 meters (5,792 ft)
Sierra de la Asamblea	Cerro Dos Picachos	1,658 meters (5,438 ft)
Sierra de Guadalupe	Monte Thetis	1,640 meters (5,380 ft)

world-class observatory, called the Observatorio Astronómico Nacional (Ensenada tel. 646/174-4580, www.astrosen.unam.mx, contacto@ astrosen.unam.mx, Sat. 11 A.M.–1 P.M., by reservation). Built in 1975, its three telescopes (2.1 meters, 1.5 meters, and 84 centimeters) assess the brightness of the sky, the state of the atmosphere, and a long list of meteorological data. This facility is regarded as one of the best places on the planet to observe the stars and planets above. It's open to the public, but hours are limited and vary by the season.

The observatory is located at the end of the park access road, also called the San Telmo de Abajo road (20 km past the park entrance). Park before the locked gate and walk the final two kilometers to the buildings.

MISÍON SAN PEDRO MÁRTIR DE VERONA

Dominican Padre José Loriente established a mountain mission (1794–1824) high in the Sierra San Pedro Mártir to serve a small population of indigenous people, but the rugged terrain and cold winter climate made for a challenging mission environment. Its 20-hectare orchard grew wheat, corn, and beans primarily. Only the faint ruins of a few walls survive

today, and access is difficult: from the observatory, it's a two-day guided horseback ride to reach the site.

HIKING AND CAMPING

Backcountry hikes and self-contained camping are permitted within the park, but infrastructure and services are limited. Few trails are marked, so you'll need to bring a GPS and topo maps (*San Rafael H11B45* and *Santa Cruz H11B55*), which Santa Barbara, California–based **Mexico Maps** (U.S. tel. 805/687-1011, www.mexicomaps.com) sells for US$15.95 per map. The easiest trails to follow are located along the northeastern edge of the park, near the observatory. If you're not confident that you can navigate the wilderness environment on your own, you can hire a guide through Meling Ranch (tel. 646/179-4106, www.melingguestranch.com) or EcoTur (www.mexonline.com/baja/ecotur3.htm).

Hunting and the possession of firearms (even with a Mexican permit) are prohibited, as is off-road driving. You can build campfires in fire rings at a few sites in the park. As with any wilderness environment, let the local rangers know the details of your trip before you head off on the trail.

Summer temps hover around 26°C during the day, dropping to 4.5°C at night. July and August also bring heavy rains and afternoon thunderstorms to the sierra. In winter, temperatures range 4.5°C to 12°C, and snowfall is common above 2,000 meters. Days are pleasantly warm in spring and fall, but night can dip below freezing.

Accordingly, the best hiking seasons are mid-April–mid-June, when the wildflowers are in bloom and fresh water is plentiful, and late September–early November, before the snows begin.

ACCOMMODATIONS
Rancho Meling

Between Km 140–141, a newly paved road goes east to the settlement of San Telmo and then climbs into the Sierra San Pedro Mártir. Along the way, 50 kilometers from the highway, the historic Rancho Meling has been entertaining and feeding adventurous guests since the turn of the 20th century.

Owned and operated by the Johnson/ Meling families since 1910, Rancho Meling (also known as Rancho San José, tel. 646/179-4106, www.melingguestranch.com, US$50 pp) was born as a base for gold-mining operations and then destroyed by bandits in the Mexican Revolution. It was rebuilt as a 4,000-hectare cattle ranch, and today, it is a haven for motorcyclists, eco-tourists, fly-in guests, and anyone seeking the solitude of a rustic getaway in the mountains.

The working cattle ranch sits at an elevation of 670 meters in a stand of pines at the base of the sierra. Its 12 rooms all have private baths, hot water, and a fireplace or wood stove for heat. For larger groups or families, there is a four-bedroom/three-bath cabin. Hearty meals (breakfast/lunch/dinner US$6/8/11) are cooked over a wood-fired stove and served at a long wooden table beside a large stone fireplace in the main house. The generator goes off at 10 P.M., but you can read by the light of a kerosene lamp after that.

The road to San Telmo comes 13.9 kilometers south of Colonet, just past a Pemex on the left. (Fill up before you head into the sierra.) Alternatively, you can fly your own plane and land on the ranch's dirt landing strip. Baja Bush Pilots members receive 10 percent off daily rates.

Mike's Sky Ranch

Just beyond Km 138 on Mexico 3, a dirt road heads 35.5 kilometers south to Mike's Sky Ranch (tel. 664/681-5514), a rustic resort in the sierra foothills (elevation 1,200 m) at the northwestern edge of the national park. Popular with off-road bikers, the ranch has been a checkpoint on the Baja 500 and Baja 1000 races for many years. Accommodations are in 27 basic cabins (US$60 pp), and the rates include family-style meals and use of the swimming pool. Campsites cost US$5 per vehicle per night (water and shower use only). Campers can pay US$12 additional for dinner and US$7 for breakfast (served 6–10 A.M. and lunch.

The road to Mike's is rough in spots and can change drastically with recent rains. Beyond the ranch, this road continues southwestward to join the newly paved road between Mexico 1 and the national park.

GETTING AROUND
Guided Trips

Ensenada native Francisco Detrell has been organizing sierra tours since the 1980s through his company **EcoTur** (Blvd. Costero #1094, Local 14, Ensenada, www.mexonline.com/baja/ecotur3.htm, ecoturbc@ens.com.mx, tours US$12–150). Guided trips include waterfall hikes, Picacho del Diablo summits, and observatory tours. Francisco speaks English and Spanish.

Meling Ranch also offers guided hikes into the sierra.

Valle and Bahía de San Quintín

South of Vicente Guerrero on Mexico 1, the wide, flat coastal plain of San Quintín begins. Two rivers, Río San Miguel and Río Santa María, provide water that fuels the local agricultural economy. Workers' camps on the outskirts of town house farm workers from mainland Mexico, who come to work the fields.

Visitors who stopover here—mainly the sportfishing set—enjoy a unique coastal environment that consists of three connected bays: narrow Bahía San Quintín and Bahía Falsa, and the larger Bahía Santa María. In between are tidal zones and marshes filled with marine life.

The town of San Quintín itself (pop. 20,000) offers some practical services for travelers (clinic, banks, Internet), but is primarily another agricultural hub. Five kilometers south of San Quintín, Lázaro Cárdenas, has Mexico's 67th Infantry battalion camp, an intercity bus terminal, and some shops and restaurants.

HISTORY

Named by Sebastián Vizcaíno, San Quintín caught the attention of foreign investors as early as the 1880s as a potentially lucrative

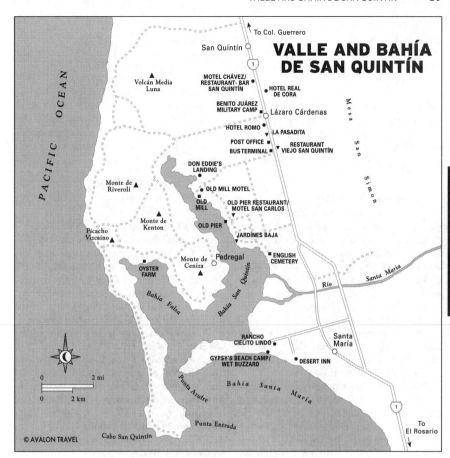

VALLE AND BAHÍA DE SAN QUINTÍN

wheat-growing area; however, early colonists, first from the United States and later from England, failed to realize the vision. Before giving up, they dredged the harbor, dug wells, laid train tracks, and set up gristmill machinery—the remains of which you can still see along the inner bay shoreline today.

In the 1950s and '60s, San Quintín captured the imagination of some pioneering anglers from the United States, and the first few resorts opened for business. Among them, the Old Mill Motel became a legend in its time.

Today, a small community of expats lives on the bayfront in a neighborhood called Pedregal, and a few fishing lodges cater to the sportfishing crowd.

SPORTS AND RECREATION
Beach and Bay Access

Follow signs to the Old Mill Motel from Mexico 1 to reac h the bay. You can launch small boats here or from the Pedregal area on the west shore of the bay. Follow a gravel road from Mexico 1 (btw the Pemex and military camp) west of Lázaro Cárdenas 14 kilometers to Bahía Falsa. When the road forks, take the left (south) branch to reach Pedregal.

Alternatively, continue west at the fork another few hundred meters to Ostiones Guerrero, where you may be able to buy fresh oysters by the dozen. The road ends at a fish camp on the ocean.

To reach Bahía Santa María, drive 16 kilometers south of Lázaro Cárdenas and turn right (west) on the paved road to Santa María. Follow signs to the Desert Inn Hotel; local clam diggers frequent Playa Santa María at low tide. It's a long, sandy beach, located just past the hotel.

Fishing and Hunting

The unique marine environment here, with the shallow bay system and several rocky seamounts just offshore in the Pacific, creates fantastic opportunities for both surf casting and deep sea fishing. Rock cod, yellowtail, and lingcod are common, and that's just the beginning of the list. Experienced anglers say they are able to catch upwards of 20 different species in one day of fishing.

The presence of several large-scale oyster farms along the inner bays shows just how clean the marine environment is. (They need pristine conditions to thrive.)

San Quintín Sportfishing (Rancho Cielito Lindo, tel. 616/165-6046, book4fish@aol. com), **Pedro's Pangas** (tel. 888/568-2252, www.pedrospangas.com), **Tiburon's Pangas Sportfishing** (near the Old Mill, U.S. tel. 619/428-2779), **Don Eddie's Landing** (tel. 616/165-6061), and **Campo Lorenzo** (tel. 616/165-6022 or Skype tel. 909/581-4140) can arrange guided fishing trips for around US$200–300 per *panga,* depending on the season.

San Quintín offers hunters the opportunity to pursue ducks and valley quail, but it's best known for the brandt hunting. Contact Lorenzo at Campo Lorenzo to arrange quail hunting. **Sporting Field International** (www.sportingfield.com) brokers pricey brandt hunts using local guides. The cost will end up being US$2,000 or so for a three-day hunt (Thursday–Sunday only). The season for brandt is January and Feburary.

Surfing

The beachbreaks along Playa San Ramón, which runs between Vicente Guerrero and San Quintín (access at Km 172), are nothing special, but they don't get crowded either. The better-known, but still uncrowded breaks are at Cabo San Quintín, with more consistent surf and longer rides. Access is difficult, via the road to Bahía Falsa and then a coastal road heading south to the point. Conditions are typically cold and super windy.

ACCOMMODATIONS AND CAMPING
Under US$50

Motel Chávez (San Quintín, tel. 616/165-2005, motelchavez@hotmail.com, US$20–30), next to a highway bridge toward the south end of town, has been a mainstay on the budget travel circuit for years. Its clean rooms have fans; cash only. Also on the highway, the **Hotel Real de Cora** (San Quintín, tel. 616/166 8576, US$32) has secure parking.

A relatively new option in town is the **Villa de San Quintín** (Av. A #5 btw 8th/9th, San Quintín, tel. 616/165-1800, www.hotellavilla. biz, US$35), an offshoot of a Tijuana hotel that was built in 2005. It has 32 non-smoking, carpeted rooms with private baths, and air-conditioning, TV, phone, and free high-speed Internet. Secure parking is designed for trailers and boats, and an on-site restaurant is open daily 6:30 A.M.–9:30 P.M.

At the northeast end of Bahía San Quintín, **Don Eddie's Landing** (tel. 616/165-6061, www.doneddies.com, US$45) has older rooms with lots of beds and sagging mattresses. Fishing packages are available and include lodging, boat, and food.

South of Don Eddie's Landing and next to the public boat launch, the **Old Mill Motel** (tel. 800/208-2154, U.S. tel. 619/428-2779, US$40–50) occupies the former gristmill site. A regular crowd of hunters and anglers frequents the place and they like to party at night. Accommodations are in cabins arranged around a courtyard, with an attached campground (US$10). Rates often include two

© PAUL ITOI

Rancho Cielito Lindo

cold beers. No heat or air-conditioning. The road out to these two places can get extremely muddy after a heavy rain; high clearance is recommended.

Next to Bahía Santa María, **Rancho Cielito Lindo** (U.S. tel. 619/593-2252, cielitolindo@ bajasi.com, US$10) is a restaurant and bar with a few rooms and a campground on the premises.

US$50-100

On Bahía Santa María, the **Desert Inn** (tel. 616/165-9008, toll-free U.S. tel. 800/800-9632, www.desertinns.com/sanquintin, US$75) was remodeled in 2004 in cool blue tones with floral spreads and drapes. Spacious rooms have remote-control heat and air-conditioning units, plus sea views and terraces. Modern tiled baths have glass shower doors; full-size bath towels are a treat. A palm-lined walkway leads to the beach. If you find yourself in the area at sundown and you don't want to shack up in a sportfishing lodge, this hotel is a good bet for a quiet night's sleep.

The newly renovated **(Hotel Jardines Baja** (U.S. tel. 619/591-8922, www.hotel-jardinesbaja.com, US$50–75) has raised the bar considerably for accommodations in the San Quintín area. It has several rooms, including a suite with its own deck and separate living room; some of the rooms have working wood-burning fireplaces. Its new restaurant opened in 2008 to rave reviews. Beds are comfortable, the grounds are beautiful, and the coffee is strong. Those who have discovered it are hoping the word doesn't get out too soon. Watch for the Jardines sign on Mexico 1, south of Lázaro Cárdenas, at the sign that points the way to Bahía San Quintín. Turn right and follow this road for about 1.5 kilometers to the sign for Hotel Baja Jardines. Turn left here and the hotel will be a few hundred meters down on the right.

Camping and RV Parks

One of the newcomers on the San Quintín scene for RV camping is **Los Olivos Family Park** (tel. 616/165-6123, US$15), popular because it is close to the highway, so you don't have to drive your big rig down a long bumpy dirt road just to crash for the night. This secure park has full hookups and a swimming pool, and hot showers were under construction at press time. It is located on the road to the Jardines Hotel and Restaurant.

If you prefer a beachside location, several places have been in business for decades: **Gypsy's Beach Camp** (no tel.) offers sites in a dirt lot for tent or RV camping for US$10 per night. Features include clean bathrooms, a two-story restaurant, and a dump station. A night watchman patrols the area 9 P.M.–5 A.M. **Rancho Cielito Lindo** (U.S. tel. 619/593-2252, cielitolindo@bajasi.com, RV/tent US$12/10) has 15 campsites—some with *palapas*—for tents or RVs.

A favorite among repeat Baja campers, **El Pabellón RV Campground** (Mexico 1, Km 16, US$5–10) is comfortably removed from the towns of San Quintín and Lázaro Cárdenas and set back from the highway. It has campsites in a large open lot fronting the beach, with water and sewer hookups, but no electricity. Restrooms are clean and have hot water. A fellow camper here once shared a delicious Peruvian-style ceviche, made of Pismo clams dug that day at the beach.

Beach camping is permitted but not recommended in the San Quintín area due to a persistent problem with theft.

FOOD

Take your pick of taco and *mariscos* stands that line the highway in both Lázaro Cárdenas and San Quintín. Clam cocktails are a local treat. **La Pasadita** (no tel., 9 A.M.–4 P.M., mains US$5) does reliable *tacos de pescado* on the plaza in Lázaro Cárdenas.

Pollos Lalos (daily 10 A.M.–10 P.M., US$5–10), on the west side of the highway in San Quintín, makes tasty *pollos al carbon*. Nearby **Tuco's Pizza** (daily 3–10 P.M., mains US$10) will satisfy your pizza cravings.

The best Mexican dining experience in the area awaits at **Restaurant Viejo San Quintín**, open daily for breakfast, lunch, and dinner (US$5–10). This friendly establishment is located between two pharmacies and across

from the post office in Lázaro Cárdenas. Order the *machaca*, chiles rellenos, carne asada, or enchiladas, and your beer will arrive in a frosted mug.

Gaston's Cannery (daily 5:30 A.M.–9:30 P.M., mains US$10–28) is part of the Old Mill complex. It serves Mexican food and seafood dinners, at relatively high prices for the area. If you're driving to the Old Mill Motel in the afternoon, make sure to pay attention to each turn along the way so you can find your way back when you drive back that evening. It's easy to get lost in the maze of sandy roads at night.

The **Hotel Jardines Baja** (U.S. tel. 619/591-8922, www.hotel-jardinesbaja.com, Tues.–Thurs. 8 A.M.–10 P.M., Fri.–Sun. 8 A.M.–2 A.M., mains US$10–15) opened its new restaurant in 2008 with a menu that features seafood, wings, and desserts.

Rancho Cielito Lindo (tel. 616/165-6046, U.S. reservations 619/593-2252, cielitolindo@bajasi.com, mains US$10) serves fresh seafood dishes at good prices (dinner only). Next door, **Wet Buzzard** (Gypsy's Beach Camp, no tel., tacos US$1 each) is known for its filling breakfasts. It also serves tacos and burritos for lunch.

Both San Quintín and Lázaro Cárdenas have *abarrotes* stores if you need to replenish food supplies.

INFORMATION AND SERVICES

There is a state tourism office between Vicente Guerrero and San Quintín at Km 178 on the west side of the highway. The office is officially open weekdays 8 A.M.–5 P.M., and weekends 10 A.M.–3 P.M., but hours tend to change with the seasons.

For medical emergencies, go to Clínica Santa María (tel. 616/165-2653, open 24 hours) in San Quintín.

GETTING THERE

San Quintín and Lázaro Cárdenas each have a Pemex station. There is an intercity bus depot in Lázaro Cárdenas, on the west side of Mexico 1; however, this area is not ideal for travelers without their own transportation, as the beaches are far from the highway.

Campo Lorenzo has a 760-meter unpaved licensed airstrip, air park, and trailer park for permanent residents. It is a private airstrip, but available to pilots who call ahead to Skype 909/581-4140 or the Mexican landline at 616/165-6022. The camp can make arrangements for transportation, and there is only a US$25 fee to land and park if you are staying at Don Eddie's.

El Rosario

Baja road-trippers tend to remember their first time passing through the commercial center of El Rosario (pop. 3,500) because it's the last chance to gas up before the long haul across the desert. As if to emphasize the point, the town has one of the largest Pemex stations in the area and it's open 24/7. There are two other reasons to hang around a while: If it's late in the day and you need a place to crash for the night, the Baja Cactus Motel has great rooms at unbelievably low prices. And if you just need a bite to eat on your way through, recently remodeled Ed's Baja's Best is a good bet.

MISÍON NUESTRA SEÑORA DEL ROSARIO DE VIÑADACO

The Dominicans established Misíon Nuestra Señora del Rosario De Viñadaco (1774–1832), the first of their nine Baja California missions, in present day El Rosario in 1774, led by Padres Vicente Mora and Francisco Galisteo. Adobe ruins of its second site are visible just off the west side of the highway at the sharp bend in the road. (Turn right at the grocery store and then left at the first road. Cross the arroyo and look for the ruins on the right.)

The standard mission crops of barley, corn, and beans grew especially well here, and the mission was able to convert hundreds of indigenous people before European illnesses began to take their toll on the population. By 1832, the mission was turned over to the local people.

ACCOMMODATIONS AND FOOD

Between the Pemex station and Mama Espinosa's restaurant, the **Baja Cactus Motel** (Km 55, tel. 616/165-8850, www.bajacactus.com) has caused quite a stir among Transpeninsular insiders in recent years. Where else in the world can you enjoy all the amenities of a four-star establishment—immaculate tiled baths, granite counters, four-poster king-size beds, luxury linens, gorgeous woodwork, 29-inch satellite TVs, purified water, air conditioning—for US$35 a night? The story goes that the son of the motel owners wanted to help his parents fix the place up. All 22 rooms are wired with Ethernet cables, so that when high-speed Internet comes to El Rosario, Baja Cactus patrons will be among the first to enjoy it. You probably won't escape the sound of trucks decelerating through town, but you'll enjoy some of the finest accommodations anywhere on the peninsula.

The dining experience at historic **Mama Espinosa's** (east side of Mexico 1, just past the large Pemex as you enter the town from the north, no tel., daily breakfast, lunch, and dinner) has slipped of late, with higher prices (US$13–20) and disappointing meals. Stop in if you want to see all of the Baja 1000 memorabilia and learn a bit about the town's matriarch, Doña Anita, but lower your expectations for a memorable meal.

On the south side of town, recently remodeled **Baja's Best Café** (no tel., daily 7 A.M.–7 P.M., mains US$7–15) serves a mean breakfast with real sausage and dependable coffee. It also runs a bed-and-breakfast on the premises. Rooms have comfortable beds and rain showers (US$50).

El Rosario has several grocery stores that carry produce, bread, and basic household supplies. **Mercado Hermanos Jaramillo,** near Mama Espinosa's, is the best of the bunch.

MEXICALI TO SAN FELIPE

Among Baja's international border towns, agricultural Mexicali strikes a balance between bustling Tijuana and quiet Tecate. Its palm-lined boulevards are cleaner and less touristy than other Baja California cities of its size (pop. 1 million). In addition to farming, state government drives much of the local economy, as Mexicali is the capital of Baja California (Norte).

Across the border from Mexicali, smaller Calexico is in every way a symbiotic community—equally dependent on agriculture and related businesses. The whimsical names of the Mexicali and Calexico border towns reflect the laid-back tone in these sister cities. Outside of the immediate border-crossing area, the focus on tourism that colors the visitor's experience in Tijuana and Ensenada is largely absent. Among other Baja cities, Mexicali is most similar to La Paz in its mixed population of mainland Mexicans and foreign immigrants and the presence of a thriving local middle class. The city welcomes visitors, but its businesses do not cater to their every need. If you've had your fill of Americanized beach resorts with their activity booths and timeshare reps, Mexicali offers independent travelers a refreshing view of life in an ordinary Mexican city.

For California and Arizona residents, Mexicali is a gateway to both the Baja Peninsula and mainland Mexico. San Felipe and the northern beaches along the Sea of Cortez are just a couple of hours away by car. Southwest of Mexicali are plenty of opportunities for desert hiking, soaking in natural hot springs, and off-road racing, as well as some of the best fishing and hunting in the country.

HIGHLIGHTS

◖ La Chinesca: Born of a lack of essential ingredients, Mexicali-style Chinese food has become a fusion cuisine all its own. Try it here, in the only true Chinatown in all of Mexico (page 100).

◖ Cañon de Guadalupe: Hot springs in the Sierra Juárez above the San Felipe desert reward backcountry explorers willing to drive the washboard access road (page 107).

◖ San Felipe *Malecón*: At night, the action in San Felipe takes place in discos and clubs along the waterfront. Start the evening off right with a seafood dinner in one of the town's open-air restaurants (page 110).

◖ Valle de los Gigantes: Between San Felipe and Puertecitos, the Valle de los Gigantes is an ideal place to snap postcard-perfect images of the world's tallest cactus species, some of which live to be hundreds of years old (page 116).

◖ Bahía San Luis Gonzaga: Popular with pilots and seasoned Baja travelers, this remote, gray-sand beach on the Gulf coast offers a slice of the old Baja (page 118).

LOOK FOR ◖ TO FIND RECOMMENDED SIGHTS, ACTIVITIES, DINING, AND LODGING.

PLANNING YOUR TIME

It takes about two hours to drive to Mexicali from the San Diego airport. Once you've arrived, you could spend just an afternoon and evening getting oriented and preparing for a trip to San Felipe, or a couple of days to explore the city's few attractions.

The most popular weekend itinerary in this area is a trip from Mexicali to San Felipe and back (two hours by car each way).

With a week or more, you could add a side trip to the Cañon de Guadalupe, and continue south of San Felipe to Puertecitos. With a four-wheel-drive vehicle, you could turn this trip into a loop, following the coastal road all the way to Gonzaga Bay and heading inland to meet the Transpeninsular Highway at Chapala. From there, you can head south to Bahía de los Angeles or turn north to Ensenada and Mexico 3, which returns to Mexicali.

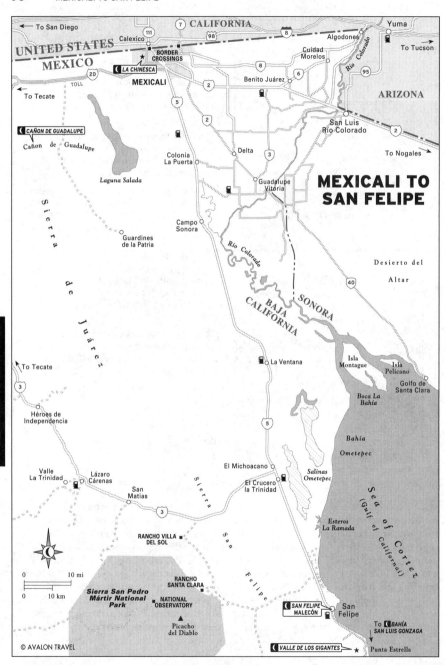

Mexicali

Founded on March 14, 1903, Mexicali has little resemblance to its border cousins, Tecate and Tijuana. As the capital of the state of Baja California (Norte) and a major agricultural hub, most of the city's one million people are too busy to take much notice of the steady stream of tourists that make their way through Mexicali to San Felipe and points south. What the city lacks in painted donkeys and street vendors, it makes up for with efficient business hotels and fine restaurants that depend on local repeat customers. The Zona Hotelera and the area along Calle Benito Juárez offer adequate nightlife with several clubs and bars.

As a visitor to Mexicali, you can choose to blend in with the locals by catching an Aguilas baseball game, watching a bullfight, or sampling *Bajanese* cuisines in La Chinesca, Mexico's only true Chinatown. If your vacation destination is beyond the city's borders, there are several hotels that cater to the guests who view Mexicali as a border staging area with secure parking and low rates.

The nicest times to visit Mexicali are any month except the peak of summer, when temperatures regularly top 38°C.

HISTORY

The Spanish first came to the Valle de Mexicali along the Camino del Diablo (Devil's Road) in the Sonora Desert. The Yumano tribes that inhabited the area grew squash, peas, melon, and corn. They also had advanced uses for medicinal herbs and used the desert flora and fauna in a variety of ways.

The Cucapá (People of the River) were a major Yumano group who traveled the Río Colorado in reed rafts. The arrival of the Spanish reduced the numbers of Cucapás to the point that today the descendents live in a small corner of the delta. Very few indigenous customs remain.

Mexicali's emergence as an agricultural center followed irrigation of the Imperial Valley on the U.S. side of the border at the turn of the 20th century.

ALTO GOLFO DE CALIFORNIA AND DELTA DEL RÍO COLORADO

Mexicali and Calexico occupy the same valley bordered by the Colorado River delta to the east and the Sierra de Cucapá to the west. Developers renamed the valley north of the border the Imperial Valley. It's also known as the Salton Sink. South of the border, it's simply called Valle de Mexicali. The entire valley was once part of the Gulf of California, before silt from the flooding of the river pushed the shoreline to the south.

The Colorado River is the deciding geographical factor in this area. For millennia, the river flowed directly to the Gulf bounded by its own natural levees, which were built up by silt. The valley itself lay underwater. Periodically, the river would break its banks and flood the Salton Sink. Over time, the break would fill back up with silt, and the temporary Salton Sea would evaporate.

In 1905, developers lost control of an irrigation project and accidentally diverted virtually the entire flow of the Colorado River into the Salton Sink. It took a railroad company's crews several years to repair the breach and correct the river's flow.

Today, the irrigation system leftover from the early 20th-century developers continues to support a vibrant agricultural economy. But 90 percent of the Colorado River is diverted prior to reaching the border. And the All American Canal north of the border might be paved, which would prevent further seepage flows south of the border.

Los Angeles Times publisher Harry Chandler was a key figure behind the irrigation of the Valle de Mexicali on the Mexico side of the border. With Chinese immigrant laborers imported to dig its canal, Mexicali became green virtually overnight. However, a 1905 storm rerouted the entire flow of the river into the valley, flooding Mexicali and filling the Salton Sea once again.

The Southern Pacific Railroad worked for several years to route the river back into the Sea of Cortez, leaving only the original channel off the main canal.

In 1911, the Magonista faction of revolutionaries briefly took control of Mexicali. To protect the border, the Mexican government moved the capital of the Territory of Baja California to Mexicali from Ensenada. With the passage of Prohibition in the United States, Mexicali experienced an influx of tourism that was made famous by the song "Mexicali Rose." Jack Tenney wrote the lyrics, originally called "The Waltz" and claimed it wasn't about a dancing girl, but was written for an elderly bar patron. Bing Crosby recorded it before Gene Autry starred in a movie by that name. Tenney went to law school and was elected to the California State Legislature. Chinese workers who had helped build the irrigation canals opened many of the area's Prohibition-era businesses.

Baja California (Norte) became a Mexican state in 1952. Cotton was initially the cash crop in the valley, but with the invention of synthetic fibers, asparagus, green onions, and other crops became more important to the economy. The Agrobaja convention (www.agrobaja.com), held in March each year, brings 50,000 U.S. and Mexican agricultural and fishery interests to town.

With the addition of a manufacturing base in the form of in-bond plants and maquiladoras, the population of Mexicali began to rise, and has doubled since the 1970s.

Mexicali's economy remains closely tied to that of the United States, and the current economic downturn has resulted in widespread layoffs at the maquiladoras. Some forays into

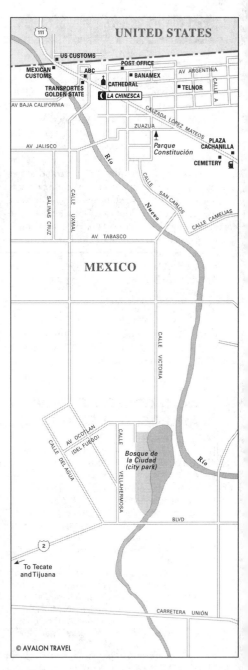

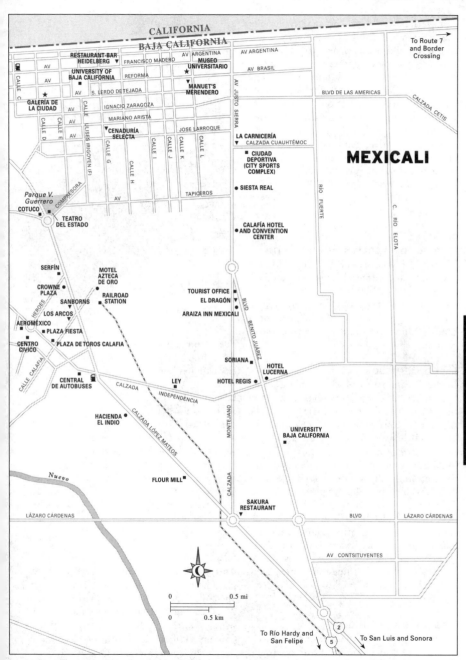

clean-tech industry may help the city through the cycle: Silicon Border is a company that is trying to build out a science park and manufacturing complex located to the west of Mexicali along the international border. The groundbreaking ceremony took place in 2005, but the park was without a tenant until 2008, when a solar-power manufacturer committed to moving in.

The Cerro Prieto geothermal power plant opened south of Mexicali in 1973. Today, it is one of the largest producers of geothermal power in the world. In early 2009, the company signed a deal with the City of Los Angeles to sell power from its plant.

SIGHTS
Centro Interactivo Sol del Niño
This children's museum (Blvd. López Mateos Blvd and Calle Alfonso Esquer, tel. 686/554-9595 or -9696, Mon.–Fri. 9 A.M.–7 P.M., Sat.–Sun. 10 A.M.–2 P.M., free), located in a former cotton seed warehouse, has more than 250 interactive science and technology exhibits.

(La Chinesca
Mexicali is home to Mexico's only distinct Chinatown. The intersection at the heart of the district is Calle Benito Juárez and Calle Altamirano close to the border crossing. The city itself boasts 100 Chinese restaurants, mostly serving Cantonese-style cuisine. Earlier in the 20th century, the percentage of Chinese residents in the city was much higher, and the only two cinemas in the city played movies in Chinese. Today, relatively few Chinese families remain, but Chinese culture and traditions live on. The signature monument to the Chinese presence in Mexicali is the pagoda on Plaza de Amistad (just outside the district). It was made entirely by Chinese craftsmen using materials shipped from China and was dedicated in 1994.

Bosque de la Ciudad
Visit Bosque de la Ciudad in southwest Mexicali (Av. Ocotlán and Calle Alvarado,

downtown Mexicali

© ANTHONY COSTELLO

Tues.–Sun. 9 A.M.–5 P.M.), when you need a break from the dusty downtown. This large city park has its own lake and zoo.

ENTERTAINMENT AND EVENTS
Baseball
Mexicali's professional baseball team, **Las Aquilas (The Eagles),** is part of the Mexican Pacific League and plays at El Nido de las Aguilas (Eagles' Nest) stadium, located in the **Cuidad Deportiva** (City Sports Complex, Calz. Justo Sierra, tel. 686/567-5129, www.aguilas-demexicali.com.mx, Nov.–Jan.). General admission tickets start at US$40.

Nightlife
Antrojo (Calz. Juárez 1807, tel. 686/568-2129) plays house music for a younger crowd. It's open Wednesday, Friday, and Saturday until 2 A.M. **La Capilla** is a music and dance club inside the Hotel Lucerna (Calz. Juárez 2151, tel. 686/564-7000, nightly until 2 A.M.). Bars at the Hotel Crowne Plaza, Araiza Inn Mexicali,

and Araiza Inn Calafía often have live music in the evening.

Teatro del Estado (State Theater)

Baja California's state theater (tel. 686/554-6419, icbcteatrodelestado@hotmail.com) occupies a 1,100-seat venue at Calzado López Mateos and Avenida Castellanos. The city tourist office also has performance schedules (tel. 888/268-8262).

Festivals and Events

Baja Prog (www.bajaprog.org) takes place in March, with four days of progressive rock band performances. Most of the festival takes place at the Hotel Araiza, but the finale is held at the Teatro del Estado (State Theatre) on Boulevard López Mateos.

In March or April, the **Mexicali 500** (www.codeoffroad.com.mx) off-road race starts in Mexicali and ends in San Felipe. The course follows the Laguna Salada dry lakebed.

In September–October, the **Fiesta del Sol** (Parque Vicente Guerrero, www.fiestasdelsol.com.mx) draws some 500,000 people over the course of 21 days to commemorate the founding of Mexicali in 1904. During the event, a festival queen is named and a number of cultural performances and art shows provide entertainment.

In November, the local chamber of restaurants, CANIRAC, holds **Muestra Gastronómica,** a food fair featuring Mexican, seafood, and Chinese cuisines (tel. 686/554-3285, www.caniracnacional.com.mx, canirac-1mexicali@prodigy.net.mx).

On Sunday afternoons, mariachi groups often play at **Parque Constitución,** a park at Avenida Hidalgo and Calle Aldama.

SHOPPING

Unless you're buying agricultural supplies or prescription medication, the visitor-oriented shopping is limited in Mexicali. The border zone along Calle Melgar has the usual shops selling kitschy souvenirs. **Plaza Cataviña** (Calz. Cetys 1800, Col. Cataviña, tel. 686/567-2896) caters to the young, upscale crowd with a modern health club and a variety of electronics, clothing, and jewelry stores.

El Armario (Calz. Justo Sierra 1700 at Blvd. Juárez, Plaza Azteca, tel. 686/568-1906) has rustic Mexican furniture, glassware, and handicrafts.

Plaza Cachanilla (Calz. López Mateos, northwest of Parque Vicente Guerrero, tel. 686/553-4177 or -4108) is a huge mall located just a few minutes away from the international border. In the summer, when the weather is hot, local families will come and spend the day inside the cool shopping mall.

ACCOMMODATIONS

Mexicali accommodations cost less than their counterparts in Tijuana and Ensenada. If you shop around when you arrive, you can often get much lower rates than if you make reservations ahead of time. The higher-end hotels cater to Mexican business travelers with meeting rooms and business centers. On the less-expensive end of the spectrum, there are a number of hotels that supply visitors with functional rooms, off-street parking, and air-conditioning.

Under US$50

Motel Reforma (Av. Reforma 625, tel. 686/533-6831, US$30) caters to budget travelers looking for accommodations near the border. It's slightly better than the **Hotel San Juan Capistrano** (Av. Reforma 646, tel. 686/552-4104, US$30) a few doors down. As you head west of boulevard López Mateos, the motels get cheaper, but they are real dives.

Motel Azteca de Oro (Calle de la Industria 600, tel. 686/557-1433, www.hotelaztecadeoro.com, US$42–60) is a typical two-story motel with air-conditioned rooms, but six rooms are combined with a private enclosed one-car garage. The rooms are standard for the price range, with older beds and shabby bathrooms. Two-story **Hotel Hacienda del Indio** (Calz. López Mateos 101 at Av. Fresnillo, tel. 686/557-2277, US$45) has 50 recently renovated rooms that surround an enclosed courtyard. **Hotel Regis** (Calz. Juárez 2150, tel. 686/566-8801, www.hotel-regis.com, US$45) is another good choice for clean, basic rooms.

US$50-100

If you're simply stopping over on your way south, or looking for a base from which to launch a fishing or hunting trip, the **Hotel Siesta Real** (Calz. Justo Sierra 899, tel. 686/568-2001, toll-free U.S. tel. 800/426-5093, www.hotelsiestareal.com, US$48–80) is a convenient option. Its 90 rooms have air-conditioning, TVs, and phones. Guests may also use a swimming pool, restaurant, and off-street parking lot.

Hotel Posada Inn (Blvd. López Mateos 939 at Calle Torneros, tel. 686/558-6100, www.hotelposadainn.com, US$63) has wireless Internet, air-conditioned rooms, off-street parking in a courtyard, and a nice sitting area on the upper walkway. It's situated on the east side of a partitioned road, so it can be difficult to get in and out by car.

The **Calafía Hotel and Convention Center** (Calz. Justo Sierra 1495, tel. 686/568-3311 or 800/026-5444, U.S. tel. 877/727-2492, www.araizainn.com.mx, US$79) houses the Calafía Steakhouse and a separate sports bar. Part of the Araiza chain, it is a clean, four-story motel with 170 rooms. The hotel caters to traveling families with a pool and secure parking. It is located next to a police station.

US$100-150

South of the Calafía along the same boulevard (which changes names en route), the **Araiza Inn Mexicali** (Calz. Juárez 2220, tel. 686/564-1100 or 800/686-5444, U.S. tel. 877/727-2492, www.araizainn.com.mx, US$70–120) has 190 rooms. The Fonda restaurant is often packed. Some of the suites have been renovated and are very nice, with flat-screen TVs, shoe-buffing machines, and spinning cycles. This hotel also has a swimming pool, coffee shop, bar, and disco.

Hotel Lucerna (Calz. Juárez 2151, tel. 686/564-7000, US$106) has 176 rooms each with air-conditioning, minibar, satellite TV, and phone. There are two pools, a fitness center, and the Restaurant Mezzosole. The tower you see when you turn left out of the reception office is worn out. For the best accommodations, ask for a bungalow. They were newly renovated, and have the feel of a W Hotel room. The family suite has a separate bedroom, spinning cycle, bathrobes, and two flat-screen TVs. Also note, this hotel has limited secured parking.

The **Fiesta Inn Mexicali** (Calz. López Mateos 1029, tel. 686/837-3300, www.fiestainn.com, US$83–135) is a newly built hotel with more than 150 rooms in a multistory white building. It's located a few minutes from the border, across from the city's bullfighting arena, and within striking distance of several shopping malls.

The **Crowne Plaza** (Blvd. López Mateos at Av. de los Héroes, tel. 686/557-3600, toll-free U.S. tel. 800/227-6963, www.crowneplaza.com, US$100–150) has most of the same amenities as the Araiza and Fiesta chains. A sports bar features pool tables and a widescreen TV. Nonsmoking rooms are available.

FOOD

Mexicali has a less-developed food scene than Tijuana or Ensenada, but it does have its own signature cuisine, Mexicali-Chinese, and plenty of places to find an enjoyable meal.

Chinese

At last count, there were just under 100 Chinese restaurants in Mexicali. The cooking is mostly Cantonese, but Mexicali-Chinese has evolved into a unique cuisine. For example, a bowl of ketchup-like sauce is commonly served as a condiment. You may also be served a bowl of jalapenos with soy sauce, limes, and salt.

Dragón (Av. Libertad 990, tel. 686/557-4425, daily for lunch and dinner, mains US$10) is an upscale Cantonese restaurant that can hold several hundred diners. The signature dish here is duck with mushrooms. Another good choice is **Fortune House** (Lázaro Cárdenas 1153, tel. 686/555-8848, daily 11 A.M.–11 P.M., mains US$10) near the exit to Mexico 2 and Tijuana.

Other International

Close to downtown, **Restaurant-Bar Heidelberg** (Av. Madero at Calle H, tel. 686/554-2022, http://restauranteheidelberg. com/index.html, Mon.–Sat. noon–1 A.M., mains US$15–25) offers German and Continental fare. The atmosphere is pleasant, but prices are high. With an attached piano bar, **Restaurant Italiano Mandolino** (Av. Reforma 1070, tel. 686/552-9544, daily for lunch and dinner, mains US$10–15) has long been popular for Italian cuisine.

Mexicali has a good option for sushi as well: **Sakura Restaurant** (Blvd. Lázaro Cárdenas 2004 at Calz. Montejano, tel. 686/566-0514 or -4848, Tues.–Sun. 8 A.M.–midnight, mains US$10–15) serves teppanyaki and sushi with the **Karaoke Video Bar** upstairs.

Mexican

In a former American-style drive-in, **Merendero Manuet's** (Calle L at Av. Pino Suárez, tel. 686/552-5694, daily 10 A.M.–1 A.M., mains US$5–10) has a full menu of *antojitos* and a full bar occupied by local ranchers and farmers in cowboy hats. The waitresses waited on the parents of some of the younger patrons that drink beer and smoke in the parking lots on weekends.

Another option for *antojitos* was brand new at press time: **Mr. Choby's** (Blvd. Benito Juárez 1199 at Calle Carranza, no tel., Sun.–Thurs. noon–10 P.M., Fri.–Sat. 10 A.M.–1 A.M.), in the Las Villas food court. Full *botana* platters go for US$22, while individual mains start at US$5. **Fonda de Mexicali** (Juárez 2220, tel. 686/564-1100 ext. 721, mains US$15 and up) in the Hotel Araiza does a huge brunch buffet on Sundays for US$15. The food is a notch above the typical hotel restaurant fare.

In business since 1945, **La Cenaduría Selecta** (Av. Arista 1510 at Calle G, Col. Nueva, tel. 686/552-4047, Mon. 7 A.M.–5 P.M., Tues.–Sun. 8 A.M.–11 P.M., mains US$12 and up) is best known for its *mole* dishes.

⟨ La Carnicería (Panamá 190 at Calz. Justo Sierra, Col. Cuauhtémoc, tel. 686/568-101, daily for lunch and dinner, mains

tacos on the outskirts of Mexicali

© ANTHONY COSTELLO

MEXICALI TO SAN FELIPE

US$18) is an elegant steakhouse that features an indoor grill and brick oven behind glass. Try the mini *al pastor* tacos to start and the very good Queso Fondido fondue platter. There is a bar attached to the restaurant with modern decor and live music occasionally on the weekends.

Seafood

Los Arcos Restaurant/Bar (Calafía 454, tel. 686/556-0903, www.restaurantlosarcos.com.mx, Mon.–Thurs. 11 A.M.–10 P.M., Fri.–Sun. 11 A.M.–11 P.M., mains US$10–15) is part of a chain of 14 restaurants scattered throughout Mexico. Located in the Centro Cívico district, it is the best place in town for fresh seafood.

Groceries

The warehouse-style **Soriana** (Blvd. Juárez north of Independencia), near the Hotel Lucerna, and 24-hour **Ley,** on Independencia or at Plaza Fiesta on Calzada López Mateos, are your best options for stocking up on food and supplies. There is a Costco (Carr. San Luis-Río Colorado, Km 7.5, tel. 686/580-4530, daily 9 A.M.–9 P.M.) on the road out of town as you drive on Mexico 5 toward San Felipe.

INFORMATION AND SERVICES
Tourist Assistance

The Mexicali Tourism and Convention Bureau (COTUCO) has offices on Boulevard López Mateos at Calle Camelias (tel. 686/552-4401 or 888/342-7323, www.mexicaliturismo.com, Mon.–Fri. 8 A.M.–7 P.M.). The information counter has friendly and helpful staff who speak English.

The state tourism department, SECTUR, also has an office in town, at Boulevard Benito Juárez 1 and Calzada Montejano (tel. 686/566-1161 or 686/558-1000, Mon.–Fri. 8 A.M.–5 P.M., Sat.–Sun. 10 A.M.–3 P.M.). The state's legal assistance department (Attorney for Tourist Protection, tel./fax 686/566-1116) is based here as well.

Money

Banks are numerous in Mexicali. Banamex, Bancomer, and Serfín each have multiple branches, most with ATMs. If you need to exchange currency, the banks offer this service only until about noon each day. Numerous *casas de cambio* on both sides of the border are another option.

Post and Telephone

Mexicali's main post and a Western Union office are located at Calzada Independencia and Calle Pioneros (Mon.–Fri. 8 A.M.–3 P.M., Sat. 9 A.M.–1 P.M.). But it's probably better to mail your postcards across the border in Calexico on Birch Street and George Avenue, four blocks west of Imperial Avenue.

Long-distance Ladatel phones can be found throughout Mexicali. Check the rate before you dial an international number. Many U.S. mobile phones continue to pick up a signal across the border into Mexicali. Beyond this zone, you'll need to set yourself up for international roaming (call your service provider before you go). Mobile phones that use the international GSM standard are the only ones that can connect reliably throughout Baja California.

Mexican Consulate

For information about immigration paperwork for traveling into Mexico, including vehicle import permits for driving on the mainland, visit the Mexican consulate on the U.S side of the border in Calexico (331 W. Second St., U.S. tel. 760/357-3863, fax 760/357-6284, Mon.–Fri. 8 A.M.–3 P.M.).

Border Crossing

The main (west) Mexicali border crossing stays open around the clock, every day. The crowds here will be considerably thinner than the crossing at Tijuana, but lines do back up during the morning and afternoon commutes. East of the main crossing, a second gateway joins Calexico East with Mexicali's industrial zone (daily 6 A.M.–10 P.M.). Wait times here are typically less half the time at the main crossing; however, if your ultimate destination is

San Diego or other points west, you'll spend a good amount of time circling east and back around to the west.

If you are a hunter coming back to the United States with game to declare, use the east crossing; the border officials at the main crossing may not know how to handle the paperwork.

If you're traveling south of Mexicali, you'll need a tourist permit, which you can pick up at the Oficina de Federal building that's marked *Migracion* or *Aduana* located to the left of the border gates as you pass through from the U.S. side.

GETTING THERE
By Air
Mexicali has an international airport, **Aeropuerto Internacional General Rodolfo Sánchez Taboada** (MXL), 20 kilometers east of the city via Boulevard de las Américas. No U.S. airlines currently serve the airport, but **Aeroméxico** (Pasaje Alamos 1008-D, Centro Cívico Comercial, tel. 686/557-2551) and **Mexicana** (Av. Obregón, tel. 686/553-5401) offer connections from Hermosillo, Sonora, on the mainland. Mexicana also flies to/from Guadalajara, Monterrey, and Mexico City.

A taxi from the airport to downtown Mexicali runs about US$15.

By Car
From the San Diego airport, take I-5 north to I-8 past El Centro, and take Route 111 south to the border. This route takes about two hours. There is parking on the Calexico side of the border at **Double AA Parking** (201 W. Second St., U.S. tel. 760/357-3213) or **Calexico Parking & Storage** (465 W. Second St., tel. 760/357-2477, Mon.–Fri. 6 A.M.–6 P.M.), where you can also store your vehicle (US$1.50/day) or trailer (US$3/day).

After passing through the border patrol, you'll reach a Y in the road. Stay right. The toll crossing is in the middle of town itself, with the usual insurance companies, fast food restaurants, and money exchangers lining the last few blocks on the U.S. side.

To reach the east crossing, take I-8 to Route 7 south. For current border wait times, visit http://apps.cbp.gov/bwt/.

Mexicali's main north–south roads are well marked. The smaller streets running north–south are named by letters in the alphabet starting with A near Route 111 and descending as you head east.

By Bus
Mexicali's **Central de Autobuses** (on the south side of Calz. Independencia btw Calz. López Mateos/Centro Cívico, tel. 686/557-2410 or -2450) offers intercity connections to Baja and the mainland. **ABC** (Tijuana tel. 664/683-5681, www.abc.com.mx) offers connections to Mexicali from Ensenada and Tijuana. **Estrellas del Pacífico** (Tijuana tel. 664/683-5022 or -6789) also runs buses to/from Mexicali and Ensenada. **Transportes Norte de Sonora** (TNS), **Transportes del Pacífico,** and **Elite** provide connections to the mainland.

To reach the bus terminal via public transportation, catch a local Calle 6 bus from one of the stops along Calzada López Mateos.

The small ABC terminal on López Mateos (btw Azueta/Madero) offers frequent service to Tecate, Tijuana, and Ensenada.

The **Greyhound** station in Calexico (123 First St., U.S. tel. 760/357-1895), right at the pedestrian border crossing, runs direct connections to San Diego and Los Angeles. From the Calexico depot, you walk across through the border gate and take a taxi to Mexicali bus depot (under US$10).

GETTING AROUND
By Bus
Mexicali's city buses are signed for their final destination (e.g., Centro Cívico, Justo Sierra). Many of these bus routes originate on Calle Altamirano downtown, close to the border crossing. Fares are less than US$1.

By Taxi
Taxis de ruta (route taxis) cover many of the same routes for a slightly higher fare. Private

taxi fare runs about US$5 downtown, US$6–8 to/from the border to the Centro Cívico area or the Boulevard Juárez hotel zone. Aside from the pedestrian border crossing, the larger hotels are good places to find an available taxi. To order a taxi, call **Radio Taxis Cervantes** (tel. 686/568-3718) or **Ecotaxi** (tel. 686/562-6565).

By Car

Aside from its many traffic circles, called *glorietas,* Mexicali is a fairly easy city to navigate by car. Street parking is readily available.

Follow Calle Juárez to find Mexico 5 south to San Felipe. There are several ways to get to Mexico 2, which goes east to Sonora and west to Tecate and Tijuana.

Pemex stations are easy to find, and these days, most offer Premium fuel.

MEXICO 5 SOUTH TO SAN FELIPE

If you want to proceed directly to Mexico 5 south toward San Felipe from the main border crossing (Route 111), keep to your right as you approach the border booths. Stop for the border light, which will flash either green or red. If it's green, you can continue. If it's red, you will need to pull over for further inspection. If you need to get a tourist visa or have an FM3 stamped, the immigration office is on the immediate right.

As you cross the border, bear to your right to get onto Boulevard López Mateos. Continue past the first traffic circle with the statue of Ignacio Allende. Get into the right-hand lane and follow the signs to San Felipe as the road forks to the right and you cross the railroad tracks. At the next traffic circle, follow the signs to San Felipe, and then take a left at the next light. This road will turn into Mexico 5 and will take you all the way into San Felipe.

Coming from the new border crossing to the east, the road will end in a T a few hundred

Mexico 5, north of San Felipe

© PAUL ITOI

meters from the border. Go right at the T, then take a left onto Boulevard Gomez Morin. This will take you straight to Mexico 5. Stay in the middle of the three lanes to avoid most of the abrupt stops.

The drive is mostly flat, but you'll have plenty to look at as you go from farmland to lakebed to desert. About an hour and half into the drive you can often see the Gulf of California in the distance. As you get closer to San Felipe, you'll encounter construction crews that are widening the road from two lanes to four. Eventually, the entire stretch from Mexicali to San Felipe with be four lanes.

The total drive time from the border to San Felipe is around two hours. For the return trip north, add at least one hour to make sure you have enough time to cross the border. During rush hour, or on holidays, the border wait can be several hours.

Mexicali to Tecate

West of Mexicali, Mexico 2 follows the northern foothills of the Sierra de los Cucapá and the top of **Laguna Salada,** a 100-kilometer-long dry salt lake. The Pemex station near Km 24 is the only option for fuel until La Rumorosa (53 km farther west). If you drive along Mexico 2-D between Mexicali and Tecate, you'll pass through two toll booths, each of which costs approximately US$2.50.

After Laguna Salada, the highway ascends the Sierra de Juárez, where several palm canyons named Tajo, El Carrizo, Guadalupe, and El Palomar offer prime hiking, off-roading, and wilderness camping. Spring-fed streams run year-round, but the time to go is between November and April. From May to October, the temperatures can get above 38°C.

◖ CAÑON DE GUADALUPE

Of the four larger canyons in this part of the Sierra de Juárez, 400-hectare Cañon de Guadalupe is the most popular among hikers and campers because of its healing hot springs. In this high-elevation oasis, granite peaks tower over a sea of blue fan palms. Waterfalls, prehistoric rock art, and solar power all are part of the experience.

Camping

Guadalupe Canyon Hot Springs and Campground (U.S. tel. 949/673-2670, www.guadalupe-canyon.com, US$50–75) is divided into two campgrounds: Arturo's Campo and Los Manantiales (Mario's Campo). The same family owns the entire valley and so far has resisted having it developed. In 2007, a fire burned most of the property, but it's in the process of being rebuilt. Arturo's campsites are arranged to afford more privacy. Each of the eight campsites features its own private hot tub made of river rock and cement, and you can adjust the temperature between 26–41°C. The sites can accommodate multiple vehicles, and there is a two-night minimum on weekends and a three-night minimum on

holiday weekends. Pets are welcome, with proof of vaccinations.

Facilities for campers include outhouses, showers, and a market that sells the basics. Refrigeration is provided by 45-kilogram blocks of ice. The owners do not want you to collect firewood or disturb any of the natural surroundings, but firewood is for sale. The canyon is popular on the holidays and the weekends, so book early.

Guided Hikes

For tours of the Cañon de Guadalupe, contact **Rupestres** (mobile tel. 044/686/158-9921, www.rupestres.com, explorandobajacalifornia@hotmail.com, US$70).

Getting There

From Mexicali, take Calle Guadalajara about eight kilometers south to Mexico 2 West and follow the highway for 32 kilometers. The first turn is labeled Cañon de Guadalupe and Laguna Salada. The road is available only from the eastbound lanes, so you'll need to pass the intersection and double back at the next U-turn opportunity. This first turn is faster and more direct, but because it uses the dry lakebed of the Laguna Salada for 40 kilometers, it will be muddy and impassable following any rain. When you drive across the lakebed, don't worry if there are multiple tracks. Follow the most worn route and keep heading south/southwest and look for the occasional sign to the canyon. If you're not comfortable navigating the lakebed, you can take the second turnoff which is 4.3 kilometers farther west and also labeled Cañon de Guadalupe. This road has a higher elevation, so it's less vulnerable to rain, but it takes longer (about 45 minutes to go 43 km) and is a less comfortable ride. Both roads merge at the opening of the canyon. The rest of the drive is increasingly winding and rocky—recommended only for high-clearance vehicles.

Eleven kilometers from the main road, a

MEXICALI TO SAN FELIPE

very rocky few hundred meters will bring you to the campground entrance.

LA RUMOROSA AND VICINITY

Heading west from Mexicali, at around Km 44, the highway climbs the steep Juárez escarpment to the town of La Rumorosa. Named for the whispering winds that blow by the 1,275-meter pass, the village is populated with the summer homes of Mexicali and Tijuana residents. The old highway was infamous for the number of fatal accidents. After the old road was closed, it was used in the filming of a James Bond movie. La Rumorosa's most famous resident might be El Diablito (Little Devil). He is a small red figure painted in a cave in the nearby El Vallecito. Only on December 21, the winter solstice, a ray of sunlight illuminates the figure. The **Museo Camp Alaska** (no tel., hours vary) is located in the middle of town in an old stone garrison and contains the history of the indigenous people of the area. For tours of El Vallecito and La Rumorosa, contact **Rupestres** (mobile tel. 044/686/158-9921, www.rupestres.com, explorandobajacalifornia@hotmail.com, US$60).

Food

Restaurant Asadero El Chipo (no tel., daily for lunch and dinner) on Mexico 2 at the west end of town serves excellent tacos for less than US$2 each.

Laguna Hanson

At Km 73, west of La Rumorsa, there is a graded dirt road that leads 63 kilometers to Laguna Hanson in the Parque Nacional Constitución de 1857. The second half of the road is for high-clearance vehicles only; four-wheel drive is recommended. The park is more easily approached via Mexico 3, southeast of Ensenada.

San Felipe and Vicinity

San Felipe (pop. 25,000) is a small coastal town on the Sea of Cortez, about two hours' drive south of the U.S./Mexico border. California and Arizona residents flock here for weekend RV and fishing trips. Punta San Felipe protects the bay from north winds. To get oriented, begin your trip by climbing the stairs to the top of the 240-meter **Cerro El Machorro** located on the point. You'll see a shrine to the Virgin of Guadalupe and panoramic views of the bay.

In the 1940s and '50s, American fishermen came down to catch the abundant *totuava,* a sporting croaker that could reach up to 115 kilograms. The tasty fish proved to be too popular and it's now on the endangered species list and off limits for any fishing. San Felipe faces a similar clash of supply and demand today. Recent fishing and shrimping practices have endangered a rare breed of small porpoise called the *vaquita.* The Zoological Society of London has designated it as one of the 100 EDGE species (Evolutionarily Distinct, Globally Endangered), which makes it a top priority for conservationists. There is a monument to the *vaquita* at the center of the *malecón* in San Felipe.

More than 250,000 tourists visit San Felipe annually. The populated area around San Felipe stretches for quite a few kilometers of coastline to the north and south. Besides fishing, there are sand dunes for ATVs and dune buggies, which are a common site around town.

The town has a splash of nightlife along the *malecón* with several clubs, bars, and the periodic S.W.A.T invasion. S.W.A.T is a tour company that brings in busloads of college students during spring break and throughout the year for all-inclusive party weekends.

Most visitors choose the months of November–April to visit the area. The temperatures are generally milder than Mexicali in the summer months, but they can still often break 38°C.

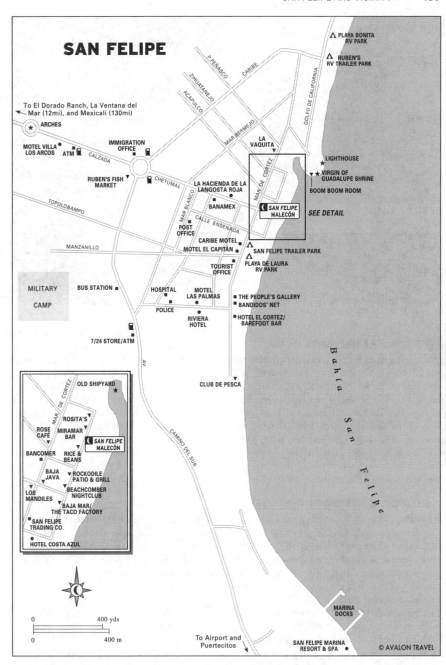

SAN FELIPE

To El Dorado Ranch, La Ventana del Mar (12mi), and Mexicali (130mi)

★ ARCHES

MOTEL VILLA LOS ARCOS

ATM

IMMIGRATION OFFICE

CALZADA

CHETUMAL

RUBEN'S FISH MARKET

TOPOLOBAMPO

MANZANILLO

MILITARY CAMP

BUS STATION

P PEÑASCO

ZIHUATANEJO

ACAPULCO

CARIBE

MAR BERMEJO

GOLFO DE CALIFORNIA

LA VAQUITA

MAR DE CORTEZ

LIGHTHOUSE ★
★ VIRGIN OF GUADALUPE SHRINE
BOOM BOOM ROOM

SAN FELIPE MALECÓN

SEE DETAIL

PLAYA BONITA RV PARK

RUBEN'S RV TRAILER PARK

LA HACIENDA DE LA LANGOSTA ROJA

MAR BLANCO

BANAMEX

CALLE ENSENADA

POST OFFICE

CARIBE MOTEL

MOTEL EL CAPITÁN

SAN FELIPE TRAILER PARK

PLAYA DE LAURA RV PARK

TOURIST OFFICE

HOSPITAL

POLICE

MOTEL LAS PALMAS

RIVIERA HOTEL

THE PEOPLE'S GALLERY

BANDIDOS' NET

HOTEL EL CORTEZ/ BAREFOOT BAR

7/24 STORE/ATM

AV

CLUB DE PESCA

CAMINO DEL SUR

B a h í a   S a n   F e l i p e

(detail inset)

OLD SHIPYARD ★

MAR DE CORTEZ

ROSITA'S

ROSE CAFÉ

MIRAMAR BAR

SAN FELIPE MALECÓN

BANCOMER

RICE & BEANS

BAJA JAVA

ROCKODILE PATIO & GRILL

LOS MANDILES

BEACHCOMBER NIGHTCLUB

BAJA MAR/ THE TACO FACTORY

SAN FELIPE TRADING CO.

HOTEL COSTA AZUL

0   400 yds
0   400 m

To Airport and Puertecitos

MARINA DOCKS

SAN FELIPE MARINA RESORT & SPA

© AVALON TRAVEL

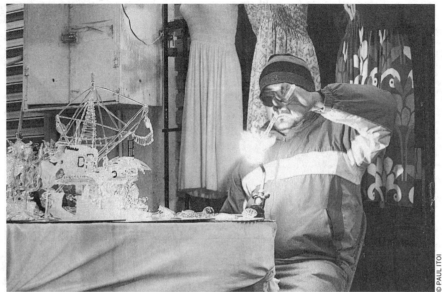

glassblower on the *malecón*

【 SAN FELIPE *MALECÓN*

Public life in San Felipe centers around the *malecón*. This waterfront promenade is a smaller version of the one in La Paz and similar to Loreto's in size. There are several bars and nightclubs that offer a scaled-down version of the Rosarito beach scene. Several restaurants and shops also line the strip. Playa San Felipe stretches the length of the *malecón* and is popular with sunbathers and **pangueros** for hire.

SPORTS AND RECREATION
Fishing

Even though you'll hear seasoned area fisherman pine for the good old days, the San Felipe fishing scene is still the big draw—for visitors and retirees alike. Croakers can be found year-round, but the peak months for cabrilla, yellowtail, sierra, and grouper are May–October. Head north above Punta San Felipe for the best onshore fishing. You can still fish from shore without a license, so all you need is a shore rod, food and water, and some lures.

There are multi-day trips available to the Midriff islands 400 kilometers to the south. These trips are usually six-day fishing marathons and involve large 100-foot-plus fishing vessels. The term "mothership fishing" refers to the 6–10 *pangas* that the larger vessels carry with them. It takes around 24 hours to reach the fishing grounds from San Felipe. From there, the *pangas* typically head out with three anglers each for a morning and afternoon run. Everyone pitches in to make bait during the night.

Tony Reyes Fishing Tours (Av. Mar Bermejo 130, tel. 686/577-1120, www.tonyreyes.com) and **Baja Sportfishing** (tel. 800/770-2341, bajasportfishinginc.net) operate these long-range trips. Prices for the week run US$1,200–1,500 and include everything but tip, drinks, and tackle.

Boating

You can launch your own boat at the Motel El Cortez, Ruben's Trailer Park, or the San Felipe Marina. **Baja Directions** (www.bajadirections.com) has an updated and detailed atlas for the

Baja sportfishing areas including boat ramps, bathymetry, and gas stations.

Golf

Las Caras de Mexico Golf Course (tel. 686/576-0517, www.lascarasdemexico.com) is an 18-hole, 7,200-yard course that opened in 2005. It's part of the El Dorado Ranch and La Ventana del Mar developments. Greens fee are US$30–85 and carts are complimentary. No need to pack your clubs; you can rent a pro bag of TaylorMades (US$30/18 holes, US$15/9 holes). The turn for La Ventana del Mar is 11 kilometers north of San Felipe at Km 176.5. A mountain course on the other side of highway is under construction.

ENTERTAINMENT AND EVENTS
Nightlife

Partying in San Felipe boils down to three main choices: Rockodile, Beachcomber, or the Boom Boom Room. **Rockodile** (Ave. Mar de Cortez 199, tel. 686/577-1219, www.4rockodile.com, rockodilemexico@aol.com, daily noon–3 A.M.) is the most popular for spring-breakers, with nearly 1,500 square meters of bars, multi-level dance floors, and a soap machine that froths the willing crowd into a slippery frenzy. **Beachcomber** (Malecón/Calz. Chetumal, tel. 686/577-1670 or 686/577-1219, www.4beachcomber.com, daily noon–3 A.M.) features live pop rock and Sinaloan bands, DJs, and professional sports broadcast on the club's 60-inch screens. The enormous **Boom Boom Room** (Calle Guaymas, northern end of the *malecón,* across the footbridge that leads to the Shrine of Guadalupe, no tel., daily noon–3 A.M.) features a high-tech sound system and stunning views.

For a less caffeinated experience, grab a drink at the relatively quiet **Club Miramar** (Av. Mar de Cortez, tel. 686/577-1192, daily 10 A.M.–3 A.M.), a San Felipe classic at the north end of the *malecón.* To get away from the crowds, head south of the *malecón* to the Hotel El Cortez's **Barefoot Bar** (tel. 686/577-1055) and enjoy the tranquil view of the sea over a cold margarita.

Festivals and Events

February and March are busy months on the San Felipe events calendar. Like Ensenada and La Paz, San Felipe celebrates **Carnaval,** usually in late February or early March. The **Tecate SCORE San Felipe 250** off-road race take place in March. The **Hobie Cat Midwinters West Regatta** (midwinterswest@cox.net, February or March) is a catamaran race on Bahía de San Felipe. U.S. college students take over the town during the latter part of March for **spring break.** Steer clear unless you want to partake in the madness.

June 1 brings a national **Navy Day** (Día de la Marina Nacional); the celebration includes a street festival with live music and dancing.

SHOPPING

Run by Steve and Linda Sullivan, **The People's Gallery** (Av. Mar de Cortés Sur 381, tel. 686/577-2898, daily 10 A.M.–5 P.M.), sells the works of local artists, including handmade furniture, jewelry, masks, paintings, and other crafts. The owners also publish the informative *San Felipe Newsletter* (sfnewsster@gmail.com).

For new and used books, try the **San Felipe Trading Company** (Av. Mar de Cortés, across from the IMSS clinic and half a block north of the Costa Azul, no tel.), or a new bookstore called **The New Bookstore** (Calzada Chetumal, no tel.), one block west of the Chinese restaurant.

ACCOMMODATIONS AND CAMPING

Given its proximity to the U.S. border, San Felipe has historically had pricier accommodations than similar Baja fishing towns. Outside of the peak months (Nov.–Apr.) though, prices may be as much as 30 percent lower. Rates shown here do not include 12 percent hotel tax or 10 percent service charge, unless specified.

US$50-100

Repeat guests continue to report satisfactory stays with the clean, friendly, and safe **Chapala** (Av. Mar de Cortés 142, tel. 686/577-1240,

US$60). It's a no-frills place, but you can't beat the price. A short walk from the beach, **Motel El Capitán** (Av. Mar de Cortés 298, tel./fax 686/577-1303, U.S. tel. 866/540-7370, www.motelcapitan.com, bsfa7@prodigy.net.mx, US$75) has 45 clean rooms on two levels surrounding a parking lot and pool. Amenities include air-conditioning and TV.

Two blocks from the beach, **La Hacienda de la Langosta Roja** (Red Lobster, Calz. Chetumal 125, tel. 686/577-0483 or 800/967-0005, www.sanfelipelodging.com, US$85) is now managed by the El Dorado Ranch. The 39 rooms in this pink two-story building were recently re-furnished, but they still feel a little Motel 6. Amenities include air-conditioning and satellite TV with 15 channels. Ask for a room in the front building.

Next to Bandodos' Net, **Hotel El Cortez** (Av. Mar de Cortés, tel. 686/577-1055 or 686/577-1056, hotelcortez1@prodigy.net.mx, US$85) has 112 basic rooms facing the beach. Take a look at one before you commit. The facilities here are in much better shape than the rooms themselves, which need an overhaul and more thorough day-to-day maintenance. The hotel has a swimming pool, boat launch, laundry facilities, *palapas,* and the Barefoot Bar. Its 112 rustic rooms come with air-conditioning, TVs, and phones.

The **Caribe Motel** (Av. Mar de Cortés at Calle Ensenada, US$40–80) opened in 2008, across from the Costa Azul, with 15 rooms. Those on the front side have decks and cost more. The motel is designed in a courtyard style, with two levels. Guestrooms are upstairs and off-street, plus there is secure parking below (each spot gets it's own light). Vinyl curtains and tile floors make for harsh acoustics, but the rooms are large and come with cable TV and air-conditioning. Hot-water issues were still being worked out when we visited.

US$100-150

San Felipe Marina Resort and Spa (Km 4.5, tel. 686/577-1569 or 800/025-6925, toll-free U.S. tel. 800/291-5397, www.sanfelipemarina.net, US$144), farther south off Avenida Camino del Sur, has rooms with kitchenettes decorated in bright colors and simple furnishings, but it's not a resort in the five-star sense. Rooms are well worn, and amenities include only TV with limited channels and phones. Wi-Fi, for an extra charge, works from the lobby only. On the premises are two swimming pools (indoor and outdoor, not heated in winter), tennis courts, a restaurant/bar, and spa that doesn't seem to offer any treatments. Service is inconsistent—sometimes attentive and others times sorely lacking. The beach is the best part about a stay here.

Overlooking the sea on the road to Puertecitos, **Las Casitas Beach and Tennis Resort** (Km 1.6, 686/577-1195 or 686/187-9422, U.S. tel. 877/270-2272, www.lascasitas.com.mx, US$110–130) has air-conditioned bungalows and studios with king-size beds and private decks.

Vacation Rentals

Condominiums Playa Bonita (U.S. tel. 626/967-8977, www.sanfelipebeachcondos.com, US$60–125) has eight one-bedroom units on the beach and an adjoining RV park.

North of town, the gated **El Dorado Ranch** (tel. 686/576-0402, U.S. tel. 877/787-2624, www.eldoradoranch.com) development often has vacation rentals available in different sizes and at varying price points. Residents and guests may use community's tennis club, restaurant/bar, *palapas,* heated pool, and hot tub. The new **La Ventana del Mar** (U.S. tel. 877/787-2624, www.laventanadelmar.com, two-bedroom units US$260–310 per night) has several two- and three-bedroom units complete and available for rent.

Camping and RV Parks

Condo developments have taken over some of San Felipe's largest campgrounds in recent years. More than 20 campgrounds remain, but of these, few, if any, are designed with big rigs in mind. Amenities are often lacking, and you'll have to battle the permanent and monthly renters to get a spot. In summer, the parks that are located along the beach north of Punta San Felipe, tend to stay cooler than those on Bahía

San Felipe. A signature feature of the nicer San Felipe campgrounds are the *palapa* structures that provide a shady kitchen area underneath and a lookout deck on top. You can park your small RV under the structure, or larger ones beside it. **Playa Bonita RV Park** (tel. 686/577-1215, U.S. tel. 626/967-8977, www.sanfelipebeach-condos.com, playabonita@aol.com, US$20–40 for full hookups), and **Ruben's RV Trailer Park** (Av. Golfo de California 703, tel. 686/577-1442, US$20, full hookups only) both offer this type of *palapa* for their guests.

North of town, past the El Dorado resort, **Big RV's Camp** (Km 174–175, Mexico 5, U.S. tel. 760/427-6469, US$10–15 per night) can accommodate big rigs with full hookups. **Pete's Camp** (Km 178, Mexico 5, U.S. tel. 951/694-6704, www.petescamp.com) has 79 sites, but no hookups, for US$15. **Playa del Sol** (Km 182.5, Mexico 5, tel. 686/576-0292, US$10–15) has *palapa*-shaded tent and RV sites that overlook the beach. Limited amenities include the proximity to El Sol restaurant (Wed.–Sun., mains US$5–10), which serves Mexican staples for lunch and dinner.

Budget camping options nearby include **Marco's** (Av. Golfo de California 788, off Av. Mar de Caribe, tel. 686/577-1875 or -1842) and **Vista del Mar** (Av. Mar de Cortés 601, tel. 686/577-1252), at US$10–15 per vehicle. The tradeoff is you won't be on the beach.

South of town, long-favored **Campo San Felipe** (Av. Mar de Cortés 301, tel. 686/577-1012, www.camposanfelipe.com, US$15–20) has 34 full-hookup sites, and Internet access too. **Playa de Laura RV Park** (Av. Mar de Cortez 333, tel. 686/577-1128) offers just the basics, but it's still a popular place. Rates are about US$10 for tents, US$16–30 for RVs, depending on how close you are to the beach. At the far south end of town, **Club de Pesca RV and Trailer Park** (Av. Mar de Cortés, tel. 686/577-1180, fax 686/577-1888, clubdepes-casf@yahoo.com, US$15–20) is removed from much of the action in San Felipe, but also close enough that you can walk to the shops and restaurants. It has 54 spots, many of them reserved for permanent residents. Call ahead.

FOOD
Seafood
Fish tacos, cold *cocteles,* and seafood platters anchor just about every San Felipe menu. **La Vaquita Restaurant & Bar** (Puerta Peñasco and Av. Mar de Cortés North, tel. 686/577-2837, Wed.–Mon. 11 A.M.–10 P.M.) serves breakfast, lunch, and dinner in an open-air setting. Seafood cocktails (US$6) are its specialty, but the menu also features fish plates (US$6–10) and tacos (US$4 per order). Close to the *malecón,* ◖ **La Hacienda de la Langosta Roja** (Calz. Chetumal 121, tel. 686/577-0484, www.sanfelipelodging.com, daily 7 A.M.–11 P.M., dinner mains US$14–26) serves Italian-style seafood (piccata, Florentine, scampi, etc.) at reasonable prices. Its sunny patio is a plus on winter afternoons.

At **Chuy's Place** (Av. Mar de Cortés, no tel., daily for dinner, mains US$15) owner Jesus Davis does an amazing shrimp entr–e with oyster sauce and ginger, as well as lamb chops with mango sauce.

Mexican
On the *malecón,* **Rice and Beans** (tel. 686/577-1770, riceybeans@hotmail.com, Mon.–Fri. 7 A.M.–11 P.M., breakfast mains US$2–6, lunch/dinner mains US$14–16) serves breakfast, lunch, and dinner with tables inside (air-conditioned) and on a street-side terrace. Fresh fish and carne asada anchor a menu of Mexican fare.

Rockodile Patio and Grill (tel. 686/577-1219, www.4rockodile.com, daily noon–midnight, mains US$10–15), on the *malecón,* serves its fish tacos with a tray of condiments. Burgers with fries are another standby. Next to Bar Miramar on the north end of the *malecón,* **Rosita's Restaurant** (Av. Mar de Cortés 381, tel. 686/540-6218, www.rositarest.com, daily 9 A.M.–10 P.M., US$6–13) is a friendly, if touristy, place with decent Mexican food, including shrimp tacos.

Also on the *malecón,* two-story **Licoraria** (no tel.) is first and foremost a place to try fish tacos, but it also serves *machaca, chilaquiles,* and other types of tacos for US$1.50 apiece.

© PAUL ITOI

Rosita's Restaurant on the *malecón*

If you're on the hunt for an authentic Mexican meal, head to **La Fonda Los Portales** (Manzanillo, one block west of the toursit office, no tel., mains US$7–12), open daily for breakfast, lunch, and dinner. It's known for its rich chicken *mole* and other Mexican classics of Aztec origin. Traditional tortilla soup and refreshing *agua de jamaica* round out the menu. The restaurant does not serve alcoholic beverages, but you can bring your own.

International

At the golf course of La Ventana del Mar Resort, **Pavilion** (U.S. tel. 877/629-2852 or 619/299-5990, Mon.–Fri. 8 A.M.–7 P.M., Sat. 8 A.M.–9 P.M. Sun. 10 A.M.–9 P.M., mains US$10–18) offers a gourmet menu with entr–es such as fricassee of veal, walnut-encrusted rack of lamb, and champagne-poached scallops.

Perched high above the town, the **Lighthouse Lounge** (Guaymas 152, tel. 686/577-2540, lighthouselounge1@prodigy.net.mx, Tues.–Sun. 8 A.M.–10 P.M., mains US$10–15) has the most unique view around

and cheerful and festive decor. On the menu are omelettes, burgers, sandwiches, and salads, plus steaks and Mexican plates for dinner.

South of the Caribe Motel, **The George** (Av. Mar de Cortés, tel. 686/577-1057, daily 6 A.M.–10 P.M., US$12–22) is a cross between a steakhouse and a diner, with leather booths and bright lighting. The menu includes Mexican fare, as well as steaks.

El Nido Steakhouse (Av. Mar de Cortés 348, tel. 686/577-1028, Thurs.–Tues. 2–10 P.M., mains US$18–25) is a Baja chain known for its Western decor and steaks grilled over a mesquite wood fire. Guests sit in tall leatherback chairs at heavy wood tables, under the dim light of red lamps.

Baja Mar/The Taco Factory specializes in shrimp dishes, and the guacamole is a standout. Tacos cost US$1–1.50 each. Entrees run US$8–20, and the seafood combo (US$48) is large enough for two. There is an enclosed dining room, but the larger dining area is outside on a large deck with a bar in the middle.

Try **Baja Burger** (Av. Mar de Cortés 162,

no tel., www.bajaburguer.com, daily for breakfast and lunch, mains US$3–9) for a quick bite, such as *chilaquiles* for breakfast or a burger with fries for lunch.

Cafés
Behind the Beachcomber Bar and on the second story of the building, **Baja Java** (Av. Mar de Cortés and Calz. Chetumal, no tel., baja_java@highes.net, daily for breakfast and lunch) is the place for espresso drinks. Enjoy the sea views from its sunny patio. Downstairs is the **Smoke Signals** (no tel.) cigar shop and lounge.

Groceries
Many of the stores you'll need for groceries and supplies are located along Calzada Chetumal on the way into town. At the entrance to town is **Ruben's Fish Market** (Mar Caribe Sur 158). Avenida Mar de Caribe also has several bakeries. Near the north end of the *malecón*, **La Vaquita Dos** (Puerto Peñasco 292, tel. 686/577-1710, daily until 11 P.M.) has meat and produce counters, as well as fresh tortillas made on-site. On the weekends, they'll barbecue your meat, free of charge. You can also pick up a variety of household supplies. Special orders are welcome.

INFORMATION AND SERVICES
Tourist Assistance
The Secretary of Tourism for San Felipe (Manzanillo 300 at Av. Mar de Cortés, tel. 686/577-1155 or -1865, turismosf@yahoo.com.mx, www.turismobc.gob.mx, Mon.–Fri. 8 A.M.–7 P.M., Sat. 9 A.M.–3 P.M., Sun. 10 A.M.–1 P.M.) distributes maps, brochures, and other visitor information.

Money
There are half a dozen ATMs around town, including a machine at the 7-Eleven/Pemex station as you enter town, a Bancomer on Avenida Mar de Cortés, and a Banamex on Calzada Chetumal. There is a *casa de cambio* on Calzada Chetumal, across from the Beachcomber.

Post and Telephone
You'll find San Felipe's post office (Mon.–Fri. 8 A.M.–1 P.M. and 2–6 P.M.) on Mar Blanco, one block south of Calzada Chetumal. For other mail and business services, try Yet Mail Etc. (Av. Mar de Cortés 75, tel. 686/577-1255).

Internet Access
Bandidos' Net (Av. Mar de Cortés, Plaza Canela 1, tel. 686/577-1600, www.sanfelipe.com.mx, Mon.–Fri. 8 A.M.–4 P.M., Sat. 9 A.M.–1 P.M., closed Sat. in summer), next to the El Cortez motel, charges US$4 per hour for high-speed wired or wireless access. At **Café Tazzo** (Av. Mar de Cortés and Calle Ensenada), next to the Caribe Moteo, you can use computer terminals or connect your own laptop via Wi-Fi while you enjoy coffee and dessert. It opens at 7 A.M. daily.

Emergencies
The **Abasolo Medical Clinic** (Calz. Chetumal, near the Pemex, tel. 686/577-1706, Mon.–Fri. 9 A.M.–2 P.M. and 4–8 P.M., emergencies any time) is run by the former head of the local hospital. He speaks excellent English and has been in the San Felipe area for two decades. He can also arrange for emergency ground or air transportation to San Diego if needed. **Hospital San Felipe** (tel. 686/577-0117 or -2849) and the **police station** (tel. 686/577-1134 or dial 060) are located next to each other on the south side of town. The Red Cross is on Puerto Peñasco.

GETTING THERE AND AROUND
By Air
San Felipe has an international airport (SFE, Mar Caribe Sur/Airport Road, tel. 686/577-1368 or -1568, danielpg60@hotmail.com, winter daily 7 A.M.–5 P.M., summer daily 8 A.M.–6 P.M.), but it isn't served by any commercial airlines. The closest major airport is Mexicali. **Grey Eagle Aviation** (U.S. tel. 760/804-8680 or 888/280-8802, www.greyeaglecharter.com) advertises an air taxi service from Long Beach or San Diego, California,

to San Felipe on Tuesday, Friday, and Sunday. Services for private pilots include aviation gas and customs clearing. The trip to town is 9.2 kilometers, and costs US$15 by taxi.

By Bus

San Felipe has a bus depot on Avenida Mar Caribe Sur, south of Calzada Chetumal and near the Pemex. It's open daily 5 A.M.– 11 P.M. (when the last bus from Mexicali arrives, tel. 686/577-1516). **ABC** offers connections to Mexicali, Ensenada, and Tijuana. You can buy your ticket an hour before the bus departs. To reach the Tijuana office, call 664/683-5681. **Estrellas del Pacífico** (Tijuana tel. 664/683-5022 or -6789) also runs buses to San Felipe from Mexicali and Ensenada.

By Taxi

Taxis congregate on Calzada Chetumal near Los Mandiles, or you can call 686/577-1293 to order one. Local trips around town should cost under US$5.

SAN FELIPE TO PUERTECITOS

South of San Felipe, the coastal road deteriorates, though it is paved as far as Puertecitos (85 km south of San Felipe). Construction had commenced in early 2009 to pave the road beyond Puertecitos; however, only the first few kilometers were underway at press time, and in the meantime, the old dirt road was in terrible shape. There is no gas until Punta Willard/ Alfonsina, so fill up your tank before leaving town, and bring some fuel to spare. Watch for *vados* (drainage dips) and potholes along the way. Accommodations are primitive camps, and supplies are few and far between.

Estero Percebú

About 16 kilometers south of San Felipe, a dirt road turn-off leads one kilometer east to a lagoon and white-sand beach with a small community of gringo homes. You can swim or kayak here, as long as you bring your own gear. The area is also known as Shell Island, which refers to a spit of land that's only accessible at low tide. Beachcombers will delight in the possibilities for collecting shells.

Rancho Percebú (Km 16, Carr. San Felipe-Puertecitos, tel. 686/577-1259, open year-round, US$10) has campsites, *palapas,* restrooms, and hot showers. There is also a restaurant/bar at the camp. The friendly Lopez family has run the ranch for several decades and counting. The campground is four kilometers east of the highway.

Valle de los Gigantes

Fifteen kilometers south of San Felipe, on the way to Puertecitos, photographers and naturalists will enjoy the chance to view the world's tallest cactus species up close. The *Pachycereus* or cardón grows to heights of more than 18 meters and can weigh up to 12 tons. Many live to be hundreds of years old.

Besides the namesake giants, the park holds ocotillo, palo verde, cholla, and many other cacti. Desert fauna includes mountain quail, eagles, owls, coyotes, road runners, and buzzards. Daytime temperatures will climb above 100°F in summer and to about 50°F in winter. Bring your own water for hiking the trails.

Look for a turnoff near Km 14 on the west side of the highway, and follow the unpaved road about 200 meters to the park entrance. The closest place to camp is Playa Punta Estrella (Km 13, Carr. San Felipe-Puertecitos, tel. 686/565-2784, US$10), with *palapas,* flush toilets, and hot showers, but no hookups. Soft sand could pose a problem for RVs here. The campground is 1.6 kilometers east of the highway.

For guided hikes in the Valle de los Gigantes, contact **Rupestres** (mobile tel. 044/686/158-9921, www.rupestres.com, explorandobajacalifornia@hotmail.com, US$60).

Camping

Continuing south, the coastline presents a series of beaches, most with primitive *campos* that charge US$5–10 a night, depending on the season and the facilities they offer. **Playa Destiny**

in the Valle de los Gigantes

(Km 71–72, Carr. San Felips-Puertecitos, no tel., US$15) has toilets, cold showers, grills, and picnic tables. **Playa Escondida** (Km 85–86, Carr. San Felips-Puertecitos, no tel., US$10) occupies a white-sand cove. Outhouses and cold showers are about it for amenities, but there are fishing *pangas* for hire.

PUERTECITOS

Civilization, such as it is, appears again at Puertecitos, but don't get too excited. This fishing village has weather-worn homes and trailers, *panga* fishing boats, and natural hot springs (US$5) to offer weary travelers. The beach is small, and the only businesses are a restaurant (Oct.–Apr. daily 6 A.M.–10 P.M.) and a grocery store *(tienda de abarrotes)*.

Accommodations and Camping

The beach camp, **Campo Puertecitos** (Km 89, Carr. San Felipe-Puertecitos, tel. 686/577-1155 or -1865) has 14 sites for primitive camping (US$20), and four barebones rooms for

rent. The property has *palapas* for shade and grills for cooking your fresh catch.

PUNTA BUFEO TO PUNTA FINAL

You need high clearance, sturdy tires, good shocks, and a lot of driving patience to continue south of Puertecitos. Plan on 5–6 hours of driving to make the 72.5-kilometer trip to Alfonsina's on Bahía Willard.

Punta Bufeo

Fishing fanatics enjoy the onshore catch off Punta Bufeo and around the **Islas Encantadas** just offshore. This group of islands provides the ideal habitat for yellowtail, croaker, corvina, and sierra.

The next settlement to the south, **Alfonsina's** (Tijuana tel. 664/648-1951) has supplies, including gas (but not diesel). Rancho Grande also may have gas if Alfonsina's is out.

ACCOMMODATIONS AND FOOD

Campo Punta Bufeo (56 km south of Puertecitos along the dirt road that parallels the coast) has campsites (US$5–10) on the beach, as well as a restaurant, toilets, showers, and simple motel rooms (US$20).

Punta Willard, the next point south, about 12 kilometers south of Punta Bufeo, has a legendary settlement called **Papa Fernández** (www.papafernandez.com). This campground on the beach has *palapa* shelters (US$5), outhouses (but no showers), a boat ramp, and *panga* fishing. The best part about Papa Fernández is its restaurant (daily dawn–dusk, and often later, mains US$6–14), which serves homemade tortillas and chile rellenos and will cook your catch.

Papa Fernández does not have its own telephone; however, in an emergency, you can dial the mini-mart at Rancho Grande on a satellite phone (tel. 555/151-4065). Leave a call-back number, as well as your name and the name of the person you are trying to contact. It's also a good idea to describe the vehicle that your contact is driving in Baja. On the message, ask

MEXICALI TO SAN FELIPE

CEVICHE GONZAGA BAY STYLE

Ann Hazard's Baja cookbooks have become a peninsular favorite, with recipes collected from many famous restaurants and devised from the author's own travels and culinary adventures. Whether you want to prepare a few of your own meals on the road, or bring the flavors of Baja back to your own home, this basic ceviche recipe is a keeper. The acid from the lime juice "cooks" the fish, so there's no need for a heat source to prepare the meal.

INGREDIENTS

- 2 lbs cubed white fish or bay scallops, raw
- 2 cups juice from *limónes* (Mexican limes)
- 5-10 fresh serrano or jalapeño chiles, diced (remove seeds if you prefer it less spicy)
- 1 red bell pepper, diced
- 1 green bell pepper, diced
- 1 onion, diced
- 3 ripe tomatoes, diced
- 2 cloves garlic, minced
- 1 bunch cilantro, with stems removed, finely chopped
- 1 tsp brown sugar
- Salt and pepper to taste
- 2 avocados, diced
- Totopos (tortilla chips) or saltine crackers

INSTRUCTIONS

In a bowl, cover the cubed fish with lime juice. Cover and refrigerate for 2-3 hours, stirring occasionally. Fish should become quite white and scallops will lose their translucent appearance. (Once this happens, you will know the lime juice has "cooked" them and they are okay to eat.)

Transfer to a larger bowl and mix with all other ingredients except avocado. Immediately prior to serving, add diced avocados and remaining cilantro. Serve in a bowl surrounded with chips or saltine crackers.

– Reprinted with permission from *Cooking with Baja Magic Dos*, by Ann Hazard (www.bajamagic.com)

Rancho Grande to contact Papa Fernández on the marine radio.

Bahía San Luis Gonzaga

Popular with private pilots and experienced Baja adventurers, the flat, gray-sand beach along remote Bahía San Luis Gonzaga is reminiscent of an earlier time. A few dozen rustic beach homes line the shore—each with its private plane, boat, or dune buggy parked outside. **Rancho Grande** (tel. 555/151-4065) offers beach camping for US$5 a night. Facilities include outhouses, showers, and a mini-market.

Punta Final is a small cape with several points and a small lagoon. It marks the south end of Gonzaga Bay and offers good views of the bay from above.

TO MEXICO 1

From Bahía San Luis Gonzaga, it's 64.5 kilometers (approximately 90 min) of graded dirt-road driving to the Transpeninsular Highway. The road intersects Mexico 1 at Km 229–230 in the town of Chapala.

About halfway from the coast to the highway, you'll come across **Coco's Corner,** a café that's famous for its beer can decor (and desert plants too). Stop here for cold beer, soda, and burritos. Camping costs US$5 a night if you've run out of daylight. Owner Coco moved to the desert from Ensenada in 1990, following an accident in which he lost one leg. He speaks some English and knows the area extremely well. When you sign his guestbook, he will draw a picture of your vehicle next to the entry.

DESIERTO CENTRAL TO BAHÍA DE LOS ANGELES

In an age of satellite TV, mobile phones, and wireless Internet, one part of Baja California continues to offer true desert solitude. This is the central peninsula, which lies between El Rosario in the north and La Paz in the south. With an average population density of just one inhabitant per 10,000 square kilometers, *cirio* cacti outnumber people here by a very wide margin. New government-sponsored ecotourism projects promise to protect this diverse and fragile ecosystem. Informative signs now lead travelers along historic trails, while training and education programs are helping local residents become knowledgeable guides and preserve their homes and natural resources rather than exploit them.

Compared to the northern and southern tips of the peninsula, Central Baja has experienced relatively little external influence to date. However, that most certainly will change as commercial development and technological progress continue their forward march. Already, power lines have been installed throughout the entire area, putting once isolated towns on the grid. Phones and even Internet access are now widely available, and newly paved roads connect many outlying areas to the Transpeninsular Highway. For the adventure traveler who wants to experience a taste of the frontier, now is the time to visit.

In order to cover this changing area in greater detail, the Central Baja region has been divided into three separate chapters: Desierto Central to Bahía de los Angeles, Guerrero Negro to Bahía Concepción, and Loreto and Bahía Magdalena.

© PABLO NOBILI

HIGHLIGHTS

Bahía
de San
Quintín
San Felipe
El
Rosario
Rancho
El Progreso
**Misión
San Fernando
Velicatá**
PACIFIC
OCEAN
*Parque Natural
del Desierto
Central*
*Sea of
Cortez*
**Valle de
los Cirios**
**Canal de
las Ballenas**
Bahía de
Los Angeles
**Sea Turtle
Research
Station**
Rosarito
San Borja
*Bahía de
Sebastián
Vizcaíno*
Guerrero
Negro
San Francisquito
0   40 mi
0   40 km

◖ **Misión San Fernando Velicatá:** Baja's only Franciscan mission settlement was active from 1769 to 1818, and remnants of the original buildings can be found in a scenic arroyo located midway between the Pacific and Gulf coasts (page 122).

◖ **Valle de los Cirios:** In an unprecedented effort to save a fragile desert ecosystem, Mexico has designated this large area between Cataviña and Guerrero Negro for ecotourism development (page 122).

◖ **Canal de las Ballenas:** If you've come to Baja for a chance to swim with a whale shark, this waterway offshore from Bahía de los Angeles has them, along with a wide variety of the largest creatures in the sea (page 126).

◖ **Sea Turtle Research Station:** In Bahía de los Angeles, a marine biologist has transformed a former turtle fishing operation into an engine of conservation (page 126).

◖ **San Borja:** Head to the Sierra San Borja for an off-road adventure along the Spanish mission trail (page 132).

LOOK FOR ◖ TO FIND RECOMMENDED SIGHTS, ACTIVITIES, DINING, AND LODGING.

In the vicinity of the Valle de los Cirios, the Velicatá Mission is the only church built by Franciscan missionaries in Baja. On the Gulf coast, Bahía de los Angeles offers a protected channel for water activities, such as snorkeling/scuba diving, sportfishing, windsurfing/kiteboarding, and kayaking—and a chance to view the majestic whale shark during its summer migration. High in the Sierra San Borja are a Spanish mission settlement and a series of prehistoric cave paintings.

PLANNING YOUR TIME

It takes about 15 hours to drive the 1,124 kilometers from El Rosario to La Paz. The stretch from El Rosario to Parador Punta Prieta is 240 kilometers, and this marks the turnoff to Bahía de los Angeles. From there, it's another 68 kilometers (about an hour of driving time) to the coast.

It's a good idea to stock up on supplies in El Rosario before making the trek across the desert, but after Km 115, a number of ranchos along the highway operate small restaurants, where you can sample a plate of basic Mexican fare.

Mission Velicatá is an easy excursion off Mexico 1. Allow a couple of days to explore the Valle de los Cirios, and three or four days for Bahía de los Angeles—longer if you are going there to dive, fish, or windsurf/kiteboard. Add another day for a side trip to San Borja.

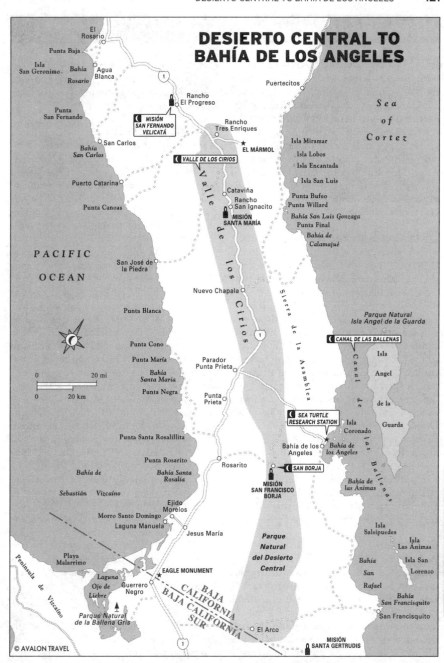

DESIERTO CENTRAL TO BAHÍA DE LOS ANGELES

El Rosario
Punta Baja
Isla San Geronimo
Bahía Agua
Rosario Blanca

Punta San Fernando

Rancho El Progreso

MISIÓN SAN FERNANDO VELICATÁ

Rancho Tres Enriques

Puertecitos

Sea

of

Cortez

San Carlos

Bahía San Carlos

VALLE DE LOS CIRIOS

★ EL MÁRMOL

Isla Miramar

Isla Lobos

Isla Encantada

Puerto Catarina

Punta Canoas

Cataviña
Rancho San Ignacito

MISIÓN SANTA MARÍA

Isla San Luis

Punta Bufeo
Punta Willard

Bahía San Luis Gonzaga
Punta Final

Bahía de Calamajué

PACIFIC

OCEAN

San José de la Piedra

Valle

de

los

Cirios

Nuevo Chapala

Sierra de la Asamblea

Parque Natural Isla Angel de la Guarda

CANAL DE LAS BALLENAS

Punta Blanca

Punta Cono

Punta María

Bahía Santa María

Parador Punta Prieta

Punta Negra

Punta Prieta

Isla Angel

de la

Guarda

0   20 mi
0   20 km

Punta Santa Rosalillita

Punta Rosarito

Bahía de

Sebastián Vizcaíno

Bahía Santa Rosalía

Rosarito

SEA TURTLE RESEARCH STATION

Isla Coronado

Bahía de los Angeles ★ *Bahía de los Angeles*

SAN BORJA

MISIÓN SAN FRANCISCO BORJA

Bahía de las Ánimas

Canal de las Ballenas

Ejido Morelos

Morro Santo Domingo

Laguna Manuela

Jesus María

Parque Natural del Desierto Central

Isla Salsipuedes

Isla Las Ánimas

Bahía San Rafael

Isla San Lorenzo

Playa Malarrimo

Peninsula de Vizcaíno

Laguna Ojo de Liebre

Guerrero Negro

EAGLE MONUMENT

Parque Natural de la Ballena Gris

BAJA CALIFORNIA
BAJA CALIFORNIA SUR

El Arco

MISIÓN SANTA GERTRUDIS

Bahía San Franciquito

San Francisquito

© AVALON TRAVEL

Into the Interior

SOUTH OF EL ROSARIO

For travelers who are making their way down the Baja peninsula, the terrain below El Rosario marks the beginning of the real adventure. The next sizable town lies a couple hundred kilometers away; meanwhile, pristine desert scenery unfolds with every turn. Around Km 62, *cirio* and *cardón* cacti begin to dot the landscape. This drive is particularly spectacular if you arrive toward the end of the rainy season in October or November, when all the desert flowers are in bloom.

(Misión San Fernando Velicatá

The Franciscans built only one mission (1769–1818) in lower California; the little that remains of it can be found relatively close to the highway (8 km to the west), off a dirt road that begins at Km 121 near Rancho Progresso. Although the Jesuits discovered the site in 1766, it was Franciscan Father Junípero Serra who established the mission in 1769. A strategic location halfway between the Pacific and Gulf coasts ensured an important, if short-lived, role. In time, some 1,500 indigenous people came to live and worship at San Fernando. The mission came under Dominican control in 1772, but would experience a rapid decline by the end of the decade due to an epidemic. Only some bits of walls and the foundation remain; the real attraction today is the arroyo setting. You'll find two ranchitos near the site. Look for petroglyphs and pictographs dating back to the 17th century in the rock cliffs above the arroyo.

El Mármol

At Km 149, a 15-kilometer graded dirt road heads east to an abandoned onyx quarry that was run by a San Diego mining company from the turn of the 20th century through the 1950s. Demand for the brown-and-tan banded mineral was highest during the art deco period, when it was used as a substitute for marble in American homes. Today, you'll find the remains of a schoolhouse made entirely of onyx, a cemetery with onyx-covered gravestones, and a scattering of onyx blocks around the site.

(Valle de los Cirios

Mexico's largest sustainable development effort, led by an agency called the Areas Naturales Protegidas (ANP) covers an area that begins just north of Cataviña and reaches almost to Guerrero Negro. According to desert plant specialist Robert R. Humphrey, the area contains one of the most interesting and varied types of desert flora in the world. This government-funded project has resulted in chain of ecologically sound cabañas throughout the area; all are rustic, solar-powered, constructed from local materials, and built to blend as much as possible with the natural surroundings. Each locale is based on proximity to longstanding ranches, and the ranchers themselves have been trained to work as hosts and guides to the surrounding area. The idea behind the project is to preserve the fragile ecosystem by empowering its few inhabitants to live off of the natural beauty around them, while also providing tourists with a low-impact way of experiencing this unique environment. The average price is $120 for two people; reasonably priced meals can be arranged through the families operating the ranches. Concepción Recoder (tel. 615/157-2849, cell tel. 646/161-8149, crecoder@conanp.gob.mx) will put interested visitors in touch with the appropriate ranch. The Valle de los Cirios office is attached to the Comisión Nacional de Areas Naturales Protegidas (CONANP) office in Guerrero Negro (Av. Profesor Domingo Carballo Félix s/n, at Calle Ruiz Cortinez, Col. Marcelo Rubio, Guerrero Negro, www.conanp.gob.mx).

CATAVIÑA

After a morning of driving the 123 hot and dry kilometers between El Rosario and Cataviña, this desert outpost emerges as a

the unique *cirio*

pleasant surprise in the midst of the protected **Parque Natural del Desierto Central.** The town itself offers a few places to stay and limited options for food and supplies. All around are giant boulders and a most impressive collection of picture-perfect desert plants. This is place to open your field guide and learn to identify *cardón* cacti, elephant trees, *cirios,* and the rest of the flora that makes the region one-of-a-kind.

Cave Paintings

For travelers making their way down the Transpennisular Highway, the first convenient opportunity to view a cave painting (origins unknown) comes at Km 176, where a large arroyo crosses the road. Park near the INAH sign on the east side of the road. Before beginning your hike, look up at the bluffs in front of you for a white wooden sign that marks the cave. Keep the sign as your directional guide and you will find a trail up the rocks once you get to the bottom of the bluffs, or you can scamper up several different ways. Once you reach the sign, you must go into the overhang behind it

to see the paintings. Unfortunately, graffiti on the rocks leading up to the cave detracts somewhat from the experience.

Misión Santa María de los Angeles

Whether you're following the Baja California mission trail, or simply want to enjoy the spectacular desert scenery, be forewarned that the 23 kilometers track that leads to the adobe ruins of the Misión Santa María de los Angeles (1767–1769) is about as rough as they come in Baja. A dirt bike or ATV may be the only motorized vehicles able to pass, and even then, you'll likely have to walk the last mile or so. A better plan would be to hire a guide and mules from Rancho Santo Inés. Though there is little to see today, the mission is significant because it was the last one the Jesuits established before their expulsion from the peninsula in 1767. The Cochimí called the site Cabujakaamung.

Accommodations

Cabañas Linda (Cataviña village, east side of the highway, no tel.), a pink, single-story motel

DESIERTO CENTRAL

© CARMEL TSABAR

a residential home in Cataviña

on the east side of Mexico 1, offers basic rooms for US$35. The proprietor, Lucy, also serves lunch or dinner daily for US$5 and coffee for US$1. A kilometer south of Cataviña, Lucy's mother Matilde offers meals, hot showers, and hostel-style rooms at **Rancho Santa Inés** (Km 181, no tel.). A room for 6–8 people runs US$35. Campers and self-contained RVers can choose a spot under any of the widely spaced mesquite trees in the dirt lot for US$6 a night. The area around the camping lot makes for incredible hiking. And the family at Rancho Santa Iné will guide hikers in the area for US$10 per group.

The recently renovated **Desert Inn** (formerly a La Pinta hotel, tel. 200/124-9123, toll-free U.S. tel. 800/800-9632, www.desertinncatavina.com, US$88) is a chain with locations in Ensenada, San Quintín, Guerrero Negro, San Ignacio, and Loreto. This one has 28 rooms with air-conditioning and a swimming pool. Long-distance telephone service is available through the front desk for guests and non-guests as well.

Cirio cacti dot the grounds of the new **Parque Natural Desierto Central de BC RV Park,** which has 66 spaces for US$6. Look for the sign on the west side of Mexico 1 before the Desert Inn.

Food

☾ Café La Enramada (daily, mains US$5–9) in front of the old highway Pemex station across from the Desert Inn, is a reliable place to fill up on large portions of inexpensive Mexican food, including its own specialties, such as Chicken a La Enramada and Chicken al Mármol. The Desert Inn has a full-service restaurant open every day for breakfast, lunch, and dinner. Rancho Santa Inés now offers Antojitos Mexicanos at the ranch instead of at a former location on Highway 1.

At any given time, there may be another taco and/or burger stand open in Cataviña. The same applies for a couple of small markets with basic groceries. It's better to come prepared to camp if that is your plan rather than expecting to find essential supplies in town.

Information and Services

Across from the Desert Inn, the old Pemex station appears to be under renovation. In the meantime, there is usually someone selling gas from a barrel here or across the street. If you've filled your tank in El Rosario before the long drive across the desert, you shouldn't need fuel in Cataviña, but it never hurts to top off whenever you have the opportunity, since it's a long way between Pemex stations in this part of the peninsula. The next closest stations are at Villa Jesús María, about 60 kilometers to the south, and Bahía de los Angeles, 170 kilometers to the southeast. Several towns—including Punta Prieta, El Nuevo Rosarito, and Chapala—do sell gas from drums along Highway 1.

SOUTH TO PARADOR PUNTA PRIETA

About 30 kilometers south of Cataviña, off the west side of the highway between Km 209 and 210, the boulders that make up the hill of **El Pedregoso** stretch 610 meters into the sky. Though they appear to be a massive manmade art installation, the rocks are actually a natural formation that has resulted from thousands of years of erosion.

Between Km 229 and 230, at Chapala Junction, you can take a graded road northeast to Bahía San Luis Gonzaga and Bahía de Calamajué on the Gulf coast. Keep an eye out for *cirio, cardón,* yucca, and cholla along the way.

At Km 280, **Parador Punta Prieta,** an abandoned rest stop, marks the turnoff to Bahía de los Angeles. Follow the east fork southeast 68 kilometers to reach the Sea of Cortez. At this junction, the basic **Loncheria Ramirez** serves coffee and *antojitos.* Gas is sometimes available from a drum.

Bahía de los Angeles

Shortly after veering southeast from Highway 1, the road to Bahía de los Angeles (called the east branch of Highway 1) crosses through the Sierra de la Asamblea. The drive is especially scenic in summer, when abundant *copalquín* (elephant trees) are in bloom. At Km 44, travelers with high-clearance vehicles can take the turnoff southwest 35 kilometers to the restored Misión San Borja. Alternatively, a better road connects San Borja to Rosarito from the west branch of Highway 1. As you descend out of the mountains to the bay and village below, the Sea of Cortez presents itself, a carpet of blue dotted with islands big and small.

Spanish explorer Francisco de Ulloa discovered the bay in 1539 during the last expedition financed by Hernán Cortés. It later became an important access point for exporting gold and silver from mines in the Sierra San Borja.

Today, watersports are the main draw at this still-remote seaside village. Adventurous anglers discovered the spot in the 1940s when thatched-roof huts were the only structures to be found. Today, kayaking, kiteboarding, and windsurfing bring tourists. A new sailboat monument on the main boulevard through town harbors the arrival of visiting yachters, though they have yet to appear in any great number.

In November 2007, power lines made their way to the bay, ending decades of reliance on a generator that shut down at night. As of spring 2009, most of the town had been connected to the new power lines, but some businesses were still awaiting the fulfillment of their promised connections, as were those along the bay just out of town.

You can pick up postcards or books on Baja at the **Museo de Naturaleza y Cultura** (on a dirt road south of the main commercial strip and west of the town plaza, no tel., daily 9 A.M.–noon and 2–4 P.M.), while you soak up some local history and culture. Inside are mining exhibits, a collection of shells and fossils, and Native American artifacts.

ISLANDS

Like La Paz and Loreto, Bahía de los Angeles is an access point to a string of 16 protected desert

DESIERTO CENTRAL

islands offshore. Sixty-eight-kilometer-long Isla Angel de la Guarda is the second-largest island in the Sea of Cortez (after Isla Tiburón), with *cirios,* sea lions, and beaches suitable for camping. Stop by the office of the **Islas del Golfo de California** (Mon–Fri 9 A.M.–2 P.M. and 4–6 P.M. and Sat. 9 A.M.–2 P.M.; permits US$4 per person per day), located in town between the Hotel Villa Vitta and the Delegacion building to obtain a permit.

C CANAL DE LAS BALLENAS

The canal that runs parallel to shore in the shelter of Isla Angel de la Guarda, teems with marine life, especially of the larger variety: Bryde's, minke, finback, blue, sperm, humpback, orca, pilot, and the occasional gray whale, as well as common and bottlenose dolphins, all pass through at various times throughout the year. The best season for spotting these pelagics is July–October, when the water is warmest (26–32°C). Visit in August for the best chance to swim with a juvenile whale shark.

California sea lions live along island shores, and northern elephant seals are sometimes seen in the spring.

C SEA TURTLE RESEARCH STATION

Until populations dwindled in the 1960s and 1970s, Bahía de los Angeles was a busy center for turtle fishing; today, it has evolved into a more sustainable center for turtle conservation because of its strategic role as a nesting ground. At the north end of the bay, marine biologist Antonio Resendiz has run a sea turtle research station since 1979, called the Centro Regional de Investigacion Pesquera (CRIP) Sea Turtle Research Station (no tel.).

Visitors are welcome to stop by Monday–Tuesday 9 A.M.–2 P.M., Thursday–Friday 9 A.M.–2 P.M., and Saturday 9 A.M.–1 P.M. to see the loggerheads and greens that are contained in its tank for tagging and observation, or to hear an occasional lecture on turtle behavior and conservation efforts. There is a US$2 admission fee.

Antonio's work received worldwide recognition in 1995 when a 97-kilogram loggerhead named Rosita, who had been released from the Pacific coast of Baja in 1994, was picked up by a fisherman in Japan. Antonio also owns the adjacent Campo Archelón.

SPORTS AND RECREATION
Hiking

From the bay, a number of arroyos lead inland to the Sierra San Borja; following one of these out and back makes for a pleasant day hike in the desert. Just be sure to keep the bay in sight so you don't get lost. Two abandoned mines are also within walking distance from the town. A trail to **Mina Santa Marta** begins at the town dump, about 3.5 kilometers south of Casa Díaz. From here, walk west until you reach the remains of a railway grade that was used to transport the gold and silver from the mines. Then continue west to the sight of the mine. One day is enough time for the round-trip hike, but you can also camp overnight at the mine.

To reach **Mina San Juan,** follow the same railway grade 17.5 kilometers southwest of the bay to Valle Las Flores. If you continue past the second mine, you can get to several cave painting sites in the Sierra San Borja. The graded road meanders through the mountains all the way to **Bahía San Francisquito,** approximately 132 kilometers south of Bahía de los Angeles.

Fishing

Onshore anglers catch sand bass, guitarfish, and triggerfish here; in spring, there are croaker and halibut at Punta la Gringa. In summer, nearby islands offer opportunities for yellowtail, white and black sea bass, dorado, tuna, and grouper. Yellowtail also sometimes run in January–March.

You can rent a *panga* for a fishing or scuba diving trip through any hotel or campground in town. **Daggett's** (about 2.5 km north of town, along the coastal road, tel. 200/124-9101, www.campdaggetts.com), **Guillermo's** (tel. 200/124-9104), **Villa Bahía** (no tel., www.villabahia.com), **Ricardo's Dive Center** (tel. 200/124-9262, www.scubabaja.com), and

BAHÍA DE LOS ANGELES AND VICINITY

Isla Coronado

Canal de las Ballenas

CANAL DE LAS BALLENAS

Punta la Gringa

Isla El Piojo

LOS VIENTOS SPA AND RESORT

Ensenada la Gringa

Isla Pata

Isla La Ventana

VILLA BAHÍA

AIRSTRIP

DAGGETT'S

CAMPO ARCHELÓN

SEA TURTLE RESEARCH STATION

PROGRAMA TORTUGA MARINA

BRISA MARINA

POSADA CERRITO

Bahía de los Angeles

SUPER XITLATI

CAMP GECKO

Punta Arena

Bahía de los Angeles

Isla Cabeza de Caballo

Punta La Herradura

Puerto don Juan

Ensenada El Quemado

Isla El Pescador

Ensenada El Pescador

Ensenada El Alacrán

0   1.5 mi
0   1.5 km

To Mina Santa Marta

To Mina San Juan and Bahía San Francisco

AIRSTRIP

© AVALON TRAVEL

Casa Díaz (tel. 200/124-9112) arrange guided fishing trips for US$150–250 a day.

Boating and Kayaking

A number of businesses, including **Guillermo's** (tel. 200/124-9104), **Villa Vitta** (tel. 200/124-9103, U.S. tel. 619/454-6108, www.villavitta.com), and **Casa Díaz** (tel. 200/124-9112), provide boat launches (US$5–10) and rent *pangas*. **Isla Angel de la Guarda** protects the channel from most high winds, except when the winter *El Norte* blows. Ask the locals for advice on the conditions before heading out to sea on your own.

When the winds subside in May–October, kayakers arrive en masse to explore the islands offshore. Popular itineraries include a paddle to **Isla Coronado** (also known as Isla Smith), three kilometers northeast of Punta la Gringa, or to the southern tip of Isla Angel de la Guarda, 19 kilometers away.

Kiteboarding and Windsurfing

Bahía de los Angeles is a good choice for beginning windsurfers and kiteboarders because the islands offshore protect it from large swells. Head to the northern parts of the bay for the strongest winds. A 10- to 12-kilometer

DESIERTO CENTRAL

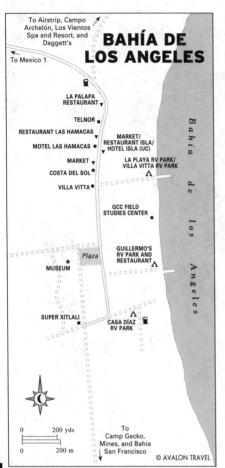

To Airstrip, Campo Archelón, Los Vientos Spa and Resort, and Daggett's

To Mexico 1

BAHÍA DE LOS ANGELES

LA PALAPA RESTAURANT

TELNOR

RESTAURANT LAS HAMACAS

MOTEL LAS HAMACAS

MARKET

COSTA DEL SOL

VILLA VITTA

MARKET/ RESTAURANT ISLA/ HOTEL ISLA (UC)

LA PLAYA RV PARK/ VILLA VITTA RV PARK

Bahía de los Angeles

GCC FIELD STUDIES CENTER

Plaza

MUSEUM

GUILLERMO'S RV PARK AND RESTAURANT

SUPER XITLALI

CASA DÍAZ RV PARK

0   200 yds
0   200 m

To Camp Gecko, Mines, and Bahía San Francisco

© AVALON TRAVEL

downwind run begins at Punta la Gringa, passes the small islands west of Isla La Ventana, and goes right in to the shore at the town's edge. Bring your own gear.

Diving

Ricardo's Diving Tours (tel. 200/124-9262, www.scubabaja.com) is run by ex-commercial diver Ricardo Arce. The center is located off the right side of the main road as you head into town. It is equipped to take groups or individuals out to the various dive sites within the bay and onto the islands as well. Prices start at US$65 for a two-tank dive to the closer destinations and go up according to distance; the longest trips take divers out to Isla Angel de la Guarda. Ricardo's also offers wildlife and fishing tours, as well as guided snorkeling (often with whale sharks, in peak season) and overnight expeditions.

Another option for a dive boat charter is to contact Jean and Roger at **Villa Bahía** (no tel., www.villabahia.com), who will rent out their cabin cruiser to a group of five or six divers for US$225 or their *panga* (which accommodates three people) for US$150; they do not have gear or tanks, but they do have a compressor.

Bird-Watching

The ecosystem around Bahía de los Angeles supports a thriving population of marine birds, among them terns, pelicans, gulls, egrets, herons, cormorants, petrels, boobies, and ospreys. Bird-watchers will find the best opportunities for observation at **Isla Partida** and **Isla Raza. Casa Díaz** (tel. 200/124-9112) and **Ricardo's Dive Tours** (tel. 200/124-9262, www.scubabaja.com) offer bird-watching tours on request.

ACCOMMODATIONS AND CAMPING
Hotels and Motels

Some longtime Baja travelers remember the days of generators and the electricity turning off at night, but mainstream power has arrived at last. Most of the town's hotels now offer 24-hour power, and around-the-clock Internet access is likely not far behind.

UNDER US$50

At the south end of town, near one of the town's two Pemex stations, family-run **Casa Díaz** (tel. 200/124-9112, US$30) offers large rooms fronting the bay. You can book fishing and bird-watching trips out to the islands, and stock up on supplies at the on-site market.

Centrally located with 30 rooms, **Villa Vitta** (tel. 200/124-9103, U.S. tel. 619/454-6108, www.villavitta.com, $45–75) is a single-story motel with a pool, restaurant/bar, boat ramp,

DESIERTO CENTRAL

and parking. Hot water does not run on electricity here, so it is always available. Fishing packages are available. An adjoining RV park and campground (US$10/night) has 25 spaces with electrical hookups and 11 without, a dump station, and bathrooms/showers.

Posada Cerrito Lindo (www.bajahostel. com, US$15) introduces the first ecologically sound accommodations in Bahía de los Angeles. Owned and run by an Italian-U.S. couple, Mauro and Patty, the posada offers a low-impact stopover (composting toilet and all-natural construction and decoration) for nature-minded travelers. Beds are arranged dormitory-style with six bunks in two rooms. The hostel offers a huge communal kitchen, Internet service, an Italian-style café and restaurant, plenty of local knowledge and, above all, the most spectacular view of the bay anywhere in town. The hostel is located on a hill on the road into town from Highway 1, about a minute before the Pemex and along a handcut and graded road.

US$50-100

North of Villa Vitta, **Costa del Sol** (tel. 200/124-19110 or mobile tel. 646/178-8167, costadelsolhotel@hotmail.com; US$65, credit cards accepted), has half a dozen large, clean rooms. Amenities include hot showers, air-conditioning, and 24-hour electricity. You can dine in the hotel's small restaurant/bar for breakfast, lunch, or dinner. Or rent a kayak for a paddle around the bay.

The rooms at **Guillermo's RV Park and Restaurant** (tel. 200/124-9104, US$50–65) each have two king-size beds and one double bed, as well as air-conditioning 24/7. Its restaurant serves seafood entrées for US$12–24 and fish tacos for US$6. You can camp on the beach here for about US$5 per person; RV hookups run US$17.

On the way to La Gringa, **❲ Villa Bahía** (www.villabahia.com, $60–95), is an interesting complex consisting of different sized buildings on the waterfront. Each unit holds at least six people, comes with a full kitchen, and includes the use of an outdoor communal

kitchen with grills. A three-bedroom, two-bath upstairs unit is great for a group stay, and features an especially intricate metal sculpture of a coral reef wall, complete with fish, by an Ensenada artist, whose works can be found all over the property. Satellite Internet is offered free to guests in the office area, and pedal boats are available for use on calm days. The Villa runs on wind and solar power, with a generator for backup when occupancy is high. Owners Jean and Roger also charter fishing, diving, and sightseeing trips on their cabin cruiser and *panga*.

US$100-150

Three miles north of town, on the way to Punta la Gringa, **Los Vientos Spa and Resort** (Ensenada tel. 646/178-1440, www.losvientosspaandresort.com, US$96–175) has a large stone fireplace in the lobby and 13 rooms and suites with air-conditioning and power 24/7. At last check, the resort was building four new rooms and a new outdoor bar. The hotel also allows each room to select 4 DirecTV channels. The management needs advanced notice to arrange a massage, since there hasn't yet been much demand. Although the property is well maintained, prices seem a bit high.

Camping and RV Parks

Across the street from its motel, **Villa Vitta** (tel. 200/124-9103, U.S. tel. 619/454-6108, www.villavitta.com) maintains 25 campsites with electrical hookups and 11 more without, plus a dump station and bathrooms with hot showers for US$10 per night.

Just south of Villa Vitta and close to the plaza, **Guillermo's** (tel. 200/124-9104, www. guillermos.net), is a longtime trailer park, motel, and restaurant with *palapas,* tent sites at US$5 per person, and full hookups for US$17 per night. Guests can use the boat launch free of charge, as well showers and toilets. There is also a small market and gift shop on the premises.

Casa Díaz (tel. 200/124-9112) has nine RV sites with full hookups for US$8.50 a night.

Just past the sea turtle station, on the way

to La Gringa, **Campo Archelón** (no tel.) has several *palapa*-roofed rock shelters for bayside camping (US$8 pp).

Another longstanding Bahía de los Angeles business, **Daggett's** (about 2.5 km north of town, along the coastal road, tel. 200/124-9101, www.campdaggetts.com) has sites with wooden ramadas and grills, as well as showers and outhouses, for US$10. You can book fishing and diving trips through Daggett's as long as you come fully equipped.

Even without hot water, **Camp La Ventana** (just south of Los Vientos, no tel.) is one of the best choices for campers. The 10 lattice-wood structures have their own grills, bathrooms are clean, and the grounds are well kept by the camp's owner, Marina, who lives just beside the property. For US$5 a person, the solitude and access to the beautiful beachfront area seem like a steal.

You can still find some sites for free camping along the graded road to **Punta la Gringa,** which marks the north end of the bay. Along the way are a number of open campsites where camping is free. East and south of the town, several sandy coves have camping areas, including **Puerto Don Juan, Ensenada del Quemado,** and **Ensenada del Pescador.**

FOOD

Given the small size of the town and relatively isolated location, food options are somewhat limited—and pricey—in Bahía de los Angeles. One alternative is to stock up on groceries and supplies in Guerrero Negro before making the journey east to the bay.

You might begin a visit to Bahía de los Angeles with a margarita under a *palapa* at **Guillermo's** (daily 6 A.M.–10 P.M.; mains US$5–10). Its menu features a number of seafood specialties. At the other end of town, **Restaurant Las Hamacas** (daily 6 A.M.–9 P.M., mains US$5–15) offers seafood and ranchero dishes.

Reyna's Place (tel. 200/124-9148, daily 6 A.M.–10 P.M., US$5–14) is the bright orange building right at the town's entrance, with the U.S., Canadian, and Mexican flags

---

THE *MICHELADA*

Mix Mexican beer, preferably Tecate, with a good amount of fresh squeezed lime juice. Add optional flavorings, such as Worcestershire sauce, soy sauce, Tabasco, and black pepper. Serve the drink in a salt-rimmed glass and you've got a Mexico original: the *michelada*, or as we like to call it, a beer margarita.

---

flying overhead. Owners Reyna and Salino (of Reyna's Tacos and La Palapa fame) cordially attend to customers from this new location, which became their business as of January 2008. Mexican *antojitos* and seafood are the main attractions; a book exchange and long-distance public phone draw information-starved travelers.

Victoria's Restaurant (daily 6 A.M.–10 P.M., US$5–15) at the Costa del Sol Hotel features reasonably priced Mexican food, with fish and shrimp specialties including *Pescado Encabronado* (Pissed-off Fish, as translated on the menu) and *Camarones a la Viagra* (Viagra Shrimp). Victoria bears more than a slight resemblance to salsa legend Celia Cruz.

Bahía de los Angeles now has a few legitimate grocery stores too. The largest, **Super Xitlali,** on the south side of town at the turnoff to head out of town, is open daily 6 A.M.–11 P.M. and has just about anything one might find in similar stores in Guerrero Negro. Also well stocked are Casa Díaz and La Isla Market, among others.

INFORMATION AND SERVICES

There are now long-distance phones at many locations around town; Internet is also available through several of the hotels and camps, including Posada Cerrito Lindo and Villa Bahía, as well as at La Isla Market, which also has stamps and a mailbox. It seems inevitable that Wi-Fi will soon become available here, as it has in most other towns in

Baja. A **TelNor** office on the main road offers long-distance phone service and Internet daily 9 A.M.–7 P.M.

Credit cards are not widely accepted; bring cash. A Bahía de los Angeles resident maintains an informative website for visitors with up-to-date business listings at www.bahiade losangeles.info.

GETTING THERE AND AROUND

The road from Highway 1 to Bahía de los Angeles was re-paved in 2005 and was still in great shape at last check. Currently, the pavement extends north along the coast, as far as Los Vientos, and plans are to continue paving all the way to Punta la Gringa. Two new Pemex stations are now in business at the turnoff to Punta la Gringa. A mechanic located behind Casa Díaz can provide minor repair services and air for tires.

Unfortunately, public transportation is not an option for travel to Bahía de los Angeles; however, once there, you can reach just about everything on foot. Taxis offer service out to Punta la Gringa.

The 1,500-meter airstrip near Punta la Gringa was recently re-paved. If you fly over the town once prior to landing, a taxi will meet you at the runway. Visit www.bajabushpilots. com for information.

South of Punta Prieta

SANTA ROSALILLITA

The kilometer-counter along Highway 1 begins anew as soon as you cross south of the Bahía de los Angeles junction. Between Km 38 and 39 a paved road heads west 13 kilometers to the fish camp of Santa Rosalillita, one of the 28 nautical "steps" in the Mexican government's Sea of Cortez Project (Escalera Nautica). As part of this initiative, the port at Santa Rosalillita is undergoing considerable expansion and the work seemed just about complete at last check. The town received electricity in March 2008, and the locals are excited about the change. A group of fishermen is forming a cooperative whose goal is to export filleted fish to the United States (at the moment, they sell everything they catch in Ensenada). Antonio at the **Tienda Comunitaria Diconsa** (tel. 615/161-1313, US$25) has four rooms with private baths for rent.

Surfing and Windsurfing

At the south end of Bahía Santa Rosalillita, off Punta Rosarito, is a surf break called **The Wall** that creates consistent, sizable, and well-formed waves in swells form any direction. When The Wall is too big, surfers in the know head 29

© PABLO NIBILI

A seashell motif adorns a Santa Rosalillita church.

kilometers north to **Punta Santa Rosalillita,** where a long right point breaks during big west and northwest swells. Windsurfers also enjoy steady winds on the bay.

DESIERTO CENTRAL

◖ SAN BORJA

Orchards planted by the Jesuits in the 18th century continue to support the family that oversees the Mission San Borja today. Located in the foothills of the Sierra San Borja, the village makes an interesting side trip for leisurely travelers who want to see some high-altitude scenery or follow the Jesuit mission trail and who are equipped for off-road driving.

There are two ways to reach San Borja, and each is about 35 kilometers long. The better of the two heads east from Rosarito on Highway 1. It should take less than an hour to reach the settlement via this route. The second, rougher option departs from the paved Bahía de los Angeles at Km 44 and takes about 90 minutes.

Misión San Francisco Borja de Adác

In prehistoric times, the Cochimí established a settlement called Adác in the foothills of the Sierra San Borja, west of Bahía los Angeles, where two freshwater springs could support a small community. The Jesuits discovered the site in the 18th century and initially built a *visita,* or subordinate mission to Misión Santa Gertrudis, which was located south of the present-day border between Baja California (Norte) and Baja California Sur. Jesuit Padre Wenceslaus Linck established Mission San Borja (1762–1818) in 1762, and the Franciscans took over five years later, in 1767, followed by the Dominicans in 1773. A stone church was completed in 1801, and in 1818, the mission was secularized. Some of the original church has been restored, and the local community uses it occasionally for services.

The mission is open daily 8 A.M.–6 P.M. Caretaker José Angel Gerardo Monteón is a fourth-generation Cochimí, and his children offer walking tours to nearby hot springs. They can also guide you on a 1.5-hour driving tour to see some of the Sierra San Borja rock art sites. Fees are by donation. The family recently built five concrete-floor *palapas* for campers (US$5–10).

Rock Art

Historian Harry W. Crosby describes the rock art in this part of Baja as the "red-on-granite" school, for their use of a single color painted on the sides of large boulders, rather than on the walls and ceilings of caves. At least two major sites are accessible from San Borja: **Las Tinajitas** (more difficult to find) and **Montevideo**. Ask around in San Borja for a guide.

VILLA JESUS MARÍA

Thirty kilometers north of Guerrero Negro, this is a great place to stop for fuel for your car or yourself if you want to bypass Guerrero Negro, or if you think you might run short before you get there. Besides the Pemex, Jesus María boasts several eating establishments. All are good and specialize in slightly different Mexican foods, from fish and shrimp tacos at **Paulina's** to tasty *desebrada tortas* at **La Casita**. The classic tamales at **La Famosa Carmelita's** have a reputation for greatness among veteran Baja road-trippers. All in all, the town makes a convenient and satisfying stop.

PARALELO 28

At Km 128 and the 28th parallel, you can't miss the giant Mexican flag and 43-meter-high steel monument that mark the state line between Baja California (Norte) and Baja California Sur. You'll pass through a military checkpoint, where you may need to show your immigration papers. The time jumps ahead an hour here, as you change from the Pacific to Mountain time zone. Kilometer markers on Highway 1 reset at Km 220 here, and count down to Km 0 at Santa Rosalía.

The town of Guerrero Negro lies seven kilometers south of this border, but before you get there, you'll need to stop at the immigration checkpoint and agricultural inspection station. In addition to checking immigration papers, officials will spray insecticide under your vehicle.

GUERRERO NEGRO TO BAHÍA CONCEPCIÓN

South of the border between Baja California (Norte) and Baja California Sur, a variety of Mexican and gringo communities invite exploration. This area begins with the saltworks town of Guerrero Negro, where you can restock supplies, get on the Internet, and spend the night to wait for daylight driving hours. Nearby, the Laguna Ojo de Liebre draws a crowd for whale-watching tours. Beyond it, the protected Desierto de Vizcaíno forms a large peninsula that juts out into the Pacific Ocean.

Continuing south, the palm oasis of San Ignacio is home to an historic Spanish mission and colonial village, as well as a launching point for more whale-watching on the Laguna San Ignacio.

Back on the Gulf coast, the river town of Mulegé and white-sand beaches along Bahía Concepción have become seasonal homes for American and Canadian snowbirds. And deep in the interior of the Sierra de San Francisco and the Sierra de Guadalupe, more historic missions and mysterious rock art sites await.

PLANNING YOUR TIME

If you're in a hurry, you can make the 990 kilometers from Guerrero Negro to Cabo San Lucas in one long day of driving, with a stop for lunch in Loreto. But if your goal is to experience a little more of the outdoors (and to have a safer drive), you'll want to take more time.

The side trip out to the Vizcaíno Peninsula takes several hours, depending on road conditions. Once there, you might spend a couple of days, up to a week, exploring the coastal towns.

© CARMEL TSABAR

HIGHLIGHTS

◖ Laguna Ojo de Liebre: Each winter, adult gray whales and their calves put on a spectacular show in this lagoon near Guerrero Negro (page 136).

LOOK FOR ◖ TO FIND RECOMMENDED SIGHTS, ACTIVITIES, DINING, AND LODGING.

◖ Reserva de la Biósfera Desierto de Vizcaíno: Mexico's largest natural reserve covers 2.5 million hectares of desert terrain and supports several hundred species of plants and mammals (page 143).

◖ Misión Nuestra Señor San Ignacio de Kadakaamán: This beautifully restored church in a pretty oasis town played an important role in Jesuit mission history (page 150).

◖ Sierra de San Francisco Rock Art: This World Heritage site contains some of the best examples of Baja's prehistoric cave paintings (page 153).

◖ Laguna San Ignacio: Playful gray whales entertain groups of ecotourists with their spouting and spyhopping during the annual winter migration along the Pacific coast (page 155).

◖ Playa El Sombrerito: Watch the sun rise and listen to the birds calling from this beach at the mouth of the Mulegé River (page 164).

◖ Playa Santispac: This beautiful white-sand beach along Bahía Concepción has *palapa* shelters for picnics and overnight camping (page 172).

◖ La Purísima and Comondú: High in the Sierra de la Giganta range, these modern-day ranching communities trace their roots back to the Jesuit mission period (page 176).

Allow 3–4 days for a whale-watching adventure in Laguna Ojo de Liebre of Laguna San Ignacio, since it can take several attempts to catch the right conditions and to see the whales up close. You can easily spend 2–3 days in and around San Ignacio; add at least two more for a trip into the sierra.

Mulegé and Bahía Concepción offer enough activities to occupy visitors for a couple of weeks—or an entire season—including hikes to nearby prehistoric cave paintings, snorkeling, scuba diving, fishing, clamming, birding, and kayaking.

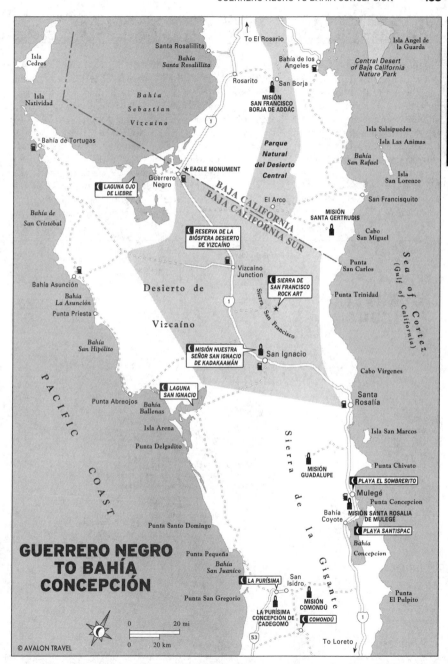

GUERRERO NEGRO TO BAHÍA CONCEPCIÓN

© AVALON TRAVEL

Guerrero Negro and Vicinity

For most Baja road-trippers making their way down the peninsula, foggy Guerrero Negro (population 12,000) looms as a stopover town for refueling vehicles, loading up on supplies, and crashing for the night. Aside from marking the halfway point of a trip from Tijuana to Cabo San Lucas, the town is known for two things: gray whales and salt.

🄲 LAGUNA OJO DE LIEBRE

Guerrero Negro is the Mexican translation for the name of a U.S. whaler, the *Black Warrior,* which sank offshore in the 1850s. After depleting the population of gray whales by the late 19th century, the hunters moved on and remarkably, the whales were able to recover. Today, whale hunting has been replaced by the far more sustainable activity of whale-watching. If you happen to visit in February or March, you'll catch the peak season for spotting—and maybe even petting—friendly gray whales. Head out to Scammon's Lagoon, known locally as Laguna Ojo de Liebre. In recent years, the whales have been arriving later

© AVALON TRAVEL

than usual (late December) and leaving later, so that the best months to watch them are now February and March; tours continue through the end of April.

There are two ways to see the whales: The first is to book a three-hour tour ($US50 pp) through an outfitter like **Malarrimo Eco-Tours** (tel./fax 615/157-0100, www. malarrimo.com; reserve a day or more in advance), **Mario's Tours** (at Restaurant Mario's, 615/157-1940, www.mariostours. com), or **Laguna Tours** (tel. 615/157-0050) on Boulevard Zapata next to Motel San Ignacio. Of these options, Mario's created a strong impression on our last visit. This operation is fully certified and has been running

THE GRAY WHALE TRAIL

Each year, the gray whale *(Eschrichtius robustus)* completes the longest known migration of any mammal in the world. It travels 16,000–19,000 kilometers round-trip from the shallow lagoons on the Pacific coast of the Baja Peninsula to the Bering Strait in the Arctic and back. The whales take about 2-3 months to complete the swim one-way. When migrating south, the gray whales cover about 161 kilometers a day, slightly less on the way north. Along the way, they stay within 3-5 kilometers of the shore.

ECOLOGY

Gray whales are the only kind of whales that feed on the ocean floor. They eat benthic (bottom-dwelling) amphipods — small shrimp-like crustaceans — by diving to the bottom, rolling on their sides, and gulping sand into their mouths. They use teeth-like baleen plates to filter water and sand out of their mouths, and then they swallow the trapped amphipods that are left behind. Adult whales eat about a ton of amphipods per day this way. They can stay underwater for 15 minutes at a time. Their natural predators are sharks and orcas.

Gray whales mate and feed primarily near the Bering Strait. Gestation takes 11–12 months, and females bear one calf every two years. They give birth in the shallow lagoons of the southern Pacific — Laguna Ojo de Liebre, Laguna San Ignacio, and Bahía Magdalena. These lagoons provide safety from orcas, as well as warmer water (important for babies that don't have much fat) and high salinity (which makes the newborns more buoyant).

Newborn whales weigh 500-680 kilograms and measure about 4.5 meters long, and they reach five or six meters in length within the first three months. Mature adults grow to about 16 meters, and weigh 36 tons. The mothers nurse their young for 6-8 months, during which time the baby whales drink 190 liters of milk per day.

Grays live to ages of 30-50 years, some as long as 60 years.

HISTORY AND CONSERVATION

The gray whale once inhabited the Atlantic Ocean, Baltic Sea, and North Sea as well as the Pacific Ocean. But Dutch, British, and American whalers hunted it to the point of extinction in the North Atlantic by the beginning of the 19th century. They almost wiped it out on the Pacific coast as well — reducing the population from 25,000 before the 1850s to just 250 by the 1930s. Charles Melville Scammon, a whaler from Boston, set the rapid slaughter in motion when he discovered the whales in Laguna Ojo de Liebre near Guerrero Negro in 1857, where he was able to trap and kill them using explosive harpoons. The introduction of floating whaling factories in the early 20th century pushed the species even closer to the brink of extinction.

Gray whales were given full international protection in 1947 by the International Whaling Commission, but many whalers didn't comply until the United States passed the Marine Mammal Protection Act of 1972.

The whale made a remarkable comeback at the end of the 20th century and now survives only in the Arctic-Pacific corridor with a population estimated at more than 26,000. It was removed from the endangered species list in 1994, but ocean pollution and fishing nets continue to pose a danger to these mammals.

tours since 1990. The staff are bilingual and include whale and bird specialists. Mario's has expanded the restaurant to include a conference room for briefings before the tours.

The second way to see the whales is to drive to the lagoon and hire a *panguero* yourself. Take Highway 1 south of town nine kilometers and look on the right for a sign pointing toward the **Parque Natural de la Ballena Gris.** Follow this road six kilometers (with heavy washboard in places) to a gate that marks the beginning of the salt company property. After an attendant opens the gate, continue across the white salt flats to the lagoon (a total of 24 km). You may be asked to pay a small fee to park here for the day. Taxis are available at the bus depot in Guerrero Negro and will drive up to five passengers to the *panga* piers and back for about US$80. (They wait for you at the lagoon.)

You can often see the whales from the shoreline, but it's best to go out with a boat tour if you want the full experience.

Whale-watching is a morning activity because that's when conditions are calmest and visibility is best. Boats typically depart 9 A.M.–3 P.M. and stay out about 90 minutes. In January–March, there are usually several boats available at the park for hire (US$25 pp).

If you have your own boat, be aware that you won't be able to use it on Laguna Ojo de Liebre when the whales are in town. *Pangueros* must apply for permits to lead tours in the bay, and they know how to maneuver the boats without scaring mothers and their calves.

Organized Tours

Every year in March, travel photographer Jim Cline leads a **Baja Gray Whales** photo tour (U.S. tel. 877/350-1314, www.jimcline.com, US$2,375) from San Diego to Laguna Ojo de Liebre. Tours include visits to Cataviña and San Ignacio, plus accommodations and seafood dinners.

Bilingual marine biologist Jose Sanchez-Pacheco offers a variety of guided trips through San Ysidro, California–based **Cedros Outdoor Adventures** (tel. 646/154-3085, cell tel. 646/193-2031, U.S. tel. 619/793-5419, www.cedrosoutdooradventures.com). Packaged trips

include whale-watching in Laguna Ojo de Liebre (5 days/4 nights from Loreto US$1,400, from the US$1,550), eco-tours to Isla Cedros and the San Benito islands (4 days/3 nights US$1,090, and sportfishing trips to Cedros, San Benito, Natividad (4 days/3 nights US$1,300). Prices include transportation from San Ysidro, California, as well as accommodations and meals.

SALTWORKS

In order to export its seven million tons of salt per year, ExportadoraSal, S.A. (ESSA) employs around 1,000 people in Guerrero Negro—far more than all of the town's tourist businesses combined. Jointly owned by the Mexican government (51 percent) and Mitsubishi Corporation (49 percent), the company owns 182 square kilometers of salt flats surrounding the lagoon. The company gives tours of the plant and its vast network of concentration ponds. Of interest are the specially designed trucks and harvesting equipment used to transport the evaporated salt from the ponds to ships that take it to Isla Cedros and eventually overseas. Tours take about three hours; for information, inquire at **Hotel Malarrimo** (tel./fax 615/157-0250, www.malarrimo.com).

DUNAS DE SOLEDAD

If the weather cooperates and you have time for a side trip, the Dunas de Soledad are worth a visit. Located north of town, four kilometers from the highway, the sand dunes reach heights of eight meters, and they face **Playa Don Miguelito,** a pristine beach on the Pacific Ocean.

BIRD-WATCHING

North of the salt plant, near an old pier and lighthouse, is a bird sanctuary, a great place to catch beautiful views of the dunes at sunset.

SHOPPING

Inside Malarrimo Restaurant, **Casa El Viejo Cactus** (tel./fax 615/157-0250, casaelviejocactus.com) is a small gift shop with a nice selection of reasonably priced handicrafts, gray whale souvenirs, and a few English-language books.

ACCOMMODATIONS AND CAMPING

Guerrero Negro has a handful of modest hotels and motels, most of which are located along Boulevard Zapata.

Hotels and Motels
UNDER US$50

Just off the main drag, the 14 rooms at **Motel Las Ballenas** (tel. 615/157-0116, US$30) are a good deal, and include TV and private bath. Near Malarrimo Restaurant, the **Motel San Ignacio** (tel. 615/157-0270, US$27) offers 24 basic rooms with a relatively late checkout time (1 P.M.).

Also in this category, the newly constructed **Baja Misión/Brisa Salina B&B, Hostel, and Camping** (Calle Emiliano Zapato, tel. 615/157-0288) adds a fresh look to Guerrero Negro's somewhat outdated image with 14 rooms priced at US$30 per night (with breakfast for an additional US$3). This place also has reasonably priced camping spots and hostel-style accommodations for travelers on tighter budgets. In the plans were a simple restaurant and bar with pool table.

Adjoining Malarrimo Restaurant, **Hotel Malarrimo** (tel./fax 615/157-0250, www.malarrimo.com, US$45) rents standard rooms with a small TV, chair, and two beds that rest on hard wooden platforms. Sloped, beamed ceilings yellow stucco walls; and cactus decor add a cheerful touch. Bathrooms have old plumbing but plenty of hot water and good pressure. Threadbare towels, bare light bulbs, and a few empty sockets remind you that this is Baja. Four new rooms were in the works at last check, and the hotel now offers free wireless Internet in its restaurant area.

New in 2006, **(Hotel Los Caracoles** (Calz. de la República, tel. 615/157-1088, www.hotelloscaracoles.com.mx, US$47) has 13 rooms, with five more in the works. You can access the Internet from the lobby only; the first 20 minutes are free. This hotel is located north of Boulevard Zapata, along one of the first cross streets as you approach the town from Mexico 1.

Motel Las Ballenas

© CARMEL TSABAR

US$50-100

If you don't need to load up on supplies in town and don't mind paying a bit extra, the **Desert Inn** (formerly La Pinta, tel. 615/157-1304, toll-free U.S. tel. 800/800-9632, www.desertinns. com, US$79) has a hotel near the state border and Paralelo 28 monument off Mexico 1.

Camping and RV Parks

The best spot for coastal camping near Guerrero Negro is inside the Parque Natural de la Ballena Gris, where you may be asked to pay US$5 per day to park. In town, **Malarrimo RV Park** (tel./fax 615/157-0100) has 40 sites with hookups and dump stations for US$18 up to 35 feet, US$20 over 35 feet, or US$14 for campers and vans. Tent sites cost US$12 per person. Rates include access to restrooms with hot showers.

The *ejido*-owned **Benito Juarez RV Park** (tel. 615/157-0025), just south of the state border, has 18 hookups (US$7–9) with restrooms and shower facilities but no shade. This place seems to be open sporadically, but probably can be counted on in the high season.

FOOD

Baja residents come from as far away as Bahía de los Angeles and San Francisquito to stock up on foods and supplies in Guerrero Negro. Most of its restaurants and supermarkets line the main avenue of Boulevard Zapata.

Few travelers make their way through Guerrero Negro without stopping at **Malarrimo Restaurant** (tel. 615/157-0100, daily 7 A.M.–10:30 P.M., mains US$10–20) for a hearty meal of fresh seafood and Mexican specialties. The adjoining gift shop has a nice selection of souvenirs.

Closer to the highway, **Puerto Viejo** (no tel., daily 7 A.M.–11 P.M., mains US$10–20) offers much of the same and free coffee with breakfast. Nearby, just inside the entrance to town, the clean **Las Cazuelas** (tel. 615/157-1303, daily 7 A.M.–11 P.M., mains US$6–12) specializes in Spanish-style *mariscadas* (seafood stews); it also serves 12 types of meat dishes and a variety of seafood platters.

Close to the Pemex on the north side of Boulevard Zapata, **Carnitas Michoacán** (no tel., daily 9 A.M.–8 P.M., tacos US$1) serves shredded pork in tacos, *tortas,* and *desebrada* styles. Across from the hospital on the north side of Boulevard Zapata, toward the salt plant, **Tacos El Gordo** (no tel., Mon.–Sat. 8 A.M.–3 P.M. and 6 P.M.– midnight, Sun. only in morning, tacos US$1–2) draws a crowd for carne asada.

On the south side of Boulevard Zapata, roughly across from the first Pemex and Tacos Gordo, **Maximo's Pizza** (no tel., Tues.–Sun. 11 A.M.–10 P.M., mains US$3–6) prepares a menu of burgers, *tortas,* pizza, and pasta. You can dine in air-conditioned comfort inside.

At the edge of town, **Paris Café** (tel. 615/157-1510, daily 7 A.M.–10 P.M.) brews espresso drinks to go with burgers, salads, and yogurt.

Groceries

La Ballena on Boulevard Zapata is the largest grocery store in town, with a variety of foods and housewares.

If you don't mind the limited selection, you can find discounted food items at the government-subsidized **Tienda ISSSTE** on Boulevard Zapata or **Tienda ESSA,** across from the main entrance to the salt plant.

INFORMATION AND SERVICES
Tourist Assistance

Stop by the small tourist office (tel. 615/157-0100, daily 10 A.M.–2 P.M. and 4–7 P.M.) in front of Malarrimo Restaurant for local information. **Mario's Restaurant and Tours** (615/157-1940, www.mariostours.com), at the northern entrance to town at the roundabout, is a reliable source of local information as well.

The Comisión Nacional de Areas Naturales Protegidas (CONANP) has an office in Guerrero Negro (Avenida Profesor Domingo Carballo Félix s/n, esquina Ruiz Cortinez, Col. Marcelo Rubio, www.conanp.gob.mx).

Money

The **Banamex** (Mon.–Fri. 8:30 A.M.–3 P.M.) at the west end of Boulevard Zapata, has an ATM and currency-exchange service.

Telephone and Internet Access

Next to Motel Las Ballenas, **Café Internet Las Ballenas** (Mon.–Sat. 10 A.M.–1 P.M. and 4–9 P.M.) offers high-speed Internet access for US$2 per hour. You can also use the public phone in front of Malarrimo Restaurant.

Laundry

You can wash your clothes across from Motel Las Ballenas on Calle Victoria at **Lavamática Express** (daily 8 A.M.–9 P.M.).

GETTING THERE
By Air to and from Isla Cedros

Aereo Servicio Guerrero (tel. 615/157-0137, toll-free 800/823-3153, www.aeroserviciosguerrero.com.mx) operates flights to and from Isla Cedros four times a week. The flight time is about 30 minutes, and a one-way ticket runs US$65; the airline office, next to the police station on Boulevard Zapata, is open Monday–Saturday 9 A.M.–4 P.M. The company also does charters upon request and flies to other destinations within Mexico.

Guerrero Negro's airfield is located north of town near the state line. Look for the turnoff between Km 125 and 126.

By Bus

Guerrero Negro's bus station is located on Boulevard Zapata across from Malarrimo Restaurant. **Aguila** and **ABC** offer daily service north to Punta Prieta, El Rosario ($40) San Quintín, Ensenada, and Tijuana, and south to Vizcaíno (US$7), San Ignacio, Santa Rosalía, Mulegé, Loreto, Ciudad Constitución, and La Paz (US$75).

GETTING AROUND

The yellow **Infonavit-Centro** city buses (US$1) run along Boulevard Zapata and Calle Madero. You can usually find a few taxis at the bus station, and a ride within the town limits will cost about US$5.

SAN FRANCISQUITO

If you have time for a day-long excursion (or more), the three- to four-hour drive east to the Sea of Cortez covers some beautiful mountain and desert scenery, ending at a seaside fishing camp on **Bahía Santa Teresa.** From Highway 1, watch for a turnoff to San Francisquito (signed for El Arco) about 30 kilometers south of Guerrero Negro. The road passes over a steep hill called Cuesta de la Ley (Slope of the Law), about 29 kilometers before San Francisquito. Some supplies are usually to be found in El Arco, 34 kilometers east of Mexico 1. A better stop is at **Rancho Piedras Blancas,** another 25 kilometers east of El Arco. Located in a spectacular setting among giant cardons, cirios, and ocotillos inside the newly designated Valle de los Cirios national park, the ranch has been selected by the government as a site for the future development of ecologically sound cabins available for tourists.

An alternative route to San Francisquito comes from Bahía de los Angeles and takes about the same amount of time. The Baja 1000 road race uses this route, and some say this wrecks the road, while others claim it helps by creating good tracks that others can follow. About 45–60 minutes into the drive from Bahía de los Angeles lies **Bahía San Rafael,** a beautiful bay with a population of one, an

© CARMEL TSABAR

the simple life in San Francisquito

ex-shark fisherman from Guaymas named Pancho who has called San Rafael home for 20 years. He's on the eccentric side but is full of great stories and can sometimes provide meals and beer to travelers for a donation. He also has a rod for fishing from shore for halibut.

Each route generally has long stretches in good condition. Remember to fill your fuel tank wherever you begin and expect to find heavy washboard and incredible scenery along either route.

The two routes to San Francisquito meet near Rancho El Progreso, approximately 21 kilometers east of Bahía San Francisquito. The roads near the ranch are sometimes difficult to navigate: To stay on track toward the bay, choose the branch that heads due east from the ranch.

Accommodations and Camping

The former San Francisquito Resort is now closed, and the entire beach was sold in 2008 to a Mexican developer who plans to build a large luxury resort. In the meantime, you can still camp on the grounds of the resort or farther on along the bay for US$5.

Vizcaíno Peninsula

South and west of Guerrero Negro, the narrow Baja Peninsula widens to form the Vizcaíno Peninsula, a vast desert, mountain, and coastal region in which average annual rainfall amounts to a mere 70 millimeters, and several years may pass without so much as a single rainstorm. And yet, despite the harsh climate, the Desierto de Vizcaíno sustains one of the most fascinating ecosystems found anywhere in the world—so much so that the Mexican government decided to protect it in 1988, well ahead of current trends in green travel. At its northernmost point, the tip of the Vizcaíno Peninsula juts out into the Pacific Ocean, framing the southwest side of Bahía de Sebastián Vizcaíno, a large bay that encompasses the Laguna Ojo de Liebre whale sanctuary. Heading south from the tip, the coastline is shaped into a series of shallow bays with four fishing towns, where you'll find accommodations, food, and basic supplies. The southernmost bay, Bahía de las Ballenas, leads to Laguna San Ignacio, another breeding ground for gray whales and other endangered marine life.

In 1993, the United Nations Educational, Scientific, and Cultural Organization (UNESCO) designated the whale sanctuary of El Vizcaíno a World Heritage site, along with the rock paintings in the Sierra de San Francisco, an area that lies east of San Ignacio.

The majority of Baja road-trippers stop to refuel in Guerrero Negro and continue their journey south along Highway 1, skipping the Vizcaíno Peninsula altogether. But there are several good reasons to add a few days, or up to a week, to explore one of Baja's last remaining frontiers. You'll find beautiful sites for coastal camping, friendly local residents, and protected plant and animal life, supported almost entirely by a nearly constant layer of marine fog. Although the Vizcaíno Peninsula has changed considerably in recent years, it remains a wild and isolated place that gives travelers the sense of being at the very edge of civilization.

Anglers generally head to the coastal stretch between Bahía Asunción and Punta Abreojos to catch halibut, corvina, and croaker, as well as sand, calico, and pinto bass.

VIZCAÍNO JUNCTION

Ejido Vizcaíno along Highway 1, offers a number of services for motorists and truckers, but the larger town of Vizcaíno Junction (pop. 2,500) is located west of the highway.

Accommodations

A couple of hotels offer reliable accommodations here. **Hotel Olivia** (tel. 615/156-4524, US$30), across from the Pemex station at Km 144, is a family-run establishment with 36 very clean rooms, each with two double beds, private hot-water bathrooms, seven channels of SKY TV, and 24-hour security.

The unique **Hotel Kadakaamán** (615/156-4112, kaadekaman@aol.com, US$40–50), on the west side of Highway 1 at Km 143, was named after the former Jesuit mission site near San Ignacio, Misión San Ignacio Kadakaamán. It also offers air conditioning, hot-water bathrooms, 10 channels of SKY TV, and Wi-Fi in its 18 rooms. The artistic grounds feature a mural of the cave paintings found in the surrounding area.

Food

Highway 1 through Vizcaíno is dotted with many good, simple eating establishments, serving mainly homemade Mexican food, roasted chicken, and tacos. At Km 140 on the east side of the highway, the very simple **Bar/Restaurant Nancy's** (no tel., hours vary) features good homemade meals at reasonable prices, with main dishes ranging US$6–9. Similar food awaits at friendly **La Huerta** (no tel., 6 A.M.–11 P.M. daily, US$5–12), located by Hotel Olivia and attached to the bus depot. **Café Restaurant/Mezquite Grill Afrodita** (daily, mains US$8–20) is the colorfully painted restaurant on the grounds of Hotel Kadakaamán, which specializes in varied cuts of steak. At Km 142 on the west side of the highway is **Maximo's Pizza** (no tel., daily for lunch and dinner, mains US$7–10), which operates a second location in Guerrero Negro.

Information and Services

Vizcaíno has a number of automotive stores (including Napa Autocar Center at Km 141 on the west side), *llanteras* (such as Llantera 2000 on the east side, 615/156-4582), as well as several long-distance phone and fax places. TelMex public phones are widely available.

Getting There and Around

An Aguila bus depot outside Hotel Olivia leads to all points on Highway 1 north and south. A van transports passengers to and from Bahía Tortugas on a daily basis for US$18 each way. Vans depart from the hotel

at 10 A.M. each day and return at 3 A.M. The trip takes three hours.

If you're driving, there are two ways to get to the Vizcaíno Peninsula's coastal attractions: You can turn off Highway 1 at Km 144 and begin a 148-kilometer journey through the desert. The road is paved for the first 75 kilometers, but the next 60 kilometers can present some heavy washboard. About 75 kilometers into the drive, the road forks, with the northern branch heading to Tortugas and the southern branch heading to Asunción. After this point, the way to Bahía Tortugas is paved and in good shape.

From the junction of Vizcaíno road and the road to Bahía Asunción, the road is paved for 12 kilometers and work is actively underway to extend the pavement all the way. After the paved bit is a generally good sandy road, with only a few small sections of washboard. Count on about two hours to go from Bahía Tortugas to Asunción, or about 30–45 minutes from the junction to Asunción.

Alternatively, if Punta Abreojos is your destination, you can turn off Highway 1 at Km 98 and follow an 80-kilometer road to the coast.

If you want to make the trip into a loop, start by heading west to Bahía Tortugas or Bahía Asunción at Km 144 on Highway 1, and then head south along the coast to Punta Abreojos, where you can turn back east and reconnect with Highway 1 at Km 98.

◖ RESERVA DE LA BIÓSFERA DESIERTO DE VIZCAÍNO

The desert that begins south of the 28th parallel is the largest such reserve in Mexico, covering some 2.5 million hectares. It holds 443 species of plants and 69 mammals, the most interesting of which is the rare *berrendo,* or desert pronghorn antelope, which gets its water only by eating succulents. An estimated 200 animals live in the reserve. Ford Motor Company has partnered with the Mexican government to sponsor a recuperation plan for the *berrendo.*

It is possible to view the *berrendos* in an area between Asunción and Abreojos, by turning

---

THE ENDANGERED PENINSULAR PRONGHORN

The *berrendo* once roamed the Baja Peninsula from San Felipe to Bahía Magdalena, but now it survives only in the Vizcaíno Reserve of the Biosphere. Sometimes confused with an antelope, the animal stands about one meter high and weighs up to 50 kilograms. It "drinks" the dew that comes with coastal fog and feeds on plants with high moisture content. The *berrendo* can run up to 95 kilometers per hour. Only about 200 pronghorn live on the peninsula today. They are protected by the government, but poachers, cattle, and periods of drought continue to threaten its existence.

---

off at a signed point on the road. Inquire at either town for specific instructions. Guided tours are also available. Chelo's in Abreojos and the SEMARNAT office in Asunción are good sources of information. There is also a CONANP office in Guerrero Negro where visitors can obtain current information.

BAHÍA ASUNCIÓN

Bahía Asunción (pop. 2,000) has undergone dramatic changes in recent years, from electricity and pavement to signed streets. It's a town that appears to be prospering and receiving considerable attention both from foreign and national interests. For this reason, its days as a quaint and quiet destination may be numbered once the pavement is complete from the Vizcaíno road.

The town's main street is Benito Juárez, on which basically all services can be found, including a Pemex, SEMARNAT office (where you can get a permit for an island tour), airstrip, two plants that process marine products, plus a clinic, library, post office/telegraph service, and a few eateries. Long-distance phones

can be found at Farmacia Eduardo's, Farmacia Rosio, and Ultramarinos Asunción.

The waterfront in Bahía Asunción is not particularly attractive, but it does have a pier and a small beach located just north of town. The annual town festival, that of the Virgen de Asunción, is held in mid-August.

Accommodations and Food

The friendly **Hotel El Verduzco** (Juárez at Calle Mantaraya, tel. 615/160-0004, US$$30) has clean, simple rooms with hot water and wireless Internet, as well as the dependable **Restaurant 3 Hermanos** (daily 8 A.M.–10 P.M., mains US$5–7), which seems to be somewhat of a hub of information in town. Next door to the hotel is the town's only Internet café, open to non-guests.

Plenty of taco and *antojito* stands line Benito Juárez, and the addition of new pavement along the beach heading out of town will probably lead to a revamping of some waterfront restaurants as well.

Getting There

There are two ways to reach Asunción from Tortugas: You can retrace your steps along the Vizcaino–Tortugas road to the fork and follow the southern branch (partially paved) southwest to the coast. Or, you can take a more scenic and shorter route via San José del Castro.

PUNTA ABREOJOS

A longtime favorite of windsurfers and surfers alike, as well as a popular spot with the fishing crowd, Abreojos somehow remains a quiet, somewhat unchartered destination. In July 2007, the town's waterfront received a makeover with the installation of new pavement and streetlamps along its *malecón*.

The town has a Telecomm office for long-distance calls, and a Western Union.

Accommodations and Food

Though most travelers who come to Abreojos choose to camp, the town does offer one good lodging, **Hotel Chelo's** (on town's main unnamed road, tel. 615/620-4515, US$35–40).

© CARMEL TSABAR

the *malecón* in Abreojos

Chelo's also has a bar/restaurant, open daily. Chelo herself is a good source of local information, as well as a key player in a local movement to improve life in Abreojos in many ways. Her organization, MEAPA (Mujeres En Acción Punta Abreojos), is active on a variety of issues, from ecological conservation and beach cleanup to women's issues and town-wide swim and surf camps. For travelers who want to donate their time or money to a good cause, Chelo is a great person to contact (tel. 615/104-2139).

Two other eateries are usually open: **Lonchería Las Palmas** (no tel., daily for lunch, mains US$5) on the *malecón,* is open during the day only and serves tasty fish tacos and other basic Mexican staples. A couple of doors down, with Speedy Gonzalez painted on the front wall, is **Antojitos Juanita** (no tel., nightly, US$5), which opens for typical *antojitos* at night.

For groceries, bread, and other basic supplies, friendly **Super Zuniga** (on town's main road, no tel., daily 9 A.M.–6 P.M.) is well stocked.

LA BOCANA

A fishing town between Bahía Asuncíon and Punta Abreojos, the settlement of La Bocana doesn't hold much to interest for travelers beside some reportedly good fishing, but it can make for a quiet rest between other destinations on the peninsula. It has one hotel, **Hotel Adriana** (on town's main road, no tel.) which is attached to **Abarrotes Adriana.** Rooms in this two-story building go for US$25, and a long-distance phone is also available. There are usually one or two eateries open for simple meals or *antojitos,* as well as gas from a barrel and a *llantera.* The road to Abreojos from here follows an unsigned mudflat; anyone in town can point you in the direction of it.

ESTERO DE COYOTE

In Bahía de las Ballenas, the next bay south of Bahía Asuncíon, anglers and bird-watchers will want to explore the Estero de Coyote, a lagoon and salt marsh area with a local *ejido.*

Campo Rene (tel. 615/103-0008 or 615/161-7360, www.camporene.com) has established itself on the estuary as a bar/restaurant/camping complex offering whale-watching, kayaking, surfing, and turtle observation. Campsites with a *palapa* and adjacent *asador* run US$15, while RV sites with power run US$10. Also available are 12 small wooden cabañas for US$20 and three trailers for US$15; all lodgings have use of shared hot-water bathroom facilities. Inquire about group and/or multiday discounts. An airstrip and *pangas* for rent (US$120 for a day's fishing trip with guide), as well as a full restaurant and bar (meals US$6–9) complete the experience. From the southern road into the peninsula, Estero de Coyote is only a 30-minute trip on a good paved road—well worth a visit.

BAHÍA TORTUGAS

The largest town on the Vizcaíno Peninsula (pop 3,000) is Bahía Tortugas, a 160-kilometer journey from Highway 1. It seems to have declined somewhat in recent years, possibly since the closure of its cannery a decade ago. Residents remain optimistic, however, that by organizing their four fishing cooperatives, they'll be able to preserve the marine life that sustains their community.

Anglers here primarily catch lobster and two species of abalone. The cooperatives, both here and in Punta Eugenia, have night vigilance teams to prevent poaching, as well as abalone cultivating centers. Tourists usually arrive by boat to stock up on fuel and supplies, or to take shelter.

The gray-sand beach closest to town was unfortunately covered with trash at last check. But near the airstrip, El Playón offers a suitable camping spot, and is also a good place for a day at the beach. To find the beach, head to the airstrip following the road to Punta Eugenia, and turn toward the ocean on any tracked road; they all funnel into a more established dirt road that leads to the beach. Once you arrive at the beach, rocky points to the left and right provide shelter from wind as well as decent breaks for surfing on occasion.

Bahía Tortugas fills during Carnaval celebrations every year (Feb.–Mar., dates vary),

as well as during its new, annual Feria del Mar (Festival of the Sea; approx. the middle of August), during which the town celebrates all facets of the sea through crafts made out of abalone and clam shells, seafood dishes, and a fishing tournament.

Accommodations and Food

Try **Motel Nancy** (tel. 615/158-0056, US$25) for basic rooms with private hot-water showers. The motel office is located inside Novedades Lupita, next door, where DVD rentals are also available. To find Nancy's, turn left as you are driving into the town onto a downward-inclined dirt street just after a big mini-market and before the curve in the road at the TelCel office. On the southwest side of town, **Motel Rendón** (tel. 615/158-0232) has rooms inside a cinderblock building for US$25–35. Rendon's office is in El Moroco restaurant, next door.

There are a variety of taco stands and *antojito* spots in town. Down the street from Motel Nancy toward the waterfront is **Taquería Delia** (no tel., daily for lunch and dinner, mains US$5–8), which offers indoor seating for its tacos and *tortas*. Farther down the same road is the **Tortillería La Trinidad** (closed Sundays) for corn tortillas, with a taco and *birria* stand in front. **Alex's Pizza** (no tel., daily for lunch and dinner, mains US$5–8), on the paved road through the center of town, is open for snacks and pizza in the afternoons and evenings daily. **Restaurant El Moroco** (no tel., daily 8 A.M.–10 P.M., mains US$7–8), near Motel Rendón, serves a variety of fresh seafood dishes.

One of the best eateries in town is **❮ La Palapa** (no tel., daily for lunch and dinner, mains US$5–10), located right in the port. Carlos and Mercedes Jimenez started serving customers a decade ago as an extension of their family gatherings for the anglers who would come ashore looking for some food and company. This is a wonderful spot to spend an hour or two having a beer or some coffee with your home-cooked meal; Carlos, an ex-fisherman, is a fantastic source of local history and makes every visitor feel welcome to this sleepy town.

On the weekends, a disco on the hill above

the Pemex is open for the younger crowd that fills the town when visiting family from school in Ensenada.

Information and Services

Services here include a Pemex station, several markets and cafés, a clinic, bakery, post office, and an out-of-use airfield. Western Union offers telegraph services, wires, and credit card advances.

Next door to the telegraph office is the town's only Internet place (no tel., Mon–Sat. 9 A.M.–1:30 P.M. and 4–9 P.M.).

There are many TelMex public phones spread throughout town for long-distance calls using public phone cards. **El Tortugo Tackle** (no tel.), right on the waterfront in the harbor, sells all manners of fishing supplies.

PUNTA EUGENIA

Follow the graded dirt road north from Tortugas for 26.5 kilometers to reach the small, picturesque village of Punta Eugenia. This is the place to plan a boat trip to Islas Natividad, Cedros, and San Benito.

The scenic cliffs along Chest Camp are perfect for solitary camping. You'll enjoy great views of Islas Cedros and Natividad in the distance, as well as Chester Rock, with the remains of a misguided shrimp boat. A local from Eugenia has constructed some palm-fringed shelters on one of the cliffs for a future tourist camp, and plans were to include a restaurant/café as well.

The drive out to Punta Eugenia and beyond is worth the extra time; the surroundings become increasingly more pristine as you get farther from Tortugas.

ISLA CEDROS

If you head northwest from Punta Eugenia by boat for 22 kilometers, you'll reach Isla Cedros (Island of Cedars). At 38 kilometers long, it's one of Mexico's largest islands, with a population of 1,350 as of 2005. Fishing and transporting salt from Guerrero Negro sustain the island's economy, but travelers also find the California juniper and Isla Cedros pine trees (mistaken long ago for cedars) of interest. The trees grow between the island's two 1,200-meter peaks.

© JOSE ANGEL SANCHEZ-PACHECO

view of Isla Cedros

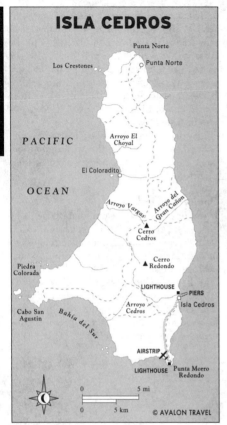

Aside from the unusual flora, there are a few beaches to explore including **Punta Prieta,** at the southwest end of the island. Look for waves at Playa Elefante, also at this end of the island.

If you travel by air, you'll arrive at the saltworks town of Punta Morro Redondo at the southern tip of the island. The largest town on the island, **Puebla Cedros,** is located on the southeast side, facing the peninsula. Services include a port captain's office, CONASUPO, fish cannery, post office, church, bank, and a few eateries and guesthouses.

You can reach Isla Cedros by chartered boat from Punta Eugenia or Bahía Tortugas, or more easily by plane from Guerrero Negro via **Aereo Servicio Guerrero** (tel. 615/157-0137, toll-free 800/823-3153, www.aeroserviciosguerrero.com. mx). A one-way ticket for the 30-minute flight runs US$65, and planes make the trip four times a week. Once you arrive, taxis are available for the short ride into town.

Note: Isla Cedros is part of the Ensenada municipality and lies above the 28th parallel, in the same time zone as Baja California (Norte). Set your watch back an hour if you arrive via Punta Eugenia or elsewhere in Baja California Sur.

ISLA NATIVIDAD
Between Isla Cedros and Punta Eugenia, tiny Isla Natividad (pop 400) was a Cochimí settlement until a Jesuit missionary convinced the group to relocate to Misión San Ignacio. The island is better known today as a world-class surf destination, with the famous Open Doors break (south swell only). Open Doors breaks on the southeast side of the island, so the same westerly winds that blow the surf out along the mainland are barrel-grooming offshore waves all afternoon. Isla Natividad is known for advanced, barreling waves and tough camping.

San Diego–based **Baja AirVentures** (toll-free U.S. tel. 800/221-9283, www.bajaairad-ventures.com) runs all-inclusive, safari-style trips to Isla Natividad from May until October, but only when a south swell is running. Trips are often planned on short notice, depending on the surf conditions. This is the way to get in and out for a surgical strike. A four-day trip costs US$1,495, and a six-day trip runs US$1,695. All trips depart from San Diego.

From Punta Eugenia, chartered boat service to Isla Natividad should cost about US$20 one-way, and the trip takes about 30 minutes. Planes also make the short trip to the island's dirt runway. Services are extremely limited here, but the island does have a clinic to handle small injuries.

ISLAS SAN BENITO
Divers who know this trio of tiny uninhabited islands say that its kelp beds are as rich with life as the Channel Islands were 75 years

ago. Purple hydrocoral grow on underwater pinnacles, abalone and lobster hide in rocky crevices, and sightings of 9- to 18-kilogram yellowtail are common. Thriving populations of California sea lions, giant elephant seals, and Guadalupe fur seals provide even more fun.

Islas Benito del Este, Centro, and Oeste are located about 80 kilometers west of Baja and about 450 kilometers south of San Diego—within reach of California-based liveaboard services. **Horizon Charters** (www.horizoncharters.com) occasionally runs an eight-day, seven-night dive trip to these islands. Boats depart from San Diego and stop at Isla San Martin on the way south.

Bilingual marine biologist Jose Sanchez-Pacheco offers a variety of guided trips through **Cedros Outdoor Adventures** (tel. 646/154-3085, cell tel. 646/193-2031, U.S. tel. 619/793-5419, www.cedrosoutdooradventures.com), which is based in San Ysidro, California. Package trips include eco-tours to Isla Cedros and the San Benito islands (4 days/3 nights US$1,090; and sportfishing trips to Islas Cedros, San Benito, Natividad (4 days/3 nights US$1,300). Prices include transportation from San Ysidro, California, as well as accommodations and meals.

San Ignacio and Vicinity

South of Vizcaíno Junction, Highway 1 begins to curve eastward on its way to meet the Sea of Cortez at Santa Rosalía. The drive presents views of the expansive Desierto de Vizcaíno to the west and the majestic Sierra de San Francisco to the east, with peaks up to 5,216 meters. In the middle of all this scenery is a spring-fed oasis surrounded by palms and the small colonial town of San Ignacio. Beyond the desert on the Pacific coast is the winter whale sanctuary of Laguna San Ignacio.

SAN IGNACIO

Experienced Baja travelers often pass straight through Guerrero Negro and push on to San Ignacio (pop. 4,000) for an overnight stop on the way to points south. With its picture-perfect oasis, restored 18th-century Spanish mission, colonial buildings, and variety of places to stay and eat, the town offers an appealing combination of scenery, history, and visitor services.

Before the Jesuits arrived, the Cochimí knew San Ignacio as Kadakaamán (Creek of Reeds). Abundant freshwater made it a prime location for growing wheat and other crops during the mission period. Today, the town consists of a small commercial and residential area surrounding the Misión San Ignacio Kadakaamán and plaza.

The weather here is moderate, compared to the surrounding Vizcaíno Desert. Nights can be chilly in the winter and all the standing water makes for a healthy population of mosquitoes.

Sights

◖ MISIÓN NUESTRA SEÑOR SAN IGNACIO DE KADAKAAMÁN

If you visit only one mission along the entire Baja Peninsula, choose this one for the quality of its restoration, accessibility, and the important role it played in Jesuit history.

The story of the Misión Nuestra Señor San Ignacio de Kadakaamán (1728–1840) begins with a visit to the arroyo in 1716 by Padre

Francisco María Piccolo, who was stationed at the Misión Santa Rosalía de Mulegé. His soldiers built a hut of sticks and leaves to serve as a chapel, and he and Padre Sistiaga returned periodically to visit the indigenous people there over the next 12 years.

In 1728, Padre Juan Bautista de Luyando came to establish a mission. He funded the effort with his own money and lived in San Ignacio for seven years, during which the original chapel became a large adobe church. All that remains of the original structure is a line of foundation stones near the base of the mesa southwest of present-day San Ignacio.

Padre Sebastián de Sistiaga became head of the mission after Luyando and was joined by Padre Consag, who began construction of the stone building that is used today. The project

© PAUL ITOI

Río de San Ignacio

was left incomplete upon his death in 1759, and Padre José Mariano Rotea became the new head of the mission until the Jesuits were expelled in 1768. With 2,000 baptisms recorded as of 1758, the Misión San Ignacio served as a base of Jesuit expansion into Central Baja.

In 1773, the mission passed from the Jesuits to the Franciscans and soon after to the Dominicans, and it was Dominican Friar Juan Crisóstomo Gómez who completed the church in 1786, following the original plans of Padre Consag.

With walls more than a meter thick made of local volcanic stone, beams of lumber from the high sierra, and six-meter-high carved doors from mainland Mexico, the church is an impressive sight to see. Decorative stonework frames windows and doors. Inside is an altarpiece made of carved wood and covered with gold leaf. The church was restored beautifully in 1976, and the present-day community holds worship services inside.

MUSEO LOCAL DE SAN IGNACIO
Next to the church, the Instituto Nacional de Antropología e História (INAH) runs a museum

(no tel., Mon.–Sat. 8 A.M.–6 P.M., free). Exhibits depict local history, including the rock art of the nearby Sierra de San Francisco. Although the exhibits have Spanish captions, a translated booklet is now available in English. The museum is open on Sundays during high season.

If you're planning a trip to the Sierra de San Francisco to view the cave paintings, stop by the **Unidad de Información y Manejo** (tel. 615/154-0222) next door to get the required permit.

Recreation
HIKING
For a good view of San Ignacio, you can hike a short ways to the top of a mesa that overlooks the town. The trail begins behind Casa Leree.

ORGANIZED TOURS
Servicios Ecoturísticos Kuyimá (Ecoturismo Kuyimá, tel. 615/154-0070, www.kuyima. com, kuyima@prodigy.net.mx) has an office facing the plaza in the old Bancomer building. Kuyimá specializes in whale-watching tours at nearby Laguna San Ignacio, but can

also arrange guided trips into the Sierra de San Francisco to view prehistoric rock-art sites. Kuyimá guides speak Spanish, English, and French.

Entertainment and Events

The residents of San Ignacio celebrates their town fiesta on July 31 with the usual lineup of traditional Mexican music, food, and games.

Shopping

Casa Lereé (Calle Madero S/N, near the plaza, tel. 615/154-0158) and **Ignacio Springs Bed & Breakfast** (tel. 615/154-0333, www.ignacio-springs.com) both carry a limited selection of English-language books about Baja.

Accommodations and Camping

UNDER US$50

A kilometer south of San Ignacio on the west side of Mexico 1, the longstanding **Baja Oasis Motel** (tel. 615/154-0111, US$35) now has air-conditioned rooms. Some have king beds, others have queens or singles. All 10 rooms include purified drinking water and hot showers. **Casa Lereé** (tel. 615/154-0158, www.prodigyweb.net.mx/janebames), a bright blue single-story building near the town plaza, was constructed around 1880 as a family home, and became the first guesthouse in San Ignacio around 1900. It has served many generations of travelers in the years since. Two small rooms (US$40) open onto a shady patio and share a bath; a larger suite (US$75) in the main house has its own bath and anteroom. Gated parking is available. Owner, Jane (Juanita) Bames has collected a number of historical sources, articles, and photos, and she offers guests and non-guests a free, self-guided tour through the house (guestrooms excepted). She also has created accurate town and hiking trail maps. Guests can use Wi-Fi inside the main house common area.

Motel La Posada (tel. 615/154-0313), a few blocks from the central plaza, and **Motelito Fong** (tel. 615/161-8573), at the entrance of town, both offer simple rooms with private bathrooms and secure parking for US$25.

US$50-100

Next to the oasis as you drive toward the town center, Canadian expats Terry and Gary have expanded **Ignacio Springs Bed & Breakfast** (tel. 615/154-0333, www.ignacio-springs.com, US$62–93) little by little during the seven years since they opened. Their accommodations now include seven yurts, some with private baths (US$87–150), others with shared facilities (US$62); one small *palapa casita* next to the river (US$80); and two block-style buildings with a shared shower facility. Each yurt is unique in style; for honeymooners, the new China Wall yurt features Chinese tapestries, lamps, and silk robes along with a whirlpool bath—for sure the only suite of its kind in Baja. Prices include tax and a big, hearty home-cooked breakfast; credit cards are accepted. Kayaks and skiffs are available for guest use. Ignacio Springs has wireless Internet access for every yurt. Terry and her staff prepare home-cooked dinner for guests and non-guests (reservations required by 2 P.M. for dinner that evening). Her prix fixe menu changes according to what's fresh and in season, but she'll take special dietary needs and allergies into consideration when planning the meal. The price of US$15–18 includes homemade pie or cake for dessert, and Terry usually has Starbucks coffee on hand to satisfy your espresso craving.

Ricardo's Rice and Beans (tel. 615/154-0283, http://ricardoriceandbeans.googlepages.com), the unofficial stopover for Baja 1000 motorheads, offers big rooms with air-conditioning and wireless Internet for US$50.

About 3.5 kilometers off Mexico 1 on the edge of town, the **Desert Inn** (tel./fax 615/154-0300, toll-free U.S. tel. 800/800-9632, www.desertinn.com, US$81) got a much-needed facelift in late 2006. It offers 28 rooms with air-conditioning, plus a restaurant, pool, and billiards room. Rates are highest during the whale-watching season.

CAMPING AND RV PARKS

You can camp at several small campgrounds set in palm groves along the Río de San Ignacio (but beware the bugs). Almost opposite the Desert Inn, **El Padrino RV Park** (tel./fax 615/154-0089) has about 100 sites (20 with hookups). RV sites cost US$18 a night. Tent camping runs US$10 a night. Amenities include a dump station and bar/restaurant. The management arranges whale-watching and cave painting tours for guests.

Camping Los Petates (no tel.) and **Camping Lakeside** (no tel.) are a step behind in terms of services, but they have the best location facing the river. Sites at Los Petates come with hot showers and electricity, and a small shop has camping supplies. Rates are US$12 for RVs and US$5 per person if you camp.

In addition to its hotel rooms, **Ricardo's Rice and Beans** (tel. 615/154-0283, http://ricardoriceandbeans.googlepages.com) has 20 RV spaces with full hookups and hot showers for US$25; tent sites are US$10.

Food

Palapa restaurant **Rene's** (cell tel. 615/103-0008, www.camporene.com, Mon.–Sat. around 8 A.M.–9 or 10 P.M., Sun. dinner only, mains US$8–12), on the east side of the San Ignacio town plaza, prepares good-value seafood dishes and *antojitos*. If it's not too hot or buggy, you can sit outside under the brick arches for a pleasant outdoor dining experience.

Antojitos Mexicanos Fong (daily 8 A.M.–11 P.M.), at the San Ignacio town entrance, has a simple menu featuring fresh ingredients. Nano Fong, who owns the restaurant and attached motel, is an ex-circus performer and marathon unicyclist (and Guinness-record holder); magic tricks and tales of his 50-hour unicycle marathons all over Mexico to raise money for various causes are free with your visit or meal. He is a living piece of Baja history.

Northwest of town, near the highway, **Ricardo's Rice and Beans** (tel. 615/154-0283, http://ricardoriceandbeans.googlepages.com, daily 7 A.M.–11 P.M., dinners US$5–15, breakfasts US$5–15) serves traditional Mexican and seafood dishes; to find it, make a U-turn at the Pemex station and follow the road parallel to the highway four blocks.

On Mexico 1, about three kilometers northwest of town, **Restaurant Quichule** (no tel., daily 8 A.M.–11 P.M., mains US$5–10) is owned by Rancho El Carricito and uses homegrown meat, milk, and cheese in its dishes. The seafood cocktails and clam cakes are particularly good here.

You can find basic supplies at a few *tiendas* and *miscelanéas* in town. Try **Mercados Mayoral López** or the **Diconsa** next to the Pemex for groceries, and **Tortillería La Misión** (near Rene's on the way to the lagoon) for flour tortillas. You can also buy dates at various stands for about US$2 per kilogram.

Getting There

Aguila and **ABC** buses stop at the bus terminal (daily 7 A.M.–11 P.M.) half a kilometer north of town. There are five buses daily in both directions.

◀ SIERRA DE SAN FRANCISCO ROCK ART

The mountains northeast of San Ignacio hold some of the most spectacular prehistoric paintings found anywhere on the peninsula. It is for this reason that historian Harry W. Crosby described the Sierra de San Francisco as a "gallery of ancient art" and UNESCO designated the region a World Heritage site in 1993.

Getting there, however, takes some planning and a willingness to rough it in the backcountry for at least a couple of days. The Mexican government requires you to obtain a permit and hire a guide before visiting these sites, which you can do at the INAH offices in San Ignacio or La Paz. Then you'll need to make arrangements to travel by mule, bringing your own food and water.

First-time visitors to the Sierra de San Francisco typically head to the Arroyo de San Pablo, where a series of five rock art sites are relatively accessible: Cueva del Ratón, Cueva Pintada, Cueva de las Flechas, Cueva de la Música (Los Músicos), and Boca de San Julio. INAH categorizes all of these sites as Level 2, meaning they are open to any visitor with a permit and guide.

You need at least one night and two days to see Cueva de las Flechas and Cueva Pintada. Departing from San Francisco, on the first morning you'll ride down to the canyon floor, a 360-meter descent, and set up camp, then visit the caves in the afternoon. On the second day, you'll climb out of the canyon and return to the village.

If you have more time, you can add up to three additional caves in the area to your itinerary: Cueva La Soledad, Cueva La Música, and Boca de San Julio.

San Francisco de la Sierra makes a good starting point for trips to rock art sites in other arroyos, including San Gregorio, El Batequí, and Santa Marta.

Cueva del Ratón

If the idea of camping overnight in the backcountry makes you uncomfortable, you might begin with Cueva del Ratón, a short hike (20 minutes) from the village of San Francisco de la Sierra. This is by far the most accessible rock art site in the Sierra de San Francisco. Measuring 12 meters long, the overhang is among the smaller canvases, but nonetheless important for its relative completeness. Images include deer, desert bighorn sheep, rabbits, human figures, and a rare mountain lion. Park in the village near the set of stairs that ascends to the site, but remember to register with INAH and hire a guide in the village before setting out to view the rock art.

Cueva de las Flechas and Cueva Pintada

Two of the most striking cave paintings in all of Baja occupy opposing walls of a deep, palm-filled canyon in the Arroyo San Pablo. If you have just one night to spend in the Sierra de San Francisco, spend it on a trip to Cueva de las Flechas and Cueva Pintada. The setting alone makes it worth the ordeal of getting into the backcountry. And the art you'll see represents some of the most dramatic and best-preserved examples of Baja's prehistoric rock art.

The relatively small canvas of Cueva de las Flechas (Cave of the Arrows) features three large human figures notable for the many black arrows that appear to pierce their bodies. Historian Harry Crosby calls them three of the most elegant monos (human figures) found anywhere. You can see parts of Cueva Pintada (Painted Cave) from Flechas.

A 30-minute scramble over to the other side of the canyon reveals Cueva Pintada, the most well-known and most-visited rock art site in Baja. Discovered in 1962 by mystery writer Erle Stanley Gardner (and also known as Gardner's Cave), the cave features 150 meters of painted walls and ceilings with remarkably well-preserved figures. The back wall alone depicts more than 40 signature red and black images of humans, deer, and sheep.

"This grand cave is the most painted place in the most painted part of the entire range of the Great Murals. It may rightly be considered the focus of the phenomenon," wrote Harry Crosby in his beautiful photography book, *The Cave Paintings of Baja California: Discovering the Great Murals of an Unknown People*. Other caves in the region are larger, but none rivals the quantity and quality of the art you'll see here.

Getting There

Look for a well-marked turnoff for San Francisco 36 kilometers northwest of San Ignacio. The rocky road climbs into the mountains and meanders along a mesa. Allow about two hours to reach the village at Km 23.5.

VOLCÁN LAS TRES VIRGENES

Approximately 30 kilometers north of Santa Rosalía, the local *ejidatarios* have come together with the Mexican government (CONANP) as part of the Reserva de la Biósfera to construct bungalows (similar in style and concept to those of Valle de los Cirios) and a lodge, all with breathtaking views of this extinct volcano and surrounding area. Until recently, this part of the interior was inaccessible to most travelers except hunters who stalked the *borrego cimarrón* (desert bighorn sheep). Licensed guides now offer a variety of ecotours, including hikes

© PABLO NOBILI

Volcán Las Tres Vírgenes

to the top of the volcano (recommended mid-Oct.–mid-Apr.), tours to Laguna San Ignacio for whale-watching (Dec.–Mar.), hikes throughout the surrounding area to view the *borregos,* and tours to the cave paintings of the Sierra de San Francisco.

When the *cabañas* are completed they will provide visitors a chance to experience true desert tranquility. Interested visitors should contact Juan Villa Vicencio or Marcial Landeros Valdez (615/155-4241, desertsheep5@yahoo.com) ahead of time, or, those with open travel plans should drive in and be prepared to stay or move on.

LAGUNA SAN IGNACIO

If you've come to Baja in the winter to witness the gray whale calving, the protected Laguna San Ignacio on the Pacific coast is a must-see destination. Discovered by whalers in 1860, Laguna San Ignacio is 58 kilometers from the town of San Ignacio and measures about 26 kilometers long and eight kilometers wide. Along with the Vizcaíno Desert, it became part of the Reserva de la Biósfera in 1988. About 100 people live beside the bay, and make their living from fishing and, increasingly, ecotourism. A major saltworks expansion effort was blocked recently by environmentalists.

Only two other bays, Laguna de Ojo Liebre to the north and Bahía de Magdalena to the south, offer comparable experiences for ecotourists. And for some reason, the whales here tend to come closer to boats and show off more for their audiences than at the other two sanctuaries (which is not to say that having an opportunity to touch one is a given).

To see the whales by boat, you need to hire a licensed *panguero.* There are two ways to do this: You can buy an all-inclusive package tour, which depart from San Ignacio or Loreto by ground transport, or from as far away as San Diego via charter plane. Independent travelers may prefer to drive directly to the bay and purchase boat fare "à la carte" from one of several outfitters (US$40 pp, min. usually 4 people). Boats typically depart at 9 A.M. and stay out for 3–4 hours. It's about a two-hour drive from the town of San Ignacio to the camps, so day-trippers need to get an early start. Stop by the plaza in San Ignacio to arrange taxi service to the lagoon for around US$50.

At the south end of Laguna San Ignacio, a peninsula sticks out into the mouth of the bay close the main calving area. This can be a good vantage point from which to see the whales. With four-wheel drive, you can drive to the point; alternatively, a *panga* driver can also shuttle you there from one of the camps at the north end of the bay.

Two dirt roads connect Laguna San Ignacio to Bahía San Juanico: One leaves from the Kuyima camp and traverses the Mesa Las Salinas, close to the coast, but may not be passable at high tide. The more reliable route is a continuation of the San Ignacio–Laguna San Ignacio road, and passes through several inland villages on the way to San Juanico.

Whale-Watching Tours and Camping

A handful of outfitters offer whale-watching tours and trips January–April. Just outside the village, **Antonio's Ecotours** (no tel., http://wildcoastecotourism.com, US$40 pp) is a popular choice for whale-watching services if you choose to arrange your own transportation to the bay.

With an office in town and a camp close to the south end of the bay, **Ecoturismo Kuyimá** (Morelos 23, San Ignacio, tel. 615/154-0070, www.kuyima.com) is a full-service operation. Its campground has hot-water showers, composting outhouses, and a *palapa*-roofed dining area. Accommodations are either in one of 30 tent sites (US$10/night without the whale-watching

package) or 10 cabins. If you don't have your own camping gear, you can rent a two-person tent, sleeping bags, and flashlights for US$40. Meals cost US$7–10. Best of all, you can often see the whale action from the shore.

If you prefer to have someone else handle more of the logistics of your whale-watching tour, Kuyimá's multi-day packages are a reasonable deal, especially when compared to the San Diego–based all-inclusive trips. For example, a four-day/three-night trip costs US$495 per person for cabin lodging, meals, and daily whale-watching excursions. Guests have use of bicycles, kayaks, a library, and video services. The packages include a trip to nearby salt fields and the expertise of the company's knowledgeable guides. Van transportation is available to/from San Ignacio for an additional US$120 for up to 10 people.

Near the mouth of the bay and even closer to the action **Baja Discovery** (U.S. tel. 619/262-0700 or 800/829-2252, www.bajadiscovery.com) has run a safari-style camp for more than 25 years. Its strategic location on Rocky Point gives visitors front-row seats to the show—in season, whales will spout and spyhop right offshore. The downside for budget-conscious travelers is that to stay here, you must buy an all-inclusive package that starts and finishes in San Diego (US$2,275 pp for five days).

The **Baja Expeditions** (2625 Garnet Ave., San Diego, tel. 858/581-3311 or 800/843-6967, www.bajaex.com) camp is nearby; its similar five-day packages cost US$2,225 per person, and include "catered camping," solar showers, and round-trip airfare from San Diego.

Santa Rosalía and Vicinity

Though it's not a top destination for most travelers, Santa Rosalía (pop. 9,700) leaves a lasting impression on those who do pass through. The reason is twofold: First, for drivers headed south on Highway 1, this former silver-mining hub is the first town you reach on the Sea of Cortez. After many hours of desert and mountain vistas, you'll likely never forget that first glimpse of ocean blue and the rapid descent to the water's edge.

Second, besides its proximity to the sea, the buildings in Santa Rosalía look very different from the rest of Baja. In contrast to the Spanish influence that dominates the peninsula, the colonial architecture here is distinctly French, thanks to the influence of a French mining company called El Boleo, which set up shop here in the 19th century and operated until 1954. Many of the original wood-frame houses are still intact. A famous French bakery and metal church supposed to be designed by none other than Gustave Eiffel complete the effect.

Crowded into the mouth of a deep arroyo, the town's main commercial area runs perpendicular to the sea, with high mesa walls on either side. Old mining equipment and machinery still are visible in many places around town.

Today, Santa Rosalía serves as a government and business hub for central Baja, as well as a convenient place for travelers to stock up on supplies. A public library in Parque Morelos displays photos from the town's historic mining days.

If you visit in June–October, be prepared for extremely hot temperatures. The town's waterfront promenade, or *malecón,* is a good place to catch an afternoon breeze.

HISTORY

Local ranchers first discovered copper deposits (called *boleos*) in the hills surrounding present-day Santa Rosalía in the late 1800s, and a French company bought rights to mine the area in 1884 and built the town that survives today. The infrastructure included 600 kilometers of

© PABLO NOBILI

a remnant of mining days in Santa Rosalía

tunnels, a large copper-smelting foundry, pier, and 30-kilometer mine railway.

By 1934, El Boleo had mined and smelted 14 million tons of copper ore. By the 1950s, the company's outdated process made the business unsustainable and El Boleo sold its facilities back to the Mexican government. A state-owned concern reopened the operation (without modernizing it) and ran it until the 1980s, when it was finally closed for good. But the story doesn't end there.

In 1992, the current management of Baja Mining Corp. briefly took control. After a decade of restructurings and changes of ownership, the mine returned to the same management team in 2001. Armed with more advanced technology, deep pockets (US$962 million in funding to date), and agreements with the Mexican government and local *ejido,*

Vancouver-based Baja Mining (www.baja-mining.com) intends to extract value from the area's mineral deposits once again, including copper, cobalt, and zinc.

The company has about 200 people on-site already, with a workers' camp, desalination plant, and cacti-relocation program in progress. Production—estimated at 56,000 tons of copper cathode, 1,500 tons of cobalt cathode, and 20,000 tons of zinc sulphate—is due to begin in 2010, with an expected life of 25 years.

SIGHTS
Iglesia Santa Bárbara de Santa Rosalía
Unlike the Spanish missions scattered across the peninsula, Santa Rosalía's church is a simple structure made almost entirely of metal. Long said to have been designed by French architect

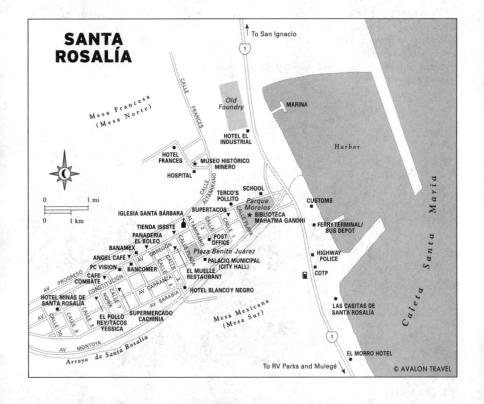

© AVALON TRAVEL

Gustave Eiffel for use in the country's African colonies, the origins of this unusual church came into question in the 1990s and the true history remains a mystery. According to the Eiffel story, the church was exhibited at the 1889 Paris World Exposition, forgotten in a Brussels warehouse, and then rediscovered by an El Boleo manager, who had it shipped to Baja.

Today, the local community uses the church for worship.

Mesa Francesa (Mesa Norte)
The mesa on the north side of town holds several well-preserved examples of French colonial architecture, including the **Hotel Frances** and the **Museo Histórico Minero de Santa Rosalía** (Mon.–Sat. 8 A.M.–2 P.M. and 5–7 P.M., US$1.30), with exhibits that depict the town's mining past.

To get to the mesa from the town center, you can climb an old set of stairs from the Iglesia Santa Bárbara, or by following Calle Altamirano.

FESTIVALS AND EVENTS
Santa Rosalía celebrates **Carnaval** usually in mid-February, and the annual **Fiesta de Santa Rosalía,** is held around September 4 in honor of patron saint Santa Rosalía. A **founder's day celebration** also occurs in mid-October.

ACCOMMODATIONS
Under US$50
Housed in one of the town's mining-era wooden buildings, the **Hotel Blanco y Negro** (Av. Sarabia at Calle 3, tel. 615/152-0080, US$18–30) has been a favorite among budget travelers for many years for basic, clean rooms with private baths. **Terco's Pollito** (Av. Obregón at Calle Playa opposite Parque Morelos, tel. 615/152-0075, US$35) has seven rooms, with air-conditioning and cable TV; its reception area is inside the adjoining restaurant (daily 7 A.M.–7 P.M.). Two-hundred meters from the ferry terminal on Highway 1, **Hotel El Industrial** (tel. 615/152-1857, US$40) has safe parking, rooms with air-conditioning and cable TV, and 24-hour reception. **Hotel**

the view from Las Casitas de Santa Rosalía

© PABLO NOBILI

del Real (Montoya 7, no tel.), is another good option for an overnight stop near the ferry terminal. New rooms on the back side of the building have air-conditioning and TV for US$35. Internet was about to be installed the last time we visited.

The business-oriented **El Morro Hotel** (tel./fax 615/152-0414, hotelmorro@aol.com, US$35–52) overlooks the Sea of Cortez about 1.5 kilometers south of town on Mexico 1 (btw Km 194/195). Its 39 spacious rooms feature ocean views and air-conditioning, and there's secure parking, a restaurant/bar, and swimming pool. Wireless Internet, included in the price, is available in the lobby area.

US$50-100
At the edge of a cliff that drops into the sea, **Las Casitas de Santa Rosalía** (tel. 615/152-3023, mariahsantarosalia@hotmail.com, US$60–70) has several modern cottages, plus a well-equipped gym, wireless Internet, and a terrace that overlooks the harbor.

In a French colonial building, the **Hotel**

Frances (Calle Jean M. Cousteau 15, tel./ fax 615/152-2052, US$85) overlooks the old copper smelting facility on Mesa Norte. Its 17 rooms have high ceilings, cable TV, wireless Internet, and air-conditioning. There is a small pool in the courtyard and the hotel restaurant is open daily for breakfast only.

FOOD

Santa Rosalía has a handful of busy restaurants—several with outdoor seating—plus a number of tempting taco stands. Most of these establishments line Avenida Obregón. **Restaurant Terco's Pollito** (Av. Obregón at Calle Playa opposite Parque Morelos, tel. 615/152-0075, daily 8 a.m.–10 p.m., mains US$5–7) does barbecued chicken right, and it's air-conditioned.

Several vendors sell tacos from carts around town. But at **Pavarotti's Tacos** (Obregén btw the church and the El Boleo bakery, no tel., daily for lunch and dinner) there are stools from which one can enjoy the town's bustle for much the same price as other taco stands.

El Muelle Restaurant Bar (Calle 9 and the plaza, tel. 615/152-0931, daily 8 a.m.–11 p.m.) is a good spot for breakfast, seafood (US$9–14), or pizza ($9–12). Outdoor seating is a plus during cooler weather.

Angel Café (Calle 5, off Obregón, no tel.) prepares tasty *tortas*, plus burgers and breakfasts for US$3–5. **Café Combate** (Obregón btw Calles 5–6, no tel., Mon.–Fri. 8 a.m.–1 p.m. and 3–6 p.m., Sat. 8 a.m.–2 p.m.) has espresso drinks.

Groceries

The government-subsidized **Super ISSSTE Tienda** (Obregón at Calle 3) is a dependable option for groceries and supplies.

A longtime favorite among locals and travelers alike, **◖ Panadería El Boleo** (Obregón, Mon.–Sat. 8 a.m.–9 p.m.) draws a crowd for its baguettes, as well as a tasty assortment of Mexican and French breads and sweets.

For fresh flour tortillas, head to **Tortillería Santa Agueda** (Av. Obregón near Calle 6, just west of the Bancomer). **Tortillería**

Ranchería, near the west end of Obregón, makes corn tortillas.

At Constitución and Calle Noria is the well-stocked **Minisuper Delya** (Mon.–Sat. 6 a.m.–9:30 p.m., Sun. 7 a.m.–2:30 p.m.), whose vividly painted walls depict a bountiful harvest.

INFORMATION AND SERVICES

Bancomer and Banamex both have branches and ATMs on Obregón (Mon.–Fri. 8:30 a.m.–3 p.m.).

Santa Rosalía's post office is located east of the plaza at Calle 2 and Avenida Constitución. You can use a public phone on the south side of the plaza for local and long-distance calls, and there are several TelMex Ladatel card phones along Obregón and elsewhere around town.

Head to **PC Vision** (on the corner of Obregón and Calle 6, daily 10 a.m.–10 p.m., US$2/hour) or air-conditioned **Dr PC** (Obregon and Calle Plaza, daily 10 a.m.–10 p.m., US$1.50/hour) for Internet service.

For repairs and supplies, there is a hardware store on the east side of the plaza (tel. 615/152-1234) and a **Go4Value** (Calle 5 and Constitución) discount store with food, cleaning supplies, and paper goods.

GETTING THERE

Domestic air service may be available from Palo Verde Airport (PVP) in San Bruno. At last check, Aéreo Servicio Guerrero (www.aereoserviciosguerrero.com.mx) was operating regular flights, as well as an air taxi service, between Baja and Hermosillo, Sonora on the mainland. Daily flights are available from Guaymas and twice a week from Hermosillo, Sonora.

Santa Rosalía's **intercity bus depot** has moved to the ferry terminal. Several buses a day travel north to San Ignacio, Guerrero Negro, San Quintín, Ensenada, Mexicali, and Tijuana, as well as south to Mulegé, Loreto, and La Paz.

A word of caution about filling up in Santa Rosalía: The Pemex station near the ferry terminal on Mexico 1 has long been known for scamming tourists. Watch the pump and count your change, or better yet fill up in San Ignacio or Mulegé instead.

Inside the harbor, **Marina Santa Rosalía** (tel./fax 615/152-0011) rents 20 moorings and sells fuel. Also here are the port captain, immigration, and customs offices.

The **Santa Rosalía ferry** (tel. 615/152-1246, www.ferrysantarosalia.com) is now running three times a week, leaving Santa Rosalía in at 9 A.M. and returning from Guaymas at 8 P.M.

SAN LUCAS COVE

The protected cove of San Lucas offers campers and travelers in small boats shelter from winter's northerly winds (small boats only, due to the shallow entrance).

Camping

This is the closest camping you can find to Santa Rosalía, 15 kilometers to the north, and it's a pleasant site. Access is via a sandy road that heads east from the highway.

San Lucas Cove RV Park (no tel.) and **Camacho RV Park** (no tel.) both offer campsites for US$7 per vehicle (no hookups). Facilities at the former include hot showers, a dump station, and a boat ramp.

SAN BRUNO

Thirty-two kilometers north of Loreto, Bahía San Bruno served as a launch pad for the first Spanish land expedition that sought to evaluate the Baja Peninsula for colonization. Padre Eusebio Francisco Kino and Admiral Isidro de Atondo y Antillón arrived in 1683 with a group of 50 soldiers and 100 loyal indigenous people from mainland Mexico and set up camp along this bay. Although they never established a permanent mission, they used the site as a base from which to explore the interior of the peninsula. And through these early efforts, they identified the future sites of the Comondú and La Purísima missions.

Modern-day San Bruno is a quaint fishing community with seemingly more *pangas* than

© CARMEL TSABAR

the office of the Hotel Costa Serena in San Bruno

residents. A new harbor and paved boat ramp were completed in 2006 with state government funding. This town also makes a good starting point for a trip to dive or fish around Isla San Marcos. Head to the harbor to charter a boat.

San Bruno celebrates its town festival in early October.

Services include gas from a drum, a bus stop, and a couple of *abarrotes* stores.

Accommodations

With prior experience at the Hotel Serenidad in Mulegé and Punta Chivato, Alberto Carrillo runs the first and only hotel in town. The new **Hotel Costa Serena** (tel. 615/153-9022, US$35) has half a dozen air-conditioned rooms in a single-story building facing the sandy beach. Each room is individually appointed with antique furnishings and named for one of Alberto's uncles. White bathrobes are a plus. Alberto is also building the first restaurant in town, and his nephew offers *panga* tours to Isla San Marcos.

Getting There

To get to San Bruno, look for a turnoff on Highway 1 at Km 173, north of the turnoff to San José de Magdalena.

ISLA SAN MARCOS

Directly offshore from San Bruno is a small island of San Marcos, known for abundant gypsum deposits and proximity to prime yellowtail fishing. Like Santa Rosalía, this is a company-built town. About 700 people live and work for the mining company, which has been in business since 1923 and for many years has been the top producer of gypsum in North America. The town's gypsum block church was built in 1954.

There are no hotels and limited supplies on the island, available from one general store and a few *tiendas*. The island also has cell phone service and Internet.

Diving and Snorkeling

Head to Punta Piedra Blanca at the northwest end of the island for the best diving and

snorkeling. On the east side, Punta Gorda and Punta La Chiva are also good sites to explore. Mulegé-based **Cortez Explorers** (www.cortez-explorers.com) runs boat trips to Isla San Marcos for US$110–135. Michael Hans Kanzler, a.k.a. **Isla San Marcos Mike** (cell tel. 415/244-8451, www.islasanmarcos. com) has run sportfishing charters on the island for nearly 20 years. Rates are US$225 for trips around Isla San Marcos and US$275 for trips to nearby Isla Tortugas. Prices cover up to three people for a half-day, starting at dawn and ending in the early afternoon. Rates are US$25 less for dive charters to the same destinations.

Getting There

The best way to get to Isla San Marcos is to hire a *panguero* at the harbor in San Bruno.

NORTHERN SIERRA DE GUADALUPE

South of San Ignacio and Santa Rosalía and west of Mulegé, the Sierra de Guadalupe rises to 1,200- to 1,500-meter peaks in a stretch of mountains that measures 128 kilometers long and 30–48 kilometers wide. The Jesuits found the terrain suitable for mission life and the Misión Nuestra Señora de Guadalupe de Huasinapi operated from 1720 until 1795 as one of the most remote settlements on the peninsula. And in the early 20th century, mining company El Boleo bought and established numerous ranches throughout the northern part of the range to support its growing community of workers.

Two scenic roads leave the highway near San Bruno, heading into the mountains, but you'll need four-wheel drive to negotiate the twists and turns and rocks along the way. At Km 188, south of the state prison, a 12-kilometer graded road heads west to **Santa Agueda.** Local ranchers may be available to guide you to some of the closer cave painting sites, such as La Candelaria, San Antonio, or Los Gatos; however, you'll need to arrange for a permit in San Ignacio before you go.

The second access road leaves Mexico 1 at Km 169, south of San Bruno, and leads to the remote farming community of **San José de Magdalena,** 14 kilometers west. After San José, the road continues another 48 kilometers to several ranchos and the mission ruins. There is little to see at the former mission site except parts of the foundation and adobe walls. This three-hour journey is best left to serious mission trail travelers.

Mulegé and Vicinity

Southbound travelers notice a distinct change in climate as they approach the mission town of Mulegé (pop. 3,300) on the Sea of Cortez. Temperatures and humidity climb to a tropical feel, and mosquitoes are ever-present. Built alongside the mouth of the Río Santa Rosalía (also known as the Mulegé River), the town consists of a small network of narrow streets lined with colonial buildings. Agriculture, tourism, and fishing support the modern-day community. With its variety of restaurants, accommodations, and services, the town serves as a stopover for some and a destination in its own right for others.

Once every 50–100 years, the river floods, as it did following Hurricane John in 2006, pushing trees, cars, and homes toward the sea. Floodwaters rose in a matter of minutes and nearly reached the first story ceilings of properties along the water's edge. Two local residents drowned, and property damage was severe. All but the hardest-hit businesses reopened by year-end

Though small in scale, Mulegé seems to have at least one of everything. There are laundry machines, auto mechanics and parts stores, grocery stores and mini-markets, restaurants, hotels, and campgrounds—and even a dive shop. And Mulegé offers enough water and land activities to keep you busy for a week or more.

SIGHTS
Misión Santa Rosalía de Mulegé

One of the earliest missions (1705–1828) established by the Jesuits in Baja California, the Misión Santa Rosalía de Mulegé was founded in 1705 by Padre Juan Manuel de Basaldúa. In 1770, a flood destroyed much of the original settlement on the Río Santa Rosalía, and the church was moved to a bluff overlooking the river. The mission continued to be active until 1828. The missions at San Ignacio and San Javier may be more elegant, but Mulegé's restored church offers great views of the town and river.

To find the church, follow Calle Zaragoza southwest under the highway bridge, then turn right to ascend the bluff by the church, about three kilometers from the bridge. It is usually locked, except when in use for services.

GUERRERO NEGRO

© CARMEL TSABAR

Misión Santa Rosalía de Mulegé

Museo Regional de Historia

The former town prison, on a hill that over-looks town, has been converted into a local museum (no tel., hours vary, admission is by donation) with a small collection of historical artifacts, including a desk used by mystery writer Erle Stanley Gardner, who researched many of central Baja's rock art sites.

ℂ Playa El Sombrerito

The Mulegé River meets the Sea of Cortez at Playa El Sombrerito, forming a large estuary that supports a wide variety of marine birds. Sea views are especially dramatic at daybreak. There are a couple of restaurants and a few places to stay near the beach.

SPORTS AND RECREATION

Mulegé offers adventure travelers a full lineup of activities, both on land and in the sea.

Diving and Snorkeling

As the Sea of Cortez becomes more tropical, the underwater environment becomes more colorful and full of warm-water life. Green moray eels poke their heads out of rocky crevices; angelfish, damselfish, and parrotfish school along the reefs while red, spiny Cortez, and slipper lobster hide in dark caves. Visibility and water temperatures are best June–November; it's not uncommon to see 30 meters at depth with temperatures of 30°C during these months. Bring or rent a full wetsuit for winter diving; in summer a Lycra dive skin is a good idea to protect against jellyfish.

The three rocky outcroppings known as **Islas Santa Inés,** offer divers and snorkelers an opportunity to observe playful sea lions, schools of anchovies, and a variety of marine life along a shallow reef. Divers can explore the boulder fields below. Farther afield, **Bahía Concepción** has more diving and snorkeling sites, including **Pelican Reef, Isla Santispac, Isla Guapa, Isla Requesón,** and **Roca Frijole.**

Under new ownership, **Cortez Explorers** (Moctezuma 75A, tel./fax 615/153-0500, www. cortez-explorers.com) has attained the highest level of PADI certification that a dive center can earn and offers a full-service operation. You can rent gear, fill tanks, take classes, and

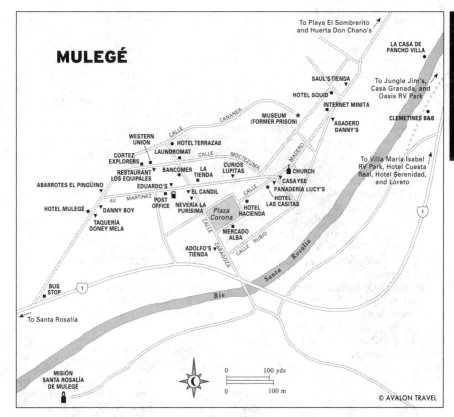

MULEGÉ

To Playa El Sombrerito
and Huerta Don Chano's

LA CASA DE
PANCHO VILLA

SAUL'S TIENDA

HOTEL SQUID

To Jungle Jim's,
Casa Granada, and
Oasis RV Park

INTERNET MINITA

CLEMETINES B&B

MUSEUM
(FORMER PRISON)

ASADERO
DANNY'S

To Villa María Isabel
RV Park, Hotel Cuesta
Real, Hotel Serenidad,
and Loreto

WESTERN
UNION

HOTEL TERRAZAS

CANANEA

CALLE

LAUNDROMAT

CALLE

MOCTEZUMA

CORTEZ
EXPLORERS

CURIOS
LUPITAS

MADERO

BANCOMER

LA
TIENDA

CHURCH

RESTAURANT
LOS EQUIPALES

ABARROTES EL PINGÜINO

EDUARDO'S

CASA YEE

PANADERÍA LUCY'S

AV MARTINEZ

POST
OFFICE

EL CANDIL

HOTEL
LAS CASITAS

HOTEL MULEGÉ

DANNY BOY

NEVERÍA LA
PURÍSIMA

Plaza
Corona

HOTEL
HACIENDA

TAQUERÍA
DONEY MELA

MERCADO
ALBA

CALLE RUBIO

ADOLFO'S
TIENDA

CALLE ZARAGOZA

Santa Rosalía

BUS
STOP

1

Río

To Santa Rosalía

MISIÓN
SANTA ROSALÍA
DE MULEGÉ

0   100 yds

0   100 m

© AVALON TRAVEL

charter boats at the shop. A one-tank guided boat dive trip costs US$70, and a two-tank trip costs US$110. Guided shore dives cost less, at US$50/90. Snorkeling gear rents for US$21 per day. Credit cards are accepted. Stop in Monday–Saturday 10 A.M.–1 P.M. and 4–7 P.M.

Kayaking

Paddlers can launch kayaks along the estuary for trips north to Bahía Santa Inés or south to Bahía Concepción; however, if Concepción is your target destination, there are better place to put in farther south. In a challenging five- to seven-day trip, you can paddle from Mulegé all the way to Loreto, 135 kilometers away. This trip is best attempted with an experienced guide or outfitter.

Fishing

Las Casitas (tel. 615/153-0019) and **Hotel Serenidad** (tel. 615/153-0530, www.serenidad.com) can arrange sportfishing charters to Punta Chivato, Bahía Concepción, and nearby islands (US$180 per day in a *panga* for up to three people, or US$200 per day for a five-person cruiser). For the best onshore fishing, head to the south side of the estuary, where you might catch yellowtail, roosterfish, mackerel, or red snapper in winter; offshore catches in summer include dorado, yellowfin, and various billfish.

Organized Tours

Salvador Castro Drew (tel. 615/153-0232, cell tel. 615/103-5081, mulegetours@hotmail.com) offers guided cave painting tours delivered in flawless English for US$40 per person, plus an additional fee charged by the rancho through which visitors must pass to get to the rock art site (US$7–10). Salvador can customize tours to include two of the following sites: Piedras Pintas, San Patricio, or La Trinidad; or he can cover all three in one day for a slightly higher fee. He also takes visitors to San Borjita, but this site requires a full day without time to see the other caves.

Salvador will pick you up in his air-conditioned van and share his knowledge of local natural and cultural history during the day. The standard tour includes stops at a local orchard, a rancho, and then the cave sites in La Trinidad. Participants need to bring photo ID to register at the INAH office, and should also have good walking shoes, a hat, sunblock, camera, and water.

Salvador also leads walking tours through the towns of Mulegé (US$10), Santa Rosalía, and San Ignacio. And he can arrange bird-watching, clamming in Bahía Concepción, snorkeling, and sportfishing outings. Overnight trips include cave paintings in the Sierra Guadalupe and whale-watching at Laguna San Ignacio. Airport transportation is also available. If you don't reach Salvador by phone, inquire at Hotel Las Casitas. As Mulegé's only guide certified to conduct all of these tours, Salvador is highly respected around town.

Baja Adventure Tours (Calle Rubio 27, tel./fax 615/153-0566, cirocuesta@hotmail.com) also leads small-group tours of the Mulegé area.

ENTERTAINMENT

Scott's El Candil (Zaragoza, a few meters from Plaza Corona, Tues.–Sat. 11 A.M.–11 P.M. or so, Sun. 11 A.M.–5 P.M. or so) is the place to watch NFL football games, NASCAR races, golf tournaments, and other sports on a big-screen TV while drinking a cold beer. It has a full Mexican menu, with good burgers for US$6–12.

Hotel Las Casitas (Madero 50 on the town's main east–west street, tel. 615/153-0019)

has invited *norteña* bands to play on Fridays and mariachis on Saturdays for many years. The small disco bar, **Danny Boy,** next to Tacos Doney, opens on the weekends 9 P.M.–3 A.M. Four kilometers east of town off Mexico 1, the **Hotel Serenidad** (tel. 615/153-0530, www.serenidad.com) hosts a pig roast with mariachis on Saturday nights.

SHOPPING

A general store in the truest sense, **La Tienda** (Martínez and Zaragoza, no tel., Mon.–Sat. 9 A.M.–1 P.M. and 3–6 P.M.) stocks fishing tackle and charts, books about Baja, gifts, swimsuits, wetsuits, and more. The Ladetel phone inside is a good place for a relatively quiet conversation. Credit cards are accepted as long as the power is on.

Adolfo's Tienda (Zaragoza across from Plaza Corona, no tel.) has a good selection of souvenirs, including hammocks and decorative crafts. **Curios Lupita's** (Martinez at Zaragoza) specializes in crafts and wearable souvenirs, such as sarongs and T-shirts.

ACCOMMODATIONS AND CAMPING

Mulegé offers several choices in modest and budget hotels, plus a few bed-and-breakfasts, and places to camp, as well. Just about every hotel in town now offers free wireless Internet service to guests; however, some have Wi-Fi only in their reception areas.

Hotels and Bed-and-Breakfasts
UNDER US$50

Centrally located on Mulegé's main east–west street, the ever-popular **Hotel Las Casitas** (Madero 50 on the town's main street, tel. 615/153-0019, fax 615/153-0190, US$39) once belonged to Mexican poet Vicente Gorosave. Its eight basic rooms have air-conditioning, and there is a pleasant patio restaurant on-site. No off-street parking.

A relative newcomer, the **Hotel Squid** (tel. 615/153-0351, US$35 and up), is located just around the corner from Minita's Internet. Completed just before the 2006 flood, it had to be rebuilt. Its nine clean, modern rooms encircle a private parking area. The hotel is adding a second level of rooms, as well as Internet service.

At the entrance to town, **Hotel Mulegé** (tel. 615/153-0090, US$44), offers clean rooms with air-conditioning, SKY TV, and parking.

On the south side of the river and about two kilometers east of town at Km 132, the **Hotel Cuesta Real** (tel./fax 615/153-0321, US$39–59) has 12 air-conditioned rooms. An archway adorns the turnoff from the highway. Amenities include a small swimming pool, restaurant/bar, and laundry service. The hotel can make arrangements for fishing and cave painting trips and tours. Credit cards are accepted.

US$50-100

Farther east along on the south side of the river, Mulegé's largest and best-known inn caters to fly-in guests. The **Hotel Serenidad** (tel. 615/153-0530, www.serenidad.com, US$85–160) has 50 rooms, several two-bedroom cottages (with a/c and parking), and nicely laid-out grounds. Wi-Fi is available in the restaurant.

Amenities include a pool and boat ramp. Its Saturday night all-you-can-eat pig roast with mariachis (US$16) is a popular affair.

Near the Oasis Rio RV Park on the south side of the river, **Clementine's Inn** (www.clementinesbaja.com, US$55–70/night or US$325–400/week) has the most comfortable beds in Baja in this price range. Owners Cliff and Judith, who also run a top-rated bed-and-breakfast on the Oregon Coast, made a speedy recovery after the flood of September 2006 and bought all new beds, linens, appliances, and artwork for their guest accommodations. Four rooms and several casitas achieve a unique balance between upscale bed-and-breakfast (luxurious sheets, tiled baths, stylish light fixtures, extra towels, tea lights) and authentic Baja (wood-paneled ceilings, basic faucets, abalone shells for soap dishes). Rooms are decorated in warm colors and set around a large, well-equipped open-air kitchen, thoughtfully designed with the culinary enthusiast in mind. Appliances include a large refrigerator, double toaster, coffee-maker, and ice machine. A

© CARMEL TSABAR

a peek into Clementine's Inn's open-air kitchen

Weber gas grill, bottled water, and bug screens for covering prepared food are also provided. Casitas range in size from a studio to three bedrooms (US$75–160/night and US$350–850/week, and the owners are building additional units on the property. Free wireless Internet is another plus. Prices vary by unit, and advance reservations are preferred.

Closer to the sea, **Casa Granada** (Estero de Mulegé 1, tel. 615/153-0500, www.casagranada.net, US$60/night or US$420/week) has the most luxurious rooms in town. Its four rooms occupy a stone building with high ceilings, tiled baths, Talavera sinks, and remote-control air-conditioning. Guests enjoy sea views and a private setting along the estuary.

Casas de Huéspedes

Mulegé supports several *casas de huéspedes,* or guesthouses, generally with accommodations around US$25. For example, **Casa de Huespedes Manuelita** (Moctezuma and Zaragoza, no tel.) offers clean rooms, with private bathrooms, and air-conditioning.

Vacation Rentals

Orchard Vacation Village (south side of Rio Mulegé, close to the highway, tel. 615/153-0516, www.bajalife.com/orchard, casitas $38–95) transformed itself after the 2006 floods. It now consists of a neighborhood of well-designed houses varying in size and amenities, sold individually and managed by the on-site office as rentals.

Camping and RV Parks

Shaded campsites for tents (US$7.50 pp) are a plus at **Villa María Isabel RV Park** (south of town, off Mexico 1, tel. 615/153-0246). It also has 30 RV campsites with full hookups for US$20. Rates include hot showers and the use of a swimming pool. The campground is located east of the highway and south of the river.

Across the river, near Playa El Sombrerito, **Huerta Don Chano's** (no tel.) offers RV and tent campsites at similar prices. **Hotel Serenidad** (tel. 615/153-0530, www.serenidad.com) has 15 RV sites with hookups for

US$16 for two people, US$2.50 per additional person.

The majority of campers spend part of a day exploring Mulegé and restocking on supplies, but set up camp farther south along Bahía Concepción, where the scenery is prettier and bugs are less of a nuisance.

FOOD
Restaurants

Mulegé's restaurants serve reasonably priced meals in an authentic setting. Don't be dissuaded by an empty dining room during off-peak months; the food is reliable any time of year.

Second-story **Los Equipales** (Moctezuma, tel. 615/153-0330, daily 7:30 A.M.–10:30 P.M., mains US$10–23) overlooks a busy street and serves the best Mexican and seafood dishes around. The name refers to a type of leather-and-wood chairs that are part of the restaurant's decor.

On the south side of the river, past Clementine's Inn, **Jungle Jim** (no tel., Mon.–Sat. for lunch and dinner, mains US$6–12) feels a bit like an eating club, with regulars helping themselves to drinks at the bar. Decent burgers and seafood are the mainstays of a changing menu.

Popular among tourists, the restaurants at **Las Casitas** (tel. 615/153-0019, daily 6:30 A.M.–9:30 P.M., breakfast mains US$4–6, dinner mains US$9–17) and **Hotel Serenidad** (tel. 615/153-0530, www.serenidad.com, daily 6:30 A.M.–9:30 P.M., mains US$10–15) offer moderately priced Mexican fare. The garden patio at Hotel Serenidad is a pleasant place to enjoy a signature daiquiri. Las Casitas also does a Friday night Mexican buffet with live music for US$10 during the high season.

Two places are worth a special trip to the beach to dine: On the beach where the road meets Playa El Sombrerito, the 21-year-old **El Patrón** (no tel., daily lunch and dinner, mains US$5–10) offers a complete menu of Mexican and seafood specialties. **Casa de Pancho Villa** (no tel., daily for breakfast, lunch, and dinner, mains US$5–10) just a few steps away on the road to the beach, is newer and funkier. Both are reasonably priced and open daily, and have spectacular views of the estuary and beach area.

Antojitos, Tacos, and Fast Food

Mulegé has several good taco stands. Try the *tacos de carne asada* or a quesadilla at **Asadero Dany's** (Romero Rubio, no tel., Thurs.–Tues 8 A.M.–4 P.M.). Better yet, **Tacos Doney Mely's** (no tel., Wed.–Mon. 7:30 A.M.–10 P.M., US$9–20), on Calle Moctezuma across from the Hotel Mulegé, makes great tacos and even better *carnes* and seafood.

Taquitos Mulegé (Plaza Corona, no tel., daily 9 A.M.–1 P.M.) serves the best fish tacos in town. Right next door, **Mr. Pizza** (no tel., summer daily 5–11 P.M., winter daily 3–11 P.M., 12" pizza US$10, 14" pizza US$15) offers pizza with additional toppings included in the price, as well as side portions of spaghetti and salad.

Eduardo's (Calle Moctezuma, no tel., US$9–15) bakes pizza Monday–Wednesday and Friday–Saturday 6:30–11 P.M. but changes the menu on Sunday to prepare family-style Chinese food.

Several ice cream shops sell *nieve* (Mexican-style, no-milk ice cream).

Groceries

Among the town's *tiendas,* you'll find the widest selection of foods—both locally grown and some prepared—at **Casa Yee** (Madero 46 near Las Casitas), **Abarrotes El Pingüino** (on the access road to/from the highway, near Hotel Mulegé), and **Mercados Alba** (on Plaza Corona, daily 8 A.M.–9 P.M.). With advanced notice, **Saul's Tienda** (on Calle Madero where it becomes Calle Playa) can get just about any gringo-requested ingredients, including a Thanksgiving turkey.

The **Hielera Mulegé** on "Ice House Road" (signed San Estanislao), just north of town and west of Highway 1, has block ice and purified water. It's open daily 24 hours. Standard business hours for most *tiendas* is 9 A.M. to 6 P.M. daily.

MULEGÉ PHONE NUMBERS

- Mulegé area code: 615
- Fire Department: 153-0079
- Highway Patrol (Santa Rosalía): 152-0839
- Hospital: 153-0298
- Immigration (Santa Rosalía): 152-0313
- Police: 153-0049
- Red Cross: 153-0110 or 153-0380
- State Tourism Office: 124-0199
- Taxi Service: 153-0420
- Tourist Assistance: 078

INFORMATION AND SERVICES

Money

The Bancomer is located on Zaragoza, between Madero and Moctezuma. **El Pez de Oro** (Moctezuma 17, daily 9 A.M.–1 P.M. and 3–7 P.M.) is a money exchange that cashes travelers checks.

Communications

The post office (Avenida Martínez, tel. 615/153-0205, Mon.–Fri. 8 A.M.–1 P.M.) is just before the Pemex station on the right-hand side of the one-way street as you come into the town center. The Minisuper Padilla (corner of Zaragoza and Av. Martínez, tel./fax 615/153-0190) has a long-distance telephone office.

Internet Minita (Mon.–Sat. 9 A.M.–9 P.M.) at the end of Calle Madero has eight desktop computers for rent for US$2 an hour. Baja Adventure Tours (Madero 3, tel. 615/153-0566) also has Internet service with printing and photocopying capabilities.

Next door to Cortez Explorers dive shop is a Western Union with telegraph service that is open Monday–Friday 8 A.M.–noon.

Laundry

Lavamática Claudia (Zaragoza and Moctezuma, tel. 615/153-0057, Mon.–Sat. 8 A.M.–6 P.M.) is the place to wash your clothes.

GETTING THERE AND AROUND

Loreto has the closest commercial airport. Mulegé does not have a bus depot or ticket office in town, so you have to buy your ticket on the bus (no reservations). Northbound and southbound ABC and Aguila buses stop twice a day at the town entrance on Mexico 1, but not at set times, and the schedule varies from year to year. Southbound buses arrive mid-morning and mid-afternoon; northbound buses arrive in the mid-afternoon and evening.

You can easily walk anywhere in town, even to or from the RV parks along the river. Mulegé's town center consists of narrow one-way streets—and not all of them are marked with arrows.

There is a Pemex station in town, on Avenida Martínez, but a more convenient alternative is the modern Mulegé Pemex Centro on Mexico 1, located about 10 minutes south of town. You can pump your own gas here, and a café and mini-market with ice are on-site.

SOUTHERN SIERRA DE GUADALUPE

The largest concentration of rock art sites are located at the southern end of the Sierra de Guadalupe range, west of Mulegé. Hotels in town can arrange guided trips to the closest ones for US$35–45 per person.

La Trinidad

In a small canyon near Rancho La Trinidad, one wall remains of a cave that was once painted on all sides. The site is known for an image of a large deer painted in a striking orange-red color. The deer is filled with a checkerboard pattern, and beside it are two fawns. According to historian Harry Crosby, the deer represents a recurring theme in Baja rock art, and the one at La Trinidad is one of the best examples found anywhere on the peninsula.

To visit the site, you must secure a permit from **INAH** (San Ignacio, tel. 615/154-0222; La Paz, Calle Aquiles Serdán 1070, tel. 612/123-0399) and hire a licensed guide, either in Mulegé or at the ranch itself. The ranch is located 29 kilometers west of Mulegé. From there, a 6.5-kilometer hike, including several river crossings, leads to the site.

Plan to carry your own water and wear submersible footwear. It takes at least half a day to hike to the cave, and the canyon is scenic enough to consume an entire day. You can also make stops at several other ranchos along the way to watch leather tanning, cheesemaking, and other ranch activities.

There are two groups of murals at La Trinidad. To reach the first, you need only cross the river once. But the second site requires several more crossings. In years when the water level is high, one of these crossings may involve swimming 100 meters through a narrow stone gorge—a true backcoun try thrill for the adventure-seeker.

Two experienced guides run half-day trips out of Mulegé: Salvador Castro Drew (tel. 615/153-0232) and Ciro A. Cuesta Romero (Calle Rubio 27, tel./fax 615/153-0566, cirocuesta@hotmail.com) of **Baja Adventure Tours.** Trips cost about US$40 per person and can be arranged through any hotel in town.

GETTING THERE

If you decide to drive your own vehicle to the ranch, you'll need high clearance and sufficient spare parts. Guides at the ranch will be less expensive, but you'll need to navigate your way there along a network of unsigned roads. Hotels in town can provide specific directions to the ranch. The route begins on Ice House Road toward San Estanislao.

San Borjitas

The best-known cave painting in the Sierra de Guadalupe—and at one time in all of Baja—was discovered by virtue of its proximity to Mulegé, a town that has existed since mission times. The cave is located on the site of an abandoned ranch that belongs to the Gorosave family. To reach it, you need to drive 23 kilometers miles north of

Mulegé to Km 157, then 30 kilometers (2 hrs) west into the interior to Rancho Las Tinajas, where you must register with INAH. Mulegé-based guides can take you to San Borjitas in a long one-day trip, or you can drive yourself and hire a guide at the ranch.

Once signed in, you must drive several more miles through two locked gates (keys will be provided when you register) to Rancho Baltasar, where the hike (less than 1 km) to the cave begins.

The San Borjitas canvas measures 30 meters long by 24 meters deep with an average height of 3.5 meters. On it are some 50 human figures, painted in a uniquely Sierra de Guadalupe style. Colors are more varied than in other parts of the Great Mural region (red, black, ochre, gray, and white). Bodies are elongated with legs spread and arms stretched out to the sides, rather than overhead. And many of the figures are filled in with vertical lines. Another unusual characteristic of this site, according to historian Harry Crosby, is the appearance of adjacent and overlapping figures painted at right angles to each other.

BAHÍA SANTA INÉS AND PUNTA CHIVATO

North of Mulegé near Km 151, a sandy road departs Highway 1 heading east toward the wide and undeveloped bay of Santa Inés—a great place for a mid-day swim or beach stroll. There are multiple ways to reach the white-sand beach that lines the bay. Follow the network of sandy roads, choosing the most-traveled branches and taking care not to get stuck in patches of loose sand. Eventually, you will end up at the low dunes that guard the beach. You can pitch a tent and spend the night here, although there are no facilities and you may be asked to pay a few dollars for overnight use of the site.

At the north end of Bahía Santa Inés (Km 156), a 20-kilometer graded road leads to remote Punta Chivato, a popular sportfishing destination and a great spot to set up camp and snorkel the rocky point. A handful of *palapas* offer shade, and the beachfront camping area can accommodate RVs as well as tents.

Accommodations and Camping

The high-end **Posada de las Flores** (off the main, unnamed dirt road that leads to Punta Chivato, tel./fax 615/155-5600, U.S. tel. 619/378-0103, www.posadadelasflores.com, US$120–800/night) group took over the historic Hotel Punta Chivato, a onetime luxury fly-in resort that opened in 1966. Like its sister properties in Loreto and La Paz, the inn has large and stylish rooms with air-conditioning, private baths, fireplaces, and garden patios. Other amenities include a boat ramp, small desert golf course, pool, and sea kayaks. Rates include breakfast, snacks, and dinner, but don't include tax or a US$18-a-day service fee. There is a small *tienda* at the hotel.

You can also camp on the beach or contact **Costa Cardonal** (www.costacardonal. com) to inquire about vacation rentals that may be coming on the market as new homes are completed.

Bahía Concepción

South of Mulegé, stunning Bahía Concepción represents the best of all that Baja has to offer. Its string of a dozen protected white-sand beaches, small islands, and steady winds create a water-sports playground for snorkelers, divers, kayakers, and kiteboarders. The mouth of the bay faces north, and a long, narrow peninsula forms the eastern shore. As a national marine preserve, the bay supports a vibrant ecosystem of creatures big and small.

Mexico 1 hugs the coastline here, and every turn reveals a new and more breathtaking vista. Generally speaking, the beaches in the north are sandier and better protected than those at the south end of the bay. Most of the beaches belong to *ejidos,* which may collect camping fees of US$6–8.

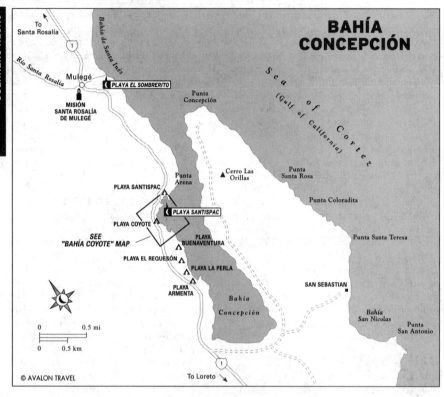

In recent years, a number of American and Canadian expats set up semi-permanent residences along several of the most protected coves. But in late 2006, local authorities asked them to remove all structures from the beach and leave the area, in preparation for sale of the property to a large Mexican real estate developer. A small development of privately owned vacation homes called Posada Concepción crowds the shoreline at Km 113. A small market may have basic supplies for sale.

PUNTA ARENA

Windsurfers, kiteboarders, and summertime campers should head to windy Punta Arena, at the north end of the bay's western shore. Follow the signed, four-kilometer road and you'll find a group of *palapas* and *palapa* huts that rent for

about US$8 a night. Look for the Punta Arena sign 13.2 kilometers from the Hotel Serenidad turnoff from the highway.

◖ PLAYA SANTISPAC

Between Km 114–115, Playa Santispac was once the most developed of the Bahía Concepción beaches; by 2008, all semi-permanent structures had been removed, leaving many ruins of small gardens, tiled floor areas, and other boundary markers created by the snowbirds who formerly made Santispac their winter home. The beachfront area and its *palapa* shelters are now accessible to campers and travelers; those who were asked to leave the area have relocated mainly to Playa El Coyote and Posada Bahía Concepción. An entrance fee of US$7 per vehicle usually is collected here, whether or not you camp.

© CARMEL TSABAR

privately owned beachfront accommodations in Bahía Concepción

Ana's Restaurant Bar (daily except Wed., winter hours 8 A.M.–10 P.M., summer hours 2–10 P.M., mains US$6–15) is a full-service operation that specializes in fresh seafood and has a full bar known for its Bloody Mary cocktails. Ana's also prepares special dishes for its Saturday night music and dancing fiestas, and continues to have a faithful following among the ex-residents of the beach. Ana's has firewood, groceries, sundries, and propane, as well as tools for repairing cars and boats. The owner, Russ, rents kayaks (US$25–35/day) and snorkeling gear (US$10/day). He can also arrange guided tours. Non-guests can use the showers for US$3.

B&B Casa de los Sueños (www.casadelossuenos.com), perched on the cliffs just north of Posada Concepción with its own clearly marked entrance, has a few rooms in its main house, as well as a separate casita. Prices vary, and the owners prefer to send quotes via email. The bed-and-breakfast faces Isla San Ramón and has kayaks as well as a skiff for guest use; air-conditioning and Internet are also part of the deal here.

PLAYA ESCONDIDA

At Km 111, an 800-meter road leads to several more beaches, ending at Playa Escondida. Larger RVs should avoid the narrow, bumpy track, which leads to a pretty, uncrowded place to lie in the sun, comb the beach, or set up camp (US$8/day).

PLAYA LOS COCOS

Just north of Km 111, Playa Los Cocos fronts a turquoise colored cove whose beautiful color is a reflection of limestone in the cliffs above the beach. You can camp here under open *palapa* structures for US$6; the only other facilities are pit toilets. Between the beach and cliffs, a small lagoon is lined with mangroves.

PLAYA EL BURRO AND PLAYA COYOTE

Continuing south along the bay, the next beach is Playa El Burro with *palapas,* trash cans, and camping for US$8 per day. The adjacent Playa Coyote has a campground with pit toilets, *palapas,* showers, and drinking water (entrance fee US$8/vehicle).

Restaurant Bertha's (no tel., daily 8 A.M.–8:30 P.M., US$5–11) serves very good, simple Mexican meals at Playa El Burro. It also has a well-stocked bar and friendly service. Across the highway is Abarrotes El Burro, a small supply store.

PLAYA BUENAVENTURA
Part coarse sand, part rock, this beach is occupied by the **Hotel San Buenaventura** (Km 94.5, www.hotelsanbuenaventura.com, US$50–70), with clean rooms and campsites (US$10 to camp or US$3 for bathroom facilities with hot shower). Rooms are set around a small courtyard and have air-conditioning and ceiling fans.

George's Olé Sports Bar and Grill (no tel., daily 8 A.M.–10 P.M., mains US$8–12) serves food and drinks; chessboards and a library of paperback books are available. The owners have a couple of *palapa* huts for rent (US$10), as well as a trailer and house.

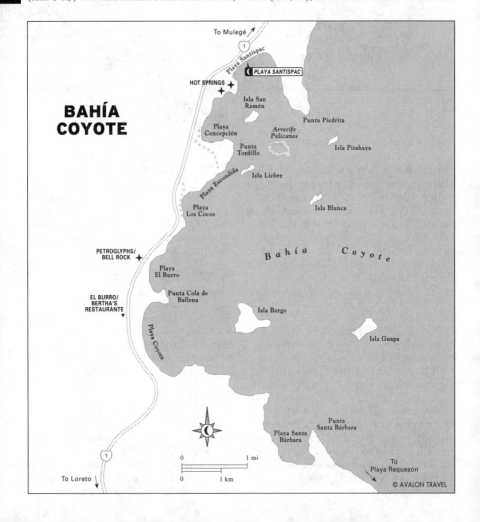

The restaurant has a pool table and kayaks for rent.

PLAYA EL REQUESÓN

A long sandbar running perpendicular to shore and connecting to a small island makes Playa El Requesón a whimsical place. Shallow coves border both sides of the sandbar. Drive your car out onto the hardened sand and the scene looks like something right out of an SUV commercial. You can camp in a tent or RV for US$6 per vehicle (pit toilets, *palapas,* no drinking water).

South of this point, the shoreline of Bahía Concepción becomes less appealing to beach-goers due to the presence of rocks and standing water. The southernmost beach on Bahía Concepción that you can reach by car is Playa Armenta, which faces northwest and has a few *palapas* and pit toilets for US$6. Look for the turnoff between Km 90 and 91. The beach is about 800 meters down this road, after the ranchito.

PENÍNSULA CONCEPCIÓN

Few travelers venture out to the peninsula that forms the east side of Bahía Concepción because you have to drive a rough 60 kilometers to reach the point, and once there, you'll find no toilet facilities or water. If you really want to explore this part of the bay, a boat from Punta Arena is a better plan.

SPORTS AND RECREATION
Kayaking

With its protected white-sand beaches, tiny islands, and shallow reefs, Bahía Concepción makes an ideal kayaking destination. Aside from a couple of weeks a year of high winds, conditions tend to be warm and calm.

Playa Santispac is a good launch point because several islands are fairly accessible offshore, including **San Ramón, Liebre, Pitahaya (Luz),** and **Blanca. Arrecife Pelícanos,** or Pelican Reef, runs between the Liebre and Pitahaya islands. Thermal springs

© PABLO NOBILI

Bahía Concepción's calm waters are ideal for kayaking.

on the point at the south end of the beach are another popular destination for kayakers.

A few hundred meters east of Playa Coyote, **Isla Bargo** has a sandy beach that makes a pleasant campsite.

Around 2.4 nautical kilometers southeast of Playa Coyote, **Playa Santa Bárbara** can only be reached by boat. This is another secluded spot for an overnight stop.

There are no kayak rentals available in the area, so you should bring your own or rent one from a neighborhing town.

La Purísma, Comondú, and Vicinity

Southwest of Mulegé, the Sierra de la Gigante range separates three fertile valleys from the Gulf coast. San Isidro, La Purísima, and Comondú are worth a visit if you want to experience a slice of Jesuit mission history and see a couple of present-day ranch communities in action. For many travelers, the desert and mountain scenery alone justifies the extra miles of off-road driving.

SAN ISIDRO

Surrounded by orchards, San Isidro (pop. 1,000) has several *tienditas,* a post office, Western Union, and café/taco stand, which seems to be open at random hours. There is also a church, clinic, and barrel gas. Aside from these services, the town offers little to warrant a lengthy stay. Continue on to La Purísima for a larger town with a colorful mission history.

◖ LA PURÍSIMA

Abundant fresh water and surrounding volcanic cliffs made the settlement of Cadegomó suitable for mission life. Padre Nicolás Tamaral established the Misión La Purísima Concepción de Cadegomó in 1720. The village was abandoned in 1822, and Mexican farmers revived it in the late 1800s. Many of the original date, citrus, and mango orchards survive today, along with the foundation ruins of the mission church (located a few kilometers north of town), which is now part of a private residence.

Services include Abarrotes Goruave, as well as a mini-market, a *llantera,* post office, pharmacy, and barrel gas at both ends of town.

A 48-kilometer graded road leads west and then north to Bahía San Juanico (Scorpion Bay), a popular surfing destination; from here, another graded dirt road connects to Laguna San Ignacio.

◖ COMONDÚ

Known collectively as Comondú, the twin towns of San José de Comondú and San Miguel de Comondú are beautiful rural communities with lively plazas and lots of architectural ruins from missionary times. Travelers are not commonly seen here, but you'll be warmly welcomed if you visit. The towns lie about three kilometers apart from each other and about 20 kilometers south of La Purísima. Date palms are abundant here; farmers also grow figs, mangoes, bananas, citrus, corn, grapes, and sugarcane.

First identified by Padre Julián de Mayorga as one of the early Jesuit mission sites in 1709, Misión San José de Comondú had several false starts, with its location and status changing from *visita* to mission and back again. Most ruins, including a stone church built in the 1750s, have been incorporated into newer buildings. San José has a small plaza lined with a number of historic stone and adobe buildings.

San Miguel has barrel gas, a post office, medical center, and limited groceries. At **Restaurant Oasis** (no tel., daily 8 A.M.–8 P.M. year-round, mains US$5–10), located a few meters south of the main plaza inside the owner's home, chef Martina serves regional dishes, or whatever she happens to have on hand—which amounted to tortillas, avocados, beans, tomatoes, and cheese on a recent visit. She knows the area well and gives reliable directions.

GETTING THERE

The easiest route to La Purísima, San Isidro, and Comondú follows a paved road north from Ciudad Insurgentes and ends a few kilometers before La Purísima. From there, you can get to San Isidro, but the unpaved road to Comondú has been impassable since Hurricane John blew through in 2006. You need to return to the paved road and look for the Comondú turn-off in Ejido Francisco Villa. This is a beautiful 40-minute drive through deep canyons, palm groves, and traditional ranchos. The unpaved road surface is suitable for just about any type of vehicle.

A more scenic (and shorter, but not faster) approach to La Purísima departs from Mexico 1 at a turnoff south of Bahía Concepción (Km 60). The branch that forks to Comondú is not recommended.

If you want to turn this side trip into a loop, you can head southeast from San José to San Javier and then on to Loreto; however, the road was in pretty bad shape as of 2009. The first 32 kilometers can take over 90 minutes due to rocks and holes, but the scenery is awesome. The last 20 kilometers improve considerably, for a total driving time of around two hours and 15 minutes.

Aguila buses travel once a day between Ciudad Insurgentes and La Purísima.

BAHÍA SAN JUANICO (SCORPION BAY)

Frequented primarily by diehard surfers, this off-the-grid bay on the Pacific coast provides access to half a dozen points that break in summer and winter swells. Novices and experienced surfers can often find suitable waves to ride, depending on the size of the swell and time of year.

Aside from a trickle of tourism revenue, fishing supports the local community. Electricity for the town comes from a combination of a diesel generator, solar power, and—in a 10-year pilot project—wind power. Services include gas, basic supplies, and an Internet café. A yoga studio called **The Jewel** holds classes twice a day for US$5 per class.

Accommodations and Food

About a 10-minute walk southwest of San Juanico, **Scorpion Bay Destination Surf Resort** (U.S. tel. 619/239-1335, www.scorpionbay.net) has a variety of accommodations. Camping is US$10 per person (free for children under age 7) and includes hot showers. *Palapas* with cots, sleeping bags, and private bathrooms for one or two people run US$45; larger three-person *palapas* cost US$60, and four-person *palapas* are US$75. Houses are available for US$150/250 per night (for up to four/eight people).

The resort has a restaurant that serves good and reasonably priced fish (US$11), burgers (US$4), and tacos (US$1.50). It's open daily 7:30 A.M.–10 P.M. You can use the Internet here for US$3 per half-hour, but it costs half that if you go into town instead.

On the main road in town, **Pizzeria Don Alakran** (no tel., mains US$5–10) is open sporadically.

Getting There

To get to San Juanico, follow a paved road out of Ciudad Insurgentes for 112 kilometers. The next 32 kilometers change to dirt and rocks, and the final 16 kilometers are paved again. You can also reach San Juanico from Laguna San Ignacio via a rough dirt road. This route takes about four hours.

LORETO AND BAHÍA MAGDALENA

Once considered just another coastal stop along the Transpeninsular Highway, Loreto has become a destination in its own right. The combination of a dramatic setting at the base of the Sierra de la Giganta and a protected marine park directly offshore facilitates a wide range of outdoor activities, from snorkeling and scuba diving to kayaking and mountain biking. With deep roots in Baja California history, Loreto serves as a gateway to the Spanish mission trail and mysterious prehistoric rock art sites located high in the sierra.

Designated for development as a government-sponsored tourist corridor in the 1970s, Loreto remained a sleepy sportfishing getaway until recently, when big-time real estate developers moved in with grand plans for a large-scale vacation community. But only a fraction of the resort has been completed to date, and compared to Los Cabos, Loreto remains relatively undiscovered.

In winter, whale-watching tours on the Pacific coast are popular excursions from Loreto-based resorts. Bahía Magdalena is one of only three places along the Pacific where you can watch gray whales up close, as they migrate into the shallow lagoon to care for their calves.

Loreto has a small international airport, a wide variety of accommodations, and a handful of good restaurants. As such, it makes an easy weekend getaway for travelers coming from the West Coast of the United States.

For diving and fishing, summer is the time to go. But temperatures are more moderate December–April. The region is quietest during the rainy season, August–November.

© PABLO NOBILI

LORETO AND BAHÍA MAGDALENA

HIGHLIGHTS

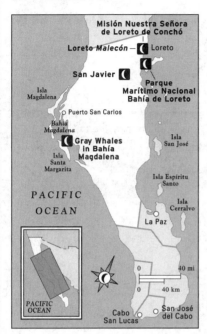

LOOK FOR ◖ TO FIND RECOMMENDED SIGHTS, ACTIVITIES, DINING, AND LODGING.

◖ **Misión Nuestra Señora de Loreto de Conchó:** Jesuit Padre Salvatierra founded the "mother of all California missions" in 1699, and visitors can tour the restored church on Loreto's town plaza (page 183).

◖ **Loreto *Malecón*:** Take a stroll along Loreto's waterfront promenade to see the sunrise, catch a breeze, or enjoy a seafood lunch with spectacular views (page 183).

◖ **Parque Marítimo Nacional Bahía de Loreto:** Mexico's largest marine preserve covers 2,000 square kilometers of the Sea of Cortez, including five major islands that are accessible from the town of Loreto (page 185).

◖ **San Javier:** One of the easiest side trips into Baja's mountainous interior is the winding road to San Javier, a former mission settlement with a beautifully restored church (page 195).

◖ **Gray Whales in Bahía Magdalena:** Gray whales frequent Bahía Magdalena in winter when they come to bear their calves in the lagoon; whale-watching tours and a traditional Mexican fiesta accompany the annual migration (page 198).

LORETO

LORETO

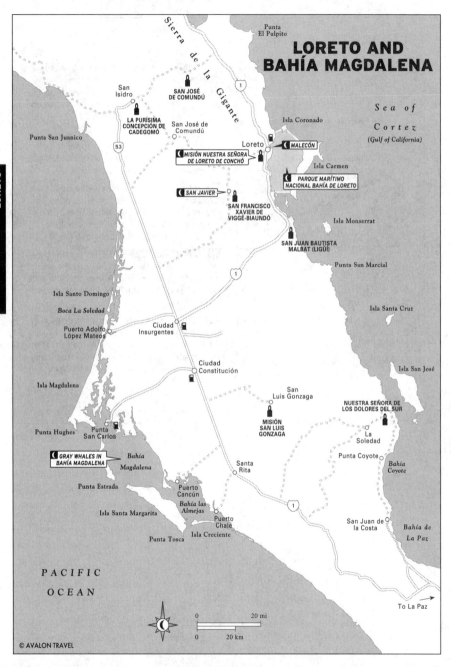

Loreto and Vicinity

For outdoor enthusiasts who would like to experience a little bit of history and culture, Loreto (pop. 15,000) makes an ideal home base. Fishing, kayaking, and diving here are all world-class; on land, town life centers around a historic plaza and mission church. With a newly restored lighthouse, Loreto's *malecón* is an attractive place to stroll. You won't have white-sand beaches, but with the National Marine Park offshore and the Sierra de la Giganta in the background to the west, the scenery is plenty dramatic.

Once sleepy Loreto has experienced a roller-coaster ride of changes in recent years. A venture between Fonatur and the American- and Canadian-owned Loreto Bay Company has changed hands several times in recent years, with Citibank and Replay Resorts the latest team to take control. Several years into the project, only a fraction of the homes have been delivered along a 27-kilometer coastal stretch, including **Nopoló** and **Puerto Escondido.** The company is far from attaining the vision put forth by the original developers. At last check, the workers' camps were empty, airlines had discontinued direct service to the local airport, and Loreto had become, once again, a quiet town with lots of appeal for independent, adventure-minded travelers.

Although the real estate market has slowed to a crawl, locals are optimistic that the town can now better prepare itself for growth and move forward with a better plan. Road and sidewalk improvements continue, with many streets torn up as of this writing. Finally, Loreto's first time-share salesperson has set up shop outside Café Ole, to the disappointment of many locals.

Beyond the town and Fonatur zones, more than 100 small ranching settlements and fishing communities remain much as they have always been.

LORETO

COURTESY OF THE LORETO BAY COMPANY

tennis courts at Nopoló

LORETO

HISTORY

Loreto holds a distinctive place in Baja California history as the site of the first permanent Jesuit mission and later as the first state capital. Its story begins with the arrival of an Italian Jesuit named Padre Juan María de Salvatierra on October 19, 1697. The Spanish had tried unsuccessfully for the preceding 167 years to establish a Baja California settlement. In a privately funded expedition conceived by Salvatierra and Padre Eusebio Kino, Salvatierra sailed from Sonora with a party of 10, landed at a place the indigenous people called Conchó and renamed it Loreto, in honor of his chosen patroness, Our Lady of Loreto. Ever the

optimist, Salvatierra prevailed where others had failed because of his prior mission experience on the mainland, boundless energy, and deep commitment. He stayed in Loreto for 20 years, developing the mission into a base of expansion throughout the peninsula and the capital of Spanish California. When Spain expelled the Jesuits from the peninsula in 1767, the padres gathered in Loreto to await their fate. Franciscan Padre Junípero Serra, who would go on to establish the first Alta California mission, arrived in Loreto a few months later with 15 Franciscan padres.

Loreto served as the religious, civil, and military capital of both Alta and Baja California

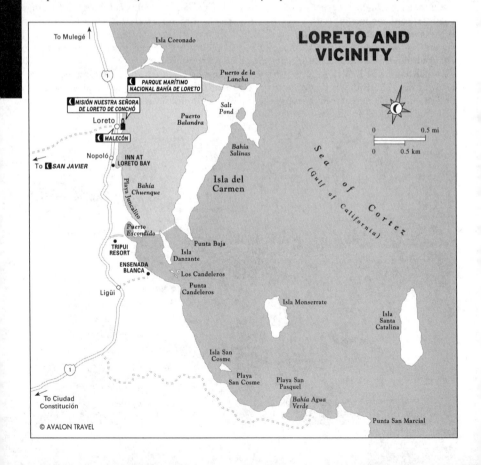

until 1776, when Monterey became the new capital. In 1829, a hurricane wiped out most of the town, prompting officials to move the regional government to La Paz. By the 1850s, the mission era had come to a close, and the town was left in ruins.

Loreto was forgotten until some Mexicans discovered its commercial fishing potential in the early 1900s. Soon after, adventurous fly-in anglers began to visit from the United States.

Present-day Loreto trace its roots to the completion of the Transpeninsular Highway in 1973. And about 60,000 tourists now visit Loreto each year. In 2008, Loreto voted in a new mayor from the left-wing PRD party, Professor Yuan Yee Cunningham, who intends to focus his administration on the needs of children and improving education.

SIGHTS
(Misión Nuestra Señora de Loreto de Conchó

Several days after landing at Conchó, Padre Salvatierra and his team erected a tent next to a wooden cross on the mesa above the arroyo where they had landed and placed the Virgen de Loreto inside. This became the first place of worship for the expedition and its converts. The settlers began to build their first permanent church in 1699, outside the walls of the presidio compound, and completed it in 1704. The building was enlarged in the 1740s to accommodate a growing population. The church survived the 1829 hurricane, as well as a devastating earthquake in 1877.

After several restorations and the addition of a bell tower in the 20th century, the church hosts regular worship services today. An inscription over the front doors to the church reads "The Head and Mother of the Missions of Baja and Alta California," with the mission founding date of October 25, 1697. The original Virgen de Loreto sits in a side room and is dressed in a new gown each year. The church also features a gilded altar restored from the mission era.

Next to the church, the tiny **Museo de los Misiónes** (tel. 613/135-0441, Tues.–Sun.

9 A.M.–1 P.M. and 1:45–6 P.M., US$4) has exhibits on life before the Spanish conquest, including arrowheads, carved volcanic stones, and large kettles made of copper and iron.

Plaza Salvatierra

The cobblestone plaza that extends southwest of the church is named for Padre Salvatierra, and a bronze bust of him sits in the center of the plaza, facing the front doors of the church. Several gift shops, restaurants, banks, and government offices border the plaza, including Loreto's city hall and tourism office.

(Malecón

Though not as impressive as its counterpart in La Paz, Loreto sports a pleasant, tree-lined waterfront promenade that runs the length of Boulevard López Mateos, connecting about 10 blocks between the marina and Hotel Oasis. This is the place for a sunrise stroll, or to catch a breeze on a hot and sticky afternoon. The west side of the street is lined with a handful of restaurants, inns, and private residences.

Nopoló and Puerto Escondido

Loreto counts itself among Cancún, Huatulco, Ixtapa, and Los Cabos as a coastal region designated by the Mexican government for development as a tourist corridor. To date, most of the development activity has focused on Nopoló, located eight kilometers south of Loreto, which now has a hotel, tennis center, golf course, and residential area—all connected by a network of wide, palm-lined boulevards with curbs (an unusual sight in much of Baja).

Over the years, various commercial entities have partnered with Fonatur in attempting to profit from Loreto's real estate opportunity. In 2008, Citibank and Canada-based Replay Resorts took the reins after the Loreto Bay Company and then a Spanish concern named Fedesa both turned their backs on the area after delivering only a few hundred homes. The Loreto Bay Company's plans had called for the building of 6,000 homes on both sides of Mexico 1. Development on this scale would likely be a mixed blessing. It remains to be seen

LORETO

LORETO

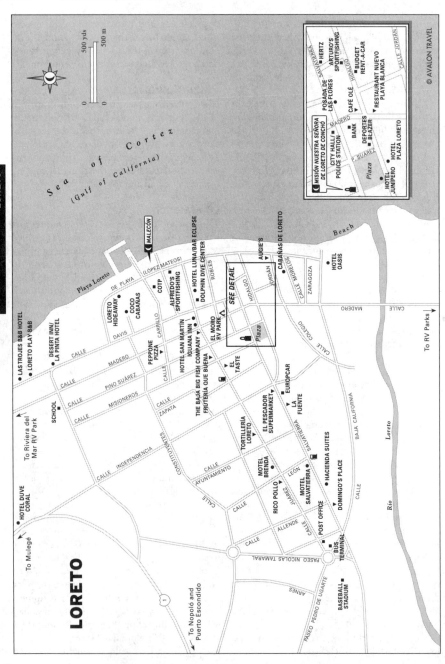

LORETO

Sea of Cortez
(Gulf of California)

Beach

Playa Loreto

MALECÓN

SEE DETAIL

Plaza

SEE DETAIL

MISIÓN NUESTRA SEÑORA
DE LORETO DE CONCHÓ

CITY HALL
POLICE STATION

POSADA DE
LAS FLORES

ARTURO'S
SPORTFISHING

HERTZ

CAFÉ OLÉ

BUDGET
RENT-A-CAR

BANK

RESTAURANT NUEVO
PLAYA BLANCA

DEPORTES
BLAZER

HOTEL
JUNÍPERO

HOTEL
PLAZA LORETO

CALLE JORDAN
HIDALGO
MADERO
P. SUÁREZ
Plaza

© AVALON TRAVEL

LAS TROJES B&B HOTEL
LORETO PLAY B&B

DESERT INN/
LA PINTA HOTEL

LORETO
HIDEAWAY

COCO
CABAÑAS

COTP

ALFREDO'S
SPORTFISHING

HOTEL LUNA/BAR ECLIPSE

DOLPHIN DIVE CENTER

CABAÑAS DE LORETO

AUGIE'S

HOTEL
OASIS

(LÓPEZ MATEOS)

DE PLAYA

CARRILLO

ROBLES

HIDALGO

JORDAN

CALLE MORELOS

ZARAGOZA

CALLE MADERO

To RV Parks

PEPPONE
PIZZA

HOTEL SAN MARTIN

IGUANA INN

EL MORO
RV PARK

THE BAJA BIG FISH COMPANY

FRUTERÍA QUE BUENA

EL
TASTE

EUROPCAR

LA
FUENTE

CALLE COLEGIO

DAVIS

CALLE MADERO

PINO SUÁREZ

MISIONEROS

CALLE ZAPATA

SCHOOL

EL PESCADOR
SUPERMARKET

TORTILLERÍA
LORETO

MOTEL
BRENDA

RICO POLLO

MOTEL
SALVATIERRA

HACIENDA SUITES

DOMINGO'S PLACE

POST OFFICE

BUS
TERMINAL

BASEBALL
STADIUM

CALLE CONSTITUYENTES

CALLE INDEPENDENCIA

CALLE AYUNTAMIENTO

CALLE

CALLE

ALLENDE

CALLE SALVATIERRA

LEÓN

CALLE

BAJA CALIFORNIA

Río

Loreto

PASEO NICOLÁS TAMARAL

ARNÉS

PASEO PEDRO DE UGARTE

To Riviera del
Mar RV Park

HOTEL DUVE
CORAL

To Mulegé

To Nopolo and
Puerto Escondido

500 yds
500 m

500 yds
500 m

© PAUL ITOI

harbor at Puerto Escondido

whether the stated goal of creating a sustainable community can be met.

The same streetlamps and curbs that are found in Nopoló line the road to Puerto Escondido, where a few older boats are moored in the protected harbor. Here, as in La Paz, Fonatur has completed a three-story gray/green building to house the marina operations.

◖ Parque Marítimo Nacional Bahía de Loreto

More than 2,000 square kilometers of waters offshore from Loreto comprise Mexico's largest marine preserve. Extending 60 kilometers from **Isla Coronado** in the north to **Isla Catalán** in the south, the Parque Marítimo Nacional Bahía de Loreto (Loreto Bay National Marine Park) is part of the federal Sistema Nacional de Areas Protegidas (SINAP), which prohibits trawling and commercial netting for 35–47 kilometers offshore along the length of the park. Five islands within the park are accessible by boat from Loreto: Coronado, Carmen, Danzante, Monserrate, and Santa Catalina.

Primer Agua

South of Loreto, an old palm oasis makes a pleasant spot for a picnic or starting point for a hike. Look for a turnoff at Km 114 on Mexico 1 and follow the graded dirt road 6.5 kilometers to the Arroyo de San Javier. Fonatur grows plants here to use in nearby real estate developments. There are picnic tables and grills available.

SPORTS AND RECREATION

Loreto offers outdoor enthusiasts a rare combination of desert, water, and mountain activities, all of which you can pursue independently or through an experienced outfitter.

Boating

Loreto offers easy access to a string of islands offshore, including Isla del Carmen (18 km from Loreto, 8 km from Puerto Escondido) with several pleasant beaches. Arrange for a *panga* through any hotel that offers fishing trips or at the harbor at the north end of the *malecón*. To launch your own small boat, head to the north end of the *malecón,* the Loreto

Shores Villa and RV Park, or Playa Juncalito or Puerto Escondido, south of Loreto. Larger boats should anchor at the deeper and protected marina at Puerto Escondido. Boat launch fees run US$3 for Loreto (through the port captain's office) and US$13 for Puerto Escondido.

The port captain's offices are located in Loreto (tel. 613/133-0656, fax 613/133-0465, VHF radio channel 16) and at Puerto Escondido.

Kayaking

From Loreto, you can easily paddle to Isla Coronado or the north end of Isla Carmen. Puerto Escondido is a better starting point for the trip to the southern or eastern shores of Isla Carmen, Isla Danzante, and Los Candeleros. Advanced kayakers might attempt to paddle all the way to Isla Monserrate or Isla Santa Catalina.

Loreto Kayak Tours (U.S. tel. 707/942-4550 or 800/398-6200, www.tourbaja.com), also called Paddling South, is a Loreto-based operation with variety of multiday trips. Co-founders Trudi Angell and Douglas Knapp have been leading trips since 1983. Trudi graduated from the National Outdoor Leadership School (NOLS) Baja course, while Doug has sailed the Sea of Cortez in a catamaran. They also organize mountain biking, horseback riding, and sailing trips.

As a safety measure, the Loreto port captain asks kayakers to file a float plan for any overnight paddling trip.

Diving

Divers visit Loreto to explore rock reefs, seamounts, underwater caves, and a few wrecks around five nearby islands (Carmen, Coronado, Danzante, Monserrate and Catalina). These waters support some 800 species, including dolphins, whales, sea lions, sea turtles, giant mantas, hammerheads, dorado, roosterfish, yellowfin tuna, and even seasonal whale sharks. Water temperatures can exceed 27°C in summer and fall, dropping to 20–23°C in winter and spring. Visibility typically exceeds 50 15 meters and can reach 30 meters on the best of days.

Several shops lead guided dive trips and offer equipment rentals and instruction. Conveniently located a half-block from the marina, **Dolphin Dive Center** (Juárez btw Davis/Mateos, tel. 613/135-1914, www.dolphindivebaja.com) is a PADI shop that leads dive tours and courses. Two-tank boat trips cost US$99–120, depending on which island you choose to visit. Rinse stations for gear and cameras and a secure room for overnight drying minimize the number of times you'll have to lug your gear across town. This outfitter also offers a special night dive to view the nearly-two-meter-long Humboldt squid, which migrates through the area in summer and early fall. These unusual underwater adventures take place in a protective cage with surface-supplied air, and cost US$200.

Arturo's Sportfishing (tel. 613/135-0766, www.arturosport.com) runs dive trips aboard a fleet of 12 *pangas* equipped with oxygen, radios, first aid, cell phone, shade, and fish finders. Boats leave at 9 A.M. Dive-and-stay packages are available at the La Pinta, Sukasa, and El Dorado hotels. Located in the Hotel Junipero, **Cormorant Dive Center** (Hidalgo at Misioneros, tel. 613/135-2140, www.loretours.com) runs dive trips to Coronado, Carmen, and Danzante islands (US$95–115), as well as SSI Discover Scuba classes and whale-watching tours.

Fishing

Anglers know Loreto first and foremost for its summer dorado catch. A number of other game fish (yellowtail, marlin, roosterfish, yellowfin tuna, cabrilla, grouper, and sailfish) are also abundant—though less so these days than in decades past. Loreto-based fishing charters visit the islands offshore for shelter from wind and to access a variety of fishing environments. A day of fishing typically begins with a 6 A.M. departure from the marina, returning in the early afternoon.

Many hotels in town arrange fishing trips and offer activity packages that include

GUIDED TOUR COSTS AT A GLANCE

GUIDED DIVE AND SNORKEL TOURS

Snorkel trip .... US$55
Two-tank dive to Coronado Island .... US$80–90
Carmen Island .... US$100
Danzante Island .... US$110
Las Ánimas .... US$200 (5 divers min.)
Extra tank .... US$45
Night dive .... US$65
Discover scuba course .... US$110–150
Open water certification .... US$400
Advanced certification .... US$250
Scuba rental package .... US$30

OTHER GUIDED TOURS

San Javier Mission .... US$120
Cave paintings .... US$115
Whale-watching .... US$120

accommodations. With more than 25 years of experience, **Arturo's Sport Fishing** (Hidalgo, tel. 613/135-0766, www.arturosport.com) has a staff of 20 and fleet of 17 boats. In 2008, it purchased new motors for its boats, upgraded its radio system, and added two new super-*pangas* to the lineup. Current prices for a day of fishing in a standard *panga* are US$170 for up to three anglers. Super-*pangas* run US$400 for four people, and cruisers run US$700 for four people. Hotel Oasis also has its own fleet and serves an early breakfast at 5 A.M. Its prices include fish filleting, vacuum packing, freezing, and taxes.

Record-setters bring their catch to **The Baja Big Fish Company** (tel. 613/135-1603, www.bajabigfish.com), Loreto's official IGFA weighing station, on Juárez, two blocks from the waterfront. Baja Big Fish leads conventional and fly-fishing trips in small groups. *Panga* fishing costs US$240 for up to two anglers, US$270–300 for up to three in a super- or deluxe super-*panga*. Half-day rates are US$150 for a standard *panga* and US$170 for a super-*panga*. This outfit also rents fly-fishing gear for US$30.

Based at the Tripui Trailer Park, **Jose Torres Fishing Charters** (tel. 613/104-4030, www.loreto.com/josetorres) is run by a local fisherman who takes anglers, divers, and snorkelers out on a fleet of three *pangas*.

Golf

After many years of neglect, the 18-hole **Campo de Golf Loreto** (Blvd. Misión San Ignacio, Nopoló, tel. 613/133-0788) is in good condition at last. Greens fees are US$58 for 18 holes, or US$40 for nine holes. An electric cart costs US$36, pull carts are US$15, and Nike clubs rent for US$30.

Guided Tours

Most of the outfitters that specialize in one activity also dabble in the others, so if you like your boat crew, you can probably go with the same shop to see the cave paintings or the gray whales. Most trips require a minimum of two or three people.

In addition to overnight paddling expeditions, **Loreto Kayak Tours** (U.S. tel. 707/942-4550 or 800/398-6200, www.tourbaja.com) offers multiday horseback, mountain biking, and sailing trips, as well as combination trips.

You can see San Javier by ATV tour through **Cormorant Dive Center/Loretours** (Hidalgo at Misoneros, tel. 613/135-2140, www.loretours.com, US$90). This outfitter also has

Mongoose bikes for guided trips to San Javier (US$123) and Primer Agua (US$55).

Desert and Sea Expeditions (Paseo Hidalgo btw Colegio/Suarez, tel. 613/135-1979, www.desertandsea.com) leads trips to San Javier, local cave painting sites, Pacific and Gulf-side whale-watching, and Coronado Island.

Once a year in April, May, or November, travel photographer Jim Cline leads a **Wonders of Baja** photo tour (U.S. tel. 877/350-1314, www.jimcline.com) of La Paz, Loreto, Mulege, Todos Santos, and Cabo San Lucas, including three boat trips to islands on the Sea of Cortez. Participants get to try their hand at capturing the seascapes, cacti, historic missions, and wildlife through the lens of their camera. Tours include accommodations and seafood dinners.

Spas

A spa has opened on the lower level of the **Hotel Posada de las Flores** (tel. 613/135-1162, U.S./Canada tel. 877/245-2860, www.posadadelasflores.com), offering massage therapy, facials, and manicures/pedicures.

SHOPPING

A handful of shops line the streets surrounding the plaza, with handicrafts, silver jewelry, home furnishings, and Mexican-style apparel for sale. In many of these stores, prices for crafts are about two or three times higher than for the same items elsewhere in Baja. In general, shop hours can vary by season and sometimes at the owner's whim.

In front of the mission, **La Casa de la Abuela** (no tel.) sells an assortment of handicrafts in a building as old as the mission itself (1744). **Artesanías Colibrí** (Salvatierra at Independencia, no tel.) carries a nice selection of ceramics, jewelry, maps, and handicrafts.

A retired school teacher from New Mexico, Jeannine Perez, opened **El Caballo Blanco** (Paseo Hidalgo 19 at Madero, no tel., jeannine1220@yahoo.com, Mon.–Sat. 9 A.M.–7 P.M.) in 2005 with thousands of used books, plus new Baja titles and art supplies for sale. Jeannine has published a personal account of Loreto history, sights, and attractions, including her own sketches.

The Baja Big Fish Company (tel. 613/135-1603, www.bajabigfish.com, Mon.–Sat. 9 A.M.–5 P.M.) on Juárez, two blocks from the waterfront, carries a wide selection of flies, plus leaders and lines. Credit cards are accepted.

One block west of the mission, **El Alacrán** (Salvatierra at Misioneros, tel. 613/135-0029) is a fine art gallery and gift shop with ironworks, jewelry, sculptures, and paintings.

Run by a young couple, Miguel and Manika, **La Biznaga** (Salvatierra 10, tel. 613/135-0961, Tues.–Sun.) is a hybrid business offering reasonably priced gifts and clothes, coffee and beer, and inexpensive bike rentals.

ENTERTAINMENT AND EVENTS
Bars

The majority of nightlife spots in Loreto are sports bars, where expats and Mexicans alike gather to watch American football and international soccer games. An open *palapa* bar on the second story of the Hotel Luna, **Bar Eclipse** (Vizcaíno btw Davis/Mateos, tel. 613/135-2288, www.hotellunaloreto.com, Wed.–Sun. 7 P.M.–midnight, Fri.–Sat. till 1 A.M.) has a 42-inch plasma screen for viewing sports events. Enjoy cocktails and espresso drinks while taking in sea and mountain views. On the same block, next to the Dolphin Dive Center, **Giggling Dolphin** (Juárez btw Calle Davis and the *malecón,* no tel.) is one of the newer establishments in town, with a bar made out of a converted boat.

You can play a round of pool over drinks at **Jarros & Tarros** (Paseo Hidalgo near Madero, no tel., daily 6 P.M.–2 A.M.).

Augie's Bar and Bait Shop (Blvd. López Mateos, tel. 613/135-1224, mains US$5–10), near the south end of the *malecón,* offers a menu of soup, salads, and burgers, as well as fresh fish and seafood dishes. Air-conditioning in the main room is a plus on hot summer days, and the second-story deck offers prime views of the bay. Augie's recently took over the space next door, formerly occupied by the Santa Lucia Café. The owners of the now-closed Santa Lucia Café have opened a new venture, **Las Mandiles Restaurant** (on the *malecón,* tel. 615/135-1846, Wed.–Mon. 8 A.M.–11 P.M.) that has live music on Saturday nights.

Festivals and Events
The **Loreto Dorado International Fishing Tournament** takes place each June. Loreto celebrates the **Virgin de Loreto** with music, food, and dancing on the first weekend of September and the **founding of the city** in the last week of October.

ACCOMMODATIONS AND CAMPING
Most visitors choose downtown Loreto for their home base in this area for access to a wide variety of travel services; however, there are a few options south of town if you don't mind the drive.

Loreto offers budget travelers several convenient options, and for those who seek a few more amenities, a number of moderately priced hotels and bed-and-breakfasts are scattered throughout the area. Some have sea views, and almost all are within walking distance of the marina, shops, and restaurants. Vacation rentals are another option as more homes come on the market.

Hotels
UNDER US$50
Rooms are barebones at the **Hotel San Martín** (Juárez 14 btw Madero/Davis near the plaza, tel. 613/135-0442, US$25) but they do come with floor fans and private bathrooms. A slight step up, the 12 rooms at **Hotel Junípero** (Hidalgo near the mission, tel. 613/135-0122, US$40) have ceiling fans, hot showers, and double beds; some rooms also have TVs.

A better deal for the price are the eight rooms at **El Moro RV Park** (Rosinda Robles 8, tel. 613/135-0542, www.loreto.com/elmoro, US$45) which include air-conditioning, off-street parking, and cable TV.

North of town, Mexican-owned **Duve**

Coral Hotel (Independencia at Arcoiris, Col. El Jaral, tel. 613/135-1037, www.duvecoral. com, US$39) has 16 doubles and 14 singles in a two-story building with satellite TV and secure parking.

US$50-100
Next door to the Hotel San Martín, **Iguana Inn** (Juárez btw Madero/Davis, tel. 613/135-1627, www.iguanainn.com, US$48–59) has four bungalows, each with its own kitchenette, two queen beds, and a large tiled shower. Rates include tax.

Hotel Plaza Loreto (Paseo Hidalgo 2, tel. 613/135-0280, www.loreto.com/hotelplaza, US$62) occupies a two-story, neocolonial building one block from the mission church. Its 29 rooms have hot water, air-conditioning, Internet, and cable TV; a small restaurant/bar is on-site.

Hotel Luna (Vizcaíno btw Davis/Mateos, tel. 613/135-2288, www.hotellunaloreto.com, US$65) has three minimally furnished rooms with queen beds, cable TV, and Wi-Fi in a convenient location.

Sukasa (corner of Paseo López Mateos and Calle Jordán, tel. 613/135-0490, www. loreto.com/sukasa, US$75), on the *malecón,* has two bungalows in a brick duplex and a main house with one bedroom and two baths. Units are furnished with king-size beds, air-conditioning, TV/VCR (Spanish channels only), and basic cooking equipment. No pool, satellite, phone, or Internet. Daily maid service is a plus.

American-owned ◖ **Coco Cabañas** (Davis 71, tel. 613/135-1729, www.coco-cabanas.com, US$70) consists of a group of well-built cottages set around a pool. Thick walls and airtight windows block the sound of wind, dogs, and roosters in the residential surroundings. Cottages come with air-conditioning, hot water, a small TV, and the best kitchenettes we've seen anywhere in Baja; new and spotless appliances include a blender, and there's matching dishware and ice cubes already made from purified water. Bathrooms are tiny but clean and functional. Beds on metal frames are a little squishy. Hand-painted vines over doorways add a nice touch. Inside the gated compound are a small swimming pool and barbecue area. It's a five-minute walk to the waterfront. Rates include tax.

At the beginning of the main drag through town, a bit far from the beach, **Hacienda Suites** (Salvatierra 152, tel. 800/224-3632, U.S. tel. 866/207-8732, fax 613/135-0202, www.haciendasuites.com, US$79) is a modern hotel with rooms set around a central courtyard and swimming pool. Amenities include air-conditioning, phones, TVs, minibars, and in-room safes. Parking is secure, and the hotel offers Wi-Fi. Rooms come with breakfast.

At **La Damiana Inn** (Madero btw Hidalgo/ Fco. Jordan, www.ladamianainn.com, US$62–75), owners Debora and Gerardo maintain six guestrooms, each with a large private shower. There is an outdoor kitchen and garden/patio area that dates back to the 1930s. Wi-Fi and secure parking are a plus; on the downside, the location can be noisy.

North along the waterfront, on Calle Davis, the **Desert Inn** (formerly La Pinta Hotel, tel. 613/135-0025 or 800/026-3605, U.S. tel. 800/800-9632, www.lapintahotels.com, US$79) offers large, air-conditioned rooms with terraces and views of the sea.

One row back from the waterfront at the southern edge of town, ▌ **Las Cabañas de Loreto** (Morelos off the *malecón,* tel. 613/135-1105, U.S. tel. 707/933-0764, www.lascabanasdeloreto.com, US$95) has four modern studios set around a small pool with comfy chaise lounges and hammocks. You can prepare simple meals in the kitchenette inside, or use the outdoor kitchen and barbecue to grill your fresh catch. The main house, also available for rent, has an ocean view from the upstairs deck; studios have garden views. A new casita was also available at last check. This place fills up well in advance; check availability online and make reservations. Studios have TV/VCR, air conditioning, free Wi-Fi, and secure off-street parking, but no satellite or phones. There's a three-night minimum.

US$100-150

A perennial favorite within the sportfishing community, **Hotel Oasis** (at the south end of Calle de la Playa/Blvd. López Mateos, tel. 613/135-0211, U.S. tel. 800/497-3923, www.hoteloasis.com, US$115–144) is the only hotel in town that has its own brown-sand beach. For anglers, the best part about a stay here is that breakfast service begins at 5 A.M. The 39 air-conditioned rooms are large but minimally furnished and not well lighted. Some rooms were freshly painted with older bath fixtures. Bright orange cotton bedspreads cover sagging mattresses. Other properties in town offer more modern accommodations at a lower price. Naturally, the Oasis has its own fishing fleet, as well as a pool, tennis court, free Wi-Fi, and a swing set for kids.

US$150-250

For elegant accommodations in a historic setting, the **Hotel Posada de las Flores** (tel. 613/135-1162, U.S. tel. 877/245-2860, www.posadadelasflores.com, US$150–180) can't be beat. Housed in a colonial building on Plaza Salvatierra, the inn has a rooftop pool with a glass bottom through which sunlight shines into the lobby below. Its 15 rooms contain antique furnishings, pottery, tile, and wrought iron from the mainland. Amenities include air-conditioning, satellite TV, wireless Internet, and a spa on the ground floor (Tues.–Sun. 9 A.M.–5 P.M.).

Loreto's newest luxury hotel, **La Mision** (Rosendo Robles, tel. 613/135-0524, U.S. tel. 877/887-2939, www.lamisionloreto.com, US$160–250) has 65 rooms and three two-bedroom suites with marble baths, flat-screen TVs, and shaded patios. Mountain view rooms face the Sierra de la Giganta, while ocean view rooms look out on the Sea of Cortez.

Bed-and-Breakfasts

Six blocks north of Plaza Salvatierra and beyond the Desert Inn, **Las Trojes Bed & Breakfast Hotel** (Davis Norte, tel. 613/135-0277, www.loreto.com/costa2.htm, US$50) offers guests a unique opportunity to sleep in converted Native American granaries that the owner originally found in the mountainous interior of the mainland state of Michoacán, transported to La Paz, and reassembled on the beach in Loreto. Amenities include air-conditioning, ceiling fans, and private showers, as well as free bicycles and Internet access. you can stroll through the cactus garden to reach the beach bar and waterfront. Rates include continental breakfast.

At the north end of the *malecón,* **Loreto Playa Bed and Breakfast** (tel. 613/135-1129, www.loretoplaya.com, US$145–195) has two suites and a beach house for rent. Accommodations come with king-size beds, bubble bath, and robes; the use of mountain bikes and kayaks; and a full breakfast.

Vacation Rentals

As new homes are constructed, a few have come on the market as vacation rentals. For example, **Stay in Loreto** (tel. 613/135-0791, www.stayinloreto.com, US$800–900/wk) manages a beachfront condo, house, and suite for weekly or monthly rentals. The newly constructed properties are located 30 meters from the water, with granite counters, seaview decks, satellite TV, and air-conditioning. **La Giganta Real Estate** (Madero 22-C, tel. 613/135-0802, www.lagiganta.com) manages a few vacation rentals in the area.

Nopoló and Puerto Escondido

For some longtime Loreto expats, poking fun at the real estate development underway in Nopoló is serious sport. But though they may have mixed feelings about the building of a 6,000-unit community, many would gladly trade beaches with the **Inn at Loreto Bay** (formerly the Camino Real, tel. 613/133-0010 or 800/507-6979, U.S. tel. 866/850-0333, www.innatloretobay.com, US$135–330). Here, guests can choose from 155 oceanfront and ocean-view rooms, all with Wi-Fi, set around a lawn and pool. New curtains and modern bathrooms make for cheerful decor, but beds are sagging; this remains a 20-year-old hotel in need of a more complete makeover. You can

book trips and rent gear for the water sport of your choice from the hotel. The **Loreto Bay Restaurant** serves breakfast 7–11 A.M., snacks, and dinner 7–10:30 P.M. Bordering the grounds are an 18-hole golf course and the Centro Tenístico de Loreto, both free for guests.

In Puerto Escondido, **Tripui Resort** (tel. 613/133-0818, U.S. tel. 512/749-6070, www.tripui.com) has a few overnight slots with hook-ups for US$17 a night for two people. This resort has a boat launch, boat storage space, pool, restaurant, laundry service, bar, and grocery store.

Camping and RV Parks

The most centrally located (and presumably one of the noisiest) option for camping is **El Moro RV Park** (Rosinda Robles 8, tel. 613/135-0542) with full hookups for US$15 per day. Stay seven nights and you'll get one night free. Hot showers are open to non-guests for US$2. El Moro also offers fishing packages.

Also close to town and near the beach, **Rivera del Mar RV Park and Camping** (Madero Norte 100, 613/135-0718, www.riveradelmar.com, US$16–18) has 25 spaces with full hookups and limited shade, plus showers, hot water, laundry, and grills. Tent camping costs US$5. This park allows pets as long as they are leashed. The atmosphere tends to be very noisy at night, especially on weekends.

South of town on the other side of the Río Loreto, **Loreto Shores Villas and RV Park** (Colonia Zaragoza, tel. 613/135-1513, www.loretoshoresvillasandrvpark.com, US$26) has 36 spaces with full hookups enclosed within a five-acre park that fronts the beach; tent camping costs US$7 per person, and includes hot showers. Wi-Fi is available for US$2 per day. Every seventh day is free. Loreto Shores has a pool, laundry service, boat launch, and *palapas* on the beach.

You can camp for free at Playa Juncalito, 22.5 kilometers south of Loreto, and the snorkeling is also good here. Look for sign on the highway.

LORETO

FOOD

Loreto's restaurants are mostly casual places that serve a variety of Mexican specialties. Seafood and steak find their way onto just about every menu.

Mexican

Though it changed names recently from El Nido to **Domingo's Place** (Salvatierra 154 at Independencia, tel. 613/104-4016, daily for breakfast, lunch, and dinner) this restaurant continues to serve tasty grilled steaks, as well as lobster, shrimp, and fish specialties. The back patio is a highlight of dining here.

Rib eye is the house specialty at **El Taste** (Juárez at Zapata, tel. 613/135-1489, mains US$20), across from the Pemex on Juárez.

La Terraza (tel. 613/135-0496, 1–10 P.M. daily), above Café Olé, overlooks Plaza Salvatierra. Order the house special if you go: grilled steaks of fresh Sonoran beef (US$10).

Under the same ownership as Domingo's, casual **La Palapa** (Paseo Hidalgo close to the *malecón,* tel. 613/135-0284, daily 1–11 P.M., mains US$7–15) burned down in 2008 but quickly reopened in its same location. Locals praise the restaurant for good seafood and Mexican dishes and great service.

Mediterraneo (López Mateos at Hidalgo, tel. 613/135-2577, www.mediterraneo-loreto.com, Tues.–Sun. 6–10 P.M., mains US$10–15) is a second-story restaurant on the *malecón,* just north of Avenida Salvatierra. It serves high-end Mexican cuisine, as well as steaks and paellas.

International

Pachamama (Zapata 3, tel. 613/135-2219, daily 5–10 P.M., mains US$7–15) is the place to sample authentic empanadas, grilled sweet peppers, thick grilled steaks, and other fare from Argentina. Credit cards are accepted.

Two restaurants in town have adopted a Spanish theme: On the plaza, **1697** (Davis 13, tel. 613/135-2538, Tues.–Sun. 6–10 P.M., mains US$10–15) does Spanish cuisine with an Italian twist. Every fourth Thursday, the menu rotates to a different cuisine. **Bar de Tapas** (Madero at Salvatierra, no tel.) specializes in small plates.

a typical Mexican platter of meat or fish, rice, beans, and tortillas

COURTESY OF WWW.DISCOVERBAJACALIFORNIA.COM

Readers recommend Mexican-owned, up-scale **Mita Gourmet** (Davis 13, tel. 613/135-2035, www.mitagourmet.com, mains US$7–15), across from the city hall building on the plaza. It specializes in seafood dishes (fish with garlic is a favorite), and hosts live guitar music most nights.

Antojitos, Tacos, and Fast Food

When it comes to fish tacos, the efficient husband-and-wife team who now run **El Rey del Taco** (no tel., mains US$5–7) have won the hearts of many a Loreto regular—some of whom place their orders before they fly into town, in case the place is closed when they arrive. Located on the south side of Juárez near the Pemex, El Rey gets high marks for *tacos de cabeza* as well as *pescado.* Those in the know say the fastest way to get your tacos is to sit down at a table, rather than waiting at the window. El Rey is open from 9 A.M. until whenever the food runs out, usually by 2 P.M.

Another longtime favorite for quick, inexpensive snacks, **McLulu's** (Salvatierra west of Colegio, no tel., daily 10 A.M.–6 P.M.) prepares *tacos de carne asada, tacos de guisado,* homemade chorizo, and *picadillo* (spicy meat-and-chili salad). The once-legendary fish tacos

FISH TRANSLATOR

albacore tuna – *albacora*
barracuda – *picuda*
black sea bass – *mero prieto*
bluefin tuna – *atún de aleta azul*
blue marlin – *marlín azul*
dolphinfish (mahimahi) – *dorado*
grouper (generic) – *garropa*
halibut – *lenguado*
hammerhead shark – *cornuda*
jack crevalle – *toro*
ladyfish – *sabalo*
mackerel – *sierra, makerela*
manta ray – *manta*
marbled scorpionfish – *cabezón*
octopus – *pulpo*
Pacific amberjack – *pez fuerte*
perch (generic) – *mojarra*
pompano – *palometa*
puffer (generic) – *bolete*
red snapper – *pargo*
roosterfish – *papagallo, pez gallo*

sailfish – *pez vela*
sea bass (cabrilla) – *cabrilla*
shark (generic) – *tiburón*
shark (small) – *cazón*
snook – *robalo*
squid – *calamar*
stingray (generic) – *raya*
striped marlin – *marlín rayado*
swordfish – *pez espada*
triggerfish – *cochi*
tuna – *atún*
wahoo – *sierra wahoo, peto*
whale shark – *pez sapo*
white sea bass – *corvina blanca*
yellowfin tuna – *atún de aleta; amarilla*
yellowtail – *jurel*

Pez is the generic word for fish. Once fish has been caught and is ready for cooking (or has been cooked), it's called *pescado*.

were on the soggy side last time we tried them. Three tacos and a soda cost US$5.

Tiny **Rico Pollo** (Juárez at Márquez de León, no tel., daily 8 A.M.–9 P.M., mains US$5) serves tasty grilled chicken.

Cafés

On the plaza, **Café Olé** (Madero 14, tel. 613/135-0495, Mon.–Sat. 8 A.M.–10 P.M., mains US$3–6) is a Loreto institution, where expats and visitors gather to dine on reasonably priced breakfast and lunch fare while watching the world go by. Seafood omelets and freshly squeezed orange juice highlight the morning menu; lunch fare includes tacos, burgers, ice cream, and the like. Check the community bulletin board for rentals, sales, and other local information.

A relatively new option for café culture is air-conditioned **Sea Coffee,** near Augie's on the *malecón* (no tel., 7 A.M.–2 P.M. and 4–7 P.M. daily).

El Mejicano (on Misioneros north of Juarez, no tel.) has the best cold treats in town, including *paletas, agua frescas,* and *nieve.*

Groceries

El Pescador, on Avenida Salvatierra, is Loreto's largest grocery store. Locals prefer to shop at the smaller but less expensive and cleaner **Chuco's** (on Madero, opposite her husband's hardware store). A government-subsidized **Tienda ISSSTE** (Mon.–Sat. 8 A.M.–8 P.M., Sun. 8 A.M.–2 P.M.) is located on Madero, north of the plaza.

Stock up on fresh tortillas and Mexican pastries at **Tortillería Loreto** (Juárez btw Ayuntamiento/Independencia). On Sunday mornings, there is a farmers market on Zaragossa.

South of Loreto

Del Borracho Saloon and Grill (no tel., Wed.–Sun. 8 A.M.–sunset, closed June–Sept., mains US$7–15) is a family-friendly place run by two hard-working Americans whose support for the local community is widely known and respected. The restaurant is located about 800 meters from the highway on the road to San Javier. Burgers, fries, and corndogs tempt

LORETO

the expat crowd. In Nopoló, the **Loreto Bay Restaurant** (tel. 613/133-0010 or 800/507-6979, www.innatloretobay.com, mains US$12–24), on the premises of the Inn at Loreto Bay, serves breakfast (daily 7–11 A.M.), snacks, and dinner (daily 7–10:30 P.M.).

INFORMATION AND SERVICES
Tourist Assistance
SEMARNAT, the government agency responsible for issuing permits to visit the protected islands near Loreto, has an office at the marina (tel. 613/135-0477, www.semarnat.gob. mx, Mon.–Fri. 8 A.M.–3 P.M.).

Loreto's **tourist office** (Salvatierra at Madero, tel. 613/135-0411, www.gotoloreto.com, Mon.–Fri. 8 A.M.–8 P.M.) occupies a street-level space in the Palacio de Gobierno on the plaza. If you are in Nopoló and need information, stop by the **Fonatur office** (tel. 613/135-0650).

Money
Loreto has three banks with ATMs. A **Bancomer** on the plaza exchanges dollars to pesos Monday–Friday 8:30–11:30 A.M. Some of the hotels can exchange currency, but at a lower rate.

Post and Telephone
Loreto's post office (Allende btw Salvatierra and Juárez) is open Monday–Saturday 8 A.M.–4 P.M. Public phones are widely available, and there are several Movistar and Telcel stores in town for mobile phone needs.

Internet Access
Many hotels now have wireless Internet for guests traveling with their own laptops, and a desktop machine or two for those who are traveling sans electronics. Internet cafés/business centers are located on Calle Madero and Calle Vizcaíno near Independencia.

Emergencies
Loreto's new **Hospital de la Comunidad de Loreto** is on the highway at the south end of town.

on the road to San Javier

© PABLO NOBILI

GETTING THERE AND AROUND
By Air
At press time, Alaska Airlines was the only major airline servicing Loreto's small international airport (LTO) from Los Angeles; however, there was talk that one or two other airlines might re-enter the market soon. Delta, Aero California, and Continental had all initiated service and then pulled out due to the depressed economic climate in 2008.

By Bus
Loreto's bus terminal is located at the intersection of Paseo Ugarte, Calle Juárez, and Calle Salvatierra. The schedule often changes, but you can usually count on about six ABC buses per day running in each direction. Fare to La Paz is approximately US$32, and about US$100 to Tijuana.

By Taxi
Head to the intersection of Calles Madero and Hidalgo to hail a cab, or call 613/135-0047

for pickups. Taxi service from the airport to Loreto or Loreto to Nopoló costs about US$15. Rides within town cost around US$5.

By Car

Loreto had three rental car agencies at last check: **Budget Rent-A-Car** (tel. 613/135-1090, www. budgetbaja.com), on Hidalgo near the *malecón;* **Hertz** (tel. 613/135-0800), on an alley between Hidalgo and Salvatierra, just off the *malecón;* and **Europcar** (tel. 613/135-2260), at the intersection of Independencia and Salvatierra, across from Win's Restaurant. These companies also have desks at the Loreto airport.

◖ SAN JAVIER

If you make only one excursion into the mountains on a drive along the Transpeninsular Highway, let timeless San Javier in the rugged Sierra de la Giganta be the one. Located 36 kilometers southwest of Loreto at an elevation of 425 meters and along the deep Arroyo San Javier, this agricultural village of thatched-roof stone and adobe houses holds one of the best-preserved Spanish mission churches anywhere in Baja. Onions are San Javier's major crop, but local farmers also grow citrus, guavas, figs, papayas, grapes, corn, chilies, and dates. December 3 is San Javier's patron saint day, and the week before this date is an especially festive time to visit.

Misión San Francisco Xavier de Viggé-Biaundó

Italian Padre Francisco María Píccolo founded the Mission San Javier (1699–1817) along the Arroyo San Javier in 1699, just two years after Padre Salvatierra established Baja's first permanent mission in Loreto. Little remains of the structures that were built on the first San Javier site, which Píccolo abandoned a few years later due to a threatened revolt. But Padre Juan de Ugarte revived the mission in 1702, choosing a new location a few kilometers downstream. He planted seeds brought from the mainland to grow a variety of fruits and vegetables and also introduced cotton and sheep, from which the indigenous people learned to weave fabrics.

© PABLO NOBILI

the Misión San Francisco Xavier de Viggé-Biaundó

The church that survives today was constructed in 1744–1758, under the guidance of Padre Miguel del Barco. It features detailed stonework around its doors and windows and a gilded altarpiece with a statue of San Javier. A glass cabinet in the sacristy displays precious vestments worn by the resident padres.

On Thursdays, a priest from Loreto holds mass. Caretaker Francisca Arce de Bastida gives informal tours of the church (daily 7 A.M.–6 P.M., by donation).

Accommodations
Most visitors spend only a day in San Javier, but if you want to stay overnight, there are a couple of options. The family that lives in the farmhouse behind the church rents a very rustic cabin for US$40. **Casa Ana** (tel. 613/135-0112, fax 613/135-0795, US$50), at the east end of the cobblestone road that leads to the church entrance, rents several *palapa*-roofed *cabañas* with

private baths. For more information, contact Ana Gloria at Hotel Oasis (tel. 613/132-4458, hoasis01@prodigy.net.mx) in Loreto.

Food
La Palapa San Javier (no tel., daily 8 A.M.–8 P.M., mains US$5) has a limited menu of Mexican staples and homegrown olives. A couple of small *tiendas* sell basic supplies.

Getting There
The road to San Javier begins at Km 118 on the highway and follows part of the original Spanish *Camino Real*. It takes about an hour to traverse the narrow road from the highway to the village. The first few kilometers are now paved, and after that, the road is suitable for just about any vehicle in dry weather, as long as you don't mind the steep grades.

If you don't have your own car, you can either rent one in Loreto or join a guided tour.

Ensenada Blanca to Ciudad Constitución

South of Puerto Escondido, Mexico 1 hugs the Gulf coast for about 20 kilometers more and then veers west across the peninsula toward Ciudad Insurgentes before turning south again to Ciudad Constitución.

ENSENADA BLANCA
About 40 kilometers south of Loreto, near the fishing village of Ligüí, Ensenada Blanca consists of a string of white-sand beaches, dunes, and estuaries that are now under development by a Mexican real estate company. The much-loved El Santuario and Danzante resorts have closed to make way for the Villa del Palmar Loreto, a luxury resort that proposes to build 2,200 rooms on its 728-hectare property.

AGUA VERDE
Between Km 64 and 63, where the highway turns west toward Ciudad Constitución, a narrow and winding gravel road heads southeast for 41 kilometers to the fish camp of Agua

Verde and a series of remote bays that make a good starting point for overnight kayak trips. The route traverses steep terrain with drop-offs of several hundred meters, frequent washouts, and no guardrails; as such, it is not suitable for trailers and RVs.

Along the way, **Rancho El Carricalito** (no tel.) offers basic accommodations and meals, and tortillas and goat cheese for sale. You can camp along the rocky shore here for about US$5, or continue on to the end of the road at Puerto Agua Verde, where the local *ejido* charges a few dollars a day to camp. Some supplies may be available at the *tienda* in the village of Agua Verde.

CIUDAD INSURGENTES
This community of about 10,000 people has fuel, supplies, and food. Although it is not a destination itself, Ciudad Insurgentes is a point of departure for excursions to La Purísima (102 km), Comondú (101 km), and Puerto Lopez

Mateos (17.7 km). Drivers should note that the kilometer markers finish their countdown from Santa Rosalía here and start over at Km 236.

CIUDAD CONSTITUCIÓN

Ciudad Constitución, the next major town along Mexico 1, gets relatively little attention from travelers, given its size (pop. 37,000). But it has plenty of hotels and restaurants if daylight is waning and you need a place to crash. As the capital of Municipio de Comondú, Ciudad Constitución is an agricultural center for the central peninsula. There are several Pemex stations, banks with ATMs, auto repair places, grocery stores, and a hospital.

Accommodations and Camping
HOTELS
◖ **Hotel Oasis** (Guerrero 284 btw Prieto/Farias, tel. 613/132-4458, hoasis01@prodigy.net.mx, US$40), located three blocks off the main drag, is one of the best hotels in town. Modern, clean rooms come with air-conditioning, phones, and TVs, and there's parking, a pool, and wireless Internet throughout.

Another good choice is the **Posada del Ryal Hotel** (Victoria btw Olochea/Lerdo de Tejada, tel. 613/132-4800 or -4690, US$40), where clean rooms have new bath fixtures. This hotel has secure parking, wireless Internet throughout the hotel, and a pleasant courtyard; there is a laundry next door.

Hotel El Tesoro (Olachea 239 at Independencia, tel. 613/132-8156, mmhotelteltesoro@hotmail.com, US$40) is conveniently located right on the main boulevard, on the south side of town. Its basic rooms come with cable TV and wireless Internet, and the hotel has 24-hour security/lobby hours, parking, and accepts Visa and Mastercard.

CAMPING AND RV PARKS
Misiones RV Trailer Park (formerly Manfred's, Km 213, tel. 613/132-1103), on the east side of Boulevard Olachea at the north edge of town, underwent a change of ownership in late 2005. The new owners have put a lot of love into the place and offer wireless Internet from the pool area, and breakfast or dinner cooked upon request. They are happy to arrange whale-watching tours for guests, and offer tourist advice in general. The park has hookups that run US$15–20 a night (dry/full), and tent camping for $6 per person. There is also a swimming pool.

Mike's Palapa 206 RV Park (tel. 613/132-3463, fax 613/132-5128), at the south edge of town but pretty much on the highway, has very little shade. Full hookups are US$15, water and electric US$14, tent camping US$7. RV storage is available, as are a couple of motel rooms.

Food
On Sunday afternoons, lines form at **Taquería Karen** (corner of Hidalgo/Olochea, no tel., mains US$5–7) for *cabeza, pescado,* and other tacos. **Tortas and Tacos Las Tortugas** (corner of Olochea/Bravo, no tel., mains US$5–7) makes *tortas, carne asada,* and Cuban sandwiches for US$2–3. At **Brismar** (Olochea at Zapata, tel. 613/137-0270, daily 8 A.M.–9 P.M., Sun. till 8 P.M., mains US$6–10), a friendly staff serves *mariscos* and *carnes* in a pleasant, clean, and air-conditioned space.

For a taste of something different, **Baja Teriyaki** (Olachea at Bellsario Dominguez, tel. 613/132-7092 or tel. 613/132-8378 for delivery from another branch on Cervantes del Rio and Morelos, daily for lunch and dinner, mains US$5–7), is a local chain that serves Mexican-style Japanese dishes accompanied by the usual Mexican salsas and pickled condiments. They have rice bowls, teriyaki of all varieties, and some sushi rolls and fried dishes.

One of the better *asaderos* in town is **Asadero Tribi** (Olachea and Suarez, tel. 613/132-7353, Tues.–Sun. 8 A.M.–midnight,) which does everything from hearty breakfasts for around US$5 to grilled meats, chicken, and seafood entrées in the US$8–12 range. Or you can order tacos with any grilled specialty for US$1.50 apiece. A clean restaurant and full bar round out the experience here.

The best options for groceries are **Super Ley** and **La Americana,** both on the main drag through town.

LORETO

MISIÓN SAN LUIS GONZAGA CHIRIYAQUI

If you're following the Spanish mission trail, Ciudad Constitución is the departure point for a trip to the short-lived San Luis Gonzaga mission (1737–1768). The site was a visita before it became a full-fledged mission in 1737 under the leadership of German Padre Lamberto Hostell. Made of sandstone, this simple but sturdy church lacks the ornate features of its counterparts located elsewhere on the peninsula. But it is well preserved, easily accessible, and a pleasant spot for bird-watching and camping. The church is used today by a local community of ranchers and farmers.

There are two turn-offs from Mexico 1 that lead to San Luis Gonzaga. The better option, signed La Presa Iguajil, begins at Km 195. Follow this road 42 kilometers to reach the settlement.

Bahía Magdalena

At the western edge of the Magdalena plain on the Pacific coast, a long string of barrier islands protects a series of shallow bays that fill with gray whales during calving season, January–March. The surrounding estuaries and mangroves support a unique and vibrant marine ecosystem. Sheltered Canal Gaviota links the two largest bays in the system, Bahía Magdalena and Bahía Almejas, to create some of the best kayaking and windsurfing conditions anywhere on the peninsula.

◖ GRAY WHALES

Just 45 minutes by car from Ciudad Constitución and about 2.5 hours from Loreto, Bahía Magdalena is the southernmost of the three main gray whale calving lagoons on the Pacific coast of the Baja Peninsula. (Laguna

It's all about the gray whales in Bahía Magdalena.

© PABLO NOBILI

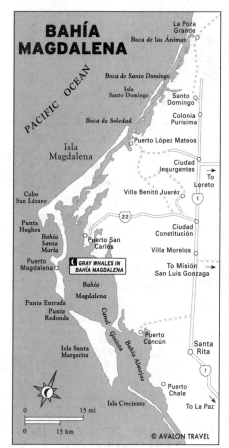

BAHÍA MAGDALENA

PACIFIC OCEAN

La Poza Grande
Boca de las Ánimas
Boca de Santo Domingo
Isla Santo Domingo
Santo Domingo
Boca de Soledad
Colonia Purísima
Puerto López Mateos
Isla Magdalena
Ciudad Insurgentes
To Loreto
Villa Benito Juárez
Cabo San Lázaro
Punta Hughes
Bahía Santa María
Puerto San Carlos
Ciudad Constitución
Villa Morelos
Puerto Magdalena
GRAY WHALES IN BAHÍA MAGDALENA
Bahía Magdalena
To Misión San Luis Gonzaga
Punta Entrada
Punta Redonda
Canal Gaviota
Bahía Almejas
Puerto Cancún
Santa Rita
Isla Santa Margarita
Puerto Chale
Isla Creciente
To La Paz
0   15 mi
0   15 km
© AVALON TRAVEL

Ojo de Liebre near Guerrero Negro and Laguna San Ignacio are the other two.) Whale-watching tours that depart from Mulegé, Loreto, or La Paz generally head for this bay.

It is possible on some days to view the whale activity from a distance on shore near Puerto López Mateos, but this doesn't compare to the experience of getting up close on a boat. Look for a viewing area with a parking lot north of the fish-processing plant.

A three- to four-hour panga tour costs about US$65 per person for up to four people, and prices are likely to change with fuel prices. It can be difficult—and dangerous—to cruise the

lagoon when the winter winds kick up, so tour operators generally recommend that you allow an extra day or two on your visit in case the weather doesn't cooperate. In addition to the whales, you'll likely spot sea lions and a variety of marine birds. Beware of any *panguero* who offers to take you out in inclement weather; your chances of seeing the whales will be slim and the danger factor will be unnecessarily high.

Boat drivers must be licensed to drive in the lagoons during the whale calving season. Ask at any hotel in San Carlos for a guide, or head down to the embarcadero on the west side of town near the lighthouse to hire someone directly.

Viajes Mar y Arena (tel. 613/136-0076, fax 613/136-0232), **Brennan's y Asociados** (tel. 613/136-0288, fax 613/136-0019, turismo@balandra.uabcs.mx), and **Unión de Lancheros y Servicios Turísticos de Puerto San Carlos (ULYSTOURS)** (tel. 613/136-0253, Crispín Mendoza) are all licensed to run guided boat tours. Readers also recommend **Mag Bay Tours** (U.S. tel. 215/667-8470, www.magbaytours.com), which started out as a surf camp and then added whale-watching and sportfishing services. It has four different base camps, two on Bahía Santa María and two on Bahía Magdalena.

In Puerto López Mateos, several operators are authorized to take tourists on whale-watching tours. They include: **Unión de Lancheros Touristicos** (tel. 613/131-5114), **Aquendi** (tel. 613/131-5164, or -5105, or -5306, US$80/hour, up to 6 people), and **Renta de Lanchas Juana Rosas III** (tel. 613/113-9195 or 613/131-5123) The offices for all of these businesses are located at the port.

Baja Expeditions (U.S. tel. 858/581-3311 or 800/843-6967, www.bajaex.com) offers week-long kayaking and whale-watching trips in Bahía Magdalena for approximately US$1,500 per person.

PUERTO SAN CARLOS

The largest town in the area is Puerto San Carlos (pop. 5,200), with the only other deep-water port on the Pacific coast of Baja besides Ensenada.

During the whale-watching season, Puerto

LORETO

LORETO

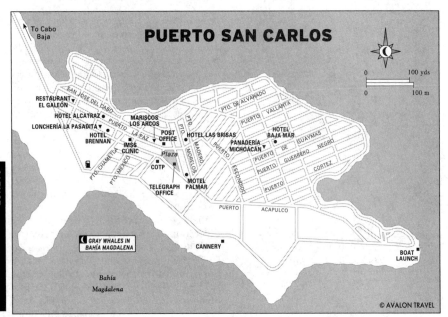

San Carlos hosts the **Festival de Ballena Gris** (Gray Whale Festival), with music, food, and crafts festivities every weekend from the middle of February through the end of March.

Puerto San Carlos has a Pemex station, several *tiendas,* a post office, and government offices for port captain, customs, and immigration. Public long-distance TelMex phones are scattered throughout the town.

PUERTO LÓPEZ MATEOS

North of Puerto San Carlos, tiny Puerto López Mateos offers a similar array of services, but on a much smaller scale. It has a cannery, post office, and Pemex, plus several *tiendas,* hotels, and restaurants. TelMex public phones are scattered throughout town.

The town celebrated its 16th **Festival Internacional de la Ballena Gris** in February 2009. It also has a local fiesta on the last weekend of April or first of May.

Several whale-watching tour operators have offices at the port, and, booths of vendors sell all kinds of *artesanías* in the high season.

PUERTO CANCÚN AND PUERTO CHALE

These two fishing camps are located in the shadow of Isla Santa Margarita. They have basic supplies, good camping, and an abundance of fresh clams, lobster, and other seafood.

SPORTS AND RECREATION
Fishing and Boating

Sportfishing remains a major attraction in the area, especially in the high season of July–November. Anglers catch halibut, yellowtail, red bass (mangrove snapper), corvina, and snook close to shore, and big game fish farther out. For clams, you cans simply walk along the shallows of either bay and dig.

San Carlos has a concrete boat ramp for launching small boats, as do Puerto López Mateos and Puerto Chale.

Kiteboarding and Windsurfing

Windsurfers and kiteboarders flock to Bahía Magdalena for the best wind conditions on the Pacific coast of the Baja Peninsula. Beginners

NORMA OFICIAL MEXICANA 029: A COMMERCIAL LONG-LINE FISHING LEGISLATION

Official Mexican Norm 029, commonly seen on bumper stickers and banners throughout Southern Baja as NOM-029, is a highly controversial legislation regulating commercial long-line fishing in the Sea of Cortez and along the Pacific coast of Mexico.

After years of opposition to the *norma* (regulation) by ex-president Vicente Fox, the legislation went into effect only five months after Felipe Calderón took office, in mid-May 2007.

Proponents hail the bill as promoting responsible fishing of sharks and rays; among other things, it restricts new shark fishing permits for the area, prohibits shark fining, and increases protected areas for sharks, sea turtles, and sea lions.

However, opponents claim that problems overlooked by the bill will actually contribute to a decline in the general health of the marine environment, especially in the Sea of Cortez. The problem is that the law legalizes the retention of incidental "by-catch" – around 80 percent of which is usually marlin, sailfish, and other fish until now officially designated to sportfishing purposes only and previously subject to much tighter bag limits. Even though more areas have been designated protected areas for marine life, the bill opens up a greater zone with closer coastal access limits than before; many activists claim that, with surveillance and enforcement being a point of weakness in Mexico, the entire sportfishing industry will

soon be wiped out by the encroaching presence of long-liners in areas once restricted for tourism.

A heated debate continues over the purpose and efficiency of achieving the stated purpose of NOM-029. Many NGOs, such as Greenpeace Mexico, IFAW (International Fund for Animal Welfare), and COMARINO (Conservation of Marine Mammals of Mexico), support the bill. They claim that its attempts at regulating the commercial fishing industry are better than nothing (though not enough), and that recognizing and protecting several species of shark – as well as prohibiting their fining, among other positive features of the bill – is a step in the right direction.

Opponents are numerous and vocal, consisting of other prominent marine ecology organizations, such as SeaWatch and Oceana, as well as local unions of sportfishing operators and hotel and restaurant unions of Los Cabos.

IGFA representative and union head Minerva Smith, who owns Minerva's Baja Tackle Shop in Cabo San Lucas, has been recognized for her conservation efforts over the years and is one of the most articulate opponents of the Shark Norma.

Both sides agree that endangered sharks and rays need government protection. Unfortunately, the argument will only be settled through a trial-and-error approach. It's quite possible that allowing commercial long-lines and gillnets so close to the coast will end the sportfishing industry as we know it.

take shelter in the relatively calm bay, while advanced boarders venture out to the *bocas*, for stronger winds and bigger waves.

Surfing

South of Bahía Magalena, committed surfers frequent remote Punta El Conejo, a point that juts far enough out into the open ocean to catch north and south swells. The left here holds the larger swells, while the right will close out. Beware the urchins on the rocks on the inside.

There are no facilities, but you can camp among the dunes here. Local lobster fishermen may come by in the evening to sell their sadly undersized catches. Normally, someone from the property will come and collect U$5 per car, in exchange for collecting garbage and maintaining the primitive but sheltered bathrooms. This land and the access to it is private, but the owners don't mind leaving it open to visitors.

With a sturdy vehicle, you can follow the coastal road south another 17 kilometers to

LORETO

reach **Punta Márquez,** another surf spot. This same road continues all the way to Todos Santos (124 km from El Conejo), passing a number of remote beach breaks along the way.

ACCOMMODATIONS AND CAMPING
Puerto San Carlos

The best place to stay in this town is 🌙 **Hotel Brennan** (Puerto Acapulco, tel. 613/136-0288, www.hotelbrennan.com.mx, US$65), where the still-basic rooms have extra amenities such as ceiling fans, air-conditioning, kitchenettes, and satellite TV. The hotel has a restaurant and bar and can arrange guided outdoor activities for guests.

A popular place for tour groups, **Hotel Alcatraz** (Puerto La Paz, tel. 613/136-0017, fax 613/136-0086, US$60–75), on the main road through town, has nicely tiled rooms set around a courtyard. In-room amenities include TVs, hot water, and mini-bars.

You can camp at the northwest and southeast ends of the peninsula for around US$5 per vehicle.

Puerto López Mateos

Hotel Posada Tornavuelta (Abelardo L. Rodríguez, tel. 613/131-5106, US$30) offers several clean rooms with private baths. Check in at the house next door. This hotel stays open year-round, and there is an adjacent restaurant in the works.

Cabañas Dunas, affiliated with the Aquendi complex which includes a restaurant, bar, and tours (tel. 613/131-5293, www.aquendi.com, cabanas_dunas@hotmail.com, US$40), is on the left as you head into the port. Its new, duplex-style *cabañas* each have private, hot-water bathrooms and small patios. **El Camarón Feliz** (Abelardo L. Rodríguez, tel. 613/131-5032) also has five rooms for rent at US$30, each with its own bath.

FOOD
Puerto San Carlos

For fresh seafood, head to **Restaurant El Galeón** (no tel., daily for lunch and dinner, mains US$10–15) close to Hotel Brennan. It serves beef and chicken dishes, as well as delicious shellfish and fish. **Mariscos Los Arcos** (Calle La Paz, no tel., daily 8 A.M.–10 P.M., mains US$5–15, lobster around US$30) prepares seafood, *antojitos,* and Mexican breakfasts. Another option for reasonably priced and delicious fresh food is **La Cocina de Tere** (no tel., mains US$5–10), just up from Hotel Alcatraz. The menu varies according to what's fresh, and your server will tell you what's available that day.

Puerto López Mateos

A few restaurants in town serve good seafood dishes, but they are usually open only January–April, when the whale-watchers are around. **El Camarón Feliz** (Abelardo L. Rodríguez, tel. 613/131-5032, mains US$5–10) is the place to stop for fish tacos. **Restaurant Ballena Gris** (no tel., mains US$10–15) on the right as you come into town, prepares fresh fish and shellfish.

GETTING THERE AND AROUND

You can drive the paved highway Mexico 22 from Ciudad Constitución to Puerto San Carlos (57 km) west in under an hour, or catch one of three buses a day that connect the two towns (US$5 pp). Bus fare from La Paz is US$34 one way.

To get to Puerto López Mateos, take the paved route west from Ciudad Insurgentes. And for Puerto Chale, turn off the highway at Km 157.

The 1:250,000-scale INEGI La Paz map (G12-10-11) will help you find roads along the coast of Bahía Magdalena and Bahía Almejas.

LA PAZ AND VICINITY

If you've been making your way down the peninsula visiting small towns, fishing villages, and remote coastal stretches, the state capital of La Paz (population 200,000) and the largest city in Southern Baja may come as quite a shock. But once you've settled in and adjusted to the sight of more cars, shops, hotels, restaurants, and people, La Paz begins to show its true colors.

For many travelers, this city achieves the perfect balance: Nestled at the southern end of the largest and one of the most beautiful bays along the Gulf coast, it is tropical and picturesque, with a five-kilometer-long bayside promenade and plenty of opportunity for outdoor adventure. Protected islands offshore entertain paddlers, snorkelers, and scuba divers. Remote beaches, mountain scenery, and even surf on the Pacific coast are all only a short drive away.

And yet, La Paz conveys the feel of a real place with real people and its own distinct history and culture. The first Europeans to set foot on the peninsula arrived at La Paz in the 16th century, and the city was a pearling center long before it became a tourist destination. It is a hub for government, commerce, education, medical services, and environmental conservation. This is not a purpose-built resort town. La Paz is ideal for the traveler who wants more than a beach-and-booze vacation; here, you'll get some history, eco-adventure, and a taste of the real Mexico. The locals go about their business, and tourists can take it or leave it. And that's exactly why many visitors fall in love with the city.

© CARMEL TSABAR

LA PAZ AND VICINITY

HIGHLIGHTS

◖ Malecón: You haven't experienced La Paz until you've strolled the waterfront promenade at sunset. Visitors and residents alike pause to watch the dramatic display of color. Take a break for a cocktail or an ice cream, and enjoy the afternoon breeze (page 209).

LOOK FOR ◖ TO FIND RECOMMENDED SIGHTS, ACTIVITIES, DINING, AND LODGING.

◖ Museo Regional de Antropología e Historia: Think you know your Baja history? Save time for a tour of the fossils, minerals, and maps of rock-painting sites in this well-run museum. Exhibits depict prehistoric and colonial life throughout central and southern Baja (page 211).

◖ Playa El Tecolote: A drive to the end of the road along Bahía de La Paz leads to this wide, sandy beach. Wade into clear, shallow waters and enjoy views of Isla Espíritu Santo across the channel. A steady breeze keeps the bugs away if you decide to spend the night (page 212).

◖ Isla Espíritu Santo: The best-known of the islands offshore from La Paz entertains paddlers, divers, and boaters with white-sand beaches and rock reefs. You can camp in several places on the island and enjoy endless opportunities for outdoor adventure (page 214).

◖ Carnaval: Like several other Mexican cities, La Paz celebrates Carnaval with great fanfare in mid-February. Time your visit with this annual event to experience the heart and soul of the city. The entertainment includes live music, colorful parades, and amusement rides, plus plenty of tequila and *cerveza* (page 226).

◖ Bahía de la Ventana: A short drive south of La Paz, this L-shaped bay offers ideal winds for kiteboarders and windsurfers, plus easy access to Isla Cerralvo for scuba diving adventures. Enjoy the remote feel while it lasts (page 243).

Marine biologists on sabbatical from universities in the United States, young professionals from mainland Mexico, vacationers cruising on their yachts, and baby-boomers looking to live comfortably in their retirement all are making La Paz their home base. If you want to move to Southern Baja yet still have some of the conveniences of urban life, La Paz may well be your place.

Despite the feverish pace of real estate activity, the city that John Steinbeck described as *antigua* has protected its deep-rooted traditions,

many of which came from the mainland along with the earliest immigrants. Then, as now, people who came over from Mexico City and other large cities were searching for a slower pace and a better quality of life.

PLANNING YOUR TIME

Allow several days to explore the city and surrounding beaches; a week or more if you plan to fish, snorkel, dive, or kayak around the islands just offshore. If you're coming to learn

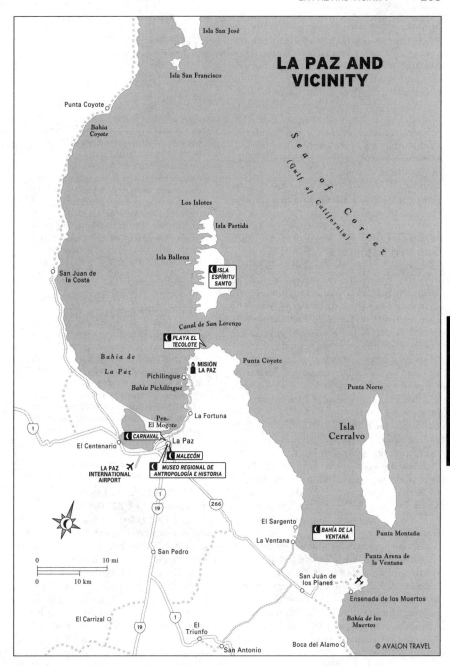

LA PAZ AND
VICINITY

Isla San José

Isla San Francisco

Punta Coyote

Bahía
Coyote

S e a   o f   C o r t e z
(Gulf of California)

Los Islotes

Isla Partida

Isla Ballena

San Juan de
la Costa

**(ISLA
ESPÍRITU
SANTO**

Canal de San Lorenzo

**(PLAYA EL
TECOLOTE**

*Bahía de
La Paz*

**MISIÓN
LA PAZ**

Pichilingue

Punta Coyote

Bahía Pichilingue

Punta Norte

Pen.
El Mogote

La Fortuna

Isla
Cerralvo

1

(CARNAVAL

La Paz

El Centenario

(MALECÓN

**LA PAZ
INTERNATIONAL
AIRPORT**

**MUSEO REGIONAL DE
ANTROPOLOGÍA E HISTORIA**

1

19

266

El Sargento

**(BAHÍA DE LA
VENTANA**

La Ventana

Punta Montaña

San Pedro

Punta Arena de
la Ventana

0   10 mi

0   10 km

San Juán de
los Planes

Ensenada de los Muertos

El Carrizal

19

1

El
Triunfo

*Bahía de los
Muertos*

Boca del Alamo

San Antonio

© AVALON TRAVEL

Spanish, local schools recommend a minimum stay of two weeks, and up to a month if you can swing it. Travelers planning to take the ferry to Mazatlán should allow an extra day or two to arrange permits and reservations.

February is La Paz's busiest month for tourists. But even then, hotel rooms are usually easy to find. One exception is when the Baja 1000 off-road race comes to town in mid-November. With the race finish just outside the city limits, every room, condo, and vacation rental books up months in advance. If you roll into La Paz without reservations, you'll likely have to continue south to Los Barriles to find a place to crash for the night.

HISTORY
Spanish Explorers
Two nomadic tribes, the Guaicura and Pericu, inhabited the area around present-day La Paz before the Spanish arrived in the 16th century. They knew the Bahía de La Paz as Airapí. In 1533, Hernán Cortés sent the *Concepcion* to sea to explore the Gulf of Mexico. After staging a mutiny and killing the ship's captain, the crew landed at La Paz in search of water, only to be attacked by the indigenous people. A few survivors were able to sail back to the mainland, and their tales of a beautiful bay filled with pearls lured Cortés himself back to Antigua California. He landed near Pichilingue in 1535 and stayed for two years, trying unsuccessfully to colonize the indigenous people.

Sebastián Vizcaíno landed next, in 1596, as part of a voyage around the entire Antigua California coast. He bestowed the name Bahía de La Paz (Bay of Peace) upon the area as a reflection of how well the indigenous people treated his crew.

Repeated attempts to establish a permanent settlement in the 17th century failed due to the scarcity of food and water and tension with the indigenous people. During this time, the bay became a hiding place for pirates seeking to attack the Manila Galleons. The Spanish needed a stronghold on the peninsula, but it would be 150 years before the first mission succeeded in Loreto in 1683.

THE PEARLS OF LA PAZ

When the Spanish began to explore the Sea of Cortez and the coastline near La Paz in the 16th century, they found abundant oyster beds near Isla Cerralvo. The pearls were well known to the indigenous people, who wore them as necklaces. Word of the treasure spread, and commercial expeditions began making the trip from the mainland to harvest saltwater pearls, which were sent back to Europe to adorn the Spanish clergy and royalty.

During the mission period of 1697-1768, the Jesuits limited pearl-diving activities, but the industry came back to life in the 19th century, when entrepreneurs contracted Yaqui divers from the mainland to dive the Gulf coast from La Paz to Mulegé.

Modern diving technology introduced in the 1870s allowed divers to reach deeper oyster beds and harvest mass quantities of the shelled mollusks. Only a small percentage of oysters harvested contained a natural pearl, and the oysters were all but depleted during this time. In the late 1930s, a disease – rumored but never confirmed to be introduced by the Japanese – attacked the few pearl oyster beds that remained, and by the time John Steinbeck arrived in La Paz, Southern Baja's world-famous pearling industry was a thing of the past.

Misión Nuestra Señora del Pilar de la Paz Airapí
Although La Paz hosted many of the first European explorers in the 16th century, it took nearly 200 years and several failed attempts for the Spanish to establish a permanent settlement. Jesuit Padres Juan de Ugarte and Jaime Bravo eventually succeeded in 1720, but their mission was short-lived. The Pericú burned the city to the ground during the rebellion of 1734, and the mission never fully recovered. The Jesuits abandoned it in 1748. The precise location of the mission is lost to

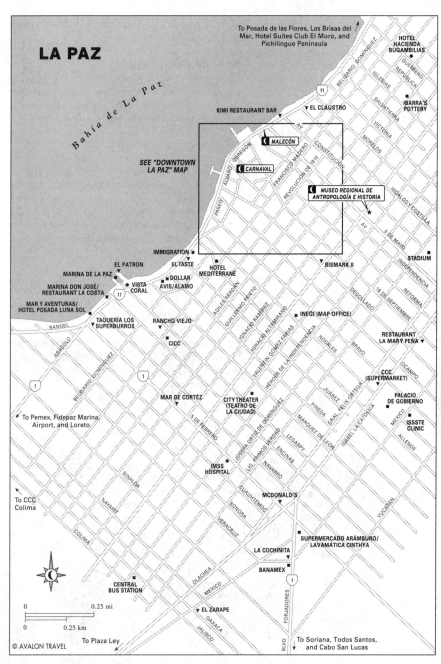

LA PAZ

Bahía de La Paz

To Posada de las Flores, Las Brisas del Mar, Hotel Suites Club El Moro, and Pichilingue Peninsula

HOTEL HACIENDA BUGAMBILIAS

GUERRERO

REPÚBLICA

IGLESIAS

SALVATIERRA

IBARRA'S POTTERY

VICTORIA

MORELOS

BELISARIO DOMÍNGUEZ

11

KIWI RESTAURANT BAR

EL CLAUSTRO

AV.

MALECÓN

CARNAVAL

FRANCISCO MADERO

CONSTITUCIÓN

REVOLUCIÓN DE 1910

HIDALGO Y COSTILLA

SEE "DOWNTOWN LA PAZ" MAP

MUSEO REGIONAL DE ANTROPOLOGÍA E HISTORIA

AV.

5 DE MAYO

ÁLVARO OBREGÓN

PASEO

IMMIGRATION

EL PATRON

EL TASTE

HOTEL MEDITERRANÉ

BISMARK II

STADIUM

INDEPENDENCIA

REFORMA

MARINA DE LA PAZ

DOLLAR

AVIS/ALAMO

VISTA CORAL

MARINA DON JOSÉ/ RESTAURANT LA COSTA

11

16 DE SEPTIEMBRE

DEGOLLADO

MAR Y AVENTURAS/ HOTEL POSADA LUNA SOL

RANGEL

TAQUERÍA LOS SUPERBURROS

RANCHO VIEJO

AQUILES SERDÁN

GUILLERMO PRIETO

IGNACIO RAMÍREZ

IGNACIO ALTAMIRANO

INEGI (MAP OFFICE)

HÉROES DE LA INDEPENDENCIA

ROSALES

BRAVO

RESTAURANT LA MARY PEÑA

OCAMPO

ABASOLO

BELISARIO DOMÍNGUEZ

1

CICC

VALENTÍN GÓMEZ FARÍAS

CCC (SUPERMARKET)

JUÁREZ

GRAL. FÉLIX ORTEGA

PALACIO DE GOBIERNO

1

To Pemex, Fidepaz Marina, Airport, and Loreto

MAR DE CORTÉZ

CITY THEATER (TEATRO DE LA CIUDAD)

JOSEFA ORTIZ DE DOMÍNGUEZ

ING. PRIMOS VERDAD

PINEDA

MÁRQUEZ DE LEÓN

LEGASPY

ENCINAS

ISABEL LA CATÓLICA

MÉXICO

ISSSTE CLINIC

ALLENDE

5 DE FEBRERO

SINALOA

NAVARRO

NAYARIT

To CCC Colima

IMSS HOSPITAL

CUAUHTÉMOC

MCDONALD'S

YUCATÁN

COLIMA

VERACRUZ

SONORA

To Plaza Ley

CENTRAL BUS STATION

OLACHEA

MÉXICO

SUPERMERCADO ARÁMBURO/ LAVAMÁTICA CINTHYA

LA COCHINITA

BANAMEX

1

EL ZARAPE

OAXACA

JALISCO

FORJADORES

BLVD.

To Soriana, Todos Santos, and Cabo San Lucas

0   0.25 mi

0   0.25 km

© AVALON TRAVEL

history, but believed to be near the modern-day Plaza Constitución and the 1861 Catedral de Nuestra Señora de La Paz. The twin towers of the church overlook the plaza. Inside, little evidence remains of the original mission.

The 19th Century

In the post-missionary period, a group of farmers and fishermen gave La Paz new life, and it ascended to a position of importance in 1829 when the municipal capital of Southern Baja was moved from Loreto to La Paz following a severe hurricane.

American forces occupied La Paz during the Mexican American War (1846–1848) until the Treaty of Hidalgo divided California into Alta and Baja territories.

In the years following the Mexican-American War, La Paz was known mainly for its pearl trade. Its economy diversified after World War II, when the government declared La Paz a duty-free port. People from mainland Mexico began traveling to La Paz to buy discounted imports, and some decided to make Baja California their home.

The 20th Century

People from the United States began arriving in the 1950s to fish the Sea of Cortez, and La Paz became known briefly as a celebrity resort town. The paving of the Transpeninsular Highway in 1973 heralded the next major change, transforming La Paz into a more accessible and popular travel destination. When Baja California Sur became a Mexican state in 1974, the government designated La Paz the state capital.

With modern transportation possible by air, land, and sea, La Paz expanded into a major center of commerce serving the greater Southern Baja region.

Tourism and Real Estate Development

Since the turn of the century, the Baja California Sur state government has invested

downtown La Paz

© CARMEL TSABAR

heavily in infrastructure improvements and tourism-related services in the area around La Paz. Former BCS Governor Leonel Cota Montaño (1999–2005) cited the development of La Paz as his personal mission and did wonders for the city, including offering the governor's mansion as the city's new aquarium.

As the real estate market becomes saturated in Los Cabos, developers are looking northward. Three large-scale resort developments are underway: Like Cabo San Lucas, La Paz now has its own hilltop Pedregal (www.pedregal.com) gated community in the making, at the northeastern edge of town on the way to Pichilingue. Cobblestone roads and utilities are the first step in the creation of a 52-hectare private, gated community of 370 lots; a 200-room hotel; condos; and a shopping plaza. Nearby, a second beach development, the 500-acre CostaBaja Resort & Marina (www.costabajaresort.com) has an operational 280-slip marina and Fiesta Inn resort. The development also includes 50 villas, plus shops, restaurants, and a golf course. Real estate fever has spread to the south as well, with five hotels, a residential neighborhood, and airport planned for the Bay of Dreams development.

Another development is taking shape on the fragile Mogote Peninsula, a spit of land edged with mangrove that juts out in the bay. Linked to the *malecón* by water taxi, the Paraíso del Mar (www.paradiseofthesea.com) project consists of two golf courses, a 535-slip marina, 2,000 hotel rooms, and 2,000 private homes. Builders say they are taking environmental precautions—by planning to build two desalination plants, for example, and designing golf greens that use native plants; however, conservationists continue to raise concerns that the development will permanently destroy hundreds of hectares of mangrove essential to the health of the local marine ecosystem. The impact remains to be seen, but regardless, the development will undoubtedly change the skyline of La Paz.

Sights

⟨ *Malecón*

The most defining feature of downtown La Paz is the five-kilometer promenade that parallels Paseo Alvaro Obregón and hugs the shoreline from Calle 5 de Febrero at the southwest end the Hotel El Moro at the northeast end. Along the way are a couple of marinas, numerous restaurants, shops, car rental agencies, hotels, a tourist pier, *panga* boats, and a small beach area. A fixture since the early days of the city, the *malecón,* is looking better than ever these days. Decorative paving, recently painted crosswalks, and white wrought-iron benches invite visitors and residents to take a sunset stroll along the Bahía de la Paz, just as the afternoon breeze kicks up. Water quality has improved too, making it possible to swim once again (though most people continue northeast to the beaches along the Pichilingue Peninsula).

gazebo on the *malecón* at sunset

© CARMEL TSABAR

LA PAZ AND VICINITY

LA PAZ AND VICINITY

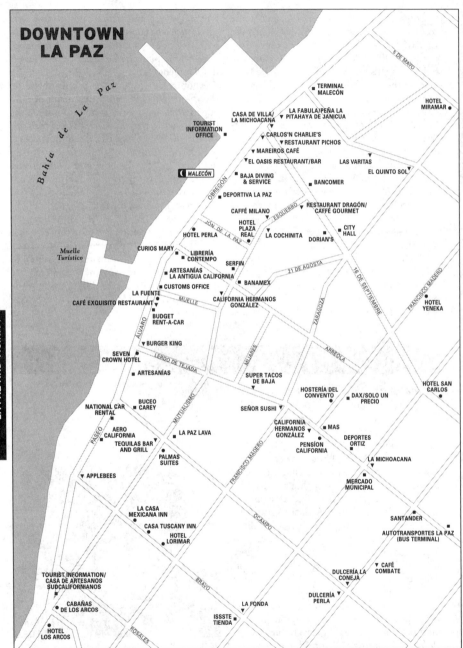

DOWNTOWN LA PAZ

Bahía de La Paz

5 DE MAYO

TERMINAL MALECÓN

HOTEL MIRAMAR

CASA DE VILLA/ LA MICHOACANA

LA FABULA/PEÑA LA PITAHAYA DE JANICUA

TOURIST INFORMATION OFFICE

CARLOS'N CHARLIE'S

RESTAURANT PICHOS

MAREIROS CAFÉ

EL OASIS RESTAURANT/BAR

LAS VARITAS

EL QUINTO SOL

MALECÓN

BAJA DIVING & SERVICE

OBREGÓN

BANCOMER

DEPORTIVA LA PAZ

RESTAURANT DRAGÓN/ CAFFÉ GOURMET

CAFFÉ MILANO

ESQUERRO

HOTEL PLAZA REAL

JÓN DE LA PAZ

CITY HALL

HOTEL PERLA

LA COCHINITA

DORIAN'S

Muelle Turístico

CURIOS MARY

LIBRERÍA CONTEMPO

SERFIN

21 DE AGOSTA

ARTESANÍAS LA ANTIGUA CALIFORNIA

BANAMEX

16 DE SEPTIEMBRE

FRANCISCO MADERO

CUSTOMS OFFICE

LA FUENTE

MUELLE

CALIFORNIA HERMANOS GONZÁLEZ

HOTEL YENEKA

CAFÉ EXQUISITO RESTAURANT

ÁLVARO

BUDGET RENT-A-CAR

ZARAGOZA

BURGER KING

ARREOLA

SEVEN CROWN HOTEL

LERDO DE TEJADA

MILARES

ARTESANÍAS

SUPER TACOS DE BAJA

HOSTERÍA DEL CONVENTO

HOTEL SAN CARLOS

BUCEO CAREY

DAX/SOLO UN PRECIO

NATIONAL CAR RENTAL

MUTUALISMO

SEÑOR SUSHI

AERO CALIFORNIA

LA PAZ LAVA

CALIFORNIA HERMANOS GONZÁLEZ

MAS

TEQUILAS BAR AND GRILL

PENSIÓN CALIFORNIA

DEPORTES ORTIZ

PALMAS SUITES

LA MICHOACANA

APPLEBEES

FRANCISCO MADERO

MERCADO MUNICIPAL

LA CASA MEXICANA INN

CASA TUSCANY INN

OCAMPO

SANTANDER

HOTEL LORIMAR

AUTOTRANSPORTES LA PAZ (BUS TERMINAL)

CAFÉ COMBATE

TOURIST INFORMATION/ CASA DE ARTESANOS SUDCALIFORNIANOS

BRAVO

DULCERÍA LA CONEJA

CABAÑAS DE LOS ARCOS

DULCERÍA PERLA

LA FONDA

HOTEL LOS ARCOS

ROSALES

ISSSTE TIENDA

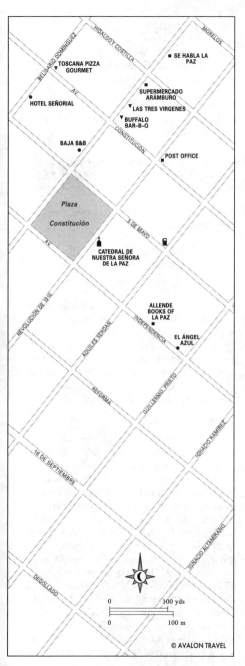

◖ Museo Regional de Antropología e Historia

As Southern Baja's cultural center, La Paz has a wonderful anthropology and history museum, the Museo Regional de Antropología e Historia (5 de Mayo and Altamirano, tel. 612/122-0162, daily 9 A.M.–6 P.M., US$2–3, free Sun. and holidays). Its three floors contain exhibits that begin with a depiction of life in Baja California before the Europeans arrived—including photos and depictions of prehistoric cave paintings—and progress all the way up through the Mexican-American War of the 19th century. Fossils and minerals tell the story of the geologic past of the peninsula. The knowledgeable and enthusiastic staff speaks limited English, and exhibit signs for the permanent exhibits are only in Spanish. The on-site gift shop has replicas of Amerindian pottery and other souvenirs for sale, as well as books, music, and guides focused on the history, geology, and anthropology of Mexico.

Plaza Constitución and Jardín Velazco

La Paz's central plaza and garden take up a full block between Avenida Independencia and Calle 5 de Mayo and between Calles Revolución de 1910 and Madero. With its gazebo and wrought-iron benches, this is a good place to get your bearings and begin a walking tour. Note the fountain with a representation of the Mushroom Rock that stands just offshore in Balandra Bay. In the evening, you might catch a live performance or a game of Mexican bingo.

On the southwest side of the plaza (Revolución de 1910 btw 5 de Mayo/Independencia) stands the 1861 Catedral de Nuestra Señora de La Paz, built by the Dominicans as a replacement for the original Jesuit mission church.

La Unidad Cultural Profesor Jesús Castro Agúndez

This cultural center (Navarro btw Altamirano/Independencia, tel. 612/125-0207, Mon.–Fri. 8 A.M.–3 P.M.) has art exhibits, classes, and the 1,500-seat city theater, which stages dance performances, concerts, and plays year-round. In the complex, **Galería de Arte Carlos Olochea** (tel. 612/122-9196) hosts temporary and permanent exhibitions by renowned national artists. The city's central library and historical archives are also located here.

Acuario de las Californias
A welcome addition to the La Paz waterfront is the long-anticipated aquarium, housed in the historic governor's mansion, three miles northeast of downtown. Built with state and federal funds as an engine for environmental education and conservation, the aquarium was just opening its first few exhibits at last check. It's open daily 10 A.M.–2 P.M., and located near the La Concha resort on the road to Pichilingue.

Beaches

BAHÍA DE LA PAZ
A series of public beaches line the Bahía de La Paz, from the city center all the way to the tip of the Pichilingue Peninsula. As a general rule, the beaches become prettier as you get farther away from the city. To find them, follow the La Paz–Pichilingue Road (Paseo Obregón becomes this road at the northeast end of the *malecón*), which is paved all the way to El Tecolote at the northern tip of the peninsula.

Palmira, El Coromuel, and Caimancito
At Playa Palmira, closest to downtown La Paz (Km 2.5), resort development has encroached on the sand—so it's best to continue another kilometer to Playa El Coromuel (Km 4.3), a small beach with a restaurant, bar, *palapa* structures for shade, and restrooms. Playa Caimancito, at the La Concha Beach Resort (Km 6), has a rock reef close to shore suitable for snorkeling.

Playa El Tesoro and Punta Colorada
Playa El Tesoro (Km 13) has *palapas* and a hit-or-miss restaurant. The dirt road that heads southwest from the beach goes to Playa Punta Colorada, a secluded swimming cove.

Playa Pichilingue
The next beach east of the ferry terminal (Km 17) has restrooms open 24/7 for visitors who want to camp. Its simple *palapa* restaurant (tel. 612/122-4565, mains US$5–10) serves reasonably priced Mexican staples. A taxi from the *malecón* to the ferry terminal will run about US$20.

Playa Balandra
The best beach for snorkeling along this stretch is Playa Balandra. Known for Mushroom Rock, which balances offshore, this sometimes-crowded beach is protected from the wind (good for calm water and chilly days, but not so good for bugs when camping). Swim out to the coral reef at the south end of the beach for the best underwater scenery. To get the best views, you'll have to scale the rock cliffs behind the beach. Look for an access road about five kilometers past the ferry terminal.

Playa El Tecolote
Continue another three kilometers beyond the road to Playa Balandra and you'll reach Playa El Tecolote, an exposed beach that faces the Canal de San Lorenzo and Isla Espíritu Santo to the north. A handful of *pangas* are moored here, and you can swim in a roped-off area, or anywhere along the beach. The slope is gentle leading into the water and the bottom is sandy, so you can wade quite far from shore before having to swim. Campers often come here to escape the bugs. Two beachfront restaurants, **El Tecolote** (tel. 612/127-9494, mains US$8–15) and **Palapa Azul** (tel. 612/122-1801, mains US$8–15), offer food and drinks—as well as rental gear (chairs, umbrellas, fishing equipment) and boat tours (US$$40–50). There are pay showers and public *palapas* for shade.

BEACHES AND ISLANDS NEAR LA PAZ

Los Islotes
Isla Partida
Isla Ballena
ISLA ESPÍRITU SANTO
Sea of Cortez (Gulf of California)
Bahía San Gabriel
Canal de San Lorenzo
PLAYA EL TECOLOTE
Puerto Balandra
Playa Balandra
Playa Pichilingue
MISIÓN LA PAZ
CLUB CANTAMAR RESORT
Pichilingue
Bahía Pichilingue
Bahía de La Paz
Playa El Tesoro
0   2 mi
0   2 km
Playa El Coromuel
Playa Palmira
MARINA COSTA BAJA/FIESTA INN
Peninsula El Mogote
ARAIZA INN
Playa El Comitán
Canal de La Paz
CLUB EL MORO
La Paz
Ensenada de La Paz
Playa Las Hamacas
FIDEPAZ MARINA
El Centenario
LA PAZ INTERNATIONAL AIRPORT
To Cabo San Lucas
© AVALON TRAVEL

Though you are well away from the city, don't leave valuables unattended. Theft is rare, but readers have reported that it happens.

Playa El Coyote

After El Tecolote, a dirt road continues around to the east side of the Pichilingue Peninsula to Punta Coyote. Coves along this stretch are rocky and sand is gray or brown instead of white. The road effectively ends here, although

the most adventurous off-roaders might attempt to find their way through a maze of sand roads to Puerto Mejia and Las Cruces.

Las Cruces

When Hernan Cortés sailed from the mainland to Antigua California in 1535, he supposedly landed at Las Cruces, about 50 kilometers southeast of La Paz on the Canal de Cerralvo. Today, three stone crosses perched on a bluff mark the historic place. The port here became a key part of the pearl trade but was abandoned by the 1930s when the oyster supply had been depleted.

Believing he had found a diamond in the rough, Abelardo L. Rodríguez Montijo, grandson of Mexico's interim president from 1932–1934, decided to invest. In 1949, he built a luxury fly-in resort on 8,000 hectares, designed to attract wealthy Hollywood celebrities—and went on to found the original Palmilla hotel in Los Cabos in 1957.

Though still a private organization, Rancho Las Cruces recently opened its guestrooms to the public (www.rancholascruces.com).

PENÍNSULA EL MOGOTE

The closest land you see when standing on the *malecón* is the thumb-shaped Mogote Peninsula. Extending 11 kilometers in an east–west direction, it joins the main Baja Peninsula via a narrow sand spit on the north side of the Ensenada de La Paz. Mangroves grow along the Mogote's southern shore, which faces the city; the opposite shore features a long, sandy beach.

Once the domain of kayakers and other adventure-seekers, the area is now under development as the US$240 million Paraíso del Mar real estate project takes shape. Plans call for two golf courses, a clubhouse, hundreds of homes, a shopping mall, church, hotels, marina, and park. Necessary infrastructure will include desalination plants, water and sewage treatment plants, and a ferry terminal. (Although there is a dirt road leading out to the peninsula from El Comitá, north of La Paz, primary access for visitors will be by water taxi, since the distance is only 800 meters from the *malecón*.)

The project has encountered criticism from environmentalists, including Greenpeace, for endangering hundreds of acres of mangroves, which provide a habitat and nutrients for thousands of marine species in the Sea of Cortez. But the developers are taking steps to protect the fragile ecosystem, for example by landscaping the golf courses with native plants.

Islands

You haven't fully experienced La Paz until you've explored the group of undeveloped barrier islands that guards the entrance to the bay. Along the shores of Isla Espíritu Santo and Isla Partida, protected coves in shallow bays provide a safe environment for swimming, rock and coral reefs attract abundant marine life, and steep cliffs lead to stunning bay views.

Isla Espíritu Santo

Closest to the Pichilingue Peninsula, Isla Espíritu Santo is 22.5 kilometers long. Its southwest side is scalloped with a series of narrow bays, each with one or more fingers reaching deep into the interior of the island. The shoreline on the northeast side is smoother, with fewer protected places to land small boats and snorkel or swim.

Formerly owned by a local *ejido,* this island was "sold" to the Mexican government in 2003 through the cooperative efforts of several nonprofits, which raised US$3.3 million to compensate *ejido* members for the land. For the traveler in search of outdoor adventure, this means the island has a good chance of remaining undeveloped, even as large real estate projects take shape on the peninsula.

Due to the presence of numerous reefs and underwater rock formations, this island is a popular stop for snorkeling and scuba diving tours. **Bahía San Gabriel** near the southwest tip of the island features ruins from a former pearl-fishing operation.

For a good hike, begin at the beach at Caleta el Candelero on the northwest side of the island. Find the arroyo and follow it inland, where a deep canyon is carved into the volcanic bluffs. Along the way are wild fig and plum trees; keep your eyes peeled for the rare black jackrabbit.

Isla Partida

The next major island heading north from Pichilingue is the much smaller Isla Partida, which has more beaches, dive sites, and opportunities for hiking and views. Fish camps at either end of the island sometimes have fresh water, but it isn't guaranteed. Plan to bring your own drinking water. If you are navigating your own boat, beware the sandbar that almost connects Isla Partida with Isla Espíritu Santo. The channel is extremely narrow.

Los Islotes

Hundreds of playful sea lions live on and around this group of small jagged rock islands north of Isla Partida. Roughly a one-hour boat ride from Pichilingue, they are a popular destination for snorkeling, scuba diving, kayaking, and sportfishing.

Camping

Because the islands near La Paz are protected by the Mexican government, a permit (US$4/day) is required to camp on them. Visit the local **SEMARNAT office** (2nd floor, Ocampo 1045 btw Rubio/Verdad, tel. 612/128-4171, www.semarnat.gob.mx, Mon.–Fri. 8 A.M.–3 P.M.) before you head out to sea. Pets are prohibited, as is harvesting wood for campfires. The availability of fresh water limits camping options on the larger islands, and camping is not allowed on Ensenada Grande or Playa Ballena.

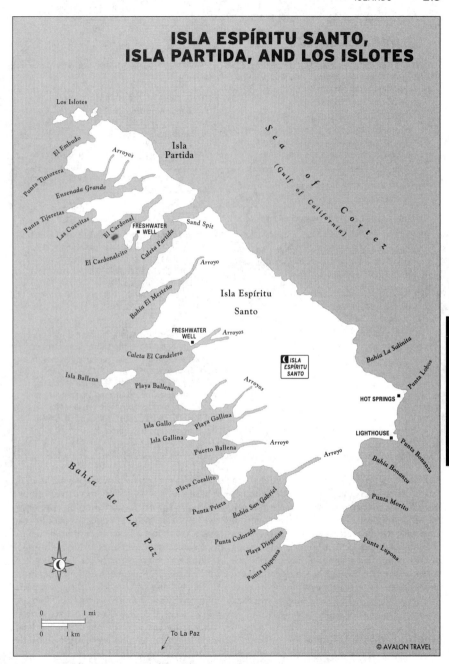

ISLA ESPÍRITU SANTO, ISLA PARTIDA, AND LOS ISLOTES

Los Islotes

El Embudo

Punta Tintorera

Arroyos

Isla Partida

Ensenada Grande

Punta Tijeretas

Las Cuevitas

El Cardonal

FRESHWATER WELL

Sand Spit

El Cardonalcito

Caleta Partida

Bahía El Mesteño

Arroyo

Isla Espíritu Santo

FRESHWATER WELL

Arroyos

Caleta El Candelero

Isla Ballena

Playa Ballena

Arroyos

Isla Gallo

Playa Gallina

Isla Gallina

Puerto Ballena

Arroyo

Playa Coralito

Bahía San Gabriel

Punta Prieta

Punta Colorada

Playa Dispensa

Punta Dispensa

Sea of Cortez

(Gulf of California)

Bahía La Salinita

Punta Lobos

HOT SPRINGS

LIGHTHOUSE

Punta Bonanza

Bahía Bonanza

Punta Morito

Arroyo

Punta Lupona

ISLA ESPÍRITU SANTO

Bahía de La Paz

0   1 mi
0   1 km

To La Paz

© AVALON TRAVEL

LA PAZ AND VICINITY

LEAVE NO TRACE

Visitors intent on setting foot on the delicate islands of the Sea of Cortez should heed the recommendations proffered by Conservation International, as follows:

- Check your equipment and provisions thoroughly before landing to avoid the introduction of rats, mice, insects, or seeds from other islands or from the mainland. Check your shoes and cuffs.

- Don't bring cats, dogs, or any other animals to the islands.

- Don't take plants, flowers, shells, rocks, or animals from the islands.

- The animals and plants that live on the islands are not used to human presence. Keep this in mind during your visit.

- Keep a minimum distance of 45 meters from all sea bird and sea lion colonies, and keep at least 300 meters away from pelicans during their nesting period (Apr.-May).

- Don't cut cacti or shrubs. Don't gather wood; plants take a long time to grow on these arid islands. Dry trunks are the home of many small animals. If you need to cook, take your own stove and avoid making fires.

- Don't make new walking paths. Don't re- move stones or dig holes; you will cause erosion.

- Don't camp on the islands unless you are familiar with low-impact techniques. Conservation International Mexico can provide you with that information.

- Help keep the islands clean. Don't throw or leave garbage on the islands or in the sea. Help even more by bringing back any garbage you find.

- To camp or even land for any activity on the islands of the Sea of Cortez you need a permit from the Secretaría de Medio Ambiente y Recursos Naturales (SEMARNAT). To obtain a permit, contact Instituto Nacional de Ecología, Dirección de Aprovechamiento Ecológico, Periferico 5000, Col. Insurgentes Cuicuilco, C.P. 04530, Delegación Coyoacán México D.F. 01049, México, www.ine.gob. mx.

For more information, contact Conservation International, Calle Banamichi Lote 18 Manzana 1, Lomas de Cortés, Guaymas, Son. 85450, México, tel./fax 622/221-1594 or 622/221-2030, m.carvajal@conservation.org, www.conservacion.org.mx, or its main U.S. office at 1919 M St., NW Suite 600, Washington, DC 20036, tel. 202/912-1000 or 800/406-2306, www.conservation.org.

Two of the bays, Caleta El Candelero on Isla Espíritu Santo and El Cardonalcito on Isla Partida, have freshwater wells where you can bathe. You'll need a bucket and five meters of rope to reach the water level. Purify the water if you must use it for drinking. (Plan to bring your own purified water and only use the well water in an emergency.) It's also a good idea to bring multi-fuel stoves for camping to increase your chances of finding the canisters you need while in Baja.

Getting to the Islands

There are several ways to reach the islands. Most visitors book a daylong kayak, snorkeling, or scuba diving tour. You can also join a guided multi-day kayak/camping trip, or arrive by private yacht. Experienced paddlers can rent a kayak in La Paz and paddle the 6.5 kilometers across the channel from Pichilingue (Playa El Tecolote is the closest launch-point) to the islands. Wind, current, and tides make this a challenging trip, even though the distance is relatively short. At Playa El Tecolote, you can also hire a *panga* for an excursion to the island. Rates are around US$150 per boat, including lunch. A one-way shuttle out to the island costs about US$75.

Sports and Recreation

FISHING

The best fishing near La Paz takes place May–November, and the typical catch includes wahoo, dorado, tuna, as well as sailfish and blue, black, and striped marlin. The El Bajo seamount is exposed to the wind, but has developed a legendary reputation for some of the biggest marlin, tuna, and dorado.

The waters around the far side of the Pichilingue Peninsula near Isla Cerralvo, Punta Arena de la Ventana, and Bahía de los Muertos have more consistent fishing than the bay and islands closer to La Paz. For this reason, many fishermen choose the relative ease of a one-hour van ride and launch at Punta Arena de la Ventana over the *panga*-pounding journey by sea to the same fishing grounds.

If the wind is blowing too hard to get to the pelagics offshore, you can try for inshore species such as barred *pargo,* snapper, mackerel, seabass, and grouper. Ceviche made from fresh mackerel is a fine consolation prize for getting blown off the big water. The norm for inshore fishing is live sardines with a few thrown in around your bait as chum.

Roosterfish *(pez gallo)* are available in the Punta de la Ventana area and can reach world-record size. The all-tackle world record, weighing 51.7 kilograms, was landed off La Paz in 1960. In 2007, a fisherman caught an estimated 54-kilogram roosterfish, but it was never weighed. Whether you are fishing or not, there is nothing more exciting than the moment when the spiked comb of the *pez gallo* breaks the surface of the turquoise waters and tears across a shallow bay on Isla Espíritu Santo. Your first instinct might be to run.

Charters

The fishing charter business in La Paz is well developed, with many professional operations, experienced captains, and well-appointed boats. Here are a few of the most popular choices: Owned by Southern California native Jonathan Roldan, **Tailhunter International** (Paseo Obregón 755, cell tel. 044/612/141-1716 (Jonathan), U.S. tel. 626/333-3355 or 877/825-8802, www.tailhunter-international. com, riplipboy@aol.com) often guides fly-fishing clients who want to catch roosterfish and dorado. It has two fleets: The La Paz boats head to Espíritu Santo and El Bajo; a separate Punta Arena fleet fishes the waters around Isla Cerralvo, Banco 88, and Bahía de los Muertos.

Jay Murakoshi's **C&J Fishing Adventures** (Flies Unlimited, U.S. tel. 559/449-0679, www.fliesunlimited.com, jaysflies@me.com) specializes in saltwater fly-fishing in tropical destinations around the world and leads charter trips to Bahía de la Ventana. Jay also sells his own saltwater and surf-zone flies.

Baja Pirates (U.S. tel. 866/454-5386, www. bajapiratesoflapaz.com, leonard@bajapiratesoflapaz.com) has a fleet of eight boats, from a standard 22-foot *panga* up to cruisers and a 26-foot Bay Liner. Boats are equipped with life jackets, marine heads (on 210 or larger), tackle, gear, and ice chests (with ice), along with breakfast and lunch. This company has package deals out of Los Angeles that include airfare out of LAX.

Other charter services include **Fishermen's Fleet** (tel. 612/122-1313, U.S. tel. 408/884-3932, fishermensfleet@hotmail.com, www. fishermensfleet.com), specializing in complete *panga* packages. Fishing destinations include El Bajo, Isla Cerralvo, and Las Arenas. Owner David Jones has lived in La Paz with his family since the 1990s. His 38-foot Hatteras cruiser is a good option for large groups and multi-day fishing trips.

The experts say, if you bring your own gear, a seven-foot rod with something like Penn 500 loaded with 30-pound test will work for most situations. You can pick up fishing tackle and related supplies at **Deportiva La Paz** (Mutualismo, tel. 612/122-7333), one block in from the Applebee's on the *malecón.*

DIVING AND SNORKELING

La Paz has one of the largest scuba diving communities anywhere in Mexico. The islands offshore from La Paz present divers of all skill levels with some of the most interesting underwater topography in the Sea of Cortez, as well as opportunities to spot some of the largest pelagics in the sea. Sea lions frolic at Los Islotes, while hammerhead sharks school around the El Bajo seamount and giant mantas cruise against the current. From the surface, you may see flying mantas, schools of dolphins, and giant bait balls.

Unlike the reef and wall diving in Cabo Pulmo and Cabo San Lucas, where dive sites are a 5- to 15-minute boat ride from shore, long, choppy boat rides (45–60 minutes) are the norm here—hence the higher rates. Remember to take your seasickness medicine the night before. (Many divers swear by Bonine, found over the counter in the United States and Mexico.)

A day of diving typically begins around 7–8 A.M. and finishes in the late afternoon. Lunch is usually included at no extra cost.

Most operators require a minimum of at least two divers to send a boat out to the islands. Some require four divers to visit the more remote sites.

Dive Sites

Most boats frequent about a dozen different sites around the islands offshore from La Paz. A sea lion colony at Los Islotes (7–15 meters) provides loads of underwater entertainment. Also suitable for beginners, the *Salvatierra* wreck (18 meters) presents an opportunity to explore the remains of a cargo ferry that sank in 1976. If conditions permit, advanced divers might request a trip to the El Bajo seamount (18–30 meters) in hopes of encountering a school of hammerhead sharks, as well as giant mantas, whale sharks, and towers of schooling amberjacks and tuna.

Day Trips

In business since 1992, **Buceo Carey** (Legaspy and Topete, tel. 612/128-4048, U.S. tel. 877/239-4057, www.buceocarey.com) is one of the more respected dive centers in town. A staff of local captains and international dive guides leads one-day and multiday dive trips to Espíritu Santo sites for US$85 a day, and to El Bajo and Isla Cerralvo for US$95. The cost includes lunch, transportation, guide, unlimited sodas and beer, weight belt, and two tanks. Rental equipment includes regulators, BCDs, wetsuits, masks, snorkels, fins, tanks, weight belts, booties, and portable air compressors. The company has a second office at Marina de La Paz. Inquire about accommodations packages: Two days/three nights at the Los Arcos runs US$317; six days/seven nights is US$773.

The largest dive operation in La Paz is Fernando Águilar's **Baja Diving and Service** (B.C.S. 11/Carr. a Pichilingue, past the ferry terminal, tel. 612/122-7010, www.clubcantamar.com). Based at the Club Cantamar Resort and Sports Centre on the Pichilingue Peninsula, the company operates a fleet of eight vessels, including some of the largest dive boats on the Sea of Cortez, holding more than 20 divers. Its custom-built 53-foot *Liberación* is the newest dive boat in La Paz, with air-conditioning and hot water, two heads, and a pleasant sundeck for warming up after each dive. The boat accommodates 30 divers for day trips and 10 divers as a liveaboard. They also run *pangas* for divers who consider the larger boats to be too much like cattle cars. Besides the sheer scale of the operation, shorter boat rides are a significant advantage of diving with the Cantamar staff. Boats typically depart at 8:30 A.M. and return by 5 P.M. For divers who aren't staying at the resort, a shuttle service is provided at no additional cost.

Dive rates are US$115 per person per day for two or three tanks, depending on conditions. Day trips include transportation, boat ride, lunch, and drinks. The resort has an ultralight plane used for spotting whale sharks (extra charge of US$20 pp). Shorter boat rides also make the more distant dive sites like Las Animas and the San Diegito Reef more accessible for day-trippers (extra charge of US$25 per diver for trips to these sites).

DIVING AND SNORKELING COSTS

GUIDED DIVE/SNORKEL TOURS
Discounts apply for multiday dives (overnight in La Paz hotel, typically the Los Arcos). Hotel/dive packages are available.

Snorkel tour (equipment included)..US$50-65

Two- or three-tank boat dive...US$85-135

Night dive..US$60

Package of two days/three nights, with accommodations and meals.........US$300-400

Package of six days/seven nights, with accommodations and meals.........US$700-800

Nondiver passenger...US$10-15

LIVEABOARD DIVE TRIPS
Types of liveaboard trips: Socorro Island, Whale Shark Expedition, Island Tour

Six days/seven nights...US$1,565

Eight days/nine nights..US$1,495-2,500

Night dive on liveaboard trip...US$30

DIVE INSTRUCTION
Open water certification (classroom and dives)..........................US$420

Discover Scuba/resort course (Introduction to scuba)....................US$110-140

Advanced certification...US$390

Nitrox certification...US$220

GUIDED KAYAK TOURS
Day trips..US$35-95

Two-day trip...US$250-300

Four-day trip..US$400-500

Six-day trip...US$1,100

10-day trip..US$2,000

DIVE AND KAYAK EQUIPMENT RENTAL
Snorkel gear (usually included with tour)...............................US$6-15

Scuba package with dives (discounts for multiday dives).................US$20-30/day

Rebreather...US$65

Airfills...US$5

Nitrox refills...US$8-12

Panga shuttle to Espíritu Santo (round-trip from Playa Tecolote)........US$200-400

Double kayak...US$60/day

Single kayak...US$40/day

Truck shuttle to Playa Tecolote..US$25

Island camping fee...US$4

Dive packages for 3–14 nights with half- or full-board cost US$373–1,580 and US$424–1,821; Nitrox and rebreather dive packages are also available at additional cost. Included are round-trip airport transfers and lunch on dive days.

Rental gear is available (snorkel set US$7/day, dive gear US$23/day). Certified divers can also get nitrox refills for US$8–12 and rent rebreathers for US$65. New divers can get certified in the resort's own pool (US$420, includes two days of open-water dives) or try an introductory Discover Scuba course (US$140). Advanced certification costs US$290. Nitrox certification is US$220. In case of a dive emergency, the Cantamar has the only recompression chamber in La Paz. For more information or to make a reservation, drop in at the Cantamar's downtown sales office (Paseo Obregón 1665-2, Plaza Cerralvo, near the Hotel Perla, tel. 612/122-1826, daily 9 A.M.–8 P.M.).

Another multiboat operation is based at the La Concha Beach Resort. **The Cortez Club Dive Center** (Km 5 Carr. a Pichilingue, tel. 612/121-6120, www.cortezclub.com) has 12 dive boats, its own classroom for dive instruction, and a private jetty and ramp. Rates are a little higher than other shops for day trips, but lower for scuba courses.

Day excursions aboard Baja Expeditions' 45-foot *Don Cano* or 48-foot *Pez Sapo* cost US$125 per day (Mar.–Dec.), which covers three dives, breakfast, lunch, snacks, and happy hour (tel. 612/125-3828, U.S. 800/843-6967, www.bajaex.com).

Liveaboard Trips

If viewing underwater marine life is the focus of your trip to La Paz, consider a multiday trip aboard one of these custom-designed dive boats. Packages typically include the first and last nights in a La Paz hotel, usually the Los Arcos. Rates shown here are for double occupancy. An additional fee often applies for single occupancy.

Baja Diving and Service (tel. 612/122-7010, www.clubcantamar.com) runs several liveaboard trips through the summer and fall months. A nine-night/eight-day trip to Socorro Island (with eight days of diving) costs US$2,500. A seven-night/six-day whale shark expedition is US$1,565. **Buceo Carey** (Legaspy and Topete, tel. 612/128-4048, U.S. tel. 877/239-4057, www.buceocarey.com) runs multiday trips on two boats: *Marco Polo* holds 6–8 divers, and offers six days/five nights for US$1,399; first and last night at the Los Arcos. **Baja Expeditions** (tel. 612/125-3828, U.S. 800/843-6967, www.bajaex.com) offers liveaboard trips on the air-conditioned, 80-foot *Don José*. Trips are booked out of the U.S. office, but you can sometimes sign up in La Paz if the boat isn't full. An eight-day trip aboard the *Don José* (offered June–Nov.) costs US$1,595 per person for superior rooms (double occupancy). Three eight-day whale shark–viewing trips take place in May and June (from US$1,895 per person). The boat holds 16 divers. The *Don José* has a loyal following, since the staff allows divers to go on their own schedule by running constant shuttles to many different sites.

Operated by a Mexican-Japanese couple, **Baja Quest** (Rangel 10 btw Sonora/Sinaloa, tel. 612/123-5320, www.bajaquest.com.mx) offers two-night/three-day dive-trip packages June–October for US$850, including hotel and airport transfers, and longer trips for US$1,040–1,190. Luxury accommodations aboard *The Sandman* cost US$993–1,395. Baja Quest also offers dive/cruise/camping combinations (Apr.–Nov. only).

Deportiva La Paz (Mutualisimo, tel./fax 612/122-7333) sells scuba diving equipment and fills air tanks but does not run dive trips.

Snorkel Tours

Most dive and kayak outfitters also run snorkel tours. Less-expensive trips visit the beaches along the Pichilingue Peninsula; the more expensive ones go to the islands for the day. For example, **Buceo Carey** (Legaspy and Topete, tel. 612/128-4048, U.S. tel. 877/239-4057, www.buceocarey.com) offers snorkeling trips for US$65 to Playa Encantada and the sea lion colony. **Baja Diving and Service** (tel.

612/122-7010, www.clubcantamar.com) at the Cantamar does local snorkel trips for US$50. One of the best values among organized trips is the snorkeling trip to Espíritu Santo run by **Azul Tours** (Paseo Obregón 774, tel. 612/122-4427, www.azultourslapaz.com, azultours@gmail.com). The staff are knowledgeable, well equipped, and safety-conscious. The adventure takes the better part of a day and includes a delicious lunch, prepared by its sister restaurant, Palapa Azul, for US$65 per person.

El Tecolote Restaurant/Bar/Playa (tel. 612/127-9494) transports snorkelers to Espíritu Santo in *pangas* for US$40 pp. The price includes gear and lunch. Boats depart between 10–11 A.M. for a four-hour tour. Stop by the booking office, just off the plaza next to the Hotel Miramar, for more information. El Tecolote also offers WaveRunners, kayaks, banana boats, and waterskiing.

WHALE-WATCHING

There are several ways to observe gray and blue whales near La Paz, and several dive and kayak outfitters offer special whale-watching tours. Some tours go to the Sea of Cortez, while others go to Laguna San Ignacio on the Pacific side of the Baja Peninsula. Some trips involve snorkeling and paddling; others are just boat cruises. You can go for one day or eight, depending on your budget and how much time you want to spend with the mammals.

Baja Outdoor Activities (tel. 612/125-5636, U.S. tel. 888/217-6659, www.kayakinbaja.com) offers a package with two three-hour boat trips plus an overnight stay and all meals for US$250 per person.

Johnny Friday and Maldo Ficher lead ecotours in the area through **Baja Adventure Company** (tel. 612/125-9081, U.S. tel. 877/506-0557, www.bajaecotours.com), a division of Mar de Cortez sports. Its marine biologists, zoologists, and other professionally trained guides lead whale-watching trips.

KAYAKING

The islands near La Paz are some of the best places in the world to kayak, and several companies provide highly recommended tours. Day trips are possible, but given the amount of gear and transportation logistics involved, many day-trippers end up feeling rushed and wish they had chosen a multiday tour instead. Most trips fall into one of two categories: a four-day paddle along the west side of Isla Espíritu Santo (usually north to south) and a seven-day (or more) paddle all the way around Isla Espíritu Santo and Isla Partida (56 km).

Overnight package trips usually include the first and last nights in hotel accommodations, with camping on the nights in between. Meals, transportation to the islands, and airport transfers are also typically covered by the price. Some trips return to a base camp every night, while others move to a new place each day. Some have motorized support boats to move camping gear from place to place and shuttle paddlers to the best snorkeling sites for the particular conditions each day. Some outfitters supply camping gear; others ask that you bring your own.

Many companies book kayak tours, but often they are brokers for the actual outfitter. In general, it's better to book directly so you can get complete information about the itinerary and equipment before you sign up for a trip. Two of the most popular operators are Mar y Aventuras and Baja Outdoor Adventure.

Owned by a La Paz native, **Mar y Aventuras** (Topete 564 btw 5 de Febrero/Navarro, tel. 612/123-0559, toll-free U.S. tel. 800/355-7140, www.kayakbaja.com), near La Marina Don José and Marina de La Paz, leads one-day and multiday trips and rents kayaks and gear to experienced paddlers (reserve well in advance if you want to rent). Its boats are a mix of doubles and singles made of fiberglass and some plastic. All have rudders. Day trips range US$35–380 per person, depending on the destination and size of the group. Two- to four-day tours cost US$425–575. Magdalena Bay whale-watching trips cost US$325–725 for 2–4 days. Longer trips to Espíritu Santo are available as well.

If you want to explore El Mogote or the islands on your own, you'll have to convince the staff that you know what you're doing. For safety reasons, they are reluctant to rent to novice and intermediate paddlers. Single kayaks rent for US$40 a day, with a PFD (personal flotation device), paddle, bilge pump, and spray deck. Double kayaks cost US$60 a day. You can also rent snorkeling gear and camping equipment. Boat shuttles out to Isla Espíritu Santo cost US$200–400 round-trip for one or two people; a truck shuttle to Playa El Tecolote for launching from the beach to Espíritu Santo costs US$25 one-way for one or two people. You can pay the US$4-per-day camping fee at the Mar y Aventuras office.

Baja Outdoor Activities (BOA) (tel. 612/125-5636, www.kayakinbaja.com) offers two different styles of kayak trips: "Cooperatively catered" trip participants carry their own gear each day and help guides prepare meals, making for a more self-sufficient experience, but with heavier boats to paddle. Others prefer a fully catered trip, in which guides prepare all meals and camping supplies are transported by motorboat. Four-day island tours range US$420–490. Daily dolphin sightings are common on the 10-day Loreto to La Paz trip (US$1,090). Participants should expect to paddle about four hours per day on this trip.

The half-day tour for US$35 is a nice way for beginners to get a feel for the sport without committing to a full-day adventure. BOA also offers a one-day tour of Balandra Bay for US$70. BOA rents sit-on-top kayaks and sea kayaks by the day or week (US$35–60/day and US$110–220/week).

Baja Expeditions (tel. 612/125-3828, toll-free U.S. tel. 800/843-6967, www.bajaex.com) has been running seven-day trips to Espíritu Santo (US$1,125) since 1985. Other destinations include Loreto to La Paz coast (10 days) and Magdalena Bay (8 days). An aggressive 10-day, open-water kayak trip hops among the islands of Espíritu Santo, Los Islotes, San José, Santa Cruz, and Santa Catalina (Oct.–Apr. only).

BOATING

With the largest bay along the Gulf Coast, La Paz is far and away the frontrunner in all of Baja when it comes to boating services and supplies. Even Cabo San Lucas pales in comparison. There are numerous public and private marinas, boatyards, and marine supply stores, with new businesses opening and old ones upgrading all the time.

Marinas

At the west end of the *malecón,* the **Marina de La Paz** (Topete 3040 at Legaspy, tel. 612/122-1646, www.marinadelapaz.com) has completed numerous upgrades in recent years: New docks and a new layout came in 2004, followed by a fixed breakwater system in 2005, and an additional 37 meters of fixed breakwater plus a new 50-meter dock for accommodating large vessels in 2006. Facilities at this floating marina now include a launch ramp, diesel fuel dock, grocery store with marine supplies, The Dock Café, water and electricity outlets, cable TV, laundry, showers, restrooms, wireless Internet, a chandlery, and boat and vehicle maintenance and storage. Local nonprofit **Club Cruceros de La Paz** (www.clubcruceros.org, Mon.–Sat. 9 A.M.–6 P.M.) has a clubhouse at the marina with a book exchange. It also provides incoming mail service.

Rates for one of the marina's 150 slips range from US$20 per day and US$375 per month for a 30-foot craft to US$95 per day and US$1,800 per month for a 90-foot craft. Discounts also apply for stays of 4–21 days, if paid in advance. Showers cost US$1.50 daily. Cable TV is US$1 per day, or US$15 per month. Parking for slip clients is US$1 daily or US$25 per month. Prices include tax.

Well known on the yachting circuit, the marina typically fills up in the high season, November–May; check for vacancies before sailing in. A US$200 deposit will hold your space on the waiting list. Reserve online, or by mailing a personal check.

Northeast of town, at Km 2.5, the **Marina Palmira** (tel. 612/123-7000 or 877/217-1513, www.marinapalmira.com) offers 186 full-service slips suitable for yachts up to 130 feet long and 12 feet deep. The marina recently reinforced its breakwater and launching ramp.

COURTESY OF PARAISO DEL MAR

boats on Bahía de La Paz

There is free wireless Internet, and a free shuttle to downtown is available at various times each day. Guests can use dry-storage facilities, laundry, water, showers, bathrooms, a pool, hot tub, and tennis court. There are also a market, two restaurants, a bar, 24-hour security, parking for one car per registered guest, a public phone, marine supplies, a fuel dock with diesel and gas, and boat launch. You can charter boats here, with or without a crew. Daily slip rates are US$12.73–25.74 according to the size of the boat; monthly rates are US$10–21 per foot for slips of 30–100 feet. Electrical service costs extra. You can rent condos and hotel rooms at several resorts nearby by the day, week, or month.

Based at the Club Cantamar Resort and Sports Centre, **Marina Pichilingue** (tel. 612/122-7010, www.clubcantamar.com) has 35 slips for boats up to 75 feet long (US$8.10/ft/month). Water, electricity, and dry storage are available.

A newcomer on the Pichilingue Peninsula, **Marina CostaBaja** (tel. 612/121-6225, www. costabajaresort.com) can accommodate mega-yachts up to 220 feet in 250 slips. Rates start at US$11.50 per foot up to 39 feet for one month, and go up to US$22 per foot for a 150- to 200-foot boat. Daily rates are subject to availability (US$1.10/ft/day up to 99 feet and US$1.65/ft/day for 100–200 ft boats). Liveaboards require special permission from the marina. Amenities include Internet, TV, and phone; at-slip pump-out service, dry storage, restrooms and showers, parking, pool, and shuttle to La Paz. Some travelers who have used this marina report problems with black soot from the nearby oil refinery damaging canvas on their boats. A reservation form is available online.

A *panga* usher guides all boats through the approach into the new **Singlar Fidepaz Marina** (Mexico 1/Constituyentes, near Km 4.5, tel. 612/124-2206), part of the Mexican government's *Escalera Náutica* Sea of Cortez Project. The marina opened in 2006 with 40 slips for boats up to 75 feet. Amenities include a restaurant, laundry, showers (US$1), rooftop lap pool and whirlpool tub, fuel dock, boat ramp, 75-ton lift, and large boatyard. There is a maximum stay of 15 days, which means this marina may have space when others are booked. Note, the location is closer to the airport than to downtown La Paz, but there is bus service to town for US$0.60.

If you're hauling your own boat, you can use ramps at Marina de La Paz, Marina Palmira, and Pichilingue. Smaller boats and kayaks can launch from any of the public beaches.

Parts and Repairs

Marina de La Paz is the one-stop-shop in town for boating questions, services, and supplies; **Ferretería Marina SeaMar** (SeaMar Marine Chandlery, Topete and Legaspy, tel. 612/122-9696, Mon.–Fri. 8:30 A.M.–1:30 P.M. and 3–6 P.M., Sat. 8:30 A.M.–1:30 P.M.), across from the marina entrance, carries basic supplies. **López Marine Supply** (Vista Coral Plaza, tel. 612/125-4160, Mon.–Sat. 8 A.M.–5 P.M.) accepts credit cards. Club Cruceros keeps a list of local marine service providers at www.clubcruceros.org/services.

Boat Charters

If you like the idea of cruising but don't have your own boat or any experience on the water, you might book a trip with **Baja Coast SeaFaris** (Dock B, Marina de La Paz, tel. 612/111-7335, www.bajaseafaris.com). This company offers full-service charters with a bilingual crew aboard two sailboats: the *Irish Mist,* a 50-foot yacht that sleeps 2–4 adults and *Tesoro del Mar,* a Beneteau 50 that is faster and roomier, with space for six adults. Privacy is the distinguishing factor with this outfitter. All trips are private, whether for a party of two or six; pricing varies with the size of the group. Multiday trips (3–5 days or longer) include stops at Espíritu Santo, Isla Partida, and Los Islotes for swimming with sea lions, scuba diving, kayaking, tubing (for kids), sailing, beachcombing, whale-watching, bird-watching, snorkeling, or fishing. Rates are US$755 per night for two persons and US$185 additional per night for additional adults on the *Tesoro del Mar,* US$115 additional per child on the *Irish Mist* or the *Tesoro del Mar.* The price covers all meals, snacks, and cocktails

while on board the yacht; a night of lodging at the Los Arcos Hotel on the final evening; and round-trip airport transfers. The boats are fully equipped with kayaks and other gear. Scuba diving and rental gear are also arranged upon request. Book well ahead (several months) for peak travel times. Inquire about a 10 percent discount for families and special occasions like honeymoons and anniversaries. "Learn to sail" trips are another option. Baja Coast SeaFaris no longer accepts credit cards or Paypal payments. Deposits must be paid by personal check, money orders, or bank wire.

The owner of Baja Coast SeaFaris has compiled a thorough list of FAQs for novice and experienced sailors that covers topics related to cruising in Baja at (www.bajaseafaris.com/cruise.html).

ATV TOURS

ATV tours have become a popular way to explore the Baja Peninsula, and La Paz now has its first tour operator: **La Paz ATV's Adventures** (cell tel. 612/131-0784, www.lapazatvs.com, US$75/90 s/d) runs three-hour tours on Honda Rancher 350 ATVs. The ride includes safety equipment, instruction, and bottled water, and the route goes from the village of El Comitán, a half-hour north of La Paz, through El Mogote sand dunes, to the end of the peninsula and back. Shuttle service is provided from La Paz to the departure site.

MOUNTAIN BIKING

Co-located in the Baja Outdoor Activities (BOA) office next to the El Moro hotel, Mexican-owned **Katún** (tel. 612/348-7758, www.katuntours.com) runs guided tours of the Sierra de La Laguna (US$1,980/two weeks, US$1,350/one week). Combination kayak/bike trips cover travel from the Sea of Cortez to the Sierra de la Laguna in 10 or 14 days (US$1,350/US$1,980). And the weeklong Jesuits trail tour traces historic routes through the Sierra la Giganta, from the Sea of Cortez to the Pacific (US$1,199).

Katún also rents 2006 Giant Yukon bikes with front suspension for US$10 an hour,

US$15 for four hours, or US$20 per day. **Azul Tours** (Paseo Obregón 774, tel. 612/122-4427, azultours@gmail.com) also rents mountain bikes for US$15 a day.

HIKING AND HORSEBACK RIDING

Antonio Moller (tel. 612/123-1370, www.bajaexplore.com) leads one-day and overnight trips into the Sierra de la Laguna from La Paz. Day trips (US$45–65 pp, min 3 people) include transportation from La Paz to the biosphere, lunch at a local ranch, and a one-hour horseback ride. Student discounts available.

SPA SERVICES

The **Hotel Los Arcos** (Paseo Obregón 498, tel. 612/122-2744, U.S. tel. 800/347-2252, www.losarcos.com) offers spa services at reasonable rates: A 45-minute massage is US$45, and a 50-minute sports massage is US$55.

ORGANIZED TOURS

Travel companies and outfitters offer a variety of guided tours and organized activities, from island kayak trips and whale-watching to language immersion and cooking classes. A number of the newer ones are committed to promoting environmentally aware tours and trips. Aside from the activity-specific outfitters mentioned earlier in this chapter, **Espíritu & Baja Tours** (Obregon #774-A btw Allende/Juárez, tel. 612/122-4427, www.espiritubaja.com, espiritubaja@gmail.com) runs professional and reasonably priced trips, such as snorkeling at Espíritu Santo (US$60 pp), whale-watching trips to Bahía Magdalena (US$110 pp), sportfishing (US$200 per boat), kayaking along the Pichilingue Peninsula (US$65 pp), horseback riding trips (US$75 pp), and airport transfer services (airport–hotel US$15, hotel–airport US$7).

Readers have reported pleasant outings with **Eduardo's Tours** (cell tel. 044/612/105-2609, eduardoviajes@hotmail.com). Eduardo Gomez provides ground transportation and leads guided trips to Los Cabos (US$99 pp), Todos Santos (US$77 pp), and El Triunfo (US$77 pp). A La Paz city tour costs US$27.50 per person. Whale-watching (US$120 pp) and snorkeling (US$77 pp) tours are also possible. **Azul Tours** (Paseo Obregón 774, tel. 612/122-4427, azultours@gmail.com) offers a La Paz city tour for US$30 per person, as well as island trips.

Mar y Aventuras (Topete 564 btw 5 de Febrero/Navarro, tel. 612/123-0559, toll-free U.S. tel. 800/355-7140, www.kayakbaja.com) offers a Spanish-language immersion and cooking class package, in partnership with Se Habla La Paz. Packages include seven nights/eight days accommodations in the Posada Luna Sol, 25 hours of Spanish classes, and three nights of cooking classes (US$495 pp, double occupancy).

Once a year in April, May, or November, travel photographer Jim Cline leads a **Wonders of Baja California** photo tour (U.S. tel. 877/350-1314, www.jimcline.com, US$2,675) of La Paz, Loreto, Mulege, Todos Santos, and Cabo San Lucas, including three boat trips to islands on the Sea of Cortez. Participants get to try their hand at capturing the seascapes, cacti, historic missions, and wildlife through the lens of their camera. Tours begin in Los Cabos and include accommodations and seafood dinners.

In addition to hiking and horseback riding tours, **Antonio Moller** (tel. 612/123-1370, www.bajaexplore.com) offers guided trips to El Triunfo and the nearby cactus sanctuary. Tours cost US$40 per person, with a minimum of three people, and last approximately six hours (8 A.M.–3 P.M.).

Entertainment and Events

NIGHTLIFE

La Paz nightlife is more diverse and vibrant than that of San José del Cabo, but not as crazy and tourist-oriented as what you'll find in Cabo San Lucas. Many Baja expats who live in surrounding towns come to La Paz for live concerts and other performances. Most venues are open nightly until at least midnight or later on weekends.

For sea views and a relaxed atmosphere, start the evening at **Bar Pelícanos** (Paseo Obregón 498, tel. 612/122-2744, www.losarcos.com, daily 10 A.M.–1 A.M.), on the second level of the Hotel Los Arcos. This large bar has an interesting collection of old photographs on its back wall, from Pancho Villa to former U.S. President Dwight Eisenhower to Clark Gable.

One of the oldest watering holes in town is **Tequilas Bar and Grill** (Ocampo 310 E. at Mutualisimo, tel. 612/121-5217) with simple decor, pool tables, and a cigar bar. It has a full kitchen and will happily cook your fresh catch for you.

Rock music plays at **El Claustro** (Paseo Obregón btw Hidalgo/Costilla, tel. 612/128-4946, Tues.–Sun.), in an unusual Italianate building on the *malecón.*

For dancing, **Las Varitas** (Independencia 111, tel. 612/125-2025, www.lasvaritas.com), near Plaza Constitución, plays recorded and live music. Wednesday is "Rock and Biker" night, and on Thursdays, a band from Sinaloa plays.

Carlos'n Charlie's, on Paseo Obregón, has an attached dance club called **La Paz Lapa** (Paseo Obregón and 16 de Septiembre, tel. 612/122-9290). Above Pizza Fabula **Casa de Villa** (Paseo Obregón and 16 de Septiembre, tel. 612/122-5799) is a rooftop bar and nightclub that's popular with locals.

The Hotel Perla's **Nightclub La Cabaña** (Paseo Obregón 1570, tel. 612/122-0777, daily 9 P.M.–3 A.M.) hosts *norteña* bands, usually on Thursdays and Sundays.

In a courtyard behind La Fabula Pizza, **Peña**

La Pitahaya de Janicua (Paseo Obregón 15) is an almost hidden spot with a bohemian ambience and live Latin folk music nightly.

CINEMA

The only cinema in town is the 15-screen **Cine Gemelos** in the Soriana shopping complex on Boulevard Forjadores at the corner of Avenida Luis Donaldo Colosio.

FESTIVALS AND EVENTS
◖ Carnaval

La Paz is known throughout Mexico for its all-out celebration of Carnaval, a six-day festival held throughout the world in mid-February on the days leading up to Ash Wednesday. Like Mardi Gras in New Orleans, Oktoberfest in Munich, or Burning Man in the Nevada desert, this is a destination event—something every traveler should consider experiencing at least once. There are daily parades along the *malecón,* brightly colored costumes, the crowning of a queen, amusement rides, fireworks, music, and food stands—with tequila and *cerveza* flowing freely all the while.

The Carnaval tradition came to Mexico from Spain, and is believed to have evolved as the last chance for Christians to party before the fasting time of Lent. Some interpret the name Carnaval as deriving from the Latin *carne vale,* which means "farewell to meat."

Fiesta de La Paz

The Fiesta de La Paz (officially known as Fiesta de la Fundación de la Ciudad de La Paz) takes place on May 3, the anniversary of the city's founding. Contact the state tourism office (tel. 612/124-0100, turismo@correro.gbcs.gob.mx), between Km 5 and 6 on Mexico 1 (Avenida Abasolo) for festival venues and events.

Baja 1000

The Baja 1000 off-road race comes to town in mid-November. Produced by SCORE International (U.S. tel. 818/225-8402, www.

score-international.com), the event is the sixth and last in a series of desert races that take place in the southwestern United States and Mexico each year. The Baja 1000 attracts more than 400 pro contestants who drive trucks, motorcycles, ATVs, and every imaginable variation of off-road vehicle. They start in Ensenada and cruise at breakneck speeds through the desert to the outskirts of La Paz. Only about half of the race entrants complete the challenging 1,000-mile course.

In its 42nd year in 2009, the race draws thousands of support crew and spectators to the most remote parts of the peninsula. The course opens for pre-running approximately three weeks before the race start. Travelers on Mexico 1 during this time will often see vehicles kicking up a cloud of dust in the distance, moving at speeds faster than highway drivers go. This is one of the only times a year you may encounter traffic on the more remote stretches of Mexico 1.

Shopping

La Paz serves as a vital commerce center for all of Southern Baja. Its many shops and department stores cater not only to local residents but also to those of towns as far away as Todos Santos and the East Cape. The result is a greater variety of items at competitive prices.

DEPARTMENT STORES

La Paz's largest department store is **Dorian's,** with two locations (16 de Septiembre at Esquerro and at the mall on Blvd. Forjadores). The original **La Perla de La Paz,** a good bet for housewares and the like, never reopened after a fire in 2006, but it does have an annex that is open for business across the street (Arrival at Mutualismo).

For clothing at discounted prices, try **MAS** (Madero at Degollado, daily 9 A.M.–9 P.M.). Next door, **DAX** (Arreola at Zaragoza, tel. 612/125-2480, Mon.–Thurs. 8 A.M.–9 P.M., Fri.–Sat. 8 A.M.–10 P.M.) has a pharmacy, cosmetics, and toiletries. And next to DAX, **Solo Un Precio** ("Only One Price," Madero btw Tejada/Arreola, daily 8 A.M.–9 P.M.) is the Mexican equivalent of the dollar store. Everything in the store is 10 pesos.

ARTS AND CRAFTS

Several tourist-oriented shops line the *malecón* between the bus terminal and the Hotel Los Arcos. They sell handicrafts, t-shirts, jewelry, and postcards. **La Antigua California** (Paseo Obregón 220, tel. 612/125-5230), has a good selection of arts and crafts made primarily in mainland Mexico. **México Lindo** (Paseo Obregón at 16 de Septiembre), next to Carlos'n Charlie's, is another option.

The government-run **Casa de Artesanos Sudcalifornianos** (Paseo Obregón at Calle Bravo, tel. 612/128-8707) next to the Tourist Information/Tourist Police office and skate park, stocks *artesanías* from all over Southern Baja.

You can watch artists at work when you visit **Ibarra's Pottery** (Prieto 625 btw Iglesias/República, tel. 612/122-0404, Mon.–Fri. 9 A.M.–3 P.M., Sat. 9 A.M.–2 P.M.) The outdoor store contains several aisles of plates, mugs, pitchers, vases, pots, and the like—mostly in bold patterns and colorful designs. **Artesanía Cuauhtémoc** (Av. Abasolo btw Jalisco/Nayarit), in a white building near the CCC, has Oaxacan-style textiles including rugs, blankets, and table linens.

Artesanías Colibrí (Paseo Obregón btw Muelle/Arreola, tel. 612/128-5833, Mon.–Sat. 10 A.M.–1 P.M. and 3–8:30 P.M.) carries a good selection of *artesanías,* rustic furniture, and decorating accessories, plus cute clothes for babies and kids.

Bargain-hunters in search of clothing, housewares, or leather goods might check out the **Mercado Municipal Francisco E. Madero** (Revolución de 1910 at Degollado). **Santander**

(Serdán and Degollado, tel. 612/125-5962) has saddles, guitars, and huaraches.

SPORTING GOODS

Deportes Ortiz (Degollado 260, almost opposite Pensión California, tel. 612/122-1209) carries basic camping, diving, and other sports gear, plus some athletic apparel.

BOOKSTORES

La Paz has a wonderful English-language bookstore, **Allende Books of La Paz** (Av. Independencia 518 btw Serdan and Prieto, tel. 612/125-9114, www.allendebooks.com, Mon.–Sat. 10 A.M.–1 P.M. and 4–8 P.M.). Open since 2007, Allende Books of La Paz carries maps, dictionaries, cookbooks, history, and contemporary fiction. The store also holds occasional events, such as book signings, children's story time, and book club meetings.

Librería Contempo (Calle Arriola at Paseo Obregón) carries Mexican newspapers as well as a few American magazines.

Accommodations and Camping

In general, rooms in La Paz are more affordable than their counterparts in most of other large Baja towns, and new options are opening all the time. There are hotels in all budget categories, many with kitchenettes, plus bed-and-breakfasts, condo complexes, and private vacation rental homes. Rates do not include tax or service fees, but many places offer discounts for stays of a week or longer.

Beach camping is available in several places outside the city limits.

HOTELS

Despite the planned construction of several large luxury hotels, most rooms in La Paz still fall in the US$50–125 range. Some of the older establishments could use a makeover, but the time warp is also part of their charm. You'll pay a bit more to stay right on the water rather than along the *malecón*. And none of the bay-front hotels are within easy walking distance of the *malecón* or downtown La Paz, although taxis are always available.

Most times of year, you can wing it and find a room when you arrive. But if you plan to visit during mid-November, check the Baja 1000 event schedule and make reservations well in advance.

Under US$50

Budget accommodations tend to be centrally located but noisy, and typically do not have air-conditioning, which can be problematic for travel during the hot weather months of July–October. A mainstay on the budget travel circuit, bohemian **Pensión California** (Degollado 209 btw Revolución de 1910 and Madero, tel. 612/123-3508, fax 612/122-2896, US$15–40) occupies a former 18th-century convent. Its basic rooms have lots of beds, peeling paint, a concrete bath area separated from the main room by a curtain, and ceiling fans, which may or may not work. Showers are hot, as long as you turn on the hot water heater well beforehand. The open-air common space has a fridge, stove, sink, and chairs, and there is a computer with Internet access at the front desk (30-min limit). Guests here tend to be young and social.

Around the corner, **Hostería del Convento** (Madero 85, tel. 612/122-3508, fax 612/123-3525, misioner@prodigy.net.mx, US$20) is owned by the same family and has similar rooms, but the scene is a bit older and quieter.

The **Hotel San Carlos** (16 de Septiembre btw Serdán/Revolución de 1910, tel. 612/122-0444, fax 612/122-3991, US$25, US$30 with a/c) has 30 basic rooms.

Posada Hotel Yeneka (Madero 1520 btw 16 de Septiembre/Av. Independencia, tel./fax 612/125-4688, ynkmacias@prodigy.net.mx, US$39) has made a name for itself among global backpackers. A courtyard filled with greenery, a rusting Model T, and collection of junk give the place a flea-market feel. Its dark rooms have little in the way of amenities, but the location is convenient, and there is a laundry facility on-site.

Around the corner from Hotel Los Arcos and a block up from the *malecón,* **Hotel Lorimar** (Bravo 110 btw Madero/Mutualisimo, tel. 612/125-3822, fax 612/125-3822, US$30–40) is a step up among hotels in this category, but still a budget operation. Hard beds, loud wall air-conditioning units, and noise from a TV in the lobby can be a nuisance. But the staff are friendly and accommodating. There are two price levels, so be sure to ask to see one of each type before you settle in.

If you're just passing through and want to bypass downtown La Paz, **Hotel Calafía** (Km 4, tel. 612/122-5811, hotelcalafia@gmail.com, US$35) is a good option for affordable rooms with secure parking and a pool. Rates include tax.

casita for rent in La Paz

© NIKKI GOTH ITOI

LA PAZ AND VICINITY

US$50–100

Under new ownership, 56-room **Hacienda Bugambilias** (formerly Las Gardenias, Serdán Norte 520, tel. 612/122-3088, www.hotelgardenias.com.mx, US$70) has a residential location (three blocks from the waterfront and six blocks north of the plaza), which makes for a much quieter night's sleep than you'll get at other downtown hotels. Rooms come with tiled floors, rustic furnishings, air-conditioning, phone, and TV. Prices have gone up with the recent change in ownership and the secure parking lot is no more, but the building and decor are still 1970s-era. The hotel restaurant serves breakfast and lunch fare. This is a popular place for Mexican visitors. Enter on Guerrero between Serdán and G. Prieto.

A block up from the *malecón,* **Hotel Miramar** (5 de Mayo at Domínguez, tel. 612/122-8885, fax 612/122-0672, hmiramar@prodigy.net.mx, US$57) sometimes has rooms available when other properties at this price level are booked. Amenities include air-conditioning (noisy units), small TVs, and secure parking. Rooms

get very little daylight, especially on the lower of its three floors. Beds rest on concrete platforms and slope a bit. Some rooms have balconies and bay views.

Above the Mar y Aventuras offices, **Hotel Posada Luna Sol** (Topete 564 btw 5 de Febrero/Navarro, tel. 612/123-0559 or 612/122-7039, www.posadalunasol.com, US$60–75) offers 14 clean rooms, all with local TV, air-conditioning, private baths, and hot water; some also have bay views. Enjoy a sunset cocktail under the rooftop *palapa.* In recent years, the property has added a new top-floor suite and a room with a small kitchen. Rates include tax, but they seem a bit high for the location and lack of services such as Internet.

The historic **Hotel Perla** (Paseo Obregón 1570, tel. 612/122-0777 or 800/716-8799, U.S. tel. 888/242-3757, www.hotelperlabaja.com, US$75–100) has been hosting foreign and domestic visitors since 1940. The building and 110 guestrooms (28 with bay views) have been well cared for over the years, but the overall impression is more business hotel than vacation destination. And rates seem to be climbing without substantial renovations in recent years. Rooms are small but very clean; decor is minimal, which means noise carries in hallways. High ceilings at least create the illusion of more space. Amenities include air-conditioning, TVs, and phones. There is Wi-Fi in the lobby only. A small pool on the mezzanine level may not be heated in winter months; the rooftop playground entertains young kids.

You can't beat the Perla's location right in the middle of the action on the *malecón*. In fact, the hotel's La Terraza restaurant is a great place to grab breakfast or lunch and watch the city life stream by. Bottom line: Stay here if a central, waterfront location and secure indoor parking are important and the price is acceptable.

Under Swiss ownership, the charming **(Hotel Mediterrané** (Allende 36, tel./fax 612/125-1195, www.hotelmed.com, US$65–75) has nine immaculate rooms in a blue-and-white stucco building just steps from the *malecón*. In keeping with the Mediterranean theme, its large and pleasant guestrooms are named for the various Greek islands. They come with air-conditioning, refrigerators, and TVs; some have bay views, but these are also the closest to the street and pick up a little more noise than those at the back of the hotel. A rooftop sundeck with lounge chairs invites visitors to catch a breeze and enjoy the bay views. The owners have loaner kayaks, canoes, and bikes available. La Pazta restaurant and café are downstairs; the café has wireless Internet.

At the northeast end of the *malecón,* on the way to Pichilingue, the **Club El Moro** (Km 2 Carr. a Pichilingue, tel./fax 612/122-4084, www.clubelmoro.com, US$80–160) is a popular choice for families and travelers planning to take the ferry across to Mázatlan. A Moorish design and nicely landscaped pool and bar area are highlights of the property. Both rooms and suites come with air-conditioning, satellite TV with HBO, reliable wireless Internet, and a private terrace. Standard rooms are a little small for the price (US$80 including tax), but at US$112, the large junior suites are a great

value. There is off-street and gated parking. The adjoining **Café Gourmet** serves great espresso, as well as breakfast and lunch every day. Hotel guests receive free coffee and a coupon for US$2.50 per day. Friendly staff and an attractive frequent-guest program bring repeat visitors back year after year. You can easily catch a city bus during daylight hours to cover the two kilometers back to the downtown area. In the evening, you'll have to walk or cab.

Next to the Baja Ferries terminal in Bahía Pichilingue, **Club Cantamar Resort and Sports Centre** (B.C.S. 11/Carr. a Pichilingue, tel. 612/122-7010, www.clubcantamar.com, US$80–120) caters to serious scuba divers and other water enthusiasts. This family business has grown steadily since it opened in 1994 with one 22-foot *panga* and an old 40-horsepower outboard engine. A boat ramp and tank-filling station paved the way to a full-scale resort.

Today, guests sleep in a four-story lodge with 45 standard rooms (11 of which were renovated in 2006), eight double condos, and two junior suites; a separate building contains four apartments, each with two bedrooms, two bathrooms, kitchenette, dining room, living room, and private balcony. Rooms are decorated in desert colors, with stucco walls and rustic furnishings. Air-conditioning and satellite TV are included, and most rooms have phones too. Other resort amenities include a 35-slip marina, swimming pool overlooking the ocean (deep enough for scuba training), bar, dockside restaurant, and swim-up bar. Other adventure-oriented amenities include a boat ramp, kayaks for rent, private beach, fishing fleet, dive shop, and recompression chamber. Proximity to the industrial ferry terminal, with semi-trucks coming and going, is one disadvantage of the location. Night owls will find the Cantamar much too remote, but for those who want to maximize their time on the water, this resort is a fine home base. Rates include breakfast and taxes.

La Concha Beach Resort and Condos (Km 5 Carr. a Pichilingue, tel. 612/121-6161 or 800/716-8603, U.S. tel. 800/999-2252, www. laconcha.com, US$90–100) has the closest beachfront location to town, but the beach itself is much less attractive than those found farther out along the Pichilingue Peninsula and the accommodations are in need of some serious attention. There are hotel rooms as well as condos with lovely bay views, and there have been some improvements such as new air-conditioners in some units; however, for the most part, the property is run-down.

US$100-150

On the *malecón* and almost as old as La Perla, the locally owned **Hotel Los Arcos** (Paseo Obregón 498, tel. 612/122-2744, toll-free U.S. tel. 800/347-2252, www.losarcos.com, US$90–125) consists of an older bungalow section (called **Cabañas de los Arcos**) with additional rooms in a tower, plus a more recent (though still somewhat outdated) hotel building next door. The hotel got its start by catering to the sportfishing crows in the 1950s and 1960s. Today, it continues to cultivate a loyal following among outdoor-adventure types, despite its aging facilities. Many outfitters place guests here for a night or two as part of their package deals. Rooms and suites have air-conditioning, and both sections have swimming pools. On-site services in the hotel section include a popular bar, restaurant, gift shop, sauna, and spa services, as well as whale-watching, diving, and sportfishing tours. Rooms at Los Arcos are slightly better than at La Perla, but also a little more expensive, and they still retain a 1970s feel. Friendly service and wireless Internet are two additional features.

Also on the *malecón,* the **Seven Crown Hotel** (corner of Paseo Obregón and Lerdo de Tejada, tel. 612/128-7787, fax 612/128-9090, toll-free U.S. tel. 800/276-9673, www.sevencrownhotels.com, US$107–153) is a modern 50-room property that has all the basics but lacks the character and history of the Los Arcos and La Perla. Amenities include a gym, parking, and wireless Internet. Suites have ocean views and kitchenettes. There is a rooftop restaurant (El Aura), bar, and whirlpool tub.

On the west side of the La Paz–Pichilingue Road, the **Araiza Palmira** (Km 2.5 Carr. a

Pichilingue, Blvd. Alberto Alvarado, Fracc. Lomas de Palmira, tel. 612/121-6200 or 800/026-5444, U.S. tel. 877/727-2492, www. araizahoteles.com, US$135) is primarily a business hotel, with conference rooms, ballrooms, and guestrooms that look out on a lush garden. Amenities include a swimming pool, tennis court, and restaurant/bar.

Across from the Araiza Palmira and next to the Club de Yates Palmira, the **Hotel Marina** (Km 2.5 Carr. a Pichilingue, tel. 612/121-6254, fax 612/121-6177, U.S. tel. 800/826-1138, www.hotelmarina.com.mx, US$115–215) has 150 suites and master suites with somewhat saggy beds and older furnishings. The resort has tennis courts, a large swimming pool, and an outdoor bar.

At the center of the new 500-acre CostaBaja Resort & Marina (www.costabajaresort. com), the **Fiesta Inn La Paz** (Km 5.5 Carr. a Pichilingue, tel. 612/123-6000, www.fiestainn.com, US$85–133) is popular with families as well as boaters, who can anchor at the on-site marina. The resort has 120 guestrooms, including some that are wheelchair-accessible; amenities include wireless Internet and a separate lap-swimming lane in addition to the main pool. To find the hotel, look for a signed entrance on a rise on the seaside of the road to Pichilingue.

US$150-250

Some of the classiest accommodations in town are found at the **❰ Posada de las Flores** (Paseo Obregón 440 btw Militar/Guerrero, tel. 612/125-5871, fax 612/122-8748, www. posadadelasflores.com, US$150–290). With its signature coral-colored building and beautiful landscaping, this property looks out on the bay from the west side of the *malecón*. Rooms are designed in a rustic Mexican style, with tile floors and marble baths. Amenities include air-conditioning, wireless Internet, cable TV, and small refrigerators. Guests can also rent a larger *casa* next door. Bikes and kayaks are complimentary, and rates include breakfast. Posada de las Flores also has sister properties in Loreto and Punta Chivato.

Southwest of town, at Km 5.5 on northbound Mexico 1 (it turns north eventually), the three-story **Grand Plaza Resort** (Lte. A, Marina Fidepaz, tel. 612/124-0830, www.grandplazalapaz.com, US$150–200) is a typical airport business hotel with 50 bayside suites. Rooms are on the dark side, and beds sag a bit, but the pool is large, and bay views are a plus (no swimming). Notable amenities include free wireless Internet in the lobby and restaurant area, plus a sauna, pool tables, gym, hot tub, tennis court, massage room, and restaurant/bar. Rooms come with air-conditioning and refrigerators. The hotel stands opposite the state tourism office and next to the Singlar Fidepaz Marina.

BED-AND-BREAKFASTS

If you like cozier accommodations and the opportunity to socialize with your host, bed-and-breakfast-style accommodations can be a wonderful way to meet Mexican and expat families.

US$50-100

A branch of the same family that runs the popular Club El Moro hotel runs **Baja Bed and Breakfast** (Madero 354, tel. 612/123-1370, www.bajabedandbreakfast.com, US$45–75) in a centrally located home just off the plaza. Two street-level rooms share a bath and a patio with a small swimming pool and barbecue. Above, a spacious first-floor apartment for rent by the night or week has a kitchen, separate bedroom, and living room. The owners completed a renovation in 2007. Next door, the owners have added four rooms with private baths. Rates include tax and wireless Internet.

Owner Cecilia Moller serves a multi-course breakfast each morning on the third-floor terrace that's attached to her own kitchen. You'll start your day with fresh breads, fruit, juice, coffee or tea, and eggs, quesadillas, *chilaquiles,* or other Mexican specialties. Cecilia is the life of the party here, so be sure to time your visit for a time when she's in the house. Some of La Paz's hottest new restaurants are less than a block away, and the *malecón* is a two-block walk.

US$100-150

A half-block off the *malecón,* **La Casa Mexicana Inn** (Bravo 106 btw Madero/Mutualismo, tel./fax 612/125-2748, www.casamex.com, US$75–135) consists of five cozy rooms in a Moorish/art deco–style home. All rooms feature remote-control air-conditioning, fans, VCRs, and private baths. Rates include a breakfast of home-baked pastries, as well as tax.

Next door, a charming couple from Down Under, Patricia and Ken Bonner, have channeled their love for all things Italian into **《 Casa Tuscany Bed and Breakfast** (Bravo 110A, tel. 612/128-8103, www.tuscanybaja.com, US$105–145). Four colorful guestrooms overlook a garden courtyard behind the main house. All around the courtyard are paintings by Ken Bonner. Each room has a comfortable queen bed, private bath, ceiling fan, and remote-control air-conditioning. Prices include tax and full hot breakfast that varies each day.

In **《 El Ángel Azul** (Independencia 518, tel./fax 612/125-5130, www.elangelazul.com, US$100–195), Switzerland native Esther Ammann has converted an abandoned 19th-century courthouse into a modern-day bed-and-breakfast, with guidance from the National Institute of Anthropology and History (INAH). The result is a living piece of La Paz history with a contemporary flair. Nine rooms and one suite are arranged around a beautiful courtyard garden designed and maintained by the owner. Brightly colored rooms have queen or twin beds, bath with shower, air-conditioning, and a radio. Locally created artwork adds to the ambience, and there is secure off-street parking for guests.

CAMPING AND RV PARKS

You can camp on the beach for free north of the ferry terminal at Playas Pichilingue, Balandra, El Tecolote, and El Coyote. Among these options, only El Tecolote has fresh water; plan to bring all of your supplies from La Paz. Two restaurants at El Tecolote sell food and drinks. Though not common, theft unfortunately does occur at these beaches. Keep valuables out of sight if at all possible.

Only a couple of RV campgrounds remain as real estate development continues in the greater La Paz area. **Oasis RV Park** (Km 15, El Centenario, tel. 612/124-6090 or 612/125-6202, open year-round, US$14) is one of the survivors. It has a good location on the Ensenada de La Paz; however, its 25 sites are best reserved for self-contained rigs, as services have been limited in recent years. Tents are welcome too.

Much closer to town and with much better facilities, popular **Casa Blanca RV Park** (Km 4.5 at Av. Pez Vela, Fracc. Fidepaz, tel. 612/124-1746, rv.casablanca@gmail.com, Nov.–May), has more than 40 full-hookup sites for US$20 per night or US$400 per month. The property is surrounded by a high white concrete wall and the park provides 24/7 security. Inside, facilities include hot showers, flush toilets, laundry, and a small convenience store—but there is no dump station. Guests may use the swimming pool, tennis court, and spa. The park does not have Internet, but there is an Internet café open to the public just a short walk away.

Food

La Paz is becoming a culinary destination of sorts, with outstanding meals to be found in every price category, from street-side tacos to fresh seafood to gourmet cuisine.

MEXICAN

A new generation of chefs up and down the peninsula are working hard to create a more distinct identity for Baja regional cuisine. La Paz enjoyed its first such restaurant debut with the opening of **Las Tres Virgenes** (Madero btw Constitución/Hidalgo, tel. 612/165-6265, Tues.–Sun. 6–11:30 P.M., mains US$10–30) in 2006. The restaurant has moved slightly up the street from its original location and is now next door to the Arámburo grocery store. Its name refers to three mountains, one of which is a dormant volcano, visible in the distance on the drive from San Ignacio to Santa Rosalía. On the menu are innovative dishes like a rose petal quesadilla with strawberry sauce to start, and mesquite-grilled baby octopus and *cabrilla* over garlic mint mashed potatoes. The restaurant gets rave reviews for the high quality of its food and a reasonably priced wine list. Indeed, local expats call it the best meal they've had in La Paz, period.

In the same category but yet not as widely acclaimed, **El Aljibe** (Revolución 385 at Constitución, tel. 612/128-8985, www. elaljiberestaurant.com, Mon.–Wed. 3–11 P.M., Thurs.–Sun. 4 P.M.–midnight, mains US$10–25) debuted with a menu of seafood specialties prepared by chef Miguel Angel Guerrero. Start with a shot of clam vodka and Baja-style tuna tartar. Unusual for an upscale venue is the menu of tacos and burritos, filled with fish, shrimp, oysters, salmon, or marinated duck. Among the more unusual main dishes are the octopus in a special house sauce and *camarones rellenos:* shrimp stuffed with *machaca de marlin* and wrapped in bacon.

Carlos'n Charlie's (Paseo Obregón at 16 de Septiembre, tel. 612/122-9290, www.car-losandcharlies.com, daily noon–1 A.M., mains US$6–17) is part of the same chain as El Squid Roe and Señor Frog's in Cabo San Lucas, but the atmosphere is less touristy and zany, so it attracts some local and visiting Mexicans as well as foreigners. The menu features traditional Mexican dishes, plus some local specialties, such as a *ceviche paceño).* There is outdoor seating on a terrace facing the *malecón,* where you can often catch the afternoon breeze.

Off the beaten track, **(El Zarape** (Av. México 3450 btw Oaxaca/Nayarit, tel. 612/122-2520, www.elzarapelapaz.com, daily 7:30 A.M.–midnight, mains US$10–15) does traditional Mexican dishes right: On Saturday evenings, the kitchen prepares a buffet of

La Paz is a great place for fresh fish.

cazuelas (large, open clay pans) filled with moles and other dishes from central and southern Mexico. Its daily breakfast buffet is also a good bet for traditional foods.

A newcomer on Madero close to the plaza is **Caprichos** (Madero at 5 de Mayo, tel. 612/125-8105, hours vary), where the owners serve reasonably priced dishes in another of La Paz's historic downtown buildings.

SEAFOOD

Ultra-fresh fish is the theme at **Restaurant La Costa** (Navarro and Topete, daily 2 P.M.–2 A.M., mains US$10–15), a waterfront *palapa* restaurant near the Marina de la Paz. From *ceviche de pescado* to *huachinango* and *albondigas de camerones,* air-conditioned **Restaurant La Mar y Peña** (16 de Septiembre btw Isabel la Católica/ Albañez, tel. 612/122-9949, daily noon–10 P.M., mains US$10) serves one of the widest ranges of fish and shellfish entrées anywhere in Baja. The decor is casual, the margaritas are fresh, and credit cards are accepted.

Once a well-kept secret, **Bismark II** (Degollado at Altamirano, tel. 612/122-4854,

daily 8 A.M.–10 P.M., mains US$10–20) has become one of the most popular tourist restaurants in La Paz in recent years, and locals no longer recommend it with as much enthusiasm. Lobster, abalone, and *carne asada* are its hallmark dishes, but the ceviche is also worth a try. On the *malecón,* **Bismarkcito** (Paseo Obregón near Constitución, tel. 612/128-9900, daily for lunch and dinner, mains US$10–15) is a waterfront offshoot of its parent restaurant. This casual eatery draws a crowd for weekday business lunches; however, when the exceptionally loud marching band starts playing on the sidewalk, conversation of any sort becomes impossible. The menu includes all manner of seafood cocktails, and fish and shellfish entrées; Peñafiel brand Mexican sodas are a treat.

On the second floor of the Hotel Los Arcos, **Restaurant Bermejo** (Paseo Obregón, tel. 612/122-2744, Mon.–Sat. 7 A.M.–11 P.M., Sun. 8 A.M.–11 P.M., US$15–20) is a good spot to watch the activity on the promenade below. Choose among seafood, steaks, and pasta dishes on the menu. If you've had a successful day fishing, the restaurant will prepare your catch.

The popular ◖ **Mariscos Moyeyo's** (corner of Paseo Obregón and Calle Héores de 47, no tel., daily for lunch and dinner, mains US$5–15), just past El Moro hotel, packs a crowd on weekend afternoons, when locals stop in for towering seafood cocktails. The floor is sand, and the tables and chairs are plastic. It takes a dozen wait staff to keep the fresh catch flowing. The restaurant has occasional live music.

Near the Posada las Flores on Obregón, **Las Brisas del Mar** (Paseo Obregón at Militar, tel. 612/123-5055, lasbrisasdelmbcs@hotmail.com, daily for dinner, mains US$13–27) serves seafood cocktails, fish *a la parilla, empanizado,* shrimp, lobster, and red meat from Sonora.

At the CostaBaja marina and resort, **Azul Marino** (tel. 612/106-7009, daily for lunch and dinner, mains US$10) does a blend of international foods, all oriented around a seafood theme.

ITALIAN

Owned and run by an Italian/Chinese husband-and-wife team, ◖ **Caffé Milano** (Esquerro 15, btw Callejón de la Paz/16 de Septiembre, tel. 612/125-9981, www.caffemilano.com.mx, Mon.–Sat. 1–11 P.M., mains US$6–18) prepares traditional Italian fare that wows discerning foodies from around the globe. Start with an order of fried oysters with caviar and move on to a homemade pasta or a hearty main dish like osso buco ord *frutti di mare.* Homemade limoncello is a fitting way to end the meal. The restaurant received a AAA diamond rating in 2006. Look for the tall, light blue wooden doors.

Decorated in pastel colors and original artwork, **La Pazta** (Allende, adjacent to Hotel Mediterrané, tel. 612/125-1195, Wed.–Mon. 7 A.M.–11 P.M., Tues. 7 A.M.–3 P.M., mains US$10–15) prepares a mix of Italian and Swiss dishes, including pastas, pizzas, and fondues. Choose from an impressive list of wines from Italy, the United States, Chile, and Baja.

Marine biologist Christian Liñan took time away from his studies to open **Toscana Pizza Gourmet** (Dominguez and Constitución, no tel., Mon.–Sat. 3–11 P.M., mains US$5–10) in 2006. This Italian pizzeria makes European-style pies for eating in or takeout; salads, pasta, and drinks complete the menu. Dine at six pine picnic tables outside or at window counter seating inside.

ECLECTIC

On the east side of the *malecón,* **Kiwi Restaurant Bar** (Paseo Obregón btw 5 de Mayo/Constitución, tel. 612/123-3282, Sun.–Thurs. 8 A.M.–midnight and until 2 A.M. Fri. and Sat., mains US$6–15) has good views and a menu of passable seafood, Mexican, and international dishes. The people-watching is better than the food, but this is not a bad choice for lobster.

El Taste (Paseo Obregón at Juárez, tel. 612/122-8121, daily 8 A.M.–11 P.M., mains US$10–20) has a longstanding reputation for good breakfasts, but the menu also has steak, Mexican dishes, and seafood. Tourists and expats are the primary clientele.

At the Hotel Perla, open-air **La Terraza** (Paseo Obregón 1570, tel. 612/122-0777, daily for breakfast, lunch, and dinner, mains US$10–20) serves everything from seafood and Mexican fare to steak and Italian dishes. The crowd is a mix of visitors and locals and the prices are reasonable.

AMERICAN

Near the plaza and across from Baja Bed and Breakfast, ◖ **Buffalo BAR-B-Q** (Madero 1420, tel. 612/128-8755, Mon.–Fri. 6 P.M.–midnight, Sat.–Sun. 2–10 P.M., mains US$10–20) gets high marks from locals for its steaks and burgers.

An upscale option on the waterfront near the Marina de La Paz, **El Patrón Bar & Grill** (Plaza Vista Coral, tel. 612/125-9977, www.elpatronbarandgrill.com, Sun.–Wed. 1–11 P.M., Thurs.–Sat. 1 P.M.–midnight, mains US$15–25) serves lamb, Sonora beef, grilled fish, tequila shrimp, and Cornish game hens in a casual indoor/outdoor setting. Some say the quality of the food doesn't match the prices.

The yachting crowd frequents **The Dock Café** (Topete/Legaspy, tel. 612/125-6626, daily

8 A.M.–10 P.M., mains US$10–15) inside the Marina de La Paz. This casual diner prepares a long list of American standbys, including fried chicken, burgers, fish-and-chips, bagels, salads, steaks—and even homemade apple pie.

Restaurant Grill Campestre (tel. 612/124-0454, daily for lunch and dinner, mains US$10–15), opposite the Fidepaz building on Mexico 1 north near Km 5.5, is popular with gringos and Mexicans alike for barbecued ribs, Cobb salad, and other American specialties.

CHINESE
A number of decent Chinese restaurants have opened around town, serving Mexicanized variations of standard Chinese fare at inexpensive prices. For example, **Jeon-San** (Revolución 1440 btw Reforma/Independencia, tel. 612/122-0606, daily noon–8 P.M., myli.wv@gmail.com, mains US$7) offers à la carte plates and combinations, all in large portions and delivered with friendly service.

ANTOJITOS AND FAST FOOD
It's easy to find 🄲 **Rancho Viejo** (Legaspy, half a block from the Marina de La Paz, tel. 612/128-4647, daily 24 hrs, dinner mains US$12–17) from the smell of the grill wafting up the street. Sit at a picnic table on the sidewalk, or in either of two dining rooms inside, to get away from the smoke. *Tacos de arranchera,* carne asada, or *pastor* arrive with the usual tray of fresh condiments. You can also order by the kilo. Service is prompt and friendly, and you can't beat the prices. Rancho Viejo has expanded to include a new space next door, and has also opened satellite location on the *malecón,* near Carlos'n Charlie's and the Thrifty Ice Cream shop. Instead of staying open round the clock, this one closes at 3–4 A.M.

A half-block from the *malecón* on 16 de Septiembre, **Restaurant Pichos** (no tel., Tues.–Sun. 8 A.M.–11 P.M., mains US$3–6) serves delicious *tortas, licuados,* tacos, burgers, and *chilaquiles.* The *Hamburguesa Mexicana* comes with carne asada instead of ground beef, bacon bits, cheese, sliced avocado, tomato, and shredded lettuce, all on a lightly toasted bun. Two people can easily have lunch here for less than US$10, including sodas.

Street vendors open in the afternoons around the plaza and along Calle 16 de Septiembre. They typically sell hot dogs, tacos, stuffed baked potatoes *(papas rellenas),* burgers, and seafood cocktails. One of the best for fish and shellfish tacos as well as *aguas frescas* is **Super Tacos de Baja California Hermanos González** on Calle Esquerro. There is a second location on Degollado at Madero, next to Pensión California, and a larger restaurant location on Degollado at Mijares. **Taquería Los Superburros** (Avenida Abasolo btw 5 de Febrero/Navarro) is another popular choice for cheap eats.

Loncherías in the **Mercado Municipal Francisco E. Madero** (Revolución de 1910 and Degollado) serve a good mix of *antojitos* and *comidas corridas.*

La Cochinita (Forjadores and Veracruz, tel. 612/122-1600, daily 10 A.M.–10 P.M., mains US$5–10) is an only-in-Mexico option for Japanese fast-food. A second branch is located on Calle Mutualismo, next to Bar El Misión.

CAFÉS
The espresso business is booming in La Paz. Several chains now have multiple locations, and new ones seem to open every month. Starbucks look-a-like **5th Avenida Coffee** has wireless Internet in various locations, including 5 de Mayo on the plaza and Avenida Abasolo near the Marina de La Paz. **Café Exquisito** has a *malecón* location with sidewalk tables (Paseo Obregón south of La Fuente, Mon.–Sat. 6 A.M.–10:30 P.M., Sun. 8 A.M.–10:30 P.M., drinks US$1–3), plus two drive-through espresso stands north and south of town on Mexico 1, and one more at the airport. **Café Combate** has at least two locations in town: Serdán between Ocampo and Degollado, and on Bravo at the southeast entrance to Mercado Bravo.

Aside from these chains, air-conditioned **Caffé Gourmet** (Esquerro and 16 de Septiembre, tel. 612/122-6037, Mon.–Sat.

8 A.M.–10 P.M.) has a counter full of sweets to go with your coffee, plus a selection of smoothies, Italian sodas, cigars, and liquors. Breakfast is served until 3 P.M. There is a non-smoking section in the back, and a newer second location on the *malecón*.

Also air-conditioned, **Mareiros Café** (Paseo Obregón,no tel., Mon.–Sat. 8 A.M.–11 P.M., Sun. 9 A.M.–5 P.M.) has sandwiches and salads to go with its full menu of hot drinks. There is outdoor seating and Internet access. **La Pazta Café** (daily 7 A.M.–11 P.M.), next to La Pazta Restaurant and Hotel Mediterrané, serves excellent espresso drinks made from imported Italian Illy brand coffee, as well as cocktails, beer, and wine. There is air-conditioning, wireless Internet is free, and a desktop computer is available.

Café Gourmet (Km 2 Carr. a Pichilingue, tel./fax 612/122-4084, www.clubelmoro.com, daily 7 A.M.–4 P.M., mains US$5–15), attached to the El Moro hotel, is a good place to stop for breakfast on the way to Pichilingue.

El Quinto Sol (Domínguez and Independencia, tel./fax 612/122-1692) prepares vegetarian *tortas, comida corrida,* pastries, salads, granola, fruit and vegetable juices, and yogurt. You can also stock up on healthy foods in the attached store. Readers also recommend **La Virtud** (Ramirez btw Bravo/Rosales, tel. 612/128-6940) for sandwiches, pastries, and healthy snacks.

GROCERIES

Vendors in the **Mercado Municipal Francisco E. Madero** (Revolución de 1910 at Degollado) sell fresh fish, meats, fruit, vegetables, and baked goods, and there is a *tortillería* at the corner of Revolución de 1910 and Bravo.

The government-subsidized **ISSSTE Tienda** (Revolución de 1910 at Bravo) has the lowest prices but limited inventory.

La Paz has two large **CCC** (Centro Comercial California) stores (Av. Abasolo at Colima and Isabel La Católica at Bravo). They stock U.S. and Mexican brands, but prices are relatively high. **Supermercado Arámburo** also has three branches in town: 16 de Septiembre at

cucumbers for sale

© PAUL ITOI

Altamirano, Madero at Hidalgo y Costilla, and Durango 130 Sur (btw Ocampo/Degollado).

For non-grocery supplies, stock up at **Plaza Ley** on the eastern edge of town (Las Garzas at Teotihuacán). Walmart- and Costco-like **Soriana** (tel. 612/121-4771) and **City Club** (tel. 612/165-4990), owned by the same company, are both in a shopping plaza on Boulevard Forjadores at the corner of Luis Donaldo Colosio.

SWEETS

A day in La Paz isn't complete without an icy treat, and the downtown area has lots of options for *nieves* (Mexican-style ice cream), *paletas* (popsicles), and the like. **La Michoacana** is a chain with branches on Paseo Obregón and Calle Madero. But the most popular stand in town by far is █ **La Fuente** (Paseo Obregón btw Degollado/Muelle), known for its long list of flavors, some of which are quite unusual. Look for a polka dot tree in front of the entrance.

A couple of *dulcerías* (sweet shops) are located at the intersection of Calles Ocampo and Serdán. **Dulcería Perla** sells traditional and modern Mexican candies, while **Dulcería La Coneja** on the opposite corner makes piñatas.

LA PAZ AND VICINITY

Information and Services

TOURIST ASSISTANCE

Baja California Sur's state tourism office, **Fideicomiso de Turismo Estatal de BCS** (Km 5.5, tel. 612/124-0100, www.explore-bajasur.com, turismo@correro.gbcs.gob.mx, Mon.–Fri. 8 A.M.–8 P.M.) is a few kilometers north of downtown on Mexico 1 (Av. Abasolo), opposite the Grand Plaza Resort. Also here is the Attorney for the Protection of Tourists. More convenient is the information booth on the *malecón* near the Los Arcos hotel, which has maps and brochures (Paseo Obregón at Allende, Mon.–Fri. 8 A.M.–8 P.M.).

MONEY

Unlike in the Los Cabos area, you will need pesos for making cash purchases at many businesses in La Paz. Three banks with ATMs are clustered near the intersection of Calle 16 de Septiembre and the *malecón*. They provide currency-exchange service Monday–Friday 9 A.M.–noon. If you need to exchange money in the afternoon or on a Saturday and you can't use an ATM, **Tony Money Exchange** (Mutualismo near La Perla, and nearby on 16 de Septiembre near the *malecón*, Mon.–Sat. 9 A.M.–9 P.M.) usually has acceptable rates. On Sundays, hotels like the Los Arcos are the only option.

POST AND TELEPHONE

The main La Paz post office is at the intersection of Revolución de 1910 and Constitución, one block northeast of the cathedral. It's open Monday–Friday 8 A.M.–3 P.M., Saturday 9 A.M.–1 P.M.

DHL (Avenida Abasolo at Nayarit, tel. 612/122-8282) offers domestic and international shipping.

INTERNET ACCESS

Many hotels and cafés now offer high-speed wireless Internet access for free. The 5th Avenida and Café Exquisito chains offer wireless access, as do most of the marinas.

LA PAZ PHONE NUMBERS

- La Paz area code: 612
- Baja Ferries Office (Pichilingue): 123-0208
- COTP (Captain of the Port): 122-0243 or 122-4364
- Green Angels: 124-0100 or 124-0199
- Highway Patrol/Federal Police: 122-0369
- Immigration: 125-3493 or 124-6349
- IMSS Hospital: 122-7377
- Police, Fire Department, Red Cross (emergency): 066
- SEMATUR Ferry Office (Pichilingue): 122-5005
- State Tourism Department: 124-0100, 122-0199

Hotels with wireless connections include the Los Arcos, Mediterrané, Fiesta Inn, Seven Crown, El Moro, and Posada de las Flores. Air-conditioned **La Pazta Café** (daily 7 A.M.–11 P.M.), next to La Pazta Restaurant and Hotel Mediterrané, has a desktop computer set up for customer use; wireless access is free if you bring your own computer.

In addition, a number of Internet cafés are still in business along the *malecón*. **Omni Services** (Paseo Obregón 460-C, tel. 612/123-4888 or 877/805-7372) has Internet, PCs, copies, and fax services. Rates in La Paz are generally a reasonable US$2 per hour.

PEMEX

The most central Pemex to downtown is located on 5 de Mayo between Serdán and Prieto. A second is 10 blocks away at the intersection of Isabel

© KATHLEEN BENNETT/COURTESY OF ALLENDE BOOKS

Allende Books of La Paz is well-stocked with books and periodicals.

la Católica, and a third is on Avenida Abasolo as you leave La Paz headed toward the airport.

LAUNDRY

Close to the *malecón,* **La Paz Lava** (Ocampo at Mutualismo, tel. 612/122-3112, daily 8 A.M.–9:30 P.M.) is a self-service or full-service facility that also can deliver your clothes to your hotel. The marinas in town have their own laundry services as well.

LANGUAGE COURSES

Swiss-run **Centro de Idiomas, Cultura y Comunicación (CICC)** (Madero 2460 at Legaspy tel. 612/125-7554, www.cicclapaz.com, Mon.–Fri. 8:30 A.M.–1 P.M., Sat. 9:30 A.M.–1 P.M.) teaches Spanish-language students of any level. Its standard program (US$780) includes four weeks of intensive study (25 hours per week); a homestay with a Mexican family costs extra. A one-week travel Spanish course costs US$99. The school also offers business-Spanish and medical-Spanish programs.

    Se Habla La Paz (Madero 540, tel./fax 612/122-7763, www.sehablalapaz.com) also offers more expensive classes and homestays for

travelers and medical or legal professionals. Costs include a US$75 registration fee that covers student/family matching for homestays and airport pickup. Lessons run US$22 per hour for a private session, US$16.50 for couples, and US$11 for group lessons. A one-week course is US$220 (20 hours), and a four-week program costs US$850 (80 hours). Payment is accepted via PayPal.

NEWSPAPERS AND MAGAZINES

La Paz has two Spanish-language dailies: *Diario Peninsular* and *El Sudcaliforniano* (www.elsudcaliforniano.com.mx). **Librería Contempo** (Arriola at Paseo Obregón) carries mostly Mexican newspapers, as well as a few American periodicals.

IMMIGRATION

La Paz has an immigration office on Paseo Obregón between Allende and Juárez (tel. 612/124-6349, daily 8 A.M.–8:30 P.M.). Another immigration office at the airport also is open daily, and a third office, at the Pichilingue ferry terminal, opens about an hour before each ferry departure.

LA PAZ AND VICINITY

Getting There and Around

GETTING THERE
By Air
Márquez de León International Airport (LAP) (tel. 612/124-6307) is located 12 kilometers south of La Paz; look for the access road at Km 9. Services include fast food (Burger King, Chili's), a duty-free shop, at least eight major car rental companies, Ladatel public phones, and a Scotiabank ATM.

Direct service from the United States has been on-again, off-again as the economy rises and falls. At last check, Alaska Air was the only airline making the trip; Delta had put its service on hold indefinitely. All other carriers required a connection in mainland Mexico, which adds significant cost and time to the trip.

Transporte Terrestre (tel. 612/125-3274) runs a shuttle service between downtown and the airport in yellow-and-white vans; prices are US$15 for *colectivo* (shared ride), US$30 for private service *(especial),* and US$56 for a larger van. A regular taxi to the airport should cost around US$20. Some hotels offer airport shuttles for US$5–10 per person. **Espíritu & Baja Tours** (Obregon #774-A btw Allende/ Juárez, tel. 612/122-4427, www.espiritubaja. com, espiritubaja@gmail.com) offers airport transfer services in addition to its other tours (airport–hotel US$15, hotel–airport US$7).

By Bus
La Paz has two bus terminals. The main one is on Calle Jalisco at Avenida Independencia, about 10 blocks inland from Avenida Abasolo. The second one, called the *terminal turistica,* is on the *malecón.* **Aguila** (tel. 612/122-3063 or 612/122-4270) has daily northbound service from the main terminal with stops at the tourist terminal to Ciudad Constitución, Puerto San Carlos, Puerto López Mateos, Loreto (US$30, twice daily), Mulegé, Santa Rosalía, San Ignacio, Vizcaíno Junction, Guerrero Negro (US$70, several times daily), San Quintín, Ensenada (US$85, four times daily), Tijuana (US$134, four times daily), Tecate, and Mexicali.

Southbound buses all depart from the **Terminal Turistica** (tel. 612/122-7898). Only one bus (5 P.M.) runs through the central Cape Region towns of El Triunfo, San Antonio, San Bartolo, Los Barriles (US$9), Santiago, and Miraflores, terminating in La Ribera/ Las Cuevas. Most run via Mexico 19 through Todos Santos (nine buses per day, beginning at 7 A.M., US$7), continuing to Cabo San Lucas (US$14) and San José del Cabo (US$17); the 3 P.M. bus continues all the way to La Ribera.

Southbound travelers have another option: **Autotransportes La Paz** (tel. 612/122-2157) has a more central terminal on Calle Degollado at Guillermo Prieto, which has several departures a day to Los Cabos via Todos Santos. Fares are competitive with the Aguila fares.

By Boat
The busy ferry port at Pichilingue lies 16 kilometers northeast of downtown La Paz via Mexico 11, also known as the Carreterra a Pichilingue. It offers passenger and vehicle service to Mazatlán and Topolobampo on the mainland through **Baja Ferries** (Pichilinque Terminal, tel. 612/123-0208, downtown office: Allende 1025 at Rubio, tel. 612/123-6600 or 800/122-1414, www.bajaferries.com, daily 8 A.M.–5 P.M.). You can book tickets in advance online, in downtown La Paz, or at the ferry terminal. (See *By Ferry from Mainland Mexico* in the *Essentials* chapter for details.)

You must obtain a **temporary vehicle import permit** (Expedición de Permisos de Importación Temporal de Vehículos, IITV, approx. US$30 payable at a Banjercito bank) in order to drive your vehicle in mainland Mexico. The purpose of this document is to make sure that you take the vehicle with you when you leave, instead of selling it illegally and avoiding the import tax. There are several ways to take care of this paperwork:

• Visit a Mexican consulate in the United States (Albuquerque, Chicago, Dallas, Houston,

Los Angeles, Sacramento, San Bernardino, San Francisco, Phoenix).

• Apply on the Banjercito website (www.banjercito.com, pages and forms are available in English), and then complete the process in person at a Banjercito branch in Mexico.

• Go to customs *(aduana)* in Tijuana, Tecate, or Mexicali when you enter Baja.

• Go to customs at the ferry terminal in La Paz.

To get the permit in La Paz, go to the customs *(Aduana Maritima)* office (Mon.–Sat. 9 A.M.–1 P.M. and 5–7 P.M.) at the ferry terminal. It's a slow and sometimes frustrating experience, and it's best to allow an extra day or two to be sure all the paperwork gets done in time for your departure.

Wherever you apply, you will need the following documentation in order to get the permit:

• Vehicle title or registration, to prove you own the vehicle: original plus three copies.

• Certificate of canceled import permit for any prior temporary import permits. a letter from the owner authorizing you to take the vehicle into Mexico (if you have leased, rented, or borrowed the vehicle).

• Major credit card (in the vehicle owner's name), for securing the temporary import deposit, which guarantees that you'll bring the vehicle out of Mexico when you leave; if you don't bring a credit card, you'll need to leave US$200–400 in cash, depending on the age and value of the vehicle; the deposit is refunded when you cancel the permit at the end of your trip).

• Valid driver's license Passport with valid Mexican visa Proof of Mexican auto insurance policy.

If you arrive with all of the requisite paperwork, the permit can usually be issued on the spot, after long waits in several lines. Once issued, the permit is valid for six months.

For travelers arriving and departing by private boat, La Paz is an official port of entry into Mexico, and foreign vessels must follow the appropriate procedures for checking in and out of the country. The port captain's office is located near the Marina Palmira. The staff at any of the major marinas in town can process paperwork required for clearing the port. The Marina de La Paz has published a detailed FAQ with information about the official entry and exit requirements at www.marinadelapaz.com.

GETTING AROUND

Except on the hottest of days, downtown La Paz is best explored on foot. Narrow one-way streets filled with people and vehicles can be intimidating to navigate for the first-time visitor, but if you stick to the perimeter streets—Avenida Abasolo, Paseo Obregón, Blvd. Forjadores, etc.—it's fairly easy to get around by car as well. City buses and taxis are readily available too.

If you are driving into La Paz from the south and want to head directly to the Pichilingue Peninsula and the ferry terminal, you can take a shortcut just after the university on Boulevard Forjadores. Look for a sign for Libramiento Norte heading off to the right. If you get to Soriana and Office Depot, you've missed the turn and it's best to continue on into the city and make your way to the waterfront.

By Bus

Municipal buses and *colectivo* shuttles congregate around the Mercado Municipal on Calle Degollado and head out in all directions from there. Routes may be indicated by he name of the street the bus will follow (e.g., G. Prieto) or the district to which it is heading (e.g., *El Centro*). To get to the Soriana mall on Boulevard Forjadores, look for buses labeled Soriana.

Frequent Aguila buses connect the downtown area to the Pichilingue Peninsula. Catch them at the Terminal Malecón (Paseo Obregón 125, tel. 612/122-7898). Buses to Playa Balandra and Playa El Tecolote depart at noon and 2 P.M., on weekends only.

By Taxi

Taxis are easily found along the west end of Calle 16 de Septiembre, and in front of the Los Arcos and La Perla hotels. Fare for rides within the downtown area should be under US$5, about US$5 to Soriana, US$15 to the airport, and US$20 to the ferry terminal. There are no meters, so be sure to agree on a price before you hop in.

By Car

A handful of international car rental agencies have airport and downtown locations in La Paz. Rates start around US$25 per day for unlimited miles, not including tax and insurance.

La Paz has numerous Pemex stations, all selling *magna sin* (unleaded), premium, and diesel.

Construction is underway to widen Mexico 19 to a four-lane highway connecting La Paz and Cabo San Lucas. So far, about 32 kilometers have been widened near La Paz.

Southeast of La Paz

Two scenic bays southeast of La Paz—Bahía de la Ventana and Bahía de los Muertos—are joined to the city via paved BCS 286, which departs Mexico 1 at Kilometer 211 and extends 43 kilometers to the farming town of San Juan de los Planes. In between, the peaks of the Sierra de la Laguna range rise to more than 1,200 meters. (The mountains here are also called the Sierra de las Cruces on the north side of the highway, and the Sierra el Novillo and Sierra la Trinchera on the south side.) The descent affords stunning views of the sea and Isla Cerralvo just 16 kilometers offshore.

Combine the culture and history of La Paz with a more rustic outdoor experience along one of these bays, and you have a near-perfect Baja itinerary.

Information and Services

La Paz has the closest hospital and other emergency services, but there is a **BlueMedicalNet** (tel. 624.104-3911, daily 24/7) clinic at Km 55, on the road from La Paz to Los Planes.

You can get gas and supplies in Los Planes; there are also a few convenience stores in El Sargento.

Getting There

Most people reach La Ventana and Los Muertos by car from La Paz. It takes about 35 minutes to get to La Ventana from downtown La Paz and about 45 minutes from the airport. Once on BCS 286, look for the La Ventana turnoff at Km 38—it's a paved road that branches northeast. Follow this road along the edge of the bay about eight kilometers to La Ventana and 11 kilometers to El Sargento.

Shuttles from La Paz to La Ventana cost around US$120 (US$350 from Los Cabos). **El Cardón Tequila Bar & Grill** (tel. 612/167-3702, U.S. tel. 619/446-6549, www.elcardon.com.mx) offers shuttle service from La Paz to Los Muertos. Pubic transportation is an option, albeit a complicated one. It's about a US$15 taxi from the airport to the La Ventana bus stop. From there, a bus leaves daily at 2 P.M. for US$5.

If you are on the East Cape heading to Bahía de los Muertos, you have two options: Follow the 47-kilometer dirt road between Los Barriles and Los Planes, or follow the Transpeninsular Highway north and use the now-paved connector between Mexico 1 and BCS 286. The dirt road begins with a relatively smooth ride, but after El Cardonal (13 km into the drive), the road narrows and ascends into the sierra, where the going gets pretty rough. You don't need four-wheel drive, but this is not a drive for those prone to vertigo or anyone in a hurry. Many of the curves have steep drop-offs, and you'll have to take it slow.

If you are coming from the south on Mexico 1, a newly paved route connects BCS 286 and Los Planes to the town of San Antonio. This road is straight and flat, and its east end begins on BCS 286 about 3.5 kilometers south of the turnoff for La Ventana and El Sargento.

The private **Aeromar las Arenas** airfield offers tie-down service and 24-hour security for guests of the Bay of Dreams resort. Currently

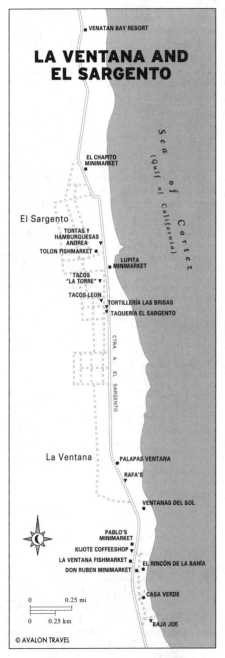

LA VENTANA AND EL SARGENTO

VENATAN BAY RESORT

S e a   o f   C o r t e z   (Gulf of California)

EL CHAPITO MINIMARKET

El Sargento

TORTAS Y HAMBURGUESAS ANDREA
TOLON FISHMARKET

LUPITA MINIMARKET

TACOS "LA TORRE"

TACOS LEON
TORTILLERÍA LAS BRISAS
TAQUERÍA EL SARGENTO

CTRA A EL SARGENTO

La Ventana
PALAPAS VENTANA

RAFA'S

VENTANAS DEL SOL

PABLO'S MINIMARKET
KIJOTE COFFEESHOP
LA VENTANA FISHMARKET
DON RUBEN MINIMARKET
EL RINCÓN DE LA BAHÍA

CASA VERDE

0   0.25 mi

0   0.25 km

BAJA JOE

© AVALON TRAVEL

1,500 meters long, the strip will be expanded to nearly 2,000 meters in the futer. Current flights must clear customs and immigration in La Paz, Loreto, or Los Cabos; however, the resort is working to get on-site customs and immigration, which would allow direct service from the United States.

☾ BAHÍA DE LA VENTANA

Once a pair of quiet fishing villages, Bahía de la Ventana and neighboring El Sargento were discovered by windsurfers in the 1990s and kiteboarders soon after. In winter months when the powerful *El Norte* winds blow through the narrow Canal de Cerralvo, sailboards fill the bay—as well as the campgrounds that surround it.

Other times of year, the towns attract scuba divers, beach-goers, and sportfishing enthusiasts.

Though it's still relatively undeveloped compared to nearby La Paz or the Los Cabos corridor, the word is out on La Ventana; the area has been experiencing a real estate boom for the last few years, with dozens of properties for sale and many new buildings taking shape each year.

Sports and Recreation
WINDSURFING AND KITEBOARDING

Windsurfers discovered the ideal conditions at La Ventana in the 1990s, but in recent years, the rising popularity of kiteboarding has brought many more adventure-seeking travelers to the area. Kiteboarders say La Ventana is one of the best places in the world to learn the sport, because the shoreline of the bay curves around to catch those who drift downwind on white-sand beaches. Experienced windsurfers say the wind at La Ventana isn't as strong as at Los Barriles, but it tends to be more consistent. The wind typically picks up around 11 A.M. and holds steady until just before sunset.

Several shops along the bay rent gear and offer lessons for windsurfing and kiteboarding. (They'll also come get you if you have trouble staying upwind.) One of the first to set up shop in the early 1990s was **Captain Kirk's Windsurfing** (U.S. tel. 310/833-3397, www. captainkirks.com), with headquarters in Los Angeles. The shop also rents several vacation

LA PAZ AND VICINITY

BAHÍA DE LA VENTANA

LIGHTHOUSE

El Sargento

BAHÍA DE LA VENTANA

La Ventana

Punta Arena de la Ventana

LIGHTHOUSE

266

San Juán de los Planes

Bahía de los Muertos

To El Triunfo

0   2 mi

0   2 km

© AVALON TRAVEL

homes, including a two-bedroom home with kitchen (US$250/day) and a *casita* with two double beds and bath (US$125/day). Rentals come with free use of mountain bikes, sea kayaks, and snorkeling equipment. A windsurfing or kiteboarding gear package is US$65.

With headquarters in Hood River, Oregon, the **New Wind Kite School** (U.S. tel. 541/387-2440, www.newwindkiteboarding.com, Nov. 15–Mar. 15) offers lessons for new and experienced kiteboarders (US$216–280/day, depending on the number of students; US$85 for a 1.5-hr session). Custom instruction runs US$76–89 for one person, with a two-hour minimum. Board rentals cost US$39 per day, kite-only rentals are US$70 per day, kite and bar rentals are US$89 per day, and a full set-up goes for US$119 per day. This school also has a beach house next door. An upstairs room has its own bath and balcony, with access to a kitchen downstairs (US$89). Store your gear and use the air compressor to inflate your kite for free.

British Columbia–based **Elevation Kiteboarding School** (Canada tel. 604/848-5197, www.elevationkiteboarding.com) began offering lessons in 2005. It offers private lessons for CDN$115 per hour (two-hour minimum),

a full day (about four hours) for CDN$325 per person, and multiday kiteboarding camp packages. The school is located at Baja Joe's Resort. **Sheldon Kiteboarding** (U.S. tel. 707/374-3053, www.sheldonkiteboarding. com) maintains summer headquarters in Rio Vista, California, and winter headquarters at La Ventana. Owner Bruce provides beds and mattresses for camping, plus a shared kitchen, and bath with a hot-water shower. Bring your own sleeping bag. Bruce offers lessons, equipment, and repairs.

Baja Adventures at **Ventana Bay Resort** (tel. 612/128-4333, www.ventanabaykiteboarding.com) is a full-service operation that provides equipment rentals and lessons. It replaces its rental gear each season, selling the previous year's equipment at reduced prices. Kiteboarding equipment includes North Rhino, Vegas, and Rebel kites and North Jamie Pros kiteboards. You can also rent K2 full-suspension mountain bikes from the shop.

SCUBA DIVING
Palapas Ventana (tel. 612/114-0198, www. palapasventana.com) has a certified PADI dive shop on-site that leads guided trips to Isla Cerralvo year-round. The 26-foot super-*panga* has a four-stroke engine and takes up to six divers per trip. Scuba certification packages are available (6 days/5 nights for US$679 pp, minimum three people). Captain Tavo is a shark fisherman and dive instructor. Several of the windsurfing and kiteboarding resorts dabble in scuba trips, as well.

FISHING
The waters surrounding Isla Cerralvo, Bahía La Ventana, Punta Arena de la Ventana, and Bahía de los Muertos offer more consistent fishing than Bahía de La Paz and the islands near the city. Many charters will drive BCS 286 from La Paz and launch at Punta Arena or Los Muertos, rather than traveling by boat across the choppy water. The Canal de Cerralvo is known for roosterfish and *pargo colorado* January–July, and for marlin and dorado in the summer months. It is also a world-class spear-

© STEPHANIE HARGRAVE

view of a windsurfer from Mokie's *casitas*

fishing destination. Contact Palapas Ventana (tel. 612/114-0198, www.palapasventana.com) for information and trips. The 88 bank area off Cerralvo is known for marlin, dorado, and yellowfin tuna. You can launch small boats easily from the beaches at Bahía de la Ventana, Punta Arena, and Bahía de los Muertos.

Festivals and Events

The **La Ventana Classic** is a fundraising kite race held in January every year. Participants start at Isla Cerralvo and finish on the shore of Bahía de la Ventana. Proceeds are donated to the town for schools and other community needs. Contact **Palapas Ventana** (tel. 612/114-0198, www.palapasventana.com) for information.

La Ventana and El Sargento celebrate their **annual town festival** in late October with three days of live music, carnival rides, and street food.

Accommodations and Camping

Located about 800 meters past El Sargento, the **Ventana Bay Resort** (tel. 612/128-4333, www.ventanabay.com, US$110–140) completed its second phase of construction in late 2006, adding accommodations, an office, shop, and bar to the premises. Guests can choose from clubhouse rooms on the beach or private bungalows set back from the beach. Amenities include tiled floors and showers, rustic wooden furniture, ceiling fans, private patios, and hammocks strung between palms on the beach. The resort offers a variety of packages that combine accommodations, meals, and windsurfing/kiteboarding or other activities. For example, a seven-day kiteboarding package includes accommodations, two meals per day, and unlimited use of kiteboarding gear for US$695–850. a "sports" package for US$625–695 includes unlimited use of mountain bikes, sea kayaks, snorkeling gear, and Hobie cats. Wireless Internet is available at additional cost. The resort also manages a few private homes as vacation rentals. Its **Cisco Restaurant** serves breakfast, lunch, and dinner. Fresh fruit margaritas are a popular way to pass the afternoon.

Between La Ventana and El Sargento, **Palapas Ventana** (tel. 612/114-0198, www.palapasventana.com) has two types of newly constructed *palapa*-roof casitas. Regular ones sleep two in a king or in two twin beds with shared shower and bath and air-conditioning (US$60 pp double occupancy). Specialty *casitas* sleep four (in one room) with private tiled bath and air-conditioning (US$77.50 pp double occupancy). Extra touches include high ceilings (with fans), Mission-style furnishings, hammocks, purified water dispensers, and rain showers. Also on-site are a dive shop, gated parking area, Internet café, and restaurant. The resort offers kiteboarding lessons and whale-watching trips in winter, and guided hikes to local cave paintings. Stay-and-dive packages include five days/four nights of accommodations; three days of diving (two tanks per day); breakfast every day and lunch on dive days; and free use of kayaks, snorkeling gear, and sailboats (US$655 pp, minimum three people).

Mokie's (tel. 612/114-0201, U.S. tel. 541/478-2199, www.mokies.com, US$550/wk or US$1,500/mo, payment via PayPal) rents studio and one-bedroom *casitas* on 1.4 fenced hectares fronting the beach. Both *casitas* come with full-size bed, kitchen (including margarita glasses), two full-size futons, bath with large shower, mountain and sea views, and an outdoor terrace. Guests store their gear in a beachfront loft just 10 meters from the water's edge, or walk to shops that rent gear and offer lessons. When not on the water, you can enjoy a partially shaded beachfront terrace that has a glass wall for shelter from the wind.

Kurt-n-Marina (tel. 612/114-0010, U.S. tel. 509/590-1409, www.ventanakiteboarding.com) offer several *casitas* with *palapa* roofs and tiled baths (US$55), as well as camping (US$15) and a shared outdoor kitchen.

Comfortable beds and very clean rooms (called *casitas*) are a plus in relatively new ⓒ **Casa Verde** (tel. 612/114-0214, U.S. tel. 509/228-8628, www.bajmahal.com, US$110). Enjoy natural light, private baths, small refrigerators, and sea views in each one. Two standalone houses on the property rent for US$170 per night. Three Native American lodges are set up for camping (US$30/40 s/d); guests may use a main kitchen or garden kitchen and shared bath with hot showers. Bikes, kayaks,

and wireless Internet are included as well. The resort has teamed up with Kitemasters to offer seven-night, all-inclusive packages that cover accommodations, all meals, and eight hours of lessons for two people, plus the use of kayaks and mountain bikes (US$1,800, including tax).

Steps from the sea, **Baja Joe's** (tel. 612/114-0001, www.bajajoe.com) has several *palapa-roof* cabins for rent (US$50–110). Some share a bath; others have their own. All have air-conditioning and a small refrigerator. RV cabanas have private kitchens, while economical bunkhouse rooms (US$30/40 s/d) have use of a shared outdoor kitchen and one of six baths on the property. Rates include mountain bikes, sea kayaks, snorkel equipment, and a storage area for gear. Baja Joe's also manages a few private beach houses (US$600–1,200/week). No children under four. Discounts for long-term stays. Baja Joe's rents windsurfing (US$25/hour or US$40/day) and kiteboarding equipment as well. Its instructors use Waverunners and helmet radios to facilitate faster learning.

La Ventana Campground, along the beach just north of the village of La Ventana, packs in the sailboarders during the windy season. This barebones campground has around 50 simple tent sites (US$7–8/night) close to the water—and the road. There are toilets and cold showers. RVs are welcome, but there are no hookups for utilities. **Yoyo's Campground** at the entrance to La Ventana, is similar, with hot showers (tel. 612/114-0015 or cell tel. 044/612/348-0004, US$8/day for up to two people and US$8/day for each additional person in the group).

Between La Ventana and El Tecolote on a remote stretch of beach accessible by private aircraft, **Rancho Las Cruces** (tel. 612/125-5639, U.S. tel. 858/764-4122, www.rancholascruces.com, hotel_las_cruces@hotmail.com), has poolside rooms (US$185–275 pp) and cabañas (US$290 pp) that are open to nonmembers. Rates include all meals, and children 5–12 are 20 percent off when they stay in the same room as their parents. (No charge for ages 4 and under.) Guests enjoy hikes on trails through the expansive property, a private golf driving range, tennis courts, and croquet courts, plus sunbathing and sportfishing. The resort is closed from mid-July–mid-October.

Food

Each winter season brings a new wave of eateries to these sleepy bayside towns. Expect to find several small grocery stores (no supermarkets), a few traditional Mexican restaurants, several newer gringo establishments, a number of taquerías, and a *tortillería* (on the paved part of the road in El Sargento). Prices are generally low, and the atmosphere is casual. Mango margaritas at the Ventana Bay Resort's Ciscos Restaurant get especially high marks. If you plan to cook most of your own meals, stock up on supplies in La Paz.

About 200 meters south of the trailer park, **Rincón del Bahía** (no tel., hours vary, mains US$7–13) serves tasty seafood and Mexican fare on the beach. Owner Joaquin will serenade you while you dine. Just south of Palapas Ventana, **Tacos Rafa** (no tel., hours vary), grills fish tacos for US$6–13. The restaurant at **Palapas Ventana** (tel. 612/114-0198, www.palapasventana.com, daily breakfast and lunch, plus Fri.–Sat. dinner and live music in winter, mains US$8–13) prepares lasagna, steaks, BBQ ribs, fresh grilled fish (all of it caught by the staff themselves). Try the coconut wahoo. Enjoy local wines, an icy margarita, or a Negra Modelo on tap (the only draught beer available in La Ventana) with your meal. Reservations are recommended.

On the beach just north of the Ventana Bay Campground, **Ventanas del Sol** (no tel., hours vary, mains US$6–12) is the place for ceviche and chicken mole, and it has a pool table, bar, and TV. It's informally known as the round restaurant. Look for **Tacos en la Torre** (no tel., hours vary, mains US$4–7) at the base of the radio tower in El Sargento, with a menu of *chilaquiles, tortas cubanas,* and *flautas.* On the west side of the road in El Sargento, **Tacos Leon** (no tel., hours vary), has hot dogs, *papas rellenas,* and enchiladas for US$4–10. Popular with RV park residents, **Viento del Norte** (mains US$4–9) serves hearty breakfasts, enchiladas, and jumbo margaritas.

In a yellow two-story building on the beach, newcomer **Las Palmas** (no tel., hours vary), is located at the end of the pavement, about a mile past La Ventana and across from the police station. It has a full bar, and the menu features seafood, Mexican plates, and a popular steak and fries. **Pizza Vela** (500 meters north of Palapas Ventana on the beach side of the road, no tel., hours vary), offers an alternative to Mexican fare; you can order a fresh salad and a glass of wine to go with your pie. At **Mariscos El Cone** (beach side of the road in El Sargento, diagonally across from MiniSuper Los Delfines, no tel., hours vary), start with the raw scallop or shrimp *aguachile* plate, and then move on to the *pescado al mojo de ajo.*

Information and Services

Many local resorts and campgrounds now have wireless Internet; some offer it for free, while others charge for access. Across from the main beachfront campground, **El Norte Restaurant** has satellite Internet for US$3 for 30 minutes. You can use the restaurant's computers or bring your own. Mobile phones work here but get spotty signals. There are public pay phones here as well; pick up a Ladatel card at one of the mini-supers. Palapas Ventana has long-distance service.

Near the end of the pavement in El Sargento are a hardware store, mechanic, pharmacy, and Internet café, as well as **Miscelania Lupita.** A couple of launderettes offer drop-off or self service. El Sargento also has a Centro de Salud (Public Health Clinic) and a place where you can buy barrel gas.

ISLA CERRALVO

Less than 16 kilometers offshore from Bahia de la Ventana is Isla Cerralvo, one of the largest islands in the gulf and once a key destination in the historic pearl-oyster trade. Few travelers make their way out to this island because it is a long boat ride from the charters in La Paz, but it has several good dive and sportfishing sites around its shores. Scuba divers can explore rock reefs, coves, and wrecks. Presently, Palapas Ventana is the only PADI-certified dive operation in La Ventana.

LA PAZ AND VICINITY

SAN JUÁN DE LOS PLANES

Los Planes, as this agricultural town is usually called, has several markets, a café, *dulcería, tortillería,* taxi stand, and around 1,500 inhabitants who make a living growing cotton, tomatoes, beans, and corn, or by fishing the nearby bays. There is a Pemex station where the road from San Antonio joins BCS 286. During the windy season, dust blowing from cultivated fields on either side of the highway can cause a complete whiteout. Once you leave the main drag in Los Planes, there is little in the way of commercial businesses until you reach the Cardon Grill on Bahía de los Muertos.

BAHÍA DE LOS MUERTOS

BCS 286 ends at Los Planes, but if you follow the graded road that continues east, you'll end up at the Bay of the Dead. The dark name of this pretty bay dates back to the 18th century, but its exact origins are unknown. At least two later incidents in history validated the name: In 1885, a Chinese ship landed and lost a crew of 18 to yellow fever after port authorities in La Paz refused to admit the ship. And in the early 1900s, when a group of farmers from the United States attempted to cultivate the land around the bay, the effort for some ended in starvation.

Long-abandoned **Ensenada de los Muertos** dates back to the 1920s, when it was used for transporting ore from mines in the Sierra de la Laguna.

Panga boats still line the shore, but the bay is changing little by little each year as a massive luxury real estate development takes shape to the south.

Bahía de los Sueños (Bay of Dreams)

When complete, the American-owned Bay of Dreams project (www.bahiadelossuenos.com) will encompass 1,700 hectares with an 18-hole golf course designed by Tom Doak, 432 homes, and 192 villas and condos. Inside the Bay of Dreams development, **Villas of Casa de los Sueños** sits on 25 landscaped acres with tennis courts, a nine-hole golf course, multiple

swimming pools, a fitness facility, and a long list of luxury amenities—including an on-site chef service and concierge. Its seven villas have king-size beds, rain showers, Viking barbecues, satellite TV, wireless Internet, private or shared pool and spa, and complimentary Internet calling to the United States. One-bedroom villas range US$350–750 per night; two-bedrooms are US$650–1,050 per night.

Food

The former Giggling Marlin restaurant on Bahía de los Muertos has changed hands and opened as **El Cardón Tequila Bar & Grill** (tel. 612/167-3702, U.S. tel. 619/446-6549, www.elcardon.com.mx, daily 7 A.M.–10 P.M.) with a diverse menu of Mexican and seafood specialties. The most popular food items include combinations of tamales, enchiladas, chiles rellenos, and quesadillas (US$12). They also offer burgers (US$7) and appetizers such as nachos, guacamole, and fresh ceviche. The kitchen will cook your fresh catch for you as well. There are fire pits on the beach, and on Fridays, the restaurants hosts live music and stays open until midnight. It is currently the only business on the bay. The management provides shuttle service from La Paz.

Information and Services

El Cardón Tequila Bar & Grill (tel. 612/167-3702, U.S. tel. 619/446-6549, www.elcardon.com.mx) has free Wi-Fi; a small convenience store; fishing and boating services; and gear rentals for snorkeling, diving, and kayaking.

PUNTA ARENAS DE LA VENTANA

About four kilometers before you reach Los Muertos, a smaller dirt road heads northeast to Punta Arenas de la Ventana (8 km), the site of an abandoned hotel and a good spot for snorkeling and fishing. Roosterfish are said to be unusually large here. You might be able to hire a *panguero* from the beach next to the former Las Arenas Resort for US$60–85 per day. Just south of the resort, snorkelers can explore the reef off **Punta Perico** (Parakeet Point).

THE EAST CAPE AND THE SIERRA DE LA LAGUNA

The promise of calm seas, steady winds, and abundant game fish lures many adventure-seekers away from the resorts of Los Cabos to the remote beaches and rocky points of the East Cape—and increasingly also to the traditional ranchos and freshwater springs hidden deep in the mountainous interior.

Some of Baja's prettiest and most secluded beaches line the Gulf coast between Bahía de las Palmas and San José del Cabo, at the southern tip of the peninsula. And along this stretch, the opportunities for deep-sea fishing, windsurfing, kiteboarding, kayaking, and scuba diving are among the best in the world. The region contains a few larger towns, such as Los Barriles, Santiago, and La Ribera, but for the most part, civilization consists of tiny fishing villages alternating with newer

gringo enclaves. The vibe is low-key and in many places, the lifestyle is still off-the-grid, with dirt roads, *palapa*-roof bungalows, solar power, and satellite-only Internet and phone service.

Coastal development began to accelerate rapidly around the year 2000 and continues along the entire coastline. Most of these developments resemble Southern California–style subdivisions, complete with signed gate, paved entrance, and concrete curbs. Unfortunately, the boom has driven real estate prices sky-high and caused inevitable tension in some communities between locals that have lived there for generations and outsiders who are moving in. On the bright side, few, if any, of the developments are fully built yet. So aside from the gates and model homes, many parts of the

© PABLO NOBILI

HIGHLIGHTS

LOOK FOR (TO FIND RECOMMENDED SIGHTS, ACTIVITIES, DINING, AND LODGING.

(Los Barriles: Anglers, kiteboarders, and windsurfers all find paradise in the Sea of Cortez near Los Barriles, the most developed town for visitors between La Paz and San José del Cabo (page 254).

(Cabo Pulmo: Reef-building corals, crystal waters, and white-sand beaches attract divers, snorkelers, and kayakers to Bahía Pulmo and Playa La Sirenita (page 268).

(Banco Gorda: Six miles from shore, this pair of seamounts offers unrivaled marlin and wahoo fishing, as well as a chance for scuba divers to see hammerheads and whale sharks (page 277).

(El Triunfo and San Antonio: These ghost towns in the mountains along Mexico 1 were once silver-mining boomtowns and the largest communities in Southern Baja (page 278).

(Arroyo San Bartolo: A freshwater spring in the sierra keeps this palm-filled riverbed lush and green (page 280).

(Santiago Town Plaza: Shaded by mature trees and lined with a row of colonial buildings, this plaza is a perfect place to relax after a trip to the nearby hot springs or waterfall (page 282).

(Cañon de la Zorra: At the edge of the Sierra de la Laguna, near Santiago, a 10-meter waterfall plunges over smooth granite rock into a swimmable lagoon (page 282).

coast still look pretty secluded; the challenge is finding access to the sea.

In September 2006, Hurricane John made landfall at Bahía de los Frailes, causing severe wind and flood damage. Although roofs and roads took a beating, the towns in its path had mostly recovered by year-end.

The East Cape, particularly along the *Camino Costero Rural,* became the center of several large land disputes during the spring and summer of 2007. Though many have by now either been resolved or forgotten, remnants of the uproar dot the landscape. Heavy barbed-wire fences, aggressive signage, and abandoned (and some still occupied) guards' camps abound, lending a somewhat hostile look and feel to the area; the reality, though, has not changed, and visitors can still feel the same pervading sense of tranquility and isolation as has always been the area's hallmark.

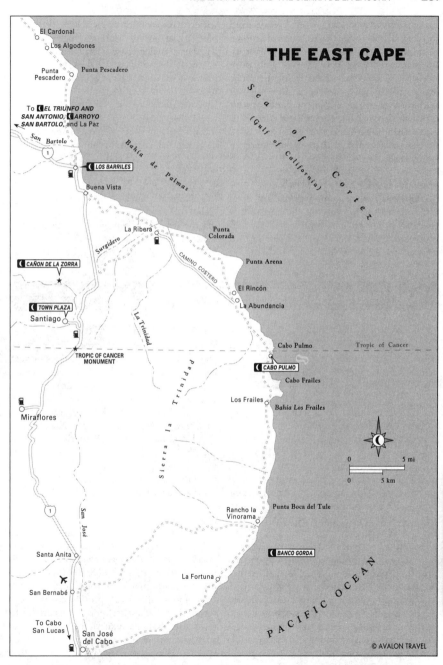

THE EAST CAPE

El Cardonal
Los Algodones
Punta Pescadero   Punta Pescadero
Pescadero

Sea of Cortez
(Gulf of California)

To **(EL TRIUNFO AND
SAN ANTONIO, (ARROYO
SAN BARTOLO,** and La Paz

San Bartolo

Bahía de Palmas

(LOS BARRILES

Buena Vista

La Ribera   Punta
                   Colorada

Surgidero

CAMINO COSTERO

Punta Arena

El Rincón

La Abundancia

(CAÑON DE LA ZORRA

(TOWN PLAZA
Santiago

La Trinidad

Cabo Pulmo   Tropic of Cancer

TROPIC OF CANCER
MONUMENT

(CABO PULMO

Cabo Frailes

Los Frailes   *Bahía Los Frailes*

Miraflores

Sierra la Trinidad

0   5 mi
0   5 km

San José

Rancho la   Punta Boca del Tule
Vinorama

(BANCO GORDA

Santa Anita

San Bernabé

La Fortuna

To Cabo
San Lucas
San José
del Cabo

PACIFIC OCEAN

© AVALON TRAVEL

THE EAST CAPE

When you've had your fill of white-sand beaches and salty air, the Sierra de la Laguna beckons, with 2,100-meter peaks and cascading waterfalls. No longer the sole domain of experienced backpackers, parts of the range are doable in a half-day excursion, with or without a guide, depending on your comfort level with navigating networks of dirt roads and missing a turn here or there. The reward is a rugged part of Baja that few travelers even know exists.

PLANNING YOUR TIME

Towns along the East Cape are small and don't take much time to explore; you could easily take in a little of each in a four- to five-day trip. However, if you've come to the East Cape for a specific activity, such as fishing, diving, or windsurfing, you'll likely want to stay in one place for awhile. If fishing is your top priority, then it makes sense to stay in Los Barriles or Buena Vista and add a day of diving. But if diving is the draw, best to head north or south to be closer to the dive sites. And if you plan to drive along the Coastal Road, as opposed to Highway 1, note that the unpaved 77-kilometer stretch between El Rincón and San José del Cabo can take up to four hours, depending on your vehicle and its ability to handle washboard roads.

Santiago, at the foothills of the Sierra de la Laguna, is an easy day trip from San José del Cabo, or a good place to stretch your legs during the drive between San José and La Paz. Allow 3–5 nights if you want to explore the backcountry of the Sierra de la Laguna.

Bahía de las Palmas

After winding its way over the Sierra de la Laguna heading southeast from La Paz, Mexico 1 reaches the Gulf coast once again at Los Barriles, more or less in the middle of the wide and exposed Bahía de las Palmas. The bay is roughly 32 kilometers long, extending from Punta Pescadero in the north to Punta Arena at its southern end. The area experienced its first heyday in the 1960s as a fly-in resort for anglers. Fishing is still a draw in summer; however, a new pair of sports have taken center stage in the winter months: Strong winds blowing out of the north combined with thermals generated by the inland peaks creates ideal conditions for kiteboarding and windsurfing.

As with the rest of the Southern Baja coastline, land development is fast changing the profile of communities beside the bay. Second homes owned by retirees from the United States rim the shore, with a few resorts mixed in. In general, the bay gets less developed the farther north you go, but even the famed Hotel Punta Pescadero is expanding to become a full-service luxury resort.

PUNTA PESCADERO

There are now two ways to reach the northern end of Bahía de las Palmas and the southern end of Bahía de los Muertos: A sandy, washboard road, narrow in parts, heads north from Los Barriles right along the water—the turnoff from Mexico 1 is signed Punta Pescadero. The road traverses two wide arroyos that could be flooded in heavy rains. Alternatively, a paved road built in 2005 continues along a scenic inland route from Los Barriles directly to El Cardonal. Watch for potholes and broken sections along this otherwise good road.

Accommodations

At the far north end of Bahía de las Palmas (13.6 km north of Los Barriles), the historic **Hotel Punta Pescadero Paradise** (tel. 612/141-0101, U.S. tel. 888/765-0653, www.puntapescaderoparadise.com, US$175–230; pets of any sort strictly prohibited) is transforming from a low-key sportfishing establishment to an exclusive luxury property, complete with timeshares, gourmet food, and guided tours. A development master plan shows

© PABLO NOBILI

Expansive views impress on the coastal route from Punta Pescadero to El Cardonal.

planned growth well beyond what is now in operation, with villas, beach clubs, "villages," spas, and a pier all included in the design. The resort has long been popular with private pilots, since it has a paved landing strip (1,065 m, Unicom 122.8, US$25 landing fee), and you'll likely hear regular fly-in guests trading stories at the bar. (As at other Baja airfields, plane theft is a very real concern here; throttle locks and prop chains are essential. Contact Baja Bush Pilots, www.bajabushpilots.com, for more information. Baja Bush Pilot and AAA discounts available.) A row of houses lines the airfield facing the sea.

Each of 21 spacious rooms comes with a view of the bay, private terrace, air-conditioning, satellite TV, and refrigerator; some have cathedral ceilings and fireplaces for keeping warm on chilly winter nights. All rooms were renovated in 2005. King-size beds are made in crisp white linens with fluffy pillows and down comforters. During the windy season, ask for a room that faces southwest for a terrace that's sheltered from the El Norte gusts. A gracious staff speaks excellent English, and

public areas include a restaurant with large picture windows, outdoor patio dining, small pool, lighted tennis court, and rental equipment for free diving (US$14/day), kayaking (US$10/hr), boating (US$15/hr), fishing (30-ft cruiser US$510/day, 28-foot cruiser US$400, super-*panga* US$300, *panga* US$250/day), and ATVs (US$20/hr).

The resort restaurant is open to the public with theme night menus—such as a traditional suckling pig roast on Saturdays, and Romantic Italian nights beachside on Fridays—and Sunday brunch. Guided trips include city tours of La Paz, a visit to the closely guarded local petroglyphs, and tours to the sites of former Spanish missions. Tour prices range from US$50–460, and range 2–8 hours in length.

The reef that extends out from the point here is among the places in the Sea of Cortez for snorkeling. Also in the works at press time was a renovation and upgrading of the resort's diving facilities; tanks and gear are being prepared to bring the dive center into use again. The resort is also gearing itself more toward

THE EAST CAPE

banquets, weddings, and other large events, and can handle groups of 50–400 people.

EL CARDONAL

A new, paved highway makes it much easier and faster to reach El Cardonal, located north of Punta Pescadero, at the south end of Bahía de los Muertos (23 km from Los Barriles). You can snorkel among the coral heads close to shore, hire a guide for a look at the local cave paintings, or simply enjoy the views from the beach.

Canadian-owned **El Cardonal's Hide-A-Way** (tel./fax 612/128-6859, www.elcardonal. net) offers six sparsely furnished suites, some of which were renovated in December 2007, for US$86/525 per night/week. There are also spaces for RV (US$13/day for full hookups) and tent (US$10–12/day) camping. Each of its large beachfront studios comes with two full-size beds, a sofa, kitchen, and ceiling fan. Amenities and services include a dump station, fishing boats, hot showers, 24-hour restaurant, laundry facilities, public telephone, horseshoe pit, volleyball net, picnic tables, ice, and rental

shop with equipment for fishing, windsurfing, diving, kayaking (free with stay), and snorkeling. You can pick up the Wi-fi signal from the restaurant/patio area. Fishing trips run US$400 for a super--panga, US$250–300 for a *panga*. The hotel can put you in contact with local guides for a two-kilometer hike to nearby cave paintings.

After El Cardonal, the road continues northward along the coast, then veers west to traverse the Sierra El Carrizalito before reaching San Juan de los Planes southeast of La Paz.

◖ LOS BARRILES

The defining image of day-to-day life in Los Barriles these days is that of early retirees happily speeding along dirt roads on ATVs, which they ride to the supermarket, the hardware store, the beach, and everywhere in between. No longer the sole domain of sports fishermen and windsurfers, the town has broadened its appeal with more guest accommodations, restaurants, and services—and a vibe that is friendly and relaxed.

El Cardonal's Hide-A-Way rooms feature beachfront patios.

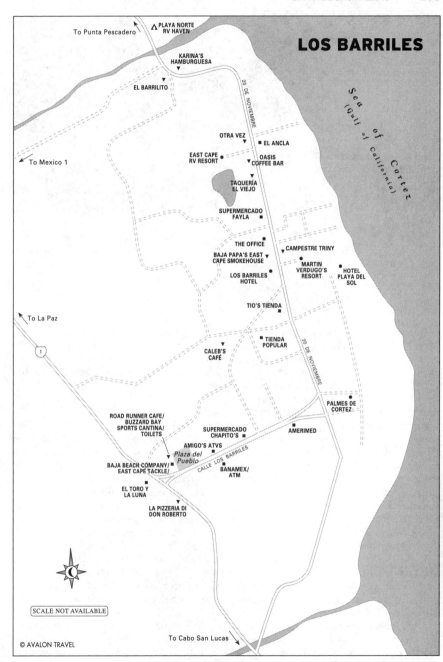

To Punta Pescadero
△ PLAYA NORTE RV HAVEN

LOS BARRILES

▼ KARINA'S HAMBURGUESA

Sea of Cortez
(Gulf of California)

▼ EL BARRILITO

▼ OTRA VEZ
■ EL ANCLA

To Mexico 1

● EAST CAPE RV RESORT
▼ OASIS COFFEE BAR

■ TAQUERÍA EL VIEJO

■ SUPERMERCADO FAYLA

■ THE OFFICE
● CAMPESTRE TRINY

▼ BAJA PAPA'S EAST CAPE SMOKEHOUSE
● MARTIN VERDUGO'S RESORT
● HOTEL PLAYA DEL SOL

■ LOS BARRILES HOTEL

To La Paz

■ TIO'S TIENDA

① 1

▼ CALEB'S CAFÉ
■ TIENDA POPULAR

20 DE NOVIEMBRE

■ PALMES DE CORTEZ

ROAD RUNNER CAFE/ BUZZARD BAY SPORTS CANTINA/ TOILETS
■ SUPERMERCADO CHAPITO'S
■ AMERIMED

■ AMIGO'S ATVS
Plaza del Pueblo

■ BAJA BEACH COMPANY/ EAST CAPE TACKLE/
CALLE LOS BARRILES
■ BANAMEX/ ATM

▼ EL TORO Y LA LUNA

▼ LA PIZZERIA DI DON ROBERTO

To Cabo San Lucas

SCALE NOT AVAILABLE

© AVALON TRAVEL

THE EAST CAPE

© CARMEL TSABAR

the rural side of sprawling Los Barriles

A strip mall on the main access road from Mexico 1 is the de facto town center, with another row of commercial businesses along Calle 20 de Noviembre, heading north to Punta Pescadero. A row of gringo McMansions front the beach behind a stone retaining wall, and several developments are in varying stages of completion in the hills above and to the north of town. However, those in search of the "real" Baja should not despair; Los Barriles retains an authentic *tortillería,* plus roosters that roam the streets, a cement factory where blocks are still made by hand, numerous taco stands, and countless other family-owned businesses. Local Mexicans know each other by their *sobrenombres* (nicknames), and the untamed backcountry is just minutes away.

BUENA VISTA

Smaller and quieter than its neighbor to the north, Buena Vista attracts a similar crowd of families, fishermen, and retirees—many of them former law enforcement professionals from Southern California. It won't be long before the two towns are connected by the homes and businesses that are spreading out between them. Southbound travelers may have difficulty finding the unsigned entrance to town: Look for the turn on a curve between Km 104 and 105.

LA RIBERA AND PUNTA COLORADA

As the last coastal town with municipal power and water heading south until San José del Cabo, La Ribera (pop. 2,000) has evolved into a busy commercial center. The town has its first ATM, an Internet café, two Pemex stations, and a few small hardware and grocery stores. There are now two large real estate developments underway. Cabo Rivera will have multiple golf courses, a large marina, plus the requisite condos and hotels. Beachfront lots (800 square meters) were going for US$500,000 and up. Nearby, Cabo Cortez, located at Bahía El Rincon, has plans to build out to 3,000 beds, four golf courses, and a marina for 400 boats.

Punta Colorada lies to the south, marking the southern end of Bahía de las Palmas. Below La Ribera, several tiny seaside communities remain off the grid—though mainstream power and phone service loom in the not-too-distant future.

SPORTS AND RECREATION
Kiteboarding and Windsurfing
The powerful sideshore winds at Los Barriles are best attempted by intermediate and advanced kiteboarders and windsurfers. In the peak season, November through April, wind speeds frequently exceed 20 knots and rarely drop below 18 knots. Beginners can usually get in the water during calmer early morning conditions. Instructors say windsurfers should know how to water-start, or plan to take a lesson to learn how when they arrive. By 11 A.M.

SURFING THE EAST CAPE

The lower East Cape gets decent waves in summer and early fall (May–Oct.), when chubascos off the mainland to the south send large swells to the region. If there is any south swell in the water, you will get waves at the lower breaks. On large south or southeast swells, you can surf as far north as Punta Colorado, but don't plan your trip around spots that far north. If it's flat, drive down to the Los Cabos Corridor or hop across to the Pacific and surf near Todos Santos. If you are day-tripping from Los Cabos for a day of surfing, make sure you stock up the night before on water, then more water, and bring your own shade, sunscreen, and food.

The closest break to San José (15 km north along the Coastal Road), called Shipwreck, is also the most consistent spot on the East Cape with the steepest waves. The point typically breaks in sections, so the crowds spread out a bit. If you like lefts, look for a small reef in the middle of the bay that breaks on the larger swells. The sandy beach out front is a good spot for spectators and post-surf picnics. Don't bother scanning the bottom for the shipwreck; it was washed away by a hurricane years ago.

Heading north, the next reliable break is Nine Palms. The palms have grown in numbers, so don't bother counting them. This is a good long-boarding wave, but can get steeper as it goes overhead. About 800 meters north of the Crossroads Country Club at Boca de la Vinorama, Punta Perfecta is a right reef break that can produce decent barrels on larger swells.

COURTESY OF THE BAJA CALIFORNIA STATE TOURISM SECRETARIAT

surf class is in session

THE EAST CAPE

most days, the winds kick up a rolling swell (no breaking waves) that is fun for jumping. Water temperatures average about 22–24°C in winter, with air temperatures around 26–27°C.

INSTRUCTION

The **Vela Windsurf Resort** (U.S./Canada tel. 541/387-0431 or 800/223-5443, Los Barriles, www.velawindsurf.com, Nov.–Mar.) provides windsurfing instruction, rental gear, and accommodations packages. At last check, it had more than 80 Starboard and JP Australia brand boards and more than 100 Neil Pryde sails—the largest stock of equipment anywhere in Baja.

Vela also has a kiteboarding program, **Dare2Fly** (www.dare2fly.com), which shares the same beach as its windsurfing school (signs attempt to keep kites and sails separate for safety). Vela provides 2008 Cabrinha gear for lessons but does not rent boards or kites for independent pursuit of the sport.

Both Vela schools are based at the Hotel Playa del Sol (tel. 624/141-0050, U.S. tel. 877/777-8862, www.vanwormerresorts.com, closed Sept.). Seven-night packages start at US$1,080–1,280 and include all gear, instruction (except for novice windsurfers), accommodations, meals, tax, and service. Guests may borrow kayaks and mountain bikes anytime during their stay for no charge. Other activities free of charge include snorkeling, tennis, and volleyball. Scuba diving, kiteboarding lessons, and horseback riding cost extra.

Fishing

Bahía de las Palmas is an exciting place to fish because the sea floor drops to great depths not far from the shoreline. The reef extending out from Punta Pescadero is great for triggerfish, barred pargo, and cabrilla. Less than a mile from land, you can find depths that exceed 100 fathoms. The popular **Tuna Canyon,** 6.5 kilometers south of Punta Pescadero, is the place to catch yellowfin tuna (YFT). Several charter services based along the bay offer trips on *pangas* (US$200–260/day) and cruisers (US$200–325/day). Bait costs around US$20–25 per day.

a successful fishing outing on the East Cape

A popular day trip when the conditions aren't too windy is to travel north by boat to Bahía de los Muertos, fish on the way, and stop for lunch at the Cardón Grill.

In Los Barriles, Martin Verdugo's Beach Resort (tel. 624/141-0054, www.verdugosbeach-resort.com) and the Hotel Palmas de Cortez (tel. 624/141-0050, U.S. tel. 877/777-8862, www.vanwormerresorts.com) offer fishing packages; the concierge at the Hotel Palmas de Cortez (tel. 624/141-0050, U.S. tel. 877/777-8862, www.vanwormerresorts.com) can arrange fishing trips for guests and non-guests. In addition, **Congo's Awesome Sportfishing** (tel. 624/141-0231, U.S. tel. 208/726-1955, www.awesome-fishing.com), headquartered at the East Cape RV Resort and run by Jeronimo "Congo" Casio, operates two cruisers, a 30-foot island hopper (US$450 for 1–4 anglers) and a 32-foot Blackfin sportfisher (US$625 for 1–4 anglers). The most popular captains in Los Barriles and Buena Vista, including Julio Cota and Chuy Cota, book a year in advance for weekend visits, so plan your trip early.

THE EAST CAPE

Juan Carlos of **La Capilla Sportfishing and Eco Tours** (tel. 624/141-0611) runs charters on a diesel-powered *panga.*

Fish With Me (toll-free U.S. tel. 800/347-4963, www.fishwithme.com, fishwithme@comcast.net) owner Jerry Hall has been fishing the East Cape since 1973 and organizes group trips several times a year.

SHORE FISHING

Since the sea floor plunges to great depths so close to shore, it's possible to catch unusually large fish simply by casting into the surf from the shoreline. Punta Pescadero, Punta Colorada, and Punta Arenas are three of the best places to try; roosterfish and jack crevalle are common catches.

KAYAK FISHING

East Cape Kayak Fishing (U.S. tel. 619/461-7172, www.eastcapekayakfishing.com) offers several guided trips a year out of the Hotel Punta Colorada and Rancho Leonero, with an emphasis on paddling and angling instruction. Owner Jim Sammons is famous for having landed a marlin from a kayak, the only person to date to have done so. An all-inclusive package including five nights and four days of fishing starts at US$1,032 per-person, all-inclusive (double occupancy). In addition to scheduled small-group trips, the staff offers private trips.

FISHING GEAR AND SERVICES

East Cape Tackle (Plaza del Pueblo, Los Barriles, www.eastcapetackle.com, Mon.–Fri. 9 A.M.–5 P.M., Sat. 9 A.M.–2 P.M.) sells bait and tackle and also rents surf rods, pole spears, and snorkeling gear; plus, you can pay with plastic. **Todo de Pesca** (20 de Noviembre, Los Barriles, tel. 624/124-8061, Mon.–Sat. 9 A.M.–2 P.M. and 4–6 P.M.), run by Ricardo Reyes, is a new fishing store well stocked with all the basics, plus some spear-fishing gear.

Baja Papa's East Cape Smokehouse (20 de Noviembre at Calle Don Pepe, tel. 624/141-0294, www.bajapapas.com, daily 9 A.M.–6 P.M.) offers processing services for your catch. Allow 48 hours turnaround time to have them smoke (US$3.50–4.50/lb of filet) or freeze (US$1.50 to flash freeze filets) and package it for your trip home. The store has started a travel club that extends discounts on auto insurance and other services to its members.

Scuba Diving

Buena Vista has a reputable dive center located on the beach, next to the Vista del Mar trailer park. **Vista Sea Sport** (tel. 624/141-0031, Buena Vista, www.vistaseasport.com) is run by two PADI-certified dive instructors from Southern California who own three super-*pangas* and one cruiser. However, boat rides to the major sites—Cabo Pulmo, Los Frailes, Punta Pescadero, and Isla Cerralvo—are long and rates are higher (US$110–125 for a two-tank dive) than at shops based in La Paz or Cabo Pulmo. Scuba gear rental is US$30 with a tour. Airfills cost US$10; snorkeling gear US$10. Look for a giant earthmover that serves as the boat launch. To find the shop from Mexico 1, take the turn across from the Calafia Hotel, then turn left at the T in the dirt road and follow the signs.

ATV Tours

ATVs are a popular mode of transportation in Los Barriles. Inquire about rentals and tours at **Amigos ATV Tours** (Calle Los Barriles near Plaza del Pueblo, Los Barriles, tel. 624/141-0430, www.amigosactivities.com) on the main access road. Tours cost US$60–70 for a single rider, and US$75–90 for a double. Rental rates are US$20 per hour, or $100 per day. Amigos also rents Wave-Runners and leads horseback rides and snorkeling tours. Other possibilities include hikes, bird-watching, mountain biking, and snorkeling. You can book any of these activities through the concierge at the Hotel Palmas de Cortez, whether or not you are staying at the resort.

Quadman (tel. 624/168-6087, cell tel. 624/168-6087, www.quadman.net), across from the Amerimed clinic on the north side of Calle Los Barriles near the T intersection at 20 de Noviembre, also rents ATVs (US$85/day) and Rhinos (US$135/day). Rhinos seat four people and you must be 35 or older to drive. ATVs have racks for fishing poles, though riders must stay at least 20 meters from the high-tide line to protect turtle nests.

Mountain Biking

Vela Windsurf Resort (Los Barriles, U.S./Canada tel. 541/387-0431 or 800/223-5443, www.velawindsurf.com) at the Hotel Playa del Sol rents Specialized mountain bikes for coastal and desert rides. Clip-less pedals are an option, so bring your shoes. They also have children's bikes, a trail-a-bike, and a kid's trailer.

Spa Services

Above the gym in the Hotel Palmas de Cortez, at the end of Calle Los Barriles, **Spa de Cortez** (Los Barriles, tel. 624/141-0050 ext. 616, spa decortez@yahoo.com) offers Swedish, therapeutic, and sports massage, plus aromatherapy, body scrubs, facials, and waxing services. A one-hour massage is US$80, and a 90-minute treatment is US$115.

SHOPPING

Los Barriles has the only real shopping in this part of Baja: **Tío's Tienda** (20 de Noviembre, Los Barriles, approximately one block north of Calle Los Barriles, daily 7:30 A.M.–10 P.M.), next door to Tío Pablo's, carries everything from fishing tackle and souvenirs to apparel, gift wrap, and office supplies. It also stocks one of the most impressive collections of books about Baja California found on either side of the border. Many of the titles are self-published memoirs written by gringo transplants; others are field guides, travel books, and novels that take place in Mexico. **Baja Beach Company** (Plaza del Pueblo 8, Los Barriles, Mon.–Fri. 9 A.M.–5 P.M., Sat. till 2 P.M.,), in the strip mall near Buzzard Bay, has ceramics, textiles, gifts, and a few books and maps. **Big Tony** (Plaza Libertad, Los Barriles, Mon.–Sat. 9 A.M.–7 P.M.) has good-quality beach clothing, shorts, bikinis, and accessories. Back on the highway, across from the main entrance to town, **El Toro y La Luna** (Mexico 1 Entrada a Los Barriles, Los Barriles,

tel. 624/141-0696, www.eltoroylaluna.net, daily 8 A.M.–5 P.M.) carries ceramic sinks, tiles, and other home furnishings. The store has a second branch in La Ribera (Av. Santa Maria, La Ribera, tel. 624/141-0698, www.eltoroylaluna.net, daily 8 A.M.–5 P.M.), at the turn for the road to Cabo Pulmo.

ACCOMMODATIONS AND CAMPING

Accommodations along Bahía de las Palmas range from all-inclusive hotels to modest hotels and RV parks to private vacation homes available for rent either by the owner or through a property manager. Los Barriles has the greatest concentration of options, but Punta Pescadero, Buena Vista, and La Ribera all have at least a couple of options.

Los Barriles
US$50-100

Martin Verdugo's Beach Resort (20 de Noviembre, approximately two blocks north of Calle Los Barriles, Los Barriles, tel. 624/141-0054, www.verdugosbeachresort.com, US$65–75) has updated air-conditioning units in each of its 29 rooms, located in a two-story hotel next to the beach. Facilities include a small pool, boat launch, and restaurant. Kitchenettes are a plus here (though not in every room). When the wind is blowing hard, the pool at the Los Barriles Hotel offers more shelter. Service was a bit gruff on a recent visit.

Off the beach but within walking distance to restaurants and shops, the exceptionally clean **◖ Los Barriles Hotel** (20 de Noviembre, approximately one block north of Calle Los Barriles, Los Barriles, tel. 624/141-0024, www.losbarrileshotel.com, US$72) looks unremarkable from the outside, but feels something like a well-kept Swiss chalet inside. It has 20 spacious rooms set around a swimming pool, each with high ceilings, two firm but comfortable queen-size beds, large tiled showers, and remote-controlled air-conditioning. Minimal but quality furnishings include rustic wooden dressers, tables, and headboards. A cedar hot tub is the latest addition to the pool

TO BUY OR NOT TO BUY: TIPS FOR PURCHASING REAL ESTATE IN BAJA

The real estate frenzy in Baja California began as a trickle at the start of the 21st century, and had progressed into a full-scale land rush by about 2003. As Mexican law and real estate services have made it easier for foreigners to own property, many Baja-bound Americans and Canadians are answering the call.

1. THE TERMS

Foreigners can only purchase coastal property (within 50 km of the coast) in Mexico through a limited real estate trust *(fideicomisos)*. Trusts are renewable every 50 years, with no limit on the number of renewals. In most cases, you will need a Mexican real estate attorney to complete a transaction.

2. FINANCING

You can finance the purchase through several lenders: Mortgages are now available for financing up to 70 percent of appraised property values with terms of 15-20 years. Lending rates run around 3 percent higher than in the United States, and closing costs for a mortgage deal are high.

Some sellers ask that the full purchase price be paid up front. Because a large number of gringos buy land in Mexico with cash, some Mexicans assume this is customary for all Americans and Canadians. Paying up-front is

not the typical procedure for Mexicans themselves, who usually make down payments and send in monthly time payments; mortgage terms similar to those found in Canada and the United States are available in Mexico, though they are difficult for non-residents to obtain. Even if you have the cash, don't hand over more than half the full amount until you have the *fideicomiso* papers in hand.

3. TITLE INSURANCE

You can purchase title insurance, previously unavailable, from several providers.

4. PRICES

Prospective buyers can find small plots in subdivisions near the beach from US$20,000. Completed small vacation homes range US$200,000-500,000, and full-scale mansions are in the millions.

5. REAL ESTATE AGENTS

Choose a reputable agent and check his or her references thoroughly. The larger tourism offices are a good place to find listings of available properties. Local residents can usually advise on the better agents to work with. Brokers do not have to get a license to operate in Mexico, so it pays to do your homework up-front before committing to real estate deals of any sort.

---

area. Popular with families, this hotel is a great value for the price.

Among the newest accommodations in town are the suites at the **Villas de Cortez** (Los Barriles, tel. 624/141-0050, U.S. tel. 877/777-8862, www.vanwormerresorts.com, US$280-600), next door to the Hotel Palmas de Cortez, which is under the same ownership. Meal packages are available through the sister resort, or you can enjoy outstanding gourmet fare in the villas' new restaurant, **La Taberna di Don Roberto**, which impressed local foodies from the get-go with its authentic Italian cuisine (tel. 624/141-0050, Tues.–Sun. 5–10 P.M.).

US$100-200

The Van Wormer family runs two all-inclusive resorts in Los Barriles, including **Hotel Playa del Sol** (tel. 624/141-0050, U.S. tel. 877/777-8862, www.vanwormerresorts.com, US$145–160, closed Sept.), on the beach off 20 de Noviembre north of Calle Los Barriles. This property has 26 air-conditioned rooms, a pool that overlooks the beach, tennis and volleyball courts, a restaurant with outdoor seating, and bar with satellite TV. The resort rents windsurfing, kayaking, and fishing gear, as well as mountain bikes. You can charter boats for a day of sportfishing (US$250–385 per day, not

© PABLO NOBILI

Hotel Palmas de Cortez

THE EAST CAPE

including fishing permits) or sign up for wind-surfing lessons.

OVER US$200

The second Van Wormer resort in Los Barriles is located on the beach at the end of Calle Los Barriles, a little south of Hotel Playa del Sol; the **Hotel Palmas de Cortez** (Los Barriles, tel. 624/141-0050, U.S. tel. 877/777-8862, www.vanwormerresorts.com, US$190–260) offers 50 poolside, oceanfront, and garden-view rooms, plus several cabanas and condos that sleep up to six guests. Rates include three meals a day. Amenities include a driving range, infinity pool, and tennis and racquetball courts. You can rent windsurfing gear and fishing equipment and charter a fishing boat (US$265–690, not including fishing permits) through the resort. The Van Wormer family also runs the Hotel Punta Colorada farther south along the East Cape.

CAMPING AND RV PARKS

A trendsetter among parks in Mexico, the **East Cape RV Resort** (20 de Noviembre at Ocean Dr., Los Barriles, tel. 624/141-0231,

U.S. tel. 208/726-1955, www.eastcaperv.com) designed its property with big rigs in mind. Located a short walk from the beach, at the intersection of 20 de Noviembre and Ocean Drive (unmarked at last check), the resort has 51 spaces with full hookups (US$25/150/525 per night/week/month). Another dozen spaces with limited hookups are located in an adjacent palm garden that sometimes floods during the rainy season (US$18/105 per night/week). Bathrooms are modern and clean, and there's a pool and hot tub. High-speed wireless Internet costs US$4/15/40 per day/week/month. Washing machines and dryers require U.S. quarters. Owner Theresa Comber is the closest thing Los Barriles has to a chamber of commerce. Ask her for advice on day trips and activities in the area.

North of Hotel Playa del Sol, **Martin Verdugo's Beach Resort** (20 de Noviembre, approximately one block north of Calle Los Barriles, Los Barriles, tel. 612/141-0054, www.verdugosbeachresort.com) caters to families and retirees with lower rates and a beachfront location. It has dump stations, flush toilets, showers, boat ramps, laundry facilities, and full hookups for US$15 for two people, plus US$3.50 for each additional person. Weekly/monthly rates are US$100/260 (credit cards are accepted). Tent sites cost US$12 per night. Kids play Marco Polo in the beachfront swimming pool, and locals gather for breakfast in the third-story restaurant. Fishing rates are US$390 for a 28-foot cruiser and US$240 for a 23-foot super-*panga*. Inquire about fishing packages that include accommodations and meals, and be sure to make reservations well in advance during the peak windsurfing season, January–March. **Juanito's Garden RV Park** (tel. 612/141-0024) in the same complex as the Los Barriles Hotel, offers permanent hookups and storage.

About five minutes' drive north of town, another big-rig- and caravan-friendly park has one of precious few remaining waterfront locations in Southern Baja: **Playa Norte RV Haven** (20 de Noviembre, Los Barriles, U.S. tel. 425/252-5952, www.playanortervpark.com, harnecker@gmail.com, US$15–29) is situated on Bahía de las Palmas between two wide arroyos, San Bartolo to the north and Buenos Aires to the south.

The park encompasses 10 hectares of landscaped property, divided into 85 sites with separate areas for tent camping, caravans (45 sites), permanent RV sites, and seasonal RV sites. A number of the sites are pull-through style for larger rigs, and many also have individual septic and power. The sites are divided into three rows that parallel the beach. The first row (24 sites) costs a few dollars more per day than the second and third rows. The owners have completed a number of improvements in recent years, including new laundry facilities, more restrooms and showers, and wireless Internet. In the works at press time was a retaining wall and pedestrian walkway along the beach, to provide privacy and hold back the sea in extreme tides.

Power and electricity cost extra (US$3 for 15–30 amp, US$5 for 50 amp). Book early if you want a site with these conveniences. There is a US$5 fee for use of the dump station (caravans and guests of longer than one week excepted). Tent sites have free access to drinking water, hot showers, parking, and Internet.

This park is a good choice for travelers with pets because they can run on the beach or in the arroyo outside the park—and there is even an on-site veterinary clinic; however, management requires pets to stay at their own site while inside the park, and it goes without saying that you should clean up after your dog.

Free primitive camping is available in the area north of these parks, usually referred to by gringos as Playa Norte.

Buena Vista
UNDER US$50
Hotel Restaurante-Bar Calafia (Mexico 1, Km 107, Buena Vista, tel. 624/141-0028, US$45) has nine basic, but new and clean rooms with air-conditioning above a simple Mexican restaurant.

US$50-150
In business since 1952, **Rancho Buena Vista** (Mexico 1, Km 106, Buena Vista, U.S. tel. 805/928-1719 or 800/258-8200, www.ranchobuenavista.com, US$105 pp) opened to host Hollywood celebrities for fly-in sportfishing vacations. Today, the scene is much less glitzy, but the fishing tradition continues. The resort has more than 50 cottage-style rooms, all with air-conditioning, ceiling fan, and tiled floor and shower. All meals are served in one restaurant; breakfast is made to order, lunch and dinner are fixed menus that rotate throughout the week. Boxed lunch is available for days on the water. The grounds include a swimming pool, whirlpool tub, and tennis and volleyball courts. The resort has fishing tackle, including fly-fishing gear, as well as its own cruisers, a boat ramp, and boat storage.

It can be difficult to find the turnoff to Rancho Buena Vista if you're heading south on Mexico 1. Watch for the entrance on the left just after a small mountain pass and a blue hotel sign on the right.

US$150-250
Popular with families and retirees, the **Hotel Buena Vista Beach Resort** (Mexico 1, Km 105, tel. 624/141-0033, U.S. tel. 619/429-8079

or 800/752-3555, www.hotelbuenavista.com, US$135–165) has 60 Mediterranean-style bungalows with air-conditioning, private baths, and private terraces. Buildings are arranged close together against a hillside, and the resort feels somewhat dated, but the location just across from the beach is ideal. A lush tropical garden surrounds the resort's two pools, one of which has a swim-up bar. If you're not fishing, activity choices include spa treatments, kayaking, horseback riding, and snorkeling. The resort organizes trips to nearby cave paintings and waterfalls, as well as bird-watching, hiking, and snorkeling tours. Most guests choose the American plan, which includes three meals a day, but European plans (meals à la carte) are available as well if you want more flexibility in where you dine. Inquire about fishing and diving packages. The fleet of boats at this hotel includes a 23-foot *panga* (US$270), 28-foot cruiser (US$415), luxury 29-foot twin-engine cruiser (US$485), and 31-foot twin-engine cruiser (US$555). (Tax, tips, tackle, bait and fishing licenses cost extra.) The resort's U.S. reservations office can arrange round-trip or one-way transportation from the airport.

Near the southern end of Bahía de las Palmas, the secluded **Rancho Leonero Resort** (tel./fax 612/141-0216, U.S. tel. 760/438-2905 or 800/646-2252, www.rancholeonero.com, US$150–250) sits on a mesa overlooking the bay. This resort was founded in the 1960s as one of the original fly-in fishing destinations in Baja, and a sense of history oozes out of the rustic, *palapa*-roofed bungalows on the property. All guestrooms have sea views, but there are no in-room TVs or phones. The grounds are well cared for, and the overall effect is something like family camp meets hunting lodge. As at Punta Pescadero, a small development now adjoins the resort, with new homes built on land sold by the owner of Rancho Leonero.

Amenities include a restaurant and bar, swimming pool with hot tub, dive center, sportfishing fleet, and a network of hiking trails. You can snorkel the rock reef in front of the hotel. Three meals a day are included in the room price. Fishing charters start at US$250 for a super-*panga,* US$385 and up for cruisers. Snorkeling equipment costs US$10 per day. The resort also arranges horseback riding, kayaking, scuba, and hiking trips.

La Ribera

At the south end of town, by near the beach, **RV Park La Trinidad** (16 de Septiembre, La Ribera, tel. 624/130-0206, rvranchtrinidad@yahoo.com, US$20–25) has more than 20 full hookups, a swimming pool, and an incredible ratio of bathrooms and showers per site (there are eight of each). There are a few tent camping sites and a restaurant/bar that serves a Mexican/seafood buffet for US$16–18. To find the park from the highway, follow the exit at Las Cuevas east to La Ribera and drive straight through town until you reach the beach road (Calle Hacienda Eureka). Turn right (south) and go about 800 meters to a Pemex station, then turn left (east) and look for the entrance on your left.

Punta Colorada
US$100-150

The southernmost of the original Baja fishing resorts was established in 1966 and overlooks Punta Colorada at the south end of Bahía de las Palmas. Friendly and unassuming to this day, the **(Hotel Punta Colorada** (tel. 612/121-0044, U.S. tel. 818/222-5066 or 800/368-4334, www.vanwormerresorts.com, US$130–140) has reputation throughout the sportfishing community as *the* place for catching roosterfish, described by veteran anglers as reel-melting fighters that will keep you coming back for more. The conditions off Punta Arena, the next point south from the hotel, are as good as it gets in Baja, as evidenced by the photo of a record-setting 42-kilogram catch on the wall in the bar. Guided fishing trips start at US$245 a day for a super-*panga* and US$330–385 for cruisers; half-day trips cost 70 percent of the full-day price. The hotel teams up with partners to offer kayak fishing and fly-fishing tours.

The hotel has 39 large rooms, all but eight of which have ocean views. About half of its rooms were renovated in 2006. Free wireless Internet is available in the lobby/courtyard area. Three meals daily are included in the price, and the locally renowned restaurant serves a Mexican buffet dinner open to the public on Wednesdays and Saturdays, as well as a seafood buffet on Sundays. Call by noon for reservations. The hotel also has an indoor/outdoor bar and its own airstrip (1,000 m, Unicom 122.8). Tap water at the resort comes from a mountain well, so you can drink it. The hotel is closed in January, February, and September through the first week of October.

Vacation Rentals

Many owners rent their Baja vacation homes by the night, week, or month. **East Cape Property Management and Vacation Rentals** (Plaza del Pueblo, tel./fax 612/141-0381, www.abajavacation.com, Mon.–Sat. 10 A.M.–2 P.M.) handles rental properties in Los Barriles, Buena Vista, Punta Pescadero, Rancho Leonero, and Los Frailes. **Sunset Rentals** (20 de Noviembre, just past the Hotel Los Barriles, tel. 624/141-0416) offers short- and long-term rentals in studios as well as one- and two-bedroom condos. All have kitchens, garages, balconies, wireless Internet, and air-conditioning. **Vacation Rentals by Owner** (www.vrbo.com) also has a few dozen East Cape listings. Rates range US$75–195 a night for one-bedroom homes.

FOOD

There are a number of casual eateries along the shores of Bahía de las Palmas, with the greatest variety in Los Barriles. Seafood takes center stage on most menus. Los Barriles also has the only large-size grocery store in the area, **Supermercado Chapito's** (daily 7:30 A.M.–10 P.M.).

Los Barriles

The number and variety of restaurants in Los Barriles is multiplying by the day. Today's menus feature grilled fish and meats, traditional Mexican *platos,* pasta, sushi, pizza, sandwiches, soups, espresso, and, of course, mouthwatering tacos.

RESTAURANTS

In a strip mall just off Mexico 1 on the access road to Los Barriles, **Buzzard Bay Sports Cantina** (Plaza del Pueblo 21, Calle Los Barriles, Los Barriles, no tel., daily for lunch and dinner, mains US$7–15) makes burgers, sandwiches, and pub fare, with tables inside and on a small sidewalk patio that adjoins the parking lot.

Tío Pablo's (20 de Noviembre, Los Barriles, tel. 612/142-1214, daily 11 A.M.–10 P.M., mains US$7–20) is popular for pizzas and does orders to go. Look for the restaurant on the west side of the main north–south street through town.

An Italian chef bakes pizzas in a wood-heated oven at **La Pizzeria di Don Roberto** (at the south end entrance to town in Highway 1, no tel., Tues.–Sun. noon–9 P.M.), open since early 2008. Variations include the simple Margarita (US$10) and a Calzone Classico (US$17).

The restaurant inside **Hotel Palmas de Cortez** (tel. 624/141-0050, U.S. tel. 877/777-8862, www.vanwormerresorts.com, Tues.–Sun. 5–10 P.M.) is open to the public for dinner. It offers a menu of pasta, fish, and seafood dishes prepared in the Italian style.

Martin Verdugo's Restaurant (20 de Noviembre, approximately one block north of Calle Los Barriles, tel. 612/141-0054, daily 6 A.M.–noon, mains US$4–7) is a third-story restaurant that serves Americanized breakfast fare. *Chilaquiles* arrive smothered in melted cheese but without the signature *queso fresco* on top. Omelets come with seasoned hash browns and a choice of toast or tortillas. Sea views and air-conditioning are the main draw. Service is friendly, though slow even by Mexican standards.

Run by the same owners as the once-famous Restaurant Balandra in Cabo San Lucas, which closed more than 30 years ago, **Campestre Triny** (20 de Noviembre across from the East Cape Smokehouse, no tel., daily noon–10 P.M., mains US$9–20) offers freshly prepared traditional Mexican fare, including specialties of *huachinango frito* (whole fried red snapper), paella, and imperial shrimp. High-quality ingredients and a somewhat upscale presentation are reflected in menu prices. This is also one of the few places in town that serves Negro Modelo beer. You can dine family-style under a canopy of trees behind the main house or at your own table on the porch. Check out the collection of arrowheads hanging on the wall while you're there.

About 400 meters farther on 20 de Noviembre, **Otra Vez** (20 de Noviembre, tel. 612/141-0249, Mon.–Sat. 5–10 P.M., mains US$8–20) is popular with local gringos, and the menu includes freshly prepared parrot fish, burgers, steaks, fresh salads, and pasta dishes.

Another favorite among locals for dinner, **☚ El Barrilito** (20 de Noviembre, no tel., daily lunch and dinner, mains US$6–15) serves large portions of fresh seafood under a large *palapa* at the bend in the road heading out toward Pescadero. Ceviche is a standout. In a smaller *palapa* next door, the same owners have opened **Kenichi Sushi & Bar** (no tel., daily for lunch and dinner) with à la carte dishes and all-you-can-eat specials for US$20. More sushi can be found at **Yako's Sushi-Bar** (tel. 624/141-0050, daily noon–7 P.M., mains US$10–20) in the Hotel Palmas de Cortez, on the beach at the end of Calle Los Barriles.

ANTOJITOS AND FAST FOOD

During American football season, you're likely to find a number of tourists watching the game at **☚ Taquería El Viejo** (20 de Noviembre near El Oasis Coffee and Baja Land Deals, no tel., daily breakfast and lunch). The restaurant has about a dozen shaded outdoor tables where you can enjoy a breakfast of eggs, omelets, or *chilaquiles* for US$5–6, tacos for US$1–2, and burgers for US$5. Lunch specials vary daily (US$7–8).

Taquería Los Barriles (no tel., daily for dinner), at the junction with the beach road, is packed all afternoon and evening for the great seafood and carne asada tacos; the breakfasts are cheap. The enormous super burros at **La Palma Taquería** (no tel., daily for dinner) are a great value, too. Look for the sign on a surfboard just off 20 de Noviembre near Tío Pablo's.

Across the street from El Barrilito, on the inside of the bend that turns to Pescadero, **Karina's Hamburguesas** (no tel., daily for dinner) serves carne asada (US$4), *papas rellenas (US$5)*, and other quick meals from a restaurant cart.

CAFÉS

Oasis Coffee Bar (20 de Noviembre, past The Office, tel. 624/141-0711, daily) serves coffee for US$2, as well as hot and cold espresso drinks and smoothies for US$2–4. It shares the space with Baja Land Deals, so you can browse pictures of real estate for sale while you wait for your drink. High-speed wireless Internet service is free, and there are a few shaded tables outside.

Road Runner Café (Plaza del Pueblo 5, no tel., daily 7 A.M.–4 P.M.) has very good coffee and espresso (US$2) and eggs any style (US$3.50–6) served at tables inside or on the patio. Free wireless Internet is a plus. **Caffe Paradise** (20 de Noviembre, across the street from Campestre Triny, no tel., Wed.–Mon. 7:30 A.M.–3:30 P.M.) has the best smoothies (US$3–5) in town, as well as coffee, espresso, sandwiches, burgers, and eggs.

GROCERIES

On Calle Los Barriles, the main access road from Mexico 1, between Plaza del Pueblo and 20 de Noviembre, **Supermercado Chapito's** (daily 7:30 A.M.–10 P.M.) is the largest grocery store in town (or anywhere on the bay for that matter), and it has a separate pharmacy inside. Newer **Tienda Popular** (daily 7 A.M.–10 P.M.), west of 20 de Noviembre, about one block north of the intersection with Calle Los Barriles, has opened just up the hill from Tío Pablo's. **Supermercado Fayla** (Mon.–Sat. 8 A.M.–6 P.M.), on 20 de Noviembre just past the Hotel Los Barriles, has basic food supplies as well as souvenirs, videos, and U.S. newspapers on Fridays. During the peak winter season, a bakery truck from La Paz visits town on Fridays and a fresh produce vendor comes on Saturday mornings.

Buy frozen or smoked fish or have yours

prepared and vacuum-packed at the **Baja Papa's East Cape Smokehouse** (20 de Noviembre at Calle Don Pepe, tel. 624/141-0294, www.bajapapas.com, smokedogg@bajapapas.com, daily 9 A.M.–6 P.M.). Allow 48 hours turnaround time.

Buenva Vista

Hotel Restaurante-Bar Calafia (Mexico 1, Km 107, Buena Vista, tel. 624/141-0028, daily 7:30 A.M.–8:30 P.M., mains US$10–20), on the west side of the highway near the local police station, makes tasty shrimp tacos and chiles rellenos, and its outdoor tables have nice views of the bay. **La Concha** (no tel., hours vary, mains US$5) at the north end of town, serves up a delicious ceviche in a taco stand environment. A **Tienda Popular** mini-market is located on the east side of the highway, north of the main entrance to town.

La Ribera

A new restaurant has opened at the Y in La Ribera, where the road turns south to Cabo Pulmo. **Lighthouse Restaurante** (south side of La Ribera Rd. at the turnoff to the Camino Rural Costero, no tel., Mon.–Sat. 9 A.M.–10 P.M., breakfast mains US$6–8, dinner mains US$7–25) offers a menu of burgers, steak, lobster, fish, shrimp, Caesar salad, and chiles rellenos. Closer to the beach and a few blocks from the Trinidad RV Park, **La Costa** (no tel., Tues.–Sun 11 A.M.–6 P.M., main US$5–10) does a good shrimp ceviche, as well as large-sized fish and scallop tacos.

Mercado Rey (daily 7 A.M.–10 P.M.) on El Camino Rural Costero, just past the Y and across from the Pemex, carries tools, propane tank parts, chains, and beer, plus basic groceries and a good selection of American liquors.

The popular **Carnitas Los Michoacanos** (no tel., www.losmichoacanos.com), a chain of five restaurants specializing in carnitas-style pork tacos (or by the kilo), has a new location in La Ribera, on the east side of the Coastal Road, just south of the Pemex. It was open Saturday and Sunday only at press time.

At the entrance to La Ribera, **Vianey's Restaurant** (La Ribera, cell tel. 044/624/158-0938, vianeyslaribera@hotmail.com, Thurs.–Tues. 8:30 A.M.–10 P.M.) does egg dishes for breakfast; tacos, meat, and fish dishes for lunch; and more elaborate meat and fish dinners. Thursday is a special pork rib and chile rellenos combo. Lunches range US$5–7, dinners US$10–15. The restaurant makes its own bread to serve with dinner entrées.

INFORMATION AND SERVICES

Most travel-related services for towns along Bahía de las Palmas are located in Los Barriles. East Cape RV Resort owner Theresa Comber in Los Barriles is the closest thing the area has to a chamber of commerce. Stop by to ask for advice on restaurants, day trips, and activities in the area. The larger resorts are also a good source of visitor information.

La Plaza del Pueblo shopping center in Los Barriles, near the highway on the main access road, has clean public restrooms and public telephones. The post office in Los Barriles closed a few years ago. Near the end of the main access road to Los Barriles, an **Amerimed Clinic** is open Monday–Saturday 8 A.M.–2 P.M. and 4–6 P.M. for medical needs. Call 624/141-0797 for emergencies.

If you don't already have a car, **National Car Rental** maintains an outpost at the Hotel Palmas de Cortez in Los Barriles, but in most cases an ATV would be a better vehicle for getting around town. The closest Pemex is just south of Los Barriles on Mexico 1. **El Lavadero/ The Washroom** (20 de Noviembre near the Los Barriles Hotel, Mon.–Sat., hours vary), and the new **Lavamatica** (Plaza Libertad, Mon.–Sat. 10 A.M.–6 P.M.) are the only places to have your clothes washed, unless you're staying at one of the full-service RV parks.

East Cape RV Park, Sunset Rentals, and many private homeowners have wireless Internet. And some keep a computer set up for guest use.

A number of businesses in these towns accept credit cards, but you'll still need cash (dollars or pesos) for tacos and the like. There is a new Banamex (Mon.–Sat. 9 A.M.–4 P.M.) in

THE EAST CAPE

Los Barriles at Plaza Libertad, which can exchange dollars to pesos, and has the only ATM in the area.

La Ribera has its own medical clinic and pharmacy, **Centro de Salud La Ribera** (tel. 624/130-0067, daily 24 hours), next to the athletic fields on the way into town, on the south side of Avenida Santa María, past the turnoff to Cabo Pulmo.

Internet Paty (16 de Septiembre at Ramon Castro, daily 9 A.M.–8 P.M.) has two PCs connected to the Internet (US$3/hour), plus photocopy, fax, and long-distance telephone services.

El Camino Rural Costero

The historic El Camino Rural Costero (Rural Coastal Road) begins south of La Ribera and follows the Gulf coast south to Pueblo La Playa, outside of San José del Cabo. The road is graded but not paved beyond the first few miles south of La Ribera. Most standard rental vehicles—and even small RVs—can negotiate the washboard and patches of soft sand, but the going will be slow, especially as you get farther south, where the road tends to be in pretty bad shape. High clearance is always helpful. During the rainy season, the road may be washed out in parts. Ask for updates before you plan your drive.

The government has had plans to pave the entire Coastal Road from La Ribera to San José del Cabo for at least a decade. So far, it hasn't come to pass. In early 2006, local government officials staged a press event to commemorate the beginning of work on a eight-kilometer-long paved road to Los Frailes; however, the earthmover that was to be the star of the show reportedly got a flat tire and the event was canceled. The machine stayed by the side of the road for weeks after, but no dirt was ever moved. Plans to pave the road have been repeatedly delayed in recent years, to the relief of local residents, who fear the arrival of mainstream power and phone service will change their towns forever.

In spite of the difficult access (or perhaps because of it), a few enclaves along the way are growing into full-scale developments. You can still camp for free on the beach in places, but as is the case all along the coast, access is becoming increasingly limited as new developments lay cinder blocks and finish their first few homes.

In the midst of all the change, a few traditional ranchos continue to raise livestock—typically without fencing to keep the animals off the road.

To reach the Coastal Road from the north, take the paved road signed La Ribera east at Km 93 off Mexico 1 (at Las Cuevas), and go 20-kilometers to a Y intersection near the Lighthouse restaurant and town athletic fields. Bear right here, and you're on the beginning of the Coastal Road. It is paved for the first few miles, then becomes dirt the rest of the way south.

PLAYA EL RINCÓN

At the point where the pavement ends on the Coastal Road is a wide, sandy beach that still feels somewhat deserted even though it's right in the middle of a major real estate project. The developers have put in an access road next to the airstrip.

⟨ CABO PULMO

About 10 kilometers from where the pavement ends, the Coastal Road climbs over a rise and presents a panoramic view of Bahía Pulmo—a shallow bay rimmed with a mix of coarse white sand and cobblestones—and the eight fingers of coral reef that are its main attraction. The road descends to parallel the beach along the bay and then passes through the center of a tiny fishing village-turned-vacation-and-retirement-community.

Modern-day Cabo Pulmo is a close-knit

community made up mostly of older expats and several branches of a local Mexican family that has fished the area for generations. The oldest vacation homes were built right on the beach, but in recent years, construction has expanded west across the road and into the hills.

Most visitors these days come to explore the reef, from above and below, and to relax on the white-sand beaches that line the bay. The surface of the beach varies with the seasons: in winter, there are usually more stones and pebbles, particularly at the north end of the bay; in summer, the sand comes back and the rocks roll back into the sea.

There are several scuba diving operations in town, *panga* fishing charters, kayak rentals, and a long list of excursions up and down the coast and into the desert.

Given its small size, proximity to the beach, and comfortable accommodations, Cabo Pulmo is an excellent place for families with young kids (though the nearest medical clinic is in La Ribera, a 15-minute drive, and the closest hospital is in San José del Cabo).

Playa La Sirenita

The most attractive beach on Bahía Pulmo goes by many names: La Sirenita (The Mermaid) seems to be the most common one, but it is also known as Los Chopitos (The Squids) and Dinosaur Egg Beach. All the more enchanting for its difficult access, the beach is hidden at the base of a cliff that frames the southern end of the bay. You can only reach it by small boat or kayak, or by walking along a path from Playa Los Arbolitos to the north, which has a small parking lot. The beach is narrow, but covered in white sand and dotted with rocks. The cove and beach are protected from winds coming out of the south, and you can snorkel around the rocks just offshore. A towering boulder pile marks the divider between Bahía Pulmo and Bahía de los Frailes; on its south-facing side lives a colony of sea lions.

To find Playa Los Arbolitos and Playa La Sirenita from Cabo Pulmo, follow the Coastal Road south about five kilometers and look for the only dirt road on the left without a fence or

ENDANGERED SEA

In 2005, the United Nations Educational, Scientific and Cultural Organization (UNESCO) added the Gulf of California (referred to in this book as the Sea of Cortez) to its World Heritage List of outstanding natural and cultural value around the globe. Citing its striking beauty and critical role as a natural laboratory for the study of thousands of marine species, UNESCO identified a site of 244 islands, islets, and coastal areas within the Gulf of California. Also important was the fact that all major oceanographic processes occurring in the planet's oceans take place in this body of water.

Environmental conservation groups heralded the designation as a critical step forward in curbing severe damage wrought by commercial fishing and bottom trawling, which destroy eelgrass beds and shellfish that sustain many other species in the sea. But World Heritage status is only the beginning of a long and costly battle. Two international organizations, Conservation International (www.conservation.org) and the World Wildlife Fund (www.worldwildlife.org) are funding projects in the area in an effort to protect the fragile ecosystem for generations to come. Meanwhile, the Mexican government is stepping up its commitment to fund marine parks and conservation activities throughout the region.

gate. The turn is the last road you can take before passing Los Frailes mountain. There may be a handmade sign that says Los Arbolitos, but they seem to come and go, so don't count on it. Occasionally, someone will be at Los Arbolitos renting snorkeling gear and kayaks.

Pulmo Reef System

The fragile hard-coral reef in Bahía Pulmo is one of only three coastal reefs in North America and the only living one in the Sea of Cortez. It plays a vital role in the health of the Sea of Cortez ecosystem, and for this reason was designated a national marine park in 1995. Commercial fishing and sportfishing are banned within the park (this means no shore fishing either), as is anchoring on the reef, or anywhere in the bay. Both foreign and Mexican residents are committed to protecting the water and land from pollution, but they worry that runoff from developments on land—especially from the mega-resorts that are just breaking ground—poses a serious threat to the reef.

The reef is made up of eight separate fingers, four of them close to shore, and the other four farther out in the bay. Depths range 4.5–10.5 meters close to shore, and as deep as 33 meters in the outer bay.

The abundance and variety of marine life here rivals anything you'll find in the Caribbean. The fact that the reef begins within a few meters from the shore makes it even more appealing. For divers, boat rides are a quick five-minute jaunt out into the bay; snorkelers can skip the boat ride altogether and hop right in from shore. You can find a wide variety of tropical fish, eels, and rays—as well as the occasional nurse shark—in waist-deep water.

Sports and Recreation
DIVING AND SNORKELING

You can dive at Pulmo year-round, but the best conditions are in summer and early fall, when water temperatures exceed 26°C, and visibility exceeds 30 meters. Guided drift diving is the norm here. Divers board a *panga* boat at the beach, zip over to the morning's dive site, and roll backwards into the water to begin the dive. While divers drift with the current along the reef below, the boat captain follows the bubbles on the surface. The sides of the reef are jam-packed with colorful marine life. Green moray eels poke their heads out of rocky crevices, schools of tropical fish dart here and there, and the occasional sea turtle cruises by. It only takes a few dives to begin to recognize the telltale pile of shells in front of an octopus's den or the antennae of a spiny lobster hiding in a cave.

Besides the natural reefs, the wreck of a tuna boat called *El Vencedor* has evolve into an artificial

© PAUL ITOI

dive center at Cabo Pulmo Beach Resort

THE EAST CAPE

reef. Dive boats also take groups to El Islote, a lone rock on the southern side of the bay, and to a sea lion colony near Bahía de los Frailes.

Three dive centers, located within 100 meter of each other, run guided tours from Cabo Pulmo. In the village center, the **Cabo Pulmo Beach Resort** (El Camino Rural Costero, tel. 612/141-0884 or -0885, U.S. tel./ fax 562/366-0398, www.cabopulmo.com) operates a PADI-certified dive center with two boats, well-maintained gear, and experienced, professional dive guides. A two-tank boat dive costs US$75 and an equipment rental package is US$20 with a boat dive. You do not need to be a guest of the resort to snorkel or dive with the shop. The dive center often hosts groups of day-trippers from resorts in the Cabo San Lucas area. These dives tend to be more crowded with novice divers. Call ahead to check the schedule if you want to do more advanced dives. Snorkeling tours are US$40 with gear, and single kayaks rent for US$35 a day.

Pepe's Dive Center (no tel., www. cabopulmo.com.mx), across from El Caballero restaurant, also offers a complete diving service, but these days the shop is open only when French divemaster Olivier is around to run the show. **Cabo Pulmo Divers** (no tel., www. cabopulmodivers.com) is another option, located in the Castro family complex, next to the Miscellanea Market. Rates at both are comparable to those at the Cabo Pulmo Beach Resort, although readers have reported higher rates (up to US$72 pp) for tours of only one or two people. It pays to shop around.

Next to La Palapa restaurant, in a blue building with a marine life mural painted on its side is **Cabo Pulmo Eco Adventures** (no tel.). Owner Juanito offers snorkel trips for US$35 and kayak rentals by the hour or day, and can arrange taxi service to La Sirenita beach. Juanito is very knowledgeable, bilingual, and the only person in town who can arrange trips to the nearby waterfall and hot springs.

The dive operators are also happy to arrange boat trips for non-divers interested in touring the bay, Playa La Sirenita, and the sea lion colony.

FISHING

Commercial fishing and sportfishing are no longer permitted anywhere in Bahía Pulmo. *Panga* boats that launch from Pulmo have to go beyond the national marine park limit (eight km from shore) before putting in lines. On land, you have to travel about eight kilometers north or south of Pulmo proper to fish from shore. Kiki and Paco Castro offer half-day (US$180) and full-day (US$260) tours in their super-*pangas,* including gear and bait. Tuna and dorado are common offshore catches. Inquire at Cabo Pulmo Divers (www. cabopulmodivers.com) behind the La Palapa beachfront restaurant.

Accommodations and Camping

As new owners build and acquire properties in Cabo Pulmo, the number of rental options has increased. Expect most high-season rates to climb even higher during the peak season around Christmas and New Year's.

For many years, **Cabo Pulmo Beach Resort** (El Camino Rural Costero, tel./fax 612/141-0244, -0884, -0885, U.S. tel./fax 208/726-1306 or 888/99-PULMO (888/997-8566), U.S. tel. 562/366-0398, www.cabopulmo. com, US$69–199) was the only option for short-term visitor accommodations in the area. The village has grown, bringing more properties and management services onto the market, but this beach resort is still a good option for beachside bungalows within steps of the water. All of its *palapa*-roofed units feature kitchenettes or full kitchens, and some have barbeque grills. Many have second-story roof decks for catching a breeze in the afternoon or watching activity on the bay. Sheets and towels are provided. Like all accommodations in the village, power here is solar, with generators for backup only.

Marly Rickers and Clint Fultz, a friendly young American couple with longtime ties to Cabo Pulmo, also manage a handful of rentals in the same group of *casitas* for US$75–150 per night. Contact **Cabo Pulmo Casas** (tel. 877/754-5251, www.cabopulmocasas.com). Across the dirt road from the Cabo

THE EAST CAPE

Pulmo Beach Resort, Kent Ryan rents **Baja Bungalows** (www.bajabungalows.com, US$45–135), with a main house that has spectacular views from the upstairs master suite, plus a two-bedroom unit on the lower level and an additional bungalow and *palapa* suite with shared bath and full outdoor kitchen. Kent recently added another house to his list of rental properties: Located on an adjacent lot, the house features two separate units (upstairs and down) and has spectacular sea and mountain views from the upstairs unit. The house once belonged to musician (and former local character) Jimmy Ibbotsen of the Nitty Gritty Dirt Band. The house has been adapted to rental standards, but holds many a good story from the musician's stay in Pulmo. The beach is a three-minute walk away.

For upscale accommodations, check out **Villa and Casa del Mar** (U.S. tel. 208/726-4455 or 888/225-2786, www.bajaparadise.com, US$170–375). This property includes a main house (US$375 per night or US$2,500 per week for two guests) and attached studio (US$170 per night or US$1,150 per week). Air-conditioning is available, although as with any Cabo Pulmo rental, it can only be used as long as there is enough power to run it. A few steps farther from the beach and centrally located in the village, the **El Nido** cottage (US$215 per night or US$1,400 per week) has a full kitchen.

El Encanto de Cabo Pulmo (U.S. tel. 619/618-1248, www.encantopulmo.com, US$90–170) brings a new standard of luxury to Cabo Pulmo. Think air-conditioning (extra cost), an espresso machine, and surround-sound entertainment with satellite TV. Designed by an artist and her husband, the home is indeed beautiful; the only caveat is that in Pulmo, there's always a chance that the power-intensive amenities won't be working when you visit. This town is an off-the-grid location that runs on solar and generator power, and when those sources of electricity run out, the air-conditioning unfortunately turns off. (Most guests find the ceiling fans adequate for cooling the home on all but the hottest of nights.) The house has three suites, two in a two-story main house and

a third in a separate *casita*. Its garden setting is lovely (though not really private if both suites and the main house are in use). This property would work best for a group of six or more that rents out the whole property together. Wireless Internet is included. Individual suites rent for US$90–170 per night, and the whole house rents for US$295 per night. There was a For Sale sign on the property at last check.

Another vacation rental, **The Jewel of Cabo Pulmo** (Cabo Pulmo village, U.S. tel. 831/440-8811), has a master bedroom in the main house and a separate garden *casita* (US$79 for the *casita*, US$119 for the house, and US$179 for both). This property is pet friendly. No smoking.

Reinhard's Rentals (www.reinhardsrentals.com, rhpulmo@gmail.com), across the street from Baja Bungalows at the metal palm-and-dolphin-sculpted gate, offers two houses each for US$85 a night, and an additional house, called Paradise with an Ocean View, for US$100 a night. These rentals are popular with the fishing crowd and owned and operated by one of the town's true characters, Reinhard and his dog Max. Another plus for pet owners: These rentals are dog-friendly.

At the other extreme, you can **camp for free** on the beach at the south end of Bahía Pulmo, or for US$5 per night at the north end.

Food

Cabo Pulmo's restaurants are notoriously understaffed, even during peak season. It can take up to 45 minutes or longer to be served, even at lunch.

Adjacent to the Cabo Pulmo Beach Resort, **Nancy's Restaurant and Bar** (no tel., Thurs.–Tues., mains US$16–20) began as a trailer and two tables 12 years ago, and has evolved into a full-scale restaurant with a rustic collection of tables beneath a *palapa* shelter. Fresh guacamole with homemade chips is a delightful way to begin the meal. Lobster enchiladas, crab cakes, and fresh catch (yours or Nancy's) are accompanied by crisp side salads.

The **Coral Reef Bar and Grill** (no tel., Wed.–Mon., mains US$10–20) is a cozy restaurant with a TV and bar located above the blue building that serves as the Cabo Pulmo Resort dive center. Head chef Jaime came to Pulmo after working at the One&Only Palmilla in Los Cabos and specializes in creative Mexican cuisine, often with an Asian flair. His specials are worth trying, as they are based on what's fresh and available that day. You can often find him zooming around the trails and backcountry of Pulmo in between shifts, searching for seasonal blooms, such as pitahaya fruit and local wild plums, to incorporate into the evening's menu.

◖ **Restaurant El Caballero** (no tel., Fri.–Wed. 7 A.M.–10 P.M., mains US$6–14), on the opposite side of the road near Nancy's, has the most varied menu in town, thanks to high-spirited Miguel Angel, a professional chef who came from San José del Cabo initially to work at the Coral Reef and then moved next door. Keep your ears open for his occasional buffet extravaganzas, held on alternating Saturdays in the yard of the restaurant, complete with fire pit and lots of dishes to try. El Caballero also has a bar and small assortment of groceries, drinks, and snacks for sale.

La Palapa (Mon.–Sat. lunch and dinner, lunch plates US$4–10, dinner mains US$8–18) offers casual beachfront dining from a menu of fish tacos, carne asada, and other traditional fare. The great family-style, traditional Mexican seafood, always fresh and simple, is served by smiling Angeles—the sister of Juanito at Cabo Pulmo Eco Adventures.

For groceries, several vendors make the rounds through town during the week. A bakery truck comes from La Paz on Wednesdays; Ysidro delivers fish, scallops, and shrimp on Tuesdays, and brings similar seafood selections on Saturday mornings. You can buy fresh tortillas (10 for less than US$2), homemade tamales (US$1), and empanadas (US$1) for takeout at **Elvira's Kitchen,** near the Cabo Pulmo Divers shop. The **Miscellanea Market** (daily 9 A.M.–7 P.M., limited summer hours), with colorful snails painted on the side of the building, is located next to Cabo Pulmo Divers and stocks basic supplies, including

dairy, juice, produce, bread, toiletries, candy, and canned goods. For a long stay, it's best to load up on groceries at Soriana or one of the other supermarkets in San José del Cabo or at Supermercado Chapitos in Los Barriles. Mexican food brands generally cost less than their U.S. counterparts. It's a good idea to buy ice, as the propane refrigerators in most Cabo Pulmo rentals cool very slowly, and a car full of groceries will take a long time to chill.

Information and Services

Internet access via satellite is possible in Cabo Pulmo, but service is by no means reliable, and it will cost you. Inquire at **The Road House** (formerly Tito's, Cabo Pulmo village, east side of the coastal road, across from Pepe's, no tel.). At last check, rates were US$2.50 for the connection and a non-fixed rate per minute. If you happen to show up when the place is open, you'll then have to cross your fingers and hope the Internet is working. A few private places throughout the village have Wi-Fi set up and you may be able to get permission to use one of those networks. In an emergency, the owners of the different rentals can usually get a message out. For casual correspondence, plan to connect in San José or Los Barriles.

There are no banks or ATMs in Cabo Pulmo or Los Frailes, and few places except the largest resorts accept credit cards. U.S. or Mexican currency is accepted, and you can load up on cash at an ATM machine in San José, Los Barriles, or La Ribera. Be sure to get plenty of small bills, as many businesses cannot change larger bills. Some places accept traveler's checks, but don't count on it.

Basic medical services are available in La Ribera and Los Barriles, and the closest hospital is in San José.

Getting There

Most visitors fly to Los Cabos, rent a car, and drive to Cabo Pulmo via El Camino Rural Costero. From San José del Cabo, follow Highway 1 north 50.6 kilometers to an overpass at Las Cuevas, and bear right (east) onto the single lane road to La Ribera. From

La Paz, pass Buena Vista heading south, and take the exit for La Ribera. As you approach La Ribera (9.6 km), turn right before the soccer field. Follow the Coastal Road 26 kilometers south to Cabo Pulmo. The drive should take about 40 minutes from the time you leave Highway 1.

If you are flying into San José and plan to drive the same day to Cabo Pulmo, aim to arrive no later than noon. By the time you get through passport control, retrieve your luggage, rent a car, and buy your groceries, several hours will have passed, and it is not advisable to drive the highway or Coastal Road after dark. If you arrive in the afternoon, consider staying overnight in San José before departing for Cabo Pulmo the next day.

The closest gas to Cabo Pulmo is at La Ribera to the north. Be sure to fill up before heading south along the Coastal Road.

Aguila bus service from San José will get you as far as Las Cuevas for about US$5 one-way, but from there, you'll have to hitch a ride or arrange in advance for someone to pick you up. Another option for traveling sans auto is to contact one of the companies that transport divers from the Los Cabos area to Cabo Pulmo for the day. For example, **Impala Transportation** (tel. 624/141-0726 or cell tel. 624/173-1476) has a van that holds 14 passengers. With notice, Cabo Pulmo Resort can arrange round-trip transportation from Los Cabos airport for a fee; a stop at a grocery store near the airport on the way up can be included.

BAHÍA DE LOS FRAILES

When winds out of the north whip Bahía Pulmo into a frothy mess, the next bay south, Bahía de los Frailes, is usually calm enough for snorkeling, diving, and fishing. The bay plunges to depths of 210 meters, which makes for slightly colder water temperatures than in Bahía Pulmo.

Following the Coastal Road, it's about eight kilometers to the turnoff for this white-sand beach. Since Los Frailes lies just outside the national marine park, the fishing onshore and inshore tends to be especially good here.

Anglers often catch roosterfish by casting into the surf; charters catch yellowfin tuna, grouper, dorado, and marlin within a couple miles of the shoreline.

Accommodations and Camping

Villa Los Frailes (El Camino Rural Costero, U.S. tel. 206/390-1700, www.bajavilla.com, US$600) is an oceanfront home that sleeps 10 people in four bedrooms and five baths with a hot tub and pool deck. Cabo Villa Rentals manages a few vacation properties along the East Cape, including **Casita Luna Azul** at

© NIKKI GOTH ITOI

a burro looking for lunch

Estancia (U.S. tel. 877/473-1946 or 310/943-7614, www.cabovillarentals.com). This one-bedroom *casita* is set on a point overlooking the sea and costs US$225 per night.

You can camp on the beach along the north end of the bay—a fee of US$2–3 per site may be charged.

SOUTH TO SAN JOSÉ DEL CABO

Below Los Frailes, the road continues to hug the coast, climbing over hills and swerving inland here and there. The scenery alternates between traditional ranchos and new gringo developments, with beautiful desert flora in between. These days, the road is in pretty good shape between Los Frailes and Boca de la Vinorama and even on to Punta Gorda, but the last few miles before La Playita will test the sturdiness of the vehicle as well as the patience of the driver.

From Los Frailes to La Vinorama, a number of small real estate development are popping up on the east side of the road: Boca del Salado has El Salado, with a row of flags along its driveway and a small group of homes up on a bluff overlooking the sea. Rancho del Sol has another 34 home sites in the vicinity.

Boca de la Vinorama

About 18 kilometers below Los Frailes and 34 kilometers up the Coastal Road from La Playita, Boca de la Vinorama refers to a river mouth, a rancho, and a growing expat community, all located just north of the Palo Escopeta turnoff, which heads west toward Mexico 1 and the Los Cabos airport. The development consists of 140 lots, and at least one gated community. The only business here is the **Crossroads Country Club Beachfront Playa** (daily 7 A.M.–9 P.M., open mic on Sat. nights), which has a bar and restaurant with Internet service, public phone, and book exchange. For breakfast, choose eggs any style for US$4. For lunch or dinner, there are fish tacos (US$6), quesadillas, sandwiches, and pasta with or without seafood (US$8–14). Jesse Ventura, of Minnesota governorship fame, lives in a beachfront mansion just up the road. **Villa del Faro** (www.villadelfaro.net, US$125–450) consists

THE EAST CAPE

of four deluxe *casitas* and a primitive stone cottage on the beach.

Palo Escopeta

Just south of the Crossroads Country Club, a graded dirt road in good shape heads west over the lower Sierra la Trinidad hills, past a series of ranchos, to the 100-person pueblo of Palo Escopeta. From there, the road continues southwest to Santa Catarina, where it joins Mexico 1, just north of San José Viejo. The total distance from the Coastal Road to Mexico 1 is 34 kilometers, about the same distance you'd travel from La Vinorama to San José del Cabo on the Costal Road. The difference is a much smoother and faster ride, plus a change of scenery from coastal desert to ranchos and sierra foothills.

The route to the East Cape via Palo Escopeta is relatively easy to find and drive, but for first-time travelers, the turns may not be as obvious as the locals would have you believe. Here is the best set of directions we've found, courtesy of Villa del Faro:

From the Los Cabos airport, head south (right) towards San José del Cabo for three kilometers and watch for the Palo Escopeta road on the left after the sign for Veterinaria Chiapa. Signs on both sides of the road here say No Tire Basura. Under each one, another small sign says Palo Escopeta. A set of topes (speed bumps) are another indication that the turn is imminent. Approaching from San José, turn right at the No Tire Basura signs. If you pass Veterinaria Chiapa, turn around. You have gone too far. Once you are off the highway, follow the paved road about 1.5 kilometers until it ends, just past a bar called Catarina Beach. The road turns to dirt and crosses an arroyo, then it becomes paved again through the town of Santa Catarina. At the town monument, the road turns left; keep going along this road until it becomes a dirt road again. From here, the road will wind back and forth. Ignore any lesser-traveled branches and stay on the main route. Approximately 8.4 kilometers after leaving Mexico 1, the road will fork. Bear left toward Palo Escopeta. If you go straight, you'll find yourself at the town dump. Continue 9.3 kilometers, staying on the road most traveled and into the village of Palo Escopeta. Veer left toward the ball court, which marks the halfway point of the route, and continue winding down the hills through the ranchos. Watch for cows in the road from here on to the coast. Keep going straight for another 14.3 kilometers until you reach the Sea of Cortez, at a "T" intersection. This is El Camino Costero Rural (Coastal Road), and you've reached Boca de la Vinorama. Turn left (north) to reach Bahía de los Frailes and Cabo Pulmo, or right (south) to Punta Gorda and Los Zacatitos.

This route is equally straightforward coming from east to west. The turns through Palo Escopeta are easy to spot; when you get close to Santa Catarina, the turns might be a bit less obvious, but you can see the highway across the arroyo and there aren't all that many options to throw you off course. When in doubt, stop and ask: *Donde está la carreterra?* The answer will likely be *todo derecho* (straight ahead).

If you opt to stay on the Coastal Road south of the Paolo Escopeta turnoff, you'll pass two more ranchos and a small dairy farm called La Fortuna. Nearby (21 kilometers north of Buzzard's Bar and Grill in La Playita), Oregonians Lloyd and Marti Miesen host a small bed-and-breakfast, **Boca de Los Palmas** (U.S. tel. 503/922-0465 or 866/781-8159, www.martimiesen.com, US$325). Accommodations are in a one-bedroom guesthouse with a king-size bed, private bath, and luxury linens; an additional guestroom is available in their home on the same property for US$150 (only with rental of the guesthouse).

Punta Gorda

About 10.3 kilometers north of Pueblo La Playa, Punta Gorda is a reliable spot for on-shore/inshore fishing, as well as surfing during the south swells of late summer and fall.

A number of new real estate projects are taking shape here. The furthest along of these is Los Zacatitos, which has a few artist residents. The development's first restaurant opened in late 2008. Run by Paul and Angel Rini, **Zac's**

GORDO OR GORDA BANKS?

The name of this prime diving and sport-fishing destination in the southern part of the Sea of Cortez has been the source of much confusion, so we attempted to get to the bottom of the issue. The word *gordo/gorda* is an adjective that means "fat" in Spanish. When used to modify feminine objects, it takes an "a," as in Punta Gorda. When used to modify a masculine object, it should take an "o," as in Banco Gordo. Not so, according to the Secretaria de Pesca (fishing secretary) of the Mexican government, whose national sportfishing map uses the name Banco Gorda. To add to the confusion, many gringos have adopted the name Gordo Banks, as in Gordo Banks Pangas. It seems in this case, either name will get you to the right place.

Bar and Grill Restaurant (no tel., Wed.–Mon. noon–8 P.M., mains US$5–15) occupies a second-story, open-air space. Check the Zacatitos homeowners association website, www.loszacatitos.net, for community news.

The Mexican resort developer Mayan Group put its plans for a new resort on hold in 2008. Pueblo Bonito also owns a large property in the area.

South of Punta Gorda, the Navarro Group owns a large chunk of coastal land and there has been talk about the potential of another marina.

On the outskirts of San José, the Laguna Hills development has views of the Estero San José and Punta Palmilla in the distance. Close to Buzzard's Bar and Grill and about three miles from La Playita, El Encanto is another group of waterfront homes and luxury condos.

After 15 years in business, Sharon and Robert Ruyg, the owners of the much-loved Casa Terra Cotta bed-and-breakfast in San José, have moved on to a more upscale and remote location: **Hacienda Soleada del Mar** (Manzana A-Lote 7, tel. 624/113-6386, www.haciendasoleada.com) is available as a bed-and-breakfast, with seven rooms for US$100–230 a night, or as a 855-square-meter vacation rental that sleeps 14 for US$1,000 a night. There is a small pool on the property, and kayaks, snorkeling gear, and beach umbrellas and chairs are provided.

◖ Banco Gorda

About 10 kilometers offshore from Punta Gorda, two seamounts known officially as Banco Gorda, but more commonly called Gordo Banks, are of interest to serious sportfishing enthusiasts and advanced scuba divers. Fishing boats head out this way in search of marlin and wahoo, while scuba divers come for a chance to see schools of hammerheads and the occasional whale shark.

If you want to fish the banks, it's best to hire a *panga* at La Playita, or book a charter out of Cabo San Lucas. For dive trips, try **Eagle Divers** (tel. 624/125-0008, www.eaglediver.com) in Cabo San Lucas.

THE EAST CAPE

Sierra de la Laguna and Vicinity

Most travelers who drive Mexico 1 from La Paz to San José via Los Barriles and the East Cape blaze right by the historic mountain towns along the way. But a quick visit to any of these communities gives you a sense of what Baja California was like during the 19th-century silver-mining boom, as well as a snapshot of present-day Mexican life in the peninsula's interior.

Fresh water is a welcome sight in Baja.

◀ EL TRIUNFO AND SAN ANTONIO

In the 19th century, these neighboring settlements in the Sierra de la Laguna formed the epicenter of Baja California's gold and silver mining boom; today, they are smaller, quieter communities sustained by agriculture and basket weaving. Miners first discovered silver in the area in the mid-18th century near present-day San Antonio (then called Real de Minas de Santa Ana). The town became the first Baja municipality founded without a mission. In 1862, better mineral deposits were discovered near El Triunfo, and the Progreso Mining Company arrived in 1878, bringing with it thousands of workers from Europe and China. A thriving company town emerged, in many ways similar to the mining town that grew at the same time around Santa Rosalía, on the Gulf coast to the north.

The two towns prospered until a hurricane flooded the mines in 1918. By 1926, the mines had closed and the towns were almost abandoned.

Today, ruins of brick buildings, a few restored colonial buildings, and walkways around the old mines are the only signs of the towns' glorious past.

San Antonio's town festival, the feast of St. Anthony, takes place on June 13 and residents from both towns show up for the celebration.

Information and Services

San Antonio (pop. 800) has a Pemex, post office, and several markets. And there are two options for basic groceries in El Triunfo:

Abarrotes La Escondida (on Mexico 1) and the **Tienda Comunitaria** (off Mexico 1 in the center of town).

Getting There

If you're driving south from La Paz, you'll encounter El Triunfo (pop. 300) first, at Kilometer 163, 48 kilometers south of La Paz, and San Antonio seven kilometers farther south.

If you're driving north along Mexico 1 from Los Barriles and want to head over to the coast at Bahía de la Ventana or Bahía de los Muertos, you can take a recently paved shortcut from San Antonio (btw Km 158/159). The road is 22 kilometers long and meets state highway BCS 286 in San Juan de los Planes. The unsigned road is easy to miss. (Look for an intersection near the school zone.) Once you reach BCS 286, turn left (north) for La Paz and La Ventana, or right (south) for Los Planes, Los Muertos, and the Cortez coast. There is a Pemex station at this intersection as well.

SAN BARTOLO

As Mexico 1 emerges from the sierra and prepares to descend to the coast once again, it passes through the farm settlement of San Bartolo (pop. 550) at Km 128. An attractive row of markets and eateries line both sides of the highway. You can buy mangoes, avocados, and other locally grown produce from markets

THE EAST CAPE

© PABLO NOBILI

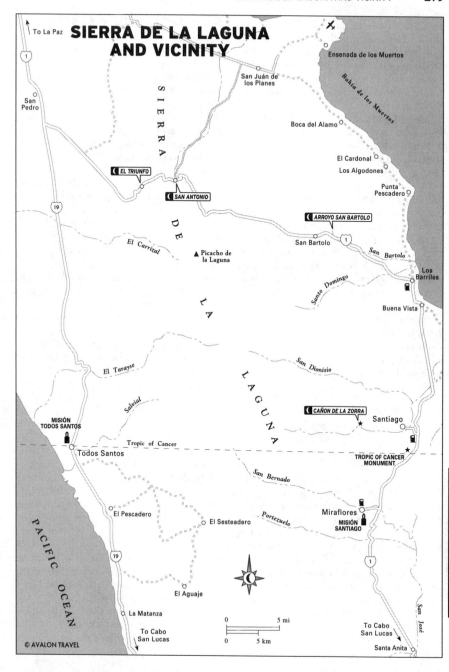

THE EAST CAPE

along the road—or pick out a bag of home-made candies. Then grab a seat on a wrought-iron bench and enjoy the vista looking down on the palm-filled arroyo. **Restaurant El Paso** (no tel., hours vary) and **Dulcería Daniela's** (no tel., hours vary), on the east side of the highway, serve simple Mexican dishes as well as sweets. **(El Oasis** (no tel., hours vary) sells fruit-filled *dulces* and other snacks.

San Bartolo celebrates its patron saint day on June 19, just a week after San Antonio's town festival.

(Arroyo San Bartolo

San Bartolo has one of the best water supplies anywhere in Southern Baja, and waterfalls along its arroyo are a popular way to cool off on balmy days. Organized tours from Los Barriles often travel here via ATV. But if you want to drive yourself to the falls, head to the village of San Bartolo and inquire at Rancho Verde for directions.

Recreation

Rancho La Venta (www.rancholaventa. com) offers guided horseback rides (up to 2 hrs US$50, up to 3 hrs US$70, overnight ride with meals and drinks US$550) and trails for hiking and bird-watching.

Accommodations and Food

Rancho Verde (Mexico 1 btw Km 143/142, tel. 612/126-9103, U.S. tel. 888/516-9462, www. rancho-verde.com) advertises itself as a private RV community with lots for sale, but it does rent sites by the night as well (RVs US$12/day, US$72/week; tents US$8/day). Set on more than 1,200 hectares of sierra wilderness, this park offers a refreshing contrast to the increasing crowds and real estate development that are overtaking much of the Baja coast. Amenities include water, sewer, hot showers, and free Wi-Fi.

Just up the road, in a historic location on the mission trail, **Rancho La Venta** (www. rancholaventa.com, US$75) offers a few *casitas* for rent, meals included. Owners Bob and Liz Pudwell ran a popular fish taco restaurant in Alaska before moving permanently to Baja. Now they grow organic vegetables on their ranch.

SANTIAGO AND VICINITY

The largest town along this stretch of Mexico 1, Santiago, was founded as a mission settlement and has evolved into a modern-day agricultural commerce center with a population of around 2,000. Located two kilometers west of Mexico 1, the town is overlooked by most Baja visitors, which allows it to retain an authentic Mexican feel despite its proximity to the Los Cabos tourist corridor.

The Arroyo de Santiago divides the town into two halves, Loma Norte and Loma Sur (North Hill and South Hill). All around the slopes are mango, avocado, and palm orchards. Local farmers now grow much of the organic produce that appears on many Los Cabos menus, and the town's palm orchards supply the palms used to make the ubiquitous *palapa* roofs used up and down the peninsula.

Set at the base of the sierra foothills, Santiago is also an access point for backpacking trips into the Sierra de la Laguna.

The town has one well-known restaurant and hotel, plus a few *tiendas* and produce markets. Santiago also has Baja's only zoo, although the animals in it are reportedly aging and the numbers dwindling.

Santiago is the last town you'll see on Mexico 1 southbound before crossing the Tropic of Cancer (latitude 23.5°N). Although the climate has likely felt tropical since Mulegé, this crossing makes it official.

Misión de Santiago El Apóstol Aiñiní

Italian Padre Ignacio María Nápoli founded the mission (1724–1795) at Santiago after attempting to build settlements on Bahía de las Palmas on the East Cape and at Santa Ana in the Sierra de la Laguna. As was the case at the other Southern Baja missions, the Pericú resisted the Catholic way of life. Santiago was the first mission attacked in the massive Pericú rebellion of 1734. Missionary buildings and possessions were burnt to the ground and the padre in residence was murdered.

Survivors began to rebuild the settlement in 1736, but uprisings and epidemics continued,

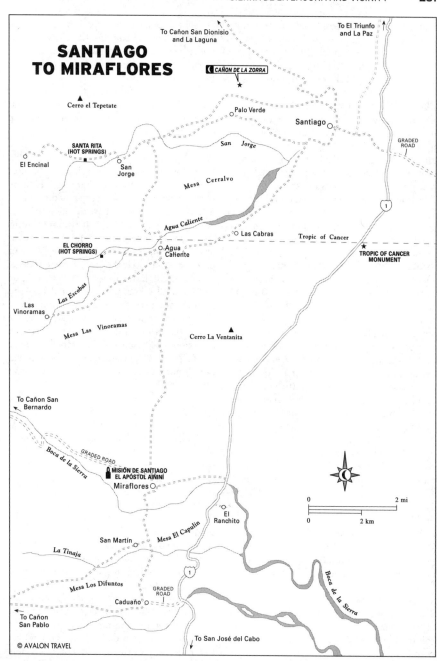

SANTIAGO TO MIRAFLORES

To Cañon San Dionisio and La Laguna

To El Triunfo and La Paz

CAÑON DE LA ZORRA ★

▲ Cerro el Tepetate

Palo Verde

Santiago

GRADED ROAD

San   Jorge

SANTA RITA (HOT SPRINGS)

El Encinal

San Jorge

Mesa   Cerralvo

1

Agua Caliente

Las Cabras   Tropic of Cancer

EL CHORRO (HOT SPRINGS)

Agua Caliente

★ TROPIC OF CANCER MONUMENT

Las Escobas

Las Vinoramas

Mesa Las Vinoramas

▲ Cerro La Ventanita

To Cañon San Bernardo

Boca de la Sierra

GRADED ROAD

MISIÓN DE SANTIAGO EL APÓSTOL AIÑINÍ

Miraflores

El Ranchito

N

San Martín

Mesa El Capulin

La Tinaja

1

Boca de la Sierra

0   2 mi

0   2 km

Mesa Los Difuntos

Caduaño

GRADED ROAD

To Cañon San Pablo

To San José del Cabo

© AVALON TRAVEL

THE EAST CAPE

and the Dominicans abandoned the site in 1795, moving the last remaining indigenous people to San José. A modern church (1958) on Santiago's Loma Sur (South Hill) is believed to have been built on the ruins of the original mission.

🔔 Santiago Town Plaza

On the north side of Santiago is the pleasant town plaza, with tall trees for shade and a handful of colonial buildings around its perimeter. The plaza makes a relaxing stop for a stroll, or a place to enjoy a picnic lunch after a trip to the hot springs or waterfall nearby. Santiago hosts its town festival on July 25, the feast day of St. James. Services on the plaza include a post office, gas station, mini-market, produce market, and a few stores.

Accommodations and Food

Decorated with local fossils, the highly regarded 🔔 **Palomar Restaurant-Bar** (tel. 624/130-2019, Mon.–Sat. 10:30 A.M.–7 P.M., Sun. 10:30 A.M.–4 P.M., mains US$11–15), south of the plaza on the east side of Calzada Misioneros, serves seafood, enchiladas, steak, and burgers. Fresh guacamole is made from avocados grown in the courtyard. Homemade soups and *pescado mojo de ajo* (fish cooked in garlic butter) are house specialties. It also offers six plain but clean rooms with air-conditioning around a shady courtyard for US$45.

Past the Hotel Palomar on the north side of town, a road heads northwest to Rancho San Dionísio (23.5 km) and the Cañon San Dionísio approach into the Sierra de la Laguna. Owner Sergio Gomez (tel. 624/130-2019) can also contact guides from Rancho San Dionísio for hikers.

Tacos La Cascada (no tel., daily for dinner) 200 meters from the plaza on the way to the waterfall, offers excellent carne asada, *mixto* (carne and cheese), and fish tacos for US$1.50 each.

Getting There

To get to Santiago, turn west off Mexico 1 at the Pemex station at Km 84/85 and follow this road for two kilometers to a boulevard that eventually meets the plaza.

Eight kilometers northeast of Santiago on Mexico 1 (around Km 93), Las Cuevas marks the exit ramp for La Ribera and El Camino Costero Rural. Services include a mini-super and bus stop.

Buses stop at Santiago, for access to the Sierra de la Laguna, and at La Ribera/Las Cuevas, Km 93, for access to Cabo Pulmo (no connecting service).

Hot Springs

Several waterfalls and hot springs are a short drive into the sierra from Santiago. Finding them involves navigating a series of turns along mostly unsigned dirt roads, although the state is beginning to make the area more visitor-friendly with more pavement and signs at each of the ranchos to indicate what they grow or produce—and what they may have for sale.

The main hot springs are called Agua Caliente, El Chorro, and Santa Rita—and all three are just a few kilometers from town. Many residents and hotel managers along the East Cape can provide accurate turn-by-turn directions to these sites. The Hotel Palomar (tel. 624/130-2019) is a good place for information. A nominal admission fee (around US$3–5) may be required to enter the sites.

🔔 Cañon de la Zorra

Fresh water is a sight to behold in the Baja desert landscape. For those travelers who would like to venture into the sierra but do not have time for a multiday hike, there is a 10-meter waterfall just 9.6 kilometers beyond Santiago that has a swimmable lagoon and is reachable by foot. At the far end of the divided avenue that leads into Santiago (as you approach the plaza), turn right and set your trip odometer to zero. At 0.48 kilometer, go straight through the dirt road intersection and head up the hill, past a sign for San Dionísio. At 1.29 kilometers and the crest of the hill, turn left. At 1.77 kilometers, turn right across a small arroyo and follow this road to 4.02 kilometers, where the road forks and there is a sign pointing to the right fork marked Cañon de la Zorra. Follow this fork to the end of the road at 9.66 kilometers

DRIVING WASHBOARD ROADS

Whether you rent a car or drive your own, exploring Baja's back roads takes a toll on vehicle and driver alike. Follow these tips to enjoy a safe and smooth ride:

- **Less is more:** Lower the air pressure in your tires for driving on softer sand.

- **Stay to the side:** You can often find a smoother track on the far left or right side of the road.

- **Pick up the pace:** Faster speeds often smooth out the bumps, but be sure to slow

down when approaching turns to avoid skids and unexpected obstacles.

- **Know your clearance:** Watch for large rocks and deep potholes that can wreak havoc on low-hanging oil pans.

- **Travel with tools:** At a minimum, a spare tire and jack are essential. Old carpet remnants work well for getting traction on soft sand.

- **Ask around:** For less-traveled routes, inquire when the road was last graded and what kind of vehicle you need to pass through safely.

---

and park at the trailhead. Small wooden outhouses are popping up in remote areas of the Cape, and you'll find one of them here. Go through the gate and follow the trail for 10 minutes down to the river bottom and the falls. The state has installed concrete steps to get to the waterfall now, instead of the rope, which used to scare off some potential visitors. And there is an entrance fee now of US$5.

MIRAFLORES

Continuing south along Mexico 1 from Santiago, the next town off the west side of the highway is Miraflores, a center for leatherwork. Follow the paved access road from a Pemex at Km 71 about 2.5 kilometers to the town center. There's not a whole lot to see here, but **Curtiduría Miraflores** (Miraflores Tannery, tel. 624/355-0254, daily 7 A.M.–7 P.M.), on the way into town, sells leather saddles and other ranching gear, as well as a limited assortment of hats, belts, and purses.

Two annual events in Miraflores would make for an especially festive visit: Fiesta Guadalupana on December 12, and the Miraflores town fiesta on July 20.

A dirt road leaves Miraflores heading northwest to the village of Boca de la Sierra (Mouth of the Sierra), which is located at the entrance to Cañón San Bernardo, an access point for hikes

into the sierra. Another dirt road southwest of town goes to Cañón San Pablo, another trail into the mountains. The leather shop is a good place to inquire about hiring a guide for a hike.

SIERRA DE LA LAGUNA

In between the tranquil Sea of Cortez and the powerful Pacific Ocean, a range of 1,500–2,100-meter granite peaks runs north to south, from the plains south of La Paz to the edge of San José, dividing the East Cape and West Cape regions of the Baja Peninsula. Its freshwater springs, unique flora and fauna, and dramatic weather patterns contrast radically with the desert-tropical environment along the coast. And yet, the access points for the Sierra de la Laguna are only minutes away from the Transpeninsular Highway and Mexico 19. There are good reasons why *Backpacker* magazine calls this area the best midwinter trail hiking on the Baja Peninsula.

There is some dispute about the highest peak in the range, but **Picacho de la Laguna** (elevation 2,161 m) is most often cited as the tallest. The meadow that stretches the 6.4 kilometers between Picacho de la Laguna and Cerro las Casitas is called La Laguna, since it used to be a lake until around 1870. (The lake was drained to support agriculture and mining operations in the late 1800s.)

THE EAST CAPE

The peaks are a genuine cloud forest in the late summer months and can receive more than 100 centimeters of rain a year.

The range's unique position between the desert to the north and the water on the other three sides creates a rare ecosystem of lush subtropical, alpine, and desert vegetation. The waterfalls that run until late spring add to the stunning scenery.

The peak hiking season here is late October through early spring, after the summer storms have subsided and the waterfalls are running. Temperatures at La Laguna can drop below freezing during the winter months, when the daytime highs range 10–20°C. In spring, daytime temperatures climb to around 25°C.

Siera de la Laguna Biosphere Reserve

Drenched with far more annual precipitation than any other part of the peninsula, La Laguna has become an isolated microclimate that sustains plants and animals long gone from the desert plains below. There are more than 900 plant species growing in the range, 70 of them indigenous. More striking than the number of species is the unusual combination of plants typically associated with opposite climates. This is a place where moss grows next to cacti and palms thrive beside willows. Naturally, the area is popular with avid bird watchers.

In 1994, the Mexican government designated the Sierra de la Laguna a "biosphere reserve," a designation long sought by local environmentalists. The reserve encompasses 11,300 hectares, divided into a core zone, in which development is prohibited, and a buffer zone, where ranchers may graze livestock.

Hiking

Hikes in these mountains typically follow canyons, trails, or cow tracks—or a combination of the three. There are three main routes into the sierra from the east side of

the range: Cañon San Dionísio, with access from Santiago; Cañon San Bernardo, with access from Miraflores; and Cañon San Pablo, with access from Caduaño (4 km south of Miraflores). The main access point from the west side is at La Burrera, between Pescadero and Todos Santos. Described here a couple of representative hikes; local guides can make additional recommendations based on current conditions and client preferences.

LA LAGUNA AND PICACHO DE LA LAGUNA SUMMIT

The most popular hike in the area is a round-trip summit of the highest peak in the range via Cañon San Dionísio, with an overnight stop to camp in the oak meadow at La Laguna. The summit is best attempted from west to east because the terrain in this direction is more direct and easier to navigate. You do not need a guide to do this hike; however, SEMARNAT, the government agency that manages the biosphere reserve, asks hikers to obtain a permit from its office in La Paz (Ocampo 1045, second floor, tel. 612/123-9313, US$1 pp).

The total distance for the hike is 24 kilometers, with 1,800 meters of elevation gain. Many people leave before sunrise under a full moon to get off the exposed face before the sun hits the west slope. There are a few forest ranger and military buildings in the meadow.

Access to this hike begins at the village of La Burrera, near Todos Santos. Look for a dirt turnoff from Mexico 19, about 100 meters south of the road to Punta Lobos. After the old water tower, take the first left and continue straight through several intersections until the road ends at a gate and parking area. From the gate, follow the dirt road all the way to La Burrera, about 25 minutes more. Continue on the same road for 20 minutes more until you reach a clearing on the right that has been used for camping; a sign here reads No Tire Basura (Don't Throw Trash). Just past the sign, the road climbs a small rise, and the trail begins from here.

Enjoy the first few steps of flat terrain because the trail gets fairly steep in a hurry. The

Sierra de la Laguna entrance
© PAUL ITOI

trail to La Laguna is 11-kilometers, which takes 5–8 hours, depending on your pace. As you approach the meadow, the dense vegetation gives way to panoramic views of the mountains and ocean below. In the southeast corner of the meadow is a waterfall and swimming pool. Pack enough drinking water to get you to La Laguna, as there is no permanent source of water along the trail.

If you need transportation to the trailhead, stop by the Siempre Vive grocery store (Juárez at Márquez de León, Todos Santos) in the late morning, or check with Todos Santos Eco Adventures (www.tosea.net) for organized trips. Taxis waiting at the taxi stand by the town park will also drive you there.

Guides are strongly recommended to do this trip from the eastern approach, due to the complex network of cow tracks. (Ask in Santiago.) Most hikers allow 3–4 days to cover the 12.8 kilometers to La Laguna. Make sure to bring enough water for the whole journey.

TRANS-SIERRA HIKE

Cañon San Bernardo presents the easiest route for crossing the range from east to west. Allow 2–3 days to complete the 22.5-kilometer hike.

THE EAST CAPE

From the village of Boca de la Sierra, you climb to an elevation of 1,000 meters over the course of about 16 kilometers, and then descend to Santo Domingo on the west side. There is drinking water in year-round pools along the way. Allow 4–5 days for this hike.

Information and Services

SUPPLIES

At a minimum, you need a reliable compass and topographic map for any of these hikes. Relevant topo maps for these hikes include El Rosario F12B23, Las Cuevas F12B24, Todos Santos F12B33, and Santiago F12B34. Pack warm layers and sleeping bags for the higher elevations, even in the spring. Long pants and sturdy footwear can protect bare skin from the getting jabbed by cactus needles.

Although some routes have water along the way, it's best to bring your own and use what's there as backup. Remember to purify any water you collect from mountain pools.

GUIDES

For hikes from the east side of the sierra, guides are recommended and readily available Santiago and Miraflores. Rates are about US$30–35 per day per person, plus an extra US$15 per day per pack animal. Rancho San Dionísio charges US$30 for a guide without mules, no matter how many people are hiking.

A guide is not essential to hike from the west side, although it helps to have someone show you to the trailhead. In Todos Santos, Fernando Arteche (sierradelalaguna@hotmail. com) has been leading trips for many years. He speaks excellent English and knows a lot about the Sierra de la Laguna. Trips are on mule or by foot. Juan Sebastián López (onejohnone@hotmail.com) runs three-day trips on horseback, with packhorses to carry your gear. At Rancho Pilar (Mexico 19, Km 73, ranchopilar@hotmail.com), artisan and amateur naturalist Cuco Moyron can arrange mule trips into the Sierra de la Laguna and is a good source of information about sierra flora. He'll need about a week to make the arrangements.

Todos Santos Eco Adventures (www.tosea. net) leads organized group trips into the sierra.

Getting There and Around

With high clearance and a sense of adventure, you can drive across the mountains from Mexico 1 north of San José del Cabo to Mexico 19 on the Pacific side via an ungraded road called Los Naranjos. The road is 42 kilometers long and ends at the village of El Aguaje, near Pescadero.

From the Los Cabos airport, head north until you pass Santa Anita and go about eight kilometers more. Turn left onto Los Naranjos road, which ascends from the flats up into the sierra.

Bring along a copy of the *Baja California Plant and Field Guide,* by Norman Roberts.

Follow the switchbacks to a plateau and then continue west until you glimpse the Pacific Ocean in the distance. At this point, the road frequently washes out and may not be passable. If it's clear, you can continue on to Pescadero.

LOS CABOS

Something magical happens at the point where the cool green Pacific Ocean crashes into the blue sapphire Sea of Cortez at Land's End. The fish that inhabit these waters drew the original visitors 30 years ago—wealthy Hollywood types who arrived by yacht or private plane to fish the Marlin Alley. Then the anglers began to bring their golf clubs, dive gear, and college-age kids. Today, stunning geography, perfect weather, endless opportunities for outdoor recreation, and federal funding from the Mexican government have transformed the area from a cluster of fishing villages into a full-scale tourist corridor.

From Cabo San Lucas to San José del Cabo, and everywhere in between, landscaped highway exit ramps are replacing dirt-road turnoffs, new resorts and condo buildings are under construction, golf courses are opening, and restaurant menu prices are reaching for the stars. Some say Los Cabos is well on its way (if not already there) to becoming Mexico's most expensive destination.

Adventure travelers, fear not: Los Cabos offers much more than nine-bedroom villas and huge yachts. Beneath the upscale veneer, quaint bed-and-breakfasts, modest hotels, free snorkeling beaches, authentic taquerías, and affordable *panga* boat tours invite exploration.

The tip of the Baja Peninsula consists of two large towns connected by a 29-kilometer-long stretch of white-sand beaches, exclusive golf courses, and luxury resorts—known as the Corridor—which the government has divided into several development zones or *fraccionamientos*. These towns and zones make up the Los Cabos *municipio* (county).

© NIKKI GOTH ITOI

HIGHLIGHTS

◖ **Plaza Teniente José Antonio Mijares:** San José del Cabo town life centers around this cobblestone plaza in front of an elegant 1940 church built on the site of the original Jesuit mission (page 294).

Plaza Teniente José Antonio Mijares

Historic Art District

Pueblo la Playa

San José del Cabo

Estero San José

CABO SAN LUCAS

Bahías Chileno and Santa María

Playa del Amor

Finisterra (Land's End)

PACIFIC OCEAN

0   5 mi

0   5 km

LOOK FOR ◖ TO FIND RECOMMENDED SIGHTS, ACTIVITIES, DINING, AND LODGING.

◖ **Historic Art District:** Historic adobe buildings in the San José Art District house a number of contemporary art galleries. More than a dozen galleries participate in Thursday evening Art Walks, which draw visitors and locals alike (page 295).

◖ **Estero San José:** Spanish colonists were originally drawn to the tip of the Baja Peninsula by the promise of fresh water. Here, a large estuary, home to hundreds of species of birds, connects the Pacific Ocean to an underground river that flows out of the sierra (page 295).

◖ **Bahías Chileno and Santa María:** Two of the Corridor's most popular and accessible beaches offer safe swimming and good snorkeling (page 318).

◖ **Finisterra (Land's End):** Every tour boat in Cabo visits Finisterra and its 62-meter-high arch. This granite rock formation marks the end of the Baja Peninsula and the point where the Sea of Cortez merges with the Pacific Ocean (page 331).

◖ **Playa del Amor:** This two-sided beach just outside the Cabo San Lucas harbor faces calm waters on its eastern Bahía San Lucas side and pounding surf on the western Pacific side (page 331).

With its signature rock arch and large, protected harbor, Cabo San Lucas is situated on the west side of the peninsula, at the place where the Sea of Cortez and Pacific Ocean meet. Cabo San Lucas is busier, noisier, more Americanized, and more touristy than unassuming San José del Cabo. On any given day, multiple cruise ships may deliver thousands of day-trippers into the Cabo San Lucas marina. They mingle with expats, snowbirds, and the adventure-seekers who come to fish, dive, cruise, and party.

On the east side of the peninsula, San José del Cabo is quieter and prettier, with a historic plaza and numerous restored colonial-era buildings. Its growing art district holds a handful of well-respected galleries, representing artists from all over Mexico, as well as some from the United States.

That said, San José is experiencing some growth pains of its own. Its new Puerto Los Cabos marina has brought power, Internet, and a modern sewage system to the village at La Playita. But with these amenities come the owners of US$80 million yachts, the noise and mess of constant construction, higher prices, and increasing traffic congestion. In many ways, San José is becoming unaffordable for the local residents whose families have lived here for generations.

The global economic recession had taken a toll on Baja-based businesses as of early 2009. Construction on just about all major developments had come to a halt, at least temporarily, and most of the workers' camps were empty. Overall, business was down an estimated 30–50 percent, depending on whom you asked. In this climate, many businesses will not be able to ride out the economic cycle and will have to close.

HISTORY

The Pericú first inhabited the Los Cabos area. They were a nomadic people whose territory extended from Cabo San Lucas to San José and up to Cabo Pulmo on the East Cape. Early Spanish explorers took interest in the vicinity of San José del Cabo when they discovered fresh water in the Río San José. While the Spanish set up camp near San José, favoring its protected estuary and abundant freshwater, English pirates, including Francis Drake and Thomas Cavendish, dominated the cape and bay at San Lucas. In a major blow to the Spanish, Cavendish captured, looted, and sank the 600-ton Manila galleon *Santa Ana* in 1578, in the same waters where modern cruisers troll for game fish.

The Pericú proved to be less tolerant of the Spanish than neighboring tribes to the north had been. Following a series of uprisings in the 1720s, Jesuit Padre Nicolas Tamarál came from La Purísima in 1930 to establish a permanent mission and military outpost that would guard the estuary from further attacks by pirates and indigenous people. He planted orchards and moved the mission site around a few times before settling on the current town center, which afforded views of the harbor without all the bugs.

Padre Tamarál baptized more than 1,000 Pericú in the first year of the mission, but peace lasted only until 1734, when the Pericú rebelled once again, this time to protest a Spanish decree against polygamy. They burned four

marina in Cabo San Lucas

© NIKKI GOTH ITOI

missions in Southern Baja and killed Tamarál in the battle.

Few of the Pericú remained by 1767 when the Jesuits were expelled from Baja California. But the mission persevered under the Dominicans. In the following decades, the Spanish built a garrison at San José, turning the mission into a military outpost that re-supplied the Manila galleons on their way to and from the Philippines.

In a rarely documented chapter of the Mexican-American War (1846–1848), a group of 20 U.S. marines from the sloop *Portsmouth* briefly occupied the city of San José from barracks in a former mission building, which is now preserved as the town's Casa de la Cultura. The U.S. forces were given a ninepounder carronade (a type of cannon) and 75 carbines to hold the town against about 150 Mexican insurgents. When Mexican lieutenant José Antonio Mijares attempted to invade the barracks and capture the cannon in 1847, he failed and was shot by the marines, but the heroic effort earned him a place in local history.

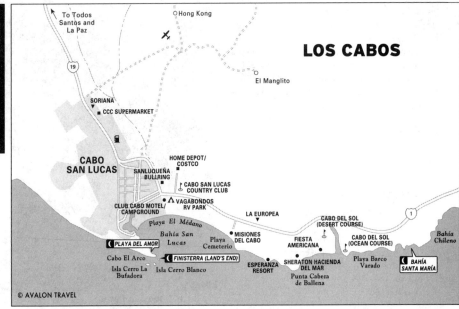

To Todos Santos and La Paz

Hong Kong

LOS CABOS

El Manglito

19

SORIANA
CCC SUPERMARKET

CABO
SAN LUCAS

HOME DEPOT/
COSTCO

SANLUQUEÑA
BULLRING

CABO SAN LUCAS
COUNTRY CLUB

CLUB CABO MOTEL/
CAMPGROUND

VAGABONDOS
RV PARK

LA EUROPEA

CABO DEL SOL
(DESERT COURSE)

Playa El Médano

Bahía San   Playa
Lucas   Cemeterio

MISIONES
DEL CABO

FIESTA
AMERICANA

CABO DEL SOL
(OCEAN COURSE)

Bahía
Chileno

PLAYA DEL AMOR

Cabo El Arco

FINISTERRA (LAND'S END)

ESPERANZA
RESORT

SHERATON HACIENDA
DEL MAR

Playa Barco
Varado

BAHÍA
SANTA MARÍA

Isla Cerro La   Isla Cerro Blanco
Bufadora

Punta Cabeza
de Ballena

1

© AVALON TRAVEL

Boulevard Mijares and Plaza Mijares are both named in his honor.

A 21-day siege of the U.S. force's barracks in San José took place in early 1848, even as U.S. President Polk was claiming victory in the Californias. The Americans were eventually rescued by a party of 102 men from the sloop *Cyane*. In the end, the Treaty of Guadalupe Hidalgo, signed on February 2, 1848, did not give the United States possession of Baja California. The U.S. forces that had held the garrison withdrew 18 months after the conflict had begun. Many expressed disappointment in the outcome, believing that the United States had abandoned its promise to take lower California under its wing and left its supporters at the mercy of their own government.

After the Mexican-American War and short-lived mining era, San José experienced a period of agriculture in the 1930s. The mission church was rebuilt in 1940, and San José began to attract its first sportfishing tourists in the 1960s.

Cabo San Lucas first became a port town near the end of the 19th century, when it began

to export the bark of the *palo blanco* tree, which was used as an agent for tanning leather. The Faro Viejo (Mexico 19, Km 2) lighthouse was built at Cabo Falso in 1890.

Next, came the era of tuna canning and the opening of the Compania de Productos Marinos, S.A. de C.V. in 1927, which spurred growth and development in the area for a couple of decades. (The pioneering company moved to Puerto San Carlos in the 1980s.) A road was constructed to join San José to San Lucas. Today, it's known as the Camino Viejo a San José (the old road to San José). The canning business declined rapidly after a severe hurricane damaged the equipment in 1941.

With an infrastructure in place, visitors began to arrive at the port after World War II, and a small tourism business evolved around sportfishing. In the 1960s, the original road was replaced by a paved highway that became part of the Transpeninsular Highway, which was completed in 1973. By this time, the population of Cabo San Lucas had grown to about 1,500.

The new highway ushered in a new phase of road travel, bringing a steady stream of visitors

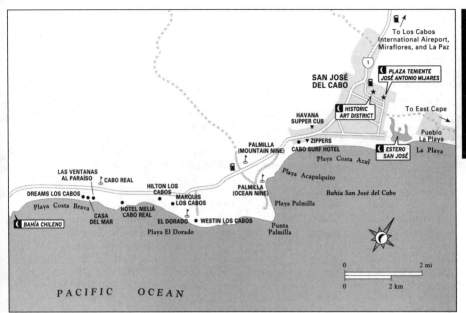

to the tip of the peninsula. Mainland Mexican residents began moving to Los Cabos in the mid-1970s, when ferry service commenced between Puerto Vallarta and La Paz. Around this time, the Mexican government designated the Los Cabos corridor for tourism investment and development, and the opening of the Los Cabos International Airport in the 1980s began to bring mainstream travelers en masse.

Today, tourism and related construction are the engines of growth for the Los Cabos economy; however, the development comes at the expense of considerable natural resources; already in short supply, fresh water remains a serious concern, as does the protection of endangered sea turtles, whose habitat continues to erode. As the ocean has become polluted and over-fished, the very ecosystem that has captured the imagination of so many visitors may disappear for good.

PLANNING YOUR TIME

In a couple of days, you can easily explore the main sections of downtown San José and sample a few restaurants, plus have time for the beach.

Add extra days for any special activities, such as scuba diving, fishing, or mountain biking. The drive from San José del Cabo to Cabo San Lucas along the Corridor takes about 30–45 minutes. Surfers and beachcombers can happily spend a full week at a resort along the Corridor. But aside from the beaches (which are spectacular) and associated activities, there is little else to see—meaning, you don't need a lot of time to cover the area if you're just passing through.

For some travelers, a half-day in Cabo San Lucas will be more than enough time; others will be content to spend a week. It all depends on whether you prefer nightlife or a more remote setting for your vacation.

CHOOSING AN ACCOMMODATION

Whether you are a first-time or veteran Los Cabos visitor, finding a place to stay involves an overwhelming variety of choices. There are all-inclusive resorts, boutique hotels, basic motels, bed-and-breakfasts, condominiums, timeshares, and villas of all sizes. (And some resorts mix and match, to give even more choice.)

You can be at the beach, on a golf course, or in town. You can book directly with a resort or private owner, or use a booking service or property management company. And you can spend US$50–950 a night, depending on your budget and the level of comfort you seek.

If you'd like a quieter location where you can look at the beach but swim in a pool, the Corridor or hotel zone of San José would be a good choice. If you want to surf, consider Playa Costa Azul, just outside of San José. For swimming and nightlife within walking distance of your hotel, head to Cabo San Lucas.

High-end resorts feature a full list of amenities, usually including air-conditioning, direct-dial phones, satellite TV, multiple swimming pools, swim-up bars, tennis courts, hot tubs, fitness centers, kids' club, and beach *palapas,* plus on-site restaurants and bars. Some resorts also have their own dive centers, spa services, horseback riding, and ATV rental services. High-speed wireless Internet, voice-over-IP phones (free long distance), and flat-screen TVs are some of the newest amenities that hotels and condo owners are adding to differentiate themselves.

Vacation rental condos or villas, or condo-style hotels, afford the most flexibility, as you can cook some of your own meals and venture out for others. Many of the newest condo complexes are concentrated near Playa Costa Azul, between San José and the Corridor. Most are on or near the beach and many have tennis courts, swimming pools, and laundry facilities; however, the persistent sound of traffic on Mexico 1 is a drawback to this location. You can rent units directly from private owners by searching for listings online (on www.craigslist.com and www.vrbo.com, for example), or by contacting a property management service. (Many of these services also advertise on the private-owner sites.)

Planning Ahead

If you are thinking about a year-end holiday vacation, book as far in advance as possible. Repeat visitors reserve many of the most popular rooms and rentals as much as a year in advance for the weeks around Christmas and New Year's. February and March are popular, too, and despite the number of choices for accommodations, there are a handful of resorts—including the One&Only Palmilla, Dreams, and Riu Palace—that seem to be full almost all the time. Flexible travelers need not plan so far ahead, and they are often rewarded with better deals.

Booking Services and Property Management Companies

If you haven't yet decided on a specific location within Los Cabos, or you have a very specific set of criteria for choosing a place to stay, contact a booking service agent, who can give you an overview of several different properties that meet your criteria and your budget. The following companies specialize in Los Cabos area bookings: **Delfin Hotels & Resorts,** also called **Cabo Hotels** (U.S. tel. 800/524-5104) lists a wide variety of villas, condos (Terrasol, Las Mañanitas, Mira Vista, Mykonos) all-inclusive resorts, and bed-and-breakfasts. It also publishes several Cabo accommodations websites, including www.cabohotels.com, www.cabocondos.com, and www.allinclusivescabo.com. **Baja Properties** (Doblado and Morelos, San José tel. 624/142-0988, Cabo San Lucas tel. 624/143-2560, toll-free 877/464-2252, www.bajaproperties.com) has 20 years of experience in Los Cabos real estate marketing, eight office locations, and a team of 25 agents.

Watsonville, California–based **Earth, Sea, and Sky Vacations** (ESSV, toll-free U.S. tel. 800/745-2226, www.cabovillas.com) specializes in luxury vacation packages to the Los Cabos area. It represents 90 villa rentals, ranging from two- to nine-bedroom units, starting at US$1,500 per night, as well as 30 resorts. For an extra fee, ESSV staff will stock your villa prior to your arrival with the foods and supplies you request. Guests can also opt for in-villa services, such as Pilates or yoga classes, spa treatments, and chef services (for one special meal or three meals daily). Since ESSV also handles activity bookings for whale-watching, fishing, and snorkeling, many travelers work with the company to coordinate group trips, such as large family vacations or small weddings.

Companies that focus exclusively on Cabo San Lucas or San José del Cabo (as opposed to the entire region) are listed in the *Accommodations* sections for those towns.

GETTING THERE

The majority of Los Cabos visitors arrive by air, but you'll meet many who have traveled by car, boat, bicycle, or even on foot. Public transportation by bus is also a possibility. Once you've arrived, you can do without a car if you plan to stay at an all-inclusive resort or at a hotel in town. Rent a car if you want to take a day trip to the East Cape or Todos Santos.

By Air

Los Cabos International Airport (SJD, Mexico 1, Km 44, tel. 624/142-5111, www.sjdloscabosairport.com) serves San José del Cabo and Cabo San Lucas. The airport does not have Jetways, so have your shades at the ready as you exit the plane and climb down the stairs to the tarmac.

The process of going through passport control and customs can take as little as 15 minutes, or more than an hour, depending on how many people are working and if other flights have arrived at the same time. After you go through passport control, you'll proceed to the baggage claim area. Claim your bags and have your paperwork ready to show the customs official. You'll be asked to run your bags through a scanner and to press a button that determines whether your bags will be randomly searched.

The airport has two terminals served by several major airlines (as well as a cargo-only termninal), including:

- Terminal 1: America West, Continental, AeroCalifornia, Mexicana, American, Aeromexico

- Terminal 2: General aviation and cargo

- Terminal 3: Alaska, Delta, Frontier, United

Both commercial terminals have a few fast-food options and souvenir shops, but seating is limited in the waiting areas for arriving flights. A new commercial terminal is under construction.

A shuttle into the San José area runs US$13 per person, US$15 per person to the Cabo San Lucas area. A private taxi from the airport to San José del Cabo costs US$50 for up to four passengers, or US$75 to Cabo San Lucas.

BY PRIVATE AIRCRAFT

Private pilots will find a 1,550-meter paved airstrip just north of Cabo San Lucas. Contact **Baja Bush Pilots** (www.bajabushpilots.com) for up-to-date information about making the trip to Los Cabos.

By Car

Most of the big auto rental agencies have desks at Los Cabos International Airport, as well as offices in or near San José and San Lucas. Rates are similar across most companies, and since car rentals don't require a deposit up front, it doesn't hurt to make a reservation in advance. You can always cancel if you change your mind. When you reserve or prepay for a car online, the price typically will not include Mexican liability insurance. Be sure to factor this cost (around US$25 per day for the minimum required coverage of US$50,000) into your travel planning. Vehicles range from standard transmission subcompact sedans to SUVs, wagons, Jeeps, pickup trucks, and vans. Independent agencies sometimes include insurance in the rates.

If you're driving yourself, there are two ways to reach the towns along the Los Cabos Corridor from the airport: Follow signs for Mexico 1 south through town, passing through several stoplights before you reach the town of San José. Continue on Mexico 1 another 10–20 minutes for destinations along the Corridor, or about 30 minutes to Cabo San Lucas. Alternatively, if you don't mind paying a toll of about US$2, you can exit the airport onto the *quota*, a fast four-lane road with no exits until you enter San José at the junction of Paseo Los Cabos and the Mega grocery store plaza. If you pick up a rental car off-site, you'll have to return to the terminal to get to the toll road.

By Bus

A steady stream of **Aguila** (tel. 624/143-5020) buses provide transportation between Los Cabos and La Paz and on to other points north. Current fares are about US$15 from Cabo San Lucas to La Paz and US$20 from San José to La Paz. Note: La Paz via Todos Santos is the shorter and less mountainous route (3.5 hours from Cabo San Lucas); the route to La Paz via the East Cape takes about an hour longer due to the terrain and number of stops. The Cabo San Lucas bus terminal is on Mexico 19, north of the Mexico 1 junction and across from the Pemex station. San Jose's main bus terminal is on Calle Gonzales near Mexico 1.

Autotransportes La Paz is another option for transportation to La Paz. Its fares are typically a little lower than Aguila's, and the Cabo San Lucas station is just across the street from the Aguila terminal.

If you're headed all the way to Tijuana (a 24-hour trip that costs US$130), you'll need to catch the 4 P.M. departure, which will stop in Ciudad Constitución, Loreto, Mulegé, Guerrero Negro, and Ensenada.

By Sea

The nearest ferry service to the mainland operates between La Paz and Mazatlán. You can book tickets in La Paz or online through **Baja Ferries** (tel. 612/123-0208, 612/123-6600, or 800/122-1414, www.bajaferries.com).

There are now two full-service marinas in the Los Cabos area. **Marina Cabo San Lucas** (Lote A-18 De la Dársena, tel.624/173-9140, www.igy-cabosanlucas.com) is still the main docking facility for those arriving by sea. But the new **Marina at Puerto Los Cabos** (Paseo de los Pescadores, Col. La Playa, tel. 624/105-6028, www.marinapuertoloscabos.com) is open and designed to hold up to 500 boats, including the largest luxury yachts.

San José del Cabo

An elevated plain above a narrow estuary at the mouth of the Río San José gave early Spanish settlers protection from pirate raids and uprisings by indigenous peoples. The first Jesuit missionaries arrived in 1730 from settlements to the north and tried several sites before choosing the current town center as the permanent location for a mission.

Surrounded by *huertas,* modern-day San José consists of a historic downtown with an attractive plaza and church, as well as many restored colonial buildings. The newer part of town includes a nine-hole golf course and new beachfront hotel zone. There is also a busy commercial area along Mexico 1. The town is the municipal seat for Los Cabos. Many expats, especially artists, have taken up residence in San José in recent years, but for the most part, they seem committed to restoring and preserving their adopted community of Josefinos, and so far, the town retains an authentic Mexican feel.

SIGHTS
◖ Plaza Teniente José Antonio Mijares

The center of all the action in San José is a wide brick plaza with a white gazebo-like structure in the middle. On the west side of the plaza, where the original mission once stood, is the 1940 Iglesia San José. Mature trees provide ample shade, while street performers entertain adults and children alike. Restaurants and shops line the plaza on Calles Zaragoza, Hidalgo, and Obregón and Boulevard Mijares. A variety of town festivals take place here, including events every Sunday evening during the Christmas season.

Misión San José del Cabo Añuiti

The Jesuit mission (1730–1840) at San José was founded in 1730 when Father Nicolas Tamarál traveled south from La Purísima and baptized more than 1,000 indigenous people in the first year.

© NIKKI GOTH ITOI

Plaza Teniente José Antonio Mijares

The current church, painted a creamy yellow color, was built in 1940 with two symmetrical towers and a mosaic over the main entrance, which depicts the murder of Father Tamarál by the Pericú who rose up against him. The church holds regular worship services for the people of San José.

Palacio Municipal

This striking 1831 building on Boulevard Mijares just off the plaza has a neoclassical facade, and a tower with a wrought-iron balcony and large clock. In the 19th century, the building housed the municipal council for San José. Today, it contains a number of local government offices.

◖ Historic Art District

About a dozen of the historic adobe buildings in downtown San José have been converted into fine art studios and galleries representing artists from all over Mexico and Central and South America, as well as the United States. Most of the galleries are concentrated in the blocks between Calles Guerrero and Hidalgo and Calles Zaragoza and Comonfort. On display are stone sculptures, paintings, pottery, and jewelry. On Thursday evenings, the galleries stay open late for the weekly Art Walk (Nov.–Jun. 5–9 P.M.). This is an unguided opportunity to visit the galleries at your own pace. Some serve refreshments, and some allow you to watch the artists at work in their studios.

Casa de la Cultura

U.S. marines stayed in this mission-era building just off the plaza in 1847–1848, during the Mexican-American War. Today, the pink building hosts art exhibits, as well as music, dance, and theater performances. The cultural center is located on Calle Obregón at the end of Boulevard Mijares, on the north side of the plaza. The building is open to the public Monday–Saturday 9 A.M.–8 P.M. Call 624/142-2960 for a schedule of events.

◖ Estero San José

The Río San José, the largest source of fresh water in Southern Baja, originates in the Sierra de la Laguna, travels about 48 kilometers

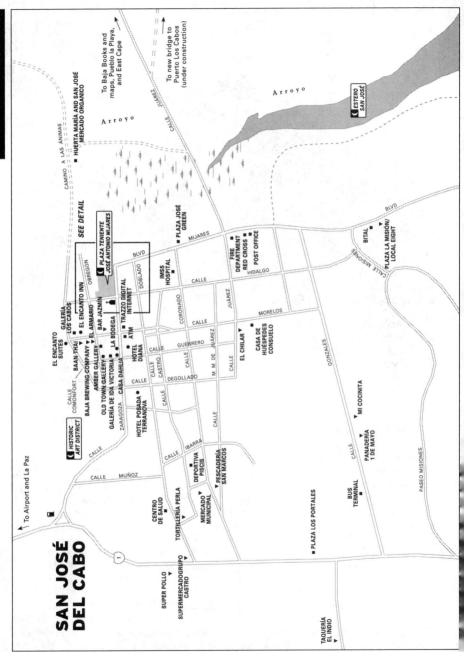

SAN JOSÉ DEL CABO

To Airport and La Paz

SUPER POLLO
SUPERMERCADO GRUPO CASTRO

TAQUERÍA EL INDIO

CENTRO DE SALUD
TORTILLERÍA PERLA
MERCADO MUNICIPAL
DEPORTIVA PISCIS
PESCADERÍA SAN MARCOS

CALLE MUÑOZ
CALLE IBARRA

HOTEL POSADA TERRANOVA

HISTORIC ART DISTRICT

EL ENCANTO SUITES
GALERÍA LOS CABOS
BAAN THAI
AMBER GALLERY
EL ENCANTO INN
EL ARMARIO
OLD TOWN GALLERY
GALERÍA DE IDA VICTORIA
CASA DAHLIA
LA BODEGA
HOTEL DIANA
ATM

CALLE COMONFORT
CALLE ZARAGOZA

PLAZA TENIENTE JOSÉ ANTONIO MIJARES
SEE DETAIL
OBREGON
BAR JAZMÍN
TRAZZO DIGITAL INTERNET

CALLE DEGOLLADO
CALLE GUERRERO
CALLE CASTRO
CALLE M. M. DE JUÁREZ
CALLE CORONADO
CALLE DOBLADO
CALLE HIDALGO
BLVD
MORELOS
CALLE JUÁREZ

EL CHILAR
CASA DE HUÉSPEDES CONSUELO

IMSS HOSPITAL

PLAZA JOSÉ GREEN
MIJARES
FIRE DEPARTMENT
RED CROSS
POST OFFICE

CALLE GONZALES

MI COCINITA
PANADERÍA 1 DE MAYO

BUS TERMINAL

PLAZA LOS PORTALES

PASEO MISIONES

BITAL
PLAZA LA MISIÓN/LOCAL EIGHT
CALLE MISIONES
BLVD

CAMINO A LAS ÁNIMAS
HUERTA MARÍA AND SAN JOSÉ MERCADO ORGÁNICO

Arroyo
Arroyo

CALLE JUÁREZ

To Baja Books and maps, Pueblo la Playa, and East Cape

To new bridge to Puerto Los Cabos (under construction)

ESTERO SAN JOSÉ

BAJA BREWING COMPANY

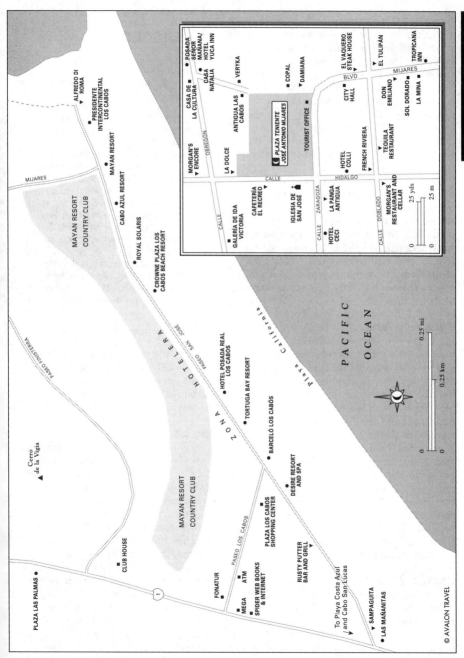

© AVALON TRAVEL

(much of it underground), and empties into a long, narrow estuary that measures 50 hectares. Sebastián Vizcaíno called the estuary Bahía San Bernabé. At the mouth of the river, a sandbar encloses a lagoon ringed by towering Tlaco palms and marsh grasses, which form a sanctuary for more than 200 species of birds.

Unfortunately, this fragile ecosystem is shrinking in size and biodiversity as the town of San José grows, the water table lowers, and the Puerto Los Cabos marina and development encroaches on the preserve.

To reach the estuary, walk or drive to the northeast end of the *zona hotelera* and park outside the Presidente InterContinental. Walk toward the beach and you'll see the estuary on the left. You can rent kayaks from **Baja's Activities** (tel. 624/142-2922, www.bajasactivities.com), next to the resort. Or follow a scenic footpath that runs parallel to Boulevard Mijares almost all the way to the intersection of Calle Juárez.

Zona Hotelera

San José's government-designated hotel zone encompasses more than 1,600 hectares that parallel the coastline from the Estero San José to Playa Costa Azul. To date, about a dozen large resorts and several condo complexes are complete. Some of the newcomers include the Royal Solaris, Mayan Grand, and Cabo Azul resorts. As more properties have opened for business, Paseo de San José has become a busy thoroughfare, with several car rental offices and a few new shops and restaurants. Condos and vacation homes surround a nine-hole golf course, now owned by Mayan Resorts. You can walk the beach all the way from the estuary to the surf break known as Zippers at Playa Costa Azul, but swimming is generally not a good idea, as the undertow is strong most of the year.

Cactus Garden

The brainchild of two cacti collectors, **Cacti Mundo** (Blvd. Mijares, btw downtown and the *zona hotelera*, tel. 624/146- 9191, www.cactimundo.org, daily 8 A.M.–5 P.M., US$3) has committed itself to the promotion,

---

THE BIG DIG

San José del Cabo's new marina has set some records in terms of its size and scale. Its 430 slips can accommodate yachts up to 180 feet long. When complete, the facility will be the largest marina in all of Mexico, with more than 21,000 linear feet of dock space at a price tag of US$50 million.

To form the protected harbor, construction crews shuttled 400,000 tons of granite blasted from a local quarry, with individual capstones weighing 60 tons apiece. They also removed some 650,000 cubic meters of earth from the site. Dump trucks were on the move six days a week for eight months straight to get the job done.

The new marina puts yachts and sportfishing boats one hour closer to Banco Gorda than the Cabo San Lucas marina, with a supposedly easier approach to navigate.

---

conservation, and reproduction of rare desert plants. It has 850 succulent species and more than 5,000 plants on display in a small public garden, most of which is visible from the street. Guided tours are available by appointment.

Pueblo La Playa

Once an isolated fishing village frequented only by *panga* fishermen and adventurous travelers, Pueblo La Playa and its sandy beach, **La Playita,** are soon to be linked to San José del Cabo via a paved road and new bridge across the wide arroyo that separates the two.

The 800-hectare **Puerto Los Cabos** project includes a new US$50 million marina designed to accommodate luxury mega-yachts, as well as a couple of designer golf courses, five-star accommodations, and beachfront lots that are selling for US$6–8 million.

At last check, the new harbor was open for business and the first few yachts were sailing into port. Pueblo la Playa had Internet access, paved streets with curbs, and a new, modern

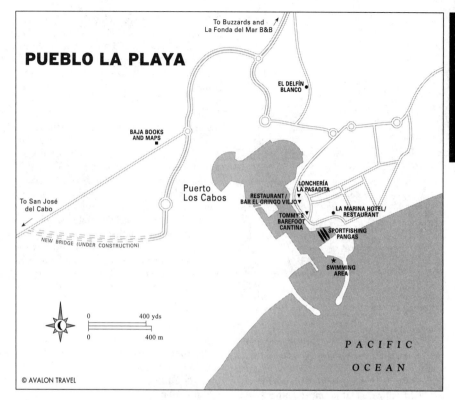

To Buzzards and
La Fonda del Mar B&B

PUEBLO LA PLAYA

EL DELFÍN
BLANCO

BAJA BOOKS
AND MAPS

Puerto
Los Cabos

LONCHERÍA
LA PASADITA

RESTAURANT /
BAR EL GRINGO VIEJO

LA MARINA HOTEL/
RESTAURANT

TOMMY'S
BAREFOOT
CANTINA

SPORTFISHING
PANGAS

To San José
del Cabo

NEW BRIDGE (UNDER CONSTRUCTION)

SWIMMING
AREA

0   400 yds

0   400 m

PACIFIC

OCEAN

© AVALON TRAVEL

sewage system in the works. A new *panga* marina and beachfront park features a play structure for kids; a roped-off, protected swimming area; clean restrooms; and the fanciest fish-cleaning tables found anywhere in Baja.

To reach La Playita, turn east off Boulevard Mijares onto Calle Juarez. Follow this road through hamlet of La Choya and turn right at the first traffic circle. Continue along the four-lane, landscaped boulevard through two more traffic circles, following signs to La Playita.

Playa Costa Azul

On the outskirts of San José, under a lookout point on the Transpeninsular Highway (Carretera Transpeninsular) near Km 28, somewhat protected Plaza Costa Azul attracts surfers, beachcombers, and occasionally swimmers who walk from the condo complexes that front the beach. For travelers coming from San José, there is a new and unmarked exit ramp just after Havanas Restaurant and before the wide arroyo. Turn left off the ramp and park in the sandy lot that divides Mira Vista condos and Zippers Restaurant.

SPORTS AND RECREATION
Fishing

Whether you're a seasoned veteran or you've never fished a day in your life, there are plenty of options near San José. For newbies, your captain and crew will find the right spot for the day, rig up the bait, and handle boating the fish. All you have to do is reel and smile for the picture. Later, top off the day by taking your fresh catch to a local restaurant to have it prepared to your liking.

© KATHRYN LATENDRESSE

entrance to the new marina at La Playita

Fishing boats for hire fall under two general categories: *pangas* and cruisers. Cruisers are the larger boats you'll see in the marina slips. They're often equipped with tuna-towers, enclosed cabins, a bathroom, and other amenities. *Pangas* are the ubiquitous open launches, powered by outboard motor and sometimes featuring a sunshade and center console. If you see a *panga* with a newer four-stroke outboard, center console, sunshade, and mounted radio, jump in—you've got a winner. The fish don't care what kind of boat you're in, but the cruisers can handle the larger game fish and a non-fishing passenger in comfort.

Don't forget to pack a hat, sunglasses, sunscreen, water, food, waterproof camera, sandals/Tevas, and windbreaker. Take motion sickness medicine the night before and morning of the trip if you are prone to seasickness (or if you aren't sure).

All hotels in the *zona hotelera* can arrange guided fishing trips. Well-known **Francisco's Fleet** (formerly Victor's Sportfishing, U.S. tel. 800/521-2281, www.jigstop.com) is based at Palmilla beach. A six-hour *panga* trip for two or three people costs US$190; bring your own food and drinks. **Gordo Banks Pangas** (Pueblo La Playa, tel./fax 624/142-1147, toll-free U.S. tel. 800/408-1199, www.gordobanks.com) launches out of La Playita and rents 22-foot *pangas* for US$210 (six hours, 1–3 anglers) or 23-foot super-*pangas* for US$250 (six hours, 1–3 anglers), and cruisers for US$350–530. **Jaime Castro** (Pueblo La Playa, cell tel. 044/624/154-9110, U.S. tel. 858/922-3355, www.caboplaya.com, US$200–280 per boat) runs *panga* fishing charters by day and manages the kitchen at Buzzard's by night. Boats depart at 6 A.M. daily from B dock at the La Playita marina and return at noon. Bait, lunch, drinks, and fishing license cost extra. Reserve online.

There are a few extra costs to factor into the planning: Tips for the captain and fish-cleaning crew are the norm. Live bait is often not included in the cost of the *panga,* so expect to pay US$20 per boat. Fishing licenses cost US$11 a day, or US$23 a week. You do not need a fishing license to fish from the shore.

For tackle, bait, and fishing books, head to **Deportiva Piscis** (Castro and Green, San José del Cabo, 1 block south of the Mercado Municipal, tel. 624/142-0332, daily 8 A.M.–7 P.M.).

Snorkeling and Diving

San José visitors must head to the East Cape, the Corridor, or Cabo San Lucas for suitable snorkeling and diving sites. Expert divers who are comfortable in strong currents and choppy seas and interested in exploring the offshore Gordo Banks seamounts may be able to hire a *panga* from La Playita; however, be aware that even groups of experienced dive instructors have run into complications when attempting to turn a fisherman into a dive-boat captain for the day. The safer approach is to book a trip through one of the PADI-certified dive shops in Cabo San Lucas.

Surfing

Summer is the peak season for catching waves in Los Cabos, but good-sized swells occasionally roll through as late as mid-November. Playa Costa Azul has three of the best-known breaks anywhere in Southern Baja. Enter from a sandy beach but beware the rocks at low tide. You scope out the scene from a lookout on Mexico 1 before taking the plunge. Longboarders and beginner surfers favor the Playa Acapulquito (Old Man's) reefbreak, in front of the Cabo Surf Hotel. Directly below the lookout, The Rock is another right. Localism is alive and well at Zippers, but only when the waves are pounding. The rest of the time, you can easily paddle out to enjoy this short and fast break. Just flash a smile and be prepared to wait your turn.

There are many lesser-known breaks along the Corridor that break on different sized swells, plus a handful of breaks on the East Cape.

EQUIPMENT

Several shops near San José rent boards and other equipment. The **Cabo Surf Shop** (Carr. Transp. Km 28, San José del Cabo, tel. 624/172-6188, U.S. tel. 858/964-5117, www. cabosurfshop.com), located at the Cabo Surf Hotel, offers private or group instruction on Playa Acapulquito through the Mike Doyle Surf School (daily 8 A.M.–6 P.M., until 7 P.M. in summer, group rate US$70 pp for 2 hrs, private lessons US$95/hr), as well as board rentals. Drop-ins are welcome. The **Costa Azul Surf Shop** (Carr. Transp. Km 28, Plaza Costa Azul, San José del Cabo, tel. 624/142-2771, Mon.–Sat. 8 A.M.–7 P.M., Sun. 9 A.M.–5 P.M.) rents short boards, hybrids, and longboards to experienced surfers, as well as beginner boards with rubber fins, and offers lessons. Stop in for beach umbrellas, beach chairs, and snorkeling gear, too. You can also rent boards right on the beach, next to Zippers Restaurant.

Golf

Centrally located in the hotel zone, the **Mayan Resorts Golf Course** (tel. 624/142-0905) is a convenient and affordable option. Rates are US$130 for 18 holes, with considerable discounts for resort guests (US$90). Discounted twilight rates (US$70) begin at 2 P.M. The clubhouse is located on the south side of Mexico 1, between Paseo de los Cabos and Paseo Finisterra.

Nearby, across Mexico 1 from the Mega grocery store, **Club Campestre San Jose Golf** (tel. 624/173-9400) is an 18-hole, par-71 course designed by Jack Nicklaus. Nicklaus is also the mastermind behind the new **Puerto Los Cabos Golf Club** (Paseo de los Pescadores, Pueblo La Playa, tel. 624/144-1200), an 18-hole, par-72 course.

Yoga

San José now has about half a dozen yoga studios, but some instructors seem to come and go each season. Caryl Leffel (tel. 624/137-3278, www.kaleidoscopeyoga.com, US$15–25 per class) teaches yoga classes in two locations: Cabo Danza (Plaza Tamarindo on Calle Gonzales, Mon., Wed., Fri. at 7:45 A.M. and 6:20 P.M.), a private dance studio, and Laguna Hills (Tues. and Thurs. at 9 A.M.), on a beachfront terrace along the East Cape. For Bikram/ hot yoga classes, try **America's Studio of Yoga** outside of town on the way to the airport (tel. 624/124-0316, www.americasstudioofyoga. com, US$12 per class). The studio is located 2.7 kilometers from downtown San José, on the east side of Mexico 1 just past the Pemex.

Spa Services

Ixchel Salon & Spa (Morelos 133, San José del Cabo, tel. 624/142-2330, www.ixchelspa.com, Mon.–Sat. 9 A.M.–8 P.M., Sun. 10 A.M.–6 P.M.), inside the El Encanto Inn, offers a full menu of treatments, including massages (50 min. for US$70), facials (50 min. for US$80), manicures, and pedicures. In addition, the Crowne Plaza, Grand Mayan, and other resorts have on-site spas that are open to the public.

Organized Tours

Most Los Cabos hotels have an activity desk with a binder full of brochures advertising guided tours, excursions, and recreational activities. You can choose from whale-watching cruises, snorkeling tours, ATV tours, horseback rides, sunset cruises, and more. Hotels do not charge an additional fee when they book these activities for their guests. Here are a few of the larger and better-known outfitters:

Located in front of the Presidente InterContinental hotel, **Baja's Activities** (Paseo del Malecón, San José del Cabo, tel. 624/142-2922, www.bajasactivities.com, daily 9 A.M.–6 P.M.) organizes horseback rides along the estuary and beach (US$35/hr, US$55/2 hrs), snorkeling tours to Santa María Bay (US$35 pp), and ATV tours of the East Cape (US$65/single, US$85/double). **Rancho Tours** (tel. 624/143-5464, www.ranchotours. com) leads walking tours of La Paz and Todo Santos for US$65 per person, as well as glass-bottom boat tours and ATV rides near Cabo San Lucas.

Ecotourism specialist **Baja Wild Outfitters** (tel. 624/172-6300, www.bajawild.com) leads a variety of adventure trips, including kayaking, snorkeling, surfing, hiking, ATV, Jeep safaris, whale-watching, and turtle-release programs. Half-day trips range US$60–98, and all-day trips are US$105–410, depending on the activity. Group and multisport packages are available.

Desertica (Carr. Transp. Km 61.8, tel. 624/146 9601, www.desertica.com.mx, US$35) has brought its amusement park style of outdoor entertainment to Baja, with canopy tours on eight different zip lines, plus trails for ATVs, buggies, and horses.

You can also tour the back roads of Baja in a fleet of Hummers with **Baja Outback** (tel. 624/142-9200, www.bajaoutback.com, US$165–220 pp). Single- and multi-day tours go to Todos Santos, Santiago, Rancho La Verdad, and Rancho Antares (between Cabo Pulmo and Los Frailes).

ENTERTAINMENT AND EVENTS
Bars and Nightclubs

San José nightlife is low-key compared to the famous clubs in Cabo San Lucas where you can dance the night away, but there are a handful of places where you can enjoy a few drinks and listen to live music.

Baja Brewing Company (Morelos 1227 btw Comonfort/Obregón, San José del Cabo, tel. 624/146-9995, www.bajabrewingcompany.com, daily noon–2 A.M., mains US$10–15) quickly became a popular watering hole when it opened next to Baan Thai in December 2007. As the only brewery in Baja California Sur, it crafts eight different artisanal beers, including a Baja Blonde and Cactus Wheat brew. Order a brew-tender and get five pints for the price of four, conveniently served from a mini-tap at your table. The brewery uses its barley, yeast, and beer to make a delicious pizza dough. Spicy chicken wings are another crowd-pleaser.

Tropicana Bar and Grill (Mijares 30, San José del Cabo, tel. 624/142-1580, Sun.–Thurs. 8 A.M.–midnight, Fri.–Sat. till 2 A.M.) has been a mainstay among gringos for many years. It plays live Cuban music Wednesday–Saturday 10 P.M.–1 A.M. and has a separate room in the back for DJ tunes.

Morgan's Restaurant and Cellar (Hidalgo and Doblado, San José del Cabo, tel. 624/142-3825, morgans@prodigy.net. mx, daily 6–11 P.M.) frequently has live jazz. Canadian-owned **Shooters Bar & Grill** (Doblado and Mijares, San José del Cabo, tel. 624/142-9900, daily for lunch and dinner, bar open until 11 P.M. nightly, later on weekends), above Tulipán Restaurant, is an open-air, rooftop bar with seating in plastic chairs and usually jazz music.

The nautical theme is a bit cheesy, and tunes are country oldies, but otherwise the **Cielito Lindo Sky Bar** (Paseo del Malecón, San José del Cabo, tel. 624/142-9292, Tues.–Sun. 5–11 P.M.), in the lighthouse tower of the Crowne Plaza, is a great place to catch the sunset.

Behind the Mega shopping center, the **Rusty Putter Bar and Grille** (Paseo del Malecón, San José del Cabo, tel. 624/142-4546, daily for lunch and dinner, bar open until 11 P.M. nightly, later on weekends) is a large sports bar and restaurant with live music on weekends, plus satellite TV and an 18-hole miniature golf course.

© NIKKI GOTH ITOI

Calle Zaragoza, opposite Plaza Teniente José Antonio Mijares

Expats who live near Playa Costa Azul convene at **Havana Supper Club** (Carr. Transp. Km 29 on the north side of the highway, tel. 624/142-2603, daily from breakfast till late night) for nightly live jazz. Across the street and a little farther west, **Zippers** (Carr. Transp. Km 28.5, tel. 624/172-6162, daily 11 A.M.– 10 P.M.) plays oldies for the baby boomer crowd on Friday and Saturday nights.

Festivals and Events

On weekend evenings during the high season, you can almost always find a fiesta in progress at Plaza Mijares, complete with music, dancing, cotton candy, mimes, and piñatas. Many art galleries stay open late for weekly **Art Walks** on Thursday evenings.

San José celebrates the **feast day of its patron saint** on March 19, a day of more music, dancing, food, games, and a parade.

On June 1, San José celebrates the annual **Día de la Marina,** a national day of honor for the Mexican navy, with great fanfare, including a fishing tournament, carnival, music, and even a greased pig.

SHOPPING

From souvenirs to collectible furnishings, you can find a little of everything along the streets of San José. And unlike in Cabo San Lucas, here you can browse at a leisurely pace without worrying about aggressive shop owners encouraging you to make a purchase.

Arts, Crafts, and Souvenirs

A handful of vendors sell inexpensive arts and crafts along the north side of Boulevard Mijares, between Calles Coronado and Juárez. These stands are open daily 11 A.M.–9 P.M. For better selection and quality, at higher prices, check out the shops that are closer to Plaza Mijares and the art district. **Antigua Los Cabos** (Mijares 5, San José del Cabo, tel. 624/146-9933, antiguabcs@yahoo.com) has some antiques, as well as handmade rugs, folk art, ceramics, and tequilas. **Sol Dorado** (Mijares 33, across from the Tropicana, San José del Cabo, tel. 624/142-1950) is a multilevel store filled with ceramics, glassware, ironworks, mirrors, and furnishings. For large or fragile items, the store ships via DHL (fully insured). It will also deliver purchases to your hotel for US$10–85, depending on the location. The smaller **Mejicanisimo** (Zaragoza 8, San José del Cabo, tel. 624/142-3090, daily 9 A.M.–10 P.M.), next to the plaza, has much of the same.

Cinthya Castro stocks **El Armario** (corner of Morelos and Obregón, San José del Cabo, tel. 624/105-2989, elarmario@gmail.com, Mon.–Sat. 10 A.M.–8 P.M.) with an artistic mix of ceramics, paintings, soaps, and other crafts made in Mexico.

Shop 12 Leather Factory (on the corner of Mijares and Coronado, no tel., daily 9 A.M.–8 P.M.) has been in business since 1927 with a large selection of leather goods, including purses, shoes, belts, and even shotgun cases.

Jewelry

Several stores sell high-quality Mexican fire opals and other gemstones. Ask to see the opals in natural light—the more "fire," the higher the price. If you don't see what you want, ask to see individual stones. Most stores offer 24-hour turnaround for custom settings, but don't plan your pickup time to the minute, or you may be late to catch your flight home.

Martha Rodriguez at **El Rincón del Ópalo** jewelry factory (Mijares 6, San José del Cabo, tel. 624/142-2566, beltran_018@hotmail.com, Mon.–Sat. 9 A.M.–9 P.M., Sun. till 2 P.M.) can help you choose a stone and setting in a pleasant gallery off the main plaza. **Jewelry Factory** (Mijares 5, San José del Cabo, tel. 624/142-6394, daily 9 A.M.–8 P.M.), on the plaza next to Antigua Los Cabos, has some of the highest-quality jewels in town, and service to match. **La Mina** (Mijares 33, San José del Cabo, tel. 624/143-3747, lamina788@hotmail.com, daily 9 A.M.–8 P.M.) displays costume jewelry on the porous walls of a small cave and has a second location in Cabo San Lucas.

Fine Art

San José has a legitimate art district that is home to a number of first-rate galleries. Run by a graduate of the Parsons School of Design in New York City and a full-time Los Cabos resident, the three-story **Galería de Ida Victoria** (Guerrero 1128, San José del Cabo, tel. 624/142-5772, www.idavictoriaarts.com, Mon–Fri. 10 A.M.–7 P.M.) has been recognized as one of the finest art galleries south of Los Angeles. State-of-the-art lighting and hanging systems were custom designed to showcase paintings, photography, sculpture, and other works of art.

The **Old Town Gallery** (Obregón 20, San José del Cabo, tel. 624/142-3662, www.oldtowngallery.net, Mon.–Sat. 10:30 A.M.–7:30 P.M., Thurs. till 9 P.M.) displays works by contemporary Mexican, American, and Canadian artists. **Galería Arenas** (Obregón 10, San José del Cabo, vicjorge71@hotmail.com, Mon.–Sat. 10 A.M.–2 P.M. and 4–8 P.M.) has original Mexican pottery.

Amber Gallery (Obregón 18, San José del Cabo, tel. 624/105-2332, www.amberart.net, daily 10 A.M.–6 P.M.) features the work of artist Ronsai, who travels to Chiapas to select raw stones to make perfume bottles, jewelry, and sculptures.

Most of the galleries in this part of town stay open late on Thursday evenings (5–9 P.M.) for a weekly Art Walk that includes wine and food.

Home Decor

Second-home owners looking to furnish their new condos and villas with authentic Mexican design elements will find just about everything they need in San José. For a rustic look, head to **Galería Los Cabos** (Hidalgo north of Obregón, San José del Cabo, tel. 624/142-0044, Mon.–Fri. 9 A.M.–8 P.M.), which has some antiques, as well as rattan pieces, and barrel-back chairs made by local craftsmen. **Casa Paulina** (Morelos at the corner of Comonfort, San José del Cabo, tel. 624/142-5555), across from El Encanto Suites, is a beautiful store to browse, even if you aren't in the market to buy. It has wood and upholstered pieces, as well as ceramics and other decorative items displayed on two levels. **Adobe Design** (Plaza San José, Carr. Transp. Km 32, San José del Cabo, tel.

624/142-4281) carries furniture and interior design materials for both antique and modern home styles.

Sporting Goods

On the north side of Mexico 1 in a small shopping plaza, the **Costa Azul Surf Shop** (Carr. Transp. Km 28, San José del Cabo, tel. 624/142-2771, www.costa-azul.com.mx, Mon.–Sat. 8 A.M.–7 P.M., Sun. 9 A.M.–5 P.M.) has board rentals and surf and snorkel maps. You can also have your board repaired after a rough day in the water.

The **Cabo Surf Shop** (Carr. Transp. Km 28, San José del Cabo, tel. 624/178-6188, www.cabosurfshop.com, daily 8 A.M.–8 P.M.), located at the Cabo Surf Hotel, offers board rentals.

Deportiva Piscis (Castro, San José del Cabo, tel. 624/142-0332, daily 8 A.M.–7 P.M.), on the south side of Calle Castro near the Mercado Municipal, has fishing tackle, bait, and fishing-related books and gear.

Bookstores

The most comprehensive selection of English-language titles related to Baja California anywhere on the peninsula is to be found at **Baja Books and Maps** (Camino a La Playa, La Choya, tel. 624/165-5596, U.S. fax 415/962-0588, Mon.–Sat. 9:30 A.M.–6 P.M.) in the pueblo of La Choya on the way to La Playita. Owner Jim Tolbert is the sole distributor of English-language books to shops throughout the central and southern peninsula. He also sells inventory online at www.bajabooksandmaps.com. A true bibliophile, Jim is a wealth of information on all things Baja.

At the conveniently located **Spider Web** (tel. 624/105-2048, bajabookcenter@yahoo.com.mx, Mon.–Sat. 9 A.M.–6 P.M.), you can trade used paperback books and browse a limited selection of new titles, including current fiction by Michael Chabon and Yann Martel. Used pocket fiction books cost US$3. There are a few PCs available for Internet access (US$4/hr). The store is located on an alley just west of the Mega shopping plaza.

Deportiva Pisces (Castro, San José del Cabo, tel. 624/142-0332, daily 8 A.M.–7 P.M.) stocks a few books related to sportfishing, **El Armario** (corner of Morelos and Obregón, San José del Cabo, tel. 624/105-2989, elarmario@gmail.com, Mon.–Sat. 10 A.M.–8 P.M.) has a small selection of design books, and the gift shop at **Buzzard's** (Laguna Hills, U.S. tel. 951/302-1735, www.buzzardsbar.com) has a few books for sale as well.

Bahías Jiromar (tel. 624/130-7524, bahiasjiromar@prodigy.net.mx), next to McDonald's in the Mega shopping plaza, also sells some English-language books.

ACCOMMODATIONS

Besides the major hotels and "condotels" in the *zona hotelera* along the beach, San José offers some smaller, reasonably priced inns in the town itself. A downtown location puts you close to shops and restaurants, with a short drive or long walk to the beach. Condos and hotels along Playa Azul are about a 5- to 10-minute drive from town, depending on traffic. Rates are given for double occupancy in the high season (holiday rates may be higher) and do not include 12 percent tax and 10 percent service charge, unless otherwise noted. Discounts may be available for stays of a week or longer.

Hotels in Town
UNDER US$50

Two budget hotels are located on Calle Zaragoza opposite the church. The accommodations are minimal and you'll hear noise from the street below, but the prices are about the lowest you'll find anywhere in town. Manager Señor Félix provides clean, if basic, accommodations at **Hotel Ceci** (Calle Zaragoza 22 opposite the church, tel. 624/142-0051, US$35). It has 14 rooms with ceiling fans, air-conditioning, TV, and hot water. The rooms at **Hotel Diana** (Zaragoza 30, tel. 624/142-0490, US$30) also have air-conditioning, TV, and hot water.

Two good-value accommodations are located side-by-side on the east side of Plaza Mijares, next to the Casa de la Cultura and at the edge

ALL-INCLUSIVE RESORTS

If making decisions about food adds stress to your vacation experience, look for a rate plan that includes meals, activities, and entertainment. The following resorts offer all-inclusive packages:

SAN JOSÉ DEL CABO

- Crowne Plaza Los Cabos Beach Resort – Business conventions

- Presidente InterContinental Los Cabos Resort – Good variety and quality of food

- Hotel Posada Real Los Cabos – Good deal for the money

- Royal Solaris Los Cabos Hotel – Families with young kids

- Desire Resort & Spa Los Cabos – Clothing optional

THE CORRIDOR

- Dreams Los Cabos – Weddings, honeymoons, anniversaries

- Meliá Cabo Real – Safe swimming beach

CABO SAN LUCAS

- Riu Palace – Largest of the all-inclusive set, with 642 guestrooms

- Tesoro Los Cabos Hotel – College students on spring break

Delfin Hotels & Resorts maintains a current list of all-inclusive resorts in the Los Cabos area at www.allinclusivescabo .com.

of town where the mango orchards begin. They shared the same name for a few years, but one has now become the **Hotel Yuca Inn** (Obregón 1A, tel. 624/142-0462, www.yucainn.com.mx, US$45), offering rooms with refrigerators, ceiling fans, and private baths. Amenities include a swimming pool and shared kitchen. Next door, **Hotel Posada Señor Mañana** (Obregón 1B, tel./fax 624/142-1372, US$40–70) has eight rooms connected by a labyrinth of ramps and ladders. Each room has a ceiling fan and private bath with hot water. When staying at either of these hotels, you can walk to the Saturday farmers market and return to cook a meal of fresh Baja ingredients in your hotel's well-equipped shared kitchen.

One of the oldest hotels in town, **Hotel Colli** (Hidalgo btw Zaragoza and Doblado, tel. 624/142-0725, US$50) has a dozen small rooms in a building just off the plaza. Its rooms come with ceiling fans, air-conditioning, and private baths. Bottled water is a plus, and the friendly service makes for a comfortable stay. As with any of the downtown hotels, noise is likely to be a minor nuisance at night, but all is usually quiet by about 11 P.M.

US$50-150

Many travelers enjoy the authentic Mexican surroundings and hospitality at **Hotel Posada Terranova** (on Degollado just south of Zaragoza, tel. 624/142-0534, www.hterra-nova.com.mx, US$60), located between Plaza Mijares and the Mercado Municipal. Over the years, this large residential property has been renovated to hold 29 guestrooms, each with two beds, air-conditioning, phone, and satellite TV. This hotel has a pleasant terrace and a dependable Mexican restaurant (daily 7 A.M.– 10 P.M., mains US$10–15).

In the heart of San Jose's growing art district, **El Encanto Inn** (Morelos 133, tel. 624/142-0388, U.S. tel. 512/465-9751, www. elencantosuites.com, US$95–144) encompasses two buildings on Calle Morelos. Fluffy towels, king-size beds, and remote-control air-conditioning are a few of the special touches at the newer property, El Encanto Suites. The two-story hacienda surrounds a small swimming pool and courtyard. More economical standard and garden suites are in the original inn. Rooms here are popular with travelers who plan a one-night stopover before heading to or from the East Cape, but recent guests have complained about duplicate charges and other complications with advanced reservation payments. Wireless Internet worked intermittently at last visit (15 minutes free, US$4 for 30 minutes, or US$10 for one hour), and there was an iMac for guest use in the lobby. A café near the pool serves breakfast and drinks, and you can park for free in a gated, but not guarded, lot across the street. The on-site Ixchel Salon & Spa offers manicures, pedicures, and massage treatments.

Behind the Tropicana Bar and Grill and set back from busy Boulevard Mijares, the American-run **Tropicana Inn** (Mijares 30, tel. 624/142-1580, US$110–160) has 40 rooms set around a relaxing courtyard, with a fountain and swimming pool. Room amenities include phones, air-conditioning, and satellite TV. Free shuttles to La Playita and Playa Palmilla are an added convenience.

OVER US$250

Internationally acclaimed **(€ Casa Natalia** (Mijares 4, tel. 624/142-5100 or 888/277-3814, www.casanatalia.com, US$230–385) sets the standard for luxury boutique hotel accommodations in Los Cabos. It has become a favorite venue for small weddings and other formal celebrations. Its 14 rooms and two suites are designed with a contemporary, European flair, including original artwork. Private (though extremely small) terraces with hammocks face a heated swimming pool. And the attached Mi Cocina restaurant (daily 6:30–10 P.M., mains US$18–32), run by owner Natalie Tenoux's husband, Loïc Tenoux, it just steps away. This is not the place for children under the age of 13.

Beach Hotels

Occupancy rates for the hotels along Playa Hotelera have been climbing in recent years to match those of their busier Cabo San Lucas peers, though you may still be able to negotiate a deal during off-peak seasons. Whether you choose a hotel or condo, beware that demolitions, renovations, and new construction are in progress all over this area, even during the peak travel season. There's a good chance you'll end up next to, above, or below a noisy construction zone. The hammering, sawing, and drilling typically begins at 8:30 A.M. and lasts till 5:30 P.M. Do your homework before you book.

OVER US$250

Situated between the Desire and Posada Real resorts along the Zona Hotelera, **Barceló Los Cabos** (formerly The Grand Baja, Paseo del Malecón l-5 D, tel. 624/146-7500, toll-free U.S. tel. 800/227-2356, www.barcelo.com, US$250 and up) has one-, two-, and three-bedroom suites and was under renovation by a new owner, Spain-based Barceló, in 2009.

At the far northeastern end of the *zona hotelera,* next to the Estero San José, the 400-room **Presidente InterContinental Los Cabos Resort** (Paseo del Malecón, tel. 624/142-0211, toll-free U.S. tel. 888/567-8725, www.ichotelsgroup.com, US$290–425) serves some of the best meals around for all-inclusive package guests.

ALL-INCLUSIVE RESORTS

Rooms at the Best Western **Hotel Posada Real Los Cabos** (Paseo del Malecón, tel. 624/142-0155, toll-free U.S. tel. 800/528-1234, www.posadareal.com.mx, US$120–210 pp) are among the better-value all-inclusive options. They come with air-conditioning, phone, and satellite TV. The property has a pool with two hot tubs and swim-up bar, plus its own restaurant. Most rooms have views of the ocean, too. Rates cover meals, drinks, tips, and tax.

Next door, the **Crowne Plaza Los Cabos Beach Resort** (Paseo del Malecón, tel. 624/142-9292, U.S. tel. 866/365-6932, www.cploscabos.com, US$220 pp and up) is one of few resorts in Los Cabos where you can enjoy a stay free of condo sales pitches, as the property does not have timeshares on-site. Large guestroom terraces and a saltwater infinity pool are two more distinguishing features. Children aged four and up can play in the kids club while adults relax by the pool. Meals are standard resort buffets, served in several

© NIKKI GOTH ITOI

view from the balcony at Crowne Plaza Los Cabos Beach Resort

on-site restaurants. High-speed Internet access costs US$15 per day. The on-site Natura Room offers a full menu of massage, body, and facial treatments (US$90–110 for 50 minutes). The resort offers free and secure parking underground.

On the northeast side of the Crowne Plaza, the **Royal Solaris Los Cabos Hotel** (Paseo del Malecón Lte. 10, Zona Hotelera, tel. 624/145-6800, U.S. tel. 866/289-8466, www.clubsolaris.com, US$145–175 pp) has a water park for kids, and serves a breakfast that's popular among resort-goers. Most of its 389 rooms have ocean views. Entertainment options include a Tehuacan dinner theater show. A free snorkeling tour comes with a stay of six nights or more.

Clothing is optional at **Desire Resort & Spa Los Cabos** (formerly the Fiesta Inn, Paseo del Malecón, tel. 624/142-9300, U.S. tel. 888/201-7551, Canada tel. 800/655-9311, www.desir-eresorts.com, US$125 pp and up). Reactions ranged from shock to awe when this couples-only establishment opened in 2006, catering to upscale, "liberated" adults. A red and dark

brown color scheme with hand-painted murals of scenes from the *Book of Kama Sutra* set the mood. A clothing-optional pool and whirlpool tub, L'Alternative Disco, and Sensuous Playroom take it over the top. The resort's 150 rooms and suites have king-size beds and flat-screen TVs, among a complete list of standard amenities. From the beach, curious onlookers can recognize the resort by shoulder-height bamboo screens on the terraces that allow for private sunbathing.

The **Grand Mayan Wyndham Alliance Resort** (Paseo del Malecón, U.S. tel. 877/999-3223, www.mexicomayanresorts.com, US$250 and up), which opened in 2007, has a stunning reception area and offers a Wednesday-evening Mayan dinner theater performance.

Pueblo La Playa and La Playita
US$50-100
At **El Delfín Blanco** (Delfínes, Pueblo La Playa, tel. 624/142-1212, tel./fax 624/142-1199, www.eldelfinblanco.net, US$49–75), Osa Franzen maintains several clean *cabañas* that are situated about 300 meters from the

beach with views of the water. The place attracts independent travelers who seek an authentic Mexican experience as well as a good value in accommodations. You may hear the wind rustling through palm-thatched roofs and dogs barking at night, but you'll also be steps away from the new marina and park at La Playita. Walk to several restaurants, or shop in town and cook your own meals in the shared outdoor kitchen.

About 6.5 kilometers past La Playita and Puerto Los Cabos, on the coastal road that hugs the East Cape, expats Judie and Denny Jones run a small solar-powered inn and popular restaurant called **(La Fonda del Mar Bed and Breakfast** (Laguna Hills, U.S. tel. 951/302-1735, www.buzzardsbar.com, US$75–95). Its three rooms have *palapa* roofs, American-style beds, and tile floors. Each has its own half-bath, but shares a shower. For families, there is a larger suite with a pullout couch and private bath. Guests may order anything off the Buzzard's menu for breakfast, including the famed eggs Benedict on Sundays. The inn is situated almost on the beach, and it's a very short walk along an arroyo to the water's edge. To find La Fonda del Mar, follow the road to La Playita and turn left at the first traffic circle and go about 6.5 kilometers, following signs for Laguna Hills and El Encanto.

Just steps from the new *panga* marina, **La Marina Inn** (formerly La Playita Inn, Pueblo La Playa, tel./fax 624/142-4166, US$69–109) has managed to stay its course through all the development and change around it. This three-story Mexican-style inn is a good choice if you are planning to fish or simply want to stay away from the hustle and bustle of downtown San José. Its air-conditioned rooms each have large showers and two queen beds. There is a small pool and an authentic Mexican seafood restaurant, La Marina.

Condominiums and Condo Hotels

Condominium complexes are sprouting up on the outskirts of San José as fast as all-inclusive resorts. Las Olas (closest to the lookout point at Zippers surf break), El Zalate (next to the

© KATHRYN LATENDRESSE

La Marina Inn at La Playita

Coral Baja timeshare resort), and Sampiguita (closer to the hotel zone) are just a few of the newcomers. Owners rent vacant units to visitors for anywhere from US$120 a night for a studio or one-bedroom to around US$450 or more for a deluxe two- or three-bedroom unit. Rates can vary quite a bit even within the same complex, depending on location and views and how the unit is furnished. Be sure to inquire how close the unit is to the highway and whether there is construction underway inside the building. At Mykonos and other complexes nearby, the persistent sound of heavy traffic on Mexico 1 can drown out the sound of waves crashing onto the beach. Discounted weekly and monthly rates are sometimes available.

The payment process for a condo is different from reserving a hotel room: Property managers typically require a deposit of 50 percent of the rental fee by check or direct deposit to a U.S. bank account, and the remaining amount by cash upon arrival. Cleaning fees are often added to the rental fee. Sometimes full payment is required before arrival—all the more reason to get the information you need before committing to a particular unit.

Mediterranean-inspired **Mykonos Bay Resort** (Km 29, tel. 624/142-3789, one bedroom US$130–290) rents one- and two-bedroom condos in three buildings, each with air-conditioning, satellite TV, kitchen, and washer/dryer. Amenities include a basic gym and lighted tennis court. Buildings B and C have larger units and are closest to the beach and quieter than Building A, which has smaller units and picks up more noise from the highway.

Within walking distance of the Mega shopping plaza as well as the beach, the sprawling **《 Las Mañanitas** complex has some of the nicest condos around for US$225–475 per night. Next door, **Sampaguita Luxury Townhouse/ Condominiums** is newer and smaller, with only 14 units in a quiet, gated complex that has a pool, hot tub, and tennis court. Two-bedroom units run about US$200–300 per night. To inquire about these properties you need to contact the individual owners through www.vrbo.com,

www.craigslist.org, a booking service, or property management company.

Booking Services and Property Management Companies

Baja Properties (Doblado and Morelos, tel. 624/142-0988, U.S. tel. 877/462-2226, www.bajaproperties.com) manages one-, two-, and three-bedroom rentals in Las Mañanitas for US$250–525 per night, as well as a few less expensive locations. **Nash Group Properties** (Paseo Finisterra #107, www.bajaholidays.com), run by the owners of the Casa del Jardín B&B, manages several rental properties in Mykonos, Las Olas, and a few other complexes. **SeaSide Vacations** (tel. 624/142-3789, Canada tel. 604/484-8488, www.sea-side.com) has a variety of units in several buildings in the area, as does **Sunshine Services** (tel. 624/142-2212, U.S. tel. 888/545-4310, www.sunshineservices.com), with an office location next to the bus terminal.

FOOD

For many travelers, San José del Cabo has become a culinary destination. Renowned chefs from Baja, mainland Mexico, and the United States are using local foods and, in many cases, organic ingredients to prepare creative interpretations of traditional Mexican cuisine. From the organic farmers market to fresh tortillas and *carnitas* by the kilo, you can find it all in and around the streets of San José.

Alta Cocina Mexicana

San José del Cabo is the epicenter of a culinary trend in Baja called *alta cocina mexicana,* or gourmet interpretations of traditional Mexican dishes. One of the trailblazers in this category was **Tequila Restaurant** (Doblado 1011 west of Mijares, tel. 624/142-1155, www.tequilar-estaurant.com, daily for dinner, mains US$20 and up). The setting is cozy, and the menu suggests Asian, Mexican, and Mediterranean influences. The restaurant cooks with organic produce, and the tequila menu is, of course, top-notch.

A member of the Slow Food movement

emphasizing locally grown and prepared foods, **Don Emiliano** (Mijares 27, tel. 624/142-0266, daily 6–11 P.M., mains US$20–36) is run by a well-known chef from Mexico City, Margarita C. de Salinas. Try the six-course tasting menu paired with Mexican wines or order à la carte. European-inspired **Mi Cocina** (Mijares 4, tel. 624/146-7100, daily 6–11 P.M., mains US$18–32), inside Casa Natalia, serves creative fare in an intimate and contemporary garden setting.

Next to the plaza, **La Panga Antigua** (Zaragoza 20, tel. 624/142-4041, www.lapanga.com, daily for lunch and dinner, mains US$20) offers colonial ambience, with a courtyard, lounge bar, and wine cellar. A menu of contemporary Mexican cuisine with a focus on seafood is prepared by a chef who is a graduate of the Culinary Institute of America.

Chilies in all their forms take center stage at **El Chilar** (1497 Juárez at Morelos, tel. 624/142-2544, Mon.–Sat. 3–10 P.M., mains US$10–30). A Oaxacan chef prepares an ever-changing menu of Mexican specialties at this small restaurant located near the Telmex tower. Cash only.

Mexican

In the art district, **Restaurant Bar Jazmín** (Zaragoza and Obregón, tel. 624/142-1760, daily 7 A.M.–10 P.M., mains US$13–40) serves *huachinango* (whole red snapper) and *carne asada a la tampiqueña* on sizzling hot platters. The atmosphere is casual, and the menu includes *licuado* and *chilaquiles* for breakfast, and *tortas,* tacos, and fajitas for lunch and dinner. Credit cards, including American Express, are accepted.

In business for more than 25 years, **Damiana** (Mijares 8, tel. 624/142-0499, www.damiana.com.mx, daily 10:30 A.M.–10:30 P.M., dinner mains US$15–20) is the place for a romantic courtyard dinner. Set in a colonial-style home on the plaza, the restaurant has two air-conditioned dining rooms, as well as candlelit patio tables in the garden. The menu features shrimp, abalone, and steak dishes.

If you don't mind the strip-mall setting,

Habañeros Mexican Bistro (Mijares in Plaza La Misión, tel. 624/142-2626, Mon.–Sat. 11 A.M.–10 P.M., lunch mains US$5–14, dinner mains US$9–18) doubles as an organic market. Dinner specials include roast pork tenderloin or surf and turf for US$20; Corona and Pacifico beers are only US$1.50.

First-time visitors to San Jose del Cabo often grab a sidewalk table at the **Tropicana Bar and Grill** (Mijares 30, tel. 624/142-1580, daily 8 A.M.–10:30 P.M., mains US$10–23) for their first meal. They can take in the scene on Boulevard Mijares as they down their first *limonada, cerveza,* or margarita. Inside and in the garden dining area behind the building, a regular clientele visits the restaurant for American-style fare and nightly live music and dancing. The menu is vast; the prices are for tourists.

Breakfast is a good value at the understated **Posada Terranova** (Degollado south of Zaragoza, tel. 624/142-0534, daily 7 A.M.–10 P.M., mains US$5–18), a family-run restaurant inside the hotel of the same name. It has indoor and outdoor tables, and the menu covers all the basics of Mexican food.

C Mariscos Mazatlán II (Km 35, Mexico 1, tel. 624/143-8565, daily for lunch and dinner, mains US$10–14), near Soriana on the way to the airport, is a favorite among expats for fresh fish at reasonable prices in a non-touristy atmosphere. Look for an orange and blue *palapa*-roof building with outdoor seating on the west side of Mexico 1. There is also a sister location in Cabo San Lucas.

American and International

El Tulipán (The Tulip Tree, Doblado at Mijares, tel. 624/146-9900, daily for lunch and dinner, mains US$10–20), below Shooter's Bar, serves casual fare such as burgers, steaks, salads, and pasta dishes. Booth seating and the varied menu make it a good place for young kids.

Regulars praise the lamb dishes at **Baan Thai** (Morelos and Comonfort, tel. 624/142-3344, daily noon–10:30 P.M., mains US$11–25). You can also order pad thai, wok-tossed salmon, and an assortment of curries. In business for many years, this restaurant draws patrons from the East Cape and beyond for a refreshing change from everyday Mexican cooking.

Dinner at **Morgan's Restaurant and Cellar** (Hidalgo and Doblado, tel. 624/143-3825, morgans@prodigy.net.mx, daily 6 P.M.–midnight, dinner till 10 P.M. only, closed Sept., mains US$20 and up) begins with a basket of homemade bread. A variety of wines from around the world complement the menu of Mediterranean entrées. **Morgan's Encore** (Morelos and Obregón, tel. 624/142-4727, daily 6 P.M.–midnight, dinner till 10 P.M. only, closed Sept., mains US$20–40), near the El Encanto Inn, can accommodate large groups in its main open air dining area. The menu includes seared scallops, grilled fish, shrimp fettuccine, and spaghetti and meatballs. This is also the kind of place where you might happily order a couple of the creative starters for your main meal.

In a relatively new plaza behind the Casa Paulina interior design store, **Voila! Bistro** (Plaza Paulina on Morelos and Comonfort, tel. 624/130-7569, www.voila-events.com, daily for lunch and dinner, mains US$10–20) serves a few wines by the glass, as well as soup, salads, and entrées like rib-eye steak.

You can watch the staff make your personal, thin-crust pizza from a patio table at **La Dolce Ristorante Italiano & Pizzeria** (Plaza Mijares, Hidalgo and Zaragoza, tel. 624/142-6621, daily 2–11 P.M., mains US$7–14). The menu includes bruschetta to start and tiramisu to finish.

Pair the meat cut of your choice with one of four house sauces, add a side or two, and you have a fantastic meal at **La Bodega Steak and Wine House** (Zaragoza btw Guerrero/Morelos, tel. 624/142-6619, www.labodegadesanjose.com, Mon.–Sat. 6–11 P.M., mains US$17–29).

New in 2008, **El Vaquero Steak House** (Mijares #31, tel. 624/105-2703, www.elvaquerosteak.com, daily 6–11 P.M., closed Sun. Aug.–Nov.) took over a long-abandoned grocery store

space just off the plaza on Boulevard Mijares. It specializes in prime rib, with three different cuts priced US$25–35. Upholstered chairs make for an elegant ambience.

Every table seems to have its own private corner at the elegant **Local Eight** (Plaza la Misión, Blvd. Mijares, tel. 624/142-6655, www.localeight.com, daily for dinner, mains US$16–24), where you dine in a second-story garden terrace located about midway between downtown and the hotel zone. Mediterranean loosely defines the cuisine, but flavors come from all over the world, with entrées ranging from Arabian snapper to gazpacho to pork tenderloin served with a tamarind sauce and fried plantains. An extensive wine list features bottles from Mexico, Chile, California, France, and Germany. Sink into the comfortable cushions, admire the unusual colored lights, and enjoy the relaxed ambience for the evening.

Taquerías and Quick Bites

Cheap eats are clustered around the Mercado Municipal and close to the highway, near Calle Doblado. Try any of the *loncherías* near the market (Mon.–Sat. 6 A.M.–6 P.M., Sun. 6 A.M.–4 P.M.). Or order *tortas* and *comida corrida* at **Mi Cocinita** (Gonzales, south of the 1 de Mayo bakery, tel. 624/142-6660, Mon.–Sat. 8 A.M.–5 P.M., mains US$5), a cute place with plastic tables and floral tablecloths. The staff here speaks English. At **Taquería Erika** (Doblado at Mexico 1, no tel., daily for lunch and dinner), where two *tacos al pastor* cost about US$2.50. Longtime favorite **Taquería Rossy** (tel. 624/145-6755, tacos US$1) is on the other side of Mexico 1, near the light for Pescador street.

Adventurous eaters should head to **Taquería El Ahorcado** (Pescadores and Marinos, tel. 624/172-2093, Tues.–Sun. 6 P.M.–midnight, mains US$5–10), in the Chamizal neighborhood across Mexico 1, for beef tongue tacos and a full menu of creative quesadillas. It's known among gringos as The Hangman, and is famous for its eclectic decor. Bring your own beer and enjoy live music while you dine.

In the same neighborhood, ◖ **Guacamaya**

(no tel., daily for dinner, mains US$8–12), off Calle Doblado, on the north side of Mexico 1, has become a local favorite for meat and fish tacos, including mouthwatering *tacos al pastor,* carved from a rotisserie spit and served with the signature toss of a pineapple slice. Huge stone bowls filled with flank steak and avocado are a super deal for US$7.

One of the most economical and tasty restaurants near the art district and plaza is ⟨ **Cafetería El Recreo** (Hidalgo btw Zaragoza and Obregón, Wed.–Mon. 7 A.M.–9 P.M., mains US$5–10). It serves tasty *tortas* and reputable fish tacos on a shaded patio next to the church. Service is friendly, and the screened-in kitchen keeps insects away from your food.

Breakfast and Cafés

It's hard to resist the strong coffee and sweet pastries once you've discovered the **French Riviera** (corner of Hidalgo and Doblado, tel. 624/142-3350, www.frenchrivieraloscabos. com, daily 8 A.M.–11 P.M., breakfast mains US$5–10, lunch mains US$10–15). Order to go from the counter or grab a table for a full breakfast.

In the art district, **Casa Dahlia Gallery** (Morelos btw Obregón and Zaragoza, tel. 624/142-2129, www.casadahlia.com) serves coffee and tea in a pleasant garden behind a 100-year-old adobe building and has wireless Internet.

Options for ice cream are surprisingly limited around town lately, but there is a **Michoacana** on Doblado at the intersection with the highway.

Groceries

These days, the best place to stock up on food and other supplies is the **Mega** supermarket (tel. 624/142-4524), at the intersection of Paseo Los Cabos and Mexico 1. Choose from a full array of Mexican and American brands, decent produce, and a wide selection of cheeses and meats. There is a well-stocked pharmacy, and those traveling with youngsters will find all manner of supplies, from pacifiers to bouncy

seats. In the adjoining plaza are a Telcel store, surf shop, public restrooms, and numerous fast-food options.

For a more authentic shopping experience, the small **Mercado Municipal** (daily dawn to dusk) between Calles Castro and Coronado in the west part of town, has separate stands for meat, fish, produce, and crafts. There is *tortillería* that makes corn tortillas next door on Calle Castro (opens daily at 5 A.M.), and another that makes flour tortillas across the street.

A half-kilometer north of town on the east side of Mexico 1, **Soriana** (tel. 624/142-6132) is a Walmart-style store with everything from beach towels to deli meats. If you are heading directly to the East Cape, this is a good place to stock up on supplies for the week.

On Calle Gonzalez, near the Corona supermarket and down the street from the bus terminal, **Panadería 1 de Mayo** has freshly baked breads and pastries with the usual tray-and-tong service.

If you're in town on a Saturday, head to the **Organic Market** (Huerta Maria, Camino a las Animas, Sat. 9 A.M.–3 P.M.), which draws some 50 vendors, many from as far away as La Paz and Todos Santos. They gather at a site located off the road to La Playita. In addition to fresh produce, you can buy cheese, ice cream, bread, books, and leather goods. There is usually music and rotating themes such as alternative medicine and eco-friendly living. Look for a sign on the left, near the beginning of the new Puerto Los Cabos bridge. It's about a five-minute walk from the plaza.

La Playita and Pueblo La Playa

Newcomer **Tommy's Barefoot Cantina** (tel. 624/142-3774, www.tommysbarefootcantina.com, Thurs.–Tues. noon–10 P.M., mains US$7–30) has taken over the old La Playita Restaurant space just steps from the new marina. Here, the gregarious TJ, originally from the San Francisco Bay Area, entertains a well-heeled clientele with a slice of the old Baja. The menu consists of fresh seafood, American-style beef, and a variety of Mexican staples. This is a good place to come in the afternoon when the fishing boats return with their catch. There is also live music and dancing on the weekends during the high season.

The friendly husband-and-wife team that previously ran Mariscos El Puerto has moved a few doors closer to the beach to open **La Marina Restaurant** (hotel tel. 624/142-4166, Tues.–Sun. 9 A.M.–5 P.M., mains US$5–10). The same colorful checked tablecloths are now clustered on a shaded patio next to the La Marina Inn lobby. Ceiling fans keep the air moving on hot afternoons. On a recent visit, the wahoo filet was extremely overcooked, but the *arranchera* tacos, served with the same signature tray of fresh condiments, were fantastic. The restaurant and hotel are located across from the *panga* marina, next to Tommy's.

For a quick bite to eat in La Playita, order a *torta* or some tacos at **La Pasadita** (no tel., mains US$5), next to Lilly's salon on the way to the beach. The decor is barebones—a *palapa* roof with a dirt floor and live chickens running about—but the food is tasty and cheap. La Pasadita is open for dinner only, and days vary; if you see the sand in front of the restaurant hosed down, that's a likely sign it will be open for business that evening.

Beyond Puerto Los Cabos on the lower part of the East Cape, **Buzzard's Bar and Grill** (Laguna Hills, U.S. tel. 951/302-1735, www.buzzardsbar.com, mains US$10–20) makes a tasty platter of coconut shrimp, as well as a popular eggs Benedict for Sunday brunch. Dinner entrées are served all day, but the side dishes may not be ready until 5:30 P.M. To find Buzzard's from downtown San José del Cabo, follow the road to La Playita and turn left at the first traffic circle, following the coastal road (it reaches the coast at Buzzard's) and signs for Laguna Hills.

Playa Costa Azul

For casual, beachfront dining, head to **Zippers** (Km 28.5, tel. 624/172-6162, daily 11 A.M.–10 P.M., mains US$10–20), where you can watch surfers try to catch the waves out front while you dine under the shade of a *palapa* roof. The menu is a mix of Mexican and pub fare. Cash only.

Buzzard's Bar and Grill

© KATHRYN LATENDRESSE

Mama Mia, at the Worldmark Coral Baja resort (Km 29.4, tel. 624/142-3939, daily for lunch and dinner, mains US$7–14) offers casual beachfront dining with friendly and attentive service. Juicy burgers come with grilled onions and lots of pickles. Chicken fajitas are accompanied by the requisite basket of warm tortillas and a healthy serving of guacamole. The menu features many organic ingredients.

INFORMATION AND SERVICES
Tourist Assistance
The Baja Sur **state tourism office** (tel. 624/146-9628, www.loscabos.gob.mx) is located in Plaza San José (Locales 3&4) on Mexico 1 near the intersection of Calle Valerio González Canseco.

Money
There are now ATMs aplenty in San José, with numerous options downtown, behind the Mega, and in several plazas in between.

Post and Telephone
The Correos (post office, Mon.–Fri. 8 A.M.–5 P.M.) is on the lower end of Boulevard Mijares, near Calle Juárez and the road to La Playita. **Mail Boxes Etc.** has a local branch in Plaza Las Palmas on Mexico 1 (Km 31, tel. 624/142-4355, fax 624/142-4360).

You can place long-distance phone calls from the **public telephone office** on Calle Doblado, across from the hospital, but there are also numerous Ladatel booths downtown. The pharmacy counter of the Mega supermarket sells Ladatel phone cards, as does Havana's Restaurant near Plaza Costa Azul. You can use a Skype account from most of the Internet cafés around town; some also allow you to plug in your own computer and voice-over-IP headset. There is a Telcel shop in the Mega grocery store plaza, and another on Zaragoza across from the plaza.

Internet Access
Trazzo Digital Internet (Zaragoza 24 btw Hidalgo/Morelos, tel. 624/142-0303, www.

SAN JOSÉ DEL CABO PHONE NUMBERS

- San José del Cabo area code: 624
- Canadian consulate: 142-4333
- General Hospital: 142-2770
- Highway Patrol: 146-0573
- Police, Fire Department, Red Cross (emergency): 066
- Police (non-emergency): 142-2835
- Taxi Service: 142-0401
- Tourism Office: 142-2960, ext. 150

---

trazzodigital.com, Mon.–Fri. 8 A.M.–9 P.M., Sat. 9 A.M.–7 P.M.) is a full-service Internet center with 15 comfortable workstations with wireless mice (US$1 up to 10 minutes, US$2.50 for 30 minutes, and US$0.30 for each additional 5 minutes). Additional services include copies, printing, and scanning. Credit cards, including American Express, are accepted. **Ciber Espacio** (no tel., Mon.–Fri. 8 A.M.–9 P.M., Sat. 9 A.M.–9 P.M., US$2/hour) has 10 computer stations in an air-conditioned space near the school. There is also wireless access at the airport.

Next to the Mega shopping center, **Spider Web** (tel. 624/105-2048) has a few computers connected to the Internet. Rates are US$1 for 15 minutes, or US$4 per hour.

Medical Services
The main *centro de salud* (hospital, tel. 624/142-2770) is located on Calle Doblado between Colegio Militar and Márquez de Leon.

For medical assistance, visit the **Walk-in MediClinic** (Km 28, tel. 624/130-7011) in the El Zalate Plaza on Mexico 1. The facility has an emergency room, lab, pharmacy, and ambulance. Two other options are **BlueMedicalNet** (tel. 624.104-3911), which operates a clinic in the Plaza Misión, next to HSBC Bank, and **Médica Los Cabos** (Zaragoza 128, tel. 624/142-2770), near the Pemex station. All will respond to emergencies 24/7.

Laundry

Blue Lavandería, on Calle Obregón near Morgan's Encore, is a full-service laundry open Monday–Saturday 8 A.M.–9 P.M. and Sunday 8 A.M.–3 P.M. A small load costs about US$5. Other laundry options are located near the Mercado Municipal (tel. 624/130-7979, daily 8:30 A.M.–12:30 P.M. and 2:30–7 P.M., US$5 wash and dry) and on Calle Green, near the art district (daily 8 A.M.–8 P.M., US$2 per load).

RV Service and Supplies

Those who drive their own home on wheels depend on **Wahoo RV Center** (tel./fax 624/142-3792, Mon.–Fri. 8 A.M.–1 P.M.) near the CFE electric utility office in Colonia Chula Vista, off Mexico 1 (turn west btw the Super Pollo and the turnoff for the Pemex station), for RV parts and accessories, as well as maintenance and repair services. It has Direct TV satellite dishes and a dump station.

Canadian Consulate

The office of the Canadian consulate is on the second floor of Plaza José Green (Blvd. Mijares near Juárez, tel. 624/142-4333, www.loscabos@canada.org.mx, Mon.–Fri. 9 A.M.–1 P.M.).

Veterinarians

San José has a number of respected veterinarians, should your pet need attention during your travels. One is usually available at the Chiapas feed store (Prolongacion Ave. Providencia, tel. 624/142-1095). And if you fall in love with one of Baja's stray animals, it may be possible to bring it home, as long as it is in good health and you can show proof of a rabies vaccinations at least 30 days prior to entry into the United States. Talk to a local vet and then contact your airline for more information.

Spanish-Language Instruction

With an office in the Mega shopping plaza, **Interlingua** (tel. 624/142-0070, www.interlingua.com.mx) offers monthly Spanish courses for small groups of students at four different levels.

GETTING AROUND

Detailed information on how to get to Los Cabos is given at the beginning of this chapter. Once you've arrived, you can get around by foot, bike, bus, rental car, taxi, or shuttle.

By Bus

The main bus station is located on Calle González (tel. 624/142-1100) near Mexico 1. Aguila/ABC offers frequent service to La Paz via Todos Santos (shorter, US$20) and Los Barriles (longer, US$15). A few buses a day from continue on to the ferry terminal on the Pichilingue Peninsula. About six buses a day go to Cabo San Lucas (US$5). The Flecha Verde and Estrella de Oro bus lines run hourly connections to Cabo San Lucas. Another option is the municipal Subur Cabo buses that connect San Jose and San Lucas. These buses stop at many places along Mexico 1, including near the Worldmark Coral Baja Resort at Playa Costa Azul, and the fare is only a few pesos (less then US$2). Buses run until 10 P.M. most nights.

By Car

You can do without a car if you plan to stay at an all-inclusive resort or a downtown hotel. Rent a car if you want the convenience of being able to drive yourself into town from a more remote location, or if you plan to take a day trip to the East Cape or Todos Santos. Most of the big auto rental agencies have desks at Los Cabos International Airport, as well as offices in or near town (many have opened new locations along the hotel zone). Note: When renting in Mexico, you must buy Mexican liability insurance (typically about US$25/day). On business days, expect heavy traffic getting into San José in the morning from points north and out of town in the evening.

By Taxi and Shuttle

Except during the hottest months, San Jose is pleasant to explore on foot. As congestion increases around the plaza, it is a convenience to leave the car behind. Cabs are available on Boulevard Mijares near the plaza, at the bus station, and along the Paseo del Malecón in the hotel zone (US$6 from the *zona hotelera* to the plaza downtown or from downtown to Pueblo La Playa, about US$40 from town to Los Cabos airport or to Cabo San Lucas). Call 624/142-0401 or 624/142-0105 for pickups.

The Corridor

In between San José del Cabo and Cabo San Lucas, a 29-kilometer stretch of beautiful coastline has evolved from a no-man's land into a luxury resort corridor. In front of and in between the resort properties are a number of sandy beaches, hidden coves, and exposed rocky points. Unfortunately for independent travelers, access to many of these prime coastal areas becomes more difficult by the month as new hotels go up; however, though builders may discourage the public from attempting to visit the beach by installing gates and security guards, they cannot legally prohibit access entirely. You may have to ask permission to pass, or park at the highway and walk, but you should be able to get to the beach, one way or another.

There aren't really separate towns along the Corridor; instead, the area is divided into several *fraccionamientos,* or districts for development, each containing several resorts, golf courses, spas, and the like. At Km 19.5, the Cabo Real development presides over scenic Bahía El Bledito and comprises the Marquis Los Cabos, Meliá Cabo Real Convention Center Beach and Golf Resort, Hotel Casa del Mar, and Casa del Mar Condos, as well as the renowned Cabo Real Golf Course and the Jack Nicklaus–designed El Dorado Golf Course. Stretching between Km 10 and Km 20, Cabo del Sol consists of the Sheraton and Fiesta America resorts and the Cabo del Sol golf course.

Driving along the Corridor is easy compared to driving around the rest of Baja. Mexico 1 is a four-lane highway between San José and San Lucas, with a mix of paved and dirt roads running perpendicular into the resorts and developments. Off-ramps are still the exception rather than the rule, so in some cases, you may have to pass your destination and make a U-turn to get to the other side of the road.

BEACHES

Pristine sunbathing beaches are the primary reason why so many high-end resorts have decided to build along the Corridor. To find the most easily accessible beaches, look for blue-and-white signs that say *Acceso a Playa* with an image of a snorkel and mask or a swimmer. (Some signs have just the picture, and not the words.) Ocean swimmers should be aware that strong undertows and rocks make many of these beaches unsafe for wading and body surfing. Playas Chileno and Santa María are two exceptions. You may also be able to get in at Playa Palmilla.

Playa Palmilla

The beautifully landscaped access road may trick you into thinking that Playa Palmilla (Km 26) is private. It's not. It does serve as the main beach for several upscale resorts, but there is a good-sized public parking lot, several *palapas* for shade, and plenty of sand to go around. The beach is pleasant for swimming or snorkeling. Palmilla is also the only place along the Corridor where you can watch the fishing *pangas* launch the old-fashioned way—without a paved boat launch or dock.

Playa El Bledito (Tequila Cove)

In front of the Hilton and Meliá resorts in Cabo Real, a breakwater protects swimmers

palapas on Playa Palmilla

from the pounding surf. You can rent personal watercraft on the beach, and the Hilton offers day passes for use of its pool and facilities. Look for an access road at Km 19.5, or enter through either of the resorts.

◖ Bahías Chileno and Santa María

If you want to swim and snorkel during your stay in Los Cabos, chances are someone will direct you to one of these two accessible beaches on the Corridor. Many land and sea tours bring groups of tourists to these bays because they are protected from the surf and have rocky points that attract a variety of marine life. Both have ample parking in dirt lots, though you may have to pay a few dollars to the security guard monitoring the lot. Shade and commercial services are lacking at both locations, though vendors seem to come and go each season. There are public restrooms at Chileno (Km 14) and snorkeling rentals at Santa María (Km 12). Both of these beaches can get crowded with shoulder-to-shoulder snorkelers when the tour boats come in mid-morning to mid-afternoon.

It's best to get an early start if you'd like to have the bay to yourself.

Playa Las Viudas (Widows Beach)

At Km 12.5, between the now-demolished Twin Dolphin and up-and-running Fiesta Americana resorts, a shallow bay with rocky points offers good snorkeling and swimming, when conditions are calm. The sand can get deep, but most vehicles seem able to traverse the access road intact.

SPORTS AND RECREATION
Surfing

Late summer storms bring a strong south swell to the Los Cabos coast, and several breaks offer fairly consistent rides. Close to Cabo San Lucas, Monuments breaks left over a rock reef located below the Misiones del Cabo condo complex at the west end of Playa Cabo Bello. Expect a crowd on good days, and beware the rocks and urchins.

El Tule is a dependable right at Km 16, and the right point break at Punta Palmilla (Km 27) may be worth the long paddle on a super big day.

Diving

Bahías Santa María (5–18 m) and Chileno (9–21 m) both have rocky reefs for underwater exploration. Due to the crowds, sea life near the shore is limited compared to what you'll see in protected marine parks elsewhere on the peninsula. These two bays are best suited for snorkeling or shallow beginner dives. Offshore from Bahía Santa María, a site called the Blowhole (12–30 m) features a wall dive where divers often see giant mantas, sea turtles, and schooling jacks and grouper.

Punta Palmilla (Km 27) is another good spot to put on your mask and fins. A zebra eel slithered about in broad daylight during a recent snorkel here.

Golf

Designer golf courses have popped up all over Southern Baja, luring players away from the competition in Arizona and California. Jack Nicklaus, Robert Trent Jones II, Tom Fazio, Tom Weiskopf, and Roy Dye all have had a hand in shaping the Los Cabos golf experience.

Gray water irrigates most of these courses, but even so, keeping all of those fairways groomed and green in a desert environment doesn't come cheap: Greens fees average US$250 for 18 holes. Discounted twilight rates begin at 2 P.M., earlier in summer. Rates typically include tax, use of a golf cart and driving range, bottled water, and club service, and prices may vary according to the travel season and day of the week.

PALMILLA

Jack Nicklaus was the mastermind behind the arroyo, mountain, and ocean courses at the **One&Only Palmilla** (Carr. Transp. Km 26, Palmilla, tel. 624/144-5250, US$200 for 18 holes), which form the center of a 384-hectare resort community. Most of its 27 holes have views of the ocean. Palmilla is known for a 440-yard, par-4 Mountain Five hole, which challenges the golfer to a long drive across two desert arroyos. Callaway rental clubs cost US$55.

CABO REAL

Open since 1989, the 18-hole, par-72 **Cabo Real Golf Course** (Carr. Transp. Km 19.5, Cabo Real, tel. 624/144-0040, U.S. tel. 877/795-8727, www.caboreal.com, US$280 for 18 holes) covers 6,400 meters with three oceanfront holes. Guests of the Westin Los Cabos, Meliá Cabo Real, and Casa del Mar resorts get 10 percent off the greens fees. King Cobra brand golf club rentals are US$50.

Jack Nicklaus designed the world-renowned 18-hole, par-72 **El Dorado Golf Club** (Carr. Transp. Km 19.5, Cabo Real, tel. 624/144-5450, US$280 for 18 holes) with an oceanfront driving range and clubhouse. Although it was initially designed as a public course, the El Dorado has now gone private, and four of the nine original oceanfront holes have been converted into home sites. It is one of only two courses in Mexico to make the *Golf Digest* list of 100 courses outside the United States in 2007.

CABO DEL SOL

The golf community at Cabo del Sol (Carr. Transp. Km 10.5, Cabo del Sol, tel. 624/145-8200, U.S. tel. 877/703-4394) includes two separate courses, with more in the plans. The ocean course (US$265–350) was designed by Jack Nicklaus and opened in 1994. Built to preserve a natural look and feel, the course extends from a kilometer and a half of oceanfront property, with seven of the 18 holes on the water. This is the only course in Mexico named to the 2007 *Golf Magazine* Top 100 Courses in the World list (#88) and one of only two courses in Mexico on the *Golf Digest* list of 100 course outside the United States (#28). The adjacent desert course (US$165–220) was designed by Tom Weiskopf, his first anywhere in Mexico. Taylor Made clubs at either course rent for US$65. Guests of the Fiesta Americana and Sheraton resorts in Cabo del Sol receive a 10 percent discount.

CABO SAN LUCAS COUNTRY CLUB

Palo Blanco trees, cardón cacti, and other desert flora form the backdrop for a challenging

18-hole course designed by Roy Dye (501 Palo Blanco, tel. 624/143-4653 or -4654, U.S. tel. 888/298-1132, www.golfincabo.com). Enjoy stunning views of Bahía Cabo San Lucas, including the rock formations at Land's End. Winter greens fees are US$105–204; summer rates are lower. The adjacent **Los Cabos Golf Resort** (tel. 624/145-7100 or 877/496-1367) has rooms with kitchenettes starting at US$235. The largest units have three bedrooms and full kitchens.

Spa Services

Most of the resorts listed in this chapter have their own spa facilities, with treatments from body wraps and massages to facials and pedicures. Services are typically offered inside or under a tent on the beach. Standouts include heavenly body wraps at **The Spa at the Westin Los Cabos** (Carr. Transp. Km 22.5, tel. 624/142-9000, toll-free U.S. tel. 800/598-1864, www.westinloscabos.com), and the indoor steam caves and waterfalls, plus holistic treatments using local fruits and vegetation,

at **Esperanza Resort** (Carr. Transp. Km 7, Punta Ballena, tel. 624/145-6400, U.S. tel. 866/311-2226, www.esperanzaresort.com), where 90-minute treatments cost US$235–250. The **Marquis Los Cabos** (Carr. Transp. Km 21.5, tel. 624/144-2000, U.S. tel. 877/238-9399, www.marquisloscabos.com) also boasts a gorgeous 929-square meter spa with six additional massage tents on the beach. A 50-minute facial runs US$100–115; deep-tissue, Shiatsu, Thai, or sports massage services are US$115–125 for 50 minutes; mud therapy treatments are US$115 for 50 minutes; and body scrubs are US$79 for 25 minutes. Non-guests can use the spa facilities (steam room, whirlpool tubs, and spa swimming pool) without reserving a treatment for US$25.

Cooking Classes

French Master Chef Jacques Chretien of the French Riviera Restaurant offers half-day introductory and advanced cooking classes (US$8–15) in which students learn the art of Mediterranean-style cooking. Visit www.

seaside massage at The Spa at the Westin Los Cabos

frenchrivieraloscabos.com for information and reservations.

SHOPPING

For jewelry, clothing, antiques, and home furnishings, head to the upscale **Shoppes at Palmilla** (Carr. Transp. Km 27.5, Palmilla, 624/144-6999, www.lastiendasdepalmilla.com) on the north side of Mexico 1 at the Palmilla Resort exit. Among other boutiques, the eclectic **Pez Gordo Gallery** (tel. 624/144-5292, www.pezgordogallery.com, Mon.–Sat. 10 A.M.–8 P.M.) represents more than 40 contemporary artists based in Baja and throughout Mexico. Works range from oil and acrylic to wax, collage, and photography. **Artesania Mágica** (Shoppes at Palmilla, tel. 624/144-6046, www.artesania-magica.com, daily 10 A.M.–8 P.M.) has a selection of upscale Mexican handicrafts. Cabo San Lucas's outstanding sushi restaurant, **Nick-San** (tel. 624/143-2491, www.nicksan.com, daily 11:30 A.M.–10:30 P.M., mains US$15 and up) has opened a second location in the Shoppes at Palmilla plaza.

At Km 16, across from the Marbella Suites Hotel, the **Regional Center of Popular Arts and Crafts** (Mon.–Sat. 9 A.M.–5 P.M.) has a small glass-blowing factory and several artisan workshops. Prices here are lower that what you'll find in San José or San Lucas.

ENTERTAINMENT

Most of the hotels along the Corridor have nightly music of some kind—though some of it can be pretty cheesy. Behind the Costco just outside of Cabo San Lucas, **Latitude+22 Roadhouse Inn** (Km 4.5, tel. 624/143-1516, www.lat22nobaddays.com, Wed.–Mon. 8 A.M.–11 P.M.) hosts live music Thursday–Saturday 7–10 P.M. It attracts Corridor residents and Baja old-timers with ocean views, reasonably priced cocktails, and giant flat-screen TVs, and offers a Croatian-influenced menu.

The Marquis, Westin, and Esperanza resorts also host musicians and vocalists from time to time. The **French Riviera Restaurant &**

ceramics at the Regional Center of Popular Arts and Crafts

© NIKKI GOTH ITOI

Beach Club at Club Ninety Six (tel. 624/144-6013) in the Villas del Mar at Punta Palmilla also has live music nightly.

ACCOMMODATIONS

Travelers with deep pockets head to the Corridor's posh resorts to see and be seen. Prices for these resorts begin around US$300–400 for the Sheraton and Hilton, climb to US$500 for the Westin and Marquis, and top out at US$700–1,000 per night or more for the Palmilla, Esperanza, and Las Ventanas. The lowest rates at each resort typically require full payment at the time of booking, and cancellation fees apply. Travel club memberships such as AAA can yield a discount of US$100 or more per night. The standard rates do not include 12 percent tax and 15 percent service, unless otherwise noted.

Cabo Surf Hotel

When the waves are rolling in at Playa Acapulquito, surfers and surfing spectators fill the 22 rooms, suites, and villas of the Cabo

Surf Hotel (Carr. Transp. Km 28, tel. 624/142-2676, U.S. tel. 858/964-5117, www.cabosurfhotel.com, US$265–625). The hotel is part of a Mexican-owned hotel company. Highlights here include marble floors, satellite TV, and in-room Wi-Fi. The largest villas accommodate up to eight guests. You can book a lesson through the Mike Doyle surf school, and when you've had enough of the action in the water, retreat to the on-site spa to recuperate. Then you can dine under an open-air *palapa* at the **7 Seas,** where choices include blue crab tostadas, fresh Baja clams au gratin, and a sea bass and spinach–stuffed chile pepper.

Sheraton Hacienda del Mar

You won't have to get up at the crack of dawn to reserve a chaise lounge at the Sheraton (Carr. Transp. Km 10.5, Cabo del Sol, tel. 624/145-8000 or 800/903-2500, toll-free U.S. tel. 888/625-5144, www.sheratonhaciendadelmar. com, from US$400); an abundance of patio furniture was part of the resort design. Even better, a poolside concierge helps guests plan the day's activities without having to leave the pool.

Mediterranean defines the look and feel of this sprawling resort, which has 270 rooms and 31 suites; the latter were renovated in late 2006. The hotel has several options for dining and entertainment. Best known among these is **Pitahayas** (tel. 624/145-8010, daily for breakfast, lunch, and dinner, mains US$15–40), which prepares variations on a Pacific Rim theme. You can also dine inside or out at the more casual **Tomates** (tel. 624/145-8000, daily for breakfast, lunch, and dinner, mains US$10–15), serving a fusion of Mexican and international dishes. Look for the beautifully landscaped Cabo del Sol exit ramp near Km 10.

Dreams Los Cabos Suites Golf Resort & Spa

A favorite among wedding parties, honeymooners, and anniversary celebrants, Dreams Los Cabos (Carr. Transp. Km 18.5, Cabo Real, tel. 624/145-7600, U.S. tel. 866/237-3267, www.dreamsresorts.com, from US$600) has 308 large and private luxury suites and all the amenities of a full-service resort. Its honeymoon packages include a champagne breakfast in bed. Book ahead if you have your heart set on a stay at Dreams; this popular resort has one of the highest occupancy rates in Los Cabos.

Hilton Los Cabos Beach & Golf Resort

Next door, the Hilton (Carr. Transp. Km 19.5, Cabo Real, tel. 624/145-6500, wwww. hiltonloscabos.com, from US$400) features Mediterranean architecture, a beautiful infinity pool, and a complete list of luxury-style amenities, plus a favorable location near Playa Bledito. Rooms were recently renovated by designer Paul Duesing and have large baths with soaking tubs, separate showers, and L'Occitane products.

Meliá Cabo Real

The Meliá Cabo Real (Carr. Transp. Km 19.5, Cabo Real, tel. 624/142-2222, toll-free U.S. tel. 888/956-3542, www.solmelia.com, from US$245) is an all-inclusive resort with more than 300 rooms situated near the Cabo Real Golf Course. Most have marble baths, balconies, and ocean views. This is one of few resorts along the Corridor that's located on a swimmable beach, thanks to a manmade jetty.

Casa del Mar Golf Resort and Spa

On a smaller scale, the 31 suites at the hacienda-style Casa del Mar (Carr. Transp. Km 19.5, tel. 624/145-7700, toll-free U.S. tel. 800/227-9621, www.casadelmarmexico.com, US$500 and up) come with ocean views, luxury bed linens, teak furniture, marble baths, and Mexican artwork. This is a boutique property with six swimming pools, four lighted tennis courts, and a European-style spa. **El Tapanco** (daily 5–10:30 P.M., mains US$10–20) serves Nuevo Mexican cuisine.

Fiesta Americana Grand Los Cabos

Adjacent to the Cabo del Sol golf course is the family-oriented Fiesta Americana Grand Los Cabos (Carr. Transp. Km 10.3, Cabo del Sol, tel. 624/145-6200, toll-free U.S. tel. 800/343-7821, www.fiestaamericana.com, US$476–662), with 250 oceanview guestrooms and suites and a secluded beach. Rooms are spread across six floors and feature private balconies. The resort's restaurant, **Rosato** (Carr. Transp. Km 10.3, Cabo del Sol, tel. 624/145-6200, daily for dinner, mains US$15–20), serves northern Italian cuisine.

Westin Resort & Spa Los Cabos

A dramatic architectural interpretation of the arch at Land's End stands at the center of the Westin Los Cabos (Carr. Transp. Km. 22.5, tel. 624/142-9000, toll-free U.S. tel. 800/598-1864, www.westinloscabos.com, US$379–705). Mexican architect Javier Sordo Magdaleno designed the hillside resort with bright colors and views from every vantage point.

The chain's signature Heavenly Beds are reason enough to stay here. Separate tubs and showers in large marble bathrooms add even more of a distinctive touch.

Several restaurants on-site provide a variety of dining experiences; they include eclectic **Arrecifes** and **La Cascada,** which serves *tapas* from around the world.

A European-style spa offers body wraps, mud baths, and massage treatments inside or on the beach. Guests have golf privileges at the Cabo Real Golf Course, about 2.5 kilometers southwest.

Marquis Los Cabos

From the inlaid turquoise stones that accent resort corridors to perfectly filtered light in the spa rooms, meticulous attention to detail and contemporary Mexican decor set the tone for a stay at the Marquis Los Cabos (Carr. Transp. Km 21.5, tel. 624/144-2000, U.S. tel. 877/238-9399, www.marquisloscabos.com, US$495–770). Opened in 2003, the Mexican-owned resort was designed to reveal ocean views from every angle. Guests can move from their room to a restaurant, the spa, or the gym without losing sight of the sea. The Marquis' 237 rooms have soaking tubs and showers, Bulgary bath fixtures, mahogany woodwork, flat-screen

TVs, and exquisite linens. Each morning, hotel staff delivers breakfast to guests through a private pass-through alcove. In addition, rooms and common areas showcase contemporary Mexican paintings and sculpture. And if you fall in love with the eclectic furnishings, as many guests apparently have, you can buy your own from a furniture store on the premises. Twenty-eight *casitas* have their own swimming pools. A 929-square-meter spa and an award-winning, 21-seat French restaurant, **Canto del Mar,** set the hotel apart. Close proximity to the highway and small balconies are the only obvious disadvantages at this resort. A service charge of US$35 per day is added to the daily room rate.

Las Ventanas al Paraíso

Romance defines the experience at Las Ventanas (Carr. Transp. Km 20, tel. 624/144-0300, toll-free U.S. tel. 888/767-3966, www.lasventanas.com, junior suites US$725–1,350), just northeast of Km 20, which celebrated its 10th anniversary in 2007. Accordingly, one of your first choices upon arrival here will be selecting bed linens from the sheet menu. Known for its underground service tunnels, designed to hide some of the infrastructure and busy staff that keep the place running, the property is run by Rosewood Hotels and Resorts. Colors are earthy and warm, for an intimate ambience.

Large guest suites feature inlaid stone-and-tile floors and adobe fireplaces. Computerized telescopes help guests find whales offshore. Three spa suites have space for in-room treatments, as well as rooftop terraces with outdoor hot tubs. Everyone else can book treatments at the on-site spa. A large infinity pool has "high-tech" pebbles that change color according to the color of the sky and sea.

A tequila- and ceviche-tasting bar hosts Friday evening Tequila Nights, open to guests and non-guests. Private movie nights on the beach, complete with wine and gourmet Mexican *botanas,* are another signature Las Ventanas diversion. Multiday spa and meal packages are available. For guests who want to

COURTESY OF ESPERANZA RESORT

Esperanza Resort

venture away from the resort, Mini Cooper S convertibles, BMW motorcycles, and off-road Hummers are available for rent.

Esperanza Resort

By many accounts, Esperanza (Carr. Transp. Km 7, Punta Ballena, tel. 624/145-6400, U.S. tel. 866/311-2226, www.esperanzaresort.com, US$675–1,325) leads the pack for outstanding guest service. Located close to Cabo San Lucas, its 50 *casitas* and six suites feature original Mexican artwork and handcrafted furnishings. A signature spa has indoor steam caves and waterfalls, with treatments that incorporate local fruits and vegetation. The oceanfront Mediterranean restaurant, the **Signature Restaurant at Esperanza,** open for breakfast, lunch, and dinner, completes the picture. Esperanza also has its own art gallery with works by contemporary Mexican painters and sculptors for sale. A four-night minimum stay is required for all weekend bookings January–April except February and March, when a seven-night stay is required.

One&Only Palmilla

The oldest resort in Los Cabos is also one of the destination's most expensive—and most popular—places to stay. Originally built in 1956 by "Rod" Rodríguez, son of former Mexican president Abelardo Luis Rodríguez, the One&Only Palmilla (Carr. Transp. Km 27, tel. 624/146-7000, U.S. tel. 866/829-2977, www.oneandonlyresorts.com, US$675 and up) has a prime location against a cliff on Punta Palmilla near San José. Over the years, it has grown from one hotel to encompass an entire resort community. Like Esperanza, this is a place for travelers who want to be pampered and are willing to pay for the personal service—which includes everything from loaner iPods and sunglasses cleaning at the pool to golf cart shuttles to get you to and from your room. The result is a private and relaxing five-star vacation. Activities include yoga, spa treatments, and golf. You can dine at Charlie Trotter's **Restaurant C** or the Mediterranean **Agua Restaurant.**

FOOD

Most restaurants along the Corridor are tucked inside full-service resorts. Expect to pay at least US$100 for two (without drinks) at most of the restaurants in this section. Here are a few stand-alone eateries and some of the resort standouts.

Seafood and International

Pecan-encrusted sea bass, mesquite-grilled prawns, and live lobster anchor the menu at **Pitahayas** (Carr. Transp. Km 10, Cabo del Sol, tel. 624/145-8010, daily 5:30–10:30 P.M., mains US$15–40), at the Sheraton Hacienda del Mar. An underground wine cellar complements the menu of fresh seafood and mesquite-grilled entrées. You'll need to wear formal resort attire if you plan to dine here.

At the Cabo Surf Hotel, **7 Seas** (Carr. Transp. Km 28, tel. 624/142-2676, www.7seasrestaurant. com, daily 7 A.M.–10 P.M., lunch mains US$7–13, dinner mains US$18–28) serves breakfast, lunch, and dinner under an open-air *palapa.* The dinner menu features Mexican, Mediterranean,

TYING THE KNOT

Destination weddings are big business in Los Cabos. Inviting your friends and family to a seaside marriage ceremony and wedding reception will create memories to last a lifetime. But the choices can be overwhelming, and there seems to be no upper limit on what you can spend. Consider these tips before you start planning the big day:

HIRE A WEDDING COORDINATOR

Different legal system, languages, and business norms can make for a difficult planning process. Do yourself a favor and get help early. Dozens of wedding specialists operate from the area and can advise on reception sites, flowers, music, and food. Some are affiliated with a particular resort; others work independently. Booking service Earth, Sea, & Sky Vacations (www.cabovillas.com/weddings.asp) works with a professional coordinator to plan weddings in the area. Baja Weddings (www.bajawedding.com) is another reputable service.

CHOOSE YOUR PRIORITIES

When planning from afar, you won't be able to oversee every last detail of the event in person. Decide in advance what matters most and focus your attention there. Leave the other details in the hands of the wedding coordinator.

FIND THE RIGHT SETTING FOR YOU AND YOUR GUESTS

An all-inclusive resort may simplify the logistics for some couples; others will prefer to select food, music, cake, photography, and flowers à la carte.

SET A BUDGET AND STICK TO IT

You may fall in love with the gourmet lunch at the One&Only Palmilla, but it may not be the place to host your 100-person event.

READ THE FINE PRINT BEFORE YOU BOOK

Are you committing to rent all the rooms in the inn? Make sure you know the terms of the deal before you pay a deposit.

DIG FOR DEALS

Join an online forum, such as CaboWeddings on Yahoo Groups (http://groups.yahoo.com/group/CaboWeddings), to learn from the experience of others. Brides report finding bands and vendors for as low as half the cost of vendors their coordinator recommended. The Los Cabos Guide keeps an online list of local wedding service providers (www.loscabosguide.com/services/weddings.htm).

and seafood entrées with a decent wine list. Seafood-stuffed poblano peppers are one of the more unusual dishes.

At the Westin Los Cabos, **Arrecifes** (Carr. Transp. Km. 22.5, tel. 624/142-9000, daily for dinner, mains US$15–25) is the more formal of the two main restaurants; jazz music plays over the sound of waves crashing on the beach below, and the menu emphasizes seafood dishes with an international twist. The other restaurant, **La Cascada** (Carr. Transp. Km. 22.5, tel. 624/142-9000, for breakfast and dinner, mains US$15 and up), underwent a US$900,000 renovation in 2006. It features illuminated onyx cube tables, a fire pit lounge, and a menu of creative *tapas del mundo,* or small plates from around the world paired with wines that match the flavors of the food.

And at the One&Only Palmilla, diners can choose between the *palapa*-style **Agua Restaurant** (Carr. Transp. Km 7.5, Palmilla, tel. 624/146-7000), featuring Mediterranean cuisine and a view of the sea, and Charlie Trotter's first overseas restaurant, called **Restaurant C** (Carr. Transp. Km 7.5, Palmilla, tel. 624/146-7000, www.charlietrotters.com, mains US$20 and up). Entrées at C include rockfish with ratatouille, quinoa, and a black olive–caper vinaigrette and steamed and spit-roasted duck with spiced carrots, parsnips, and a tangerine-merlot reduction. Both restaurants are open for breakfast, lunch, and dinner.

The Mediterranean-inspired **French Riviera** in San José has a new branch in the exclusive Club Ninety Six beach club at Punta Palmilla (Carr. Transp. Km 27.5, Palmilla, tel. 624/144-6013, www.frenchrivieraloscabos.com, daily noon–11 P.M., mains US$33).

Italian and Continental

In the Misiones del Cabo complex, **Sunset da Mona Lisa** (formerly Da Giorgio, Carr. Transp. Km 5.5, tel. 624/145-8160, www.sunsetmonalisa.com, daily 8:30 A.M.–11 P.M., mains US$18–35) draws a crowd for sunset views and Italian fare. A multilevel patio overlooks the bay and Cabo San Lucas.

Dinner at the award-winning French restaurant **Canto del Mar** (Carr. Transp. Km 21.5, tel. 624/144-2000, dinner only, prix fixe US$60 pp), inside the Marquis Los Cabos resort, is an Old World affair, complete with acoustic guitar music and a collection of masks from Florence on the walls. There are just 21 seats in the house for the nightly six-course tasting menu. An adjoining cigar room has a hardwood floor and ornate upholstered armchairs.

Mexican

Close to Cabo San Lucas, **◖ Puerta Vieja** (Carr. Transp. Km 6.3, tel. 624/104-3252, www.puertavieja.com, mains US$13–23) offers a fantastic view and hearty fare like Sonora beef and fresh shellfish, prepared with Asian accents and offered at incredibly reasonable prices—a rare find along the Corridor. One more kilometer east, the same owners run the popular **Villa Serena Restaurant** (Carr. Transp. Km 7.5, tel. 624/145-8244, daily 7 A.M.–10 P.M., mains US$12–25) next to the Villa Serena RV Park. Tasty seafood platters or beef and chicken dishes are a great deal.

Groceries and Supplies

If you want to stock up on fine wines, spirits, and gourmet foods, **La Europea** (Carr. Transp. Km 6.7, tel. 624/145-8755, Mon.–Fri. 9 A.M.–8 P.M., Sat. 9 A.M.–9 P.M.) is the place to shop. Look for the main store at the first stoplight as you enter Cabo from the east. Credit cards are accepted. **Costco** (Carr. Transp. Km 4.5, tel. 624/146-7180, daily 9 A.M.–9 P.M.) and **Home Depot** (Carr. Transp. Km 6.5, tel. 624/105-8600) have also opened stores close to Cabo San Lucas.

INFORMATION AND SERVICES

Pemex stations are located at Km 5 just outside of Cabo San Lucas and near the Westin between Km 24 and Km 25. Most of the resorts offer Internet access and phone services for guests.

For medical needs, see *Information and Services* in the *San José del Cabo* and *Cabo San Lucas* sections.

GETTING AROUND

Resorts along the Corridor are a 30- to 60-minute drive from the airport. Many, including the Westin, offer shuttles to San José del Cabo and Cabo San Lucas for guests who want to see a little more than their hotel grounds. Car rental agencies have offices at many of the larger resorts.

Cabo San Lucas

Baja travelers tend to love or hate Cabo San Lucas (pop. 56,800) with great passion. Some relish the crowded beach clubs, two-for-one happy hours, all-you-can-drink sunset cruises, and late-night dance clubs. The scene is anything but Mexican, but the energy and pure silliness are infectious, and with all this partying going on, it would seem impossible not to have a good time.

For other travelers, the intensity is too much, the timeshare sale pitches too aggressive, and the overall experience far too Americanized to be enjoyable.

Whether you love it or hate it, there's no denying Cabo San Lucas is one of a kind. Its natural beauty is hard to beat: the dramatic arch stands at Land's End; Playa del Amor, which connects the Pacific Ocean to the Sea of Cortez; and the peaks of the Sierra de la Laguna rise in the distance.

The town attracts a surprising variety of visitors, from partying singles to thirtysomethings with kids, and from cruise ship passengers to scuba divers and sportfishing enthusiasts. Food and accommodations are correspondingly diverse. Cabo has luxury resorts and vacation rental villas, as well as modest condos, budget motels, and trailer parks. You can eat world-class sushi, shrimp by the kilo, or simple Mexican *antojitos*. The downtown shopping plazas sell everything from Sergio Bustamante sculptures to hand-embroidered dresses. Venture away from the immediate tourist area, and you'll find a grid of dirt roads lined with ordinary Mexican homes and small businesses.

As the second-largest municipality in Baja California Sur after La Paz, Cabo San Lucas has struggled to cope with fast-paced growth over the past two decades. Most of the development has centered around the hillside Pedregal neighborhood, along Playa El Médano, and most recently on the Pacific coast north of Playa Solmar.

In 2008, the town embarked on a series of infrastructure improvements. Several of its main

Cabo San Lucas Marina

© KATHRYN LATENDRESSE

streets were temporarily torn up in preparation for new road surfaces, sidewalks, traffic lights, and signage. The goals are to increase safety, provide new green spaces, and ease the congestion that has overtaken the town in recent years. Services related to tourism and the construction business drive the local economy today.

CABO SAN LUCAS MARINA

Much of the Los Cabos tourist activity takes place at or near the Cabo San Lucas Marina and along a wide boulevard that wraps around the harbor. A number of the most popular bars and restaurants are clustered here along the waterfront. You can hire water taxis and book all kinds of recreational tours from the many vendors who compete aggressively for your business. Many snorkeling tours and sunset cruises depart from the Main Dock, located on the southwest side of the marina, near the mouth of the inner harbor.

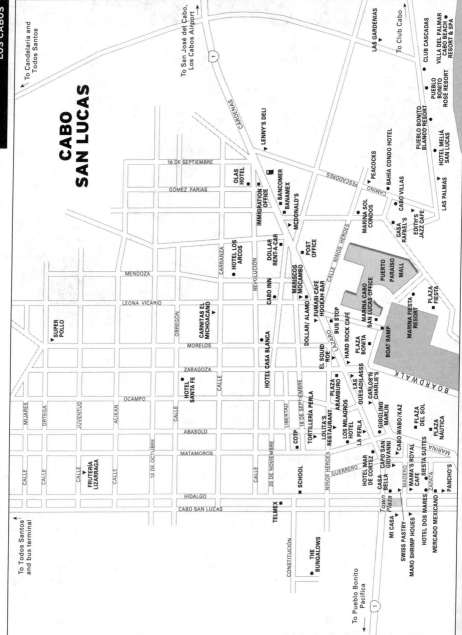

CABO SAN LUCAS

To Candelaria and Todos Santos

To San José del Cabo, Los Cabos Airport

To Club Cabo

LAS GARDENIAS

CLUB CASCADAS

VILLA DEL PALMAR

CABO BEACH RESORT & SPA

PUEBLO BONITO ROSÉ RESORT

PUEBLO BONITO BLANCO RESORT

HOTEL MELIÁ SAN LUCAS

LAS PALMAS

CAMINO PESCADORES

CARDENAS

LENNY'S DELI

16 DE SEPTIEMBRE

GOMEZ FARIAS

OLAS HOTEL

IMMIGRATION OFFICE

BANCOMER

BANAMEX

McDONALD'S

PEACOCKS

BAHIA CONDO HOTEL

CABO VILLAS

MARINA SOL CONDOS

CASA RAFAEL'S

EDITH'S JAZZ CAFE

CARRANZA

HOTEL LOS ARCOS

DOLLAR RENTA-CAR

POST OFFICE

CABO INN

REVOLUCIÓN

MARISCOS MOCAMBO

CALLE NIÑOS HEROES

PUERTO PARAISO MALL

MARINA CABO OFFICE

MARINA CABO SAN LUCAS OFFICE

PLAZA FIESTA

MENDOZA

LEONA VICARIO

OBREGON

CARNITAS EL MICHOACANO

MORELOS

FUMARI CAFÉ HOOKAH BAR

BUS STOP

HARD ROCK CAFÉ

LAZARO

SUPER POLLO

DOLLAR / ALAMO

EL SQUID ROE

PLAZA BONITA

MARINA FIESTA RESORT

BOAT RAMP

ZARAGOZA

HOTEL CASA BLANCA

CALLE

HOTEL SANTA FE

OCAMPO

CALLE

16 DE SEPTIEMBRE

LIBERTAD

PLAZA ARAMBURO

LAS QUESADILLASSS

CARLOS'N CHARLIE'S

BOARDWALK

MIJARES

ORTEGA

JUVENTUD

ALIKAN

ABASOLO

TORTILLERIA PERLA

LOLITA'S RESTAURANT

LOS MILAGROS HOTEL

LA PERLA

GIGGLING MARLIN

CABO WABO/KAZ

PLAZA DEL SOL

PLAZA NAUTICA

COTP

MATAMOROS

SCHOOL

CALLE

HOTEL MAR DE CORTEZ

CASA BELLA

CAPO SAN GIOVANNI

SIESTA SUITES

MADERO

MARINA

ZAPATA

PANCHO'S

FRUTERÍA LIZARRAGA

CALLE

12 DE OCTUBRE

20 DE NOVIEMBRE

NIÑOS HEROES GUERRERO

MAMA'S ROYAL CAFÉ

HIDALGO

CABO SAN LUCAS

TELMEX

CONSTITUCIÓN

THE BUNGALOWS

Town Plaza

MI CASA

SWISS PASTRY

MARO SHRIMP HOUES

HOTEL DOS MARES

MERCADO MEXICANO

To Todos Santos and bus terminal

To Pueblo Bonito Pacifica

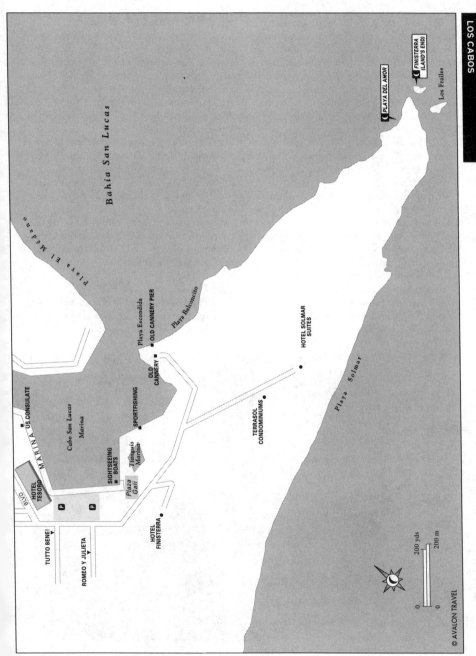

© AVALON TRAVEL

Several plazas along the marina contain a variety of cafés, shops, and service businesses. At the north end of the harbor, the **Puerto Paraíso Mall** is a three-level shopping center, with a cinema, bowling alley, art galleries, boutiques, and American food chains such as Häagen-Dazs and Johnny Rockets. Plaza Bonita has an outdoor coffee stand and Internet café, as well as a Sergio Bustamante sculpture gallery.

The Hotel Tesoro Los Cabos, with its labyrinth of hallways and passages, occupies a long stretch of the marina on the southwest side of harbor.

A gray five-story cinderblock building remains an unfortunate eyesore on Boulevard Marina. It was abandoned in the late 1980s and has been in an ownership dispute ever since.

On busy days, multiple cruise ships shuttle thousands of passengers into this downtown area. They wander the streets looking for souvenirs and familiar shops like Diamonds International. But at day's end, they return to their cabins, leaving the nightlife to those who've arrived by air and car.

PLAZA AMELIA WILKES

Set back a few blocks from the tourist corridor, the original town plaza (between Calle Hidalgo and Avenida Cabo San Lucas, cross streets Madero and Lázaro Cardenas) has a pretty gazebo and several benches, where you can enjoy a break from the frenzy at the marina. The plaza hosts various festivals, often with live music and dancing.

It is also home to a small **natural history museum** (tel. 624/143-0187, Tues.–Sun. 10 A.M.–2 P.M. and 5–8 P.M.) that opened in 2006. Exhibits trace the natural and cultural evolution of Baja California Sur. Admission is by donation.

Across from the plaza on Avenida Cabo San Lucas is the unassuming Iglesia de San Lucas, which dates back to the 18th century and holds regular worship services today.

PLAYA EL MÉDANO

Cabo San Lucas offers the rare combination of a large tourist destination with a well-developed beach area within walking distance

view of Playa El Médano from the bay

© 123RF.COM/ALYSTA INC.

El Arco rock formation, part of Finisterra

of the town, plus several pristine beaches just minutes away by boat. And when you've exhausted all of these possibilities, the beaches along the Corridor and closer to San José are only a short drive away.

The partying crowd congregates at beach clubs along Playa El Médano (Dune Beach) beginning in the late morning. This long, sandy beach starts at the entrance to the inner harbor and parallels the old road to San José (Camino Viejo a San José) for several kilometers heading northeast. You can swim here any time of year, though the water is warmest July–October. On busy days, keep an eye out for boats landing on the beach. You can book just about any water activity from the beach, including rental of personal watercraft, kayaks, and snorkeling gear. The Manta dive shop (tel. 624/144-3871, www. caboscuba.com) is just a few buildings away from the beach on Camino Pescadores. Options for food and facilities at the beach include *palapa* bars, beach clubs, and resort restaurants.

◖ FINISTERRA (LAND'S END)

You know you've reached the end of the road in Baja when the towering granite rock

formations and signature arch at Finisterra, or Land's End, come into view. Just about every tour boat that departs the Cabo San Lucas Marina heads to the 62-meter El Arco to stage a postcard-perfect photo op. In most conditions, the boat captain can pull right up to the arch. On rare exceptionally low tides, sand appears under the arch and you can walk through the passage. Nearby rocks host a colony of sea lions, while pelicans congregate at the Roca Pelican, a popular snorkeling and scuba diving site.

If you're the sort of traveler who avoids the well-beaten tourist path, consider making an exception for this sight. It's generally not as crowded as you might expect, and the dramatic effect of sunlight dancing on the cliffs and wildlife playing in the sea spray is truly spectacular.

◖ PLAYA DEL AMOR

At the southernmost tip of the cape, Playa del Amor (Love Beach), also known as Playa del Amante (Lover's Beach), offers a rare opportunity to dip a toe in two different bodies of water from the same beach. This two-sided beach touches both the Sea of Cortez in the Bay of San Lucas and the Pacific Ocean. The beach is narrow on the bay side and opens into a wide, sandy expanse on the ocean side. You can swim and snorkel on the bay side, but heavy surf pounds the exposed western shoreline, creating a dangerous undertow.

Water taxis and glass-bottom boats from the Cabo San Lucas marina shuttle passengers to and from the beach for US$8–12 round-trip. (Ask to see the boat before you pay, as some are in much better shape than others. Should the engine fail and cut your trip short, the person you paid will likely be nowhere in sight.)

There are no docking facilities at the drop-off point, which is on the narrow bay side of the beach. *Panga* drivers drift as close as possible to shore, but passengers inevitably get wet on the way in and out. Wear water shoes and protect any electronic gear. Shade is limited to a few rocky overhangs (get there early to claim a spot, or bring your own umbrella), and there are no commercial services at the beach, except for an occasional vendor selling cold drinks. Bring a cooler and pack your own lunch.

Another option for getting to Playa del Amor is to rent a kayak (US$10 pp/hr) on Playa El Médano and paddle across the bay. It's best to go in the morning, when the water is calm; the paddle takes about 40 minutes one-way.

PLAYA SOLMAR

To escape the crowds or cool off in an ocean breeze, head to Playa Solmar on the Pacific Coast. This exposed beach has a steep slope and strong undertow, making it unsafe for swimming. But for sunbathing and whale-watching, it's a find. Follow Boulevard Marina to the sign for the Hotel Solmar on the right, and park at the resort.

SPORTS AND RECREATION
Fishing

Fish counts may not what they used to be a few decades ago, but recreational fishing remains a popular activity throughout the Los Cabos area, and Cabo San Lucas has the widest variety of charters and related services. The legendary Bisbee Tournament takes place each October, with thousands of boats on the bay.

In the peak season, hundreds of boats depart the Cabo San Lucas marina each morning in search of prized billfish (blue, black, and striped marlin and sailfish), plus tuna, wahoo, and dorado. It's not uncommon for boats to hook 1,000-pound marlin and multiple billfish in one outing. Depending on the season, you might also catch red snapper, yellowtail, sierra, jack crevalle, roosterfish, and grouper.

Cabo San Lucas boats report an average of almost one billfish per departure, and multiple catches are not unusual. Fortunately, the boats also report a high release rate (95 percent or better), meaning they return the fish to the water to fight another day. A universal system of flags reveals the action that took place on any given boat that day: A red flag with a T means the boat caught and released a billfish, while a blue triangular flag means the crew caught and killed a billfish. Boats may legally keep one billfish per boat, but most charter operations strongly discourage the practice.

For marlin fishing, captains generally head to San Jaime Banks, 29 kilometers southwest of Cabo Falso, or Golden Gate Banks, 31 kilometers west of Cabo Falso. Anglers frequently catch dorado and wahoo as well in these areas.

There are three ways to fish the waters near Cabo San Lucas: by cruiser (motorboat equipped with fish-finders, tackle, captain's chairs, and wells for live bait), in a *panga* (simple aluminum skiff), or from shore (surf casting).

SPORTFISHING CRUISERS

Numerous outfitters arrange sportfishing trips aboard cruisers (US$350/day on a 28-foot boat with up to four anglers; US$550/day on a 36-foot boat with up to six anglers). A few outfits charge extra for the license, gear, tax, and ice, but most include these items in the daily fee. Bait, however, always costs extra. **Pisces Fleet** (Blvd. Marina at Madero, tel. 624/143-1288, U.S. tel. 619/819-7983, www.piscessportfishing.com) is one of the oldest and most conservation-minded fishing operations in Cabo. It offers two different rates: Bareboat prices, in which customers bring their own lunch and handle their own catch when they return, are US$445 for a 28-foot cruiser for up to four people, US$580 for a 31-foot Bertram for up to six people, and US$900 for a 31-foot Cabo Express (up to six people). The bareboat rate includes crew, ice, tackle, coffee, and sweet rolls before departure. All-inclusive packages add drinks, box lunches, fishing licenses, live bait, plus filleting and freezing services for your catch, The fleet includes yachts of every size, all the way up to the 111-foot *Crystal* (US$9,500 for up to 12 anglers). Half-day rates are available for many boats.

After many years of fishing the Baja Peninsula from a home base in the United States, "Renegade" Mike moved to Cabo San Lucas, bought a 31-foot Bertram, and set it up the way he wanted to fish. He has earned a reputation for top-notch service and high-quality gear, including two-speed reels and bamboo gaffs, which he makes himself. Within his first few months of operation, Mike had completed several days of two-digit marlin releases. Contact him at **Renegademike Sportfishing Charters** (tel. 624/129-9581, U.S. tel. 619/591-8969, www.renegademikesportfishing.com, renegademikesportfishing@hotmail.com, US$550/day).

Dream Maker Sportfishing (Locale 20, Hotel Tesoro complex, tel. 624/143-7266, www.dreammakercharter.com) leads five-hour and eight-hour trips with a fleet of nine boats that includes everything from a 22-foot *panga* (US$175/5 hrs) to a 42-foot sportfisher (US$1,250 all-inclusive or US$1,050 boat only).

Located at the Bahía Hotel, **Gaviota Sportfishing** (toll-free U.S. tel. 800/932-5599, www.gaviotasportfishing.com) has experienced captains and 11 boats ranging from 26- to 36-foot cruisers. All-inclusive packages for four (US$755 including tax or US$595 boat charter only) come with tackle, bait, lunch, and a case of beer, soda, or bottled water. The same package for two aboard a 26-foot cruiser is US$440 (US$360 boat charter only). Boats leave at 7 A.M. and return at 3 P.M.

If you don't want to contact an outfitter directly, you can arrange guided fishing trips through any major hotel. A few, including the Solmar and Finisterra, run their own fleets.

First-timers are sometimes surprised and frustrated by the amount of time it takes before they actually have lines in the water. Getting bait, cruising out to the banks, and returning to the harbor are all part of the time that will be spent on a day of fishing. You can save time by buying bait in advance and requesting to fish destinations closer to shore.

PANGA FISHING

The most economical—and exhilarating—way to plan a Baja fishing adventure is to hire a local *panguero* for a few hours; however, options for these simple skiffs are limited in Cabo San Lucas, where most visitors prefer the luxury cruiser experience. The best bet is to head to La Playita near San José del Cabo. If you can find one, a day of *panga* fishing will cost around US$175 for five hours in a three-person, 22-foot boat. **Dream Maker Sportfishing** (Locale 20, Hotel Tesoro complex, tel. 624/143-7266, www.dreammakercharter.com) is one of the few outfitters that has a *panga* in its fleet. Typical catches include cabrilla, grouper, and sierra, but even marlin are possible with the right captain in the right place at the right time. Prices won't include rental gear or fishing licenses. Some will fillet the fish you catch for no additional cost. Be forewarned, if you happen to go out on a *panga* when the fish are on, you may well tire of the action long before your captain is ready to return to shore. As one *panguero* told us in the midst of a prolonged fishing frenzy, "When the fish are here, you fish!"

SURF CASTING

If you want to fish without parting with the cash of a full day aboard a cruiser, you might try casting into the surf from shore. You don't need a license, and your catch might include sea bass, sierra, and red snapper. Playa Solmar offers the best conditions, but it is a dangerous location because of the strong undertow.

Sleeper waves often strike here, catching even the most experienced anglers off-guard. A safer place to try is the old pier at the entrance to the harbor. Fishing is permitted at the northeast end of Playa El Médano.

BAIT, TACKLE, AND FISH PROCESSING

Minerva's Baja Tackle (Blvd. Marina at Madero, tel. 624/143-1282, Mon.–Sat. 9 A.M.–7 P.M.), next door to Pisces Fleet, carries a wide selection of gear and tackle for your fishing adventure. It is also the designated Los Cabos representative to the International Game Fish Association (IGFA).

You can buy fresh bait at the docks along the marina for a few dollars and hire local pros to clean and fillet your catch. Another option for cleaning, processing, vacuum-packing, and freezing is **Gricelda's Smoke House** (Loc 19 & 20 in the Tesoro Hotel complex, tel. 624/143-7266, www.dreammakercharter. com) on the marina.

Diving and Snorkeling

Cabo San Lucas offers a variety of unique opportunities for underwater exploration. A strategic location between tropical and temperate zones and the presence of a vast submarine canyon bring large pelagics such as giant mantas, hammerhead sharks, and amberjacks very close to shore, along with a colorful mix of tropical species. Boat rides are relatively short (as little as 5 minutes to the closest sites), and the terrain is dramatic. There are wall dives, submerged boulder fields, drift dives, and a one-of-a-kind dive that begins in the Sea of Cortez, rounds the point at Land's End, and ends in the Pacific Ocean.

Playa del Amor is a great place to snorkel on your own, or with a guide. Just offshore from this beach, Pelican Rock is another good snorkeling site, though given its proximity to the harbor, it can get crowded during the high season. Boats out of San Lucas make the trip to Bahías Chileno and Santa María on the Corridor for snorkeling and shallow diving, but you can also reach these sites yourself by car.

Guided scuba dives tour many of the same sites as snorkelers, making it convenient to

---

SAND FALLS

Many scuba divers come to Cabo San Lucas hoping to see the unusual sand falls – rivers of sand flowing between rocks and over the edge of a canyon wall beginning 30 meters below the surface. The sand falls lie within the national marine preserve, close to Playa del Amor.

The Scripps Institute of Oceanography first discovered the phenomenon in 1960, and Jacques Cousteau later made the sand falls famous in his television series.

Divers should note that the sand rivers typically run in stormy weather; during extended periods of calm seas, when diving conditions are otherwise best, you may not be able to see the falls in action. But there is plenty to see at the site, whether or not the sand is flowing. The canyon walls support marine life big and small. Graceful eagle rays, good-sized grouper, and tiny zebra eels are just a few of the sightings divers may experience on these dives.

---

accommodate mixed groups (but also making it more crowded, both above and below the surface). Also, given the proximity of these dive sites to the harbor, the loud and constant rumble of boat traffic overhead makes for an annoying distraction.

The most popular dive sites in the Cabo Marine Preserve include Pelican Rock, Neptune's Finger, and the point at Land's End. Pelican Rock and Neptune's Finger begin at shallow depth (6–8 m), and then descend over boulders or along a wall into a vast submarine canyon, as diver skill, air consumption, and visibility allow. All of these dives take place in a protected marine preserve, an unusual feature to have so close to a town the size of Cabo San Lucas.

The Land's End dive begins in the surge under a sea lion colony on the bay side of the point and ends with an underwater swim

DIVING AND SNORKELING COSTS

GUIDED DIVE AND SNORKEL TOURS *Discounts apply for multiday dives.*

Snorkel tour (equipment included) .... US$25-45
One-tank boat dive .... US$45-65
Two-tank boat dive .... US$70-85
Night dive.. US$50-65
Cabo Pulmo day trip ....US$120-155
Gorda Banks day trip...US$120-185
Nondiver passenger .... US$10-15

SCUBA INSTRUCTION

Open Water referral (four dives, for students who have
completed classroom and pool work prior to arrival)......................... US$210-250
Open water certification (classroom and dives)............................US$375-430
Discover Scuba/resort course (introduction to scuba)........................ US$90-100
Refresher dive...US$100
Advanced certification ....US$280-330
Rescue diver course .... US$300

EQUIPMENT RENTAL

Snorkel gear .... US$4-12 (usually included with tour)
Scuba package with dives .... US$20-25/day (discounts for multiday dives)
Weight belt and weights.. US$8
Regulator .... US$12
Tanks... US$12
BCD .... US$12
Wet suit... US$8
Airfills .... US$45

around to the Pacific side, covering varied underwater topography along the way. Guitar fish, schooling amberjack, green sea turtles, and countless other species are likely to make an appearance on this dive.

Cabo San Lucas dive shops can also arrange trips to Cabo Pulmo on the East Cape for reef dives in a protected marine park and the Gordo Banks, where advanced divers with experience in deep dives and strong currents have the opportunity to view hammerheads, whale sharks, and giant mantas, among other pelagics. The dive usually circumnavigates the top of a seamount at a depth of about 41 meters.

DIVE GUIDES AND OUTFITTERS

Just about any local resort or hotel can arrange guided dive trips and equipment rentals for their guests. Some have their own shops on-site, while others book through one of the many independent shops in town. Dive operators typically organize two outings per day, weather permitting. Morning boats leave the harbor around 9 A.M., and the afternoon shift departs around 1 P.M. Mornings tend to be less crowded above and below the surface. In the afternoon, the wind kicks up and boat traffic increases, making water entries and exits a little trickier.

Manta (tel. 624/144-3871, www.cabos-cuba.com) is a professionally run PADI shop conveniently located at Playa El Médano. Its custom-designed 35-foot boat holds 15 divers comfortably; additional 28-foot and 26-foot boats accommodate up to 10 divers each. All three boats are equipped with radios, first-aid kits, and oxygen. For local dives in the Cabo Marine Preserve, advanced and novice divers often share the same boat, but have separate dive guides, since easy and advanced dives start at the same points. (Experienced divers go deeper and stay under longer than beginner groups.) Knowledgeable boat captains and a friendly international guide staff make for a safe and enjoyable dive experience. An earlier morning start at 8:30 A.M. helps avoid the crowds. Rental gear is in good shape, with Sherwood regulators; Aqualung and Genesis BCDs; and Akona, Body Glove, and Scuba Pro wetsuits. In addition to standard 80-cft tanks, smaller (63 cft) and larger (100 cft) sizes are available. A two-tank dive costs US$85.

Underwater Diversions (tel. 624/143-4004, U.S. tel. 949/226-8987, www.dive-cabo.com) is another reputable shop in the Plaza Marina. **Blue Adventures** (U.S. tel. 877/267-8958, www.aventurasazul.com), also in the Plaza Marina, takes divers to sites in the Cabo Marine Preserve and along the Corridor. Longer trips to the Gordo Banks and Cabo Pulmo are also possible. Non-divers can ride along for US$10 with a reservation.

Local dive instructors prefer PADI-certified **Eagle Divers** (Plaza Embarcadero Local 3, tel. 624/125-0008, www.eaglediver.com) for advanced diving. A trip to Gordo Banks runs US$165. This shop also offers scuba courses for kids aged eight and up.

LIVEABOARDS
Amigos del Mar (tel. 624/143-0505, toll-free U.S. tel. 800/344-3349, fax 624/143-0887), next to Solmar Fleet on the west side of the harbor, arranges luxury liveaboard dive trips to the Socorro Islands, Guadalupe Island, Gordo Banks, Los Frailes, El Bajo, Cabo Pulmo, and

other more remote sites aboard the 112-foot *Solmar V* (www.solmarv.com, US$2,100/8 days). The boat holds a maximum of 22 divers and 10 staff members.

Blue Adventure (tel. 624/144-4680, U.S. tel. 877/267-8958, www.aventurasazul.com) also runs custom multiday trips to La Paz, Cabo Pulmo, and Gordo Banks for US$385 per person per day.

SNORKEL TOURS
Pez Gato (Camino Del Cerro 215, El Pedregal, tel. 624/143-3797, www.pezgatocabo.com, daily tours 10 A.M.–2 P.M., US$45) organizes four-hour sail and snorkeling tours to Bahía Santa María, along the Corridor, aboard one of three catamarans. The tour includes two hours of water exploration at Santa María, plus lunch and cold drinks. Kids under 12 are free.

SunRider Adventure (tel. 624/143-2252, U.S. tel. 619/240-8669, www.sunridertours.com) has a 60-foot vessel with a restaurant onboard. A snorkeling lunch tour to Playa Santa María for US$45 per person includes a Mexican buffet and open bar. Cash only.

EQUIPMENT
Most dive shops rent snorkel and dive equipment in packages or à la carte, so if you forget your fins or your mask strap breaks, you'll be able to borrow a replacement for the day. Repairs are a different story, however. If you're bringing your own gear, have it serviced before you leave home; check your computer batteries and bring spare parts. Despite the number of dive shops, replacement parts are difficult, if not impossible, to come by in Baja.

RECOMPRESSION
Clinica de Especialidades (Lopez Mateos btw Morelos/Vicario, tel. 624/143-3914 or 624/143-2919) has a hyperbaric recompression chamber that is available to recreational divers for emergencies.

Surfing
Cabo San Lucas is not a surf destination, though the action isn't far by car. In summer,

there is surf along the Corridor and in winter, the closest action is north along the Pacific near Todos Santos.

Kayaking

Playa El Médano is calm enough most of the time for launching kayaks easily, and you can rent from a number of vendors along the beach for US$10 per person per hour or US$50 for a half-day.

The water is calmest in the morning, and it takes about 40 minutes to get to Playa del Amor, so it's best to get an early start. Beware of larger watercraft on the bay, and if you are a beginning paddler, stick close to the beach, regardless of the conditions.

Boating

The **Cabo San Lucas Marina** (Lote A-18 De la Dársena, tel. 624/173-9140, www.igy-cabo-sanlucas.com) is now owned by Island Global Yachting, a company that develops and manages luxury marinas around the world. Its 380 slips line the inner harbor and can accommodate yachts up to 200 feet in length. Services include 24-hour security, wireless Internet, and a desalination plant for water. There is a swimming pool, laundry facilities, hot showers, storage, a two-lane boat ramp, and state-of-the-art fuel dock with both diesel and gasoline. The on-site boatyard and 75-ton lift can handle just about any standard repair. Rates are US$340 per week or US$1,250 per month for a 20-foot boat, up to US$2,814 per week or US$10,325 per month for a 79-foot boat. Reservations are accepted online. Office hours are Monday–Saturday 9 A.M.–5 P.M., Sunday 10 A.M.–3 P.M.

Cabo San Lucas offers a greater variety of shops, restaurants, and services within walking distance of the marina than the new Puerto Los Cabos marina at La Playita near San José. As an official port of entry into Mexico, Cabo San Lucas has a port captain's office (Calle Matamoros at 16 de Septiembre).

Cape Marine (Plaza Marina, Local J2-3, tel. 624/143-4970, Mon.–Sat. 8 A.M.–6 P.M.) carries hardware, apparel, yachting supplies

one of the Pez Gato catamarans

© NIKKI GOTH ITOI

and tools, and fishing equipment. Credit cards are accepted.

Cruises

An abundance of glass-bottomed tour boats depart frequently from the marina and from Playa El Médano 9 A.M.–4 P.M. each day. The standard 45-minute tour costs US$8–12 per person and covers Pelican Rock, the famous Land's End arch, and the sea lion colony. For no extra charge, the crew will let passengers off at Playa del Amor near the arch; you can flag down any passing boat from the same fleet and catch a ride back to the marina later in the day. Be sure to see the boat you will board before you pay, as engines can be old and unreliable, and you may not get your money back if the trip is aborted due to engine failure. **Dos Mares** (tel. 624/143-4339) is one of the oldest fleet operators; **Esperanza's Fleet** (tel. 624/144-4666, US$12 or US$22 with snorkeling gear rental) is another option.

A handful of larger boats head out of the harbor in the late afternoon to catch the sunset

The *Caborey* cruise ship is available for sunset cruises.

over the Pacific Ocean. The usual route is to head out to the arch and around the point, up as far as the Hotel Solmar and Pueblo Bonito hotels. These sunset cruises usually include all the beer and margaritas you can drink, which can make for an entertaining boat ride. You can make reservations directly through the cruise companies, or at any hotel in town (for no extra charge).

The all-the-margaritas-you-can-drink sunset cruise aboard one of the **Pez Gato** (Camino Del Cerro 215, El Pedregal, tel. 624/143-3797, www.pezgatocabo.com, Mon.–Sat.) catamarans is a memorable experience. The tunes are all from the 1980s—from Toto and Abba to Bon Jovi—and the crowd is a mix of older couples and families. A hard-working staff from the mainland sees that drinks are replenished and no one falls overboard. **Jungle Cruise Tours** (tel. 624/143-7530, www.caboboozecruise.com, US$35 pp) does a similar cruise, except it's adults-only. Boats leave from the marina at 6 P.M. in spring and summer and 5 P.M. in fall and winter.

A larger cruise ship, **Caborey** (tel. 624/143-

8269, U.S. and Canada tel. 866/460-4105, www.caborey.com) runs a dinner cruise for US$89 per person and a margarita cruise with appetizers for US$55.

Two modern-day pirate ships take passengers back to the days when the English stalked the Spanish Manila galleons from hiding spots behind the rocks at Land's End. The 29-meter **Buccaneer Queen** (tel. 624/144-4218, www.buccaneerloscabos.com, US$50–78 pp) races around the bay and heels like it's racing in the America's Cup (passengers must wear life preservers). The **Sunderland** (www.pirateshipcabo.com.mx) is a historic tall ship built in 1885. Tours are family-friendly, except for the loud noise from the cannon.

Whale-Watching

During the winter months, adult and juvenile gray whales entertain resort-goers all along the Los Cabos coast with their spouting and breaching. Many of the glass-bottom boat operators also offer whale-watching cruises to get you a little closer to the action; however, note that these are not the close encounters that you can have in the breeding grounds farther north. If you are determined to touch a whale, you'll need to head to Bahía Magdalena, Laguna San Ignacio, or Laguna Ojo de Liebre near Guerrero Negro.

Swimming with Dolphins

At **Cabo Dolphins** (tel. 624/173-9500, www.cabodolphins.com, Mon.–Fri. 10 A.M., noon, 3 P.M., and 5 P.M., Sat.–Sun. 10 A.M. and noon), you can spend a half-hour swimming alongside playful bottlenose dolphins for US$165 per person. Children under 10 must be accompanied by a paying adult.

ATVs and Personal Watercraft

When you've had enough of the water, you might begin to explore the area's kilometers of open beaches and inland attractions via ATV (not permitted near swimming or turtle-nesting areas). A number of outfitters offer these tours, and any hotel or activity stand along the marina can make a reservation. Current prices are around US$60 per person single/US$80 double. **Baja's Activities** (tel. 624/143-2050, www.bajasactivities.com) has locations at the Presidente InterContinental, Hilton, Tesoro, and Villas de Palmar hotels, plus an outpost on Highway 19 on the way to Playa Migriño. It allows two riders per ATV at a discounted rate.

On a calm day, a WaveRunner or Jet Ski can be a fast and fun way to explore the bay and Playa del Amor, and you don't have to be a speed demon to enjoy the ride. A number of vendors along Playa El Médano offer rentals for around US$70 per hour.

Horseback Riding

Several stables offer horseback tours along Playa El Médano and into the mountains nearby. The going rate is about US$30 per hour. **Red Rose (La Rosa) Riding Stables** (Km 4, across from Cabo San Lucas Country Club, tel. 624/143-4826) offers custom trips and lessons. **Rancho Collins** (Camino Viejo a San José, tel. 624/143-3652, daily 8 A.M.–noon and 2–6 P.M.), across from Club Cascadas, has

45 horses that are healthy and in good shape. Look for a pretty palomino near the road.

Skydiving and Parasailing

Look for **Skydive El Sol** (tel. 624/129-7173, www.skydiveelsol.com, daily year-round), a relative newcomer to Cabo San Lucas, near Club Cascadas on Playa El Médano, where the going rate is US$250 for a tandem jump that includes one minute of freefall time. Plan on a two-hour outing, from start to finish. For an additional US$130, you can return home with a video and photographs of the entire experience. Skydive El Sol needs at least two jumpers to book a trip.

The *Caborey* luxury cruise ship (tel. 624/143-8260, www.caborey.com) offers parasailing trips at a rate of US$35 for an eight- to ten-minute ride.

Golf

Just beyond the Cabo San Lucas city limits, the 300-hectare **Cabo San Lucas Country Club** (501 Palo Blanco, tel. 624/143-4653 or -4654, U.S. tel. 888/298-1132, www.golfincabo.com, US$105–204) is one of the more reasonably priced courses in Los Cabos. There are many other more exclusive and more expensive options along the Corridor.

Yoga

Cabo Mind Body Fitness offers Pilates and Bikram yoga sessions in the privacy of your own villa, but prices are correspondingly steep: Pilates sessions run US$125–225 per person per hour (or US$45 per person per hour for groups of seven or more). Yoga classes cost US$110–160 per person per hour (or US$30 per person for groups of 10 or more). Discounts apply for pairs and triples too, so it pays to buddy up. Visit www.cabovillas.com for details.

Spa Services

Most of the larger Cabo resorts have their own spas on-site. One of the nicest is the **Armonia Spa** (tel. 624/142-9696, www.pueblobonito.com) at the Pueblo Bonito Pacifica resort, which offers 50-minute massage treatments for

US$110. Choices include hot stone, Shiatsu, four hands, deep tissue, Swedish, and pregnancy massage. Located in the basement of the hotel, the spa setting is a bit cave-like, but quiet and peaceful with a friendly and professional staff. The find the resort and spa, follow the main street through Cabo San Lucas (Lazaro Cardenas), past the plaza and up the hill. The road will curve to the right and back to the left, and the name will change to Boulevard Herrera. Keep going up the hill about a kilometer and a half until you reach a stop sign with the Pueblo Bonito entrance and sign on the left. Currently, the sign says Pueblo Bonito Sunset Beach, but this is also the entrance for the Pueblo Bonito Pacifica.

ENTERTAINMENT AND EVENTS

With an emphasis on booze and music, Cabo nightlife begins early and ends late. On any given night, there are dozens of options for entertainment. The drinking begins at the bars along the marina and moves to the dance clubs around midnight. The clubs stay open until 3 or 4 A.M., at which point the party moves to any hotel that will tolerate the noise.

Bars

You won't have any trouble finding a watering hole in Cabo—there are far too many for a comprehensive list here. One of the most famous is the **Giggling Marlin** (Matamoros at Blvd. Marina, tel. 624/100-6956, www.gigglingmarlin.com) with a nightly dance show and signature block-and-tackle hoist from which well-imbibed patrons hang upside down, like hooked marlins. **Carlos'n Charlie's** (Blvd. Marina, tel. 624/143-1280, daily 11 A.M.–midnight, mains US$10–20) is a tourist-oriented chain with a popular bar and decent Mexican food.

Among the row of bars and restaurants along the marina in Plaza Bonita, **The Nowhere Bar** (tel. 624/143-4493, www.nowherebar.com, daily 11 A.M.–1 A.M., margaritas US$5) is a popular stop, especially during March madness NCAA basketball championships. At

happy hour (5–9 P.M.), you'll get two drinks (served in glasses, not plastic) for the price of one, whether you need them or not.

For a taste of Manhattan, **Red** (Zaragoza, around the corner from Squid Roe, tel. 624/143-5645, Mon.–Sat. 6 P.M.–3 A.M.) is an open-air wine and martini lounge.

At **Hemingway's** (Guerrero btw Cardenas/Madero, tel. 624/143-9845, www.jnjhabanos.com), you can order a sip of tequila for US$150 (the bottle costs more than US$1,000). Or the knowledgeable bartenders can help you taste a variety of high-end tequilas in the range of US$7–10 per taste. There are more than 345 tequilas from which to choose. The immense walk-in humidor has a full selection of Cuban cigars from Cohiba, Montecristo, and Partagas. A cigar roller, or *torcedor,* rolls well-made cigars for US$11–15.

Fumari Café Hookah Bar (Lázaro Cardénas across from the Paraíso mall, Mon.–Thurs. 4–11 P.M., Fri.–Sat. 4 P.M.–2 A.M., drinks US$2–4) is a cozy second-story café with several tables inside and a large roof deck outside. Curl up on a sofa and play a game of chess while you smoke a flavored hookah (US$13) or sip a chai tea.

Friday is tango night at super-chic **Barometro** (tel. 624/143-1466, daily 10 P.M.–2 A.M.) on the Plaza Marina.

For nightly jazz music, try **Edith's** (tel. 624/143-0801, www.edithscabo.com, daily 6 P.M.–1 A.M.), a block from Playa El Médano on the west side of Camino de los Pescadores.

Dance Clubs

Cabo's discos are empty before 11 P.M. and packed from midnight on. Among them all, none embodies the party-till-you-drop Cabo spirit better than **El Squid Roe** (Lázaro Cárdenas at Zaragoza, tel. 624/143-0655). Giant margaritas and piña coladas appear two at a time to set the mood. Balloons and confetti fall from the sky, while staff and patrons climb on tables, form 50-person centipedes, and whoop it up on the dance floor.

Rock'n'Roll music artist Sammy Hagar celebrated his 60th birthday in 2008 by performing at the club he owns, **Cabo Wabo** (Guerrero btw Madero/Lázaro Cárdenas, tel. 624/143-1188, www.cabowabo.com, daily 7 P.M.–2 A.M.). Open since 1992, the club plays recorded and live music. The birthday performance is an annual tradition, and Hagar often makes a New Year's Eve appearance as well.

Among the newer clubs targeting a younger crowd is **Zoo Bar & Dance** (Blvd. Marina across from Plaza Bonita, tel. 624/143-5500, daily 9 P.M.–4 A.M.).

Cinema

On the second floor of the Puerto Paraíso mall, **Cinema Paraíso** (tel. 624/143-1515) with 10 theaters shows a mix of blockbusters and independent films from Mexico, the United States, and elsewhere around the world. The VIP area has comfortable reclining leather seats.

Festivals and Events

Bike races, fishing tournaments, music festivals, and national holidays are just a few of the gatherings that take place in Cabo San Lucas each year. The Los Cabos Guide (www.loscabosguide.com) has the most up-to-date listing of events online. The largest of the fishing tournaments is **Bisbee's Black and Blue Marlin Jackpot Tournament** (tel. 624/143-1622, www.bisbees.com), held for three days each October.

The **San Lucas Fiesta** takes place on October 18 and includes a traditional mix of music, dancing, crafts, and foods.

SHOPPING

The streets of Cabo are chockablock with places to buy souvenirs, apparel, fine art, tequila, cigars, and more. A number of new, upscale shops line the Plaza Fiesta, near the Marina Fiesta hotel, and most of the luxury stores inside the Puerto Paraíso mall are open for business.

Arts, Crafts, and Souvenirs

Across from the main dock, the **Marina Mercado** (Cabo San Lucas Marina, Lot 4, daily 9 A.M.–5 P.M.) is an arts and crafts market with

© KATHRYN LATENDRESSE

hand-embroidered dresses on display at the Marina Mercado

dozens of vendors selling embroidered dresses, carved ironwood figures, ceramics, and jewelry. Sellers expect to bargain. Inquire about prices at several places before you decide to buy.

Taxco (Guerrero and Blvd. Marina, tel. 624/143-0551, daily 9 A.M.–6 P.M.) has a good selection of silver jewelry. **Joyería Albert** (Matamoros btw Niños Héroes and Lázaro Cárdenas, daily 9 A.M.–6 P.M.) is a satellite of a well-regarded Puerto Vallarta jeweler.

Dos Lunas (Plaza Bonita and Puerto Paraíso locations, tel. 624/143-1969, daily 9 A.M.–6 P.M.), has pretty sundresses, handbags, and the like, and **Cartes** (tel. 624/143-1770, Mon.–Sat. 9 A.M.–9 P.M., Sun. 9 A.M.–4 P.M.) carries rustic furniture, Talavera pottery, and classy accents for the home.

Across from Mi Mariscos restaurant at the corner of Paseo a la Marina and Camino Viejo a San José, **Chile & Anis** (tel. 624/143-7454, Mon.–Sat. 9 A.M.–8 P.M.) is a Baja arts and crafts store with silver jewelry, wood crafts, mirrors, and ceramics for sale. Upscale crafts line the shelves of **Mi Mexico Magico** (Loc. 52, tel. 624/143-5153, daily 8 A.M.–9 P.M.) in the Marina Fiesta plaza.

Puerto Paraíso

Upscale Puerto Paraíso (tel. 624/144-3000, www.puertoparaiso.com), a shopping mall on the east side of the marina, is the first of its kind in Southern Baja. Most stores are now open, and the mall contains a mix of luxury boutiques, international chains, and entertainment venues. You'll find everything from Sergio Bustamante artwork to Diamonds International, and many familiar brands such as Tumi, Kenneth Cole, and Nautica. There is even a Curves exercise center. Food options include Ruth's Chris Steak House, Häagen-Dazs, Houlihan's, and Johnny Rockets. There is also a bowling alley on the third level. Clean public restrooms and underground parking are added conveniences.

Fine Art Galleries

In the lobby of the Tesoro Los Cabos Hotel, a photography gallery displays prints by

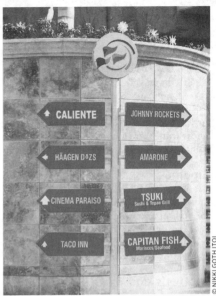

Puerto Paraíso shopping mall

Tomas Spangler (www.fotomas.com), whose work depicts images and scenes unique to the Baja Peninsula. A representative is available Monday–Saturday 10 A.M.–2 P.M.

Golden Cactus Gallery (Guerrero and Madero, tel. 604/628-2233 or 624/143-6399, www.goldencactusgallery.com) features the works of artist Chris MacClure in a second-story studio. MacClure's work captures local Baja imagery, and he has created commissioned paintings of yachts, airplanes, and the like for celebrity clients including John Travolta.

Cigars

Many stores sell Cuban cigars in Los Cabos, but fakes are rampant. Buy from a reputable merchant if you want the real thing. And remember, Cubans never go on sale. **La Casa del Habano** (formerly J&J Habanos, Blvd. Marina near Madero, tel. 624/143-6160 or 877/305-6242, www.jnjhabanos.com) has a walk-in humidor and a few tables inside. Prices are steep, but you can be confident that you're getting what you pay for. The owners have also opened a new cigar bar called **Hemingway's** (tel. 624/143-9845, www.jnjhabanos.com) across from the entrance to Cabo Wabo.

Wine and Liquor

La Europea (tel. 624/145-8755, Mon.–Fri. 9 A.M.–8 P.M., Sat. 9 A.M.–9 P.M.) has opened a small street-level store in the Puerto Paraíso complex. This satellite of the larger, main store on the Corridor has the best selection and most competitive prices on wines from around the world, plus a fairly complete list of liquors and gourmet foods.

Sporting Goods

Head to **Cabo Sports Center** (Plaza Náutica, tel. 624/143-4272, daily 9 A.M.–7 P.M.) for beach gear, water shoes, and basic supplies for golf, swimming, surfing, snorkeling, boogie-boarding, and mountain biking. **Minerva's Baja Tackle** (Blvd. Marina at Madero, tel. 624/143-1282, Mon.–Sat. 9 A.M.–7 P.M.), next door to Pisces Fleet, is the one-stop shop for lures and tackle.

Books and Magazines

Cabo San Lucas does not have a dedicated English-language bookstore; however, several shops in town stock a few titles. They include **Minerva's Baja Tackle** (tel. 624/143-1282, www.minervas.com) for fishing books, and **Bahías Jiromar** (Puerto Paraíso Local #284, tel. 624/144-3250) for newspapers, magazines, and some books. In addition, most of the larger resorts carry at least a few pocket fiction titles.

ACCOMMODATIONS AND CAMPING

You can find just about any type of accommodations in Cabo San Lucas, from simple and reasonably priced motels to boutique inns and luxury resorts. There are condos and villas for rent as well. The one exception is camping, for which there are relatively limited options. Most visitors prefer to stay at the beach, but the better values are downtown or on the outskirts of town, away from the water.

Downtown and Marina

UNDER US$50

Near the bus terminal, **Hotel Casa Blanca** (Revolución at Morelos, tel. 624/143-5360, US$45–50) has 20 recently updated rooms with king-size beds and air-conditioning. In the same vicinity, **Olas Hotel** (Revolución at Gómez Farías, tel. 624/143-1780, fax 624/143-1380, US$55) feels more like a hostel, with 35 rooms (some with one king-size bed, others with two single beds). Amenities include cable TV, fan, fridge, microwave, and patio. Budget travelers might also check out relative newcomer **Hotel Oasis** (US$35–45), across from the CCC (Centro Comercial California) on the west side of Mexico 19 just north of the junction with Mexico 1.

US$50-100

City Siesta (formerly Hotel Dos Mares, Zapata, btw Hidalgo and Guerrero, tel. 624/143-0330, reservationscitysiesta@hotmail.com, US$55–69) has 37 guestrooms with air-conditioning, TV, and phone. Amenities include a swimming pool, Wi-Fi, and parking.

You can easily walk to the marina and the Puerto Paraíso mall from the two-story **Cabo Inn Hotel** (20 de Noviembre btw Vicario/Mendoza, tel. 624/143-0819, U.S. tel. 619/819-2727, www.caboinnhotel.com, US$58–120), but with the central location comes a whole lot of noise, and readers have shared disappointing experiences in staying here. Here are some factors to consider before you book: Its 22 rooms are mostly small and dark, especially the ones without windows. Beds have foam mattresses and baths have curtains instead of doors. Air-conditioners are old and often loud. Some rooms have refrigerators. Two rooftop *palapa* rooms give travelers a sense of the real Baja; one has its own whirlpool tub and both come with bug nets over the beds. There is a full kitchen and shared TV in the common area, as well as a very tiny "social" pool. The managers do ask guests to adhere to a number of house rules, which are reasonable, but the tone in which they are presented may not sit well with some travelers.

LOS CABOS TIMESHARES

Few visitors board their flight to Los Cabos intending to buy a timeshare. Yet the timeshare market is booming as the destination evolves. Timeshares now command higher prices and higher occupancy rates than hotels. Nearly six million people now participate in fractional ownership vacation models (also called vacation clubs), and they spend US$1 billion a year on their condos and villas. How do so many travelers come to change their minds between arrival and departure?

LOS CABOS IS A BEAUTIFUL PLACE

It's a lot easier to pack up and head home when you know you can return again and again.

THE PITCH IS ALL AROUND

Timeshare salespeople disguise themselves as activities coordinators, concierges, restaurant hosts, rental car agency staff, and even grocery store clerks. Their goal is to draw unsuspecting visitors into a friendly conversation – *Is this your first time in Los Cabos? Where are you staying? Would you like to go whale-watching today? Can I help you find the sugar?* – and then invite them to a 90-minute presentation over breakfast in exchange for any number of giveaways. With prices ranging US$15,000-25,000, "owning" a timeshare in a world-class destination can be an attractive proposition. Why not hear what they have to say?

THE FREEBIES ARE ENTICING

Salespeople may offer US$200 in cash, free whale-watching or snorkeling tours, sunset horseback rides, restaurant coupons, and more. The deal gets better the longer you resist. Not a bad way to finance part of your trip if you don't mind giving up part of a day.

Everyone thinks they can work the system, and many who participate in a presentation do resist the temptation to buy. Some even sign up for a second pitch on their next visit. But here's the catch:

TIMESHARES ARE NOT REAL ESTATE

They are vacations. When you buy a timeshare, you prepay for vacations at a discounted rate. If you like the idea of returning to a familiar place in Los Cabos for one or two weeks each year, this model can make a lot of sense.

The owner has installed wireless Internet throughout the property. Credit cards are accepted for advanced reservations only; you'll need cash if you show up unannounced.

A much better deal in this category is the ▧ **Siesta Suites Hotel** (Zapata btw Guerrero/Hidalgo, tel. 624/143-2773, U.S. tel. 866/271-0952, www.cabosiestasuites.com, US$69), which completed a top-to-bottom remodel in 2007. Highlights include granite counters, new bath fixtures, and new queen beds. In business since 1992, it is owned by a couple originally from Southern California who converted an old apartment building into the hotel. Several of Cabo's best restaurants are steps away. The hotel has 15 suites with kitchenettes (including microwaves and toaster ovens) and separate bedrooms and five hotel-style rooms. All are air-conditioned and come with satellite TV. Repeat guests enjoy the sundeck, BBQ, and "social" pool; secured parking is another plus. Wi-Fi for guests costs a one-time US$5 fee, and several PCs in the lobby are available to guests and the public for US$3 an hr. Salvatore's Italian Restaurant now offers rooftop dining under a *palapa* roof on the top floor of the hotel.

The **Hotel Los Arcos** (Vicario and Revolución, tel. 624/143-0702, hotelplazalosarcos@hotmail.com, US$55) opened in December 2005 with 32 clean rooms in a two-story building with cable TV, air-conditioning, and wireless Internet.

The centrally located and well-worn **Hotel Mar de Cortez** (Blvd. Lázaro Cárdenas at Guerrero, tel. 624/143-0032, toll-free U.S. tel. 800/347-8821, www.mardecortez.com, US$60–80) has seen better days, but it is much-

IT'S HARD TO SAY NO

Sales reps choreograph every aspect of the pitch, from the upbeat music to the champagne and cheers of congratulations echoing around the room. They face intense pressure to sell, so if the first approach doesn't win you over, there will be one or two more pitches as you attempt to leave the room. (Biannual weeks? Off-season weeks? Trial membership? Free Jet Ski tour? Take our survey before you go?) As prices come down, the deal gets sweeter, and suddenly you either begin to feel guilty for accepting all the freebies or you think you're crazy for not taking advantage now that you've negotiated the terms so low. Bottom line: That 90-minute breakfast presentation could result in a US$10,000 charge on your credit card.

YOU MAY NOT GET WHAT YOU PAID FOR

Timeshare developments typically begin selling when construction has just begun – sometimes they don't get finished, or when they do, they don't always shape up as promised. Stories abound of frustrated timeshare purchasers who don't get the weeks they originally bought, or whose reservations seem to get lost every time they book. Services may not be available as promised, and the quality of the accommodations may change as the years go by.

Also, because timeshare owners aren't year-round residents, they usually lack both a sense of community and a sense of responsibility toward the local environment. For the developer, timeshares mean huge profits, as the same space is sold repeatedly in one-week segments. Because land in Baja is relatively inexpensive, considering the charming scenery and climate, it seems to attract get-rich-quick developers who show a decided lack of respect for the fragile Baja environment.

PROCEED WITH CAUTION

Timeshares are not all bad, and attending a presentation may be a worthwhile experience for a variety of reasons. Just be sure you know what's coming before you give away any of your precious vacation time. And don't buy without considering all the options.

---

loved by its loyal patrons, many of whom return for the same week year after year, and still manages to stay full in the high season. Its *muy tranquilo* setting provides a welcome respite from the noisy, crowded streets of downtown Cabo San Lucas—yet puts guests conveniently close to all the action (except the beach, which is a 20-minute walk). Clean, air-conditioned rooms each have one queen and one twin bed, some with a bit of a slope, and dimly lighted baths. There are no TVs and no phones. Guests can enjoy the small pool and patio area, which are shaded by date palms, or dine in the on-site restaurant and outdoor bar.

Friendly and attentive service makes for a memorable stay at 🄲 **Los Milagros Hotel** (Matamoros 116, tel. 624/143-4566, U.S. tel. 718/928-6647, www.losmilagros.com.mx, US$75–115), which has a dozen large rooms with air-conditioning and private baths; a few rooms include kitchenettes as well. There is a cactus garden on the roof, a tiny pool in the courtyard, and free Wi-Fi.

Now owned by The Villa Group (www.villagroupresorts.com), **Hotel Santa Fe** (southwest corner of Zaragoza and Obregón, tel. 624/143-4401, U.S. tel. 877/845-5247, gerenciasantafe@prodigy.net.mx, US$74–95) is a well-maintained property with 46 studios surrounding a pool. Each studio has a sliding glass door, tile floor, recently renovated bath, kitchenette, and relatively new furnishings, as well as air-conditioning, satellite TV, and phone. Amenities include wireless Internet, off-street parking, 24-hour security, a small counter restaurant with outdoor seating (daily 7 A.M.–7 P.M.), laundry, and a mini-super (daily 7 A.M.–7 P.M.). A free beach shuttle service is provided.

One block off the marina on the second floor of Plaza de la Danza, **Viva Cabo Hotel** (Blvd. Marina, Plaza La Danza, tel./fax 624/143-5810, US$90–100) has eight studios, each with two double beds or one king, kitchenette, air-conditioning, and satellite TV. Guests have access to a pool and fitness center next door.

On the east side of the marina, next to the Marina Fiesta Hotel, between downtown and the beach, the **Marina Cabo Plaza** condominium hotel (Marina Blvd. 39, tel. 624/143-1833, US$100/day or US$700/week) has 63 rooms with tiled floors and balconies with impressive views of the marina below. Guests share a swimming pool.

It's impossible to miss the sprawling **Tesoro Los Cabos Hotel** (tel. 624/173-9300 or 800/716-8770, toll-free U.S. tel. 800/543-7556, www.tesororesorts.com, US$165–176 European plan or US$183–194 American plan) on the west side of the marina. It is the most basic all-inclusive resort you'll find in Los Cabos. All 286 rooms have air-conditioning, phone, and refrigerator, and the hotel has a beach club on Playa El Medano.

Not quite as large as the Tesoro, but still an imposing presence on the marina, is the **Marina Fiesta Resort & Hotel** (tel. 624/145-6020, U.S. tel. 866/998-3767, www.marinafiestaresort.com, US$200–330). This property gets high marks for a central location, but the noise coming from nearby bars and round-the-clock construction has bothered many recent guests. Amenities include a swimming pool and views of the marina, but guestrooms could use a cosmetic overhaul. The timeshare pitch comes on strong from the moment you walk in the door. The resort seems overpriced at its current rates.

US$150-250

Elegant 【 **Casa Bella** (Hidalgo 10, tel. 624/143-6400, U.S. tel. 626/209-0215, www.casabellahotel.com, Oct. 1–July 31, US$160–190) brings a San José del Cabo feel to downtown Cabo San Lucas. Its 11 rooms are set in a restored colonial-style home across from the town square and Mi Casa restaurant. Rooms have ornate wooden doors, antique-style furnishings, oversized tiled showers, and remote-

© KATHRYN LATENDRESSE

Casa Bella balcony

control air-conditioning. An enclosed patio has a small pool with several chaise lounges. You will be hard-pressed to find this kind of intimacy and elegance so close to the marina and nightlife anywhere else in town.

Playa El Médano
US$50-100

East along Playa El Médano, and set back a ways from the beach, clean and cozy **Club Cabo Hotel and Campground Resort** (tel./fax 624/143-3348, www.clubcaboinn.com, US$65–95) is also dog-friendly. It has a handful of suites and bungalows, some with *palapa* roofs, all with air-conditioning and king-size beds. Owners Irene and Martin Rozendaal, a Mexican and Dutch husband-and-wife team, have been in business since 1992. Their property borders the only remaining expanse of mesquite forest in the area, which is also a bird sanctuary. On the grounds are laundry machines, a large fridge for storing freshly caught fish, and a swimming pool with an attached whirlpool tub. The hotel provides wireless Internet and a shuttle to town (a 15–20 minute walk).

Once a single-family residence, **Casa Rafael's** (Pescador at El Médano, tel. 624/143-0739, www.casarafaels.com, US$75–100) has been expanded over the years to encompass 10 rooms above a public restaurant on the main level. The aquamarine building is just a couple of blocks from the beach. You'll be greeted by Spanish-speaking parrots and a friendly staff. A recent problem for all hotels in this area has been the construction next door of the Casa del Dorado building, which was nearly complete at press time.

US$150-250

Families particularly like **Villa del Palmar Cabo Beach Resort & Spa** (Km 0.5, tel. 624/145-7000, U.S. tel. 877/845-5247, www.villadelpalmarloscabos.com, junior suites US$200–400 inc. tax, three-night minimum), with 458 junior suites and one- to three-bedroom oceanview deluxe suites. Each unit has a kitchenette, marble bath, and balcony. There are two pools (one with a bar), two lighted tennis courts, a fitness center, and restaurants. Some units are available only by the week. The on-site Spa at Villa del Palmar offers individual and package treatments in a European-style spa.

OVER US$250

Next door to the Villa del Palmar, **Villa La Estancia** (Km 0.5 Camino Viejo a San José, tel. 624/143-8121, U.S. tel. 619/683-7883, www.villalaestancia.com) has 156 units ranging in size from one bedroom (US$550–650) to three bedrooms, as well as standard guestrooms (US$301–370) and junior suites. Brand new **Villa del Arco** (tel. 624/145-7000, U.S. tel. 888/880-8512, www.villadelarcocabo.com, US$250–400) has three buildings with junior suites, as well as one- and two-bedroom units. Prices at both of these resorts include tax, and there is a three-night minimum.

The **ME Cabo** (Playa El Médano, tel. 624/145-7800, U.S. tel. 800/336-3542, www.solmelia.com, US$335–796) is a Spanish-owned Sol Meliá property with 88 recently remodeled rooms and suites built in a horseshoe shape around a large pool and patio area. Distinctive touches include an adults-only floor, free preloaded iPods, and home theaters. Most rooms have ocean views.

The Pueblo Bonito chain has four properties in Cabo San Lucas. The original **Pueblo Bonito Los Cabos** (tel. 624/142-9797, toll-free U.S. tel. 800/990-8250, www.pueblo-bonito-loscabos.com, US$400 and up) is a white adobe, five-story building designed in a Mediterranean theme. From the tiles on the roof to the chaise lounges, blue and white form the dominant color scheme. Its 148 junior and luxury suites surround an attractive freeform swimming pool. Room features include kitchenettes and views of the bay.

Farther away from downtown along the beach, the **Pueblo Bonito Rosé** (tel. 624/142-9898, toll-free U.S. tel. 800/990-8250, www.pueblobonito-rose.com, US$400 and up) has a striking Baroque-themed lobby, but its 260 suites leave less of a dramatic impression. Not-especially-new rooms have decent beds, private balconies, and hand-painted terra-cotta floors.

About five kilometer east of Cabo San Lucas, beachfront **Riu Palace** (Km 5.5, Camino Viejo a San José, tel. 624/146-7160, U.S. tel. 888/666-8816, www.riu.com, US$248–310) comprises a town unto itself, with 642 guestrooms—booked almost all of the time, according to travel agents—and all-inclusive (only) meal plans. Part of a large international hotel chain, the lively Riu has so many dining and entertainment options that many guests never leave the resort during their visit. Rates include taxes.

Pacific Beach
US$150-250

One of the oldest hotels in Cabo, the **Hotel Finisterra** (tel. 624/143-3333, toll-free U.S. tel. 800/347-2252, www.finisterra.com, US$175–225) stands on a ridge overlooking the Pacific Ocean. There are two parts to this resort: an original building built into the hillside but set back from the beach,

and two newer towers collectively called the Palapa Beach Club, which are on the beach and overlook the pool. A well-equipped business center makes for a comfortable office away from home. It has leather chairs, five flat-screen TVs, and several Dell computer stations. Wireless Internet costs US$10 a day. A 1,040-square-meter swimming pool with whirlpools and swim-up bar sits on the beach at the foot of the Palapa Beach Club. Beds are on the firm side, and there are a variety of views on the older Finisterra side of the resort. Be sure to request city, marina, garden, or ocean views when you book. Guests can use lighted tennis courts, sauna, and swimming pool. There is a spa and wedding chapel on-site.

Another historic property close to Land's End is the **Hotel Solmar Suites** (tel. 624/143-3535, U.S. tel. 310/459-9861 or 800/344-3349, www.solmar.com, US$189–330), which features 180 rooms and suites on the beach with separate timeshare/condo units overlooking the beach. An older section of units directly on

Condominiums can be a budget-friendly lodging option for small groups and families staying in Cabo San Lucas.

© NIKKI GOTH ITOI

the beach has lower ceilings and less natural light; newer units are set back from the sand but have high ceilings, better lighting, and newer furnishings. Amenities include tennis courts, an aquatic center, and two heated pools with swim-up bars and hot tubs. The hotel's La Roca restaurant (daily 6 A.M.–10 P.M., mains US$6–15) cooks your fish any way you like it. The Solmar is well known among anglers for its fishing fleet and among divers for its luxury liveaboard boat, the *Solmar V* (www.solmarv.com).

OVER US$250

Open since 2002, the **Pueblo Bonito at Sunset Beach** (Cabo Pacifica, tel. 624/142-9999, toll-free U.S. tel. 800/990-8250, www.pueblobonitosunsetbeach.com, US$394–550) has 327 suites on a 20-hectare hillside overlooking the Pacific, behind the Pedregal development. Amenities include a hilltop "sky pool," a main pool that overlooks the beach, tennis courts, and a free shuttle into town (drop off at the Pueblo Bonito Blanco on Playa Medano). Fitness facilities cost extra (US$15/day) and massages run a steep US$130 at the Spa at Sunset Beach (daily 8 A.M.–7 P.M.). Two-for-one happy hour lasts exactly one hour, so it's best to load up on beverages during that time. Eat tacos and chicken sandwiches and the like poolside, or enjoy sushi in the bistro.

In the vicinity, the newest Pueblo Bonito property, **Pueblo Bonito Pacifica** (Cabo Pacifica, tel. 624/142-9696, toll-free U.S. tel. 800/990-8250, www.pueblobonitopacifica.com, US$400–494), opened in 2005. Couples in search of a romantic getaway like the no-kids factor at this boutique-style resort. Its 154 rooms, including 14 suites, are appointed in minimalist fashion, with a sand and ivory color scheme. Those who want a little more nightlife find the location a bit too remote. Strolling along the beach is discouraged due to heavy surf; you can, however, rent a bed on the beach for US$20 an hour. There is a free shuttle to town, or cabs for US$10 one-way. Meals at **Siempre,** the resort's main restaurant, are pricey, and food quality gets mixed reviews.

The on-site **Armonia Spa** offers a variety of massage treatments, including hot stone, Shiatsu, four hands, deep tissue, Swedish, and pregnancy massage (US$100 for 50 minutes).

To get to any of the Cabo Pacifica resorts, including the forthcoming Ritz-Carlton Quivira, follow Lázaro Cardenas, the main boulevard through town, west past the Plaza Amelia Wilkes, until it curves to the right and becomes Herrera. Go through a traffic circle and continue following this street around a few "S"-turns and up the hill toward the Pacific Ocean. Along the way, two blue-and-white signs indicate the way to Cabo Pacifica. At the stop sign, turn left into the driveway that says Pueblo Bonito Sunset Beach. This is the entrance for all of the Cabo Pacifica resorts at this time. Tell the attendant at the gate which resort you want to visit, and then proceed along a long, landscaped boulevard that descends down the ridge to the resorts and beach below.

Bed-and-Breakfasts
US$50-100

A few blocks from the town center, **Casa Pablito Bed and Breakfast Hotel** (Hidalgo and Ortega, tel. 624/143-1971, U.S. tel. 866/444-1139, www.casapablitoloscabos.com, US$90–110) is a new property opened by the owner of Club Cascadas. Originally built to house employees of the condo resort, the building has been converted into a traditional Mexican hacienda-style inn with 14 suites set around a pool and *palapa*-shaded breakfast area. Rooms have either one queen or two twin beds, plus kitchenettes, air-conditioning, and cable TV. This location will work for you if you don't mind a fairly long walk to most of the shops and restaurants downtown.

US$100-150

Another place that's removed from most of the action downtown is **The Bungalows Breakfast Inn** (Dorado and Lienzo Charro, tel. 624/143-5035, U.S. tel. 888/424-2226, www.cabobungalows.com, US$135–185), a good option for small groups, or any travelers who like to stay off the beaten path. Its eight suites have separate sleeping areas, air-conditioning, kitchenettes, and TVs. A honeymoon suite has its own terrace with city views. Six two-bedroom bungalows, can accommodate 4–6 guests each. There's no smoking, inside or out. The small but nicely designed grounds hold a swimming pool, hot tub, and BBQ. Full breakfast is a treat to start the day. Guests here unanimously praise owner Eric for his personal service and attention to detail.

US$150-250

About one and a half kilometers east of Cabo San Lucas and 800 meters above Mexico 1, **Casa Contenta** (tel. 624/143-6038, www.cabocasacontenta.com, US$160–195/day or US$1,050–1,300/week) has five air-conditioned rooms with private baths in a three-story home with a swimming pool and wireless Internet throughout. Take a yoga class, book a spa treatment, or simply enjoy the view of Land's End on the rooftop terrace. There's a three-night minimum.

Condominiums and Condo Hotels

Condos are a good deal for families and small groups because you don't pay for the overhead of resort services and amenities and you can cook some or all of your meals yourself. Some condos take reservations directly, while others have booking services (some do both). And many different property management companies may have listings in the same complex. Rates do not include tax and service unless otherwise noted.

US$100-150

Bahía Condo Hotel (tel. 624/143-1888, toll-free U.S. tel. 800/932-5599, www.grupobahia.com, US$129–149), just off Camino de los Pescadores above Playa El Médano, has lost most of its ocean views due to construction of the El Dorado complex right in front. Its studios feel more like basic hotel rooms than condos, but for the price, you can't beat the proximity to the beach and friendly service. Units have minimally equipped kitchenettes, air-conditioning, satellite TV, and direct-dial

phones. Giant sculpted concrete shells frame the beds as headboards, and bamboo doors enclose the bathroom and closet. Faucets and tiling have aged a bit. The property includes laundry facilities, a decent restaurant, pool with hot tub and swim-up *palapa* bar, and free parking in a gated lot. Rates here include tax. Like many affordable Cabo San Lucas locations, the place is overrun with college students on spring break during the month of March.

Close to downtown but also within easy walking distance of Playa El Médano, **Marina Sol Condominiums** (tel. 624/143-3231, U.S. tel. 877/255-1721, www.marinasolresort.com) has basic one- and two-bedroom condos arranged around a pretty courtyard and swimming pool. A wheelchair-accessible room is available. The lobby has several independently operated businesses, including a convenience store, day spa, and laundry service.

US$150-250

Part of the Trading Places International network of timeshares, **Club Cascadas de Baja** (Camino Viejo a San José, tel. 624/143-1882, toll-free U.S. tel. 800/365-9190 ext. 400, www.clubcascadasdebaja.com, one bedroom US$199–525), at the east end of El Médano, has 110 thatched-roof villas, plus two swimming pools and tennis courts. You can make reservations online.

Near Edith's on Camino de los Pescadores and a short walk up from Playa El Médano, **Cabo Villas** (tel. 624/143-9166, fax 624/143-2558, cabovillasresort@prodigy.net.mx, US$180–330) has one-bedroom, one-bath units and two-bedroom, two-bath units in two white towers.

Next door to the Hotel Solmar and walking distance to the beach, **Terrasol Condominiums** (tel. 624/143-1803, toll-free U.S. tel. 800/524-5104, www.terrasolcabo.com, one bedroom US$130–250) has studio, one-bedroom, and two-bedroom units. Each has a full kitchen, ocean view, and wireless Internet access. Amenities include two pools, a tennis court, a swim-up bar, and a snack bar.

Luxury Villas

As the new Pedregal development takes shape on the west side of town, a number of large, luxury beach homes have come on the rental market in Cabo San Lucas. Ranging in size from two to five or more bedrooms, these townhouses or private homes accommodate small groups with a creative list of in-villa services. For an extra fee, the property manager will stock your villa prior to your arrival with the foods and supplies you request. (You can also head to Costco and buy w hat you want when you get there.) Guests may schedule Pilates or yoga classes, spa treatments, and chef services (one special meal or three meals daily). Prices start at about US$1,500 per night for a three-bedroom villa.

Booking Services and Property Management Companies

Delfin Hotels & Resorts (toll-free U.S. tel. 800/524-5104) has condos in the Terrasol complex. It also books for Casa Contenta B&B and most of the all-inclusive resorts. **Cabo Villa Rentals** (U.S. tel. 877/473-1946, www.cabovillarentals.com, daily 8:30 A.M.–5 P.M.) manages condos in the Terrasol and Villa La Estancia complexes and three- to five-bedroom villas in the Pedregal development. **Earth, Sea, and Sky Vacations** (toll-free U.S. tel. 800/745-2226, www.cabovillas.com) represents 90 luxury villa rentals, ranging from two- to nine-bedroom units, with a starting price of US$1,500 per night, as well as 30 resorts. **Pedregal Escapes** (Camino de La Plaza 145, Fraccionamiento Pedregal, tel. 624/144-3222, www.pedregalescapes.com) is the vacation rental division of the company that developed the Pedregal gated community on the west side of Cabo San Lucas. It manages two- to five-bedroom villas, plus even a few larger homes. Prices start at about US$450 per night, and some properties require a security deposit.

Camping and RV Parks

Three kilometers northeast of Cabo San Lucas off Mexico 1, the Mexican-owned **Vagabundos del Mar RV Park** (Km 3, tel. 624/143-0290, www.vagabundosrv.com) has 52 slots with full hookups but no dump station. Rates are US$22 per day or US$130 per week, with a 10 percent discount for members of the Vagabundos del Mar travel club. The park is not on the beach; however, campers return year after year to enjoy the peaceful surroundings, comfortably away from the frenzy of activity in downtown Cabo San Lucas. There are four double-size pull-through spaces, and more than half of the spaces are designated annual rentals with *palapas.* Book early if you want to get a spot at this popular park. No caravans. Facilities include a restaurant, bar, flush toilets, *palapas,* showers, a pool, and new laundry machines.

In the same vicinity, the campground part of **Club Cabo Hotel and Campground Resort** (tel. 624/143-3348, www.clubcaboinn.com, US$20) has 10 sites for tent camping and another 10 for small RVs. Guests may use clean restrooms, hot showers, and a hot tub. There is a lounge area with hammocks, table tennis, a swimming pool, wireless Internet, and secure parking.

Villa Serena RV Park (Km 7.5, toll-free U.S. tel. 800/932-5599, www.grupobahia.com, US$21/day, US$112/week, US$391/month) has 54 spaces with full hookups but no shade, as well as laundry, restrooms, and hot showers. In the adjacent *palapa* restaurant, a La Paz native serves delicious food (coconut shrimp, whole *huachinango/*red snappper) at reasonable prices (tel. 624/145-8244, daily 7 A.M.–10 P.M., mains US$12–25).

For primitive camping on the beach, you need to head out of town to the Pacific beaches along Mexico 19 or the Gulf Coast along the East Cape.

FOOD

Cabo San Lucas offers a wide range of culinary delights, including some world-class dining; however, many of its restaurants are expensive tourist-oriented establishments, rather than authentic local eateries. You'll have to venture away from the marina district to find enjoy real Mexican food at un-inflated prices.

Mexican

Located in one of the oldest adobe buildings in town, **Mi Casa** (Ave. Cabo San Lucas opposite the plaza, tel. 624/143-1933, www.micasarestaurant.com, dinner daily 5:30–10:30 P.M., lunch Mon.–Sat. noon–3 P.M., mains US$15–30) prepares authentic Mexican specialties, including *chile en nogada* (a traditional Independence Day dish) and *cochinita pibil* from the Yucatán.

The restaurant has its own tortillas station and makes its own *mole poblano* from scratch, and it takes a staff of 15 cooks to keep up with the demand. The ambience is festive, with hand-painted murals on the walls of an indoor/outdoor dining area, primary colors for chairs and tables, and mariachi groups passing through all evening long. In recent years, though, many readers have reported underwhelming and inconsistent dining experiences here.

The more contemporary **O Mole Mío** (Plaza del Sol, Blvd. Marina, tel. 624/143-7577, daily 11:30 A.M.–11:30 P.M., mains US$10–20) specializes in various kinds of chicken mole. An artist from Guadalajara designed the unique interior of the restaurant with glass and metal accents.

At **Edith's** (tel. 624/143-0801, www.edithscabo.com, daily 6 P.M.–1 A.M., mains US$10–20), near Playa El Médano on the west side of the Camino de los Pescadores, you can enjoy views of Bahía Cabo San Lucas and Land's End as long as the sun's up, and a hearty dinner of prime rib, rack of lamb, or any number of regional specialties through the evening hours.

Join the locals at **La Perla** (Blvd. Lázaro Cárdenas at Guerrero, no tel., Mon.–Sat. 9 A.M.–4:30 P.M., mains US$4–5) for inexpensive and tasty burritos, enchiladas, *chilaquiles,* tacos, *licuados,* and *comida corrida* (1–4 P.M., US$5). Another option for real Mexican food is **Lolita's Restaurant** (Niños Héroes near Matamoros, no tel., Mon.–Sat. 7 A.M.–7:30 P.M., mains US$7–13), where you can order *huachinango* and *champurrado* (hot chocolate made with cornstarch).

Family-run **《 Las Gardenias** (Camino al

WABORITA, THE SIGNATURE CABO WABO DRINK

The signature Cabo Wabo drink looks like a tropical fish, blue on the bottom and green on top. Here's how to make one when you get home:

1 oz tequila
½ oz Damiana liquor
½ oz orange liquor
½ oz lime juice

Shake and serve straight up with a dash of blue curaçao.

Hacienda at Niños Heroes, no tel., Tues.–Sun. 8 A.M.–5 P.M., tacos US$2, mains US$10–25) is a mainstay that attracts a loyal following of visitors and locals. Plastic tables and chairs and minimal decor put the emphasis on the food: tacos of nearly every kind, including *barbacoa* (lamb), *nopales,* and *cochinita pibil,* and the house specialty, shrimp *molcajetes* served in a mortar.

Portions are large at **Pancho's Restaurant and Tequila Bar** (Hidalgo off Blvd. Marina, tel. 624/143-0973, daily 7 A.M.–11 P.M., dinner mains US$18–40) but prices still seem high. Breakfast is a slightly better deal, and the bar pours hundreds of different kinds of tequila. English is spoken.

Casa Rafael's (Pescador and Médano, tel. 624/143-0739, Mon.–Sat. 6–10 P.M., mains US$20 and up) takes the tropical theme to the extreme, from the aquamarine exterior to shells and fish painted on the walls. The menu features shrimp scampi, Cornish game hens, and rack of lamb. There are 10 guestrooms above the restaurant, plus a piano bar and cigar room.

Amber glassware and a free pomegranate tequila aperitif are nice touches at **Los Garcia** (tel. 624/143-4601, mains US$8–15), one of the newer restaurants located at the street level of the Puerto Paraíso mall, serving upscale tacos, barbecued ribs, lobster salad, and other Mexican fare.

Tequila shrimp, made with the restaurant's own label, and lobster burritos are standout entrées at Sammy Hagar's **Cabo Wabo Restaurant** (Guerrero btw. Madero/Lázaro Cárdenas, tel. 624/143-1188, www.cabowabo. com, daily 11 A.M.–11 P.M., mains US$17–28). Try the Waborita cocktail to start the meal off right. Downstairs, the Cabo Wabo Cantina serves a more casual menu.

Known for its signature salsa bar, which has some 20 different variations on the theme, **Felix** (Zapata and Hidalgo, tel. 624/143-4290, 4–10 P.M., mains US$15–20) began serving tacos and has expanded to a full menu over the years. The restaurant shares its indoor and outdoor space with Mama's Royal Café during the day.

Seafood

Just about every Cabo San Lucas restaurant offers seafood on the menu, but a few make it their focus. Casual **Mocambo de Los Cabos** (Vicario and 20 de Noviembre, tel. 624/143-6070, daily noon–10 P.M., mains US$10–20) has an extensive menu of seafood cocktails, plus fish and shellfish entrées like a fish fillet gratin and a grilled pargo (red snapper) fillet.

Try the *pescado zarandeado* (red snapper served whole in a tomato-based broth) or grilled fish *meniore* style (in a sauce of garlic, butter, white wine, and capers) at **Mariscos Mazatlán** (Mendoza and 16 de Septiembre, tel. 624/143-8565, daily for lunch and dinner, mains US$10–15). The menu also includes 12 different preparations of shrimp. This restaurant has a second, less touristy location in San José del Cabo, on the west side of Mexico 1 on the way to the airport. Near the Ace Hardware store at the corner of Camino Real and Paseo de la Marina, **Mi Casa de Mariscos** (tel. 624/143-1858, salesmicasa@gmail.com, daily 1–10:30 P.M., mains US$13–29) has a raw bar with shrimp, scallops, oysters; "barely touched" dishes like ceviche and seared fresh catch; and fully cooked entrées like *huachinango frito a la*

shellfish for dinner at The Shrimp Factory

© KATHRYN LATENDRESSE

talla (fried whole red snapper). The restaurant is located in a striking hacienda-style building, and it's owned by the same folks who operate Mi Casa and Peacock's.

Japanese and Mexican flavors meet at ◖ **Nick-San Restaurant** (Lte. 10, Blvd. Marina, tel. 624/143-4484, www.nicksan. com, Tues.–Sun. 11:30 A.M.–10:30 P.M., mains US$20 and up), and sushi connoisseurs cannot rave enough about the results: tuna tostada, pulpo carpaccio, cabrilla misoyaki, hamachi curry, and sashimi serranito are just a few examples. The restaurant ranks among the world's best in its class. Plan to spend about US$50–100 per person.

On the marina near the Marina Fiesta hotel, the old El Shrimp Bucket was under renovation at press time and planning to reopen as the **Baja Lobster Co. Seafood Grill** (formerly El Shrimp Bucket, Blvd. Marina Locals 37–38, tel. 624/143-2598, daily 6 A.M.–11 P.M., mains US$20 and up). At **The Shrimp Factory** (Blvd. Marina at Guerrero, tel. 624/143-5066, daily noon–11 P.M., mains US$10–20), you can order shrimp or lobster by the kilo (US$20–30 per half-kilo)—served with bread, salad, and crackers—and go to town.

For upscale dining on the beach, you can't beat **Las Palmas** (Playa el Médano, a few buildings northeast of Camino de los Pescadores, tel. 624/143-0447, laspalmas-cabo@hotmail.com, daily 10 A.M.–11 P.M., mains US$10–15). Choose a table on the raised patio or on the sand below, order the signature shrimp carousel dish, and enjoy the views.

On the marina, family-oriented **Solomon's Landing** (tel. 624/143-305, daily 7 A.M.–11 P.M., mains US$10–30), behind the Tesoro Hotel, prepares a variety of tasty shellfish entrées.

The shrimp and lobster combo (US$17) is the way to go at ⬛ **Maro's Shrimp House** (Hidalgo btw Madero/Zapata, tel. 624/355-8060) where you can order fresh shellfish by the kilo and enjoy friendly service in a small open-air restaurant located across the street from La Dolce and Mama's Royal Café. A half-kilo of shrimp costs US$16, and a half-kilo of lobster is US$20.

On the marina next to Pisces Fleet and near the Tesoro Resort, **Captain Tony's** (tel. 624/143-6797. daily 6 A.M.–9:30 P.M., mains US$11–30) will cook your fresh catch. A bucket of five beers goes for US$10.

Italian and Continental

Southern Italian defines the hearty fare at **Capo San Giovanni** (Guerrero at Madero, tel. 624/143-0593, Tues.–Sun. 5–11 P.M., mains US$13–32). The restaurant is located roughly across from Cabo Wabo.

Near the Solmar and Finisterra hotels, **Romeo & Julieta** (Camino al Pedregal, tel. 624/143-0225, daily 4–11 P.M., mains US$10–20), aims to create a Spanish/Mediterranean feel with a menu of mesquite wood–fired pizza and homemade pasta dishes. In the plaza below the Puerto Paraíso mall, **Amarone** (Store #107, tel. 624/105-1035, daily for lunch and dinner) prepares starters like antipasti or prosciutto and melon for US$12 and lobster or veal filet for US$38. Also downtown, **La Dolce Italian**

Restaurant & Pizzeria (Hidalgo and Zapata, tel. 624/143-4122, daily 6–11 P.M., mains US$10–20) serves a full menu of pastas and pizzas, plus Italian starters and desserts.

The appetizer list at **Peacocks Restaurant and Bar** (Camino de los Pescadores at Vicario, tel. 624/143-1858, daily 6–10 P.M., mains US$20–30) demonstrates the creative powers of its chef: salmon tartar tower, calamari fusilli in a cilantro pesto, and sautéed lobster dumplings. Combined with the lovely garden setting, the menu makes for an enchanting evening.

Olé Olé (Plaza Bonita Loc. 3A, tel. 624/143-0633, daily 7 A.M.–11 P.M., mains US$15–40) faces the marina at Plaza Bonita. The large outdoor tapas bar features Spanish cuisine and dinner combos. Paella (US$22) is served from 1 P.M. on Sunday (and sometimes on Friday).

American and Eclectic

Popular with Corridor residents and Baja old-timers, **Latitude 22+ Roadhouse** (Km 4.5, tel. 624/143-1516, www.lat22nobaddays.com, Wed.–Mon. 8 A.M.–11 P.M., mains US$10–20) prepares a Croatian-influenced menu of slow-roasted prime rib, steak, burgers, ribs, shrimp, fish, chicken fried steak, and pastas. Ocean views, reasonably priced cocktails, and giant flat-screen TVs add to the dining experience. Formerly a downtown hangout, "Lat 22" is now located next Costco and behind the power plant.

Serious carnivores should head to **Brasil Steakhouse** (Zapata at Hidalgo, tel. 624/143-8343, daily 5–11 P.M., US$25 pp) for an all-you-can-eat feast of top sirloin, New York strip, *arranchera,* sausage, ribs, and more. The chef slices meats from a serving skewer at the table, while the waitstaff delivers fresh salads and vegetables. The chicken wings that come as an appetizer rival the best you can find in the United States. Try the *caipirinha* cocktail to start—essentially a mojito without the mint.

The English-speaking staff at the **Stop Light Bar and Grill** (Lazaro Cárdenas and Morelos, tel. 624/143-4740, daily for breakfast, lunch and dinner, mains US$6–19) serves a decent breakfast of eggs, pancakes, and *chilaquiles.*

© KATHRYN LATENDRESSE

Brasil Steakhouse, one of many options for dinner

Portions are large, and cocktails are served in glasses, not plastic. Dinner fare includes ceviche, snails, sandwiches, salads, and enchiladas, as well as lobster, steak, and pasta.

Enjoy a sunset meal at the aptly named **Sunset Grill** (Callejon del Pesdacor, tel. 624/143-9199, 8 A.M.–10 P.M.) atop the Cabo Villas complex at Playa El Médano. The restaurant serves breakfast (mains US$5–10), lunch (mains US$5–9), and dinner (mains US$13–22) daily. Empanada appetizers come with a side of guacamole; fish ceviche goes well with a martini. Cash only.

Taquerías and Quick Bites

To find the local fast-food options, you need to venture away from the marina. Calles Morelos and Ocampo are good bets for tacos, *tortas,* seafood cocktails, and the like. The **Carnitas Los Michoacanos** chain has two locations in town (Vicario btw Carranza/Obregón, tel. 624/105-0713, and on Mexico 19 across from Soriana, tel. 624/146-3565). For tacos *al pastor* (shepherd's style, served from a rotisserie grill), try **El Palacio del Taco** (16 de Septiembre btw Morelos/Vicario, cell tel. 044/624/147-6894, daily 8:30 A.M.–3 A.M.).

Las Quesadillasss (Blvd. Marina at Lázaro Cardénas, tel. 624/143-1373, daily 7 A.M.–2 A.M., mains US$6–13), opposite Arámburo Plaza, is a good bet for late-night dining.

In the plaza below Cabo Wabo, **Taco Loco** serves bean, chicken, pork, and shrimp tacos for US$1 each. **La Luna** (tel. 624/105-0132, Tues.–Sat. noon–10 P.M., Sun. noon–6 P.M.), behind the Pueblo Bonito Rosé resort, serves wraps, burgers, and tacos.

Delicatessens

Across from the City Club on Paseo del Pescador, **Lenny's Deli** (tel. 624/143-8380, daily 7 A.M.–4 P.M.) bakes fresh bagels, sourdough, and rye breads daily and prepares authentic New York and Philly-style subs. Its box lunches are good sustenance for a day of fishing. You can also order sandwiches at **La Europea** (no tel., daily 9 A.M.–6 P.M., mains US$5–12) just outside the Puerto Paraíso mall. There are a few tables out front, overlooking the marina. Air-conditioned booths are a comfortable place to grab a sandwich (and check your email with free Wi-Fi) at **Señor Greenberg's Mexicatessen** (tel. 624/143-5630, daily 24 hours, mains US$5–12), which has several locations, including a new deli next to Johnny Rockets in the Puerto Paraíso mall.

Breakfast and Cafés

One of the best places to get breakfast in Cabo San Lucas these days is ⒸMama's **Royal Café** (Av. Hidalgo btw Zapata and Madero, tel. 624/143-4290, daily 7:30 A.M.–2 P.M., mains US$7–15). Brightly colored woven linens serve as tablecloths in this small indoor/outdoor café. Start with the signature mango mimosa, served in a giant sundae glass. Then move on to the traditional breakfast burrito or the chef's creative interpretation of *chilaquiles,* in which the tortillas are cut in strips instead of wedges and served with a medley of seasoned vegetables (avocado, mushrooms, spinach, and tomato) instead of smothered in sauce. The menu features exceptionally fresh ingredients. The only downside: no espresso drinks.

Starbucks has finally made an appearance in Cabo (Plaza Bonita), but so far, the cafés are holding their own. **Theory Café** (tel. 624/143-5518, daily from 10 A.M., mains US$8–12) in the center of Plaza Bonita serves lattes, mochas, and frappucinos, and plays music like the Red Hot Chili Peppers. Use your laptop or theirs for wireless Internet. **Cabo Coffee Company** (tel. 624/105-1130) has expanded to a new Internet café with high-speed wireless connections on the corner of Hidalgo and Madero, across from its original roasting facility. This is your stop for 100 percent organic brews. A satellite location is also available outside the Giggling Marlin. **San Francisco Coffee Company** (Blvd. Marina 38, tel. 624/144-4387, www.sanfranciscocoffeecompany.com) brews hot and cold espresso drinks (US$2.50–5.50) and blends smoothies (US$4.50–5.50). It also has wireless Internet (US$2 for up to 15 minutes), DVD rentals, and English-language books.

Among the many dockside restaurants by the marina, **Baja Cantina** (Dock L–M, tel.

624/143-1591, mains US$7–15) serves tasty jalapeño poppers, artichoke and spinach dip, and other starters for US$5–8, as well as fish, burgers, and Mexican plates for dinner. Wireless Internet is a plus. Look for a second location at Playa El Médano (tel. 624/143-9773).

Palapa Restaurants

Several *palapa* bars and restaurants scattered along Playa El Médano—including **Billygan's Island** (tel. 624/143-0402, daily for lunch and dinner), **The Office** (tel. 624/143-3464, daily for lunch and dinner), and **Las Palmas** (tel. 624/143-0447, daily for lunch and dinner)—offer cold beverages, as well as burgers, seafood, and Mexican plates (lunch mains US$8–15; dinner menus are more expensive).

Groceries

Most visitors these days buy supplies for their stay at **Soriana** (Mex. 19/Carr. Todos Santos and Calle Guajitos, tel. 624/105-1290, www.soriana.com), a Walmart-esque superstore, or at the Costco on the Corridor. But there are some smaller options right in town that carry brands from Mexico and the United States. They include **Almacenes Grupo Castro** (southwest corner of Morelos and Revolución, tel. 624/143-0566), **Supermercado Sánliz** (three locations: Blvd. Marina at Madero, Ocampo at Matamoros, and Vicario at López Mateos), and **Supermercado Arámburo** (Arámburo Plaza, Lázaro Cárdenas at Zaragoza, tel. 624/143-1450). There is also a **CCC** (Centro Comercial California, tel. 624/146-7200) on the east side of Mexico 19 just north of the junction with Mexico 1 and before the Soriana. On the east side of town, warehouse-style **City Club** (Blvd. Lázaro Cárdenas at Paseo del Pescador, tel. 624/143-9492, www.soriana.com) has groceries, produce, and baked goods.

Pescadería El Dorado (5 de Febrero btw Abasolo/Ocampo, tel. 624/143-2820), is a good bet for fresh fish and shellfish. You can buy fresh tortillas at **Tortillería Perla** (Morelos btw Hidalgo/Matamoros, tel. 624/143-1381).

Next to the entrance to the Pedregal

community, **La Baguette** (Blvd. Lázaro Cárdenas, tel. 624/142-1125, Mon.–Sat. 8:30 A.M.–7:30 P.M.) specializes in pastries, bagels, and breads from Europe and the United States. For a sweet tooth, the **Swiss Pastry** (Hidalgo at Lázaro Cárdenas across from the plaza, tel. 624/143-3494, Mon.–Sat. 7 A.M.–4 P.M.) has homemade chocolates and candies, as well as a variety of pastries.

For fresh fruits and vegetables, head over to **Frutería Lizarraga** (Matamoros at Av. de la Juventud, tel. 624/143-1215). And for organic produce and imported wines, try **Tutto Bene!** (Blvd. Marina opposite the Tesoro Hotel, daily 9:30 A.M.–9 P.M.).

INFORMATION AND SERVICES
Tourist Assistance
The **Los Cabos Tourism Trust** (Fideicomiso de Turismo de Los Cabos) has an office on Lázaro Cárdenas Edificio Posada (tel. 624/143-4777, U.S. tel. 866/567-2226).

Money
There is no shortage of ATMs in Cabo San Lucas, and U.S. currency is accepted just about anywhere; however, in most cases, you'll get a better deal if you pay in pesos. You can exchange money Monday–Saturday 8:30 A.M.–noon at **Bancomer** (Hidalgo at Guerrero), **Banamex** (Hidalgo at Lázaro Cárdenas), and **Santander Serfín** (in Arámburo Plaza). Avoid exchanging money at the airport or other money-change stands in town, as the will always charge you more.

Post and Telephone
The local post office (Lázaro Cárdenas at 16 de Septiembre) is open Monday–Friday 8 A.M.–4 P.M. and Saturday 9 A.M.–noon. Public telephone booths are scattered around town, and long distance services are often found inside Internet cafés. A few places are beginning to offer Internet phone services as well.

Mail Boxes Etc. (Blvd. Marina 39-F, Plaza Fiesta, tel. 624/143-3033, fax 624/143-3031)

CABO SAN LUCAS PHONE NUMBERS
- Cabo San Lucas area code: 624
- Amerimed: 624/105-8500
- Hyperbaric chamber: 143-3666
- Immigration: 143-0135
- Emergency: 066
- Police (non-emergency): 143-3977 or 143-5123
- Red Cross (non-emergency): 143-3300
- Taxi service: 143-2221
- U.S. Consulate: 143-3566

carries mailing supplies, postage stamps, and magazines.

Internet Access
Cabo San Lucas has experienced a proliferation of Internet cafés, although they seem to come, change hands, and go as fast as taco stands. Coffee shops and real estate offices are good places to check. Prices have come down quite a bit in recent years, settling at about US$2–6 per hour. If you travel you're your own computer, wireless Internet access is also widely available in Los Cabos hotels and campgrounds—and many also have public computers available for guest use. The following list is by no means exhaustive.

Internet Café Cabo Mail (Arámburo Plaza, tel. 624/143-7797, Mon.–Fri. 9 A.M.–9 P.M., Sat. 9 A.M.–6 P.M., Sun. noon–6 P.M.) offers Internet calls to the United States for US$2 per 10 minutes. At **Cabo Clipper Internet & Computers Business Center** (Level 3 Puerto Paraíso Plaza, tel. 624/105-0482, caboclipper@gmail.com, daily 10 A.M.–10 P.M.), you'll pay US$2 for up to 15 minutes or US$6 for one hour. You'll pay the same prices if you bring your own laptop. Credit cards are accepted.

The lobby of the Siesta Suites Hotel also has three fast PCs (with USB ports) for US$3 per hour.

There are several places in town where you can enjoy a latte or cappuccino while you check your email: **Theory Café** (tel. 624/143-5518), in the center of Plaza Bonita, opens at 10 A.M. daily. **Cabo Coffee Company** (tel. 624/105-1130, U.S. tel. 619/819-7953, www.cabocoffee.com) has expanded to a new Internet café with high-speed wireless connections on the corner of Hidalgo and Madero, across from its original roasting facility. A satellite location is also available outside the Giggling Marlin. **San Francisco Coffee Company** (38 Blvd. Marina, tel. 624/144-4387, www.sanfranciscocoffeecompany.com) has wireless Internet for US$2 for up to 15 minutes. **Baja Cantina** (Dock L–M, tel. 624/143-1591) offers wireless Internet along with a full lunch and dinner menu.

Laundry

Cabo has a number of self-serve and full-service laundry facilities scattered about town. One of the most reputable is **Lavandería Evelyn** (Matamoros and Mijares, tel. 624/143-0920, daily 7 A.M.–7 P.M.), which has a self-serve option. The Marina Sol resort has an on-site laundry and dry cleaning service with quick turnaround times: same day for laundry and next day for dry cleaning (tel. 624/143-5430).

Magazines and Newspapers

The online *Los Cabos Guide* (www.loscabosguide.com) contains overviews of many Los Cabos businesses, including hotels, restaurants, and outfitters; much of its content is promotional in nature and some of the information is several years out of date, but the listings are fairly thorough. Pop into any real estate office or large hotel for a free copy. Another handy resource is the *Los Cabos Gringo Pages* (tel. 624/104-3887, www.thegringopages.com), an annual yellow pages listing covering the entire Los Cabos region, with some listings for Todos Santos and the East Cape as well.

The local Spanish-language newspaper is *El Heraldo de los Cabos.* The *Gringo Gazette,* aims to get the inside scoop on all things Baja for an audience of expats and frequent visitors.

Destino is another promotional paper that is available or free. The bilingual *Los Cabos News* reports on happenings from Cabo San Lucas to San José.

Bahías Jiromar also carries some English-language periodicals (Puerto Paraíso Local #284, tel. 624/144-3250).

Spanish-Language Instruction

California Conexion (tel. 624/108-2095, thecaliforniaconexion@hotmail.com) holds Spanish classes for beginners and intermediate students.

Medical Services

Dial 066 for emergency situations. Check the *Los Cabos Gringo Pages,* available in many hotels, for English-speaking doctors and clinics. **AmeriMed** (Pioneros Building Loc. 1, Blvd. Lázaro Cárdenas, tel. 624/143-9670) has a bilingual staff trained to handle emergencies, along with OB/GYN care and a family practice. The clinic is open 24/7, and accepts most insurance policies. **BlueMedicalNet** (tel. 624/104-3911, daily 24/7) operates a clinic in the Plaza del Rey, across from Home Depot.

Immigration

Cabo's *migración* office is on the north side of Boulevard Lázaro Cárdenas between Gómez Farías and 16 de Septiembre across from the Banamex.

U.S. Consulate

The U.S. consular agency in Cabo San Lucas is at Plaza Náutica (C-4, Blvd. Marina, tel. 624/143-3566, usconsulcabo@hotmail.com, Mon.–Fri. 10 A.M.–1 P.M.). This is the place to go if you lose your passport or for other emergencies.

GETTING AROUND

The majority of Cabo San Lucas visitors get around by foot and by cab. A taxi ride around town should cost around US$5, but it's always a good idea to ask for a quote before you hop in.

You can hire water taxis from the marina in front of the Tesoro Hotel to Playa El Médano

© NIKKI GOTH ITOI

the Cabo San Lucas harbor

(US$3) and Playa del Amor (US$8–12, round-trip only).

For trips to the Corridor and beyond, a rental car comes in handy. Rates are lower from the airport, but if you only want the car for a day or two of a longer trip, then renting in town makes sense. Brands include Budget (Hotel Tesoro complex, Blvd. Lázaro Cardenas), Dollar (tel. 624/143-1250, www.dollarloscabos.com), Avis (Blvd. Lázaro Cardenas at Vicario), and Thrifty (ME Cabo).

Other ways to get around include mopeds and ATVs. Look for vendors advertising these services along Marina Boulevard.

THE WEST CAPE AND TODOS SANTOS

A few hundred meters past the modern Soriana shopping complex in Cabo San Lucas, the urban sprawl abruptly ends, cows reclaim the road, and the Pacific Ocean eventually pops into view. A lone trailer or two has set up camp along the shore, but you can't quite tell which dirt road they drove to get there. If it's late fall or early winter, wildflowers may still dot the landscape with a splash of color.

Don't get too lost in the scenery, however, or the Aguila bus driver tailgating you might very well decide to pass on a blind turn just as an 18-wheeler approaches from the opposite direction. Welcome to the West Cape, the least developed stretch of coastline on the lower part of the Baja Peninsula. Although paved, two-lane Mexico 19 connects Cabo San Lucas to Todos Santos and meets Mexico 1 just south of La Paz,

housing developments are still few and far between. Several large real estate projects are in the early stages near the farming community of El Pescadero and close to Cabo San Lucas, leaving the middle stretch to the pelicans, rancheros, fishermen, and the occasional ATV tour.

Once considered a stopover on the drive from La Paz to Cabo San Lucas, bohemian Todos Santos has become a destination in its own right. Surfers, artists, retirees, exotic bird rescuers, and yoga students all cross paths here, and at least several hundred of them are permanent expat residents. Over the last few years, Todos Santos has basked in the attention of its recent designation as a Pueblo Mágico—one of only 23 small towns in Mexico given government funding to make their culture and history more accessible to tourists and travelers.

HIGHLIGHTS

LOOK FOR  TO FIND RECOMMENDED SIGHTS, ACTIVITIES, DINING, AND LODGING.

THE WEST CAPE

 **La Candelaria:** Experience the rancho way of life in this rural village set in the foothills of the lower Sierra de la Laguna. Plan a day hike or a scenic drive from Cabo San Lucas on the way to Todos Santos (page 364).

 **Playa Los Cerritos:** Popular with novice surfers, swimmers, and sunbathers, this gently sloped beach lies comfortably protected from winter's northwest swell. Eagle rays, puffer fish, and other marine life await discovery (page 365).

 **Playa San Pedrito (Playa Las Palmas):** Rock cliffs at either end of the beach frame your view of the Pacific at this beach near Todos Santos. Bring a picnic and enjoy the secluded setting (page 367).

 **Historic District in Todos Santos:** The most memorable postcards of Todos Santos depict rows of colorful, century-old facades with the signature large windows and doors of the Andalusian architecture style. Spend an afternoon exploring the town's galleries, shops, and restaurants on foot (page 374).

 **La Poza:** A small, freshwater lagoon within walking distance of Todos Santos is home to many types of waterfowl, as well as the area's finest boutique hotel, Posada La Poza (page 375).

Foreign and Mexican locals alike remain optimistic that the town will be able to preserve its artsy character even as the number of visitors increases.

The economic recession in the United States is taking a toll, however, and these days Todos Santos is experiencing a bit of a hangover from all the fast-paced growth. Too many businesses sharing too few visitors have resulted in a more sober mood around town.

PLANNING YOUR TIME

The drive from Cabo San Lucas to Todos Santos via Mexico 19 and the West Cape takes approximately one hour—making it an easy day trip for visitors who are staying in the Los Cabos area, or a slightly longer drive (90 minutes) directly from the airport.

You can take in most of what Todos Santos has to offer in a full day of sightseeing, covering the historic buildings and galleries in town and a beach or two along the coast. But as with most other towns in Baja, you'll enjoy the West Cape infinitely more if you stay long enough to wander kilometers of virgin, as-yet-undeveloped beaches stretching north and south from Todos Santos along the Pacific, explore the steep western escarpment of the Sierra de

THE WEST CAPE

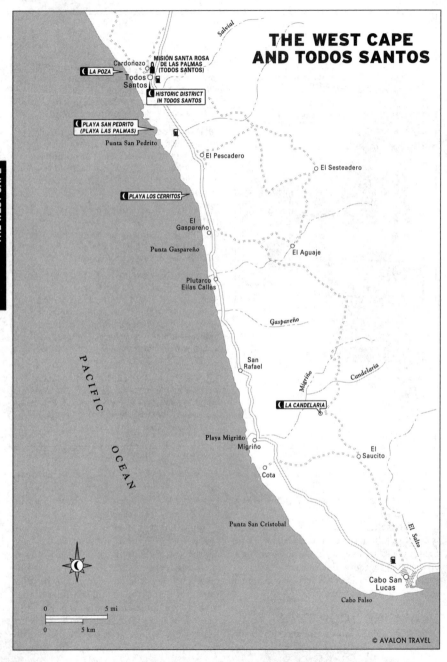

THE WEST CAPE AND TODOS SANTOS

Saleial

Cardoñozo

Todos Santos

MISIÓN SANTA ROSA DE LAS PALMAS (TODOS SANTOS)

LA POZA

HISTORIC DISTRICT IN TODOS SANTOS

PLAYA SAN PEDRITO (PLAYA LAS PALMAS)

Punta San Pedrito

El Pescadero

El Sesteadero

PLAYA LOS CERRITOS

El Gaspareño

Punta Gaspareño

El Aguaje

Plutarco Elías Callas

Gaspareño

PACIFIC

San Rafael

Migriño

Candelaria

LA CANDELARIA

OCEAN

Playa Migriño

Migriño

El Saucito

Cota

Punta San Cristóbal

El Salto

Cabo San Lucas

Cabo Falso

0   5 mi

0   5 km

© AVALON TRAVEL

© PABLO NOBILI

Modern Todos Santos still retains its small-town feel.

la Laguna, or simply hang out and soak up the small-town ambience.

Backpackers often plan multiday trips into the sierra from the West Cape. If that sounds too challenging, guides also run half-day hikes, as well as trail rides on ATVs. A day of fishing or surfing could also lengthen your stay. Of course, if you're into these activities, a day probably isn't enough. Surfers can easily spend a week or a month trying to master the winter breaks here. And the fishing—whether by boat, surf rod, or hand line—is just as addictive.

GETTING THERE AND AROUND
By Air
Todos Santos is more or less equidistant from the Los Cabos and La Paz airports. A shuttle from Los Cabos costs approximately US$150, while a shuttle from La Paz runs US$200–300.

By Car
Though not essential, most travelers will want to have a car while staying in the West Cape and Todos Santos, as the beaches and sights are spread out from the two small towns. If you don't rent a car at the airport or drive your own from the United States, you can rent one in Todos Santos. **Budget Car Rental** (Márquez de León 4, tel. 612/145-0062, egarcia@budget-baja.com) has opened an office in Todos Santos next to the church and main plaza, and a second location inside the Milagro Real Estate office on Juárez.

Mexico 19 connects Todos Santos to Cabo San Lucas to the south and La Paz to the north. From the Los Cabos airport, follow the Transpeninsular Highway (Mexico 1) toward Cabo San Lucas, and take the turnoff for Todos Santos/Mexico 19. From La Paz, follow Mexico 1 south to the turnoff for Mexico 19. There are numerous Pemex stations in La Paz, Todos Santos, Pescadero, and Cabo San Lucas. If you need a mechanic during your visit, there are a couple of options in Todos Santos, but you may have to head south to Cabo San Lucas for complicated transmission work.

By Taxi
A small fleet of blue vans parked next to the park in Todos Santos can provide taxi service around town for US$2 a trip. A van all the way to Los Cabos International Airport will cost around US$150; vans can hold 8–15 people with luggage. Call 612/145-0063 for more information.

By Bus
Nine Aguila buses a day connect Todos Santos to La Paz and Cabo San Lucas. The La Paz and Cabo San Lucas bus trips take about two hours and cost about US$7 per person; a bus all the way around to San José del Cabo costs US$10. Tickets are sold on the buses, which arrive at and depart from Colegio Militar and Zaragoza (for San José del Cabo and Cabo San Lucas), or in front of Karla's Lonchería (for La Paz). In Pescadero, buses stop across the street from the Pemex.

THE WEST CAPE

The West Cape

A handful of beach communities fronting the Pacific Ocean comprise the sparsely populated West Cape. In the shadow of the more established Todos Santos, El Pescadero is emerging as a small center for commerce and tourism.

CABO FALSO TO PLAYA MIGRIÑO

Early explorers once believed that a cape three kilometers west of Cabo San Lucas marked the southern tip of the peninsula. Later cartographers discovered the mistake, and named the cape Cabo Falso. Today, the wide, sandy beach is protected so that sea turtles can lay their eggs undisturbed; once a popular destination for ATV tours from Cabo San Lucas, the dunes are now off limits as well, due to pending development. An abandoned lighthouse, **El Faro Viejo,** was in operation from 1895–1961; some years back, the original lens was moved to a modern lighthouse located higher on the beach.

Inland from Cabo Falso, Mexico 19 enters the foothills of the Sierra de la Laguna and reaches the village of Migriño. The coast here consists of a long, sandy beach dotted with rocks and a small estuary at the mouth of Río Candelaria.

In winter, surfers can find a right point break at the north end of the beach, but the camping is no more. Rancho Migriño has moved in, with new home sites for sale.

Playa Migriño is easily accessible from Cabo San Lucas (about 15 minutes by car), with access roads at Km 94 and Km 97. The beach is about 2.5 kilometers west of the highway on either road.

◖ LA CANDELARIA

A small ranching settlement in the sierra foothills, La Candelaria is worth a side trip if you want to get away from the crowded beaches and have an off-road adventure. Known for its pottery and *curanderos* (healers who specialize

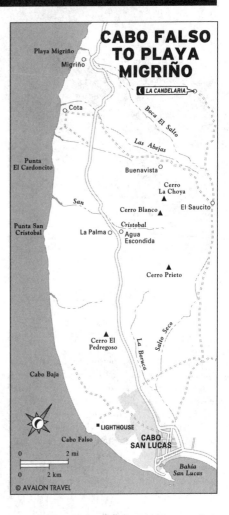

in herbal treatments), the town is most often visited by guided ATV tours, which stop to buy the inexpensive ceramics and swim in the palm oasis. Fewer than 100 people live here year-round, raising livestock and tending to crops of citrus, avocado, and mango. The village itself consists of simple homes with *palapa* roofs, a church, and school.

Getting There

There are two ways to reach La Candelaria if you want to drive yourself. The most direct, via Migriño, requires four-wheel drive. The longer route has more turns and forks, but you can make it in most regular vehicles.

FROM PLAYA MIGRIÑO

The route follows the Río Candelaria 9.1 kilometers southwest from Mexico 19 near Playa Migriño. The turnoff is not signed. Look for a dirt road three kilometers south of Km 94, or about a half-kilometer north of the main Playa Migriño turnoff (Km 97). The road is sandy and narrow in places. Do not attempt the drive in the rainy season.

FROM CABO SAN LUCAS

From downtown Cabo San Lucas, drive along Boulevard Lázaro Cárdenas east toward San José and turn left at Boulevard Constituyentes (also labeled Ave. Reforma on some maps) and the sign for La Paz Via Corta. Follow this street northwest toward Todos Santos and La Paz, past a soccer field on the left. At the power plant on the right side, turn onto a wide, dirt road (1.7 km from the intersection of Blvds. Lázaro Cárdenas and Constituyentes).

From here, La Candelaria is 22 kilometers away, assuming you manage to find all the correct turns on the first try. Turn right 4.3 kilometers from the highway at the sign for La Candelaria and Los Pozos. Pass through the fence and cattle guard—an attendant may be on guard to prevent livestock theft. Watch for cattle in the road from here on.

Twelve kilometers from the highway, the road forks. Stay left, ignoring the right branch, which goes to San Felipe and El Sauzal. Next come the ranches and adobe ruins of Los Pozos. There is a small chapel 14 kilometers into the drive (measuring from the highway). Keep following signs for La Candelaria and La Trinidad, ignoring any smaller branches off the main road.

Soon, the Pacific Ocean comes into view. About 21 kilometers from the highway is a turnoff for Rancho San Ramón, after which

is another fork. Both branches will get you to La Candelaria, but the right fork is quicker. It crosses an arroyo, passes a turn to La Trinidad, and then arrives in La Candelaria.

ATV TOURS

An easy way to visit La Candelaria is by guided ATV tour. Contact **Baja's Activities** (Km 104–105, tel. 624/143-2050, www.bajasactivities.com).

PESCADERO AND VICINITY

In recent years, the area around El Pescadero has seen the rise of many new homes and businesses. Although there has been some development, you can still get lost in the maze of unmarked dirt roads that lead from the highway to the beach.

Playa Los Cerritos

A new official road sign points the way to Playa Los Cerritos at Km 64 (12.8 km south of Todos Santos). From the turn, follow a dirt road 2.7 kilometers southwest until you reach the sandy parking area. Sheltered by Punta Pescadero at its north end, the beach is usually safe for swimming, though you should ask at the surfs shops about currents and riptides before getting in the water. Throw on a pair of goggles and you may even catch a glimpse of a spotted eagle ray gliding by just offshore. Boogie boarding is another popular activity.

This is generally a good beginner surf spot, but it can get big in the right conditions. The Costa Azul Surf Shop and El Diablo Blanco rent boards at the beach dawn till dusk.

Campers note: Change is afoot at this much-loved beach. Having received its title to the land, the local *ejido* has been selling property near the beach. Campers and RVers who set up camp were asked to leave in late 2006, and the **Los Cerritos Club** bar and beach restaurant (restaurant cell tel. 044/624/129-6315, office tel. 624/143-4850) opened in 2007. Next to the restaurant, some people had started camping again at last check.

About five kilometers south near Km 75, a new real estate development, **Tortuga del Sol**

THE WEST CAPE

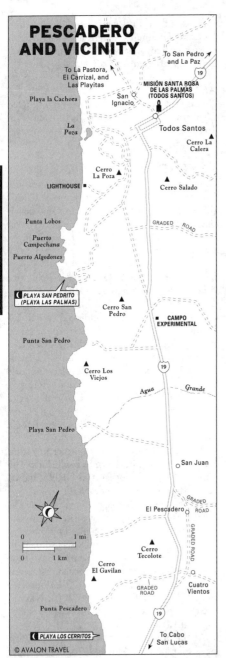

PESCADERO AND VICINITY

To San Pedro and La Paz

To La Pastora, El Carrizal, and Las Playitas

Playa la Cachora

San Ignacio

MISIÓN SANTA ROSA DE LAS PALMAS (TODOS SANTOS)

Todos Santos

Cerro La Calera

La Poza

Cerro La Poza

LIGHTHOUSE

Cerro Salado

GRADED ROAD

Punta Lobos

Puerto Campechana

Puerto Algodones

PLAYA SAN PEDRITO (PLAYA LAS PALMAS)

Cerro San Pedro

CAMPO EXPERIMENTAL

Punta San Pedro

Cerro Los Viejos

19

Agua Grande

Playa San Pedro

San Juan

GRADED ROAD

El Pescadero

GRADED ROAD

0   1 mi
0   1 km

Cerro Tecolote

Cerro El Gavilan

Cuatro Vientos

GRADED ROAD

Punta Pescadero

19

PLAYA LOS CERRITOS

To Cabo San Lucas

© AVALON TRAVEL

(www.tortugadelsol.net) is taking shape with 123 home sites.

El Pescadero

As you approach El Pescadero from the south (Km 62), hilly terrain gives way on the west side of Mexico 19 to a series of flat, cultivated fields, most of which are bordered by a single row of tall corn stalks. Between fields of cherry tomatoes and basil, a number of palm-lined dirt roads meander to the water's edge. Though still much smaller and more spread out than its neighbor to the north, Pescadero has evolved in recent years from a cluster of simple *tiendas* and *loncherías* into a more developed business center with its own Pemex and Oxxo convenience store. The first major real estate development underway in the area is the 20-hectare gated community of **Playa Agave Azul.** More development is underway at nearby Playa Los Cerritos.

Local expat residents here are getting involved with turtle conservation efforts, through egg collection and baby turtle release programs, as well as the building of an educational amphitheatre, designed in the shape of a turtle, to promote ecological awareness. Visit www.bajaturtle.com for more information.

Dirt roads heading to the beach can be a bit tricky to navigate. There are no street names or signs, and many roads dead-end at someone's driveway. The easiest way to find most of Pescadero's waterfront attractions is to follow a wide dirt road with a row of palms in the median that meets Mexico 19 just across from the Sandbar restaurant. If you've rented a place along this stretch of coast, be sure to get specific directions to find it.

Playa San Pedro

Playa San Pedro (former site of the now closed San Pedrito RV park) extends north from El Pescadero to Punta San Pedro. It is filled with cobblestones near the point, but sandy the rest of the way south. Surfable waves break along the north end of the beach. Follow the access road 3.1 kilometers west from Km 59 to the beach.

◖ Playa San Pedrito (Playa Las Palmas)

Harder to find, Little San Pedro Beach (Km 56–57) also goes by the name of Palm Beach. With its fan palms and salt march, you might forget you're in the desert here. Enclosed by rocky points at either end, the beach can offer good swimming, shore fishing, and surfing, depending on the swell. Watch for riptides near the points. Beach camping is permitted on the sand. The access road to San Pedrito is across from the Campo Experimental buildings on Mexico 19. Stay left when you reach the ruined mansion and you'll arrive at the south end of the palm orchard. From here, it's a short walk to the water's edge.

Sierra de la Laguna

East of Pescadero, you can navigate a network of dirt roads up into the foothills to palm-filled arroyos, remote ranches, and stands of *cardón* cacti. A high-clearance vehicle is a necessity; better yet, park in the foothills and hike in. It's easy to become lost here, so consider hiring a guide in Pescadero or Todos Santos. At Rancho Pilar (Mexico 19, Km 73, ranchopilar@hotmail.com), artisan and amateur naturalist Cuco Moyron can arrange mule trips into the sierra and provides interesting information about the local plants and animals. He'll need about a week to make the arrangements for your trip. In Todos Santos, **Todos Santos Eco Adventures** (Juárez and Topete, tel. 612/145-0780, www.tosea.net) arranges one-day and multiday hikes.

The rugged, and often impassable, Naranjos road heads southeast from a point near Playa Los Cerritos and crosses the Sierra de la Laguna to join Mexico 1 between Santa Anita and Caduaño.

SPORTS AND RECREATION
Surfing

Surfable waves pound the West Cape in winter, from Playa Migriño all the way to Punta Márquez, north of Todos Santos. Beginning in the south, Migriño has an exposed right point and hollow beach break. Punta Gaspareño, a

© PABLO NOBILI

fair warning at the Pescadero Surf Camp

rock-bottomed right point break at Km 73, break best in large west or northwest swells. Playa San Pedro (Km 59, site of the former San Pedrito RV park) offers fairly consistent right reef and beach breaks; paddle out from the beach to avoid urchins on the reef. A little farther north, Playa San Pedrito has another beach break, best enjoyed during a west or north swell. Popular with novice surfers, Playa Los Cerritos has several left and right beach breaks. Ask the local shops about currents and riptides before you hop in for the first time. Experienced surfers will enjoy the right break off the point on larger northwest and south swells. Vacation rentals in the Pescadero area are popular with some surfers, while others prefer to camp north of Todos Santos. The **Pescadero Surf Camp** (Km 64, www.pescaderosurf.com) offers cabanas, campsites, board rentals, and instruction.

Skate Park

Also at Km 64, the **Pescadero Surf and Skate Camp** (Barrio Las Palmitas, tel. 612/141-9440, camping US$10) has a skate park (Tues.–Fri. 1–6 P.M., Sat.–Sun. 11 A.M.–6 P.M., US$2) that was in great shape on our last visit.

Yoga

Yandara Yoga Institute (Mexico 19, Km 73, www.yandara.com) offers yoga instructor courses several times a year. Students prepare most of their meals from the house *huerta*. At Km 73, take the dirt road toward the beach until it ends and then turn left. Another studio at the Mini Super Los Arcos across from the Pemex offers Hatha yoga classes taught in Spanish with instructor Mayra Torres (tel. 612/130-3006, Mon., Wed., Fri. 9 A.M.–10:30 A.M., US$5/class).

Swimming

Most of the beaches along the West Cape are exposed to heavy surf; however, on calm days Playa Los Cerritos and Playa Las Palmas offer sheltered conditions for an ocean swim. At Las Palmas, the middle section of the cove is usually the safest. Toward the north and south ends, the water looks shallow and inviting, but riptides pose a danger.

Spa Services

In a brick building three rows in from the beach, **Los Bules Day Spa** (Playa Congrejos, El Pescadero, tel. 612/118-1062, www.pescadise.com) offers deep tissue, hot stone, or Swedish massage (US$50), body wraps (US$45), and facials (US$40–70)—plus a Native American *temazcal,* or sweat lodge (US$20). The proprietor, Maria, is also a gourd artist. Her gallery on the property contains pitchers, bowls, animals, candles, and teacups—all crafted from hard-shelled bottle gourds.

ENTERTAINMENT

These days, when Todos Santos residents want to go out for a night on the town, they head to Pescadero. Todos Santos may have more shops and restaurants, but Pescadero has the **Sandbar** (Km 63, tel. 612/130-3209, Mon.–Sat. 3 P.M. till late, Sun. 1–10 P.M.), with a pool table, live music, and daily happy hour specials, as well as occasional cook-your-own kebab dinners.

SHOPPING

A string of *artesanías* selling colorful Mexican blankets, hammocks, and pottery lines the highway in the Pescadero area.

A handful of Candelaria artisans make pottery, baskets, and *palo escopeta*-style chairs. At Km 69, **The Blanket Factory** is a popular stop for organized tours. Shop here for handmade rugs, blankets, clothing, and hammocks (US$60–80), or request a custom design.

Rancho Pilar

Originally from La Paz, Cuco Moyron (Mexico 19, Km 73, ranchopilar@hotmail.com) is an artist, craftsman, and naturalist who uses recycled tire-rubber soles to make custom-fit sandals (US$35 a pair). He and his wife, Pilar, also make pottery, jewelry, and hats of woven grass. They have campsites available on their property. Cuco leads informative trips through the Sierra de la Laguna. Allow a week to make arrangements. At Km 73, take the dirt road toward the beach until it ends and turn left. Continue straight past Yandara Yoga Institute until you reach the Rancho Pilar gate.

ACCOMMODATIONS AND CAMPING

Several longtime Pescadero inns have changed hands in recent years, and new places are opening with each season. A number of private homes are also coming on the market as vacation rental properties.

US$50-100

On the beach in Pescadero, 3.5 kilometers from the wide dirt road that leaves Mexico 19 across from the Sandbar, the **San Pedrito Surf Hotel** (www.sanpedritosurf.com, US$65–170) is a remodel of the former Casa Cyrene. Now owned by two families from Hawaii, the property has five *casitas*. The surf bunkhouse has been converted into a two-bedroom family *casita*. All have full kitchens and king-size beds. Other amenities include bottled water, basic cooking utensils and spices, and linens. There is a washer/dryer on the property.

Also in a beachfront location and a little south of the San Pedrito Surf Hotel, **Casa Simpatica** (http://todossantos.cc/casasimpatica. html, casasimpatica@yahoo.com, US$65, three-night minimum) features four clean *casitas,* each with a queen-size bed and private bath; guests share an outdoor kitchen. A new main house was under construction at press time, and owner Gary Faulk provides Internet access.

At the San Pedrito surf break, **Las Palmas Tropicales** (www.tropicalcasitas.com, US$75–140) has five *palapa*-roof *casitas* (four with kitchens) with tiled baths and wireless Internet. Also close to the San Pedrito surf break, friendly Rob and Lorinda Costa from Santa Cruz, California, own **Sierra de la Costa** (rcliv2surf@aol.com, US$70, three-night minimum), super-clean beach bungalow rentals with queen-size beds, tiled baths, private patios, and gas barbecues.

A little farther away from the beach and the surf breaks, **Rancho de las Olas** (Mexico 19, Km 63, tel. 612/111-7121, ranchodelasolas@ yahoo.com, www.bajacasitas.com, US$65–75) has three minimally furnished *casitas.* One is a stand-alone unit, while the others are second-story apartments. Weekly rates and longer-term discounts are available.

US$100-150

Near the San Pedrito Surf Hotel, **El Pozo Hondo** (pozohondobcs@yahoo.com, US$100–110) is a bed-and-breakfast with two *palapa*-roof bungalows surrounded by mango, avocado, and citrus trees. Guellermo prepares excellent coffee for guests every morning.

US$150-250

Marble floors, robes, Egyptian cotton sheets, and fluffy towels are just a few of the luxury amenities at **La Alianza** (tel. 612/118-3423, www.bajaturtle.com, US$130–240), a five-room property located between Cerritos and San Pedrito point. Guests share a third-floor *palapa*-roof deck and common kitchen. A separate, two-bedroom *casita* has two

bedrooms, one bath, and a kitchen for US$150. Commissioned works from local artisan Cuco Moyron add an authentic Baja twist to the grounds and home. This is the place to stay if you want privacy and that extra special touch. Owner Debora McIntire is involved with local sea turtle conservation activities to protect the leatherbacks and olive ridleys that nest on the beach in Pescadero. Inquire about participating in a baby turtle release August–December.

Vacation Rentals

The Todos Santos community website, www. todossantos.cc, keeps a list of vacation rentals in the area. Here are a few of the most popular homes: For kids (and the young at heart), the highlight of a stay at **Villa del Faro** (U.S. tel. 707/468-0876, www.villadelfarobaja.com, US$4,000/week) is the curved waterslide that deposits swimmers into a 12-meter saltwater pool rimmed with fiber-optic lights that glow after dark. Located at the south end of Pescadero Beach, the villa was built to handle a crowd, with three kitchens, five bedrooms, and a hot tub, plus massage, maid services, and catering available by request. For more entertainment, there are a ping-pong table, volleyball court, and 52-inch Sky TV.

As the name implies, the **Beachfront Family Hacienda** (jarmour@bajalifecamp. com, US$300/night or US$1,800/week), near the San Pedrito surf break, is a family-friendly 280-square-meter redbrick building with three bedrooms, two indoor baths, an outdoor shower, and a full kitchen. This home also comes with a washing machine and dishwasher, swing set, and beach gear, and a full playground for kids.

Between the Los Cerritos and San Pedrito surf breaks, **Alhaja de Baja** is a recently remodeled two-bedroom house with king-size beds (www.alhajadebaja.com, US$990/week). **The Great Escape Ranch** at Los Cerritos (Mexico 19, Km 66–67, 240jordi@gmail.com, US$150/night or US$850/week) has three rustically furnished bedrooms in a solar-powered home. Amenities include laundry, Internet, and satellite TV.

For luxury accommodations in a more re-mote location, **Noche de las Estrellas** (www. nochedelasestrellas.com, US$350/night or US$5,000/week) sits on a bluff overlooking a sand beach at Elias Calles, 16 kilometers south of Pescadero. Four suites have private sitting areas, granite baths, and guest robes (for walking to the pool and hot tub). A shared living room has satellite TV and Wi-Fi, and the tiled kitchen has granite counters, an island and window bar with stools, and a table that seats eight. An outdoor kitchen is available for grilling. During the low season, they also operate as a bed-and-breakfast for only US$195 per night.

Also in the Elias Calles area, **Casa Aqua Brillante** (Mexico 19, Km 82, www.todossantos.cc/casaaquabrillante.html, US$3,500/week) is a luxury villa that sleeps six in three suites. Liberal use of marble, onyx, and granite set the stage. A 10-person dining table has ocean views. A fully equipped kitchen, satellite TV, and Wi-Fi complete the experience. The villa is off the grid, using solar power and propane for power and heat. Daily maid service is included in the rate. Inquire about food-stocking service and airport shuttles.

Surf Camp

On the east side of the highway at Km 64, **Pescadero Surf Camp** (tel. 612/134-0480, www.pescaderosurf.com, US$30–60) is a good place for diehard surfers to meet kindred spirits. Options for lodging include a *cabaña* for six with its own kitchen and bath, or camping under a *palapa* (US$7–10 pp/night). Guests may use the swimming pool, hot showers, and shared outdoor kitchen.

Camping and RV Parks

RV Park Baja Serena (tel. 612/130-3006, US$12) in Pescadero offers eight spaces with water and sewer hookups (no electricity) that can be rented by the day, week, or month. The entrance is on Mexico 19 just south of Mini Super Los Arcos, and guests check in at the Los Arcos. Rancho Pilar (Km 73, no tel., rates vary) has several campsites on his property. The

Pescadero Surf and Skate Camp (tel. 612/141-9440) at Km 64 has camping for US$10.

Camping at Playa Los Cerritos has been on again off again in recent years as developers prepare to begin work on a new oceanfront resort. You may be able to stay overnight here (self-contained camping only), but don't count on it.

Free beach campsites along Mexico 19 await at the ends of several dirt roads that leave Mexico 19 between Km 89 and Km 70—though these are fast disappearing as developers move in.

FOOD

Restaurant Migriño (Mexico 19, Km 102, no tel., hours vary), on the west side of the highway, serves basic *antojitos* and refreshingly cold beer. Another road stop is the dirt-floored **Los Idolos de Mexico** (Mexico 19, Km 79, no tel., hours vary). They keep it simple but tasty with carnitas and tacos *de pescado* and *de camarón*.

Lonchería Rosita (tel. 612/130-3094, daily 8 A.M.–8 P.M.), on the east side of Mexico 19 near the Pemex, is small with a *palapa* roof. Try its pork tamales or *machaca* burritos.

The friendly **Marina's** (Km 62, no tel.) offers a nice variety of fish and shrimp tacos, plus quesadillas, a soup of the day, and the huge cheese/carne asada mixto (US$3).

Popular with locals and expats alike for its casual fare, ◖ **Felipe's Restaurant** (Mexico 19, Km 61, no tel., Wed.–Mon., hours vary, mains around US$8) makes delicious Mexican and seafood dishes at nongringo prices for breakfast, lunch, and dinner. This place serves an excellent shrimp chile relleno and even better *arrachera*. Closed on Tuesdays.

Grill your own kebabs at the **Sandbar** (Mexico 19, Km 63, tel. 612/130-3209, Mon.–Sat. 3 P.M. till late, Sun. 1–10 P.M.), or just pop in for daily happy hour specials, as well as weekly all-you-can-eat pizza. Show up for all-you-can-eat spaghetti on Thursdays, reggae night with live music on Fridays (for which there is a $2–3 cover charge), and disco nights on Saturdays.

The **Los Cerritos Club** (Mexico 19, Km 66.5 at Playa Los Cerritos, restaurant cell tel. 044/624/129-6315, office tel. 624/143-4850, daily 7 A.M.–8 P.M., mains US$5–20) opened with multiple large-screen TVs and outdoor tables arranged around a few firepits. This is the perfect place for a beer and a burger after a good surfing session, and/or to enjoy the sunset. Live music plays Friday and Saturday nights.

Regulars praise **Art & Beer** (Mexico 19, Km 69, no tel., hours vary) for large signature cocktails—creative variations on the Bloody Mary—which comes generously garnished with all manner of shellfish. You must agree to buy a drink or a meal in order to view the art on display. When it's time to go, your eccentric hosts, Alfredo and Lourdes, may offer up a beer for the road. Fish dishes cost US$20.

Groceries

Mini Super Los Arcos on Mexico 19 stocks the basics, and the owners welcome special orders. **Mini Super Los Cerritos** (Mexico 19, Km 63) sells cold beer and ice, as well as some arts and crafts. At Km 61, you can buy strawberries direct from the farmers at US$1–2 per basket.

INFORMATION AND SERVICES

Pescadero has the only Pemex between Cabo San Lucas and Todos Santos, as well as an Oxxo convenience store. For emergencies, call 612/145-0445, or head to Todos Santos or the Los Cabos area for medical services. Buses en route to La Paz and Cabo San Lucas stop across from the Pemex. Many places in the Pescadero area now have wireless Internet; otherwise the new **Gonver's Coffee Shop** (located exactly across from the Pemex, no tel.) charges US$2 per hour for the use of one its computers, and the service is free if you buy a coffee or a muffin. This place makes great smoothies.

Todos Santos

About halfway from La Paz to Cabo San Lucas, at a kink in the highway, Mexico 1 passes through the 18th-century mission town of Todos Santos (pop. 5,000–7,000, depending on the season). When they discovered fresh water in an underground spring here at the base of the Sierra de la Laguna, the Jesuits developed this arroyo settlement, about two kilometers inland from the coast, as a farming supply station. When the silver mines were active on the east side of the sierra, wealthy families from El Triunfo began making Todos Santos their weekend getaway town.

After a period of booming sugar production in the early 20th century, the town became once again an agricultural center, supplying restaurants in Los Cabos and markets as far away as the United States with organic fruits and vegetables year-round. The spring keeps Todos Santos lush and green, especially around the *huerta* (orchard) on the north side of town.

In recent decades, Todos Santos has become a haven for artists, retirees, snowbirds, and yogis who either live here permanently, or return year after year to soak up the sun and the bohemian vibe. It is also a popular weekend place for La Paz residents looking to escape the summer heat.

The downtown area consists of a grid of mostly paved though dusty streets, many lined with 100-year-old brick buildings. There is a town plaza with a historic church, but it doesn't feel like the center of the action in modern-day Todos Santos. Most visitors congregate along the central blocks between Avenida Juárez and Calles Centenario, Obregón, and Márquez de León.

Beyond the immediate downtown area are sandy beaches with surf breaks and a freshwater lagoon called La Poza that supports a healthy population of birds.

As a newly designated Pueblo Mágico, Todos Santos has received access to

THE WEST CAPE

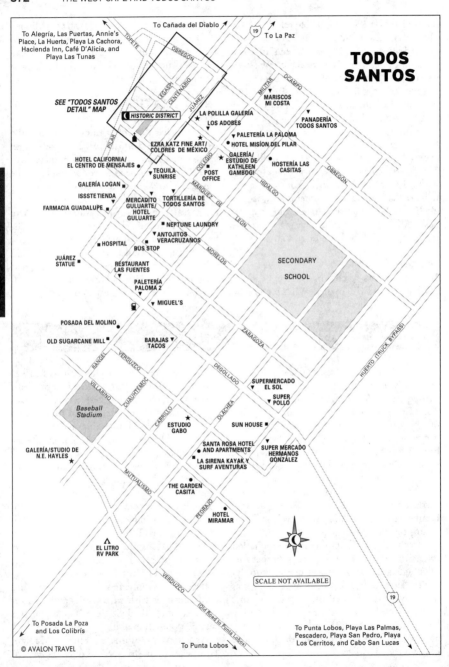

TODOS SANTOS

To Cañada del Diablo

19 To La Paz

To Alegría, Las Puertas, Annie's Place, La Huerta, Playa La Cachora, Hacienda Inn, Café D'Alicia, and Playa Las Tunas

TOPETE

OBREGÓN

LEGASPI

CENTENARIO

JUÁREZ

SEE "TODOS SANTOS DETAIL" MAP

■ HISTORIC DISTRICT

PILAR

MILITAR

OCAMPO

MARISCOS MI COSTA

LA POLILLA GALERÍA

LOS ADOBES

PANADERÍA TODOS SANTOS

PALETERÍA LA PALOMA

EZRA KATZ FINE ART/ COLORES DE MÉXICO

HOTEL MISIÓN DEL PILAR

COLEGIO

GALERÍA/ ESTUDIO DE KATHLEEN GAMBOGI

HOSTERÍA LAS CASITAS

HOTEL CALIFORNIA/ EL CENTRO DE MENSAJES

TEQUILA SUNRISE

POST OFFICE

OBREGÓN

MARQUEZ DE

HIDALGO

GALERÍA LOGAN

ISSSTE TIENDA

FARMACIA GUADALUPE

MERCADITO GULUARTE/ HOTEL GULUARTE

TORTILLERÍA DE TODOS SANTOS

LEÓN

NEPTUNE LAUNDRY

ANTOJITOS VERACRUZANOS

HOSPITAL

BUS STOP

JUÁREZ STATUE

RESTAURANT LAS FUENTES

MORELOS

SECONDARY SCHOOL

PALETERÍA PALOMA 2

MIGUEL'S

POSADA DEL MOLINO

OLD SUGARCANE MILL

BARAJAS TACOS

ZARAGOZA

HUERTO (TRUCK BYPASS)

RANGEL

VERDUZCO

VILLARINO

CUAUHTEMOC

DEGOLLADO

OLACHEA

SUPERMERCADO EL SOL

SUPER POLLO

Baseball Stadium

CARRILLO

ESTUDIO GABO

SUN HOUSE

GALERÍA/STUDIO DE N.E. HAYLES

SANTA ROSA HOTEL AND APARTMENTS

SUPER MERCADO HERMANOS GONZÁLEZ

LA SIRENA KAYAK Y SURF AVENTURAS

MUTUALISMO

THE GARDEN CASITA

PEDRAJO

HOTEL MIRAMAR

EL LITRO RV PARK

19

VERDUZCO (Old Road to Punta Lobos)

To Posada La Poza and Los Colibrís

To Punta Lobos

To Punta Lobos, Playa Las Palmas, Pescadero, Playa San Pedro, Playa Los Cerritos, and Cabo San Lucas

SCALE NOT AVAILABLE

© AVALON TRAVEL

THE WEST CAPE

© CARMEL TSABAR

sunset at Playa Las Pocitas

government funding for improving infrastructure and developing cultural tourism. To date, the money has been used to remodel the park and repair the auditorium. Next on the project list: burying wires and cables in the town center, repairing the theater, and protecting the oasis and lagoon.

In recent years, the town has buzzed with talk of real estate development. One project near La Poza ran into problems with water and sewer rights; another at San Pedrito changed hands three times in less than a year. There has been talk of a fishing village at Punta Lobos. And new homes have popped up at the other end of town, along Playa Las Tunas, as power and water infrastructure creep northward. Locals remain optimistic that Todos Santos will retain its small-town feel, even in the wake of increased development—with Carmel and Santa Fe as models, rather than Los Cabos or Cancún.

HISTORY

Spanish Jesuit Padre Jaime Bravo arrived in the Todos Santos area in the early 18th century to find the nomadic Guaicura tribe living off abundant freshwater and shellfish in a coastal oasis environment. He promptly set up a *misión de visita* (visiting mission) in 1724 as a support station for the struggling settlement at La Paz. Within a few years, Todos Santos was sending 200 burro-loads of *panocha* (raw brown sugar) a year, along with figs, pomegranates, citrus fruits, and grapes to La Paz.

Misión Santa Rosa de las Palmas

Todos Santos' mission history begins with the founding of a *visita* by Jesuit Padre Jaime Bravo in 1724. The visiting station became a full-fledged mission called Misión Santa Rosa de las Palmas in 1733, with Padre Sigismundo Taraval in charge. A year later, the Pericú rebelled, destroying four southern Baja missions, including Todos Santos. Taraval, however, escaped to Isla Espíritu Santo. Missionary activities resumed a year later, but the Pericú continued to resist conversion, and a number of epidemic began to wipe out the population. When the mission in La Paz closed in 1748, Todos Santos was

THE WEST CAPE

renamed Nuestra Señora del Pilar de Todos Santos. In 1768, the Franciscans moved several hundred Guaycura to Todos Santos from other missions in the central peninsula. The population continued to drop until the mission was secularized in 1840.

The earliest mission buildings were located about a kilometer and a half north of the current town center. A modern church and private residence are located on top of the ruins. The Iglesia Nuestra Señora del Pilar stands on the southwest side of the Todos Santos town plaza. Originally built by the Dominicans in the mid-19th century, the building was expanded in 1967. It contains a statue of the Virgin of Pilar, whom the town honors with a festival each year in October.

Sugar Mills

Following the mission period, Todos Santos built an economy based on sugarcane production. By the late 1800s, there were eight sugar mills in the area, and the town grew rapidly. The sugar market crashed after World War II in the face of lower prices and lack of fresh water, and by 1965, all of the mills closed. Todos Santos was virtually abandoned until the end of the century.

Around 1981, the spring filled once again with freshwater, and land became arable again. In 1984, the government paved Mexico 19 from San Pedro (out of La Paz) and Cabo San Lucas, leading the way to an economy built on tourism and permanent expat residents.

SIGHTS
Historic District

A stroll along streets near the historic town plaza reveals hundred-year-old homes made of brick and some adobe, many of them now owned by outsiders and carefully restored in an array of pastel colors. Oversized windows and doors framed by decorative pilasters (rectangular supports that look like flat columns) are a signature design, borrowed from the classic revival style of architecture. The present-day Café Santa Fé on Calle Centenario, facing the plaza, is the largest adobe structures left standing in

town. The facades on the surrounding streets are likely to look more homogenous in coming years, as a uniform appearance is one of the contingencies of funding made available through the Pueblo Mágico program. Check *El Calendario* (www.elcalendariotodossantos.com) for the timing of the annual historic home tour, when owners open their doors to visitors.

Centro Cultural Profesor Nestor Agúndez Martínez

To immerse yourself in Todos Santos past, visit the Centro Cultural (Ave. Juárez at Obregón, Mon.–Fri. 8 A.M.–5 P.M., Sat.–Sun. 9 A.M.–1 P.M., free admission), which covers the anthropology, ethnography, and history of the area, including a few examples of modern art and handicrafts. Named for a local high school teacher who passed away in 2009, the museum is housed in a restored brick building. Its pottery display has examples of local ranchware, as well as older pieces created by the native Pericú.

BEACHES

Just about every dirt road heading west from Todos Santos ends at the beach. But few of them are paved or signed, which means you may be in for an adventure when you try to find a particular spot along the coast. Ask for directions before you set out and remember that routes often shift a little with each successive season of rain. With the exception of Los Cerritos near El Pescadero and sometimes Playa Las Palmas/San Pedrito, beaches near Todos Santos are not swimmable because of strong currents, heavy surf, and rocky bottoms. (The exception may be in summer when the swell subsides for long periods of time.) Plan to sunbathe, fish, stroll the beach, or surf, but save the splashing around for the pool.

Punta Lobos

Starting south of town, local fishing boats launch out of Punta Lobos, marked by a rocky point and sea lion colony on the south side of a sandy cove. The *pangas* return to shore around 3 P.M.; watch the captains time the waves so that they can safely run the boats onto the beach. You can often buy fresh catch directly from the *pangueros*. If you walk north along the beach past the lighthouse, you'll reach **Playa Las Pocitas** and **Playa La Cachora.**

The signed access road to Punta Lobos leaves Mexico 19 about two kilometers south of Todos Santos at Km 54. As you near the beach, you'll see the ruins of an old turtle cannery. To walk to Punta Lobos from town (20–30 minutes each way), follow Calle Pedrajo southwest one long block to a wide, dirt road. Turn left and follow this road until you can see the lighthouse on your right; take the next dirt road west to Punta Lobos.

Puerto Algodones

Between Punta Lobos and Playa San Pedrito, an old port bound by cliffs was used reportedly in the early 20th century to ship fresh produce, sugarcane, and canned fish. Climb (carefully) out to the old pier or to the summit above it for some of the most memorable views. You can swim here, but pay attention to currents and tides.

The access road to this secluded bay is rough and steep in parts. Turn off Mexico 19 toward Punta Lobos and turn left when you pass the cannery ruins (before the beach). You probably won't be able to make it all the way to the port. Alternatively, leave your car at Punta Lobos and it will take about an hour to get there by foot.

◖ La Poza

Bird-watchers rejoice in this freshwater lagoon located west of the *huerta* and south of La Cachora road—and just beyond the tideline. With dunes in front and palms behind, La Poza provides ideal habitat for a long list of birds including pelicans, herons, egrets, gulls, frigate birds, ibis, ducks, cormorants, sandpipers, and stilts. The beach in front of the lagoon is called Playa Las Pocitas, and it meets Playa La Cachora to the north, where La Cachora road meets the coast.

A word of warning: The lagoon appears to be shallow but is in fact very deep. Most of the time, it is separated from the ocean by a high sand dune; however, the dune occasionally breaks in large swells, and when this happens, a trickle of water out of the lagoon can turn into a towering wall of water almost instantly. Unsuspecting visitors have drowned in these situations. Stay back from the water's edge and monitor the wave patterns at all times.

To reach the beaches and the lagoon from downtown, start on Calle Topete near the Galería de Todos Santos and follow it north, down a small hill and around to the west, across the orchard. Turn left at the first sand road, which comes immediately before a low rock wall. If you start going uphill, you've gone too far. La Cachora road heads west to

COURTESY OF POSADA LA POZA, TODOS SANTOS

La Poza

the beach passing a few homes and an inn or two along the way.

Playa La Pastora

If you skip the turnoff to La Cachora and drive past the rock wall up the small hill, you'll find yourself in the *otro lado* (other side) of Todos Santos, with yet more beaches at the end of unnamed dirt roads and a few housing developments in various states of completion. Follow this coastal road about 5.6 km farther northwest to a wide arroyo that leads to a sandy beach. Resist the urge to drive all the way up onto the sand to check the surf from your car. Chance are, you will get stuck. The break is a right point in a northwest swell and occasionally also a beach break in a south swell.

North to Punta Marquez and Punta Conejo

If you're up for some serious off-road exploration, continue north along the coastal road. After Playa La Pastora, the road veers east and reaches a T, from which you can turn right to get back to Mexico 19 or turn left to

continue northwest more or less parallel to the coast. At Rancho los Inocentes (57 km from La Pastora), you can once again head inland (straight) to rejoin Mexico 1 north of La Paz (29 km from Rancho los Inocentes), or turn left to stay on the coast. This road eventually reaches Punta Marquez (24 km north of Rancho el Tomate) and Punta Conejo (18 km north of Punta Marques), two well-known points for surfing. This entire stretch of the Pacific coast is lined with sandy beaches and, in winter, surfable breaks on a succession of reefs and points. You can camp anywhere along the shore, just be sure to bring all of your supplies, as the nearest commercial outposts are a long drive away.

SPORTS AND RECREATION
Fishing

Since it lacks a marina or protected harbor (other than the abandoned pier at Puerto Algondones), Todos Santos does not have much of a charter fishing business. However, if you speak Spanish, you can talk to the *pangueros* to arrange a day of sportfishing. Prices average

© NIKKI GOTH ITOI

surf casting near Todos Santos

about US$30 per hour, usually with a three-hour minimum.

Playas San Pedrito (Palm Beach), San Pedro, and Los Cerritos are among the easiest (and safest) places for fishing from shore. Experienced locals also head to La Pastora and points north. The catch from shore includes *sierra* (mackerel), *cabrilla* (sea bass), *pargo* (snapper), and *robalo* (snook).

Ferretería Oasis de Todos Santos (Rangel at Zaragoza, tel. 612/145-0754, Mon.–Fri. 8 A.M.–3 P.M. and 4–7 P.M., Sat. 8 A.M.–4 P.M.) carries some fishing supplies. You can buy live bait from the local fishermen at Punta Lobos.

Whale-Watching

Whale-watching from Todos Santos is from a distance, compared to the up-close encounters you can have in the birthing lagoons farther north. But an afternoon spent watching juvenile gray whales breach and slap their tales offshore while you sip margaritas on a rooftop deck makes for great entertainment nonetheless. December–April are the best months for catching the whales on their journey to the Sea of Cortez.

Pangueros at Punta Lobos may be willing to take passengers out to see the whales for about US$25 an hour; book at the beach or through any of the hotels in town.

Surfing and Kayaking

Winter months are best for surfing the Todos Santos area when the local breaks catch the strong northwest swell. In summer, the action moves south to the Corridor between Cabo San Lucas and San José del Cabo, or to lesser-known spots around the east side of the Cape.

The **Los Cerritos Surf Shop** (at Playa Los Cerritos, no tel., hours vary) has opened its physical storefront. You can contact owner/instructor Mario Becerril directly (tel. 612/142-6156, mariosurfing@hotmail.com) for lessons, rentals, and ding repair. He is a highly reputable instructor and has lots of experience with the local breaks.

Costa Azul Surf Shop (on Juárez, no tel.) is an extension of the same store at Playa Costa Azul in San José del Cabo, and they have also set up a mobile board rental/lesson kiosk on the north end of Cerritos beach.

La Sirena Kayak y Surf Aventuras (Olachea off Degollado, tel. 612/145-0353, www.lasirenakayaksurf.com) rents surfing equipment and supplies, offers surfing instruction (US$50/hour), and leads local kayak tours (US$50).

Hiking

You can arrange guided day or overnight hikes into the Sierra de la Laguna at **Todos Santos Eco Adventures** (Juárez and Topete, tel. 612/145-0780, www.tosea.net) or **La Sirena Kayak y Surf Aventuras** (Olachea off Degollado, tel. 612/145-0353, www.lasirenakayaksurf.com).

Yoga, Meditation, and Martial Arts

Hatha and Ashtanga yoga classes meet several times a week at the La Arca building on Topete (US$4 per class). In the same location,

THE WEST CAPE

El Dharma de Todos Santos (tel. 612/145-0676, www.eldharma.com) holds dharma talks and *vipassana* meditation classes Sundays 10–11:30 A.M. And Carlos Martinez Hererra offers Aikido classes to beginners and experienced students (cell tel. 612/018-1052, ranchaiki@aikifarms.com, US$4 per class).

Tai chi chuan classes take place at the Centro Cultural Monday, Wednesday, and Thursday, October–June, for around US$6. Hours vary with the season.

The Elephant Tree (Obregón btw Centenario/Juárez, tel. 612/145-0299) offers yoga, tarot, and writing workshops.

Spa Services
Kathleen Nelson offers massage treatments through **Todos Santos Oasis** (19 Legaspi at Hidalgo, tel. 612/145-0545, US$35/hr).

Organized Tours
Todos Santos Eco Adventures (Juárez and Topete, tel. 612/145-0780, www.tosea.net) leads half-day outings to nearby waterfalls, cliff walks, and La Candelaria for US$55, as well as overnight trips to the Sierra Laguna, fishing trips (US$275 per boat for up to 6 hrs), and horseback riding (US$45/hr). A 90-minute walking tour of historic sites in Todos Santos is US$15 per person. The Eco Adventures office is also a friendly source of tourist information.

La Sirena Kayak y Surf Aventuras (Olachea off Degollado, tel. 612/145-0353, www.lasirenakayaksurf.com) leads similar trips, including whale-watching (US$35 pp for two hours), fishing (US$50/hour), and waterfall hikes (US$40 pp).

SHOPPING
Todos Santos has a growing collection of boutiques that are fun to browse if you want to return home with gifts or something special for yourself. The quality is generally high, but note that most of the inventory in these stores comes from the mainland, not from Baja. Most of the shopping centers around the historic district near the plaza.

Home Furnishings and Gifts
In business since 1994, **Fénix de Todos Santos** (Juárez at Hidalgo, tel. 612/145-0808, Mon.–Sat. 10 A.M.–5 P.M.) has a selection of hand-blown glass, Talavera pottery, *equipal* pig skin furniture, and decorative tinware.

Emporio Hotel California (Juárez btw Morelos/Márquez de León, tel. 612/145-0217, daily 10 A.M.–7 P.M.) has a variety of apparel, jewelry, ceramics, and other gifts on display in a large storefront adjoining the hotel.

Mangos Folk Art (Centenario btw Topete/Obregón, tel. 612/145-0451, Tues.–Sat. 10 A.M.–5 P.M.) specializes in folk art from mainland Mexico and Guatemalan textiles.

Also on Centenario at Topete, **Manos Mexicanas** (tel. 612/145-0538, Mon.–Sat. 10 A.M.–5 P.M.) has arts and crafts from Guadalajara and Michoacan on the mainland, plus ceramics created by local artist Ruben Gutierrez.

Joyería Brilanti (Centenario 24 btw Topete/Obregón, tel./fax 612/145-0799, www.brilanti.com, Mon.–Sat. 10 A.M.–5 P.M.) has a distinctive history as one of the earliest silver designers from Taxco on the mainland. Today, the business is run by the son of the original founder, Ana Brilanti. In addition to a beautiful selection of silver pieces, the gallery has sculptures and paintings for sale.

Clothing
Owned by the Brilanti family of jewelers, **El Perico Azul** (Topete at Centenario, tel. 612/145-0538, Mon.–Sat. 10 A.M.–5 P.M., Sun. 11 A.M.–4 P.M.), sells handwoven cotton clothing for men and women. **Sisy's Boutique** (Hidalgo and Colegio Militar, no tel.) sells beachwear and T-shirts, as well as imported perfumes.

Arts and Crafts
For less expensive souvenirs, several vendors usually are set up near the plaza, though their names change frequently. **La Iguana** and **Artesanías El Cardón**, on the northwest corner of Márquez de León and Juárez opposite the church, have been around a while. Next

door, **Bazar Agua y Sol** (tel. 612/145-0537) has jewelry, sculptures, pottery, and paintings. Credit cards are accepted here.

Pintoresco (Colegio Militar at Zaragoza, tel. 612/145-0222, cell tel. 044/612/158-8457, Mon.–Sat. 10 A.M.–7 P.M.) is divided into two locales in the same shopping gallery: The first features more tourist-oriented crafts from various parts of Mexico, including textiles, jewelry, and decorations; the second is next door and features fine art, all of Mexican origin. The gallery is at Local #5 in the shopping gallery on Colegio Militar at the corner of Zaragoza.

La Polilla (Hidalgo and Juárez, tel. 612/161-4840) offers paintings, furniture, and decorative items selected by owner José Ramirez. He has a second, mainly furniture-related store on the highway near Pescadero's Pemex (on the other side of the road.) La Polilla is also a studio/gallery for a family of artists from Guadalajara, and José Luis Malo offers dynamic crash courses in modern painting in which students complete a canvas of their own within a few hours to take home.

Books
El Tecolote Books/Libros (Juárez and Hidalgo, tel. 612/145-0295, fax 612/145-0288, janethowwey@yahoo.com, Mon.–Sat. 10 A.M.–5 P.M., Sun. 11 A.M.–3 P.M.) is a book lover's shop—the kind of place that makes you want to run an independent bookstore in your retirement. The owner stocks the shelves with a mix of foreign and Mexican periodicals, new and used paperback fiction, and hardcover design and coffee-table books, plus maps and a good section of Baja-related titles. It's no Borders or Barnes&Noble, but whether you want to read Tom Clancy or Graham Greene, chances are you'll find something you like at this shop. Bilingual children's books make a nice gift for kids. You can also buy books on tape and rent or buy movies. Besides the books, the store carries some art supplies.

Artist Studios and Galleries
The art scene in Todos Santos has come of age in recent years, with more than a dozen galleries representing internationally known artists from the United States and Mexico. For historical value alone, the **Charles Stewart Gallery & Studio** (Centenario and Obregón, tel./fax 612/145-0265, www.charlescstewart.com, Mon.–Sat. 11 A.M.–4 P.M.) merits a visit by anyone interested in the development of Todos Santos' art culture. Known as the founder of the now-prolific artist colony here, Stewart bought the only house for sale in town in 1983. His gallery was the first and only one until the mid-1990s, and his work has been catalogued by the Smithsonian and the Fine Arts Museum of Houston, Texas.

Galería On cé (Hidalgo 11, tel. 612/145-0550, variable hours) opened in 2006 to showcase the photography of Howard Ekman and Jack Hamilton.

Galería de Todos Santos (Legaspi 33 at Topete, tel. 612/145-0500, www.galeriadetodossantos.com, Mon.–Sat. 11 A.M.–4 P.M.), established in 1994, is one of the few in town representing both local and foreign artists and, accordingly, diverse styles. Among those represented here are owner Michael Cope himself, celebrated local artist Erick Ochoa, and the whimsical style of Jennifer Power.

Jill Logan creates the original oils and mixed media works featured in the **Galería Logan** (tel. 612/145-0151, www.jilllogan.com, Mon.–Sat. 11 A.M.–4 P.M., Sun. by appointment). Logan has an extensive education in fine art, and her work has been exhibited across the United States, as well as in Mexico.

La Paz native Ezra Katz, known for murals and etchings featured in a number of Cabo San Lucas restaurants and hotels, has opened **Galería Indigo** (Juárez at Hidalgo, tel. 612/137-3473, Mon.–Sat. 10 A.M.–5 P.M., or by appt.), featuring John Comer, Lindy Duncan, Lesley Rich, and others, in addition to his own artwork.

Galería/Studio de N. E. Hayles (Cuauhtémoc, tel./fax 612/145-0183, www.mexonline.com/hayles.htm, Mon.–Sat. 11 A.M.–4 P.M.) displays unique paper-tile mosaics, multimedia art, and tables fashioned by the artist/owner. **Galería Wall** (Hidalgo and Colegio Militar, a few feet away from Café Brown, tel. 612/145-0527, www.catherinewallart.com, Mon.–Sat. 11 A.M.–4 P.M.) shows Mexican-themed original oils by artist Catherine Wall.

Gabo Galería (Márquez de León, btw Juárez and Colegio Militar,, tel. 612/145-0514, gaboartist@hotmail.com, Mon.–Sat. 10 A.M.–4 P.M.) features paintings by Gabo, who was born in Mexico, studied in Europe, and settled in La Paz in 1978. In the years since, he has played a major role in the art scene in La Paz and Todos Santos. His works are known for their bright colors and humorous style. Tours of his studio are by appointment only, while the gallery keeps regular hours.

Colores de México (Juárez at Hidalgo, tel. 612/145-0106, omommag@aol.com, daily 9 A.M.–6 P.M.), across from Los Adobes, is a family-owned gallery specializing in photographic art. All of the photographs featured here are the work of Pat Gerhardt, a longtime resident of Todos Santos, and her daughter, Christiana Parsons.

ENTERTAINMENT AND EVENTS
Bars
La Iguana Disco Bar (Zaragoza and Rangel, no tel., Fri.–Sat. nights) hosts live reggae and rock bands. In the gardens of the Todos Santos Inn, **La Copa** (Legaspi 33, tel. 612/145-0040, daily 5–9 P.M.) is a classy wine bar with romantic appeal. Michael Cope has added a tapas menu Wednesday–Friday evenings (US$10/plate). The entrance is on Calle Topete.

The bar in the Hotel California's uniquely decorated **La Coronela** (Juárez btw Morelos/Márquez de León, tel. 612/145-0525), frequented by local expats as well as the hotel's guests, is a fun place to have a few drinks. There's live music on Saturday evenings.

Theater
The restored **Teatro Márquez de León** (Legaspi at Márquez de León, no tel.) hosts music and dance performances, often during the annual October town fiesta. Before La Paz

city theater was built, Todos Santos had the only true theater in the state.

Festivals and Events
Fiesta Todos Santos takes place in October each year, around the feast day of the Virgen del Pilar (October 12). This four-day extravaganza begins on the second Saturday of the month and involves dances, sports competitions, horse races, theater performances, and amusement-park rides. Most of these events center around the town plaza.

The Christmas holidays are especially festive in Todos Santos, where for 12 days beginning on the **Día de Guadalupe** (December 12), local residents hold nightly candlelight processions to the Iglesia Nuestra Señora del Pilar. The season culminates in a midnight Mass worship service on **Christmas Eve.**

In late January or early February, the government-funded **Todos Santos Art Festival** takes place with sculptures, paintings, ceramics, and other visual works by local artists. Performing arts groups also arrive from out of town to participate in the event. Then, in early March, the **Todos Santos Latin Film Festival** comes to town.

Also once a year, usually in February or March, historic homes in Todos Santos open to the public. Check *El Calendario* (www.todossantos-baja.com) for more information.

ACCOMMODATIONS AND CAMPING
Overnight guests in Todos Santos can choose from a variety of modest hotels, bed-and-breakfasts, and private vacation rentals. As more visitors arrive each year, new properties are opening, old ones are renovating, and others are just raising prices without making significant improvements. Many properties are now up for sale, and if water and sewer rights are worked out, several large resorts may be coming to the area in the not-too-distant future.

The principal complaint that many first-time visitors express is frustration with the noise that comes with staying in a non-resort town. From the rumble of 18-wheelers to the persistent dog-barking and chicken-clucking, Todos Santos can feel like a town that doesn't sleep. In general, places closer to the beach are quieter (though not silent, and farther from town). It's a good idea to bring earplugs, and ask your host what to expect at night.

There are three accommodations in town with "Todos Santos" in their name: The Hacienda Todos Los Santos is located in the palm grove at the end of Avenida Juárez; the Todos Santos Inn is on Calle Topete, with its own wine bar; and the Hacienda Inn Todos Santos is north of town. Details for each are given in this section.

Hotels, Inns, and Bed-and-Breakfasts

UNDER US$50

Large, clean rooms are centrally located at **Motel Guluarte** (Juárez and Morello, tel. 612/145-0006, US$30). This place is well-known among budget travelers.

US$50-100

The former Hotel Misión del Pilar got a fresh coat of paint inside and out in 2006 and opened under new ownership as the **(Maria Bonita Hotel** (Colegio Militar at Hidalgo, tel. 612/145-0114, US$50–60). The office and 12 guestrooms are all on the second floor, above the popular Café Brown. Though rooms are plain, the clean off-white walls, new curtains and bedspreads, and comfortable mattresses make for a pleasant stay. Small but clean bathrooms have shower stalls with glass doors and hot water aplenty. A great value, this hotel is a wise choice for budget travelers who need a place to crash for the night. Through-traffic on Mexico 19 passes right by the hotel entrance, so expect to hear trucks and car radios unless you crank the fan on the air-conditioner. Rates include tax.

At **Bed and Breakfast Las Casitas** (Rangel btw Obregón/Hidalgo, tel./fax 612/145-0255, www.lascasitasbandb.com, US$60–100), Canadian artist Wendy Faith has lovingly restored four *chiname* adobe cottages and one four-person suite over the last decade. Set among lush landscaping, rooms are small with low ceilings, one bed, and brightly colored walls and ceilings. Accommodations here are basic but artsy, with hand-painted murals in some rooms and the artist's own glasswork in others. Breakfast includes the bed-and-breakfast's own blend of coffee. An authentic *palo de arco casita* houses the owner's studio. This property was up for sale at last check.

To get to the **Hotel Santa Rosa** (tel. 612/145-0394, www.hotelsantarosa.com.mx, US$70), go three blocks south of the Pemex station, turn right on Calle Olachea, and go two blocks. There are eight spacious units with kitchenettes and queen beds, plus a well-maintained pool, hot tub, and enclosed parking. The hotel offers a 5 percent discount for weeklong stays, 10 percent off for two weeks, and 33 percent off for a month-long reservation.

US$100-150

Set among towering palm, mango, and banana trees, **Jardin de Pilar** (Pilar btw Topete/Hidalgo, tel. 612/145-0386, www.jardinde-pilar.com, US$105–120) has two beautifully appointed *casitas* for rent. Details include colorful high-end linens and bamboo accents, as well as wireless Internet and swimming pool.

A few meters from La Cachora road, **The Hotelito** (tel. 612/145-0099, www.thehotelito.com, US$90–145) is an elegant and enchanting boutique-style inn, with four cottages that blend a modern Mexican and European style.

Much-loved for its location, sparkling pool, and friendly service, **(Hacienda Todos Los Santos** (Juárez, tel. 612/145-0547, www.mex-online.com/haciendatodoslossantos.htm) has updated and expanded with eight new rooms in its four guesthouses. Each room has its own unique personality, but all have air-conditioning, private terraces, and spacious bathrooms. Casa Santa Luz (US$195) has a queen-size bed, TV/VCR, and fireplace. Casa del Palmar (US$165) is a studio suite with multiple terraces, king-size bed, and TV/VCR. Casita del Encanto (US$125) is a studio suite complete with two patios, queen-size bed, and seating area. Casa de los Santos, a new four-bedroom and six-bath at Hacienda Todos Los Santos, opened in 2007. It has one room (US$125) and three suites (US$185–225), and the whole house rents for US$850 a night. The upstairs suites have great views of the surrounding farmland. Owner Karen Rodriguez also rents a two-bedroom brick house with a *palapa* roof, **Casa San Vicente,** on the corner of Pedrajo and Mutualismo.

US$150-250

On the road to La Pastora, the **Hacienda Inn Todos Santos** (tel./fax 612/145-0193, US$110–140 with continental breakfast) is about two kilometers from the center of town—not ideal unless you have your own car. The inn has a swimming pool and restaurant with a bar. All 14 rooms and suites have air-conditioning, cable TV, and comfy bathrobes. Turn right at the El Sol II grocery store to find the inn.

A stay at the elegant **Todos Santos Inn** (Legaspi 33 at Topete, tel./fax 612/145-0040, www.todossantosinn.com, US$125–225) takes visitors back to the town's sugarcane era in the 19th century. Housed in a restored brick building, the inn is beautifully designed and appointed with high ceilings, antique furnishings, and tile floors. Amenities include private terraces, ceiling fans, and air-conditioning. Guests enjoy use of a small pool and the on-site La Copa Wine Bar. Spanish-language instruction is available, either separately or as a package with accommodations (10 hours for US$200).

Last renovated in 2003, two-story **Hotel California** (Juárez btw Morelos/Márquez de León, tel. 612/145-0525, hotelcaliforniareservations@hotmail.com, US$125–200) has 11 suites, a small swimming pool, and courtyard garden. It also has its own restaurant, **La Coronela,** and a gift shop called **Emporio Hotel California.**

Posada La Poza (tel. 612/145-0400, www.lapoza.com) blends the relaxed pace of life in Baja with a Swiss sensibility for quality and efficiency. Hosts Jörg and Libusche Wiesendanger opened the hotel in 2002. Guests stay in one of four garden suites (US$200), two

Posada La Poza

junior suites with private hot tubs (US$325), or the honeymoon suite (US$480). Suites here come with views of the lagoon and ocean beyond, plus air-conditioning, a CD player, and Swiss bed linens. Guestrooms and common areas also feature Libusche's oil and acrylic paintings. You can splash around in a large saltwater swimming pool, soak in the new saltwater 10-person whirlpool tub, watch for whales from the deck, or borrow a bicycle for a ride into town. And when you've had your fill of the great outdoors, you might give yourself an aromatherapy treatment in the on-site sweat lodge, which is filled with heated lava rocks topped with eucalyptus leaves, rosemary, or other herbs. Internet access is available. Rates include continental breakfast, and **El Gusto!** restaurant serves hearty Mexican and international dishes like pork loin, rib-eye, and lobster. The road to La Poza is well marked: Turn southwest off Degollado (Mexico 19) onto Calle Olachea or Calle Carrillo and follow the blue-and-white signs.

Guesthouses and Vacation Rentals
US$50-100

The **Garden Casita** (Olachea and Mutualismo, tel./fax 612/145-0129, www.todossantos-baja.com/gardencasita.htm, US$85/395 day/week) is a unique redbrick guest house with a *palapa* roof. The *casita* has a living area, separate bedroom, and patio with enclosed courtyard. Wireless high-speed Internet is included and the long-term rates include weekly maid service.

In roughly the same neighborhood, **Las Flores Posada** (formerly Jane's Place, Pedrajo and Villarino, tel. 612/145-0216, www.todossantos.cc/lasfloresposada.html, US$55) has four cozy but well-worn casitas on an acre of property centered around a courtyard with a fountain. There are three studio bungalows, each with private bath and kitchen and a main bungalow with two-bedrooms, kitchen, and living room.

Across the *huerta,* north of town near Café D'Licia, a fun-loving retired Italian couple,

Sandra and Enrico Ugolini, have built several charming one-bedroom *casitas* (US$75–100) with separate kitchens, beautiful landscaping, and fabulous ocean views. Gourmet potluck dinners are a tradition for guests and friends alike. They prefer to not publicize their email or telephone number. To inquire about availability you have to stop by or ask around town.

Located in the middle of a trailer park near the sugarcane mill ruins, the **Posada del Molino** (off Rangel, tel. 612/145-0233, www.todossantos.cc/posadadelmolino.html, US$90–110) has four well-appointed and air-conditioned studios next to a swimming pool. Each studio has a queen-size bed, wireless Internet, satellite TV, and fully equipped kitchenettes.

US$100-150

At **Los Colibrís** (tel. 612/145-0780, www.loscolibris.com, US$115/night, US$700/week), the proprietors of family-run Todos Santos Eco Adventures have built three guest *casitas* on their hillside property, with stunning ocean views overlooking the freshwater estuary and Posada la Poza resort. Two twin beds in each *casita* can be arranged as a king. Meticulously tiled baths have rain showers and sculpted concrete countertops. Lampposts made of decorative tree trunks, colorful linens, and hummingbird feeders are few of the special touches. Rooms have ceiling fans (no air-conditioner), bottled water, and CD players. Outdoor space is limited given the steep incline of the property, but the upper unit has its own balcony, and two others share a furnished patio. Downstairs, the owners have set up a new movie room with a decent list of titles and board games. Two generations of the Jáuregui family attend to guest needs. (They also manage Casa Colina, a separate stand-alone house with two bedrooms and a kitchen.) Breakfast room service and afternoon margaritas are available upon request.

The same family has also built **Casa Colina** (tel. 612/145-0780, www.casacolina-ts.com, US$200/night, US$1,000/week), a two-story, two-bedroom home located below Los Colibris *casitas* and above Posada la Poza. Large picture windows in the bedrooms and kitchen open to ocean views, while balconies on both bedrooms face the mountains. Each bedroom has a king-size bed with luxury linens, ceiling fan, and its own bath. The casa also has a fully equipped kitchen.

Another longtime Todos Santos property now up for sale, **Annie's Place** (tel. 612/145-0385, anniesplacebaja@yahoo.com, US$135–185/day, US$800–1,100/week, three-night minimum) is tailored for the creative getaway. The large main house, Casa Amplia, has a high *palapa* roof over two bedrooms, a fireplace, and fully equipped kitchen. The tree house is a three-story structure, with a kitchen on the first floor, two twin beds on the second, and an open patio on the third. Long-term stays are welcome. Both structures are ensconced in a grove of mature coconut palms and mango trees.

On the road leading to Playa la Cachora, **Las Puertas** (tel./fax 612/145-0373, www.alaspuertas.com, US$135–175) offers a large two-bedroom guesthouse, a one-bedroom guesthouse, and a suite with ocean views. All of the structures are nicely furnished, private, and built in classic Baja style with *palapa* roofs and adobe walls. The ocean-view suite is the newest edition and has the nicest furnishings, a fireplace, and exceptional views. Daily maid service is included.

In addition to the guesthouses already listed, many part-time Todos Santos residents turn their homes into vacation rentals for guest use. Current lists of these places are usually kept at **El Centro de Mensajes** (The Message Center), in the Hotel California (Ave. Juárez, tel. 612/145-0525, fax 612/145-0288, messagecenter1@yahoo.com), **Su Casa** (Degollado btw Pedrajo/Olachea, cell tel. 612/157-5519, www.sucasa.cc), or **Como El Sol** (11 Hidalgo, tel./fax 612/145-0485, comoelsol@prodigy.net.mx, Mon.–Fri. 10 A.M.–2 P.M.) in the back of Colores de México.

These rentals generally cost US$400–700 a month for small, local-style cottages with few amenities, up to US$1,000–3,000 a month for larger houses with the works.

Camping and RV Parks

El Litro RV Park has only five short-term camping sites, since it is nearly full of permanent residents. RV sites are in a large dirt lot surrounded by palm trees, south of Mexico 19 at the end of Calle Olachea. Full hookups cost US$15 a night or US$250 a month, including hot showers, clean bathrooms, and laundry facilities. The park also has 30 tent camping sites (US$8 per night). The beach is a 15-minute walk. The owners can store your rig for US$40 a month.

The beaches north of town offer good camping, but no facilities. The farther north you go, the more remote and secluded it gets.

FOOD

With the wide variety of cuisines at just about every price point, you'll be hard-pressed to go hungry in Todos Santos.

Alta Cocina Mexicana

On the back patio of a beautifully restored adobe house, **Los Adobes** (Hidalgo btw Juárez/Colegio Militar, tel. 612/145-0203, www.losadobesdetodossantos.com, Mon.–Sat. 11:30 A.M.–9 P.M., mains US$15–22) prepares gourmet Mexican cuisine with prices to match. The menu includes grilled fish entrées, chicken mole, and steak fajitas.

El Gusto! at Posada la Poza on Playa La Cachora (tel. 612/145-0453, Fri.–Wed. 11:30 A.M.–4 P.M. and 6–9 P.M.) is the only beachfront restaurant in Todos Santos. A tapas menu is available on the Whale Terrace. The menu changes based on what organic produce is available, but there is usually a wide variety of seafood and meat choices. El Gusto! is a popular spot for sunset margaritas.

Mexican

Made famous by a *New York Times* write-up several years ago, **Miguel's** (Degollado and Rangel, daily 8 A.M.–9 P.M., mains US$6–10) became famous for lightly battered chiles rellenos smothered in sautéed tomatoes and onions. But on a recent visit something had changed, and the signature dish came up short. On the plus side, though, the new bypass through town has diverted most of the truck traffic away from this corner, making for a much more pleasant dining experience. A dozen tables are arranged on a sand floor under a *palapa* roof. The garrulous proprietor, Miguel, speaks excellent English and usually takes time to chat with repeat and first-time visitors. The menu also features enchiladas, burritos, and cheeseburgers.

You'll be hard pressed to find anything on the menu over US$7 at **Restaurant la Ramada** (Militar and Obregón, no tel., Mon.–Sat., mains US$3–6). This relative newcomer serves tacos, tostadas, and the like in a clean kitchen with friendly service; it's open for breakfast, lunch, and dinner.

Pueblo Mágico, on Juárez at Ocampo, at the north entrance/exit to town (Tues.–Sun. 8 A.M.–10 P.M.) offers standard Mexican dishes, including a wide variety of tacos (US$1–2), which can also be made into combination plates that include rice and beans (US$5–10). The restaurant is colorfully decorated and has foosball and pool tables.

Seafood

The friendly **Mariscos Mi Costa** (Colegio Militar at Ocampo, no tel., daily 10 A.M.–8 P.M., mains US$8–15) is a simple seafood restaurant with a raked sand floor. Its *sopa de mariscos* and *camarón al ajo* are especially good.

Located a few doors down from the Tecalote bookstore, **Fonda El Zaguán** (no tel., Mon.–Sat., US$6–15) is an open-air restaurant that offers seafood specialties. If *robalo* (snook) is available, get the fish tacos or order it as a filet. Daily specials are usually offered on a chalkboard out front.

Restaurant las Fuentes (Degollado and Colegio Militar, tel. 612/145-0257, Tues.–Sun. 7:30 A.M.–9:30 P.M., mains from US$6) is a large, open-air restaurant that has benefited from the rerouting of truck traffic away from the downtown area. The house special, *pescado empapelado,* is fish baked in paper with tomatoes and mild chilies.

AGUAS FRESCAS

Ladeled out of large glass jars, refreshing *aguas frescas* are made of still water infused with fresh fruit and sweetened with sugar. Popular flavors include *fresa* (strawberry), *jamaica* (hibiscus flower), *melón* (cantelope), and *sandía* (watermelon). Although technically not an *agua fresca, horchata,* rice milk flavored with cinnamon and sugar, is often served alongside the fruit drinks. Look for *aguas frescas* at taquerías, *licuados* stands, and Mexican restaurants up and down the Baja Peninsula.

International

Hotel California on Calle Juárez boasts the atmospheric **La Coronela** restaurant/bar (Juárez btw Morelos/Márquez de León, tel. 612/145-0525, daily 7 A.M.–1 A.M., dinner mains US$8–20). Prepared by a Belgian chef, the international menu has some creative dishes, such as almond-crusted Pacific oyster tacos and yellowtail in an opal basil/ginger/coconut sauce. Visa and MasterCard are accepted.

One block south of the park, **Ana San Sushi Bar** (tel. 612/137-9856, Tues.–Sat. 1–9 P.M.) prepares sushi, sashimi, soups, and salads.

Suki's (Hidalgo btw Rangel/Cuauhtemoc, no tel., Tues.–Sat. 5–9 P.M.) prepares a moderately priced menu of pan-Asian cuisine, with pad Thai, teriyaki, and Korean specialties. The owners were rebuilding the dining room at press time.

Italian

For high-end Italian food, **Café Santa Fé** (Centenario 4, tel./fax 612/145-0340, Wed.–Mon. noon–9 P.M.) is probably this town's most frequently recommended restaurant. It offers a broad menu with wood-fired pizzas, ravioli, fish crudo, and fresh pasta. With entrées starting at more than US$20, its reputation for being overpriced is understandable.

Around the corner from Todos Santos Eco Adventures, **Tres Gallines** (Topete and

Juárez, tel. 612/145-0274, Mon.–Sat. noon–10 P.M.) serves northern Italian fare at more reasonable prices, including homemade pasta (US$13–18) and imported espresso. New in 2007, **Buena Vida** (Calle Centenario next to Mangos, no tel.), in a historical brick building, opened to rave reviews for its dinner menu of pizzas (US$10), salads, and wines. Another popular newcomer is **Il Giardino** (Degollado btw Olochea/Carrillo, no tel., Tues.–Sun. 1–10 P.M.), serving wood-fired thin-crust pizza (US$18) and other casual Italian fare.

Antojitos and Fast Food

Tres Hermanos at the corner of Márquez de León and Juárez (daily 8 A.M.–2 P.M.) is among the best taco stands in town. Try the clam tacos for something different. Local Mexican residents praise **◖ Barajas Tacos** (Wed.–Mon. 8 A.M.–11 P.M.), on Degollado (Mexico 19) toward the south edge of town, for serving authentic *carnitas* and *tacos de pescado y camarones* during the day and *tacos de carne asada* and *papas rellenas* at night.

Cafés

Attention to detail and a love of improvisation set **◖ Café Brown** (Hidalgo and Colegio Militar, tel. 612/145-0813, Tues.–Sun. 7:30 A.M.–9 P.M., mains US$4–9) apart from your average small-town café. Enjoy a limited menu of home-style cooking made from quality ingredients (Sonora beef, breads from a bakery in La Paz) while you check your email on the fastest wireless connection in town (US$2/hr). Friendly and attentive service sets the tone; good music completes the experience. Art that doesn't have permanent gallery space often finds a home here. And from informal cooking classes and independent films to percussion instruction and salsa dancing, owners Ekerd and his wife love to throw a good party. Look for Café Brown in the back of the María Bonita Hotel (formerly Hotel Misión del Pilar) complex.

Vonn Café's new location (Colegio Militar and Zaragoza, no tel., Mon.–Sat. 9 A.M.–8 P.M.) hasn't changed the good coffee, and excellent sandwiches. Organic salads play an important role on their new menu.

Above the Costa Azul Surf Shop, **Café Felix** (Juárez near Hidalgo, no tel., hours vary, mains US$4–6) is a second-story café with a small patio overlooking the busy street below. It offers good coffee and a small sandwich menu, with reliable Wi-Fi access.

The smell of homemade bread wafts out of **Caffé Todos Santos** (Centenario 33, tel. 612/145-0300, Mon. 7 A.M.–2 P.M., Tues.–Sun. 7 A.M.–9 P.M., mains US$6–12) in the morning. This is the place to get your espresso fix, with fresh pastries, waffles, and omelets to boot.

On the plaza next to Café Santa Fé, the **Santa Fé Deli** (tel./fax 612/145-0301, Wed.–Mon. 8 A.M.–3 P.M., mains US$4–9) serves waffles for breakfast, and Cobb salad, soup, and other light fare for lunch. The deli/gourmet market stays open till 6 P.M. Walk through the Galería Santa Fe to get to the deli.

Worth a two-kilometer drive to the other side of town, **◖ Café D'Alicia** (tel. 612/145-0862, Thurs.–Sun. 8:30 A.M.–3 P.M., mains US$5–9) in the Las Brisas area off Calle Topete, serves the best homemade cinnamon rolls and sticky buns on the peninsula. There's also a full menu of breakfast and lunch specials, from eggs and pancakes to enchiladas and chiles rellenos. Drinks include smoothies, espresso, and fresh-squeezed juice. Breads, salsas, and sauces are all homemade. Enjoy the all-you-can-eat buffet on Sundays. This is a great place to bring young kids who like animals, as the owners rescue exotic birds, some of which have learned to speak a few words of Spanish. To find D'licia, follow Calle Topete past the Todos Santos Inn, across the lush *huerte,* past the primary school and into the dirt road that leads to Playa La Pastora. After the El Sol II market, look for a sign and driveway on the left.

Five minutes from town on the way to La Pastora, **◖ La Esquina** (no tel., daily 7 A.M.–7 P.M.) offers good coffee, build-your-own sandwiches with three different kinds of homemade bread, excellent soup of the day, a huge variety of fresh fruit juices and smoothies, as well as a great selection of loose and bagged

the entrance to La Esquina in Todos Santos

teas. There's free wireless—and they do occasional movie screenings in the evenings as well as hosting eco-café nights, featuring discussions on local ecological issues.

If all you need is a cup of coffee, look for **Café Combate** (Juárez, Mexico 19, no tel., hours vary) on the way to La Paz.

Groceries

Basic food supplies line the shelves of several markets in town, including **Mercadito Guluarte** (next to Hotel Guluarte), **Tienda Disconsa** (Calle Colegio Militar), **Super Mercado Hermanos González** (Calle Pedrajo), and **Supermercado El Sol** (Calle Degollado, open till 10 P.M. nightly). A second El Sol is on the road to Playa La Pastora one block west of Hacienda Inn Todos Santos.

La Siempre Viva (Juárez and Márquez de León, open from 7 A.M.) sells meats, cheeses, produce, and honey from local farms and ranches. It usually opens an hour or two earlier than the competition, and it carries some household goods and ranch supplies in addition to groceries.

The government-subsidized **ISSSTE Tienda** (Juárez btw Zaragoza/Morelos) offers an ever-changing selection of inexpensive groceries and holds a fairly well-stocked pharmacy.

Panadería Todos Santos (Rangel and Ocampo, Mon.–Sat. 2–8 P.M. or until sold out) sells a full lineup of Mexican breads, including *bolillos* and *pan dulce*—all baked in a wood-fired oven. The bakery occupies an unsigned two-story brick building at the north end of Calle Rangel near Ocampo. Bread lovers enjoy it, as there aren't many places like this one around.

You can buy fresh *tortillas de maíz* for about US$1 per kilo at the **Super Tortillería de Todos Santos** (Colegio Militar btw Morelos/Márquez de León). Head to Punta Lobos to buy fresh seafood directly from the *pangueros*. **Bodega Lizarraga**, at Colegio Militar and Obregón, has the biggest selection of fruits and vegetables in town, and it's without question the cleanest.

Homemade ice cream awaits at **Paletería la Paloma** (daily 8 A.M.–9 P.M.), on Colegio Militar next to Hotel Maria Bonita, along with icy fresh fruit *paletas* (popsicles). Pushcart vendors sometimes sell *paletas* around town. A second location, **Paletería la Paloma 2,** is opposite the Pemex. **Nevería Rocco** (Hidalgo btw Centenario/Juárez), a small shop in a pink house, sells Carnation ice cream and *paletas.*

INFORMATION AND SERVICES
Tourist Assistance

Todos Santos does not have an official tourist office, but several businesses in town are usually able to answer visitor questions. They include El Tecolote Libros, El Centro de Mensajes at the Hotel California, and Todos Santos Eco Adventures. If you speak Spanish and want information on the sierra backcountry, go to La Siempre Viva, which is where the ranchers often come to stock up on supplies.

The monthly *El Calendario de Todos Santos* (www.todossantos-baja.com) publishes current events listings and short articles on local culture; it's distributed free at various locations around town.

Medical Services

For police, fire, and Red Cross call 612/145-0445. The Centro de Salud (tel. 612/145-0095, open 24/7 for emergencies) is located on Mexico 19, at the corner of Juárez and Degollado.

Pharmacies

Farmacia Guadalupe (Av. Juárez, tel. 612/145-0300) fills prescriptions 24/7. Two other options include **Farmacia Hipocrates** (Morelos across from Mercado Guluarte) and **Farmacia Similares,** in the Hotel Maria Bonita complex.

Money

BANORTE (Juárez at Obregón, Mon.–Fri. 9 A.M.–4 P.M.) will cash travelers checks or exchange dollars (passport required). It also has an ATM outside. **Bancomer,** at Juárez and Zaragoza, is another option.

Post and Telephone

The post office in Todos Santos is literally a one-person operation. Located on Colegio Militar (Mexico 19) between Hidalgo and Márquez de León, it's supposed to open Monday–Friday 8 A.M.–1 P.M. and 3–5 P.M., but the hours can be erratic, since the manager is often out delivering mail.

Long-distance phone calls can be made from several Ladatel phones around town, including one on Hidalgo near Tecolote Books. **El Centro de Mensajes Todos Santos (The Message Center),** on Juárez in the lobby of Hotel California (tel. 612/145-0033, fax 612/145-0288, messagecenter1@yahoo.com, Mon.–Fri. 8 A.M.–3 P.M., Sat. 8 A.M.–2 P.M.) offers long-distance service at reasonable rates. The office also provides fax, DHL, mail forwarding, travel, and answering services.

For mobile phone needs, two Telcel stores are located on Militar, between Hidalgo and Degollado.

Internet Access

Many Todos Santos guesthouses and hotels now have wireless Internet service. In addition, **Café Brown** (Hidalgo and Colegio Militar, tel. 612/145-0813, Tues.–Sun 7:30 A.M.–9 P.M.) in the Hotel María Bonita complex has high-speed access on its own PC or via a wireless connection. The **Todos Santos Internet Café** (Juárez at Topete, tel. 612/145-0219, Mon.–Sat. 9 A.M.–5 P.M.), in the Milagro Real Estate office, has five desktop stations and two Ethernet connections for laptops. At the *papelería*/business center on Rangel and Márquez de León, you can use one of three PCs, as well as a fax and photocopy machine.

Pemex

There is a Pemex in town located at the intersection of Militar and Degollado (Mexico 19), and one at Km 50–51 on the way north to La Paz.

Laundry

The *lavandería* (tel. 612/145-0006, daily 8 A.M.–6 P.M.) on Juárez in the Hotel Guluarte provides laundry service for about US$4 per load, or less if you do it yourself.

Language Courses

Guillermo Bueron (tel. 612/145-0119, g_bueron@yahoo.com) teaches Spanish-, English-, and French-language classes at the Centro Cultural, using the Berlitz approach. He offers group and individual classes at all levels.

Hardware Store

Ferre Todos Santos (Zaragoza at Rangel, tel. 612/145-0565, Mon.–Sat. 8 A.M.–2 P.M. and 3–6:30 P.M.) has employees who speak English, and stocks a decent selection of hardware goods. **Ferreteria Oasis de Todos Santos** (Rangel at Zaragoza, tel. 612/145-0754, Mon.–Fri. 8 A.M.–3 P.M. and 4–7 P.M., Sat. 8 A.M.–4 P.M.) has fishing supplies, as well as plumbing and electric parts.

Volunteer Opportunities

Todos Santos has a few well-organized non-profit organizations working towards the betterment of the community that accept temporary volunteers—as well as a wide variety of donations, from sheets and pillows to toys and books for children. Those traveling with some extra time and/or the desire to integrate themselves into the community might like to hook up with some of those organizations and leave the place a little better than they found it.

Fortalecer, in operation since 2005, strives to provide a nontraditional classroom environment to the children of migrant agricultural camps near the town. Volunteers go to the camps and set up art project centers; organized games and puzzles; creative play centers; music, math, and literacy activities; and other hands-on projects for the children of the workers. Contact Aaron Balducci (612/135-4856, balducciaaron@gmail.com) to get involved.

La Palapa Society (Obregón 15, tel. 612/145-0299, palapasociety@yahoo.com), founded in 2003, is another non-profit based in the town of Todos Santos. It provides programs, events, and activities for children in the area—as well as medical services, educational scholarships, English-language instruction, and environmental education. Visitors can get involved by mentoring a child in English for a day, assisting local artists in mural painting workshops, or visiting the Todos Santos library.

BACKGROUND

The Land

GEOLOGY

The Baja Peninsula separated from mainland Mexico and opened up the Sea of Cortez some 5–10 million years ago in the Cenozoic Age, as the result of a gradual shifting of land masses called plates. The process, called plate tectonics, began as far back as the Mesozoic Age (63–230 million years ago), when the North American and Pacific Plates began to collide, pushing up mountains from Alaska to the tip of Baja. As the collision took place, the thicker North American Plate rode over the thinner Pacific plate, forming a new landmass prone to volcanic activity along volatile faults, such as the San Andreas, which runs through the middle of the Sea of Cortez. Over a period of tens of millions of years, the Pacific Plate drifted northward, tearing Baja from the mainland of Mexico. About five millions years ago, Baja pulled far enough away from the mainland to open up the Sea of Cortez. Many of the islands we see today were formed during the last ice age, when low-lying valleys filled with water, leaving only the highest points along the coast exposed.

Baja continues to drift northward today as part of the Pacific Plate, and geologists predict it will eventually become an island, proving the early Spanish explorers right.

© KATHRYN LATENDRESSE

Land's End rock formations

GEOGRAPHY

The lower California peninsula stretches 1,300 kilometers (806 mi) from top to bottom. It begins at Tijuana at the border with the U.S. and extends 193 kilometers (120 mi) east to Mexicali and south to the cape at San Lucas below the Tropic of Cancer. Baja lies 250 kilometers (155 mi) west of mainland Mexico at its greatest distance. In between is the Golfo de California (Gulf of California), more commonly known as the Mar de Cortés (Sea of Cortez). On the west coast of the peninsula is the Pacific Ocean. At its narrowest point, between Bahía de La Paz and the Pacific Ocean, the peninsula measures just 45 kilometers (28 mi) across.

Numerous mountain ranges (23 to be exact) run the length of the interior, from northwest to southeast, with the highest peak, Picacho del Diablo, rising more than 3,000 meters (10,000 ft). The longest and highest ranges include the **Sierra Juárez** and **Sierra de San Pedro Mártir** in the north, the **Sierra de la Giganta** in the central peninsula, and the **Sierra de la Laguna** in the south.

At the foot of the sierras are vast desert areas comprising about 65 percent of the peninsula. The San Felipe Desert covers much of northeastern Baja, while the Gulf Coast Desert extends from Bahía de Los Angeles to San José del Cabo in the south. The Vizcaíno Desert, in the west-central part of the peninsula, is Baja's largest desert area and has been designated a protected Biosphere Reserve by the United Nations. South of this area, the Magdalena Plains (Llano Magdalena) border Bahía Magdalena, the largest bay on either side of the peninsula. Together, these two desert areas are often called the Desierto Central.

In addition to these extremes, the peninsula features coastal wetlands, sandy beaches, more than 100 islands (most of them located along the Gulf coast), and deep canyons filled with palms.

THE SEA OF CORTEZ

The Mar de Cortés (Sea of Cortez) was originally named for the legendary Spanish explorer, Hernán Cortés, in the 16th century, and was sometimes also called the Mar

ECOTOURISM

In recent years, the number of low-impact activities and accommodations throughout the peninsula has increased, giving travelers a way to experience Baja without wreaking havoc on its fragile desert and marine ecosystems. From Bahía de los Ángeles to Loreto to Cabo Pulmo, you'll find solar-powered *casitas*, organic produce, self-sufficient resorts, and proprietors who put the environment first. Bird-watching near San Ignacio, whale-watching in Bahía Magdalena, and sea turtle conservation efforts at Bahía de los Ángeles and around the Cape Region are just a few of the ways to get involved.

Vermejo (Vermillion Sea) on early maps— a name that referred to the massive schools of pelagic red crabs that float on the water's surface in the spring. The Mexican government changed the official name to the Golfo de California (Gulf of California) in the early 20th century. Both names are used on maps today.

The sea is 669 miles long, extending from the mouth of the Colorado River to the cape at San Lucas. The northern section of the sea is shallow, the result of silt deposits from the river. Tidal fluctuations are extreme, as much as six meters near San Felipe.

Around the Midriff Islands near Bahía de los Angeles, the sea gets deeper and colder, and strong currents bring more nutrients, which sustain a phenomenal diversity of life—more than 900 species of marine vertebrates and more than 2,000 invertebrates. It's an environment that Jacques Cousteau once called the aquarium of the world.

South of La Paz, the gulf becomes more like an ocean, with deep trenches, submarine canyons, and towering seamounts.

The Sea of Cortez meets the Pacific Ocean below the tip of the Baja Peninsula, offshore from the rocky point known as Finisterra (Land's End).

ENVIRONMENTAL ISSUES

The rapid growth of tourism and real estate development, especially in the Los Cabos area, has strained fragile ecosystems up and down the Baja Peninsula. Coastal development threatens mangrove habitat on the Mogote Peninsula near La Paz and the Estero San José. The delicate coral reef offshore from Cabo Pulmo could deteriorate rapidly if the water gets polluted from ongoing beachfront development. Even the pristine islands offshore from La Paz are showing early signs of stress from the increase in camping and organized trips.

On both sides of the peninsula, endangered sea turtles face poaching and loss of habitat for laying eggs. Commercial fishing has taken a toll on other species as well, with prize billfish reportedly now much smaller in size than in the early years of Baja's fishing camps.

In the long term, the scarcity of freshwater and ability of municipalities to keep up with water and sewage treatment needs pose another concern. The Escalera Náutica project, through which the Mexican government plans to build a network of 10 new ports and expand a dozen existing ports, may further disrupt ecosystems and local communities.

Residents and visitors, both Mexican and foreign, are getting involved to help conserve the environment for years to come. For example, Grupo Tortuguero (www.grupotortuguero.org) runs a turtle conservation program in Baja, and Pro Peninsula (www.propeninsula.org) publishes an informative website and quarterly newsletter about Baja's environmental concerns.

CLIMATE

The most important feature of Baja's climate for most travelers is its abundance of warm, sunny, dry days. In fact, your chances of enjoying a winter beach vacation without rain are higher here than in Hawaii or Florida. (Wind is another matter, however.) Across the entire peninsula, the climate ranges from Mediterranean to desert to tropical. In general, the mountains are cooler than the coast, the Pacific coast is cooler than the Gulf coast in summer (but can be warmer than the Gulf coast in winter), and the northern part of the peninsula is cooler than the southern part. But within these guidelines are numerous microclimates, caused by the interplay of mountains, bays, currents, fog, and winds.

In summer and fall, tropical storms called chubascos can bring rain and high winds for a few hours to a few days at a time. Hurricanes are less common, but they do occur every few years. The most recent one to strike Baja was Hurricane John in 2006, which made landfall at Cabo Pulmo bringing heavy rains and 150-mph winds all the way to Mulegé and Santa Rosalía.

Flora

According to botanist estimates, the unique ecosystems of the Baja Peninsula and its islands support more than 4,000 varieties of plants. For an introduction to about 550 of them, consult the *Baja California Plant Field Guide,* by Norman C. Roberts. Here are some of the highlights:

CACTI

Scientists have identified 120 species of cactus here, and the majority of them live only on this peninsula or its offshore islands. Many of them flower after summer and fall rains, painting the desert in splashes of bright color for a few weeks of the year. One of the most common cacti in Baja is the *cardón (Pachycereus pringlei),* the tallest of them all, which is especially prevalent in the Valle de los Gigantes (Valley of the Giants) south of San Felipe. They can grow to heights of 18 meters (60 ft) and weights of 12 tons (not counting the roots), and they live for hundreds of years.

Less common but also unique to Baja, the *biznaga (Ferocactus),* or barrel cactus, lives only on a few islands in the Sea of Cortez. It has red-tinged spines and blooms in yellow and red flowers in the spring.

The indigenous Pericú treasured the *pitahaya dulce,* or organ pipe cactus, for its watermelon-like fruit. During the late summer-early fall harvest, the Pericú ate the abundant fruit until they fell asleep, waking only when they were ready to eat some more. The species lives south of the Sierra de San Borja in Central Baja and on a few islands in the Sea of Cortez. A related

© PABLO NOBILI

A crested *caracara* perches atop a *cardón.*

species, *pitahaya agria* (galloping cactus) has a less sweet but still edible fruit.

Multiple kinds of cholla and nopal (prickly pear), both part of the *Opuntia* species, grow throughout the region. The nopal is an edible cactus, common on menus up and down the peninsula.

AGAVES

Nineteen types of agave are found in Baja, including several varieties of yucca. Agaves are pollinated most commonly by bats and flower only after several years. Many of them are edible. The tree yucca, or *datilillo* (little date) looks a lot like a date palm and thrives on the west side of the Vizcaíno Desert, among other places. You can eat its fruit and flowers, boil its roots to soften soap or leather, and weave the leaves into sandals, baskets, or mats. Maguey, or century plant, flowers only once in its lifetime, sending up a tall, slender stalk after maturation. It was another major source of food and fiber for the indigenous people that inhabited the peninsula.

FOUQUIERIACEAE

The most striking plant in this family of succulents is easily the most distinctive in all of Baja. Indeed, the tall and lanky *cirio* (candle) or Boojum tree looks like an upside down carrot—something right out of a Dr. Seuss story. Almost as tall as the *cardón*, it grows about three centimeters a year and lives for hundreds of years. In order to see this unusual plant, you have to venture into central Baja. It only grows between the southern end of the Sierra de San Pedro Mártir and the Sierra Tres Vírgenes and on Isla Angel de la Guarda near Bahía de los Angeles. If you're driving the Transpeninsular Highway south, your first glimpse of the species comes as you enter the desert below El Rosario.

Also part of the same family, the *ocotillo* and *palo adán* (Adam's tree), are found throughout the peninsula and often used to make fences.

TREES
Palms

A universal symbol of the tropics around the globe, palm trees are used as landscaping in warm climates all over North America. But there is something spectacular about seeing them grow in the wild, especially when they are clinging to the walls of a deep canyon high in the sierras. Seven varieties live in the Baja California wilderness. Besides providing shade and an overall tropical aesthetic, they are used to make woven baskets, thatched roofs, and

construction materials such as roof beams or rails for fences.

The endemic blue fan palm (also called the Mexican blue palm, and in Spanish, *palma ceniza* or *palma azul*,) has bluish-colored leaves and grows from the canyons and arroyos of the Sierra Juárez in the north to San Ignacio in the south, reaching heights of 24 meters (79 ft).

The smallest palm found in Baja is the *tlaco* palm (also called the *palma palmia* and the *palma colorado*). It's found south of Loreto. The tallest palm in Baja, also with fan-shaped leaves, is the Mexican fan palm (Baja California fan palm, skyduster, or *palma blanca*). It tops out at 27–30 meters (90–100 ft).

Spanish Jesuit missionaries brought the feather-leaf date palm to Baja, and it continues to thrive near Loreto, Comondú, Mulegé, San Ignacio, and San José del Cabo. And the coconut palm *(cocotera),* the only other feather-leaf palm in Baja, grows south of Mulegé.

Elephant Tree

Part of the sumac family of trees that emit a milky sap, the *Pachycormus discolor* (*copalquín* or *torote blanco* in Spanish) has a gnarled trunk and branches covered in a gray-white outer layer that peels off, exposing a smooth blue-green inner bark. It's most common in the Desierto Central. This tree is often confused with *Bursera odorata* (*pachycormus,* also called *torote blanco* in Spanish), a member of the torchwood family, which has a yellow inner bark and grows south of Bahía Concepción.

Conifers

An unexpected delight when exploring the interior of the peninsula is the wide variety of conifers that grow in the high sierras. Cypress, cedar, juniper, white fir, and lodgepole pine are just a few examples. The Tecate cypress grows on the western slopes of the Sierra Juárez and north to Orange County in Alta California, while the San Pedro Mártir cypress lives on the eastern escarpment of the Sierra de San Pedro Mártir. Cedros Island in the Pacific Ocean has its own endemic conifer, the Cedros

Island pine, as does Isla Guadalupe, with the Guadalupe Island pine.

Ironwood

If you browse any of Baja's arts and crafts markets, you'll often see shelves filled with animals carved out of wood. The raw material for these crafts comes from the ironwood tree (*palo fierro* or *tesota* in Spanish). A hard, hot-burning wood, it has been logged extensively on the peninsula and is no longer as common as it once was.

Mimosas

Mimosas are a subfamily of the pea family (*Leguminosae*), all of which have linear seedpods and double rows of tiny leaves. Within this subfamily, mesquite and acacia occur throughout the peninsula. Baja's indigenous people had many uses for mesquite wood, from construction materials to herbal remedies, and the traditions are carried on today by those who live in the most rural parts of the peninsula.

When it blooms in the spring, the small white blossoms of the *palo blanco* tree are a sight to behold. The Sierra de la Giganta near Loreto is one of the best places to find it.

Wild Figs

Even figs grow wild in Baja. Called *zalates,* they tend to prefer the rocky areas of Southern Baja, below La Paz.

HERBS

A number of herbs used in cooking and alternative medicine thrive in the hot, dry Baja climate. For example, white sage is found on the rocky hillsides in northern Baja. Another type of sage, the rare chia, grows only in the desert areas of Baja, Sonora, and the southwestern United States. But the herb most commonly associated with Baja California is damiana (*Turnera diffusa),* consumed either as a tea or in a liqueur and believed to be a powerful aphrodisiac. When you see a Baja margarita on the menu, it usually contains damiana liqueur instead of triple sec. This shrub prefers the rocky areas of Southern Baja, near the capes.

Fauna

LAND MAMMALS

Baja's marine and animal life is just as diverse as its plant life. More than 100 mammals inhabit the peninsula, two dozen of which are considered endemic. The extreme terrain and climate has made for some interesting adaptations. Among the list of carnivores that live in the wilderness are coyotes, mountain lions, foxes bobcat, and raccoons. Mule deer live below 1,500 meters (5,000 ft), while fewer white-tailed deer live in the higher elevations.

Desert bighorn sheep (*borrego cimarrón*) have yet to recover from excessive big-game hunting of the early 20th century. And the endangered peninsular pronghorn (*berrendo),* survives only in the protected preserve of the Vizcaíno Desert. Also on the endangered species list is the endemic black jackrabbit.

GRAY WHALES

Before it was over-hunted by Dutch, British, and American whalers in the 19th century, the gray whale inhabited the Atlantic Ocean, Baltic Sea, and North Sea, as well as the Pacific Ocean. Today, it lives only in the Pacific. The object of many organized trips to Baja, gray whales migrate around 19,300 kilometers (12,000 mi) a year from the Arctic Circle, where they feed, to the shallow lagoons on the west side of Baja California, where they give birth to their calves. Adults measure 10–15 meters (35–50 ft) long and weigh 20–40 tons. Their skin is almost black at birth, but the growth and scarring of barnacles over the years makes them look more gray than black.

There are three lagoons along the central Pacific coast of Baja where visitors can observe the gray whales up close: Laguna Ojo de Liebre

© PABLO NOBILI

friendly neighborhood cows

near Guerrero Negro, Laguna San Ignacio, and Bahía Magdalena.

OTHER MARINE MAMMALS

Besides the social gray whale, Baja's Pacific and Gulf waters host two dozen species of whales and dolphins, including the endangered vaquita dolphin, which once thrived in the northern Sea of Cortez near San Felipe.

The elephant seal and Guadalupe fur seal have made a recent comeback on Isla Guadalupe and nearby islands, where they were hunted nearly to the point of extinction in the 19th century. More common California sea lions, or *lobos marinas,* live on and around several islands in the Sea of Cortez, including Isla Ángel de la Guarda near Bahía de los Angeles and Isla Espíritu Santo near La Paz.

FISH

Marine biologists have labeled the Sea of Cortez the richest body of water in the world. Diverse marine environments along both sides of the Baja Peninsula support thousands of species of fish. There are sailfish and marlin (collectively called billfish); corvinas and croaker, including the protected totuava; yellowtail, amberjack, pompanos, and roosterfish; dorado (mahimahi), wahoo, and bluefin, albacore, and yellowfin tuna (YFT), which can grow to sizes exceeding 180 kilograms (400 lbs); various types of sea bass, including *garropa* (grouper) and *cabrilla;* flounder and halibut; snappers (*pargo,* including the red snapper, which is called *huachinango* in Spanish. More than 60 types of sharks live here, among them the hammerhead, thresher, bonito (mako), bull, whitetip, sand, blue, blacktip, and whale shark—the world's largest fish at 18 meters (59 ft) and 3,600 kilograms (almost four tons).

Eagle rays, guitarfish, sting rays, and other rays often rest on the sandy bottom of the sea, offshore from the southern part of the peninsula. Divers and snorkelers are sometimes lucky enough to see the Pacific manta glide by. With a wingspan of up to seven meters (23 ft), it can weigh nearly two tons.

The Humboldt squid is another unusual deepwater creature. It grows to 4.5 meters (15 ft) long and weigh up to 150 kilograms (330 lbs).

Barracuda are found in both the Pacific and the Sea of Cortez. And in Southern Baja, the flying fish puts on a good show as it leaps out of the water offshore.

Abundant shellfish are found all along the coast, including clams, oysters, mussels, scallops, and shrimp, and spiny lobster.

BIRDS

With this great variety of plant and fish life comes an equally fantastic bird population. Ornithologists have identified at least 300 species, but unfortunately no one has published a Baja-specific field guide to date, though several Mexican bird guides include the species found on the peninsula and its islands.

Coastal Birds

The Midriff Islands in particular provide habitat for many rare and endangered species, and the Mexican government protects 49 of

pelicans near the shores of Playa Palmilla

these islands as wildlife preserves. Well known among birders, Isla San Pedro Mártir has the blue-footed booby, as well as the brown booby and masked booby. Tiny Isla de Raza is another popular birding destination.

Brown pelicans are common in Baja, but gone from the coastal islands of California and the U.S. shores of the Gulf of Mexico. Other noteworthy birds include the frigate, fisher eagle, cormorant, egret, gull, heron, loon, osprey, plover, sandpiper, and tern.

Boaters sometimes see pelagic birds such as the albatross, black-legged kittiwake, red phalarope, shearwater, surf scoter, south polar skua, storm petrel, black tern, and red-billed tropic bird.

Freshwater Birds

The inland ponds, springs, lakes, streams, and marshes of Baja support two species of bittern, the American coot, two species of duck, the snow goose, the northern harrier, six species of heron, the white-faced ibis, the common moorhen, two species of rail, five species of sandpiper, the lesser scaup, the shoveler, the common snipe, the sora, the roseate spoonbill, the wood stork, three species of teal, the northern waterthrush, and the American wigeon.

Birds of the Sierra

The golden eagle, western flycatcher, lesser goldfinch, black-headed grosbeak, red-tailed hawk, pheasant, yellow-eyed junco, white-breasted nuthatch, mountain plover, acorn woodpecker and canyon wren live in the peaks and valleys of the sierras, along with two species of hummingbird, four species of vireo, and eight species of warbler.

Desert Birds

Falcons, flycatchers, hawks, hummingbirds, owls, sparrows, and thrashers live in the hot, dry desert environment, along with the American kestrel, merlin, greater roadrunner, vernon, turkey vulture, ladder-backed woodpecker, and cactus wren.

The largest bird in North America is the endangered California condor (*Gymnogyps*

© NIKKI GOTH ITOI

californianus), which weighs up to 11 kilograms (24 lbs), with a wingspan of nearly 3.6 meters (12 ft). A group of U.S. and Mexican scientists plans to release captive-bred condors in Baja's Sierra de San Pedro Mártir, in hopes that the more limited human presence will permit the bird to survive in the wild.

REPTILES AND AMPHIBIANS

Thirty types of lizards live on the Baja Peninsula, including the large chuckwalla, which inhabits several islands in the Sea of Cortez and can grow to one meter (3 ft) long. The desert iguana and the endemic coast-horned lizard are also noteworthy species.

Turtles

Five sea turtles live in Baja waters: the leatherback, green, hawksbill, western ridley, and loggerhead, which swims 10,460 kilometers (6,500 mi) between the island of Kyshu in Japan and the Sea of Cortez. All of these turtles are endangered, and it's illegal to hunt any of them or collect their eggs, but enforcing the law has been a challenge.

Many organizations are involved in turtle conservation efforts in Baja. One of the largest is Grupo Tortuguero (www.grupoturtuguero.

org), which holds its annual meeting in late January–early February in Loreto. A who's who of Baja influencers usually attends.

Snakes

There are 35 species of snakes *(serpientes)* in Baja, about half of which are poisonous, although they rarely come into contact with people.

Non-venomous kinds *(culebra)* include the western blind snake, rosy boa, Baja California rat snake, spotted leaf-nosed snake, western patch-nosed snake, bull snake, coachwhip, king snake, Baja sand snake, and California lyre snake.

Among the poisonous types *(víbora)* are the yellow-bellied sea snake, which resembles a floating stick in the water; and 18 species of rattlesnake *(serpiente de cascabel* or *cascabel),* including the common Baja California rattler, red diamondback, and western diamondback, which is the largest and most dangerous of Baja's snakes and lives in the canyons of the northern sierras.

The only rattler that's endemic to Baja California is the rattleless rattlesnake *(Crotalus catalinensis),* which lives only on Isla Santa Catalina in the Sea of Cortez.

History

PRE-CORTESIAN HISTORY

The Asians who crossed the Bering Strait land bridge beginning around 50,000 B.C. most likely migrated as far south as the Baja Peninsula, but relatively little archeology has been done to test the theory. About 7,000 years ago, a group called the San Diegito moved south into Northern Baja and lived near the peninsula's freshwater sources. Next came the Yumanos, around 2,500 years ago, who painted much of the peninsula's rock art—the only aspect of the culture that survives today. Yumano tribes included the Cucapá, Tipai, Paipai (or Pa'ipai), Kumyai, and Kiliwa.

Historians believe that the indigenous people who lived in Central and Southern Baja at the time of the Spanish conquest were more primitive than the Yumanos, who engaged in more advanced hunting, fishing, and cultivation. But it is difficult to know for sure because the missionary histories—the only documentation available—were written with a strong bias against the indigenous people, whom they sought to convert. According to the missionaries, the Cochimís inhabited the central peninsula and Comondú, while Guaycuras (consisting of the Pericú, Huchiti, and Guaicura tribes) lived in Southern Baja near the capes.

THE SPANISH CONQUEST

Following its conquest of Mexico and Central America in the early 16th century, Spain turned its attention farther west. Early explorers believed the Baja Peninsula was an island and that the present-day Sea of Cortez was a northwest passage to the Atlantic. Legendary conquistador Hernán Cortés directed four voyages into the Sea of Cortez beginning in 1532. In 1534, the first Europeans set food on the peninsula, landing at La Paz, but most were promptly killed by the indigenous inhabitants. A few survivors returned to the mainland with stories of rich pearl oyster beds on a big island. Cortés himself landed in the Bahía de La Paz in 1535, but he failed to establish a permanent colony. He sponsored a fourth voyage in 1539, led by Captain Francisco de Ulloa, who explored the entire perimeter of the Gulf of California and then continued north along the Pacific coast, as far north as Isla Cedros. Ulloa is credited with naming the Mar de Cortés.

Cortés returned to Spain in 1541, and was replaced by a Portuguese explorer named Juan Rodríguez Cabrillo, whose expedition explored the Pacific coast, as far north as Oregon.

Manila Galleons

When the Portuguese conquered the Philippines, they quickly established a trade route from Manila to the New World, following the Japanese Current across the Pacific Ocean. The ships that made this arduous journey were called the Manila galleons; in order to make it safely to Asia, their crews needed a place to stop for fresh water, and a protected harbor to hide their treasure from enterprising pirates like the famous Sir Francis Drake. Baja's fate as a target for European colonization was sealed.

As English and Dutch privateers began to raid Spanish ships with increasing frequency and success, the Spanish got more serious about settling Baja. Sebastián Vizcaíno landed in Bahía de La Paz in 1596, encountered friendly indigenous inhabitants, and named the place La Paz. From there, he traveled north along the Gulf coast and then

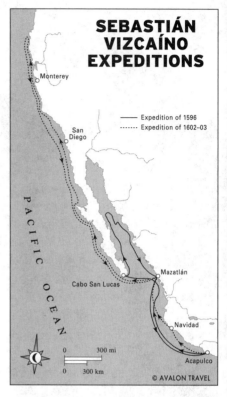

SEBASTIÁN VIZCAÍNO EXPEDITIONS

——— Expedition of 1596
········· Expedition of 1602–03

Monterey
San Diego
Cabo San Lucas
Mazatlán
Navidad
Acapulco

PACIFIC OCEAN

0   300 mi
0   300 km

© AVALON TRAVEL

returned to mainland Mexico. He returned in 1602 and sailed around the cape and up the Pacific coast to Mendocino, California, renaming the islands, bays, and points along the way. But the Spanish would not prevail in Baja for another 80 years.

The next expedition, led by Admiral Isidor Atondo y Antillón and Jesuit Padre Eusebio Francisco Kino, landed first at La Paz and later at San Bruno to the north, where they established a mission that lasted less than two years. Lack of food and freshwater forced the colonists to head home to the mainland.

THE MISSION ERA
The Jesuits (1697-1767)

Padre Juan María Salvatierra established Antigua California's first permanent Spanish

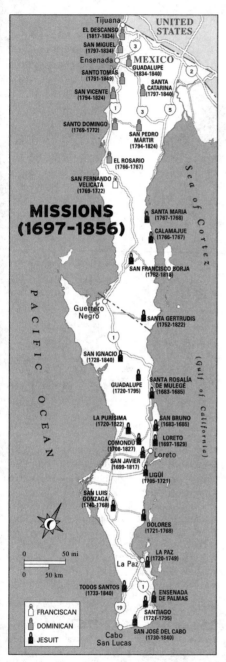

**MISSIONS
(1697–1856)**

Tijuana
EL DESCANSO
(1817–1834)
SAN MIGUEL
(1797–1834)
Ensenada
SANTO TOMÁS
(1791–1849)
SANTA
CATARINA
(1797–1840)
SAN VICENTE
(1794–1824)
SANTO DOMINGO
(1769–1772)
SAN PEDRO
MÁRTIR
(1794–1824)
EL ROSARIO
(1766–1767)
SAN FERNANDO
VELICATÁ
(1769–1772)
SANTA MARÍA
(1767–1768)
CALAMAJUE
(1766–1767)
SAN FRANCISCO BORJA
(1762–1818)
Guerrero
Negro
SANTA GERTRUDIS
(1752–1822)
SAN IGNACIO
(1728–1840)
SANTA ROSALÍA
DE MULEGÉ
(1683–1685)
GUADALUPE
(1720–1795)
LA PURÍSIMA
(1720–1822)
SAN BRUNO
(1683–1685)
COMONDÚ
(1708–1827)
LORETO
(1697–1829)
Loreto
SAN JAVIER
(1699–1817)
LIGÜÍ
(1705–1721)
SAN LUIS
GONZAGA
(1740–1768)
DOLORES
(1721–1768)
LA PAZ
(1720–1749)
La Paz
TODOS SANTOS
(1733–1840)
ENSENADA
DE PALMAS
SANTIAGO
(1721–1795)
Cabo
San Lucas
SAN JOSÉ DEL CABO
(1730–1840)

GUADALUPE
(1834–1840)

UNITED
STATES

MEXICO

Sea of Cortez

(Gulf of California)

PACIFIC OCEAN

0   50 mi
0   50 km

FRANCISCAN
DOMINICAN
JESUIT

mission in 1697. He landed in San Bruno but promptly found a more reliable source of freshwater 24 kilometers (15 mi) south of the original mission, and proceeded to establish the mission that would become "the mother of all California missions," Nuestra Señora de Loreto. Historians estimate the indigenous population at about 50,000 at the time of Salvatierra's arrival.

Over the next 70 years, the Jesuits established 22 settlements and supporting *visitas* (visiting missions), creating a mission trail south to the cape at San José and north to Cataviña in the Desierto Central. The missionaries introduced the indigenous people to the "civilized" Spanish way of life and offered food and water, in exchange for labor. The indigenous people planted crops, dug waterways, and built churches. But they did not always welcome the missionary efforts to change their ways, particularly when it came to the decree against polygamy.

Uprisings were a frequent occurrence during the missionary period. The Pericú rebellion of 1734 caused extensive damage, destroying four missions in the southern part of the peninsula and killing two of the padres. Through the rest of the 18th century, the indigenous population decreased rapidly due to epidemics of European-borne diseases such as smallpox and measles. By 1748, more than 80 percent of the population estimated at Salvatierra's arrival had perished. With no one left alive to convert, the missions began to close. By 1767, only one member of the entire Huchiti branch of the Guaycura nation survived.

In the wake of disease and death, the missionaries pressed northward, always seeking more "neophytes" for their religious activities.

On June 15, 1767, King Charles III of Spain issued the Jesuit Expulsion Decree, requiring the 16 missionaries left in Antigua California to return to the mainland, where they were shipped back to Europe and imprisoned or exiled. Historical accounts of the reason for the expulsion differ. One theory says the Jesuits were accused of stealing the hidden treasures of Antigua California from the crown; others believe the Jesuits were punished to speaking out against government corruption. In any case, they were replaced immediately by the Franciscan Order.

The Franciscans and Dominicans

Fourteen Franciscan padres landed in Loreto in 1768, including Padre Junípero Serra, who carried the mission torch north to Alta California. The Franciscans established one mission in Northern Baja, San Fernando Velicatá, before crossing into the present-day U.S. state of California to establish a mission at San Diego and a new mission trail that would extend as far north as Sonoma.

With his attention on Alta California, Serra transferred the Baja missions to the Dominican Order in 1772, and the first of nine Dominican missions (and one *visita*) was established at El Rosario in 1774, which became the official boundary between Alta and Baja California in 1777. In 1776, Monterey replaced Loreto as the capital of the two Californias.

By 1800, only 5,000 indigenous people survived on the peninsula, and the Spanish government could no longer justify support of the missions.

THE 19TH CENTURY

Mexico's revolt against the Spanish crown began on September 16, 1810, a date celebrated annually as Día de la Independencia, or Mexican Independence Day, in a climate of social and economic instability. In an attempt to regain control over the powerful Catholic Church, the Spanish government had seized all church funds, which left the local economy in turmoil. Padre Miguel Hidalgo y Costilla issued the call for independence from the mainland city of Dolores, Guanajuato. It would take more than a decade, but Mexico would finally emerge independent from Spain in 1821. According to the Plan de Iguala treaty, the Catholic Church would remain the dominant force in Mexico, a constitutional monarchy would rule, and mestizos and Mexican-born Spaniards would gain equal rights under the new regime. Former viceroy Agustín de

Iturbide became emperor of the new republic, but only for two years. In its first 30 years of independence, Mexico would weather 50 changes in government.

In 1830, the capital of Baja California moved from Loreto to La Paz following a severe hurricane, and in 1834, the last Dominican mission in Baja was established at Guadalupe, northeast of Ensenada.

The Mexican-American War

In 1833, Antonio López de Santa Anna, a powerful general who had enforced the expulsion of Spain's troops from Mexico, seized power, revoked the Constitution of 1824, and set in motion the chain of events that would lead to independence for Texas, war with the United States and the loss of vast territories in the north.

The United States declared war on Mexico in 1846, following a series of skirmishes over the border with the newly established U.S. state of Texas. In Baja, Mexican and American forces confronted each other at Santo Tomás, Mulegé, La Paz, and San José del Cabo. Mexico City surrendered to the United States in March 1847, and the two countries signed the Treaty of Guadalupe Hidalgo in 1848, in which Mexico conceded the Rio Grande area of Texas as well as part of New Mexico and all of Alta California in exchange for US$25 million and the cancellation of all Mexican debt. The treaty moved the border between Baja California and Alta California from El Rosario to Tijuana, establishing a new international border zone.

In 1849, many Baja California residents left the peninsula to pan for gold in the California gold rush of 1849. As Baja's population dwindled, it became a land of bandits, pirates, outlaws, and misfits.

The latter part of the 19th century brought more turbulence for Mexico. In 1853, Mexico sold Arizona and southern New Mexico to the United States for US$10 million, and American military "freebooter" William Walker invaded La Paz with 45 mercenaries and declared himself president of the Republic of Lower California. The Americans fled when he heard that Mexican troops were en route to La Paz. Walker was tried and acquitted in the United States for violating neutrality laws, but he was subsequently executed for a similar attempt in Nicaragua two years later.

The War of Reform

The Mexican people overthrew General Santa Anna in 1855, and he was replaced by a Zapotec lawyer named Benito Juárez. In 1858, a civil war called the War of Reform broke out on the mainland, with the wealth of the church at the root of the conflict. The liberals, led by Juárez, drafted a new constitution to limit the powers of the church, while the opposition seized control of Mexico City. The liberals declared victory in 1861, and Juárez became president.

The French invaded Mexico the following year, after Mexico failed to pay its debts to France. Napoleon III captured Puebla and then Mexico City, where he placed Austrian Ferdinand Maximilian as emperor of Mexico. The United States pressured France to withdraw, Maximilian was executed by a Juarista firing squad, and Juárez resumed control of the nation in 1867.

The end of the decade brought a series of reforms to strengthen the Mexican economy and its educational system. Juárez died in 1872 and his political opponent Porfirio Díaz took over, continuing the program of reform, but with a much more authoritarian approach. Díaz ran the country for nearly three decades, and during this time, he improved its transportation and education systems, but at the expense of political freedom.

Foreign Investment

Díaz promoted aggressive foreign investment in Baja, selling large tracts of land to U.S. and European corporations. The peninsula's gold- and silver-mining era began in 1878, with the arrival of the American Progreso Mining Company. In 1883, the International Company of Mexico, a joint venture among U.S., British, and Mexican investors, bought the rights to develop more than seven million hectares (18 million acres) of land south of Tijuana. The British would build a pier and flour mill near San Quintín, but colonization efforts would end without success. A French mining company named Boleo & Cie commenced mining operations and built the town of Santa Rosalía, beginning in 1885. In 1889, the discovery of gold near Ensenada triggered a rush to Santa Clara.

The Territory of Baja California was divided into two districts, north and south, at the 28th parallel, in 1885.

THE 20TH CENTURY
The Mexican Revolution

Several decades of political oppression under Díaz and an ever-widening gap between rich and poor sowed the seeds for a full-scale revolution. The country's underrepresented workers and peasants—led by liberal Francisco Madero and aided by a bandit named Pancho Villa and a peasant named Emiliano Zapata—rose up against Díaz. The rebels prevailed, but through the course of the conflict, they divided into factions, one of which, the Magonistas, took control of Tijuana in 1911. Madero was executed in 1913.

Following several more years of instability, revolutionary Venustiano Carranza became president and drafted the Constitution of 1917, which returned lands to the peasants as cooperatively owned *ejidos*. Three years later, supporters of Carranza's political opponent, Álvaro Obregón, overthrew Carranza.

Obregón stayed in office four years and initiated more educational reforms. Plutarco Elías Calles, who succeeded him in 1924, redistributed three million hectares (7.5 million acres) of land and helped establish the National Revolutionary Party (PNR), a regime that would maintain a tight grip on the country for the next 70 years.

U.S. Prohibition

Northern Baja began to develop a tourism-driven economy around the time of the U.S. Prohibition, in 1920. With alcoholic beverages illegal north of the border, U.S. residents flocked to Tijuana and Mexicali to drink and gamble in newly opened casino resorts. Flush with cash, the cities began to invest in manufacturing and agricultural infrastructure. Building of the Transpeninsular Highway began in 1927. The repeal of Prohibition in 1933 caused a deep recession just a few years later.

Nationalist Reforms and World War II

In 1938, PNR candidate Lázaro Cárdenas, a mestizo, became president of Mexico and enacted far-reaching social reforms. He redistributed 18.6 million hectares (46 million acres) to the *ejidos* and established Petróleos Mexicanos (Pemex), as a government-owned oil monopoly. Foreign investors fled the country as a result. Under Cárdenas, the PNR became the Partido Revolucionario Institucional (PRI), which would control the Mexican government until 2000.

In 1942, the United States allowed Mexican citizens to work north of the border for short periods of time under the Bracero Program, which stayed in place until 1962 and contributed to rapid urban development along the international border.

Statehood

Following World War II, Mexico enjoyed steady growth in its manufacturing and agricultural sectors. Northern Baja became Mexico's 29th state in 1952, with a population of 80,000 (the minimum required for statehood). Southern Baja remained a sparsely populated territory of isolated ranches and fishing settlements. A small number of Mexicans from the mainland visited La Paz to shop in the duty-free zone. But commerce by land was difficult because it took 10 days to drive the rough road from Tijuana to La Paz. A paved highway was needed to link the prosperous border zone with the rest of the peninsula. Construction of the 1,700-kilometer (1,054-mi) Transpenisular Highway (Mexico 1) was completed in 1974, opening the door to greater commerce and tourism. Baja California Sur became Mexico's 30th state less than one year later. In 1975,

the government decided to invest in tourism infrastructure along the corridor between San José del Cabo and Cabo San Lucas, setting the stage for the destination resort we know today as Los Cabos.

Baja California (Norte) and Baja California Sur are socially more progressive than the majority of mainland states. In 1989, BCN elected a National Action Party candidate as governor, becoming the first state in the nation to vote in an opposition party to the PRI. For its part, BCS voted in a leftist coalition party consisting of the PRD (Partido Revolucionario Democrático, or Democratic Revolutionary Party) and the PT (Partido Trabajadores, or Workers Party). These victories represented major milestones in Mexican politics, long notorious for election fraud and corruption.

From Devaluation to Democracy

Mexico experienced another period of instability under President Ernesto Zedilo when the North American Free Trade Agreement (NAFTA) took effect in 1994. Indigenous uprisings in Chiapas on the mainland, the assassination of PRI presidential candidate Luis Donaldo Colosio in Tijuana, and the exposing of systemic corruption at the highest level of government scared investors out of the country, triggering a currency crisis and severe recession in early 1995.

But in the final years of the century, a grassroots movement succeeded in gradually and peacefully transforming the country into an open, multi-party democracy. In July 2000, the Mexican people elected the first non-PRI candidate in 70 years to the presidency, Vicente Fox of the National Action Party. *Opening Mexico: the Making of a Democracy,* written by *New York Times* reporters Julia Preston and Samuel Dillon, chronicles this period of change in an engaging, narrative format.

With its close ties to the U.S. economy, Baja California emerged from the currency crisis stronger in many ways than the mainland. But it faces grave challenges today in the form of organized crime, human trafficking, and corruption among law enforcement officials.

In July 2006, Felipe Calderón (PAN) was elected President of Mexico in a contentious election by a margin of only 0.56 percent over López Obrador (PRD). Amidst allegations of voting irregularities by the losing party, the initial election results were challenged. The ghosts of Mexico's past civil unrest hung in the air during the months it took to confirm the initial results.

Since taking office, Calderón has taken on the drug cartels and corruption at the city level. Most notably, the Tijuana city police force had its guns confiscated and officers temporarily armed themselves with slingshots.

Government and Economy

GOVERNMENT
Political Boundaries
The 28th parallel divides the Baja California peninsula into two states, Baja California (BC) north of the parallel and Baja California Sur (BCS) to the south. The northern state is sometimes called Baja California (Norte) or BCN, to distinguish the state from the entire peninsula.

Mexicali is the capital of Baja California (Norte), and the state consists of five *municipios* that are similar to U.S. counties: Tijuana, Rosarito, Ensenada, Mexicali, and Tecate. The state shares an international northern border with the United States. To the east, on the other side of the Colorado River, is the mainland state of Sonora.

Baja California Sur also consists of five *municipios:* La Paz, Los Cabos, Mulegé, Loreto, and Comondú. La Paz is the state capital.

Political System
The 31 United Mexican States form a representative democracy, which functions according to a constitution that was ratified in 1917. There are three branches: executive, legislative, and judicial. Presidents serve for six-year terms with no re-election. The legislature consists of two houses, the Senate and the Chamber of Deputies. States and municipalities (counties) have some independence, but each one must follow a republican form of government based on a congressional system.

Three parties dominate Mexican politics today: The National Action Party (PAN), the Party of the Democratic Revolution (PRD), and Institutional Revolutionary Party (PRI), which was the single reigning party through most of the 20th century.

The present governor of BCN is José Guadalupe Osuna Millán (PAN), an economist and former representative in the federal Chamber of Deputies. He took office in 2007. The current governor of BCS is Narciso Agúndez Montaño (PRD), who took office in 2005, following the term of his cousin, Leonel Cota Montaño, who served from 1999–2005.

ECONOMY
Tourism, commercial fishing, large-scale agriculture, and manufacturing in the border zone drive the economy of the Baja Peninsula. The mining of salt and other minerals plays a lesser role in the state of BCS. Organic agriculture is on the rise, with peppers, tomatoes, mangoes, basil, asparagus, and oranges among the crops that are being grown without the use of pesticides.

In the border region, hundreds of maquiladoras produce airplanes, electronics, automobiles, and medical devices. This part of the Baja economy is inseparably tied to that of the County of San Diego in the United States. People on both sides of the border regularly cross to the other side to work, shop, and travel.

Income and Employment
People who live in Baja are well-off, compared to the majority of their fellow citizens on the mainland. Per-capita income in both states ranks higher than the national average, while

Tourism remains a large part of Baja's economy.

unemployment is the lowest in the country. Workers employed by the in-bond plants earn higher wages than at comparable jobs elsewhere in the country, though the pay is far less than what their U.S. counterparts would make on the other side of the border.

Recent Economic Conditions

President Calderón has spent the first two years of his term fighting the drug cartels and ridding the government of corrupt officials at every level. To date, he has placed 45,000 troops and 5,000 federal police around the country to uphold the rule of law. But immigration, corruption, and narco-terrorism continue to pose grave challenges to the Mexican economy. Some see these problems as isolated border issues, and they say that the increase in violence is a sign that the strategy to prevent the flow of illegal drugs is working. Others believe the entire country could be on the brink of collapse if it doesn't stop the violence soon.

Calderón met with newly elected U.S. President Obama in early 2009 and reiterated the Mexican point of view that the drug problem has roots on both sides of the border. Stuck between a rock and a hard place, he needs to make a strong case for increased financial assistance without sending a message that will frighten foreign visitors and investors.

People and Culture

The people of Baja California are a diverse mix of farmers, fishermen, laborers, entrepreneurs, students, and professionals. Some belong to families that have lived on the peninsula for generations; others arrived more recently from mainland Mexico, the United States, Canada, or Europe. But regardless of their line of work and heritage, Baja's residents tend to share a common outlook on life: Somewhere along the line, they decided to search for—and found—a better way of life, albeit one that requires resourcefulness. Mainland Mexicans tend to regard Baja California in the same way that Americans view Hawaii or Alaska—as a faraway place that captures the imagination.

POPULATION

The current population of the Baja Peninsula is between 3–4 million people, most of whom reside above the 28th parallel in Baja California (Norte). More than half the population lives in Mexicali or Tijuana. The rest of the peninsula is sparsely populated, with an average density of less than one person per 26 square kilometer (one person per 10 sq mi).

Mexico's population growth rate is estimated at 1.16 percent per annum for 2006. The average for Baja California is probably somewhat higher than the national average because of immigration. Baja California Sur is Mexico's least-populated state.

ORIGINS

When the Spanish missionary period began in 1697, historians estimate the indigenous population of Baja was about 50,000. Less than 100 years later, only 20 percent of the population survived. Today, very few people of the central and northern Cochimí and Yumano tribes live in the valleys and sierras of Northern Baja.

True *bajacalifornianos* are a multicultural lot, with a much more diverse heritage than

a catholic church in Mulegé

BAJA FESTIVALS AND EVENTS

In addition to celebrating Mexico's national holidays as well as the major Catholic religious holidays, every town in Baja that is named after a Catholic saint holds an annual fiesta on the feast day of its namesake. Add to this seasonal festivals that celebrate lobster, gray whales, wine, etc., and you stand a pretty good chance of happening upon an event of one sort or another on your trip. Here are some of the highlights:

JANUARY

- **New Year's Day,** January 1, is a national holiday.

- **Día de los Santos Reyes** (Day of the King-Saints), January 6, is a Catholic religious holiday, the conclusion of Las Posadas.

FEBRUARY

- **Constitution Day,** February 5, is a national holiday.

- **Carnaval** takes place in late February or early March before Lent. La Paz and Ensenada put on the biggest celebrations in Baja.

- **Flag Day,** February 24, is a national holiday.

MARCH

- The **Birthday of Benito Juárez,** March 21, is a national holiday.

- **Spring Break** is not a Mexican festival, but a time when U.S. college students invade Rosarito, Ensenada, San Felipe, and Cabo San Lucas to party.

APRIL

- **Semana Santa** (Holy Week) takes place during the week leading up to Easter. After Christmas, it's the most important holiday of the year for Mexicans, and a time when many popular resorts are likely to fill up with visitors from the mainland.

- **The Rosarito-Ensenada 50-Mile Bicycle Ride** takes place on a Saturday in April and attracts thousands of cyclists. It is sponsored by **Bicycling West** (P.O. Box 9441, San Diego, CA 92169-0441, U.S. tel. 858/483-8777, www.rosaritoensenada.com).

- **The Newport-Ensenada Yacht Race,** one of the largest international yachting regattas in the world, takes place on the last weekend in April (U.S. tel. 949/644-1023, www.nosa.org).

MAY

- **International Workers' Day,** May 1, is a national holiday.

- **Cinco de Mayo,** May 5, honors the defeat of the French at the mainland city of Puebla, in 1862.

JUNE

- **Día de la Marina** (Navy Day), June 1, is a national holiday, celebrated most enthusiastically in San Felipe and La Playita near San José del Cabo.

SEPTEMBER

- **Día de Nuestra Señora de Loreto,** September 8, is a special day in Loreto, when the community honors the founding of the first Spanish mission in the Californias.

- **Fiesta Patria de la Independencia** (Mexican Independence Day), September 16, is also called Diez y Seis, referring to the date. This is Mexico's celebration of independence from Spain, which dates back to 1821. Mexicali and La Paz put on fireworks, parades, *charreadas*, music, and folk-dance performances.

- The **Rosarito-Ensenada 50-Mile Bicycle Ride** is held again on the last Saturday in September.

(continues on next page)

BAJA FESTIVALS AND EVENTS (continued)

OCTOBER

- **Día de la Raza,** October 12, commemorates the arrival of Christopher Columbus in the New World and the subsequent founding of the Mexican race.

NOVEMBER

- **Día de los Muertos** (Day of the Dead), November 1-2, is Mexico's third-most important holiday after Christmas and Easter. It is similar to the European All Saints Day, except that in Mexico, the celebration lasts two days.

- The **Baja 1000** off-road race takes place during the second or third week of November between Ensenada and La Paz. On alternate years, the course is shorter and limited to Northern Baja only. The event is sponsored by SCORE International (U.S. tel. 818/225-8402, www.score-international.com).

- The **Anniversary of the 1910 Revolution,** November 20, is a national holiday.

DECEMBER

- The Virgen of Guadalupe, also called Our Lady of Guadalupe, is one of the most important religious and cultural symbols in Mexico. The feast day for this patron saint, **Día de Nuestra Señora de Guadalupe,** takes place on December 12.

- **Las Posadas,** December 16-January 6, are nightly candlelight processions to local nativity scenes.

- **Día de la Navidad** (Christmas Day), December 25, is the most important holiday period in Mexico, as well as the United States. Resorts book well in advance around this time, and rates go up accordingly.

Mexican people from the mainland. Many are a mix of the Spanish and Indian cultures, but others descend from British, French, German, Dutch, Chinese, Russian, and other roots.

In addition to the families that have been in Baja since the early days of colonization, the peninsula has attracted a sizable population of U.S. and Canadian retirees, as well as increasing numbers of younger professionals from Mexico City and groups of migrant workers from Oaxaca.

RELIGION

The Spanish missionaries first introduced Catholicism to Baja California, and it remains the dominant religion today. Like the rest of Mexico, Baja's Catholics celebrate Our Lady of Guadalupe as an icon of the Virgin Mary on December 12. Baja has fewer churches per capita than the mainland, so in order to accommodate demand for worship services, some churches (*iglesias*) hold a dozen or more masses a day.

LANGUAGE

Latin-American Spanish is the primary language spoken in Baja California. People who work in the tourism industry tend to speak at least some English, especially in the larger cities, but a little Spanish goes a long way in day-to-day interactions with the local residents. Learning and using the basic greetings and a few essential phrases will show respect and build trust with the people you meet, which will likely result in a better overall travel experience.

ESSENTIALS

Getting There

BY AIR

Baja California has several international airports with direct connections to cities in the western United States. By far the busiest of these is the Los Cabos International Airport (SJD), with flights originating in Atlanta, Chicago, Dallas, Denver, Houston, Los Angeles, New York, Oakland, Phoenix, San Diego, San Francisco, and San Jose. You can also get to Los Cabos via connections on the mainland. La Paz (LAP) and Loreto (LOR) offer fewer direct connections to the United States but frequent flights to/from the mainland. Alaska Airlines is the only U.S. carrier that has offered direct service

consistently from the United States to these airports in recent years. American, United, and Delta have offered on-again, off-again connections.

Flying out of Tijuana International Airport (TIJ) is an economical way to get to Southern Baja. A new discount carrier called Volaris offers luxury bus service from downtown San Diego to the Tijuana airport and competitively priced flights on new planes to La Paz.

Private Planes

Private pilots can fly their own planes over the border to remote destinations all over the peninsula. The majority of landing fields in

© NIKKI GOTH ITOI

Baja are unattended dirt strips. Contact **Baja Bush Pilots** (U.S. tel. 480/730-3250, www.bajabushpilots.com) for up-to-date information about flight routes, entry requirements, insurance policies, landing fees, paperwork, and runway conditions.

BY BUS
To Tijuana
Greyhound Bus Lines (U.S. tel. 619/515-1100, www.greyhound.com) offers frequent service from San Diego (120 W. Broadway) to Tijuana (both the downtown bus terminal and the Central de Autobuses (for southbound connections). Fares are about US$12 one-way. You can also take Greyhound from Los Angeles (1716 E. 7th St., U.S. tel. 213/629-8401, US$26 one way), which is a four-hour trip. There's no extra charge for boxed bikes.

The easiest way to get from downtown San Diego to the border is the **Tijuana Trolley**, which departs every 15 minutes (U.S. tel. 619/685-4900 for general info or U.S. tel. 619/233-3004 for schedule and stops, daily 5 A.M.–1 A.M., Sat. "night owl" service 2–5 A.M., US$1–2.50). The trip takes about an hour. You can bring your bike along.

The most economical bus from downtown San Diego to the border at San Ysidro is city bus 932 (U.S. tel. 619/685-4900, www.sdcommute.com, US$2.25), with daily departures every half-hour, beginning around 6 A.M. to 11 P.M. every day. The trip takes about 80 minutes one-way.

Once you've reached the border, **Mexicoach** buses (tel. 664/685-1470, U.S. tel. 619/428-9517, US$5) leave every 30 minutes 8 A.M.–9 P.M. for the Terminal Turística Tijuana (Av. Revolución btw Calles 6/7).

To Mexicali and Calexico
Greyhound (Mex. tel. 800/710-8819, www.greyhound.com.mx) and its Mexican partner Crucero offer daily bus service from Los Angeles (US$37) and San Ysidro (US$31) to Calexico (1st St. at the border). A short walk from the station gets you through the border gateway and into downtown Mexicali.

Buses from Mainland Mexico
Transportes Norte de Sonora (TNS, Tijuana tel. 664/688-1979) and **Autotransportes Estrellas del Pacífico** (Tijuana tel. 664/683-5022) run long-distance express connections to Mexicali and Tijuana from various mainland destinations.

Green Tortoise
Budget travelers who like the idea of exploring Baja with a organized group might consider Green Tortoise (U.S. tel. 415/956-7500 or 800/867-8647, www.greentortoise.com). It offers nine-day (from US$466) and 15-day (US$729) trips to Baja November–April that begin in San Francisco (pickups in L.A. and San Diego are possible) and go as far south as Cabo Pulmo. Prices include transportation, accommodations (on the bus), guided hikes, and side trips to the beach.

BY CAR
Driving into Baja
It's easy to drive yourself across the border for a Baja adventure. There are several places to cross (the busiest is San Ysidro/Tijuana), and you don't need a permit for your vehicle unless you plan to continue on to the mainland. You do need a validated tourist permit if you plan to go south of Maneadero or stay longer than 72 hours anywhere on the peninsula.

Mexican Auto Insurance
There is a lot of confusion and misinformation in travel circles about why and how to insure your vehicle when driving in Mexico. Whether you are driving your own vehicle into Mexico, renting a car to drive over the border, or renting within Mexico, read this section carefully:

Before driving into Baja, all drivers should arrange for Mexican vehicle insurance. Why? Mexican law requires drivers to have proof of financial liability (a minimum of US$50,000 worth) for any property damage or bodily injury they cause to other parties in an accident. Unless you have a bond with a Mexican bank or cash in hand at the time of an accident, the only practical way to comply with the law is to

DRIVING DISTANCES

Distances from Tijuana, along the Trans-peninsular Highway, using the Tijuana-Ensenada toll road:

Ensenada	109 km (68 mi)
San Quintín	301 km (187 mi)
El Rosario	359 km (226 mi)
Cataviña	481 km (298 mi)
Punta Prieta	599 km (371 mi)
Bahía de los Ángeles	654 km (405 mi)
Guerrero Negro	714 km (443 mi)
San Ignacio	856 km (531 mi)
Santa Rosalía	928 km (575 mi)
Mulegé	990 km (614 mi)
Loreto	1,125 km (698 mi)
Ciudad Constitución	1,268 km (786 mi)
La Paz	1,483 km (919 mi)
Cabo San Lucas	1,704 km (1,056 mi)

purchase an insurance policy underwritten by a Mexican company. Without it, a minor traffic accident can turn into a nightmare, involving jail time and steep financial penalties. *No matter what your own insurance company may tell you, Mexican authorities do not recognize foreign insurance policies for private vehicles in Mexico.*

If you are planning to drive your own vehicle, you can purchase short-term insurance—as little as one day's worth—from one of 20 or so online vendors of Mexican Tourist Auto Insurance. Simply request a quote, complete an application, pay by credit card, and print a certificate from home before you leave for your trip. (You can purchase a policy in advance, and set it to begin on the day you plan to cross the border.) Policy terms and quality of service vary significantly, so be sure you are dealing with a reputable broker before you buy. A good way to tell is to call and speak to a live person, then complete the process online.

If you're not the plan-ahead type, or you prefer to deal in person, you can stop in several agencies found in nearly every border town between the Pacific Ocean and the Gulf of Mexico. Again, read the terms carefully before paying.

The first decision you'll need to make is between a liability-only policy (to comply with the law) or full coverage (to protect your vehicle). Liability-only policies typically cover third-party liability from a minimum of US$50,000, up to US$300,000, plus legal expenses (levels range widely from US$500 to US$30,000), medical payments for you and your passengers (US$2,000–5,000 per person; US$19,000–25,000 per accident), and some form of roadside assistance. Higher-end policies may include medical evacuation and a flight home if your car is stolen or not drivable. Standard deductibles begin at US$500 and scale to 2–10 percent of the value of the vehicle, or a flat US$5,000 for motorcycles.

Full coverage adds physical damage and theft coverage to the list. Since the cost of upgrading from liability-only to full coverage amounts to a few dollars more per day, it usually makes sense to add the theft coverage and enjoy the peace of mind. Theft coverage typically carries a higher deductible than just liability.

In business since 2001, Santa Cruz, California–based **Adventure Mexican Insurance** (U.S. tel. 831/477-0599 or 800/485-4075, www.mexadventure.com) provides daily, monthly, and annual Mexican auto insurance to individual travelers, as well as travel organizations. The company's website clearly explains Mexican insurance options and allows you to compare various policies from its three underwriters; well armed with information, you can then purchase online in a matter of minutes. For a long weekend trip to Baja, you'll pay around

MEXICAN AUTO INSURANCE POLICY CHECKLIST

Consider the following criteria before buying Mexican insurance for your private vehicle:

- Look for a U.S.-based claims office.

- Deductibles should be clearly stated, typically a minimum of $500 or 2 percent of the value of the vehicle.

- The better policies include legal coverage, roadside assistance, plane tickets home if your car cannot be driven, and medical evacuation.

- Some premium policies include extra coverage for uninsured drivers.

- Policies with a "combined single limit" (CSL) for bodily and property damage are preferred over "split limits," which are less flexible.

- The policy should allow you to handle repairs in the United States or Canada.

- The policy should clearly state an hourly labor rate high enough to cover the cost of repairs in the United States (the US$15/hour standard in Mexico will not be sufficient).

- Keep one copy of your policy in the glovebox and another in your wallet (in case the car is stolen).

- Call your claims number when you cross into Mexico to verify that it works.

- If you have a claim, report it before you leave Mexico within the time limit specified in your policy; some companies will not honor the policy once you have left the country.

- Claims adjusters can reach most parts of Baja within two hours.

- Driving on the beach is considered a non-conventional road: If you get stuck and the tide comes in and floods your car, it's probably not going to be covered.

- Any roads that require four-wheel drive are probably not covered.

When shopping online:

- Websites should display an insurance license logo.

- Check that the site is secure before you transmit personal data.

- When in doubt, call the vendor to verify services.

US$30 for liability only, and US$40 for full coverage (both at the minimum liability level of US$50,000). Full coverage monthly rates range US$200–350, depending on the value of the vehicle. Its policies cover repairs in the United States and include a bundled travel assistance package for medical evacuation of up to four passengers and plane tickets home if your vehicle is undrivable. Call toll-free for detailed information about insuring an RV, trailer, or other special circumstances. Short-term policies cover travel in all of Mexico, but for long-term policies, customers have the option of a regional North West policy covering Baja as well as the mainland states of Sonora, Chihuahua, and Sinaloa, at a reduced rate.

Several travel clubs offer discounted rates to members: For example, **Discover Baja Travel Club** (toll-free U.S. tel. 800/727-2252, www.discoverbaja.com) offers liability insurance for only US$77 per year and full coverage starting at US$140. AAA members can purchase Mexican auto insurance through the travel club website (www.aaa.com) or by phone.

If you forget to purchase insurance before you leave or prefer to purchase your policy in person, try **Instant Mexico Insurance Services** (223 Via de San Ysidro, U.S. tel. 619/428-4714, or 800/345-4701, www.instant-mex-auto-insur.com, open 24 hrs daily) at the last exit before the San Ysidro/Tijuana border crossing. You can also purchase tourist cards, fishing permits, maps, guidebooks, and other Baja requisites here.

Once you've purchased a policy, make several copies of it and put the originals in a safe place, separate from the copies. You should also carry a copy of the first page—the "declaration" or "renewal of declaration" sheet—of your home country insurance policy, since Mexican law requires drivers to enter the country with at least six months' worth of insurance in their home country.

Temporary Vehicle Import Permits

If you plan to head to the mainland from Baja (via ferry from Southern Baja or via land in Northern Baja), you'll need to obtain a temporary vehicle import permit from a Mexican customs office at any of the border crossings or in La Paz at the ferry terminal. Bring a valid state registration for the vehicle (or similar document certifying legal ownership), driver's license, and major credit card (not debit card) issued outside Mexico.

If you are leasing or renting the vehicle, you'll also have to present the contract you've signed that allows you to bring the vehicle into Mexico. If you are borrowing the vehicle, you'll need a notarized letter from the owner giving you permission to take the vehicle to Mexico.

Once Mexican customs officials have approved your documents, you'll be directed to pay by credit card at an adjoining Banjército office (US$17). (If you don't have a credit card, you'll have to post a bond (1–2 percent of the vehicle's blue-book value) issued by an authorized Mexican bond company, a time-consuming and expensive procedure.

Permits are valid for the same period of time shown on your tourist card or visa. You can drive back and forth across the border—at any crossing—as many times as you wish during the this time; however, you need to cancel the permit at the completion of your trip, or the government will presume that you've permanently imported your vehicle (illegally)

in Mexico and forbid you from obtaining another temporary vehicle import permit, should you need one for a future trip. (We've seen this happen to an unsuspecting motorcyclist.) For more information on this process, call U.S. tel. 800/922-8228.

BY FERRY FROM MAINLAND MEXICO

If you are on the Pacific coast of the mainland and want to get to Baja, you can take a modern passenger or car ferry service from Mazatlán or Topolobampo/Los Mochis to La Paz or from Guaymas to Santa Rosalía. Routes and schedules change periodically, so double check the current service offerings a week or so before you want to cross. At last check, **Baja Ferries** (Pichilingue Terminal, tel. 612/123-0208, U.S. tel. 915/833-3107, downtown La Paz office: Allende 1025 at Rubio, 612/123-6600 or 800/122-1414, www.bajaferries.com, daily 8 A.M.–5 P.M.) was running two routes: La Paz–Topolobampo (6 hrs, US$75 per seat), La Paz–Mazatlán (12 hrs, once daily Tues.–Sun., US$83 per seat). Cabins (US$76) and cars (US$105–215) cost extra. Baja Ferries has another ticket office at the Mega grocery store in San José del Cabo (Mexico 1 at the traffic circle). If you're starting from Topolobampo, the local number is 668/862-1003.

Transportación Marítima de California (TMC) (La Paz office tel. 800/744-5050, Mazatlán office tel. 800/700-0433, www.ferrytmc.com) also runs a car ferry between La Paz and Mazatlán (15.5 hrs). A car and driver cost US$280; RVs up to 10 meters (about 33 ft) cost US$670.

The **Santa Rosalía ferry** (tel. 615/152-0013, www.ferrysantarosalia.com) is now running several times a week, leaving Santa Rosalía in the morning at 9 A.M. and returning from Guaymas in the evening at 8 P.M. To book vehicle passage, you must hold a valid temporary vehicle import permit (best obtained at least a day before your departure). Show up three hours before the scheduled departure to board the ferry.

Getting Around

Most Baja visitors navigate the peninsula by car—either their own vehicle or a rented one. If you stay at a large resort and don't want to venture far from it, you may be able to rely on shuttles and taxis to get around. Other ways to get around include domestic flights, such as from Tijuana to La Paz or Los Cabos, as well as intercity and municipal buses.

BY BUS
Intercity Bus Service

Several companies offer connections between northern and southern Baja towns. It takes about 30 hours to complete the journey from Tijuana to Cabo San Lucas by bus with **Autotransportes Aguila** (tel. 612/122-4270, US$134). Many travelers divide the trip into two parts by stopping overnight in La Paz.

Transportes Norte de Sonora (TNS, tel. 664/688-1979) operates buses in Northern Baja, connecting Tijuana, Tecate, and Mexicali with the mainland state of Sonora.

Buses are modern, comfortable, and usually air-conditioned for longer trips. Schedules vary (this is not Switzerland), and prices are reasonable. You don't usually need reservations (stop by the day before just in case), and in many cases, it's not possible to make them.

The Spanish word for ticket is *boleto*. Fares are usually posted on the wall inside the depot.

Municipal Buses

Tijuana, Ensenada, Mexicali, San Quintín, and La Paz have city bus systems that cost a dollar or two per trip (pesos only). The route or destination (a street name or district) usually is posted on the front of the bus.

BY TAXI

Taxis wait at the larger hotels and designated taxi stands in most of the larger towns along the peninsula. There are no meters; you pay a set fare based on the distance you are traveling.

An Aguila bus waits for passengers in San José del Cabo.

© NIKKI GOTH ITOI

Ask around for the going rate to your destination and negotiate the fare with the driver before you hop in. Even the smaller towns often have a few taxis for hire near the town plaza.

Larger cities with their own bus systems (Tijuana, Rosarito, Ensenada, and Mexicali) also have *taxis de ruta* (route taxis), which follow a set route, like a bus, but stop wherever someone flags them down or a passenger asks to get off. These taxi services use large American station wagons that hold up to 12 passengers. Fares tend to be marginally higher than comparable bus fare.

BY CAR

Driving the Transpeninsular Highway and the few other paved routes in Baja is fairly straightforward. Road conditions can vary, though—with potholes, speed bumps *(topes)*, livestock, construction, rock slides, and other unexpected obstacles possible around every bend. Among the greatest challenges are the deep *vados,* dry river beds that fill with water after heavy rains; the narrow width of the road, and the fact that it has no shoulder in many places; and the 18-wheelers that barrel along at high speeds, often passing on blind turns.

Other than the four-lane toll roads between Tijuana and Ensenada and between San José del Cabo and Cabo San Lucas, these highways are two-lane roads. Several dirt roads have been recently paved, connecting inland communities such as San Javier, near Loreto and Los Planes, near La Paz, to the Transpeninsular Highway. But aside from those developments, all other roads in Baja are gravel, dirt, or sand.

Off-Highway Travel

The condition of Baja's unpaved roads varies widely, from smooth graded paths to heavy washboard, soft sand, and steep grades with frequent washouts. Good road maps categorize dirt roads to give you an idea of what to expect, but it's best to ask about current road conditions before embarking on an off-highway excursion.

Travelers who aren't intending to venture into the backcountry often get stuck in the sand the moment they pull off the coastal road to check

ROADTRIPPER'S CAR KIT

Automotive fuel and supplies are much easier to come by these days than in the past, especially if you stick to paved Mexico 1; however, extra supplies for your vehicle can save precious time and money, should things go awry. Here's what to pack:

- air filters
- battery cables
- brake, clutch, steering, and transmission fluids
- eight-meter tow rope
- emergency flares
- fan belts
- fire extinguisher
- fuel filters
- fuses
- lug wrench and jack
- one five-gallon water container
- one or two five-gallon gas cans
- radiator hoses
- spare tire
- spark plugs
- tire gauge
- tube-repair kit (if appropriate)
- 12-volt air compressor
- water filters

the surf or park at the beach. Carry a shovel for digging yourself out, plus something to put under the wheels to provide traction, like a piece of wood or ribbed plastic. It also helps to let some of the air out of your tires, but bring a compressor for pumping the tires back up.

Driving Precautions

Common sense and a few additional precautions will get you safely from one town to the next in Baja. Wherever you go, plan the driving so that you are not on the road at night. The biggest danger after dark is animals: cows, burros, and dogs, which appear in the road more frequently than you'd think. Other concerns include local vehicles without headlights, brake lights, or tail lights; drivers under the influence of alcohol; and the lack of lighting or reflectors on most of these roads.

Follow the speed limits, even though the locals often drive much faster (they know the road, you don't). Taking it slow gives you a little extra time to react in an emergency situation, and also reduces the chance that you'll inadvertently commit a traffic offense. Plus, it's a better way to enjoy the scenery.

Note that *topes* and *vados* are not always marked, so pay attention and be ready to slow down immediately upon spotting them. We've seen cars take particularly bad speed bumps at full speed and launch themselves in the air to reveal the undercarriage of the vehicle. Measure the depth of water in any *vado* before driving through.

Highway Signs

Highway signs in Baja are usually self-explanatory, with symbols or pictures are well as words. Some of the more useful road signs include:

- *Curva Peligrosa* (Dangerous Curve)

- *Despacio* (Slow)

- *Zona de Vados* (Dip Zone)

- *Desviación* (Detour)

- *No Tire Basura* (Don't Throw Trash)

- *Conserve Su Derecha* (Keep to the Right)

- *Conceda Cambio de Luces* (Dim Your Lights)

- *No Rebase* (No Passing)

- *No Hay Paso* (Road Closed)

Kilometer Markers

Baja's major highways feature kilometer markers that count up or down between cities, depending on which direction you are heading. People often use these markers when measuring distances and giving directions (e.g. "Turn off at Km 171"). In Baja California (Norte), the markers start at zero (Km 0) in Tijuana and ascend heading south. Starting at the state line with Baja California Sur, the markers descend as you continue south, beginning with Km 220 in Guerrero Negro.

Traffic Offenses

In the larger cities, it can be difficult to navigate busy streets and unfamiliar intersections; foreign motorists do get pulled over for running hard-to-see (or nonexistent) stop signs and other legitimate (though understandable) violations. The best way to prevent this kind of incident is to drive slowly, and assume you must stop at every urban intersection, whether you see a sign or not.

If you're stopped, respond kindly and respectfully, and you may be let go without a ticket. If the officer persists, you'll need to proceed to the nearest police station to pay the fine. If the officer asks you to pay on the spot, you're being targeted for *la mordida,* a minor bribe.

In Baja, these incidents tend to happen in Tijuana, Rosarito, Ensenada, and La Paz. If it happens, you should insist on going to the nearest station to pay the fine, and when you pay, ask for a receipt. The charges may well be dropped at this point.

Something many drivers don't know that could invite trouble with the police is that in Mexico, it's illegal to display any foreign national flag except over an embassy or consulate—this includes small flags flying from the antenna of your vehicle.

Fuel

Motorists fill their tanks in Mexico at government-owned Pemex stations, which are common in the larger towns, and less prevalent as you get into the more remote parts of the peninsula. Barrel gas is sometimes available in rural settlements. You can choose among regular unleaded fuel (*magna sin,* octane rating 87), a.k.a. *verde* (green); a high-test unleaded (premium, octane rating 89), a.k.a. *roja* (red); and diesel. Rates are the same from station to station (but exchange rates offered may vary if you pay in dollars). At press time, a gallon of *verde* in Baja was US$1.40 cheaper than the same fuel in the state of California. The price should always be marked in pesos on the pump.

Most Pemex stations are full-serve (though Los Cabos now has the first self-serve station on the peninsula), and a visit begins with two questions: How much and what type of gas do you want? *"Lleno con premium (roja)/magna (verde), por favor"* is the usual answer. Leave a small tip (up to US$1) for window washing or other extra services.

An early 2007, a National Public Radio segment in the United States reported that Mexican authorities had determined that 9 out of 10 gas stations in the country were rigging their pumps, costing drivers some US$1 billion per year. Pay attention at the pump, but don't assume every attendant intends to rip you off. Here are some precautions to avoid problems at the Pemex:

• Check to make sure the pump is zeroed before the attendant starts pumping your gas.

• Get out of your vehicle to watch the pumping procedures.

• Carry a hand-held calculator to check currency conversions.

• When paying in large bills, tell the attendant what denomination you are handing him and make sure he acknowledges the amount, then count your change carefully. A common scam happens when you hand over a 500-peso bill, expecting change, and the attendant comes back to say you only gave him a 50.

Cash is the only way to pay for gas in Mexico. Some stations near the border and in the Los Cabos Corridor will accept dollars, but they are notorious for offering below market exchange rates. At press time, many were following the old 10/1 rule, while the exchange rate had shot up to 14/1.

Parts and Repairs

Just about every town has a *llantera* (tire repair). Experienced mechanics are harder, but not impossible, to come by. Try any of the larger towns and cities. For those used to the systematic process of a large U.S. auto shop, the Baja approach might seem haphazard, but they do seem to get the job done most of the time. For extensive driving in remote areas, bring your own spare parts.

Roadside Assistance

If you have a breakdown while traveling in Mexico, chances are one of the **Angeles Verdes** (Green Angels) will come to the rescue. Sponsored by the Secretaría de Turismo, these green trucks patrol the highways in Baja twice a day, and offer roadside assistance to anyone with car troubles. Trucks are equipped with first-aid kits, shortwave radios, fuel, and spare parts. Drivers will can do minor repairs for the cost of the parts and/or provide towing for distances up to 24 kilometers (15 mi). If they can't solve your vehicle's problem or tow it to a mechanic, they'll arrange for other assistance. They can also radio for emergency medical assistance if necessary.

Military Checkpoints

When driving the Transpeninsular Highway, you'll encounter numerous military checkpoints *(puestos de control),* or roadblocks at which uniformed officials search vehicles for drugs and firearms. Although the concept is foreign to many U.S. and Canadian residents, the soldiers are courteous (and often just curious about your travels) and it rarely takes more than a few minutes. If you have any concerns about a search, discreetly record information such as badge numbers, names, or license numbers, and file a report with the Mexican Attorney General for Tourist Protection.

CAR RENTALS

ACE Rent a Car (tel. 624/146-1839, www.acerentacar.com)

• Los Cabos International Ariport (SJD)

Advantage (tel. 624/143-0466 or 624/146-5500):

• Cabo San Lucas

• Los Cabos International Ariport (SJD)

Alamo (tel. 800/849-8001, www.alamorentacar.com.mx):

• Los Cabos International Airport (SJD)

• San José del Cabo

Avis (tel. 624/146-0201, U.S. tel. 800/331-2112, www.avis.com):

• Cabo San Lucas (three locations: Ave. Lázaro Cárdenas, Hotel Pueblo Bonito Rosé, and Pueblo Bonito Pacifica)

• Los Cabos International Airport (SJD)

• La Paz (downtown at Paseo Obregón)

• La Paz International Airport (LAP)

• Tijuana (downtown in the Zona Río)

• Tijuana International Airport (TIJ)

Budget (tel. 624/146-5333, U.S. tel. 800/527-0700, www.budget.com):

• Los Cabos Corridor (Marquis Hotel)

• Los Cabos International Airport (SJD)

• Loreto International Airport (LOR)

• Mexicali International Airport (MXL)

• San José del Cabo (Crowne Plaza)

• Tijuana International Airport (TIJ)

• Todos Santos (Marquez de Leon 4)

Dollar Rent A Car (tel. 624/105-8410, U.S. tel. 866/434-2266, www.dollar.com or www.dollarloscabos.com):

• Cabo San Lucas (four locations: downtown at Blvd. Marina, and at Club Cascadas, Hotel Finisterra, and Hotel Meliá Cabo Real)

• Los Cabos Corridor (Hotel Fiesta Americana)

• La Paz International Airport (LAP)

• La Paz/Pichilingue (La Concha Hotel)

• Mexicali downtown (Blvd. Benito Juárez)

• San José del Cabo (two locations: downtown at Blvd. Castro and at the Presidente InterContinental)

• Tijuana downtown (Zona Río)

Europcar (tel. 612/124-7011, U.S. tel. 877/940-6900, www.europcar.com):

• La Paz (downtown at Obregón)

• La Paz International Airport (LAP)

• Loreto (downtown)

• Loreto International Airport (LOR)

• Los Cabos International Airport (SJD)

Hertz (tel. 624/146-1803, U.S. tel. 800/821-1727, www.hertz.com) with locations in:

• Cabo San Lucas (Ave. Lázaro Cárdenas 6)

• Ensenada (downtown at Ave. Alvarrado 143)

• La Paz (downtown at Obregón 2130-D)

• La Paz International Airport (LAP)

• La Paz/Pichilingue (Marina Costa Baja, Km 61, Carr. a Pichilingue)

• Loreto (downtown on Calle Romanita)

• Loreto International Airport (LOR, Km 5, Mexico 1)

• Los Cabos Corridor (Westin Los Cabos)

• Los Cabos International Airport (SJD)

• Mexicali (two locations downtown: Blvd. Benito Juárez and at Hotel Araiza Inn)

- Mexicali International Airport (MXL)
- Tijuana (four locations downtown: Camino Real, in the Zona Río 9575, and at Grand Hotel and Hotel Pueblo Amigo)
- Tijuana International Airport (TIJ)

National (tel. 624/142-2424, U.S. tel. 877/567-3572, www.nationalcar.com):

- Cabo San Lucas (two locations: Ave. Lázaro Cárdenas and at the Riu Palace)
- Los Cabos Corridor (four locations: Hilton Los Cabos, Hotel Casa del Mar, One&Only Palmilla, and at the Sheraton Hacienda del Mar)
- Los Cabos International Airport (SJD)
- La Paz International Airport (LAP)
- La Paz (downtown at Obregón)
- Los Barriles (20 de Noviembre)

- San José del Cabo (Posada Real Los Cabos)
- Tijuana (Ave. Nezuhuatcoyotl 1640)
- Tijuana International Airport (TIJ)

Payless Car Rental (tel. 624/105-8411, www.paylesscarrental.com):

- Cabo San Lucas (two locations: ME by Melia Cabo, in Cabo San Lucas, and Melia Cabo Real, along the Los Cabos Corridor)
- La Paz International Airport (LAP)
- Los Cabos Corridor (two locations: Dreams Los Cabos and at the Westin Resort)
- San Felipe
- San José del Cabo (two locations: downtown at Blvd. Mijares and Nissan and at the Crowne Plaza Hotel)
- Tijuana International Aiport (TIJ)

Recreational Vehicles

Baja has long been popular with RV travelers because it offers so many beautiful and accessible places to camp; however, driving a big rig along the narrow and winding stretches of Mexico 1 can be a white-knuckle experience for first-timers. One way to learn the ropes is to join an organized caravan, which leads a group of RVers along a set itinerary down the peninsula and back. These trips cost around US$100 a day, not including meals and fuel.

Car Rental

You can rent cars in Tijuana, Rosarito, Mexicali, Ensenada, Loreto, La Paz, Los Barriles, Todos Santos, San José del Cabo, and Cabo San Lucas. In general, larger cities offer the least-expensive rentals. Most of the international chains offer economy/compact cars for around US$30–45 a day with unlimited miles or US$60–75 for an SUV or Jeep. Rates in La Paz are slightly lower than in Los Cabos.

Mexican liability insurance costs an additional US$25 a day with these companies, and deductibles are often high (US$1,000 and up). It pays to shop around. Book ahead online, or comparison shop when you arrive.

Online discount car rental services, such as Hotwire (www.hotwire.com), offer substantially lower rates than the major brands by selling excess inventory for their partner companies. Rentals through Hotwire come from names like Avis, Hertz, or Budget, but you won't know which company until you agree to purchase the rental. The other difference is that you prepay for the rental at the time of reservation, so you won't be able to change your mind once you get to Baja.

Independent agencies are another option, sometimes at lower cost but often with per-kilometer charges in addition to the daily rate.

Rentals out of San Diego are sometimes a bit cheaper, but most agencies that allow their cars into Mexico won't allow them any farther south than Guerrero Negro. Some only allow travel 40 kilometers (25 mi) into Baja. If you drive beyond these limits, you won't be covered. They often add mandatory collision damage waivers to the cost as well. If you're planning to rent in San Diego, note that even though Avis and other companies allow you to drive across the border, Hotwire's contracts with its partners stipulate no cross-border travel. Go directly to the rental car provider if you want to rent from San Diego.

California Baja Rent-A-Car (9245 Jamacha Blvd., Spring Valley, CA 91977, U.S. tel. 619/470-7368 or 888/470-7368, www. cabaja.com) specializes in vehicle rentals for driving the Baja Peninsula. Internet discount rates start at about US$60 a day plus US$0.32 per mile beyond 100 miles per day for a subcompact. A Wrangler rents for US$120 a day plus US$0.32 per mile (100 free miles per day), while a Landrover Discovery II 4X4 costs US$130 daily plus US$0.38 per mile (100 free miles per day). Mexican insurance is included in these discounted rates. Drop-offs in Cabo San Lucas can be arranged for an extra charge. Optional accessories include satellite phones, Sirius satellite radio, and coolers. Note: This agency is located about 20 minutes from the San Diego airport, and did not have a shuttle at press time, so customers need to take a US$40–45 cab to the pickup location.

Insuring Your Rental Car

The Mexican proof of financial responsibility law applies to drivers of rental cars in Mexico, except in this case, you don't get to choose a specific policy—rather, you agree to pay an additional US$25–40 per day for whatever coverage the rental car company provides. The exact amount depends on the size of the rental car and how far into Baja you drive it (if you rent from San Diego). Terms and coverage limits vary among the various agencies, and they don't make it easy to see the fine print before you arrive at the counter. To learn about the policy before you agree to rent the car, call the local office for the company you are considering. Read the contract carefully at the rental car counter, and be sure you understand the terms. If you drive farther than the contract permits, fail to report an accident within the time specified, or violate other clauses, your coverage may be nullified.

Avis (U.S. tel. 619/688-5000 or 800/852-4617) allows renters to drive inside the Free Trade Zone area which is up to 40 kilometers (25 mi) from the U.S. border. **Hertz** (U.S. tel. 619/767-5700) allows customers to drive a rental car from the San Diego airport location only into Baja. Mexican insurance costs US$25 a day for an economy- to regular-size car, US$35 a day for a premium car or mini-van, up to 40 kilometers (25 mi) south into Mexico (which won't get you very far); and US$35–40 a day for travel between 41–400 kilometers (26–250 mi) south of the border. Coverage limits are US$25,000 for collision, US$25,000 for theft, US$50,000 for liability; legal and medical are not specified.

Deductibles at Thrifty were as high as US$2,500 at last check.

BY MOTORCYCLE

The open roads of Baja have captured the imagination of many a motorcyclist. The **Adventure Rider Motorcycle Forum** (www. advrider.com) has some of the best motorcycle trip reports around.

Motorcycle mechanics are even harder to come by in Baja than auto mechanics, so you'll need to be self-sufficient in handling equipment problems. Mid-day travel may be impossible in some parts of the peninsula due to intolerably high temperatures. Factor this into your trip planning.

Chris Haines Motorcycle Adventure (P.O. Box 966, Trabuco Canyon, CA 92678, U.S. tel. 866/262-8635, www.bajaoffroadtours. com) operates four-day rides from Ensenada to Mike's Sky Ranch for US$2,100 and seven-day rides from Ensenada to Cabo San Lucas for US$4,550, including equipment and road support. Custom itineraries are also possible. **Baja Off-Road Adventures** (www.bajaoffroad.com) offers similar trips.

BY BICYCLE

It's not unusual to meet cyclists riding their way down the Transpeninsular Highway, often as part of longer coastal journeys from Alaska all the way to Panama. While we understand the attraction of this epic cycling tour, we believe the dangers of riding along the highway have been downplayed for too long. In the early days of the paved road, when traffic was lighter, cycling may have been a safer option, but today, motorists, RVers, and truckers drive at faster speeds and in greater numbers. The problem is the width of the road. When two 18-wheelers approach from opposite directions, they pass with inches of pavement between them. If the driver must choose between colliding with an oncoming truck or pushing a cyclist off the road, the cyclist is inevitably going to lose out. Shoulders and guardrails are non-existent on many of the most dangerous stretches of road.

If your dream is to ride your bike the length of Baja, consider an off-road route à la the Baja 1000. This way, you can enjoy more of the coastal and mountain scenery and avoid putting yourself in danger on the highway.

Some of the best trail riding in Baja awaits in the Parque Nacional Constitución de 1857, close to the international border. The Cataviña Boulder Field in the Desierto Central also has some good off-road riding. In Southern Baja, the Camino Rural Costero between San José del Cabo and Cabo Pulmo is a fantastic route along the coast, as is the dirt road between Los Barriles and Bahía de los Muertos.

Equipment and Repairs

Many cyclists have never completed an overnight bike trip before planning a ride through Baja. Here are some of the basics you'll need:

- Camping gear
- Helmet
- Rearview mirror
- Locking cable
- Removable handlebar bag for valuables
- Four one-liter bottles of water per day (puncture resistant)
- Heavy-duty tires (including one spare) and, preferably, slime tubes (2–3 spares)
- Tire gauge
- Complete tire repair kit.
- Basic first-aid kit, including duct tape and moleskin
- Spare parts and tools to work on them

The larger towns in Baja all have bicycle repair shops.

Bicycle Transportation

Bikes are permitted on the **Tijuana Trolley** (U.S. tel. 619/233-3004), and they may be checked as luggage (if boxed) for no additional cost on **Mexicoach** and **Greyhound** buses.

Guided Bicycle Trips

Pedaling South (U.S. tel. 707/942-4450 or 800/398-6200, www.tourbaja.com), offers a number of multiday cycling tours: Sierra Ridge Ride (nine days, US$795), San Javier Singletrack (eight days, US$795), Oasis Bases (seven days or eight days, US$695), and Cross Baja/Whale Watch (nine days, US$995). Combo sea kayak/mountain bike trips are also available at US$795 for seven days. If you bring your own bike, Pedaling South deducts US$95 from the tour rates. Included in the price are accommodations, ground transport, meals on tour days, camping gear, tents, guides, tracking vehicles, and first aid.

Visas and Officialdom

ENTRY REGULATIONS
Passports and Tourist Permits

Under the Western Hemisphere Travel Initiative, as of January 2007, anyone traveling by air between the United States, Canada, Mexico, Central and South America, the Caribbean, and Bermuda is required to present a valid passport (including infants). The same applies to anyone traveling by land or sea as of January 2008.

Citizens of the United States or Canada (or of 42 other designated countries in Europe and Latin America, plus Singapore) who are visiting Mexico as tourists do not need a visa. They must, however, obtain validated tourist cards, called *formas migratorias turistas,* or FMTs, available at any Mexican consulate or Mexican tourist office, on flights to Mexico, and at any border crossing. The tourist card is valid for 180 days and must be used within 90 days of issue. It expires when you exit the country. If you are planning to enter and leave Mexico more than once during your trip, you can ask for a multiple-entry tourist card, which is available at Mexican consulates.

To validate the tourist card, you need to present proof of citizenship to a Mexican immigration officer, either at the border or in the airport. Acceptable documentation includes a birth certificate (or certified copy), voter's registration card, certificate of naturalization, or passport. Your driver's license won't suffice.

In 1999, the Mexican government instituted a tourist fee (currently around US$22), which is factored into your airfare if you fly, but must be paid separately at a bank in Mexico if you cross the border by land or sea. The immigration office you visit will direct you to the nearest bank. Once you've paid, you'll get a receipt, which you can bring back to the immigration office in exchange for validation of the tourist card. If you do not plan to travel south of Ensenada or San Felipe, you are not required to pay this fee.

Tourist Visas

Tourists from countries other than the 45 countries referenced earlier must obtain visas before arriving in Mexico. Apply in person at a Mexican consulate and expect about a two-week turnaround. The Mexican Consulate General in San Diego can often issue same-day tourist visas. Required documentation includes a valid passport, valid U.S. visa for multiple entries, form I-94, proof of economic solvency (such as an international credit card), and a round-trip air ticket to Mexico. The visa fee costs about US$40.

Foreign visitors who are legal permanent residents of the United States do not need visas to visit Mexico for tourism. You can get a validated tourist card by presenting your passport and U.S. residence card at the airport or border control.

Pets

Dogs and cats may be brought into Mexico with proof of current vaccinations and a **health certificate** issued within 72 hours before entry into Mexico and signed by a registered veterinarian.

BORDER CROSSINGS

Baja California's international border with the U.S. has six official crossings:

- San Ysidro/Tijuana (daily 24 hrs)
- Otay Mesa (daily 24 hrs)
- Tecate (daily 5 A.M.–11 P.M.)
- Calexico East (daily 6 A.M.–midnight)
- West/Mexicali (daily 24 hrs)
- Los Algodones (daily 6 A.M.–10 P.M.)

Tijuana is the largest and busiest of the bunch, with waits up to two hours, but even the less-crowded ones have lines during morning and afternoon commute hours and on weekends. The pedestrian crossing is a great way to avoid the lines. Public and chartered buses are also allowed to jump to the front of the lines.

Mexican Consulate in San Diego

San Diego's Mexican Consulate General (1549 India St., San Diego, CA 92101, U.S. tel. 619/231-8414, www.consulmexsd. org, Mon.–Fri. 8 A.M.–1:30 P.M.) is 30–45 minutes by car from the Tijuana border crossing. The office can help with visas, immigration problems, special-import permits, and questions concerning Mexican customs regulations.

CUSTOMS
Entering Mexico

Mexico allows tourists to enter the country with personal items that they will use during their trip and additional merchandise worth less than US$75 per person if arriving by land, or US$300 if arriving by air. There are official limits for the number of electronic devices (2 cameras, 2 mobile phones, 1 laptop), musical instruments (2), liters of liquor (3), cartons of cigarettes (20), fishing rods (4), and other recreational sports equipment you may bring. For the most part, as long as it doesn't look like you are sneaking in items that you intend to resell, or bringing bags of professional equipment for business instead of tourism, you'll be able to enter without declaring anything. In addition, you may carry up to US$10,000 in cash without paying a duty. Do not under any circumstances attempt to bring firearms without a permit (issued for hunting only) or illegal substances. For the latest information in Spanish, visit www.aduanas.sat.gob.mx.

Returning to the United States

The process of returning to the United States almost always takes longer than leaving. U.S. customs officials may ask to search your luggage, and they'll ask a few routine questions. Sometimes they also use dogs to inspect luggage and/or vehicles for illegal substances and undocumented immigrants.

Many items made in Mexico may be imported duty-free. Adults may bring only one liter (33.8 fluid ounces) of alcohol and 200 cigarettes (or 100 cigars) per person. Remember that it is illegal to import Cuban cigars into the United States. You can bring US$400 worth of purchases within any 31-day period without declaring the goods.

Here is a list of prohibited items. Regulations change occasionally so check with a U.S. consulate before crossing or visit www.cbp.gov for the latest information:

- oranges
- grapefruits
- mangoes
- avocados
- potatoes
- straw
- hay
- unprocessed cotton
- sugarcane
- any plants in soil (including houseplants)
- wild and domesticated birds (including poultry, unless cooked)
- pork or pork products
- eggs

Returning to Canada

Duty-free items for travelers returning to Canada include 200 cigarettes (or 50 cigars or 200 grams of tobacco) and one bottle (1.1 liters) of liquor or wine, 24 cans or bottles (355 ml) of beer or ale, and gifts up to C$60 per gift (other than alcohol or tobacco). Exemptions run C$50–750 depending on how long you've been outside the country. To obtain the maximum exemption of C$750, you must travel outside of Canada for at least one week.

LEGAL MATTERS

The Mexican legal system differs from the U.S. system in several ways. It does not provide for trials by jury; rather, a judge decides the fate of the accused. The Mexican system also does not provide the writ of habeas corpus, although it does stipulate that you must be charged within 72 hours of incarceration or set free. Arrested foreigners rarely are granted bail, so once you are in jail, it can be very difficult to get out. You do have the right to notify your consulate if you are detained. You can also contact the local state tourism offices for help in emergencies.

Sports and Recreation

Travelers to Baja California pursue a long list of recreational activities in water and on land. Most of these can be pursued independently or as part of an organized trip. Here is a summary of the highlights; specific routes and outfitters are covered in the respective destination chapters.

HIKING AND BACKPACKING

Hiking in Baja can range from desert walks to high-sierra summits. You might spend half a day on trails in the coastal hills, or a full week in the backcountry. It all depends on your experience level, preferred wilderness environment, and amount of time you have. Some of the top places to hike in Baja include the two national parks in the north (Parque Nacional Sierra San Pedro Mártir and Parque Nacional Constitución de 1857), the desert trails near Cataviña in the Desierto Central, and the Sierra de la Laguna in Southern Baja. Facilities are minimal in all of these places, so hikers should expect primitive camping and plan to be self-sufficient.

Trails, if they exist, are often not well marked, so bring the appropriate topo maps for the area you plan to hike. **Mexico Maps** (U.S. tel. 805/687-1011, www.mexicomaps.com) offers GPS maps and digital maps for some areas, as well as printed topo maps.

The **Instituto Nacional de Estadística, Geografía e Informática** (INEGI, www.inegi.gob.mx)—with offices in La Paz (Plaza Cuatro Molinos, Calle Altamirano 2790, Col. Centro, tel. 612/123-1545 or 612/122-4146, www.inegi.gob.mx), Mexicali (Calzada Independencia 1086, Centro Cívico, tel. 686/557-5883 or 686/556-0995), and Tijuana (Av. Via Rapida Oriente 9306, Zona Río, tel.

664/979-7900 or -7909)—sells topo maps at a much lower cost.

What to Bring

Protective footwear and plenty of water (2–5 liters per person per day, depending on the season) are the two most important items for any Baja hike. Bring layers of clothing for overnight trips in the sierras. Pack a first-aid kit with an elastic bandage for sprains, snakebite treatment, and pair of tweezers for removing thorns and cactus spines. Other essentials include a flashlight, compass, waterproof matches, knife, extra batteries, rain gear, and signal device (mirror or whistle). Consider a telescoping fishing rod with light tackle if you are hiking near the shore. Don't count on mountain springs to re-supply your water. Purify any water you use from these sources.

Camping Tips

Avoid setting up your tent under the shade of a coconut palm or in arroyos. Open fires are permitted most remote places in Baja, but keep them small. Dried ocotillo and cactus skeletons burn well. Follow basic low-impact camping guidelines: Pack out all trash, including cigarette butts. Bury human waste 15 centimeters (six inches) down, and don't use soap in streams or springs.

FISHING

Baja's tourism industry was largely built by the will and frontier spirit of the traveling anglers. Baja offers an unparalleled variety of species and fishing styles. Whether it's bluewater billfishing, fly-fishing for roosters, or spearing wahoo, the fisheries of Baja still have more fish and fewer crowds than just about

© NIKKI GOTH ITOI

bait for sale in Bahía San Lucas, Los Cabos

anywhere other than Alaska. If you plan to freelance your way through fishing in Baja, pick up a copy of the longtime bible of Baja fishing, *Baja Catch* or the newer *Angler's Guide to Trailer-Boating.*

There are endless ways to fish in Baja, but if you have never fished here before, one of the best ways to get started is to hire a *panga* for the morning. Prices vary depending on location and season, but the captain should have extensive knowledge of the hotspots as well as where the bite was on in the days leading up to your trip.

If you decide to fish while on a trip, you can buy a surf casting rod and some tackle and fish from shore without a license. Corvina, sierra mackerel, and snapper can all be caught in the surf.

If you are targeting trophy billfish, you will want to visit the Los Cabos or East Cape region of Southern Baja. Los Barriles, San José del Cabo, Cabo San Lucas, and La Paz all host numerous sportfishing fleets for hire.

Seasons

The ebb and flow of the various fish populations in Baja are difficult to generalize in a simple calendar. The *Angler's Guide to Baja California* has a calendar for each of 10 fishing zones, but you should always check with the locals before getting your heart set on a certain species. As a rule of thumb, April–October offer the warmest water and the greatest variety of fish, but there are year-round species, including yellowtail and rockfish.

Tackle

A good selection of high-quality tackle is increasingly available in the larger Baja fishing towns, but you are better off assembling your gear before your trip since supplies can still vary. Given the variety of species, there is no single ideal Baja rod. Since airlines currently allow up to four rods as "personal gear," consider packing two trolling rods with 60-pound test, one shore rod with 25-pound monofilament, and a light six-foot rod for bait fishing.

Remember that you are only allowed to fish with one rod at a time.

Licenses and Regulations

It's worth noting up front that even if you have fished for years in Baja without ever hearing anyone mention a fishing license, the times have changed. There have been numerous reports of poles and coolers of fish being confiscated at the airport from travelers without a license. The best practice today is to obtain a Mexican fishing license before going on your trip and to keep it until you get back home.

A fishing license is required for anyone over 16 years old fishing from a boat. Anyone on a boat that is equipped for fishing (whether or not you intend to fish) is required to have a license, but as of January 2008, a boat permit is no longer required. Single-day fishing licenses are often sold at marinas and sometimes by the fishing guide. At last check, a one-day license was US$13, US$25 for a week, US$37 for a month, and US$48 for the year.

The easiest way to obtain your license is through the mail before you leave for your trip. You can send in your request to the **Mexico Department of Fisheries (PESCA)** (2550 Fifth Ave., Suite 101, San Diego, CA 92103-6622, U.S. tel. 619/233-4324). You can also buy one at the Mexican insurance companies near the border, from some outfitters, or in some tackle shops in Baja.

For the most recent fishing regulations for Mexico, check www.conapescasandiego.org before going on your trip. The daily limit is 10 fish per person, including no more than 5 of any one species. Some species have lower limits, but they also count towards the 10 fish limit: The big game species—including marlin, sailfish, and swordfish—are limited to one per day, and it should be noted that most anglers release these fish unless it's obvious the fish will not survive. Dorado, roosterfish, halibut, shad, and tarpon are limited to two fish per day per person.

You can only have 30 fish in possession on a multi-day fishing trip and you cannot filet the fish while you are on the boat.

The same limits apply to spearfishing. Spearfishing is limited to free-diving, so tanks and hookas are off-limits. Gas-powered spear guns and powerheads also are prohibited.

Although the harvesting of any species of shellfish by a non-citizen of Mexico is officially prohibited, very few people would consider it a citable offense if a tourist were to dig up a few clams. That does not apply to abalone or lobsters.

Taking live fish for your tank at home is also strictly prohibited and you shouldn't try to sell anything you catch.

U.S. Customs and State of California Regulations

Keep your Mexican fishing license or the receipt if you've purchased seafood. U.S. regulations mirror the Mexican bag limits, but make sure to keep the species of the fish the filet comes from identifiable by leaving the skin on. For more information, contact the California Department of Fish and Game (1416 9th St., Sacramento, CA 95814, U.S. tel. 916/445-0411, www.dfg.ca.gov).

HUNTING

Upland hunting for pheasant, dove, and several species of quail draws hunters, primarily from Southern California and Arizona. Duck hunting near San Quintín was once popular, but now it's viewed primarily as a brandt hunting area. The seasons are similar to those in the United States, starting in October and extending into February for some species. Most hunters head toward Mexicali, Ensenada, and San Quintín.

Guns and ammunition are highly regulated in Mexico. Getting caught with either without the proper paperwork will involve serious consequences, including jail time and fines. The fee for having the outfitter register your gun for the season is typically over US$350, so almost all outfitters rent guns for a daily fee. The quality of available guns varies, but make sure to inspect the barrel of any rental gun for kinks and obstructions. Also make a point to ask about the choke installed on the gun and if alternate chokes are available. A hunting license and game tags are also required.

Recent changes to the regulations require that any non-citizen hunter be accompanied by a licensed hunting guide while in the field. There is a list of licensed outfitters at www.discoverbajacalifornia.com/hunting/outfitters.htm. Most outfitters employ "bird boys" to act as blockers and retrieve the game. To bring your dog with you, make sure you have up-to-date vaccination records and a health certificate from your veterinarian, issued within 72 hours of your departure. Many outfitters discourage or prohibit dogs, since there are risks associated with snakes, cacti, and burrs. If you do decide to bring your dog, make sure to have a full field first-aid kit.

Questions to ask your outfitter include:

- What type of species are available in the region and during that part of the season?

- Are dogs or bird boys used?

- What is the type of terrain and what will the weather typically be like during that time of year?

- What does the package include? Lodging, license, guide fee, gun rental, bird tags, bird cleaning, shells, meals, drinks, transportation?

- What is a typical day like (e.g., start time, finish time)?

- What type of guns are available, and how old are they?

- If you are left-handed, it can't hurt to ask if there are any left-handed or straight-stocked guns.

Keep in mind that there is no hunter safety course requirement to obtain a license in Mexico, so you may be paired with an inexperienced hunter. If you are uncomfortable with the situation, speak up and request to hunt on your own.

BOATING

Popular since the 1950s, recreational boating remains one of the most pleasurable ways to experience Baja's marine environments. Some people cruise all the way down from California, following the path of John Muir; but the vast majority haul their boats down the peninsula via Mexico 1 and launch from one of Baja's many well-developed marinas. The Sea of Cortez offers safer conditions and more protected places to anchor than the exposed Pacific coast, which gets pounded with big swells and high winds. Types of recreational boats suitable for use in Baja vary from lightweight car-toppers and inflatables to large trailered boats and multimillion-dollar mega yachts.

Nautical Charts and Tide Tables

Charlie's Charts: The Western Coast of Mexico (Including Baja) is a compilation of all U.S. nautical charts from San Diego to Guatemala, updated with anchorages, boat ramps, hazards, and fishing and diving spots. The 11th edition is available in many U.S. marine supply stores and from the company's website (www.charliescharts.com).

Other options include waterproof, tear-resistant, double-sided plastic charts published by **Fish-n-Map** (U.S. tel. 303/421-5994, www.fishnmap.com, US$8 per sheet) and **Gerry Cruising Charts** (U.S. tel. 520/394-2393, www.gerrycruise.com, US$32–55). Gerry Cruising Charts also has tide tables for the Pacific and Gulf coasts.

Port Check-Ins

Several Baja towns have port captain's offices, where you must check in upon arrival by boat. These include Ensenada, Guerrero Negro, Bahía Magdalena (San Carlos), Cabo San Lucas, San José del Cabo, La Paz, Puerto Escondido, Loreto, Mulegé, Santa Rosalía, Bahía de los Ángeles, and San Felipe. You don't need to check out each time, except when leaving your port of origin.

Fuel, Parts, and Repairs

Several full-service marinas are open year-round in Ensenada, Cabo San Lucas, San José del Cabo, La Paz, Puerto Escondido (south of Loreto), and Santa Rosalía. Bring extra fuel

© NIKKI GOTH ITOI

Playa Palmilla *pangas*

containers in case you need to ask for fuel at a boatyard or fish camp when a marina is not in range.

Marine supplies and places for repairs are hard to come by in Baja. Ensenada, Cabo San Lucas, and La Paz are your best bets. Bring plenty of spare parts.

SEA KAYAKING

Kayaking expeditions in the Sea of Cortez have become increasingly popular as more visitors look for eco-friendly ways to travel the peninsula and more marine preserves come under government protection from commercial exploitation. Paddlers can get to remote coastal and island beaches that are inaccessible to larger boats or those traveling by land. There are appropriate destinations for all abilities, from Bahía Concepción for beginners to the Loreto/La Paz route for advanced kayakers. (The Gulf Current makes north to south itineraries the most logical approach.)

Kayaking on the Pacific side requires more experience. Punta Banda, south of Ensenada, is popular with San Diego residents. Bahía Magdalena in Southern Baja draws a crowd of paddlers in winter for whale-watching, but you shouldn't venture out into the bay during the season without a guide.

Organized Kayak Trips

Paddling South (U.S. tel. 707/942-4550 or 800/398-6200, www.tourbaja.com) leads multiday trips out of Loreto. **Baja Expeditions** (U.S. tel. 858/581-3311 or 800/843-6967, www.bajaex.com) offers kayaking trips to Bahía Magdalena and the Midriff Islands in the winter. **Sea Trek** (U.S. tel. 415/488-1000, www.seatrekkayak.com, US$1,150/8 days) is another well-established outfitter.

KITEBOARDING AND WINDSURFING

November–March is the season for kiteboarding and windsurfing in Baja. The two main destinations for these sports are Los Barriles on the East Cape and Bahía de la Ventana, southeast of La Paz. Which one you choose depends on your level of experience and what kind of post-recreation scene you prefer. La Ventana generally provides more consistent conditions and a safe place for beginners to learn, with rustic accommodations in a more remote setting. The stronger winds at Los Barriles appeal to advanced kiters and sailors. Los Barriles also is more developed as a tourist town, with a broader mix of accommodations and restaurants. You can take lessons and rent gear at either destination.

SURFING

At even the most remote spots in Baja, the chances you're the first one to surf a break are low, but with an empty lineup and not a building in sight, you can get the full surf pioneer experience within a few hours of the California border.

The variety of surf experiences you can have in Baja runs the entire spectrum. You can ride your first wave on a longboard with the Pescadero Surf Camp or you can win US$50,000 for charging down an 18-meter (60-ft) face at Islas Todos Santos. The saturated breaks along the northern beaches from Rosarito to Ensenada can feel like extensions of the localized and aggro scene in Southern California. Those willing the walk to the next point, or drive a little farther, can quickly fall off the known surf map and find their own mecca. Perhaps the biggest threats to Baja surfing aren't the fleets of Honda Elements or the longboarders poaching waves on the outside, but the accelerating development along the coastline and the drive to close off beach access along both sides of the peninsula.

There are more than 75 named breaks along the Pacific coast, across the corridor between Cabo San Lucas and San José del Cabo, and up the lower East Cape. Some, of course, are more accessible than others. Which region you choose depends on the time of year, your surf ability, and how much time you have. Some of the top surfing destinations in Baja include the coast near Ensenada, Islas Todos Santos, Scorpion Bay, and the beaches near Todos Santos and El Pescadero on the West Cape.

There are more than 25 known point, reef, and beach breaks around the cape alone. Stop by the **Costa Azul Surf Shop** along the Corridor at Playa Costa Azul or in Todos Santos for a map with descriptions of the breaks, or buy a copy of the incredibly detailed *Surfer's Guide to Baja California,* by Mike Parise.

Water temperatures on the Pacific side are only slightly warmer than Southern California until you get south of Bahía Tortuga. In fact, at Punta Banda near Ensenada, the water is actually colder than San Diego, due to the proximity of the California Current, which causes upwelling of colder waters from below. You'll need several millimeters of neoprene to be comfortable in temperatures that range from as high as 21°C (70°F) in the early fall to the 10–11°C (low 50s°F) in the spring. The southern Pacific coast warms to highs of 24°C (about 75°F) in the fall and drops to 15–20°C (in the 60s°F) in the spring. The Corridor gets even warmer, with temperatures often exceeding 26°C (80°F). A shortie-style wetsuit works well in these warmer waters.

Equipment

Experienced surfers bring as many boards as possible for their Baja expedition, plus wax and a patch kit for repairing dings. A cooler and first-aid kit will come in handy as well. Surf shops in Ensenada, San José del Cabo, and Todos Santos sell boards, apparel, and accessories.

Airlines have made it more expensive these days to fly with your quiver; check the going rate before you head for the airport. Renting a board sounds pretty good when checking it costs US$100 each way. For longer trips, buying and reselling a board while you're there is another option.

Organized Trips

Baja Surf Adventures (BSA, toll-free U.S. tel. 800/428-7873, www.bajasurfadventures.com) runs a surf camp in Northern Baja that welcomes novice to advanced surfers. Other surf camps are located in El Pescadero (West Cape) and Bahía Magdalena.

SCUBA DIVING AND SNORKELING

Baja California offers several different types of marine environments for underwater exploration. The northern Pacific coast features a number of islands surrounded by rock reefs, seamounts, and kelp forests. The water here is cold (wear lots of neoprene or, preferably, a dry suit), visibility is often limited, and conditions favor advanced divers. But for those who make the trip, the marine life is fantastically unusual and diverse, and the spearfishing is excellent. La Bufadora and the Islas Coronado and Todos Santos are the top dive destinations in this region.

At the other end of the spectrum, the southern Sea of Cortez along the East Cape offers tropical conditions for diving and snorkeling, with drift diving over a living coral reef, sea lion colonies, dozens of islands, secluded coves, and white-sand beaches. A few sunken ships have formed artificial reefs over the years. The most popular dive destinations in Central/Southern Baja are Loreto, La Paz, and the Los Cabos Corridor. Water temperature ranges 20–30°C (from the high 60s to the 80s°F), and visibility often exceeds 30 meters (100 ft). July–October is the best time to go.

Baja's only dive shops are located in Ensenada, Mulegé, Loreto, La Paz, Buena Vista (East Cape), Cabo Pulmo (East Cape), San José del Cabo, and Cabo San Lucas. Most of these shops offer guided dive and snorkel tours, rental gear, and lessons. Note, when diving in the protected marine parks near Cabo Pulmo, Loreto, and Cabo San Lucas, diving with a guide is required by law. For this reason, the shops in Cabo Pulmo do not offer airfills to independent divers.

The *Solmar V* (www.solmarv.com, tel. 866/591-4906) and the *Nautilus Explorer* (www.nautilusexplorer.com, tel. 888/434-8322) both offer liveaboard diving, to the Socorro Islands, Guadalupe Island, and Sea of Cortez, among other trips.

Scuba gear is hard to buy in Baja, even in the resort areas. Bring your own, or plan to rent. On that note, it's a good idea to bring your own spare parts kit and safety equipment, even when diving with a guide. You don't want to sit out a dive when your mask strap breaks or the o-ring on your tank blows. Likewise, a safety sausage, whistle, and dive knife are must-have accessories.

Recompression Chambers

Cabo San Lucas (**Buceo Medico Mexicano,** Plaza Marina, tel. 624/143-3666, cabo@sssnetwork.com), La Paz (**Baja Diving and Service,** tel. 612/122-7010, www.clubcantamar.com), and Playas de Tijuana (**Centro Hosp. Internacional Pacifico,** CHIP, tel. 664/685-2566) have the only recompression chambers on the peninsula. In San Diego, head to the **Hyperbaric Medicine Center** at the University of California Medical Center in San Diego (U.S. tel. 619/543-6222, Mon.–Fri. 7:30 A.M.–4:30 P.M. and for emergencies).

Accommodations and Camping

First-time Baja travelers faces some tough choices when it comes to deciding where to sleep. Remote or central? Luxury or rustic? Mexican or foreign-owned? These are just some of the considerations. Self-sufficient travelers can camp for free most of the way down the peninsula and back, or step it up a notch, and camp at designated campgrounds, which offer varying levels of service and facilities. If you want a roof over your head, there are budget motels, rental condos, boutique inns, and large international chain hotels. You can spend US$10 or US$1,000 per night, depending on your means and the level of comfort you seek.

RATES

Prices range from US$30 per night at the low end to US$200 and up for an upscale room to

US$1,000 or more for a luxury resort experience. In most towns, you can find something basic for under US$50 a night. Rates may drop considerably midweek versus weekend, and in the low season (winter for Northern Baja, summer for Southern Baja). Many of the larger hotels add 12 percent tax and 10 percent service charge to the rate. Prices given in this book reflect double-occupancy, high-season (but not holiday) rates. Discounts are often available for longer stays.

MAKING RESERVATIONS

People who book their accommodations in advance almost always pay more than those who book in person when they arrive. It takes more time to shop around, but the reward is often lower prices and the opportunity to inspect a room before you commit. (Website photos can be deceiving.) It's also difficult to get deposits back from the smaller inns and motels if you pay upfront and then your plans change.

If you are planning a short trip to a popular resort in the peak season, you may not have the flexibility to wait and see what's available. In this case, it makes sense to shop around online and go with a name you trust. When visiting hotels in person, don't be afraid to ask to see more than one room. Mexican hotel managers have a funny habit of offering the less-desirable rooms in the building first, even if the cost is the same and the rest of the rooms are empty.

HOTELS AND MOTELS

Hotels and motels come in every shape and size in Baja, from 10-room family-owned establishments with basic but clean rooms to sprawling corporate complexes with hundreds of rooms and long lists of amenities. Rooms often are arranged around a central courtyard for added privacy and security. Most towns have at least one option with secure parking (gated and/or monitored by a security guard). Multistory properties may not have elevators, so consider the ground floor if you have a lot of luggage to transport to the room.

BAJA'S BOUTIQUE HOTELS

Once confined to the Los Cabos area of the peninsula, boutique hotels are popping up from Ensenada to El Pescadero. Here are some of the highlights:

- **La Villa del Valle** (Valle de Guadalupe): Tuscan-style accommodations atop a hill on 70 acres with sweeping views of surrounding vineyards, orchards, and gardens.

- **Casa Natalie** (Ensenada): Five suites and three newer rooms, all furnished to a level rarely seen in Baja. The ideal home base for a weekend of wine-tasting in the Guadalupe Valley.

- **Clementine's Inn** (Mulegé): The most comfortable beds in Baja in a moderate price range. The owners made a speedy recovery after the flood of September 2006 and bought all new beds, linens, appliances, and artwork for their guest accommodations.

- **Posada de las Flores** (Punta Chivato, Loreto, La Paz): Among the most charming properties found in Baja. Rustic Mexican furniture and tile are used throughout, and all-marble bathrooms feature large bathtubs and extra-thick towels.

- **Posada La Poza** (Todos Santos): Enjoy the relaxed pace of life in Baja with a Swiss sensibility for quality and efficiency.

- **La Alianza** (El Pescadero): Marble floors, robes, Egyptian cotton sheets, and fluffy towels in a five-room property near San Pedrito point.

- **Casa Natalia** (San José del Cabo): A contemporary European-style boutique hotel with rooms set around a small pool and individually decorated with authentic artwork from San Miguel de Allende, Oaxaca, and Puebla.

BOUTIQUE HOTELS

A growing number of higher-end places in Baja offer a distinctive and more intimate lodging experience in restored historic buildings and/or striking natural settings with exquisitely appointed guestrooms. They include La Villa del Valle in the Northern Baja wine country; Casa Natalie in Ensenada; Clementine's Inn in Mulegé; Posada de las Flores in Punta Chivato, Loreto, and La Paz; Posada la Poza in Todos Santos; La Alianza in El Pescadero; Casa Bella in Cabo San Lucas; and Casa Natalia in San José del Cabo.

FULL-SERVICE RESORTS

$:Many Baja hotels, motels, and campgrounds call themselves resorts, but in this book, we reserve the term for the large, full-service establishments that pamper guests with gourmet meals, spa treatments, golf clubs, fitness programs, infinity pools, swim-up bars, and the like. Meals are often but not always included. Rates for this type of accommodations vary from around US$200 a night at the Tesoro Los Cabos in Cabo San Lucas to more than US$1,500 a night at the exclusive One&Only Palmilla on the Los Cabos Corridor.

BED-AND-BREAKFASTS

For a more personal stay—often at a good value too—consider one of Baja's many bed-and-breakfast inns, where you'll likely meet the owner(s) and learn a bit about the surrounding community. Cabo San Lucas, La Paz, San José del Cabo, Todos Santos, Loreto, Mulegé, and San Ignacio all have bed-and-breakfasts at varying price points.

VACATION RENTALS

Independent travelers planning a stay of a week or more who like the flexibility of preparing some of their own meals tend to prefer vacation rentals over the hotel experience. Whether you are stretching a budget or need to accommodate the needs of small children, the convenience of a kitchen makes it easy to avoid pricier restaurant fare, especially in the larger towns. Rental condos and villas are

© NIKKI GOTH ITOI

resort living at the Crowne Plaza Los Cabos Beach Resort on Playa California

usually foreign-owned and easy to find online via sites like Vacation Rental by Owner (www.vrbo.com) and Craigslist (www.craigslist.com). They often are part of vacation communities with many of the same amenities as a mid-sized hotel, such as fitness centers, swimming pools, maid service, and restaurants. The tradeoff is that vacation rentals are managed by individual owners, so it can be hard to know in advance what kind of service you'll get, especially if there are maintenance issues or other problems when you arrive.

CAMPING AND RV PARKS

There are hundreds of places to camp in Baja, ranging from isolated fish camps to high-sierra campsites to fancy big-rig RV parks. Fees range from around US$5 for a place to set up a tent to US$30 or more for RV spots with full hookups and access to recreational facilities. Many of these campgrounds feature some of the best views anywhere on the peninsula. Best of all, you don't need four-wheel drive to reach the majority of these campgrounds.

Food and Drink

Fresh seafood, hearty ranch-style foods, organic produce, and the fusion of culinary influences from around the world are some of the delights of eating your way through Baja California.

FOOD SAFETY

First-time Baja travelers tend to share two concerns about the food in Mexico: Will I get sick from the food? And can I drink the water?

The answer to the first is, most likely not, but the dreaded *turista* does happen. Here's how to avoid overtaxing your system: Go easy at first—lots of heavy, spicy foods combined with alcoholic drinks and desert heat are a recipe for digestive trouble. If you're prone to food illness, or especially worried about getting it, avoid street food, raw fruits and vegetables (except the ones you wash and peel yourself), and fresh salsas—at least until your stomach has had a few meals to adjust. (Many of these foods are fine to eat, but if there's going to be trouble, they are a likely source.) Some people swear by Pepto-Bismol tablets as preventative medicine.

If you do get a case of the runs, drink lots of purified water and revert to a diet of bland foods. The symptoms usually go away within a few days. Unfortunately, this can also be the duration of your visit.

As for the water, it's not recommended. Use purified water to brush your teeth and rinse fruits and vegetables before consuming them. Most tourist-oriented restaurants and hotels use only purified water and ice in their kitchens. When buying *licuados* (Mexican-style smoothies), *aguas frescas,* and drinks with ice from street stands, try to do your own inspection first. Many, but not all, use purified water, but asking whether they use *agua purificada* will most likely elicit an affirmative, whether or not it's true. Some hotels and vacation homes are equipped with water filtration systems; most just provide bottled water.

For extended stays, economical 20-liter (approx. five-gallon) plastic jugs called *garafónes* are sold in most Baja towns. They cost about US$6 for the first container, which includes a deposit on the jug, then US$2 for each refill.

WHERE TO EAT

Travelers generally have many choices at mealtimes in Baja, although in more remote areas or off-peak seasons, you may have to settle for any place that's open. Restaurants vary from traditional Mexican establishments that seat a dozen patrons in plastic chairs around metal tables on a raked sand floor to culinary destinations that offer creative dishes in a white-linen and candlelight setting. You could make your way down the peninsula searching for the best *taquería* in every town. Or plan an itinerary

BAJA CULINARY GUIDE

For those who like to travel from one meal to the next, Baja presents a lot more than Tecate beer and fresh fish tacos (although both of these are must-taste delights). Use the list below as a culinary guide to the peninsula.

1. Ceviche – many different styles; often served as a seafood cocktail in a martini glass with red sauce

2. California lobster platters – in Puerto Nuevo, Baja's lobster capital

3. Fish tacos – made everywhere, but especially tasty at the Mercado de Mariscos in Ensenada

4. Mexicali Chinese – Cantonese cuisine with a Mexican twist

5. The best *bolillos* – at El Mejor Pan in Tecate

6. Freshly made tortillas – corn *(maiz)* or flour *(harina)*, buy them hot off the press at any *tortillería* for about US$1 per dozen

7. Abalone sausage – from Isla Cedros

8. Clamato cocktail – a meal in a cup that is nothing like its American counterpart

9. Award-winning red wines – made in the Valle de Guadalupe

10. *Alta cocina mexicana* – served at upscale restaurants in San José del Cabo, La Paz, and Tijuana

To find the best *taquería* in any given town, stroll near the plaza in the evening and look for the longest line. Locals eat tacos for the evening meal *(cena)*, not for lunch *(comida)*. Casual places may be called *loncherías, cafés, cenadurías,* or restaurants. Most will serve a variety of Mexican *antojitos,* such as tacos, burritos, enchiladas, quesadillas, tamales, *flautas,* and the like, plus main dishes emphasizing meat and/or seafood. Some offer *comida corrida,* affordable multicourse meals for a fixed price of US$5–7. In more remote places, restaurants serve whatever they happen to have on hand.

Aside from these eateries, one of the real pleasures of traveling around Baja is the chance to shop in local markets and create your own meals using the variety of fresh ingredients on hand, including tortillas, shellfish and seafood, chiles, avocado, mango, cheese, limes, and more.

WHAT TO EAT

Centuries ago, Spanish, Asian, French, and indigenous foods met in Mexico to form a distinctive—if varied—cuisine. Far removed from the culinary traditions of such mainland states as Oaxaca Puebla, Veracruz, and Yucatán, Baja California was known only for its fish tacos, until the turn of the 21st century, when celebrated chefs from the mainland and overseas began bringing their talents to the Los Cabos Corridor, La Paz, and Valle de Guadalupe wine Country. The Baja California cuisine that is emerging today blends fresh seafood from the coast with ranchero staples from the interior and organic produce from the fertile valleys in between. The flavors are fresh and unique, reflecting influences from around the world.

Antojitos

The majority of menus in Baja feature a long list of *antojitos* ("little whims"), or traditional Mexican fast-food fare, such as tacos, *tortas* (sandwiches), *flautas* (stuffed and fried corn tortilla roll), chiles rellenos (stuffed, breaded, and fried poblano peppers), enchiladas, and quesadillas.

around the top five or ten chefs that are defining contemporary Baja California cuisine. Serious foodies find some of the most exciting options in Tijuana (La Diferencia), Ensenada (Laja) and the Valle de Guadalupe wine country, La Paz (Tres Vírgenes), San José del Cabo (El Chilar), and Cabo San Lucas (Nick-San Sushi).

a typical *mercado municipal* in San José del Cabo

© NIKKI GOTH ITOI

When ordered as main dishes, these items typically come with rice and beans on the side.

Meats

Beef appears in many forms on Baja menus, including as steak *(bistec),* carne asada (in tacos), and hamburgers *(hamburguesas).* Chicken *(pollo)* and pork *(puerco)* are the next most common meats. Worth seeking out in Rosarito, La Paz, or San José del Cabo, *carnitas* (sold by the kilo) is a slow-braised pork dish originally from the mainland state of Michoacán.

Seafood

A trip to Baja isn't complete without a sampling of fresh fish and shellfish. Order the *pescado del día* and enjoy the fresh catch of the day, which may be mahimahi *(dorado),* seabass *(cabrilla),* or red snapper *(pargo). Huachinango* is a whole red snapper cooked over an open flame. Mackerel *(sierra)* is commonly used in ceviche (raw fish "cooked" in lime juice). Puerto Nuevo between Rosarito and Ensenada is the

self-proclaimed lobster capital of the region, although these days, most of its lobsters come from Southern Baja. Oysters, shrimp, scallops, and clams also make their way onto many seafood menus.

But the simplest and tastiest seafood delight in Baja is the fish taco—small filets of white fish breaded and fried, topped with shredded green cabbage, raw onion, fresh cilantro, and a squeeze of fresh lime, then wrapped in a tortilla and devoured. The variations are infinite, but the result is always delicious.

Fruits and Vegetables

Given the dry climate, Baja does not have the same variety and abundance of fresh produce as mainland Mexico. In fact, most of what you'll find in the larger grocery stores is imported from the mainland. However, in Southern Baja, a handful of boutique growers are farming organic produce and supplying it to local restaurants. The Saturday farmers market in San José del Cabo is a good place to buy from these growers.

BAJA'S GOURMET RESTAURANTS

Gourmet restaurants are no longer just in Los Cabos. You'll now find gourmet eats in towns such as Tijuana, Ensenada, and La Paz. Here are some of the highlights:

- **La Diferencia** (Tijuana): Seasonally available *chile en nogada* or duck with a hibiscus flower-based sauce stand out on an all-around excellent menu. Attentive service and a contemporary setting make the meal.

- **El Taco de Huitzilopochtli** (Ensenada): No other restaurant in the area serves more authentic Central Mexican food.

- **Restaurant Laja** (Valle de Guadalupe): The brainchild of former Four Seasons chef Jair Téllez prepares farm-fresh cuisine on par with California's celebrated Chez Panisse and French Laundry restaurants.

- **Nick-San Restaurant** (Cabo San Lucas): The best food in Cabo San Lucas, period.

- **Don Emiliano** (San José del Cabo): A member of the Slow Food movement and run by Margarita C. de Salinas, a well-known chef from Mexico City.

- **Las Tres Virgenes** (La Paz): Local expats call it the best meal they've had in La Paz.

True vegetarian cuisine is difficult but not impossible to find; you'll often find a restaurant or two, plus a few natural foods stores, in the larger cities.

Salsas and Condiments

Many restaurants in Baja distinguish themselves by the variety and presentation of condiments that accompany their meals. Trays of ceramic dishes containing half a dozen salsas, plus guacamole and *crema* (thinned sour cream) are common. Most places make their own original salsa recipes, with varying levels of spiciness, so no two will taste alike.

Beverages

Soft drinks like Coca Cola tend to taste better in Mexico because they contain cane sugar instead of high-fructose corn syrup, which is what is used in the U.S. versions, and the beer in Mexico is a bit stronger than in the United States. Tecate in the north and Pacífico in the south are the local beers of choice. When you've had enough *cerveza* and tequila, try some of the local non-alcoholic treats: Refreshing *agua de jamaica* (hibiscus) is an iced-tea-like drink served from large glass jars; other flavors of *agua fresca* include strawberry *(fresa),* watermelon *(sandia),* and lime *(limón).* A *limonada natural* is freshly squeezed lime juice mixed with sparkling water and a simple syrup.

If you're particular about coffee, you may want to bring your own; the larger towns have decent coffeehouse chains, but the stuff you get in ordinary hotels and restaurants is pretty weak; often times it's instant.

BUYING GROCERIES

If you're traveling on a tight budget or you have dietary restrictions, preparing your own food will be easier and more economical. You can shop at large supermarkets, smaller *abarrotes* stores, or municipal markets called *mercados.* You'll find a mix of familiar international brands, as well as local Mexican foods, which generally cost less. For the most interesting, authentic, and cost-effective food-shopping experience, seek out the *mercados,* which typically have a butcher, fish market, and several produce stands.

Conduct and Customs

TIME AND APPOINTMENTS

Whether you are waiting for your meal to arrive at a restaurant or waiting to board a ferry to the mainland, it helps to know that things happen at a slower pace in Baja than you may be used to at home. Dubbed the "*mañana* attitude" (as in, everything gets done tomorrow), this flexibility with time is deeply rooted in the Mexican culture. But it doesn't mean that everyone you meet in Baja will be late to scheduled events, or that you should show up two hours late for a scheduled tour. Many businesspeople in Baja know that foreign visitors expect a more punctual approach and will be there on time. If you come with patience and an understanding of the culture, you'll have a better time when the day doesn't go exactly as planned.

YES OR NO?

A related cultural difference between Mexico and the United States is the tendency to avoid answering in the negative to any direct question. This practice can cause confusion for visitors in a variety of situations. For example, when confirming a reservation, you might ask, "Are we confirmed on this flight?" The answer may be *"Sí,"* even if there is a problem with the reservation. You won't know until you show up at the airport.

Likewise, if you invite someone to a social engagement, the person may accept, even if they are not able to come because it is better to accept and not show up, than to decline the invitation at the outset.

To avoid getting a false "no," try to avoid asking yes/no questions, or rephrase the question giving the person the opportunity to answer in the affirmative: "Do we need to do anything else to confirm our reservation?"

SIESTA

Many small businesses close for a few hours in the middle of the day, between 2–4 P.M., when the owners eat lunch and take care of personal business or relax. The trade-off is they often stay open much later at night than their U.S. counterparts, until 7–8 P.M.

Hours tend to vary day-by-day as well. Banks and post offices are the exception, which follow regularly scheduled hours.

DRESS

Many of the larger tourist centers in Baja are used to seeing visitors strolling around town in their swimsuits, sarongs, and flip-flops, but this doesn't mean that anything goes. Outside of Rosarito, Cabo San Lucas, and San Felipe, beachwear should be confined to the beach. If you visit any church or chapel, even for a quick look, you should wear close-toed shoes and long-sleeve shirts and remove your hat.

Health and Safety

A trip to Baja California exposes travelers to relatively few health risks compared to mainland Mexico. Driving and recreational activities pose the greatest danger, which you can minimize through common-sense precautions.

SUNBURN AND DEHYDRATION

Most people worry about drinking the water in Baja, but the most common afflictions are sunburn and dehydration. Get used to carrying a bottle of water and sunscreen at all times.

Most visitors aren't used to the intensity of the tropical sun in Baja. Use sun protection in all of its forms even if you aren't prone to sunburn. Even mild sunburn can sap your energy and make sleeping and showering painful.

Hats, sunglasses, light long-sleeve shirts, and sunscreen are essential. Apply sun block of at least SPF 25 to any skin exposed to the sun—especially

IS BAJA SAFE?

If you've read any of the news headlines coming out of Mexico in the past year, you have to wonder, Is it safe to visit Baja right now? It's a fair question that's difficult to answer. Here's the context:

When he took office in December 2006, President Felipe Calderón vowed to crack down on the country's drug traffickers and refused to negotiate with the cartels. While necessary and admirable, the policy has led to a dramatic increase in violence and corruption throughout the border region. Warring cartels are battling each other for power and testing the government in an unprecedented stand-off that was ongoing as of June 2009. The facts alone are gruesome enough, but when the U.S. media begins to sensationalize them, it can be difficult to uncover the truth.

Visitors need to remember that tourists are not the target in this fight, although they certainly can get caught in the crossfire. The kidnappings and shootouts have taken place primarily in the northern and eastern parts of Tijuana, which are not places tourists frequent. And statistically, Tijuana is safer than several U.S. cities, based on the number of homicides per capita.

That said, there is another, likely related trend playing out: The entire northwestern Baja California region has experienced a rise in armed robberies of a more professional nature than the petty theft that might have occurred in the past. From surfers and RVers to veteran Baja 1000 participants, foreigners have been pulled over, held at gunpoint, and robbed of their possessions. The victims represent a tiny percentage of all the visitors who make their way through Baja, but it's enough of a shift to give cause for concern.

Those who are studying the problem believe the trend is connected with rising drug use within some Baja communities. In the past, drugs flowed through the peninsula but were too expensive for most residents to buy. That apparently has begun to change, and the result is troubling.

For every local and traveler who tells you it's business as usual in Baja, there are others who counter with a well-intentioned warning to take precautions. We can't rule one way or the other, but we do advocate a few basic guidelines that have always applied to travel in this part of the world: Drive only during daylight hours, travel in groups whenever possible, and keep a low profile at all times.

---

the face and neck region, as well as the scalp if it is exposed. Bring sun block with you and reapply it after swimming or perspiring.

Familiarize yourself with the signs of heat exhaustion and heat stroke. The symptoms include flushed face, excessive perspiration and then the inability to perspire, headache, and dizziness. If you suspect heat exhaustion, the first priority is to get the victim in the shade and cool them with a wet towel and rehydrate them. Heat stroke can be fatal, so if the symptoms persist, get to a doctor.

MOTION SICKNESS

Some say the best views of Baja are found from the gently rocking bow of a *panga*. Unfortunately, that rocking can cause many people to get seasick. If you haven't been on a small boat, it's better to assume that you are one of the 60 percent of people who will experience motion sickness on a rocking boat, even if you've never been carsick.

Preventing seasickness seems to be more art than science, since a drug that works for one person might not work for the next. The main side effect of motion-sickness medications is drowsiness. There are over-the-counter drugs such as Dramamine, Bonine, Meclizine, and Marezine; prescription drugs include Antivert, Phenergan, and Transderm Scopolamine. Transderm Scopolamine, popular with boaters, is a dime-sized patch worn behind the ear for 72 hours. The most important thing is to take the medication well before boarding the boat. These drugs do not work after you have begun to feel sick.

Yawning and drowsiness are the earliest signs

of seasickness. Try to stay alert, stand or sit as close to the center of the boat as possible, and get a view of the horizon. Some people swear that lying down and closing their eyes is the best remedy, while others guarantee that will cause the condition to get worse. Stay in the fresh air and avoid exhaust fumes if at all possible.

BITES AND STINGS
Mosquitoes and *Jejenes*

Mosquitoes and *jejenes* (gnats or no-see-ums) can pose a minor or major nuisance, depending on the time of year you travel (times of rain and little wind are the worst), where you go (oasis towns like San Ignacio and Mulegé are the worst), and how susceptible you are to insect bites. Malaria is not a concern, however. Use liberal amounts of insect repellent and wear lightweight clothes that cover your arms and legs. Bring Caladryl or another brand of calamine lotion to relieve itching.

Scorpions

Scorpions are common throughout the peninsula, especially in thatched-roof shelters and buildings. The sting is rarely dangerous, but it can be painful. Check showers and avoid walking around barefoot or sticking your bare hand in damp, dark, warm places. Shake out your shoes and always check bedding in the desert before climbing in. If you do get stung, lie down to avoid spreading the venom. Use ice packs to prevent swelling. Seek medical attention for small children (under 13 kg/30 lbs).

Poisonous Sea Creatures

Jellyfish, Portuguese man-of-war, cone shells, stingrays (in sandy areas), sea urchins (in rocky areas), and fish with poisonous spines present a potential danger when swimming, snorkeling, or diving. Look before you leap, and you'll be able to avoid most of these marine creatures. Scan the surface for jellies before hopping off the dive boat, wear a Lycra dive skin and water shoes even in warm water, and learn to do the stingray shuffle when entering the water to send any rays resting in the sand scurrying away.

If you do get stung, don't scratch the area with your hands, since you'll spread the poison wherever you touch next. Seek immediate medical attention for any allergic reactions.

MEDICAL ASSISTANCE

You can find knowledgeable medical practitioners in just about every sizable town on the peninsula. Facilities range from hospitals (in Tijuana, Mexicali, Ensenada, Guerrero Negro, Ciudad Constitución, San José del Cabo, and La Paz) to Red Cross stations and private and public clinics. There are public IMSS clinics or Red Cross (Cruz Roja, tel. 066) stations in nearly every other town.

Emergency Evacuation

Several companies offer emergency evacuation services from Baja via land or sea, but read the fine print before you buy a policy. Providers include **Aeromedevac** (Mexico tel. 800/832-5087, U.S. tel. 619/284-7910 or tel. 800/462-0911, www.aeromedevac.com), **Air Evac Services, Inc.** (U.S. tel. 602/244-9327 or 800/321-9522, www.airevac.com), **Advanced Aeromedical Air Ambulance Service** (toll-free U.S. tel. 800/346-3556, www.aeromedic.com), and SkyMed (tel. 866/805-9624, toll-free U.S. tel. 800/475-9633, www.skymed.com).

SAFETY

Outside of the border zone, Baja California is a relatively crime-free place; even in Tijuana, where drug-related violence has gripped the city of late, the statistics are lower than comparable figures for many U.S. cities. Tourists are rarely, if ever, the targets in these incidences, though it is possible to get caught in the crossfire.

Precautions

Common sense and keeping a low profile are the best ways to prevent being the victim of crime. Leave valuables at home, and safely stow the ones you must bring. Experts disagree on the relative safety of using in-room hotel safes; in theory, anyone can call the number on the box to get the combination and remove your money. We prefer a strategy of hiding money and electronics in unlikely places, such as hard-to-find luggage compartments or simply the dustiest place in the room. When out and about, keep your belongings close to you, especially in busy tourist areas, to avoid tempting a pickpocket. Use the locks on your hotel room and vehicle, but don't leave any valuables in clear view. Call the **SECTUR** (State Secretary of Tourism) hotline (tel. 555/250-0123 or 800/903-9200) for emergencies of all kinds.

Information and Services

MONEY
Currency
The Mexican currency is called the **peso,** which is abbreviated as MXN and uses the same symbol ($) as the U.S. dollar. It's printed in denominations of Mex$20, Mex$50, Mex$100, Mex$200, and Mex$500. There are also 5, 10, 20, and 50 centavo coins, and Mex$1, Mex$2, Mex$5, Mex$10, Mex$20, and Mex$100 coins. If you see the abbreviation *m.n.* next to a price, it stands for *moneda nacional* (national money), which is another term for pesos.

Dollars vs. Pesos
U.S. currency is accepted in many places on the peninsula, but you may not always get the current market exchange rate. It's better to bring an ATM card and withdraw pesos from a Mexican bank when you arrive. You can also use a major credit card at many businesses in the larger towns and cities.

If you need to exchange currency, banks offer the best rates, but have limited hours (in the mornings only).

CHANGING CURRENCY EXCHANGE RATES

For a number of years, the ratio between the Mexican Peso (MXN) and the U.S. dollar (USD) hovered near 10/1, making it easy to do the math when reading prices in local currency and paying in foreign denominations. Recently, however, turbulence in global markets has pushed the dollar up in value versus the peso (to more than 14/1 at press time), which means a hotel room priced at MXN 900 a night should cost US$62 instead of US$90 – a significant savings.

But there's a catch: Many businesses in Baja have begun pricing their goods and services in dollars instead of pesos. This has made for some rather steep hikes. Others keep their prices in pesos, but if you pay in dollars, they offer only the old 10/1 conversion. Pemex stations in particular are known for this practice.

There are several steps travelers can take to navigate the more complicated and volatile currency exchange environment:

• Take your time when negotiating prices and making purchases, and be sure you understand the real price of any item or service before you commit.

• Only spend money at places that you believe are charging a fair price relative to the market; if you think it's over-priced, then go elsewhere.

• Carry a calculator for computing exchange rates on the fly.

• Carry some of both currencies to avoid situations in which a merchant might offer a below-market exchange rate.

• Remember that many business owners in Baja are dependent on revenue from tourism to make ends meet, and they are feeling the effects of the global recession just the same as you.

WHAT TO TAKE

Seasoned Baja travelers pride themselves on the detailed nature of their packing lists. Spreadsheets with multiple tabs for each kind of gear are not unheard of. These are some of the items you should consider:

Gadgets: A camera is a must-have for any trip to Baja. A GPS, laptop, cell phone, and portable music player may also come in handy while on the road, but the more electronics you pack, the heavier your bags will be, and the more you'll have to keep track of your belongings. Even if you don't plan to camp, a headlamp is useful in remote places where there are no streetlights for getting around at night.

Toiletries and First Aid: You can buy just about anything you need in major cities and larger towns, but bring any favorite specialty items from home, just in case. Tums and Pepto-Bismol come in handy when you OD on the hot sauce. Bug repellent and anti-itch lotion help prevent and soothe insect bites. Hand sanitizer is always a good idea.

Shoes, Clothes, and Accessories: Bring sturdy footwear for walks and hikes, and Tevas or other water-friendly footwear for the beach. A sunhat, sunglasses, and sunscreen are essential. Layers come in handy. Also pack your reading material of choice — English-language books and magazines are hard to find and more expensive in Baja.

Sports Equipment: Consider the size of your vehicle when packing up the sports closet. Camping equipment, fishing rods, scuba gear, and surfboards take up lots of room. Bring straps for securing gear on the roof and repair kits for fixing dings and leaks. Renting equipment is an option in the more developed towns. Even out-of-the-way places sometimes have kayaks and scuba gear available for rent.

Tipping

Tips of 10–15 percent are the norm at restaurants, unless a service charge appears on the bill. Tip bellhops about US$1, maids US$1/day, and Pemex attendants US$1 if they wash your windows or check your oil.

BUSINESS HOURS

Standard business hours for small businesses in Baja are Monday–Friday 9 A.M.–2 P.M. and 4 or 5 P.M. until 7 or 8 P.M. Many open on Saturday as well. Government offices are generally open 8:30 A.M.–3:30 P.M., although hours do vary day-to-day.

Bank are usually open Monday–Friday 8:30 A.M.–3 P.M., but the foreign exchange service usually closes around noon.

TOURIST INFORMATION

Mexico's national Secretaría de Turismo (SECTUR) has an office in La Paz that distributes free brochures, maps, hotel and restaurant lists, and information on local activities (Km 5–6 Mexico 1 or Av. Abasolo, tel. 612/124-0100, Mex. tel. 800/903-9200, toll-free U.S. tel. 800/482-9832, www.sectur.gob.mx, turismo@correro.gbcs.gob.mx). It's located outside of town on the way to the airport and new Fidepaz marina.

SECTUR maintains Mexican Tourism Board (www.visitmexico.com) offices in the United States and other countries to market the country's tourist destinations.

Travel Clubs

A few Baja-specific travel clubs offer information, services, and discounts to members. For example, **Discover Baja Travel Club** (3089 Clairemont Dr., San Diego, CA 92117, U.S. tel. 619/275-1836 or 800/727-2252, www.discoverbaja.com, US$39/yr) has a conveniently located San Diego office, which many members visit for the latest information before entering Baja.

MAPS

The best roadmaps currently available for the Baja Peninsula debuted in 2008 from

National Geographic (*Baja North and Baja South Baja Adventure Travel Map,* www.natgeomaps.com, US$19.95). They are printed on waterproof, tear-resistant paper and feature insets of the larger cities, with most of the popular dive, fishing, sailing, and surfing locations identified. We used these maps for much of the research this edition and found them to be a significant improvement over previously published maps by AAA and ITM.

Guia Roji (www.guiaroji.com.mx), the largest map publisher in Mexico, publishes city maps (scale 1:20,000) for Tijuana (2007, US$11.95) and La Paz (hasn't been updated since 2004), plus state maps for Baja California Sur (scale 1:350,000) and Baja California (Norte) (scale 1:1,000,000). The complete *2008–09 Mexico Tourist Road Atlas* (English edition, paperback, US$38.95), is invaluable for extended trips that include the mainland.

Topographical Maps

For serious off-road exploration, topographic maps are essential. Order them before your trip, unless you're going to be in the La Paz area, where the **Instituto Nacional de Estadística Geografía e Informática** (INEGI, in Plaza Cuatro Molinos at Calle Altamirano 2790, Col. Centro, tel. 612/123-1545 or 612/122-4146, www.inegi.gob.mx) sells them.

WEIGHTS AND MEASURES

Mexico uses the metric system for measuring weights, volumes, temperature, and distances. Driving directions are given in kilometers (1 km is 0.6 mi), meat is bought by the kilo (1 kg is 2.2 lbs), temperature is measured in degrees Celsius (27°C is 80°F), and Pemex stations sell gas by the liter (1 liter is 0.26 gallons).

In this book, distances are given in kilometers, often followed by miles in parentheses. Most other measurements are given in the metric system, except for boat lengths and fishing line tests, which are given in feet and pounds in Baja.

Time

Baja California (Norte) follows Pacific time, whereas Baja California Sur follows Mountain time. Don't forget to adjust your clocks when you cross the state line. Daylight saving time takes effect in both states from the first Sunday in April to the last Sunday in October.

Electricity

Mexico uses the same electrical system as the United States and Canada: 110 volts, 60 cycles, and alternating current (AC). U.S.-style outlets work with appliances that have standard double-bladed plugs. This means you can recharge your electronics without bringing an adapter.

Communications and Media

TELEPHONE SERVICES

You can make local calls from public phones in most towns, for just a few pesos. It's almost always more expensive to make local phone calls from your hotel, which adds a surcharge. The larger cities also have public TelMex offices. Private telephone services, often available at Internet cafés and office/business centers, are another place to make calls. Yellow Ladatel pay phones accept TelMex phone cards for local or long-distance calls. You can buy these cards in many grocery stores, pharmacies, bus depots, and airports in 20-, 30-, 50-, and 100-peso denominations.

Area Codes and Local Numbers

Phone numbers in Mexico follow the same format as U.S. numbers, with a three-digit area code (except for Mexico City, which is 55/), followed by a seven-digit local number. The difference is that numbers are not hyphenated according to any standard format. In this book, we've adopted the U.S. convention of a slash after the area code and a dash between the middle three and last four digits. Prior to 2001, numbers followed an older format, which some businesses still use.

To dial long-distance within Mexico, use 01 before the area code. Calling cards from Sprint, AT&T, MCI, Bell Canada, and British Telecom can also be used. Each has its own access code (usually toll-free) in Mexico for direct dialing. To reach toll-free 800 numbers in Mexico, dial 01 first.

Mobile Phones

Most of the Baja Peninsula now enjoys reliable mobile phone access through two competing companies: Telcel and Movistar. Telcel has better coverage and lower rates. For extended stays in Baja, during which you plan to make a number of local calls, buying a low-cost GSM phone and prepaid cards can make sense. Using it to call the United States, however, will cost a fortune, unless you are an AT&T customer in the United States.

Two U.S. carriers offer North America plans that include calling to/from Mexico and the United States: AT&T charges US$4.99 a month and US$0.59 per minute, or no monthly fee and US$0.99 per minute, for roaming in Mexico. There are plans that offer data services for smartphones, such as Blackberries and iPhones, that start at US$25 a month and US$5 per MB transferred. If you travel with your phone, make sure to disable the features on your phone that automatically check email and download data, or you may find yourself with a sky-high roaming bill. SMS messages cost US$0.50 to send; receiving them is free. Picture or video messages cost US$1.30 to send. You can activate the international service over the phone, but you need to call before you leave the country.

Verizon (www.verizonwireless.com/international) partners with Movistar to offer North America calling for US$60 a month for 450 minutes, and US$0.45 per minute after

the monthly allowance. International roaming on a standard U.S. plan through Verizon costs US$0.99 per minute. Remember to call Verizon before you leave the United States to check if international roaming is activated on your phone. SMS charges are US$0.50 for each message sent and US$0.05 for each one received.

In 2007, rates for calling a Mexican cell phone from the United States jumped about US$0.17 cents a minute, due to changes in the Mexican government's regulation of the telephone industry. Also, a caller-pays policy began in 2006. When calling a Mexican cell phone number from the United States, it's now necessary to add a 1 after the country code: 52 1 612/xxx-xxxx. Within Mexico, you need to add 044 before the area code: 044 612/xxx-xxxx.

International Calls

To dial an international number from Mexico to the United States or Canada via TelMex, dial 001, then the area code and number. Rates are about US$0.25 per minute. For international calls to other countries, dial 00 followed by the country code, area code, and number. To make an operator-assisted call, dial 09 before the country code.

Internet Phones

In areas with Internet access, voice-over-IP (VoIP) calling is fast replacing the need for satellite phones and Ladatel cards. Skype (www.skype.com) and Gizmo VoIP (www.gizmovoip.com) are two of the many service providers out there. Rates are about US$0.01–0.03 per minute, plus an account setup fee of around US$10. Some companies include a free U.S. number for family and friends back home to dial while you are on the road.

Long Distance the Old-Fashioned Way

If you don't have access to the Internet, you can dial access numbers to reach operators from AT&T, MCI, or Sprint for calling-card or credit card calls. Beware the no-name phone companies that try to get you to call the United

States collect or via credit card. They are notorious for overcharging, and some have forged partnerships with hotels that get a cut when guests use their inflated services.

Satellite Phone

For the many areas of Baja where there are no regular telephone lines, no radio phones, no Internet, and no cellular phone service, the only solution is satellite phone—assuming you *have* to stay in phone contact at all times. **California Baja Rent-a-Car** (9245 Jamacha Blvd., Spring Valley, CA 91977, U.S. tel. 619/470-7368 or 888/470-7368, www.cabaja.com) rents GPS-satellite phones, as does **Discover Baja Travel Club** (3089 Clairemont Dr., San Diego, CA 92117, U.S. tel. 619/275-1836 or 800/727-2252, www.discoverbaja.com).

EMAIL AND INTERNET ACCESS

To the surprise of many first-time visitors, high-speed Internet access is almost ubiquitous in Baja these days. Hundreds of miles of fiber-optic cable were buried alongside the Transpeninsular Highway in 2002–2003, replacing the need for slow dial-up connections in most towns, and connecting Baja residents and visitors to computers and websites around the world.

Reliability is another matter, however. Even the most well-equipped business centers have trouble keeping their connections up 24/7. If all you need to do is check your email now and then, this won't be a problem. But if you intend to run business processes remotely while on the road, it may be difficult to find a good setup.

Five-star resorts, espresso bars, marinas, and RV parks all have set wireless antennas for guests who travel with their own laptop or other Internet-enabled devices. Some charge extra by the hour or day; others throw it in for the price of a latte. In the larger condo complexes, you may be able to find an open (unsecured) Wi-Fi network to use. And for those traveling sans computer, there are dozens of Internet cafés in hotels, real estate offices, and business centers with desktop machines, as well as printers, copiers, and scanners for imaging needs.

Rates vary widely, from free with a food or beverage purchase to US$8 an hour at one of the hotels in San José del Cabo.

In more remote areas of the peninsula, some residents and RV owners have costly satellite Internet service through providers like HughesNet (formerly Direcway) and Starband.

POSTAL SERVICES

The Mexican postal service, **Correos de México** (www.correosdemexico.gob.mx), is slower than you're used to at home, though letters and postcards do arrive eventually (usually within 10 days).

Most towns in Baja have a *correo* (post office), where you can receive general-delivery mail. Correspondents should address letters in your name (capitalize the last name), followed by a/c Poste Restante, Correo Central, the town name, the state (BC or BCS), and the country (Mexico). For example, Nikki Goth ITOI, a/c Poste Restante, Correo Central, Loreto, Baja California Sur, Mexico. Mail sent this way is usually held up to 30 days. If you know the postal code for the town or city, add it after the state name.

Many visitors who are seasonal Baja residents forward their mail to a hotel or RV park. You can rent a post office box at the larger post offices, but the application process may take several weeks. Some of the larger towns also have private mail companies that rent boxes to visitors.

The Mexican post office offers express service (domestic and international) called Mexpost. UPS, Airborne Express, DHL, FedEx, and other courier services operate in some of the larger cities.

MEDIA

A few English-language newspapers are published regularly in Baja, but they tend toward tourism marketing. For real news, you'll need to read Spanish or visit the Internet. In Southern Baja, the *Gringo Gazette* (www.gringogazette.co) has a long and colorful history of covering local news and issues from the expat perspective. *El Calendario de Todos Santos* (www.todossantos-baja.com/elcalendariotodossantos.htm) covers the West Cape. In Northern Baja, the *Baja Times* (www.bajatimes.com) is a free biweekly, also published online.

In tourist hotels, you may be able to find day-old copies of the *San Diego Union-Tribune, Los Angeles Times,* or *USA Today.*

RESOURCES

Glossary

abarrotes groceries

aduana customs service

alta cocina mexicana Mexican food prepared in a "high cuisine," or gourmet, style

antojitos literally "little whims," quick Mexican dishes like tacos and enchiladas

aparejo burro saddle

bahía bay

basura trash or rubbish; a sign saying *No Tire Basura* means Don't Throw Trash

BCD buoyancy compensation device

BCN the state of Baja California (Norte)

BCS the state of Baja California Sur

boca literally "mouth," a geographic term describing a break in a barrier island or peninsula where sea meets lagoon

calle street

callejón alley or lane

cañon canyon

cardón *Pachycereus pringlei,* the world's tallest cactus

casa de huéspedes guesthouse

cerro mountain peak

cerveza beer

charreada Mexican-style rodeo

charro/charra horseman/horsewoman

colectivo van or taxi that picks up several passengers at a time for a standard per-person fare, much like a bus

correo post office

corrida de toros "running of the bulls" or bullfight

COTP captain of the port, *capitanía del puerto* in Spanish

curandero traditional healer

Diconsa Distribuidora Conasupo, S.A., a government-subsidized food distributor

efectivo cash payment

ejido collectively owned agricultural lands

ensenada cove or small bay

Fonatur Fondo Nacional de Fomento del Turismo (National Foundation for Tourism Development)

Gral. abbreviation for General (rank)

hostería hostelry, inn

IMSS Instituto Mexicano del Seguro Social (Mexican Social Security Institute)

INAH Instituto Nacional de Antropología e Historia (National Institute of Anthropology and History)

indios Mexicans of predominantly Amerindian descent; **indígenas** (indigenes is the less common, but more politically correct, term) indigenous people

INEGI Instituto Nacional de Estadística, Geografía e Informática (National Institute of Statistics, Geography, and Information)

ISSSTE Instituto de Seguridad y Servicios Sociales para Trabajadores del Estado (Security and Social Services Institute for Government Workers)

laguna lagoon, lake, or bay

llano plains

lleno full

malecón waterfront promenade

maquiladora or maquila a "twin-bond" or "in-plant" manufacturing enterprise where foreign components may be imported and assembled, then exported to a foreign country, free of customs duties in each direction

mariscos literally "shellfish," but often used as a generic term for seafood

mercado market
mochila knapsack or backpack
mochilero backpacker
nopalitos strips of cooked or pickled prickly-pear cactus
PADI Professional Association of Dive Instructors
palacio municipal literally "municipal palace," equivalent to city or county hall in the United States
palapa thatched, umbrella-like shade shelter or roof
PAN Partido Acción Nacional
panadería bakery
panga aluminum skiff used for fishing and diving in Baja
panguero captain of a *panga*
parrada bus stop
Pemex: Petroleos Mexicanos (Mexican Petroleum)
pensión boardinghouse
playa beach
plazuela smaller plaza
PRD Partido Revolucionario Democrático
pre-Cortesian a reference to Mexican history before the arrival of Spanish conquistador Hernán Cortés, i.e., before 1518; other terms with the same meaning include pre-Columbian (before Columbus's arrival) and pre-Hispanic (before the arrival of the Spanish)

PRI Partido Revolucionario Institucional
punta point
ramal branch road
rancheria a collection of small ranching households, most often inhabited by *indios*
ranchito small ranch
SECTUR Secretaría de Turismo (Secretariat of Tourism)
SEDESOL Secretaría de Desarrollo Social (Secretariat of Social Development)
SEMARNAT Secretaría de Medio Ambiente y Recursos Naturales (Secretariat of the Environment and Natural Resources)
tienda store
tinaja pool or spring
topes speed bumps
ultramarinos minimarket/delicatessen

ABBREVIATIONS
Av. Avenida
Blvd. Boulevard
Calz. Calzada
Col. Colonia (neighborhood)
Fracc. Fraccionamiento
nte. *norte* (north)
ote. *oriente* (east)
pte. *poniente* (west)
s/n *sin número* ("without number," used for street addresses without building numbers)

Spanish Phrasebook

Your Mexico adventure will be more fun if you use a little Spanish. Mexican folks, although they may smile at your funny accent, will appreciate your halting efforts to break the ice and transform yourself from a foreigner to a potential friend.

Spanish commonly uses 30 letters – the familiar English 26, plus four straightforward additions: ch, ll, ñ, and rr, which are explained in "Consonants," below.

PRONUNCIATION
Once you learn them, Spanish pronunciation rules – in contrast to English – don't change.

Spanish vowels generally sound softer than in English. (*Note:* The capitalized syllables below receive stronger accents.)

Vowels
a like ah, as in "hah": *agua* AH-gooah (water), *pan* PAHN (bread), and *casa* CAH-sah (house)
e like ay, as in "may:" *mesa* MAY-sah (table), *tela* TAY-lah (cloth), and *de* DAY (of, from)
i like ee, as in "need": *diez* dee-AYZ (ten), *comida* ko-MEE-dah (meal), and *fin* FEEN (end)
o like oh, as in "go": *peso* PAY-soh (weight),

ocho OH-choh (eight), and *poco* POH-koh (a bit)

u like oo, as in "cool": *uno* OO-noh (one), *cuarto* KOOAHR-toh (room), and *usted* oos-TAYD (you); when it follows a "q" the **u** is silent; when it follows an "h" or has an umlaut, it's pronounced like "w"

Consonants

b, d, f, k, l, m, n, p, q, s, t, v, w, x, y, z, and ch
pronounced almost as in English; **h** occurs, but is silent – not pronounced at all.

c like k as in "keep": *cuarto* KOOAR-toh (room), Tepic tay-PEEK (capital of Nayarit state); when it precedes "e" or "i," pronounce **c** like s, as in "sit": *cerveza* sayr-VAY-sah (beer), *encima* ayn-SEE-mah (atop).

g like g as in "gift" when it precedes "a," "o," "u," or a consonant: *gato* GAH-toh (cat), *hago* AH-goh (I do, make); otherwise, pronounce **g** like h as in "hat": *giro* HEE-roh (money order), *gente* HAYN-tay (people)

j like h, as in "has": *Jueves* HOOAY-vays (Thursday), *mejor* may-HOR (better)

ll like y, as in "yes": *toalla* toh-AH-yah (towel), *ellos* AY-yohs (they, them)

ñ like ny, as in "canyon": *año* AH-nyo (year), *señor* SAY-nyor (Mr., sir)

r is lightly trilled, with tongue at the roof of your mouth like a very light English d, as in "ready": *pero* PAY-doh (but), *tres* TDAYS (three), *cuatro* KOOAH-tdoh (four).

rr like a Spanish r, but with much more emphasis and trill. Let your tongue flap. Practice with *burro* (donkey), *carretera* (highway), and Carrillo (proper name), then really let go with *ferrocarril* (railroad).

Note: The single small but common exception to all of the above is the pronunciation of Spanish **y** when it's being used as the Spanish word for "and," as in "Ron y Kathy." In such case, pronounce it like the English ee, as in "keep": Ron "ee" Kathy (Ron and Kathy).

Accent

The rule for accent, the relative stress given to syllables within a given word, is straightforward.

If a word ends in a vowel, an n, or an s, accent the next-to-last syllable; if not, accent the last syllable.

Pronounce *gracias* GRAH-seeahs (thank you), *orden* OHR-dayn (order), and *carretera* kah-ray-TAY-rah (highway) with stress on the next-to-last syllable.

Otherwise, accent the last syllable: *venir* vay-NEER (to come), *ferrocarril* fay-roh-cah-REEL (railroad), and *edad* ay-DAHD (age).

Exceptions to the accent rule are always marked with an accent sign: (á, é, í, ó, or ú), such as *teléfono* tay-LAY-foh-noh (telephone), *jabón* hah-BON (soap), and *rápido* RAH-pee-doh (rapid).

BASIC AND COURTEOUS EXPRESSIONS

Most Spanish-speaking people consider formalities important. Whenever approaching anyone for information or some other reason, do not forget the appropriate salutation – good morning, good evening, etc. Standing alone, the greeting *hola* (hello) can sound brusque.

Hello. *Hola.*
Good morning. *Buenos días.*
Good afternoon. *Buenas tardes.*
Good evening. *Buenas noches.*
How are you? *¿Cómo está usted?*
Very well, thank you. *Muy bien, gracias.*
Okay; good. *Bien.*
Not okay; bad. *Mal or feo.*
So-so. *Más o menos.*
And you? *¿Y usted?*
Thank you. *Gracias.*
Thank you very much. *Muchas gracias.*
You're very kind. *Muy amable.*
You're welcome. *De nada.*
Goodbye. *Adios.*
See you later. *Hasta luego.*
please *por favor*
yes *sí*
no *no*
I don't know. *No sé.*
Just a moment, please. *Momentito, por favor.*
Excuse me. *Disculpe or Con permiso.*
I'm sorry. *Lo siento.*

Pleased to meet you. *Mucho gusto.*
How do you say…in Spanish? *¿Cómo se dice…en español?*
What is your name? *¿Cómo se llama usted?*
Do you speak English? *¿Habla usted inglés?*
Is English spoken here? (Does anyone here speak English?) *¿Se habla inglés?*
I don't speak Spanish well. *No hablo bien el español.*
I don't understand. *No entiendo.*
How do you say…in Spanish? *¿Cómo se dice…en español?*
My name is… *Me llamo…*
Would you like… *¿Quisiera usted…*
Let's go to… *Vamos a…*

TERMS OF ADDRESS

When in doubt, use the formal *usted* (you) as a form of address.

I *yo*
you (formal) *usted*
you (familiar) *tú*
he/him *él*
she/her *ella*
we/us *nosotros*
you (plural) *ustedes*
they/them *ellos* (all males or mixed gender); *ellas* (all females)
Mr., sir *señor*
Mrs., madam *señora*
miss, young lady *señorita*
wife *esposa*
husband *esposo*
friend *amigo* (male); *amiga* (female)
sweetheart *novio* (male); *novia* (female)
son; daughter *hijo; hija*
brother; sister *hermano; hermana*
father; mother *padre; madre*
grandfather; grandmother *abuelo; abuela*

TRANSPORTATION

Where is…? *¿Dónde está…?*
How far is it to…? *¿A cuánto está…?*
from…to… *de…a…*
How many blocks? *¿Cuántas cuadras?*
Where (Which) is the way to…? *¿Dónde está el camino a…?*
the bus station *la terminal de autobuses*

the bus stop *la parada de autobuses*
Where is this bus going? *¿Adónde va este autobús?*
the taxi stand *la parada de taxis*
the train station *la estación de ferrocarril*
the boat *el barco*
the launch *lancha; tiburonera*
the dock *el muelle*
the airport *el aeropuerto*
I'd like a ticket to… *Quisiera un boleto a…*
first (second) class *primera (segunda) clase*
roundtrip *ida y vuelta*
reservation *reservación*
baggage *equipaje*
Stop here, please. *Pare aquí, por favor.*
the entrance *la entrada*
the exit *la salida*
the ticket office *la oficina de boletos*
(very) near; far *(muy) cerca; lejos*
to; toward *a*
by; through *por*
from *de*
the right *la derecha*
the left *la izquierda*
straight ahead *derecho; directo*
in front *en frente*
beside *al lado*
behind *atrás*
the corner *la esquina*
the stoplight *la semáforo*
a turn *una vuelta*
right here *aquí*
somewhere around here *por acá*
right there *allí*
somewhere around there *por allá*
road *el camino*
street; boulevard *calle; bulevar*
block *la cuadra*
highway *carretera*
kilometer *kilómetro*
bridge; toll *puente; cuota*
address *dirección*
north; south *norte; sur*
east; west *oriente (este); poniente (oeste)*

ACCOMMODATIONS

hotel *hotel*
Is there a room? *¿Hay cuarto?*

May I (may we) see it? ¿Puedo (podemos) verlo?
What is the rate? ¿Cuál es el precio?
Is that your best rate? ¿Es su mejor precio?
Is there something cheaper? ¿Hay algo más económico?
a single room un cuarto sencillo
a double room un cuarto doble
double bed cama matrimonial
twin beds camas gemelas
with private bath con baño privado
hot water agua caliente
shower ducha
towels toallas
soap jabón
toilet paper papel higiénico
blanket frazada; manta
sheets sábanas
air-conditioned aire acondicionado
fan abanico; ventilador
key llave
manager gerente

FOOD

I'm hungry Tengo hambre.
I'm thirsty. Tengo sed.
menu carta; menú
order orden
glass vaso
fork tenedor
knife cuchillo
spoon cuchara
napkin servilleta
soft drink refresco
coffee café
tea té
drinking water agua pura; agua potable
bottled carbonated water agua mineral
bottled uncarbonated water agua sin gas
beer cerveza
wine vino
milk leche
juice jugo
cream crema
sugar azúcar
cheese queso
snack antojo; botana
breakfast desayuno

lunch almuerzo
daily lunch special comida corrida (or el menú del día depending on region)
dinner comida (often eaten in late afternoon); cena (a late-night snack)
the check la cuenta
eggs huevos
bread pan
salad ensalada
fruit fruta
mango mango
watermelon sandía
papaya papaya
banana plátano
apple manzana
orange naranja
lime limón
fish pescado
shellfish mariscos
shrimp camarones
meat (without) (sin) carne
chicken pollo
pork puerco
beef; steak res; bistec
bacon; ham tocino; jamón
fried frito
roasted asada
barbecue; barbecued barbacoa; al carbón

SHOPPING

money dinero
money-exchange bureau casa de cambio
I would like to exchange traveler's checks. Quisiera cambiar cheques de viajero.
What is the exchange rate? ¿Cuál es el tipo de cambio?
How much is the commission? ¿Cuánto es la comisión?
Do you accept credit cards? ¿Aceptan tarjetas de crédito?
money order giro
How much does it cost? ¿Cuánto cuesta?
What is your final price? ¿Cuál es su último precio?
expensive caro
cheap barato; económico
more más

less *menos*
a little *un poco*
too much *demasiado*

HEALTH

Help me please. *Ayúdeme por favor.*
I am ill. *Estoy enfermo.*
Call a doctor. *Llame un doctor.*
Take me to . . . *Lléveme a . . .*
hospital *hospital; sanatorio*
drugstore *farmacia*
pain *dolor*
fever *fiebre*
headache *dolor de cabeza*
stomach ache *dolor de estómago*
burn *quemadura*
cramp *calambre*
nausea *náusea*
vomiting *vomitar*
medicine *medicina*
antibiotic *antibiótico*
pill; tablet *pastilla*
aspirin *aspirina*
ointment; cream *pomada; crema*
bandage *venda*
cotton *algodón*
sanitary napkins use brand name, e.g.,
  Kotex
birth control pills *pastillas anticonceptivas;*
  píldora
contraceptive foam *espuma anticonceptiva*
condoms *preservativos; condones*
toothbrush *cepillo dental*
dental floss *hilo dental*
toothpaste *crema dental*
dentist *dentista*
toothache *dolor de muelas*

POST OFFICE AND COMMUNICATIONS

long-distance telephone *teléfono larga*
  distancia
I would like to call . . . *Quisiera llamar a . . .*
collect *por cobrar*
station to station *a quien contesta*
person to person *persona a persona*
credit card *tarjeta de crédito*
post office *correo*

general delivery *lista de correo*
letter *carta*
stamp *estampilla, timbre*
postcard *tarjeta*
aerogram *aerograma*
air mail *correo aereo*
registered *registrado*
money order *giro*
package; box *paquete; caja*
string; tape *cuerda; cinta*

AT THE BORDER

border *frontera*
customs *aduana*
immigration *migración*
tourist card *tarjeta de turista*
inspection *inspección; revisión*
passport *pasaporte*
profession *profesión*
marital status *estado civil*
single *soltero*
married; divorced *casado; divorciado*
widowed *viuda/o*
insurance *seguros*
title *título*
driver's license *licencia de manejar*

AT THE GAS STATION

gas station *gasolinera*
gasoline *gasolina*
unleaded *sin plomo*
full, please *lleno, por favor*
tire *llanta*
tire repair shop *vulcanizadora; llantera*
air *aire*
water *agua*
oil (change) *aceite (cambio)*
grease *grasa*
My...doesn't work. *Mi...no sirve.*
battery *batería*
radiator *radiador*
alternator *alternador*
generator *generador*
tow truck *grúa*
repair shop *taller mecánico*
tune-up *afinación*
auto parts store *refaccionería*

VERBS

Verbs are the key to getting along in Spanish. They employ mostly predictable forms and come in three classes, which end in *ar*, *er*, and *ir*, respectively:

to buy *comprar*
I buy, you (he, she, it) buys *compro, compra*
we buy, you (they) buy *compramos, compran*

to eat *comer*
I eat, you (he, she, it) eats *como, come*
we eat, you (they) eat *comemos, comen*

to climb *subir*
I climb, you (he, she, it) climbs *subo, sube*
we climb, you (they) climb *subimos, suben*

Here are more (with irregularities indicated):

to do or make *hacer* (regular except for *hago*, I do or make)
to go *ir* (very irregular: *voy, va, vamos, van*)
to go (walk) *andar*
to love *amar*
to work *trabajar*
to want *desear, querer*
to need *necesitar*
to read *leer*
to write *escribir*
to repair *reparar*
to stop *parar*
to get off (the bus) *bajar*
to arrive *llegar*
to stay (remain) *quedar*
to stay (lodge) *hospedar*
to leave *salir* (regular except for *salgo*, I leave)
to look at *mirar*
to look for *buscar*
to give *dar* (regular except for *doy*, I give)
to carry *llevar*
to have *tener* (irregular but important: *tengo, tiene, tenemos, tienen*)
to come *venir* (similarly irregular: *vengo, viene, venimos, vienen*)

Spanish has two forms of "to be":

to be *estar* (regular except for *estoy*, I am)
to be *ser* (very irregular: *soy, es, somos, son*)

Use *estar* when speaking of location or a temporary state of being: "I am at home." "*Estoy en casa.*" "I'm sick." "*Estoy enfermo.*" Use *ser* for a permanent state of being: "I am a doctor." "*Soy doctora.*"

NUMBERS

zero *cero*
one *uno*
two *dos*
three *tres*
four *cuatro*
five *cinco*
six *seis*
seven *siete*
eight *ocho*
nine *nueve*
10 *diez*
11 *once*
12 *doce*
13 *trece*
14 *catorce*
15 *quince*
16 *dieciseis*
17 *diecisiete*
18 *dieciocho*
19 *diecinueve*
20 *veinte*
21 *veinte y uno* or *veintiuno*
30 *treinta*
40 *cuarenta*
50 *cincuenta*
60 *sesenta*
70 *setenta*
80 *ochenta*
90 *noventa*
100 *ciento*
101 *ciento y uno* or *cientiuno*
200 *doscientos*
500 *quinientos*
1,000 *mil*
10,000 *diez mil*
100,000 *cien mil*

1,000,000 *millón*
one half *medio*
one third *un tercio*
one fourth *un cuarto*

TIME
What time is it? *¿Qué hora es?*
It's one o'clock. *Es la una.*
It's three in the afternoon. *Son las tres de la tarde.*
It's 4 A.M. *Son las cuatro de la mañana.*
six-thirty *seis y media*
a quarter till eleven *un cuarto para las once*
a quarter past five *las cinco y cuarto*
an hour *una hora*

DAYS AND MONTHS
Monday *lunes*
Tuesday *martes*
Wednesday *miércoles*
Thursday *jueves*
Friday *viernes*
Saturday *sábado*

Sunday *domingo*
today *hoy*
tomorrow *mañana*
yesterday *ayer*
January *enero*
February *febrero*
March *marzo*
April *abril*
May *mayo*
June *junio*
July *julio*
August *agosto*
September *septiembre*
October *octubre*
November *noviembre*
December *diciembre*
a week *una semana*
a month *un mes*
after *después*
before *antes*

(Courtesy of Bruce Whipperman, author of *Moon Pacific Mexico*.)

Suggested Reading

TRAVELOGUES

Amey, Ralph L. *Wines of Baja California: Touring and Tasting Mexico's Undiscovered Treasures.* San Francisco, CA: Wine Appreciation Guild, 2003. A compilation of historical information and winery profiles covering the Valle de Guadalupe and other regions in Northern Baja.

Berger, Bruce. *Almost an Island: Travels in Baja California.* Tucson: University of Arizona Press, 1998. Berger, a pianist, poet, desert aficionado, and keen observer of human behavior, surveys Baja's social landscape, with a special focus on La Paz.

Mackintosh, Graham. *Into a Desert Place.* New York: W. W. Norton & Co., 1995. One of the most widely read accounts of a gringo discovering Baja for the first time. With no wilderness experience, Graham decides to walk the entire coastline of Baja California.

Mayo, C. M. *Miraculous Air: Journey of a Thousand Miles through Baja California, the Other Mexico.* Milkweed Editions, 2007. Poignant, contemporary memoir by a fiction writer originally from the United States, who is now a Spanish/English translator and editor living in Mexico City.

Miller, Max. *Land Where Time Stands Still.* Gleed Press, 2007 (paperback). A classic 1940s travelogue that recounts the author's trip from San Diego to Cabo San Lucas.

Salvadori, Clement. *Motorcycle Journeys Through California and Baja,* 2nd Ed. North Conway, NH: Whitehorse Press, 2007. A well-known motorcycling journalist advises kindred spirits on the best way ride the Baja Peninsula.

Steinbeck, John. *The Log from the Sea of Cortez.* New York: Penguin USA, Viking, 1951. This classic armchair travel read tells of Steinbeck's journey with marine biologist Ed Ricketts from Monterey, California, down the Pacific coast, around the tip of Baja, and up the Sea of Cortez.

HISTORY AND CULTURE

Crosby, Harry. *Antigua California: Mission and Colony on the Peninsular Frontier, 1697–1768.* Albuquerque: University of New Mexico Press, 1994. A well-written academic account of the Jesuit mission era in Baja California, from planning through expulsion.

Hazard, Ann. *Cooking with Baja Magic Dos.* Renegade Enterprises, 2005. A collection of updated recipes drawn from conversations with restaurant owners and other Baja characters, plus the author's own experience of living in La Bufadora and Buena Vista.

Niemann, Greg. *Baja Legends.* San Diego, CA: Sunbelt Publications, 2002. A light read that bring the ghosts of Baja past alive, one town at a time.

NATURAL HISTORY AND FIELD GUIDES

Case, T. J., and M. L. Cody, eds. *A New Island Biogeography in the Sea of Cortez,* 2nd Ed. Oxford University Press, 2002. An interesting read if you want to learn more about conservation efforts in the Sea of Cortez.

Edwards, Ernest Preston. *The Birds of Mexico and Adjacent Areas.* Austin: University of Texas Press, 1998. This field guide may come in handy, but is not Baja-specific, and birders find it frustrating that birds of the same species are illustrated on different color plates.

Gotshall, Daniell W. *Sea of Cortez Marine Animals: A Guide to the Common Fishes and*

Invertebrates Baja California to Panama. Sea Challengers, 1998. A good reference guide to divers, sailors, and snorkelers.

Peterson, R. T., and E. L. Chaliff. *A Field Guide to Mexican Birds.* Boston: Houghton Mifflin Co., 1999. The closest thing to a Baja-specific bird-watching guide lacks Spanish names for the birds.

Roberts, Norman C. *Baja California Plant Field Guide.* Natural History Publishing Co., 1989. The must-have field guide to Baja's desert and sierra flora.

SPORTS AND RECREATION

Eckardt, Dave. *The Guide to Baja Sea Kayaking: The Sea of Cortez and Magdalena Bay.* Paddle Publishing, 2008. The newest resource for kayakers covers San Felipe to Los Cabos and all the islands in between, plus Bahía Magdalena on the Pacific coast. Includes GPS coordinates and color maps.

Kelly, Neil, and Gene Kira. *The Baja Catch: A Fishing, Travel & Remote Camping Manual for Baja California,* 3rd Ed. Valley Center, CA: Apples and Oranges, 1997. The undisputed bible of Baja fishing has a lot of information on camping as well.

Lehman, Charles. *Desert Survival Handbook,* Revised Ed. Phoenix: Primer Publishers, 1998. Practical information for surviving in the desert—essential for any serious Baja exploration.

Parise, Mike. *The Surfer's Guide to Baja.* Surfpress Publishing, 2007. A must-have resource for Baja-bound surfers, the guide includes detailed directions to more than 75 breaks along the peninsula, plus maps and wave height charts.

Williams, Jack. *Baja Boater's Guide, Vols. I and II.* Sausalito, CA: H. J. Williams Publications, 2001 (Vol. I, 3rd Ed.) and 2003 (Vol. II, 4th Ed.). These ambitious guides, one each on the Pacific Ocean and the Sea of Cortez, contain useful aerial photos and sketch maps of Baja's continental islands and coastline.

REAL ESTATE AND LIVING ABROAD

Luboff, Ken. *Living Abroad in Mexico.* Berkeley, CA: Avalon Travel, 2005. This resource gives advice and tips for Americans thinking of moving from the United States to Mexico.

Peyton, Dennis John. *How to Buy Real Estate in Mexico.* San Diego: Law Mexico Publishing, 2006. If you've decided you want a place of your own in Baja, read this book first. It will answer many of your questions, saving time and minimizing frustration in the process.

Internet Resources

The Internet has become an invaluable resource for Baja-bound travelers. Most out-of-the-way establishments have at least a basic website with directions and current pricing. The most technologically savvy ones use the Google Earth application to show visitors exactly where they are located. When it comes to directory-type sites, you need to be careful what you read. The vast majority of these sites are advertising engines with unedited and out-of-date information. Here is a short list of some of the most useful all-Baja sites:

Baja Books and Maps
www.bajabooksandmaps.com

Online bookstore with a comprehensive collection of Baja-related titles. This company is also the sole distributor of Baja-related titles to English-language bookstores throughout Southern Baja.

Baja Bound
www.bajabound.com

One of many businesses that offers Mexican auto insurance policies for travelers driving their own vehicles to Baja. Lots of related travel information too.

Baja Bush Pilots
www.bajabushpilots.com

A must-read for pilots interested in flying a private aircraft to Baja.

It costs $50 a year to access the forums, which might be worth it even if you're not a pilot.

BajaInsider.com
www.bajainsider.com

Comprehensive online publication for visitors and residents with news, weather, and commentary.

Baja Nomad
www.bajanomad.com

An interactive forum with extremely active participants, many of them veteran Baja travelers and local business owners. If you have the time to read through all the threads, you'll find a wealth of information about border crossings, road conditions, restaurant and hotel reviews, and more. If it's not on Baja Nomad, it probably hasn't happened yet.

Baja Times
www.bajatimes.com

Online version of the biweekly English-language newspaper serving tourists and residents of the main Northern Baja communities with news, real estate, and travel information.

Border Wait Times
http://apps.cbp.gov/bwt

Real-time border crossing times from the U.S. Customs and Border Protection. Scroll down to find the list of Mexican Border Ports of Entry.

In Search of the Blue Agave
www.ianchadwick.com/tequila
A good start for tequila aficionados, however the content appears to be out of date.

Instituto Nacional de Estadística, Geografía e Informática
www.inegi.gob.mx
INAH is a Mexican government agency that publishes statistics on population and economics for the entire country, as well as topographical maps. It also has an interactive map of Mexico, including Baja California. Spanish only.

iWindsurf.com and iKitesurf.com
www.iwindsurf.com and www.ikitesurf.com
Daily Baja wind forecast and reports for windsurfers, plus a whole range of consumer weather delivery services, from the parent company WeatherFlow.

Los Cabos Guide
www.loscabosguide.com
Relatively up-to-date, advertiser-driven listings of hospitality and tourism businesses in the Los Cabos area, with some coverage of the East Cape and Todos Santos. Useful restaurant reviews and hotel listings. Fairly comprehensive.

Mexico Fishing News
www.mexfish.com
Weekly fishing report that covers the entire peninsula with conditions, regulations, catches, and photos.

Olsen Currency Converter
www.xe.com/ucc
This online tool for currency conversions comes in handy now that the dollar-to-peso exchange rate is no longer an easy 1/10 ratio.

Sunbelt Publications
www.sunbeltpub.com
This book publisher specializing in upper and lower California has an online catalog of its Baja titles.

U.S. Embassy
http://mexico.usembassy.gov
Visit the U.S. Embassy in Mexico City online, with information on services for U.S. citizens, plus current State Department travel warnings.

Index

A

accommodations: all-inclusive resorts 13, 306, 307-308, 432; Bahía de las Palmas 260-265; Bahía de la Ventana 245-247; Bahía de los Angeles 128-130; Bahía Magdalena 202; beach hotels 307-308; booking services/property management 292-293, 310, 351; Cabo Pulmo 271-272; Cabo San Lucas 343-351; Cataviña 123-124; Ciudad Constitución 197; Corridor 321-324; El Rosario 93; Ensenada 67-69; Guerrero Negro 139-140; La Paz 228-233; Loreto 189-191; Los Cabos 291-293; Mexicali 101-102; Mulegé 166-168; Parque Nacional Sierra San Pedro Mártir 87-88; rates 430-431; reservation services 431; romantic resorts 27; Rosarito 45-46; San Felipe 111-113; San Ignacio 152-153; San Javier 196; San José del Cabo 305-310; San Quintín 90-92; Santa Rosalía 159-160; Tecate 53-54; Tijuana 36-37; Todos Santos 380-384; Valle de Guadalupe 78-79; West Cape 368-370; see also vacation rentals
Acuario de las Californias: 212
Aeropuerto Internacional General Rodolfo Sánchez Taboada: 105
agaves: 393-394
Agua Caliente: 38, 282
aguas frescas: 385
Agua Verde: 196
air travel: general discussion 409-410; Ensenada 72; Guerrero Negro 140-141; La Paz 240; Loreto 194; Los Cabos 293; Mexicali 105; San Felipe 115-116; Tijuana 39-40; Todos Santos 363
all-inclusive resorts: 13, 306, 307-308, 432
Alto Golfo de California: 97
Amerindian cultures: 97, 398, 406, 408
amphibians: 398
Ángeles Verdes: 39, 417
animals: general discussion 395-398; Bahía de los Angeles 126; Islas San Benito 149
antiques: Corridor 321; La Paz 227
appointments: 437
aquariums: 212
area codes: 442-443
Arrecife Pelicanos: 175
Arroyo San Bartolo: 250, 280
art galleries: general discussion 27; Cabo San Lucas 342; Ensenada 66; La Paz 212; San José del Cabo 304; Todos Santos 25, 379-380
arts and crafts: see handicrafts; shopping
Art Walk: 28, 303
astronomical observatories: 85-86
ATMs: Cabo San Lucas 357; Ensenada 71; Guerrero Negro 140; La Paz 238; Loreto 194; Mexicali 104; San Felipe 115; San José del Cabo 315; Tecate 55; Tijuana 39; Todos Santos 388
ATVs (all-terrain vehicles): Bahía de las Palmas 259-260; Cabo San Lucas 339; La Candelaria 365; La Paz 224
Avenida Constitución: 36
Avenida López Mateos: 26, 65-66
Avenida Revolución: 34, 36, 37-38

B

backpacking: 424
Bahía Asunción: 144
Bahía Chileno: 288, 318
Bahía Concepción: 13, 18, 23, 164, 171-176
Bahía de La Paz: 19
Bahía de las Palmas: 252-268
Bahía de la Ventana: 20, 204, 242-247
Bahía de los Angeles: 13, 125-131
Bahía de los Frailes: 274-275
Bahía de los Muertos: 248
Bahía de los Sueños: 248
Bahía La Paz: 212-213
Bahía Magdalena: 13, 179, 198-202
Bahía San Francisquito: 126
Bahía San Gabriel: 214
Bahía San Juanico: 177
Bahía San Luis Gonzaga: 12, 95, 118
Bahía San Quintín: 12, 88-93
Bahía San Rafael: 141-142
Bahía Santa Inés: 171
Bahía Santa María: 288, 318
Bahía Santa Teresa: 141
Bahía Tortugas: 146-147
Baja 500: 53, 65
Baja 1000: 65, 226-227
Baja Studios: 17, 30, 47
Banco Gorda: 250, 277
banks: Cabo San Lucas 357; Ensenada 71; La Paz 238; Loreto 194; Mexicali 104; Mulegé 169; Tijuana 39; Todos Santos 388
Bar Andaluz: 62

List of Maps

Acknowledgments

This edition of *Moon Baja* was written while braving winter's El Norte winds along the Gulf coast, living large in San José del Cabo, driving Pedro the pickup to the most remote corners of the peninsula, finding hammerhead sharks at Gorda Banks, and hanging with local outfitters in Mexicali.

Carmel Tsabar and Pablo Nobili shared a discerning traveler's eye, vast knowledge of the desert and ocean environments, and their love of all things Baja. They pointed the way toward sustainable eco-initiatives and interesting personalities in some of the fastest changing parts of Central Baja.

Kathryn LaTendresse indulged her newfound passion for photography as we traipsed around the greater Cabo area, while Tom Goth donated hotel points that landed us in the lap of luxury for a week.

Paul Itoi, Anthony Costello, and Shannon Painter got the scoop on Mexicali and San Felipe. Jim Tolbert of Baja Books and Maps gave generously of his time and expertise, helping to polish the Southern Baja chapters. Many other friends and acquaintances shared their local knowledge and travel experiences along the way.

And the professional team at Avalon Travel transformed the resulting collection of notes and impressions into a workable manuscript.

I am indebted to all.

www.moon.com

DESTINATIONS | ACTIVITIES | BLOGS | MAPS | BOOKS

MOON.COM is all new, and ready to help plan your next trip! Filled with fresh trip ideas and strategies, author interviews, informative blogs, a detailed map library, and descriptions of all the Moon guidebooks, Moon.com is all you need to get out and explore the world—or even places in your own backyard. As always, when you travel with Moon, expect an experience that is uncommon and truly unique.

MAP SYMBOLS

▦▦▦	Expressway	**(**	Highlight	✕	Airfield	⌐	Golf Course
▦▦▦	Primary Road	○	City/Town	✈	Airport	**P**	Parking Area
▦▦▦	Secondary Road	◉	State Capital	▲	Mountain	▰	Archaeological Site
⸱⸱⸱⸱	Unpaved Road	⊛	National Capital	✛	Unique Natural Feature	▮	Church
- - - -	Trail	★	Point of Interest			▯	Gas Station
⋯⋯⋯	Ferry	●	Accommodation	⥿	Waterfall	◯	Glacier
⬟⬟⬟	Railroad	▼	Restaurant/Bar	▲	Park	▱	Mangrove
▦▦▦	Pedestrian Walkway	■	Other Location	▣	Trailhead	▨	Reef
▥▥▥	Stairs	⋀	Campground	⅀	Skiing Area	▭	Swamp

CONVERSION TABLES

°C = (°F - 32) / 1.8
°F = (°C x 1.8) + 32
1 inch = 2.54 centimeters (cm)
1 foot = 0.304 meters (m)
1 yard = 0.914 meters
1 mile = 1.6093 kilometers (km)
1 km = 0.6214 miles
1 fathom = 1.8288 m
1 chain = 20.1168 m
1 furlong = 201.168 m
1 acre = 0.4047 hectares
1 sq km = 100 hectares
1 sq mile = 2.59 square km
1 ounce = 28.35 grams
1 pound = 0.4536 kilograms
1 short ton = 0.90718 metric ton
1 short ton = 2,000 pounds
1 long ton = 1.016 metric tons
1 long ton = 2,240 pounds
1 metric ton = 1,000 kilograms
1 quart = 0.94635 liters
1 US gallon = 3.7854 liters
1 Imperial gallon = 4.5459 liters
1 nautical mile = 1.852 km

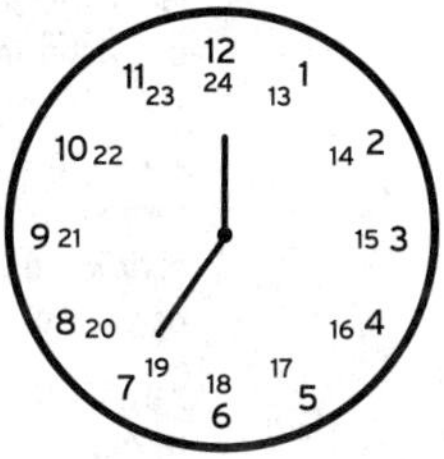

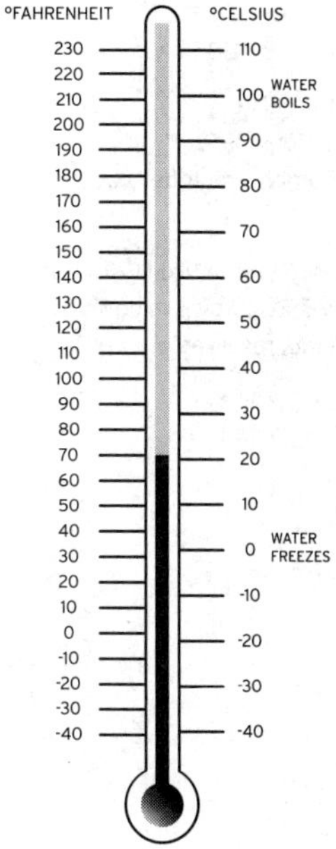

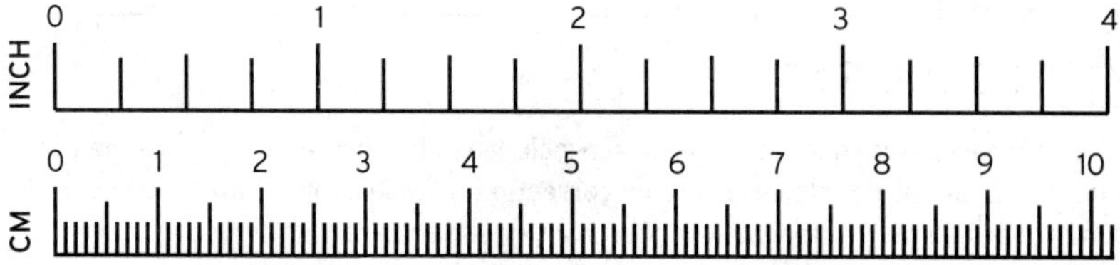

24-hour clock face

Fahrenheit / Celsius thermometer: WATER BOILS (100°C / 212°F), WATER FREEZES (0°C / 32°F)

INCH ruler 0–4, CM ruler 0–10

MOON BAJA

Avalon Travel
a member of the Perseus Books Group
1700 Fourth Street
Berkeley, CA 94710, USA
www.moon.com

Editor: Erin Raber
Series Manager: Kathryn Ettinger
Copy Editor: Ellie Behrstock
Graphics and Production Coordinator:
  Domini Dragoone
Cover Designer: Domini Dragoone
Map Editor: Albert Angulo
Cartographer: Kat Bennett
Indexer: Judy Hunt

ISBN: 978-1-59880-177-4
ISSN: 1098-6685

Printing History
1st Edition – 1992
8th Edition – October 2009
5 4 3 2 1

Some photos and illustrations are used by permission and are the property of the original copyright owners.

Front cover photo: © Blaine Harrington III/Corbis, sea kayaking in El Cardonal Bay.
Title page photo: © Carmel Tsabar, beachfront living in Bahía Concepción.
Interior color photos: pgs. 8 and 15 (bottom) © Paul Itoi; pgs. 9 (left and right), 10 (top), 11 (bottom right), 23, and 24 © Carmel Tsabar; pgs. 9 (center), 15 (top), 19 (bottom), 21, and 22 © Pablo Nobili; pgs. 10 (bottom), 11 (top left, bottom left), 14, 20, 25, and 27 © 123rf.com/Carlos Sanchez Pereyra; pg. 11 (top right) © 123rf.com/Derrick Neill; pg. 12 © 123rf.com/Connie Wade; pg. 16 (top) © 123rf.com/Alysta, Inc.; pgs. 16 (bottom), 17, 19 (top), 26, and 28 © Nikki Goth Itoi.

Printed in Canada by Friesens Corp.

KEEPING CURRENT

If you have a favorite gem you'd like to see included in the next edition, or see anything that needs updating, clarification, or correction, please drop us a line. Send your comments via email to feedback@moon.com, or use the address above.